Encyclopedia of
Children's
SEWING
COLLECTIBLES

IDENTIFICATION & VALUES

Sewing Sets
Dolls
Books
Patterns

Darlene J. Gengelbach

COLLECTOR BOOKS
A Division of Schroeder Publishing Co., Inc.

On the front cover:

The composition doll with four Dolly Dress Patterns in a Fairy Tin is by Transogram Company, Inc. (plate 44), $100.00 and up. The paper doll on the cover is Pretty Things for Baby #68 by Ontex, Canada (plate 125), $25.00 and up. Books are *Sue Sew-and-Sew* by Flavia Gàg (plate 578), $100.00 and up; *Mary Frances Sewing Book* by Jane Eayre Fryer (plate 574), $50.00 and up. The presentation needlework box, titled La Tapisserie, was made in France and was sold in the store "Au Bonheur des Enfants Chaufour" (plate 314), $1,000.00 and up. The Dolly's Dressmaker #1 pattern was published in London by Joseph Myers & Company and in Berlin by Winckelmann & Sons in the early 1860s (plate 518), $300.00 and up.

On the back cover:

Top: Trade card for Doll's Dress Patterns Kindergarten Pleasant Hour by Mrs. M.S. Schafor (plate 524), $300.00 and up. The hat making set is titled Modiste and was made in France by an unknown maker (plate 228), $700.00 and up. The mannequin set is Peggy McCall (hat box) made in 1942 by Dritz-Traum Company, Inc. (plate 156), $500.00 and up. The dolls from Daisy Kingdom Dolls are Daisy Dolly in back and from left to right Rosie and Daisy Baby (plates 512 and 514), each, $5.00 and up. The last item is Little Traveller's Sewing Kit #1567 made by Transogram. Company, Inc. in 1947 (plate 55), $75.00 and up.

Cover design by Beth Summers
Book design by Mary Ann Hudson

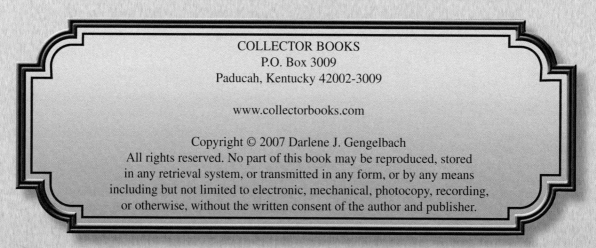

COLLECTOR BOOKS
P.O. Box 3009
Paducah, Kentucky 42002-3009

www.collectorbooks.com

Searching for a Publisher?

We are always looking for people knowledgeable within their fields. If you feel that there is a real need for a book on your collectible subject and have a large comprehensive collection, contact Collector Books.

Proudly printed and bound in the
United States of America

Contents

Dedication

This book is dedicated to my grandchildren who are the sunshine of my life. They have kept me happy, young, creative, and always on the move. All of them have shared time with me to stitch on a "project" or two. Their curious minds, eagerness, and willingness to learn is amazing, so I dedicate this work to Ian, Christina, James, Amanda, and Meghan.

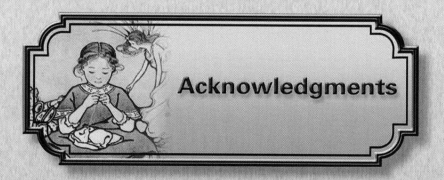

Acknowledgments

My first thanks goes to my husband who has suffered through many hardships to allow this book to be written; it would take another book to elaborate. He was my number one man when computer problems arose and I couldn't have written this book without him. I also want to thank the rest of my family for understanding when I couldn't visit or spend the time I would have liked to with them. They are the best!

When it comes to friends, there are so many who have supported me and cheered me on. They know who they are and my heartfelt thanks goes out to each and every one of them. I also would like to give special thanks to Pat Burns who started the ball rolling after seeing my Children's Sewing Collectibles program, and who generously supplied pages of FAO Schwarz catalogs for my research. To Bill Tribelhorn for his time and shared photography expertise. To Agnes Sura who was so generous with her knowledge about Bleuette and Marilu and who let me take pictures of her collection. To Atha Kahler for sharing her information about Lettie Lane's Daisy Doll and for all the effort she has put into researching.

To Patricia Hogan, for her support, her advice, and most of all for her editing of my first attempts at query letters. And to Carol Sandler, Strong National Museum of Play chief librarian, who put up with me on a regular basis for over two years. Both Carol and Strong National Museum of Play's wonderful library are a wealth of information. Thanks to Collector Books and my editor Gail Ashburn and her assistant Amy Sullivan.

And finally, I can't begin to express my gratitude for the expertise and generosity of my dear friend Helene Marlowe, my right arm in writing this book. Her memory and knowledge of dolls, both old and new is amazing. It has been an interesting ride and I am glad she was at my side.

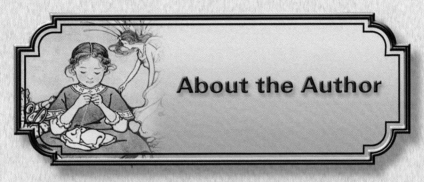

About the Author

Darlene Gengelbach has served as doll and textile conservator for the last 20 years to the more than 15,000 dolls in the collection of the Strong National Museum of Play in Rochester, New York. She has also traveled to a number of other museums and institutions in the United States for consultations, restoration, and appraisals of their doll collections. Darlene has been published in *Doll Reader* as well as being featured in an article in the magazine. She has been a member of the United Federation of Doll Clubs for more than two decades during which time she has studied and researched dolls and toys extensively. She has been collecting and researching children's sewing books, sets, dolls, and patterns for 20 years.

Her collection of children's sewing collectibles has been featured in exhibits at numerous museums and was also showcased at the 1999 National Convention of the United Federation of Doll Clubs in Washington, DC. She is a much sought-after speaker and has presented numerous lectures on dolls, teddy bears, children's sewing sets, and children's sewing books at various museums and conventions on both national and local levels. She also worked as a needle arts instructor for 27 years at the Monroe County Office for the Aging.

Darlene is presently a member of the UFDC (United Federation of Doll Clubs), the Margaret Woodbury Strong Doll Study Club of Rochester, New York, and, due to her interest in needlework, she is also a member of the Flower City Rug Hookers.

Darlene lives with her husband Robert in Rochester, New York, where they raised their two children. She and Robert are now the proud grandparents of five wonderful grandchildren who look forward to visits from "Nanny" with her "Craft-Case" filled with kid-type projects, which naturally include some sewing projects too. Thus, she perpetuates the sewing instruction tradition.

Preface

I began collecting children's sewing sets with a new passion about four years ago, and I soon realized that when I found a set that had been used or played with, I had nothing with which to compare it and no way of knowing if it was complete. How nice it would be if somewhere there was a book with plates so that I could compare and identify the sets. There was not one book on the market that had even a chapter about children's sewing sets. There were a few reprints of early toy catalog pages showing the French presentation sets. But the early sets are so hard to find that the chances of finding one that is actually in these catalogs are few and far between.

I started hunting down old catalogs and vintage women's magazines and began photocopying pages that had advertisements for children's sewing books, patterns, and sewing, knitting, or tapestry sets, anything I could find on children and sewing. I also printed out every set that I could find on the Internet. I put this information into notebooks and, as the information grew, I started new notebooks using categories such as bisque-doll sewing sets, composition-doll sewing sets, and so on.

As I hunted for the information on the sets, I started finding wonderful early children's activities and amusements books that contained chapters on sewing. Some chapters were entirely devoted to sewing for a favorite doll. And then there were patterns; patterns made especially for children to make complete wardrobes for their dolls with little or no help. This was so exciting! I was finding books and patterns I never knew existed. It wasn't long before I realized I had a book waiting to be written. Writing this book has been an experience — an experience I am glad to have undertaken. I have learned so much in doing so. There were times I may have wished I had my old life back (the life that I thought was so busy), but at no time, have I ever been bored or dreaded sitting down to the computer to write. The reading that was required to research how sewing has impacted not only young girls' and women's lives, but has also played a part in our economy in the past hundred or so years, was a pure delight to me.

My original purpose in writing this book was to illustrate the various sewing sets so one could compare the contents. I have seen many sets that were sold with added or missing components. I have tried to include as much information as possible in the captions and, hopefully, I have provided you enough information to identify your set and its contents. In order to be certain of a set's content, I studied advertisements and catalogs or documented at least three or more examples of the same set to verify an item or doll was correct. I am always seeking information, so if any of you out there know more about these sets or any other information concerning children and sewing I would love to hear from you. I can be contacted through the publisher.

I found that the dolls were often interchanged in the sewing sets as many dolls were cheaply made and sold in large lots to manufacturers to use where needed. It is difficult to research and document the early bisque-doll sewing sets. The boxes are not marked and sometimes were not even named. Occasionally there is a clue: the presentation, the doll's manufacturer, a company's or a country's name printed on the wrappers of thread or trims. All these things play an important part in identification, but since some materials were imported, even these clues are not foolproof. The best way to identify the content of a child's sewing set is to document it in a trade catalog, but even manufacturers sometimes slightly changed the content before it entered the market. Another frustrating problem is finding sewing sets without dates. There are ways of dating these sets if you become a sleuth. One of my sewing sets had an undated advertisement for new children's books included with its contents. I went on a book search, found one of the books and the date it was published, and had a clue of an approximate date for the set. Sometimes it's possible to estimate the date by the style of the clothing. One example is the Gold Medal Needlecraft #521 (plate 15). Some of the clothing in this set is labeled "Hooverette." Some garments were known to be named after Herbert Hoover during World War I, so if the clothing looked original to the doll and set, it would date the set to that period. However doll clothing didn't always keep pace with the latest fashions.

Another way to date a set is by the thread; some sets have the thread manufacturer's name on the thread. J.P. Coats has been in the loom and thread business in Scotland since opening their first cotton thread factory in 1812. Clarks opened a cotton thread mill a few years later. By the 1840s, both companies had sent family members to sell thread in America as well as other countries. In 1896, the Coats' and Clark's interests were consolidated, however they continued to sell the thread under two names. The Spool Cotton Company became the sole selling agent for both companies. In 1953, J.P. Coats and the Clark's Thread Company merged to become Coats & Clark's Inc. After 1952, their thread was marketed as Coats & Clark's. Of course this isn't a foolproof way of dating a set unless the thread is secured and there is proof it wasn't added at a later date.

Graphics are another clue to the age of the set. Methods

of printing improved. The styles in type, art, and graphics changed with the times just as did fashion. I have tried to be as accurate as possible in identifying the sets and their content, but if your own set looks to be untouched and complete, please leave it that way until it is documented otherwise. Throughout the book, I have stated when I have found a set in a catalog or dated advertisement.

I have found many reasons for collectors to collect children's sewing sets: sometimes it is for the dolls, such as Madame Alexander's Little Genius or Effanbee's Wee Patsy,"other times it's for the patterns. Men are collecting sets for the graphics, some especially seek out the comic book and Disney characters. In an effort to make this book as user-friendly as possible, I have arranged every chapter in the book in chronological order. I have also indexed all the sewing sets, books, and patterns alphabetically at the back of the book. My hope is that reading and using this book will bring you the same joy that it has brought me in writing it.

Little Genuis Sewing Basket, see page 61 for more information.

Walt Disney's Sleeping Beauty Sewing Set #3595, see page 58 for more information.

Introduction

It's funny how something becomes so ingrained in your mind you don't even notice it. About three years ago, I met up with an old friend. In our conversation I was asked what was new in my life and I replied that I was enjoying myself making doll clothes. My friend's reply was, "I remember when our daughters were in dance class together; you were sewing doll clothes then." I had forgotten that I had spent hours working on doll clothing while waiting with other mothers in the waiting room. Back then I wasn't a doll collector, more of a soccer mom, spending most of my time driving my two children to dance lessons, soccer, scouts, or whatever was in vogue at the time. The doll clothing I was working on years ago was a Christmas gift for my daughter Suzanne.

Looking back, I realize sewing has always been a significant part of my existence. I guess I never noticed it because I adapted sewing to meet whatever needs I had at the time. The first time I remember sewing was in the 1950s with a little plastic doll sewing set. It probably was a Junior Miss Sewing Kit or Little Traveler's Sewing Kit, since they were the most common. All I really can remember was the bright pink doll and dresses cut out to sew up the sides. I also remember my first real sewing class in junior high. I made an apron, pajamas, and a cotton jumper. When I was trimming threads on the jumper, I accidentally cut a hunk right out of the center back. Our home economics class had a fashion show scheduled to model our garments for our parents and friends, so my teacher made me put a square patch on the back where I had cut into the fabric. I hated that patch! I can still remember modeling my patched jumper for the whole world to see; it was so embarrassing. Another sewing experience I will never forget is when I cut a strip of fur from my mother's fur coat to trim a skating skirt. (The coat was just hanging in the closet and I never saw her wear it that much.) Needless to say, I didn't do much skating that year.

I remember sewing clothes for myself when I was in high school, and sewing curtains and a bedspread for our first apartment when I was newly married. My first born, a son we named Robert Jr., had clothes like John F. Kennedy Jr. because I could sew. I would clip pictures of John-John and find patterns I could alter to make Eaton suits and short pants just like his. It didn't stop with my son; my daughter was always in lace and eyelet. Both my children wore handmade sweaters and coats. I made pillows, wall hangings, cushions, and anything else my first homes needed. As the children got older, they wanted designer jeans and polo shirts (not what Mom made), I went back to sewing for myself, and my own wardrobe started expanding. I always found a reason for sewing: a charity bazaar, hospital bears, and special Christmas presents, (all of my daughter's dolls had large wardrobes).

After my children grew up, I started collecting antique dolls. What a bonanza for sewing! If there wasn't a garment to be made, there certainly was something to be mended. As I learned more about the hobby of doll collecting, a whole new aspect of sewing came into focus. The books, the vintage patterns, and the wonderful early presentation sewing sets were of another world. I remember the first time I ever held a presentation sewing set with a china doll. It was at Francis Walker's house, sometime in the 1980s. I had never seen anything like it, and at that time, thought I never would again. Never even in my wildest dreams, did I think I would actually write a book about children's sewing sets.

My first children's sewing set was one of dear Frances's. When she passed, I went to an auction of her estate and bought Schnittmuster Baby-Kleid shown in plate 2. This book is the ultimate outcome from that first presentation set purchase. Thank you, dear Frances. Frances was a wonderful lady that loved dolls along with sewing. Frances collected dolls that related to sewing among many others. Frances and Margaret Whitton were responsible for the book *Playthings by the Yard*, a wonderful book about printed cloth dolls.

Learning to sew has served me well; both my jobs involved sewing. I worked for Monroe County in New York for 27 years and taught sewing and needle arts to senior citizens. I loved the job; the government had to cut the program to get rid of me. I have also worked at the Strong National Museum of Play in Rochester, New York, for 23 years in the conservation department as conservator of dolls, conserving and taking care of the dolls and their clothing. I hope to continue doing so for a good while yet. I feel truly blessed in having had two jobs and a hobby that I have truly enjoyed.

Sewing and Embroidery Sets for Bisque Dolls

For centuries little girls were taught to sew as soon as they were capable of holding a needle. Mothers, family members, or family friends usually taught the child her first lessons. Home sewing was a necessity for many families and considered an essential skill for a girl. In the eighteenth century, families often provided in their will for their daughters to be taught sewing as well as reading. It was a great attribute to be able to handle a needle well and this assured a meaningful life for a woman.

In *Sewing Illustrated*, written in 1881, Louise Kirkwood wrote:

If girls of but one grade — say from nine to twelve years — could be afforded the opportunity of becoming familiar with the use of the needle, it would be a telling step in the right direction, putting them in possession of a most valuable art, which would prove an armor of defense against temptation to idleness, which leads to want and so often to crime.

Sewing was woven into daily life; projects were given to the child to complete by a given time, scheduled a few hours each day until the piece was finished. Often women and children brought their sewing workbags when visiting, sharing their ideas and instructions, making it a social time as well as a duty.

The first sewing a young girl was taught was plain sewing, also known as common sewing or useful work. The stitches included basting, seaming, overhanding, hemming, gathering, darning, and patching. Many times she was given the household mending, and when she became practiced, the making of plain baby clothing or underwear. Diaries of young girls sometimes complained of the dull boring hours of plain sewing.

Families, who could afford it, sent their young girls to sewing schools to be taught the art of plain sewing. At the schools each girl made a sample or model book, filling it with models of her various construction procedures such as seams, hemming, methods of applying trims, adding plackets, and other applications of plain sewing. The books were very important to the girls for they could refresh their memories by referring to them when needed. After the basic stitches were perfected, the girls would move on to ornamental work. They would learn the stitches of the alphabet so that they might mark the linens in the family. Many times this would be done in a sampler that would hang on the wall, showing the talents of young lady who signed it.

Victorian children were the first to grow up with the new sewing machines, however in the beginning, these machines were not readily accepted in most homes. They were very expensive; so expensive that *Godey's Lady's Book* suggested that families pool their money together and buy a machine and share it, working out a plan where each home uses it equally.

Not only were the new sewing machines expensive, but families who could afford them also could afford seamstresses to come into their homes. If the ladies in the family had a machine to do their work, there would be no need for a seamstress and this, of course, would add more work to their already busy lives. So promoters often appealed to middle class families to buy a sewing machine to save their women from the drudgery of sewing by hand. The New Home Sewing Machine Co. published a trade card showing on one side a woman, unkempt, bent over her hands, sewing, and on the other side, the same woman, well dressed, smiling, sitting up straight, happily working on her new sewing machine.

As hard as it was to introduce the new sewing machine to the general adult public, it didn't take long for the new sewing machine to be miniaturized and introduced into the children's toy catalogs. Grands Magasins du Printemps along with the Louvre were the first Christmas catalogs in 1875 in France, according to Francois Theimer, who had the catalogs reprinted in 1996. Toy sewing machines were already in these 1875 French toy catalogs, along with tapestry sets. The largest and most complete children's sewing sets came from France and Germany during the golden age of toys from 1875 to 1889. Most of these were needlework sets with embroidery, tapestry, lace-making, and Berlin work. Usually these sets did not contain a doll but often held, tucked in among the array of threads and accoutrements, doll's collars or collar and cuff sets, to be embroidered.

In the nineteenth century, a doll was more than just a favorite toy, it was often the instrument of motherhood. It was used to teach a child to love, care, and especially to sew. Mothers gave their child a doll, along with all the materials to cut, fit, and sew a complete wardrobe for it, knowing that the skill learned would surely serve them in later life. The early boxed sewing sets, so carefully arranged, must have been a treasure to the child that received them, with all the implements made just for their little fingers.

Sewing and Embroidery Sets for Bisque Dolls

An excerpt from *Queen of Home* written in 1888 states:

Through her doll, the miniature woman learns to sew, to plan, to make, to mend; and many a mother can trace present ease of performance of some daily task, back to experience gained in caring for her doll. Let them have all the belongings for their baby that you can afford. Give them a bed and bedding, and let them make their own sheets, and pillow cases. Provide them with all material, but let them do their own work, and no mother will ever regret the time spent in teaching her daughter to sew for her doll.

In the early nineteenth century, the sewing sets with dolls that were available on the market might have been considered toys, but surely they were also meant to teach. If examined carefully, you will find materials and threads of the finest cotton.

The accoutrements were small (for small hands), but precise and sharp, surely as nice as any adult lady's work box. It was especially nice for the children to find doll patterns selected to accompany sewing sets as shown in The Little Dressmaker (plate 3). In many sewing sets however, there were no patterns, only the materials to use for dolly's clothes.

It is hard to find information on these early sewing sets. Usually the only documentation we have are the few early catalogs that have survived. It is fortunate today that people who have obtained these early toy catalogs have realized the value and have reprinted them in English as well as other languages for others to research and enjoy.

One such catalog is Der Universal-Spielwaren-Katalog 1924 – 1926, a German toy catalog reprinted in 1985 by Hobby House Press, Inc. It lists two doll-related sewing sets:

• "Cardboard boxes containing articles for doll's tailoring with dolls with rigid joints in good style."

• "Embroidery casket covered w/striped mull, cross embroidery for doll's things, with pearl thread."

France, always the leader in luxury, had the most extravagant, detailed sewing sets. France's presentation sewing boxes were draped in silk ribbons, flowers, and lace, had little gilt-trimmed, glass-lid boxes filled with bright glass beads, and everything was arranged in the most pleasing manner.

Shown in the 1906 French catalog Au Bon Marché, reprinted by Denys Ingram in 1981, was one sewing set, La Petite Couturiere:

• "Sewing arrangement in box. A jointed bisque head doll in a complete sewing set containing sewing machine, threads, fabrics, accoutrements, and patterns."

Marshall Field & Company's 1914 catalog Kringle Society Dolls, reprinted by Hobby House Press in 1980, listed three doll outfits for sewing.

• "C68057 – Doll's Outfit: complete with material and trimmings for the little dressmaker; also fine baby doll, with bisque head, closing eyes, mohair wig, jointed limbs, in leatherette covered box, 2½x9x12½" each in box. Dozen, $8.00."

• "C68058 – Doll's Outfit: with 6½" jointed doll and material and patterns for dressmaking; doll with bisque head, turning neck and moving eyes, mohair curls, lace-trimmed chemise, hat, silk ribbon, 1 bunch of braid, 3 patterns dress goods, 2 bunches of lace, 1 piece cambric, 1 card of silk thread, 1 spool of cotton, buttons, hooks, and eyes, 1 bunch of ribbon, 1 card of complete dressmaker's patterns in display box. 2½x8½x11½". Dozen, $17.00." Similar to (plate 2) in this chapter.

• "C68059 – Doll's Outfit: fine doll, with bisque head, closing eyes, mohair curls, jointed limbs; complete with material and trimmings for the little dressmaker; also a number of patterns to work by; in handsome box, 2½x11½x14". Dozen, $24.00." Similar to (plate 3) in this chapter.

Toilette de ma Poupée (plate 1) is one early set that I have found which yields some clues to its origin. Agnes Lucas and S. Barazetti created the set. I have no information on S. Barazetti at this time, but I do know a few things about Agnes Lucas. She was drafting her patterns from approximately 1895 to 1910 and she used the publishing house of Otto Maier in Ravensburg, Germany. I have seen Agnes Lucas patterns paired with sewing sets with bisque head dolls with names such as Toilette de ma Poupée (my doll's attire dress), Puppenmütterchens Nähstube (doll mothers sewing room), Die Kleine Puppenschneiderin (the little doll seamstress). I have not seen Puppenmütterchens Nähstube advertised with a doll; it was shown alone in a tied folder. The book *German Doll Studies* by Cieśliks tells of another little book by Agnes Lucas circa 1910 with the name of *Puppenschneiderei für Baby und Charakterpuppen* (doll dressmaking for baby and character dolls). The Children's Sewing Patterns chapter in this book has an additional Agnes Lucas pattern set translated into English, Dolly's Dress Patterns to Dolly's Wardrobe (plate 526).

In most of this book we will be focusing on sewing sets in the United States, however in the early 1900s Americans could buy few American-made sewing sets. Most toys, including dolls, were imported from Germany, Schnittmuster Baby Kleid and Armand Marseille Sewing Set (plates 2 and 5), and France, The Little Dressmaker, and French Doll with Sewing Machine (plates 3 and 4). These sets continued to be imported until the outbreak of World War I. During the war, imports were halted and the toy industry in the United States faced the challenge of filling the toy shelves of America. Our toy industry rose to this challenge and flourished. By the end of World War II, the United States toy industry had become the leader in its home market. Toy imports in the United States in 1914 had reached 50% of all toys that were sold in the United States. By 1939, we imported only 5%.

By the 1920s, young women were breaking free from the domestic role they had once played. Many were now working girls and used their wages to enjoy some of the things the 1920s had to offer. Ready-made clothing was easily attainable and sewing was no longer considered a necessity. The new housewife was enjoying all the new appliances on the market and household chores were becoming less of a burden. Little girls mimicked their mothers with miniature toy washing machines, toy refrigerators, toy gas stoves, and sewing sets, such as My Dolly's Work Box (plates 7 and 8).

Life seemed to be less of a chore; it was indeed the "Roaring Twenties." But alas, the good life was short lived. The stock market crash of October 1929 wiped out 40% of the paper value of common stocks. People lost great amounts of money and as the depression continued many banks failed, factories shut down, and businesses closed. One out of four Americans had lost their jobs by 1932. Close to 100 toy companies went out of business. Those that survived had to cut costs drastically, often using cheaper materials and imports from Japan to keep their prices down. By the 1930s, children's sewing sets had drastically changed. They were no longer the well-equipped and beautifully arranged sewing boxes that would teach children the fine art of sewing. They became toys.

Most of the sewing sets available in the 1930s were offered by American toy manufacturers. The new sets came in cardboard boxes with bright lithographed lids reflecting the period. The dolls were cheap all-bisque imports, predominantly Japanese.

Some sets still contained patterns, but most had very simple pre-cut dresses having only side seams to sew, such as Sewing Set (plate 10). The array of fine threads and packs of assorted needles of the past were replaced with heavy rayon floss and a large needle. Most of the sets had a thimble but instead of the fine little scissors of the earlier sets, the new sets had safety scissors with blunt flat medal blades that wouldn't cut fabric and couldn't even cut the thread without chewing it. These inexpensive sewing sets were still pretty to look at with their colorful lids and contents. Most sets had all the little dresses lined up along the sides with the doll in the middle. Many toy companies cut back on the contents but offered brighter oversized boxes, spreading the content over a large area. The new trend was to make toys easier to use, less tedious, and to offer instant gratification.

The new sets did little to really teach sewing and may have defeated the purpose with the thick threads, large needles, and scissors that didn't cut. The cheaper quality of these new sets didn't seem to bother either the children or adults. They sold well and by the 1930s had become a staple in the toy catalogs.

At this same time, new methods of communication were emerging. Almost every home now boasted a radio. Magazines and newspapers were delivered to people's doors and by 1926, there were "talkies" — movies with sound. The toy companies realized it was now possible to direct their advertising to the children and use celebrity children to promote their products.

The earliest licensed child celebrity sewing sets I have found thus far, are the sets Standard Solophone produced. These sets were the brainchild of Sol Luber, then president of Standard Solophone. In 1931 Mr. Luber accompanied his children to the film, *The Adventures of Tom Sawyer*, the first talkie version of Mark Twain's beloved story showing at the Paramount Theater in New York. Looking around, he realized that the audience was composed mainly of children and that these children were mesmerized by the film and the child stars that played the roles. He realized the child stars were the children's heroes and those stars would make perfect marketing agents for selling his toys. He left with the idea of printing child actors' pictures on his box tops, using them as spokesmen for his line of toys. Using children for advertising was not entirely new, in a 1928 *Playthings* article, Sol Luber had used his daughter Sydelle in a picture for Standard Solophone sewing sets. But using child celebrities was a revolutionary idea.

He contacted Paramount for permission to use the film child stars to endorse Standard Solophone's products. A deal was struck and child stars in *Tom Sawyer* like Jackie Coogan, Mitzi Green, and Junior Durken were licensed to sell his painting, sewing, and embroidery sets. Jean Darling, the little blonde bombshell of the famous Our Gang comedies, was also signed exclusively to pose for and endorse the Standard Solophone toys.

The Jean Darling sets were the most popular and lasted the longest. Jean's first sets, in the early 1930s, show a picture of her holding her sewing set on the box top of Jean Darling's Art Needlework Outfit #2D (plate 21). Late in 1935, after the company name changed from Standard Solophone Company to Standard Toykraft Products, Jean Darling's picture was replaced on the box top with a picture of a castle and renamed Jean Darling and Her Sewing Outfit (plates 22 through 29). Later yet, came the luggage-style boxes found in chapter 2. After *Our Gang*, Jean continued her career in show business, singing and dancing in vaudeville, traveling all over the United States, to make public appearances at children's hospitals and orphanages. The Jean Darling sets were produced for 18 years, from 1931 through 1949.

Five little celebrities were brought into the world on May 28, 1934, near Corbeil, Ontario, Canada. The Dionne Quintuplets were the world's first set of quintuplets to survive beyond a few days. The Dionnes were popular magazine and newspaper copy for years. Madame Alexander secured the exclusive rights to the Dionne Quintuplets name for dolls. Many other companies used just the name quintuplets. One such company was J. Pressman and Company, founded in 1922. Using at least three different box tops with two different type bisque dolls, Pressman marketed sets with the titles of Quintuplet Sewing Set Complete with Dolls and Dresses #1705 (plate 32) and Quintuplets Play & Sewing Outfit #1715 (plate 33). I have come across three different lithographed box tops for J. Pressman and Company, and one for American Toy Works, which used "quintuplets" in their sewing set titles.

Celebrities were not the only selling tools that toy manufacturers had at their fingertips. There were also comic strips. Little Orphan Annie, drawn by Harold Grey, began as a comic strip in 1924. Most newspapers quickly picked it up; all over America children read Annie. In December of 1930, *Adventure Time with Orphan Annie* was first aired on WGN radio in Chicago with 12 year old Shirley Bell as the voice of Annie. The program was soon picked up for network radio syndication on ABC. Annie, solving mysteries on her harrowing adventures,

Sewing and Embroidery Sets for Bisque Dolls

kept American children glued to the airwaves for 12 years. Sponsored by Ovaltine chocolate drink mix, Annie was the first radio serial to offer premiums successfully; most being Ovatine mugs and Annie's Secret Society decoder badges. In the late 1930s J. Pressman and Company came out with Little Orphan Annie sewing, knitting, and embroidery sets. J. Pressman & Company, along with Standard Solophone Company, were among the first toy companies to begin licensing. To date, I have seen seven different sets, all with different graphics. They are very hard to find and considered rare. Two are shown in this chapter — Little Orphan Annie Embroidery Set #1645 (plate 30) and Little Orphan Annie and Her Sewing Outfit #1680 (plate 31).

For the most part, all of the bisque doll sewing sets come from the first 30 years of the twentieth century. There are a few exceptions, one being Bisque Doll Joan Walsh Anglund (plate 35). Joan Walsh Anglund, born in 1926, became successful in 1958 with her first book, *A Friend Is Someone Who Likes You*. Both illustrator and author, she has been writing and drawing her round-faced, mouth-less children in books and on cards ever since. In 1958, the same year her first book was published, Determined Production manufactured their sewing set titled Bisque Doll Joan Walsh Anglund. It was designed around her character "Friend."

Today seems devoid of bisque doll sewing sets. Only occasionally will you find a modern doll artist that will offer a new bisque doll in a sewing set. For the most part, the bisque doll sewing sets ended in the 1930s to make way for the new, unbreakable composition dolls and their sewing sets.

Plate 1. Toilette de ma Poupée, ca. 1900 (My Doll's Attire), is a German-made sewing set for the French trade. The set is signed by Agnes Lucas and S. Barazetti and was published by Otto Maier of Ravensburg, Germany. The paper-lace-lined cardboard box measures 13" x 10½" x 4". Inside the box is a bisque-head Armand Marseille doll marked "Made in Germany///390n///A.4/0X.M." In the set are two books *Feuilles DEPatrons pour Toilette de ma Poupée* and *Toilette de ma Poupée*. The first is a book of patterns and the second tells the history of dolls and how to assemble the clothing cut from the patterns. There is also a small box titled "Outils pour coudre" (Sewing Implements) that contains metal scissors, a metal thimble, three wooden spools of thread, two tiny cards of pearl buttons, a package of needles, and a card of glass-head pins. The patterns included in the set are Feuille (sheet) I, dress, chemise, bonnet, and nightgown; Feuille drawers, half-slip, full slip, dress and jacket, socks and shoes; Feuille III, boy's sailor suit and a girl's gathered dress; Feuille IV, skirt with straps, pinafore, and full apron; Feuille V, dress with bonnet; Feuille VI, apron and dress; Feuille VII, short coat and bonnet; and Feuille VIII, baby dress, two bibs, and carrying pillow. **Complete: $1,000.00 and up.**

Note: See plates 522, 523, and 526 on pages 273 and 275 for more pattern sets made by Agnes Lucas.

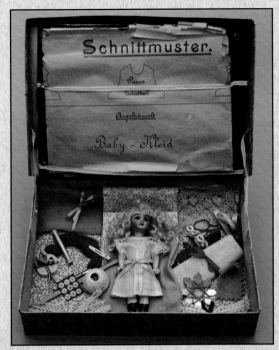

Plate 2. Schnittmuster Baby-Kleid translated from German to English is Baby Dress Pattern. The box measures 11½" x 8" x 2½". An allover tan mottled decorative paper covers this hard-sided sewing box. A small lithograph picture of two sweet children is applied in the center. It is circa 1910. Inside the cotton-tape-hinged lid is a paper pattern marked *Schnittmuster Baby – Kleid* containing 30 pieces. In the center of the set is a 6" bisque-head doll with a five-piece jointed composition body, black painted stockings, tan two-strap shoes, stationary blue glass eyes, open mouth with two teeth, and a mohair wig. She is marked with the sun type mark of "Gebrüder Kuhnlenz" with numbers "44 – 15" and is dressed in a gauze chemise trimmed with lace. Tied securely to the bottom of the box are numerous fabrics, laces, buttons, threads, and miniature sewing accoutrements including a wooden measuring stick, a bone ribbon threader, a tiny button hook, a metal needle holder, a tiny metal thimble, and tiny silver scissors marked "Germany." The lace on the doll's chemise is the same type of lace that is also tied into the box for trimming. **Complete: $1,000.00 and up.**

Plate 3. *The Little Dressmaker ///GE///B* is stenciled in gold on the lid of this plain black cardboard-boxed set. The interior is done in the French presentation manner, but has patterns printed in English. My guess is that it was made in France for the American market circa 1905. The box is 15" x 12" x 2½". Inside the center recess, surrounded by pink cloth flowers, is a 7" Simon and Halbig bisque-head doll, marked "S & H" on the back of her head. She is dressed in a white chemise and a large white mobcap hat. Both are trimmed in lace and red ribbons. She has blue sleep eyes, an open mouth with four teeth, a silk fiber wig pulled into two braids, and a five-piece composition body with painted two-strap orange shoes. Still attached to the lid is the original pattern sheet that reads, *Dressmaking pattern for dolls size 5½" – 6½".* In early doll clothes patterns only the body was measured, omitting the head. The pattern sheet has patterns for 12 articles of clothing. Securing the pattern to the lid are cloth flowers, hanks of lace, ribbon, metal and glass buttons, 5/9 needles, and a cloth tape measure. On the platforms on either side of the doll are eight lengths of fabric and pieces of lace, buttons, spools of thread, a wooden needle holder, a metal thimble, snaps, and a miniature drop spindle. The fabric and the doll are still tied in with the original red silk ribbons. **Complete: $1,000.00 and up.**

Sewing and Embroidery Sets for Bisque Dolls

Plate 4. French Doll with Sewing Machine. This varnished, wooden box, circa 1900, is 11" x 6½" x 3½". A picture of children sewing is secured on the inside lid of the box, as well as the outside. The children are using the same type of little machine as is contained in this set. Also secured on the inside lid is a 5½" bisque-head doll with a five-piece composition body, marked "SFBJ / 301 / Paris." She has stationary glass eyes, a mohair wig, open mouth with teeth and painted shoes and socks, and is jointed at neck, shoulders, and hips. The doll is dressed in her original pink voile dress and hat with tan lace trim. Fitted into the opposite side of the lid are three boxes, one of buttons, the other two smaller boxes depicting children, contain needles and pins. Printed in French on the boxes is: "Accourez, Joyeux dégourdis; Ecoutez mon expérience; Je vais vous causer, mes amis, De ce mot profond: Patience, LI faut être Patients; Toute chose vient en son temps." It advises the child that with patience they will succeed. Below the boxes are a card of pearl buttons and a small buttonhook. Nestled in the tray on the side of the sewing machine are four lengths of fabric tied with pink silk ribbon and three more cards of white pearl buttons in different sizes. Resting underneath the tray are two clamps to secure the sewing machine to a table and the manual for operating the machine, that reads "Jours sur taile Muller's Machine Kinder Nähmaschine DR. PAT #4157." **Complete: $1,000.00 and up.**

Note: I have seen this same box with the same graphics and sewing machine with a slightly smaller doll and different sewing fittings in the lid.

Plate 5. Armand Marseille Sewing Set, circa 1910, is housed in a paper-lace-trimmed, 10" x 9½" x 2¼", thin plain cardboard box. This set is untouched and is in excellent condition. The doll is 6¼" and is incised "Armand Marseille//390//A10/0M" on the back of her head. She has a mohair wig, glass stationary eyes, closed mouth, and painted multi-stroke eyebrows and lashes. Her composition five-piece jointed body has white socks and one-strap shoes painted on. On one side of the doll is her ready made dress trimmed with lace and silk ribbons, just below is her lace trimmed muslin underwear. On the other side of the box are four pieces of fabric rolled onto wooden dowels. Tied to the insert below are five miniature spools of thread, a tiny pair of scissors, a card of tiny buttons, and a straw hat trimmed with ribbons and silk flowers. The box is stamped "Made In Germany" on the bottom. **Excellent condition: $300.00 and up.**

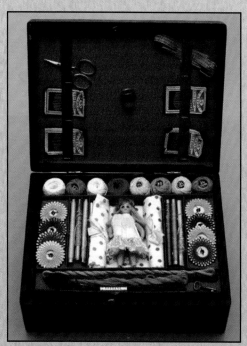

Plate 6. This **Bisque Doll Sewing Set**, circa 1910, is not marked. It is housed in a 9½" x 7" x 3½" leatherette-covered box and it still has its own little key. Opening it reveals a bright red interior. The lid is fitted with two leatherette straps that are holding four packs of 5/9 gold eye sharps, an oilcloth measuring tape, gold-plated scissors, and a thimble. The tray has seven compartments, one holds eight spools of cotton and two others hold five thread wheels each. In the center there is a 4" unmarked German, all-bisque doll. She has stationary glass eyes, mohair wig, five-piece jointed body strung with elastic, and painted two-strap shoes. She is tucked among three pieces of polka dot cotton fabric. On each side of her are long cardboard spools of thread and along the bottom are skeins of Perlene embroidery cotton. The tray lifts out for an ample area of storage. **Complete: $700.00 and up.**

Plate 7. This small circa 1920 faux snakeskin box measures 7½" x 3¾" x 1½" and has **My Dolly's Work Box** stamped in gold script across the top. It has a snap closure and is marked "Made in Germany" on the bottom. The 3¾" all-bisque doll is wire jointed at the shoulders with stationary legs. She has painted features and hair, blue boots, and green banded socks. There are numbers incised on her back, but they are so faint I can't make them out. On the inside lid of the box is a written Christmas tag: "To Marion from Sis B." In the center inside of the lid is a single tab that holds a packet of needles with the silhouette of a deer printed on the front. The bottom of the box has four compartments. Four wooden spools of thread line the back, with the doll and her homemade two-piece white cotton outfit resting in the front. The rest of the contents are four cardboard thread wheels, metal thimble, card of buttons, snaps, and a piece of pinked felt for the pins. **Complete: $100.00 and up.**

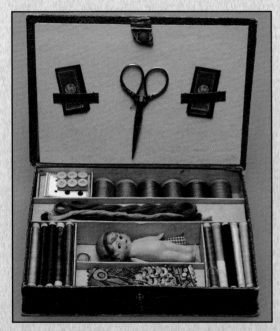

Plate 8. This larger **My Dolly's Work Box** is stamped in gold script on the top of this 8¼" x 5¾" x 1½" faux snakeskin pasteboard box with a snap closure. It is from circa 1920 and marked "Germany" on the bottom. The little 3½" doll, jointed at the shoulders only, is also marked "Germany." She has molded painted hair with a headband and painted features with side-glancing eyes. A simple little gingham dress is lying underneath her. The inside lid includes two needle packs with the silhouette of deer printed on the front and a pair of silver metal scissors. The interior is arranged with a number of sewing threads; there are six wooden spools, ten paper tubes, and three hanks, all in different colors. Accompanying the thread are cards of snaps and buttons, cotton felt-lined needle strip, and a metal thimble. **Complete: $100.00 and up.**

Plate 9. Bisque Baby Set. What a surprise to open up this un-adorned cardboard box to find an all-bisque baby set circa 1930 in a presentation box! It comes decorated with pinked color papers and white paper lace frame and the box measures 13½" x 9½" x 1". The only marking is a triangle with 14/0695 below it on the bottom of the box. The painted bisque baby measures 4", has painted features with an open mouth, and jointed arms and legs. Accompanying the baby is a layette stamped for embroidery. A bib, romper, and one dress also need to be cut out and assembled. The dress the baby is wearing, along with a pillow, a blanket, and a cape are already sewn and waiting only for the embroidery. A celluloid rattle and two hanks of embroidery cotton finish off this wonderfully presented set. **Complete: $100.00 and up.**

Sewing and Embroidery Sets for Bisque Dolls

Plate 10. Sewing Set, circa 1930, is marked "Made in U.S.A. American Toy Works." The box measures 20" x 9½" x 2". The graphics on this set look earlier than most of the others with this type of doll. Furthermore the graphics don't match the contents. The picture shows a boxed sewing set below the girls in the scene, and the contents show embroidery and spool-knitting. Indeed, that is what the girls in the picture are working on. But upon opening the box, we find a 5½" all-bisque doll with an array of dresses all neatly displayed with titles. The dolly has nicely painted features and a bow loop in her blonde painted hair. She is dressed in a manufactured pink rayon dress with a matching hair bow. The box was arranged with six cut out dresses that were ready to sew, the original owner has previously stitched three of them. Also included are two printed dresses, "Dolly's Party Dress" and "Dolly's Dress," to embroider cut out and sew. To complete the set is a wooden hoop, metal blunt-nose scissors, two hanks of cotton thread, a packet of sharps, and a tiny metal thimble. **Complete: $100.00 and up.**

Note: I am convinced this set has the correct contents, everything fits so perfectly in the box. Box graphics were sometimes used for more than one set within a company to save on cost. This leads me to conclude, that at an earlier date the box graphics were used for a needlework set, and then recycled later with above contents.

Plate 11. This box top is as busy as its namesake, **Fifth Avenue Dress Shop for Little Dolls #549**. Transogram Company manufactured it, circa 1930. The box is 13½" x 10½" x 2" Inside is a 5" Japanese-made painted all-bisque doll jointed at the shoulders and hips. She has a molded bow loop in her hair, painted features with very thick and long black lashes. The doll is dressed in a manufactured rayon dress, her original bow, and painted shoes and socks. On either side of her are thin fabric squares, six in all. The set also includes metal blunt-nose scissors, a metal thimble, needles, rayon rope floss, a cardboard hoop, and "Patterns for Dollies Clothes." The patterns include an apron with pockets, dress and collar, coat, collar and belt, playsuit with pocket, pajamas with belt, handkerchief, and handbag with instructions to sew garments on the doll with floss or thread. **Complete: $100.00 and up.**

Plate 12. Dolly Dressmaker #3520 is the name of this little Transogram Company set, a Gold Medal Sewing Outfit, circa 1930. The box is 9½" x 6½" x 1¼". Inside we find a 3½" painted, all-bisque doll jointed at the shoulders and hips. The Japanese-made doll has very poorly painted features and is dressed in a manufactured rayon dress. The contents in the box include a paper pattern for a coat, apron with pockets, and dress, four pieces of thin cotton fabric, metal blunt-nose scissors, metal thimble, needles, and a hank of sewing thread. The first owner of this set has already used the pattern to make the doll an apron, hood, and a dress using some of the same fabric as shown in the box. She also "enhanced" the box's graphics with crayon. **As shown: $75.00 and up.**

Note: The Gold Medal label was used often by Transogram Co. In 1915 the Friction Transfer Pattern Co. won a gold medal at the Panama Pacific Exposition. Later the company name was changed to Transogram, but they still proudly used the Gold Medal label on their box tops.

Plate 13. Moderne Sewing for Little Girls #417 is a product of American Toy Works, circa 1930s. The box measures 16" x 12" x 2" The little all-bisque doll in this set is 6" tall, has painted features, and a molded bow in the hair. She has movable arms, is marked "Made in Japan," and is dressed in a striped bathing suit. Below the doll is a small metal thimble, a wooden embroidery hoop, needle, and metal blunt-nose scissors. Flanking the doll on both sides is her clothing. One side contains three uncut outfits to embroider, cut out, and sew. On the other side are four cut-out ready-to-sew dresses in rather large prints. **Complete: $100.00 and up.**

Note: American Toy Works also used the above graphics on the box tops of a composition doll and paper doll sewing set.

Plate 14. What child wouldn't be thrilled with this **Doll House Dress Shop #555**, circa 1930. This set is an actual dollhouse, sewing set, dollhouse furniture, and doll all in one. The box measures 16" point to bottom, 14" across, and 2" deep. Transogram Company manufactured this Gold Medal Toy. The box top makes the front of the house; a tray with the doll and fabric lifts out, and the bottom of the box makes the back of the house. The two sides, a roof, and furniture are hidden under the tray. The furniture is cardboard, and everything, including the house, is assembled with paper fasteners. The furniture includes a fireplace, bookrack, occasional chair, wing chair, radio, davenport, davenport table, easy chair, and end table. In the point of the box are two cards of American-made pearl buttons, four wood spools of buttonhole twist, Elliptic large eye sharps, and a plastic thimble. The tray holds a 7" Japanese all-bisque doll with jointed arms and a molded hair ribbon. On the sides of the tray are six lengths of cotton fabric, a wooden hoop, paper fasteners, metal blunt-nose scissors, a metal clothes rack with wooden spool feet, and a wire hanger for dolly's clothes. Also included is a paper pattern for dolly's clothes. The pattern includes an apron with a pocket, pajamas, playsuit with straps and pocket, coat with collar and belt, handbag, and a dress. **Complete: $200.00 and up.**

Plate 15. Gold Medal Needlecraft #521, "The Smartest Sewing Outfit for the Modern Little Girl," was manufactured by Transogram Company, circa 1930. The box is 12¾" x 9½" x 2". The 5½" all-bisque doll with jointed arms, painted features, hair band, and sun suit is waiting to be dressed. All the clothing in this set is printed in three colors, green, yellow, and red. The clothing is labeled and includes a "Hooverette" scarf, pajamas, slippers, handkerchief, and six dresses. Also included in this set is a wooden embroidery hoop, silk floss, needles, metal blunt-nose scissors, thimble, and a booklet "My First Lesson in the Art of Embroidery." The booklet also tells us about Gold Medal Toys. The slogan "Playthings that serve a purpose" is doubly true, for not only do Gold Medal Toys keep the kiddies busy, happy, and amused, but they teach the child some useful art. The scissors in this set are much better quality than in most of the sets from the 1930s.
Complete: $100.00 and up.

Note: I have seen Gold Medal Needlecraft #521 with the same graphics and doll, but with printed fabric, stamped only with black outlines to cut out and sew. These same graphics are also on another sewing set manufactured by Transogram titled Dolly Debby and her Newest Clothes #527. It contains the same type 5½" all-bisque doll as above and printed clothing. The above Hooverette is a double-breasted dress named for Herbert Hoover during World War I when Hoover was food administrator.

Sewing and Embroidery Sets for Bisque Dolls

Plate 16. Measuring 14½" x 11" x 1¾" is the **Young Folks Fashion School for Sewing #301**, with cutout windows in the lid. American Toy Works manufactured this set circa 1930. Resting on the original tissue in the center of the box is a 5½" all-bisque doll with molded, painted features and hair. She is jointed at the arms and has a molded ribbon in her hair. The doll is wearing her original manufactured rayon dress and cape. Colorful arrays of precut dresses in large prints are shown along the sides along with a wooden hoop. In the top recess is heavy floss for sewing, a packet of needles, a thimble, and a pair of metal blunt-nose scissors. **Complete: $100.00 and up.**

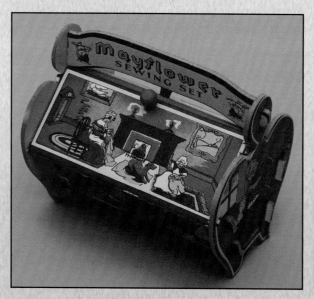

Plate 17. Mayflower Sewing Set #S50, circa 1930, was manufactured by Gropper Toys. The box measures 14" x 10" x 5". The little Japanese all-bisque doll with molded, painted features and hair and a painted-on sunsuit is 4½" tall and is jointed at the arms. She comes with her own little sewing box, which is a delight in itself. It is made of heavy paperboard with a handle and is covered with lithographed paper depicting people dressed in pilgrim costumes, going about their daily chores. It measures 6½" x 5½". Also contained in the set are two squares to embroider, a wood-grained cardboard hoop, pink and blue floss, metal blunt-nose scissors, a thimble, and brown thread on a spool. There are four squares of dress fabric. Also included is a printed paper pattern in an envelope labeled, "Complete Dress Patterns for Dolls." The pattern sheet includes a dress with belt, collar, and pocket; a hat with a tassel; a cape with a belt and pockets; a nightgown with a ribbon belt; and an apron with a pocket. **Complete: $100.00 and up.**

Note: This is the smaller of two Mayflower sets that I have found with the same graphics and all-bisque doll. See Mayflower Sewing Set #S100 (plate 18) and Mayflower Sewing Set #200 (plate 124) manufactured by Concord Toys for a set with a paper doll.

Plate 18. Mayflower Sewing Set #S100 is in a rather deep box, 15½" x 12½" x 4½". Gropper Toys manufactured this set circa 1930. Inside there is a tray with an assortment of fabric squares, a set of doll napkins, four net tapestries, and three hanks of wool yarn. Under the tray is a raised platform with embroidery and sewing thread, pearl cotton, sewing needles, metal blunt-nose scissors, plastic thimble, tapestry needles, directions for tapestry, and a colored embroidery piece on a cardboard hoop. But best of all are the two gems in recessed areas in the center of the box. The little flip-lid sewing box is made of thick pasteboard and decorated with people dressed in pilgrim costumes, going about their daily chores. The decorated handle shows the Mayflower and "Mayflower Sewing Set" written in script. In the compartment below it is a 7¾" all-bisque doll, with molded, painted features and jointed at the shoulders. She has a very colorful bathing suit painted on and a matching ribbon in her hair. She is marked "made in Japan." The sleeves on the wool yarn have the Gropper label, as does the little sewing box. This is a beautiful untouched set. **Complete: $200.00 and up.**

Note: See plate 17 for the little flip top paperboard sewing box inside.

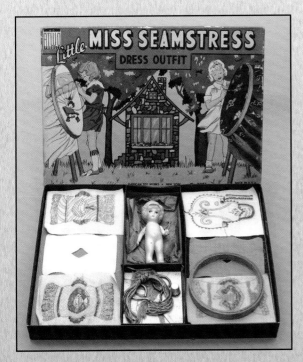

Plate 19. Little Miss Seamstress Dress Outfit #3061 was manufactured by American Toy Works. The box measures 13" x 9½" x 1½". This circa 1930s set contains a 4¼" all-bisque doll, jointed at the shoulders, with molded, painted features and a pink band in her hair. There are six pre-cut garments to sew; two are plain cotton dresses and four are three-color, preprinted outfits that are marked, "Dolly's Sweater Outfit," "Dolly's Apron," "Dolly's Dress," "Dolly's Party Dress." In the center recess above Dolly are metal blunt-nose scissors, a hank of threads, and a metal thimble. A wood-grained cardboard embroidery hoop completes the set. **Complete: $100.00 and up.**

Note: I have also seen this same size set (#3061) with the same graphics and doll but with eight dresses all pre-cut floral (no preprinted) outfits and yet another set (#3063) with a little larger box and a 6½" all-bisque doll. Also see Little Miss Seamstress Dress Outfit #3063 (plate 51) in chapter 2 for a set with the same name and graphics but with a composition doll.

Plate 20. Dollies Dress Shoppe #533 was manufactured by Transogram Company, circa 1930s. The box is 14½" x 12½" x 2½". The box top graphics are the same as set #3548 with the same name, except this set has all the windows and doors cut out and cellophane covers the contents. This set is more challenging as all the clothing needs to be cut out and most outfits have separate pieces to sew together. The box has seven sections. The first section holds a pair of metal blunt-nose scissors, a pink plastic thimble, American-made pearl buttons, and Peerless Elliptic large eye sharps. The second section has a red and blue stamped dress in a wooden hoop to embroider. Next to that is Premier rayon embroidery-rope, a dozen wood clothespins, and pink clothesline. The all-bisque doll rests in the center, she is 7½" tall with molded, painted hair, features, and a hair-bow loop. She is jointed at the shoulders and hips with painted shoes and socks. The doll was made in Japan, and wears a manufactured dress. She is chubbier than the doll in Dollies Dress Shoppe #3548. On either side of the doll is her clothing. On one side is material, stamped with black outlines to cut out, that includes an apron with pockets and straps and a Hooverette to be embroidered on the front. The other side has red and blue preprinted clothing to cut out and assemble, including a coat, pajamas with a belt and hanky, a bonnet, coat collar, and handbag. All pieces are marked with instructions. Also in the set is a booklet "My First Lesson in the Art of Embroidery." **Complete: $100.00 and up.**

Note: See Dollies Dress Shoppe #3548 (plate 34) on page 26 for a different version of this all-bisque doll set.

Plate 21. The first Jean Darling sewing sets had not just her name, but also her picture on them. Standard Solophone Company copyrighted **Jean Darling's Art Needlework Outfit #2D** in 1931. A large box, measuring 18" x 13½" x 2½", contains a 7" all-bisque Japanese-made doll with a molded bow loop in her hair, molded, painted features, and shoes and socks. She is jointed at the shoulders and hips and is wearing her manufactured rayon dress. In the recessed area beside her is a pair of metal blunt-nose scissors and a metal thimble. Below her are embroidery floss, sewing thread, cardboard hoop, and sewing needles. She has a large wardrobe waiting to be sewn consisting of ten outfits. On one side are four stamped dresses and a romper to embroidery, cut out, and sew. The other side has five outfits preprinted in three colors of red, green, and yellow to cut out and sew. Two nightgowns and two rompers are marked "Jean Darling" in the neck selvage. **Complete: $200.00 and up.**

Note: There were also Jean Darling Embroidery sets using these same graphics and title, but in a smaller box and offering only napkin and embroidery squares. See Jean Darling & Her Embroidery Outfit #200-10 plate 268.

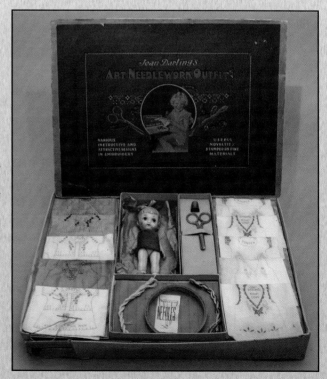

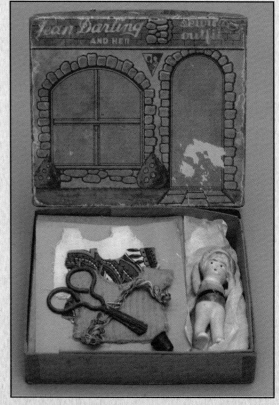

Plate 22. Jean Darling and Her Sewing Outfit #100-10 was manufactured by Standard Toycraft Products, Inc., circa 1934. The small box measures 7" x 6" x 1¼". Inside is a recess with a 3½" all-bisque, Japananese-made doll with molded, painted features, a painted bathing suit, and jointed arms. On the insert next to her are three pre-cut dresses. Included in the set are metal blunt-nose scissors, a small metal thimble, and a twist of sewing thread. **Complete: $50.00 and up.**

Note: The original price for this little set was ten cents.

Plate 23. Jean Darling and Her Sewing Outfit #100-25 was manufactured by Standard Toykraft Products, Inc. and copyrighted in 1934. The cellophane-windowed box is 12¾" x 8½" x 1½". Inside in the center recess is a 4½" all-bisque Japanese-made doll with molded, painted features and hair and a painted bathing suit and hair band. The seven outfits are lined up on either side of her and are all preprinted in three colors, red, yellow, and green. The labeled outfits include two sets of pajamas, two party dresses, afternoon dress, novel dress, and frock. Also included in the set are a pair of metal blunt-nose scissors, a metal thimble, needle. and three skeins of Gold Medal embroidery floss. **Complete: $100.00 and up.**

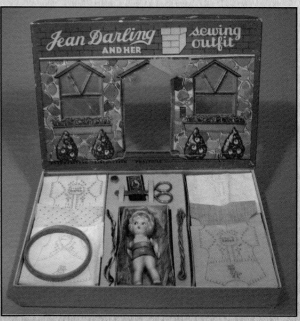

Plate 24. Jean Darling and Her Sewing Outfit #100-50 was copyrighted in 1934 by Standard Toykraft Products, Inc. The cellophane-windowed box measures 16" x 10½" x 1½". The all-bisque Japanese-made doll inside is 5½" tall with jointed arms. The doll has molded, painted features and hair and a painted bathing suit. Above the doll are metal blunt-nose scissors, a package of Standard Highgrade needles, and a metal thimble. The side inserts hold two skeins of thread, four printed outfits to cut, embroider, and sew, and two pre-cut dresses to be stitched up the sides. **Complete: $100.00 and up.**

Sewing and Embroidery Sets for Bisque Dolls

Plate 25. Standard Toycraft Products, Inc. copyrighted **Jean Darling Sewing Outfit #110** in 1936. This box top with a printed castle measures 8½" x 5¾" x 1½". Inside in the center recess is a 4¼" Japanese all-bisque doll with molded, painted features and hair with a bow. She has a painted bathing suit and jointed arms. The platforms at her sides hold four pre-cut print dresses in two styles. Included in the set are two hanks of floss, a needle, metal blunt-nose scissors, and a thimble. **Complete: $75.00 and up.**

Plate 26. Jean Darling Sewing Outfit #135 was manufactured by Standard Toycraft Products, Inc., circa 1936. The windowed box measures 13½" x 9¼" x 2". Inside in the recess is a 5½" Japanese all-bisque doll with molded, painted features, hair, and hair bow. She is dressed in a ribbon dress and has jointed arms. Above her in the insert are two wooden flowerpots with silk flowers. On the sides of the box are seven pre-cut dresses and two ropes of thread. To complete this outfit are metal blunt-nose scissors, a packet of needles, and a metal thimble. **Complete: $100.00 and up.**

Note: The box in this image is quite damaged, however since it was different, I chose to include it.

Plate 27. Jean Darling Sewing Outfit #150 was copyrighted in 1936 by Standard Toycraft Products, Inc. The box measures 16" x 10½" x 1¾". The doll in this set is incised "Nippon," and is very well painted with molded features, hair, and hair bow. She is 5½" including her bow and has jointed arms. There are four pre-cut dresses on one side of the box, three have been finished, one is unfinished. On the other side are another three dresses to be embroidered and cut out. To complete this set, are three spools of thread, two twists of floss, a package of needles, blunt-nose metal scissors, and a metal thimble. **As shown: $100.00 and up.**

Plate 28. The Jean Darling Sewing Outfit #150 has a box that measures 16" x 10½" x 2" and was copyrighted in 1936 by Standard Toykraft Products, Inc. There were many sets using Jean Darling's name manufactured by Standard Toykraft Products Inc., but this is the only set that I have found that had a doll that actually resembled the child star of Our Gang films. The little painted all-bisque Japanese-made doll is 5½" tall, with molded curly blond hair and a puckered mouth. She is jointed at the shoulders and hips, has molded, painted features, painted shoes and socks, and a manufactured pink rayon dress. The box contains six dresses, cut in three different shapes to stitch, three cardboard spools of thread, metal blunt-nose scissors, a metal thimble and a package of needles. The doll is in a center recess with a rope of cotton sewing thread on each side and three wooden pots of fabric flowers in recesses over her head. The flowerpots are a mystery. When Jean Darling was asked, "Why the flowerpots?" She had no idea she only remembered the rainy day in New York, when she was asked to pose with Sol Luber (president of Standard Solophone Co.) and one of her sets for a press release. The first sets in the early 1930s have a photograph on the cover of Jean working with her sewing set. **Complete: $200.00 and up.**

Note: Jean Darling Sewing Outfit #150 with the same graphics slightly altered is also found with a painted all-bisque doll that looks very much like Wee Patsy (plate 29). Were the popular dolls of the 1930s being copied and the above doll not a Jean Darling, but instead a Shirley Temple look-alike? These are questions that might never be answered.

Plate 29. Jean Darling Sewing Outfit #150 windowed box measures 16" x 10½" x 2". It is dated 1936 and was manufactured by the Standard Toykraft Products, Inc. The doll in this set looks remarkably like an EF-FanBEE Wee Patsy. She is a 6" tall painted, all-bisque doll, with molded, painted features and jointed at the shoulders and hips. She is wearing a manufactured pink rayon dress and has painted shoes and socks. The doll is stamped "Japan" on her foot and incised "Made in Japan" on her back. The set's center insert contains three wooden flowerpots, each with a silk flower and two leaves, the doll rests below in a recess. There are two twists of thread on each side of the doll. The remainder of the set includes six pre-cut dresses, three cardboard spools of thread, a needle pack, blunt-nosed metal scissors, and a tiny thimble. **Complete: $200.00 and up.**

Plate 30. Little Orphan Annie Embroidery Set #1645 graphics show Annie doing her embroidery with her doll at her feet. J. Pressman and Company is the maker of this circa 1935 set. The box is 13" x 14" x 1¾". Inside we find a 5½" all-bisque doll, jointed at the arms with painted features and a molded blue bow in her hair. She has a pink ribbon gathered around for a dress. There are also four preprinted dresses and a romper to sew. They are printed in yellow, pink, and blue, and all marked at the edges "JP & Co." Also included is a 5" cloth doll of Little Orphan Annie to sew that is signed "Pressman NYC, Copyright Harold Gray." The previous owner has stitched together one dress and the romper. The remainder of the contents includes a pair of metal blunt-nose scissors, Standard Highgrade sharps, four skeins of silk floss, a cardboard hoop, and a thimble. **As shown: $300.00 and up.**

Note: See Little Princess Embroidery Set #21 (plate 180) for a cloth doll sewing set.

Plate 31. J Pressman and Company, Inc. manufactured **Little Orphan Annie and Her Sewing Outfit #1680**, circa 1935. The box measures 16" x 10" x 2". The box lid has cutout cellophane-covered windows and a colorful lithograph of Little Orphan Annie signed by Harold Gray. There is a preprinted Little Orphan Annie doll to cut out, sew, and stuff. "J. Pressman" is printed on the selvage. There is also a 4¾" all-bisque Japanese-made doll jointed at the shoulders, with molded, painted blonde hair and blue hair bow. The doll looks nothing like Annie, but is original, as the same doll is repeated in other Annie sets I have seen. The set also contains metal blunt-nose scissors, a metal thimble, Dix & Rands high-grade sharps, four skeins of Royal Society Perle cotton, and a cardboard hoop. The clothing consists of three dresses and a romper all preprinted in pink, blue, and yellow and printed on the selvage is "JP & Co." **Complete: $300.00 and up.**

Note: See Little Princess Embroidery Set #21 (plate 180) for a cloth doll sewing set.

Plate 32. Quintuplet Sewing Set Complete with Dolls and Dresses #1705. The box is 14" x 9½" x 1", manufactured by J. Pressman and Company, circa 1936. This totally untouched quintuplet set contains five little 3⅝" all-bisque dolls jointed at the arms, each with molded, painted hair and features, green or blue sunsuits, and red or blue bands in their hair. The dolls are marked "Made in Japan" on their backs. Arranged above them are five pre-cut dresses, a pair of blunt-nose medal scissors, boil-proof floss, and a needle. This set #1705 seems to be the most elusive of all the Quintuplet sets. **Complete: $200.00 and up.**

Plate 33. Quintuplets Play Set & Sewing Outfit #1715. The graphics on this brightly colored circa 1936 cardboard-boxed set closely resemble the Dionne Quintuplets. J. Pressman and Company in New York manufactured it. The box measures 18½" x 13¾" x 1¼". There are five 6½" all-bisque dolls dressed in pink and blue play suits, each with a blue bow in her hair. They are marked "made in Japan," have molded painted features and hair, and are jointed at the shoulders only. There are ten dresses pre-cut to be sewn; four are made up in this gently used set. The set also contains metal blunt-nose scissors, a packet of needles, and assorted sewing floss. **As seen: $300.00 and up.**

Plate 34. Dollies Dress Shoppe #3548 was manufactured by the Transo-gram Company in 1937. The box is 16" x 12" x 2". The brightly colored lid shows three little girls sewing and a larger-than-life mannequin standing in the doorway. The inside of the set is done in blue with black decorations. The set contains an all-bisque doll with molded hair and hair bow. She is 6", jointed at the shoulders, has painted features, and one-strap shoes, and is marked "Made in Japan." This lucky little doll has a manufactured dress 16 dresses pre-cut to be made just for her. The set also has 12 Gold Medal Magic Transfer Patterns to make your own dresses by rubbing the transfers onto cloth with the wood paddle and cutting them out on the transfer lines. The set also contains assorted colored thread, metal blunt-nose scissors, a thimble, two needles, and instructions. **Complete: $100.00 and up.**

Note: See Dollies Dress Shoppe #533 (plate 20) for a different version of this all-bisque doll set.

Plate 35. Joan Walsh Anglund offered this **Bisque Doll Joan Walsh Anglund** sewing set in 1958. The 7½" x 4¾" x 2" armoire opens to reveal Joan Walsh Anglund's love-able little character, Friend an all-bisque 3½" doll. The doll has molded hair and features, jointed arms and legs, painted underwear, and is stamped on the back "Joan Walsh Anglund." The set is manufactured by Determined Production. Also included are scissors, a square of red gingham, small piece of tan fabric, two buttons, two snaps, plastic thimble, plastic tape measure, pin cushion with pins, a hank of red ribbon, lace, a cardboard thread spool, and a dress and apron pattern with instructions. **Complete: $100.00 and up.**

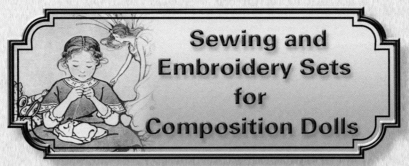

Sewing and Embroidery Sets for Composition Dolls

It's hard to say just when composition dolls were first made, as there is but a fine line between paper maché and composition. In America, composition came on the market around the beginning of the twentieth century. E. I. Horsman Company made one of the first American composition dolls, Billiken, in 1909. Billiken had a composition head and a cloth body. It was part doll and part teddy bear. Billiken's "only job in life was to make you smile."

Doll manufacturers all tried to create the ultimate composition doll, using sawdust, glue, flour, and whatever their secret ingredient happened to be. By 1910, composition heads on cloth bodies and all-composition dolls were advertised in magazines and periodicals as the new "Unbreakable Dolls." The larger toy companies, such as Ideal Toy and Novelty Corporation, EffanBee Doll Corporation, American Character Doll Company, and Madame Alexander Doll Company not only manufactured, but clearly marked, their composition dolls, sometimes both the doll and clothing alike. In 1910 E. I. Horsman Company introduced the Campbell Kids with composition heads and cloth bodies. Many smaller toy companies jumped on the bandwagon and produced composition dolls, but never marked them. For the most part, the unmarked dolls were generally a cheaper made doll. By the 1930s, the more fragile bisque dolls were losing the battle and more and more American composition dolls were showing up on the toy shelves.

The middle 1930s was the golden age of American composition dolls. The composition doll had all but taken over the market. They were cheap to make and a bright spot in the slow economy. Many composition dolls portrayed celebrities and movie stars. Shirley Temple, Deanna Durbin, Baby Sandy, Princess Elizabeth, and the Dionne Quintuplets all graced the shelves of department stores along with cheaper unmarked dolls.

As in the past, parents were still the audience for toy companies advertising, most of the toy advertising was found in adult-oriented magazines such as, *Ladies' Home Journal*, *Saturday Evening Post*, and *Parents Magazine*. Even when advertising was aimed at the children, the ads were careful to make the parent a part of the picture. Mom or Dad were often in the background, sometimes in the foreground, sharing the joy the selected toy might bring. The preferred toys remained traditional: American-made baby dolls, farm toys, trucks, paint sets, and sewing sets.

Standard Toykraft Products was still successfully selling their Jean Darling sewing outfits and by 1936 they had changed their dolls from bisque to composition, but retained the castle printed box top. However there were no more window box tops, color printed dresses to cut out, or even stamped dresses to be embroidered. The new sets still had the metal blunt-nose scissors and metal thimbles, but all the clothing was now pre-cut, all ready for the child to sew, as in the bisque Jean Darling Sewing Outfit #150 (plate 29). However, a new paper pattern had been added to Jean Darling Sewing Outfit #1100 (plate 39). The set also contained seven pre-cut dresses. There were two pieces of fabric and the paper pattern with a dress, coat, bib shorts, and hat. The instructions in the pattern sheet read:

In this sewing set you have a very attractive 'glamour' doll and the dresses, patterns, and materials to dress her as a 'glamour' doll should be dressed. Some of the dresses in your sewing set are all ready cut out ready to sew. And for more sewing fun you can make a complete wardrobe and outfit your doll. By following the patterns, you will be able to make a dress, coat, hat, and handbag for 'special occasions,' such as parties and holidays. There is also a pattern for making your doll a pair of shorts for romping around the house and everyday wear.

First decide what garment you wish to clothe your doll in. Suppose you choose shorts. Take a piece of tissue paper and with a pencil, trace over the heavy lines in the pattern marked 'shorts' and 'bib top for shorts.' Cut out the tracing along the heavy lines and pin the tracing on to the material included in the set. Cut the material by following the outlines of the tracing paper. Now, sew the cut out shorts along the dotted line (as shown in the pattern), sew on the reverse side of the material. Trim the excess material after sewing and turn the shorts right side out. Sew the 'bib top' onto the shorts.

The same procedure should be followed when making all of the doll's clothes. A small hem should be sewn on the bottom of the dress, around the dress collar, and around the bottom of the coat.

The hat is an open crown 'glamour' hat, and if you wish, a small hem can be sewn around the edge also, in that case, cut the pattern a bit oversized.

A pretty pouch bag can easily be made by following the pattern and directions written on the pattern.

Wasn't it easy? Wasn't it fun? You can make many more ensembles of matching materials, or contrasting materials. There may be some extra material pieces around the house, but ask for permission before using them — won't you?

This is the only Jean Darling Sewing Set I have found with a pattern. I have always felt children's sewing sets with patterns were the best, not only did they teach a child how to work with a pattern, they allowed the child to progress beyond what was in the set. With a pattern she could make a whole wardrobe for her doll and try different fabrics and trims.

Sewing and Embroidery Sets for Composition Dolls

One of the nicest composition doll sets had a larger doll than most — Dolly Dear Sewing Kit #5321 (plate 40) by Transogram Company. The kit has an 8½" unmarked composition doll, jointed at the shoulders and hips. The pattern in this set has six outfits, and each is illustrated as to how it is made. There is ample fabric to make each outfit, thread to match, and even buttons. The child that received this set must have been delighted. She very carefully traced around the edges of the patterns onto wax paper and cut out the wax paper pattern to make up the overall outfit. She didn't use any of the materials in the set, but left them all in place.

Little girls that were happily sewing with their composition doll sewing sets as the decade of the 1930s came to an end were blissfully unaware of the turmoil that was about to come. World War II actually started September 1, 1939, but it was in 1941 that it became real to the people of the United States. In a famous radio broadcast on December 8; President Franklin D. Roosevelt told the United States:

Yesterday, December 7, 1941 — a date that will live in infamy — the United States of America was suddenly and deliberately attacked by naval and air forces of the Empire of Japan.

The 1940s are pretty much defined by World War II. The war in some ways put the toy industry on hold. In *Playthings* magazine, articles began to appear on government restrictions. The National Defense Program started to have an effect upon the toy industry. There were delays in securing materials, and sometimes there was even difficulty in acquiring labor. In an October 1943, *Playthings* magazine John M. Cloud wrote "Toy Makers Up in the Front Line-With American Industry." He wrote:

From tools for youth to tools for war is the transition that has taken place in many toy factories. Manufacturers, who normally produce a varied list of playthings designed to entertain, educate, and aid in the normal development of children, now produce an equally varied list of war materials as their contribution to the effort to sustain the American way of life. It is estimated that toy manufacturers are producing as many as 5,000 different war items. The little boys who not so long ago played with their trains, rode on their wheel toys, and built new worlds from blocks and construction sets are the young men today who fight with equipment from the factories that once made their toys in order that another generation of children may be free to play and grow unhampered by the shackles of dictatorship.

There were many full-page ads taken out in *Playthings Magazine* from toy manufacturers stating that they were using their toy manufacturing plants for war purposes. Another problem in the industry was the manpower it took to run the factories. As the men went off to war, the women stepped in and filled the jobs when they could, but they were also needed to work in the manufacturing plants that were supplying war materials. For these reasons there were many cutbacks in the toy industry.

Written up in a 1942 Montgomery Ward Christmas Catalog were three composition-doll sewing sets. They were marked "Good, Better, and Best." Two of the three sets are shown in this chapter. The sets were advertised as:

Good — *Doll's Sewing Set in Case. 6¼", composition doll, movable arms. Set includes 4 cut dresses, 4 pcs. material, 4 dress patterns, play scissors (cut fairly well), lace, ribbon, buttons, needles, thread, thimble. In Metal case, removable tray. Ship. Wt.13 oz. 48 T 984-21-pc. Sewing Set..............98c.*

See Fair Tin (plate 44).

Better — *Doll's Sewing Set. Made by Effanbee. 5¾", composition doll, movable arms, painted features. Wears panties, shoes, socks, painted on. Includes materials and trimming for making slip, bathrobe, dress and coat. All materials cut out ready to sew and trim. In hinged cardboard box. Ship. wt. 13 oz. 48 T 982-Better Quality Sewing Set...$1.10.*

See Dolly's Dressmaker Set (plate 45).

Best — *Doll's Sewing Set. Made by Effanbee. Much better material than sets above. 9½". composition doll; movable head, arms, legs. Wears panties, housecoat, slippers. Complete Nurse's uniform, cut and ready to sew. Buttons, needles, thread, thimble, measuring stick, shoes, stockings. In hinged box. 48 T 983-Best Set. Ship. wt. 1 lb. 12oz....$2.39*

All the pieces in each set were out of the boxes and shown in the illustrations. The good set had all the items in the set listed in its write-up, however the better and best sets didn't. In the better set, the measuring stick, needles, and thread were forgotten. The write up for the best set eliminated a dress, matching panties, and a cape and hood. The doll offered in the best set looked a lot like an Effanbee Patsy, however it was not a Patsy. It was very similar, but unlike Patsy, had just a bit of curl in her hair at the ears. The 6¼" unmarked doll in the good set was used by most of the toy companies in their sewing sets through the 1940s. Kaye Novelty Company, manufacturers of Kanco Products, ran a full-page ad in the 1940s showing this unmarked doll as the #19 doll for a retail price of 19c. Unmarked, #19 doll was a cheaply made doll and many times the seams were rough and unfinished. The dolls were dipped in paint and sometimes there were drips still attached to an arm or shoe, and some arms didn't get completely covered in the paint at the top. The painted features were not always on the mark and some had hair color spray painted only in the back. The molds for the dolls were used so many times that even though the doll was supposed to have molded shoes and socks, on some dolls they are barely visible.

During the war there was a demand for war toys, especially for little boys, who played with soldiers, tanks, planes, and battleships. Little girls had war nurse sets and even a war sewing set. Junior Waacs Sewing Set #136 (plate 46) was made by New York Toy and Game Company, circa 1942. The set was printed with a tan and dark blue military theme. The content of the box is very sparse with just enough materials to make one WAAC military uniform for the doll. There is also a little booklet, *Facts About the Waacs*, which gives a little history:

On May 14, 1942, President Roosevelt created the W. A. A. C. Its members have the very important task of replacing men in the Army who do non-combatant work, and in that way release our soldiers needed urgently on the far-flung fighting fronts.

The W. A. A. C. is rapidly growing from its first few hundred women to the 150 thousand authorized by the President's original order. W. A. A. C. units composed of 50 or more members serve the Army at home or abroad.

To join, a woman must be a U. S. citizen between the ages of 21 and 44, and have good character. She must pass mental alertness and physical tests before being accepted. A married woman can join too, if she doesn't have any children under 14.

Once a woman has become an Auxiliary (that's like an Army Private) she will be given basic training that lasts four weeks. At the end of that time a test is given so that her officers can learn what kind of work she is best fitted for. Based on these tests a member may be assigned to one of many classes of duty. The W. A. A. C. may learn to be a baker, clerk, lab-assistant, mechanic, radio operator, weather observer, truck driver, just to mention a few. Or, if she is capable, she may be sent to school for eight weeks more and at the completion of that course become an officer herself.

The term of service in the W. A. A. C. is for the duration of the war plus a period of not more than 6 months thereafter. The range of pay starts at $50 a month paid to an Auxiliary, but if she becomes a 3rd Officer in 8 weeks, she will receive $150 a month.

WAACS live in comfortable and attractive quarters, especially planned for women. Each of the W. A. A. C. barracks has a pleasant, well-furnished day room where they may enjoy games and music when off duty. Appetizing, well-balanced meals are prepared by women cooks trained in the W. A. A. C. When meals are not furnished, a cash allowance is paid.

Medical and dental services, hospitalization, medicines, and other health services are provided at Government expense for all members of the W. A. A. C.

Members of the Women's Army Auxiliary Corps wear distinctive uniforms, with insignia and accessories, all supplied by the Government. These include summer and winter uniforms, and special clothing for athletics, mechanical work, bakers and cooks, and other duties.

The fact that this sewing set was for Junior W.A.A.C. and not W.A.C. helps to date the set. May 1941, Congress authorized the W.A.A.C. and President Roosevelt created the W.A.A.C. a year later in May of 1942. Just a year later in July 1943, the Women's Army Corps "W.A.C." was formed as part of the United States Army, and absorbed the W.A.A.C. That means this set was made sometime between these dates. I have only seen this set twice, could it be because of the name change to W.A.C.?

In *Playthings* magazine, New York Toy and Game Company, the maker of Junior W.A.A.C.s Sewing Set, is listed as making sewing and embroidery sets from 1940 until 1953.

In October of 1978, the Army disestablished W.A.C. as a separate corps of the Army. Women are still in the Army, but are no longer segregated or identified as W.A.C., they are now known only by their rank. This sewing set will always be a part of history, reminding us of World War II and the first proud women who served beside their men.

Jean Darling sets made by Standard Toykrafts Products, were some of the few children's sewing sets that were dated. I have found sets dated 1936, such as Jean Darling Sewing Outfit #150 (plate 38) and Jean Darling Sewing Outfit #1100 (plate 39), but did not find any new sets during the war years. After 1936, the next sets are dated 1949. One of the 1949 sets, Jean Darling Doll Sewing Kit #1100 (plate 60), had a message from Jean on the inside of the lid, telling how to sew the dresses for her composition doll included in the kit. It shows Jean as a little girl sitting at a table and sewing for her doll. I thought this was quite interesting because five years earlier, during the war, Jean was not sewing, Jean was all grown-up and doing her part for our soldiers. Jean Darling took a 21 week tour to perform for our troops. A letter written to Jean Darling in 1944:

Headquarters Services of Supply
North African Theater of Operations
United States Army
Special Service Section
Army Post Office 750
September 13, 1944

Dear Miss Darling:
I wish to take this opportunity to thank you for the splendid work you have done as a member of USO-Camp shows Unit No. 209. During your tour of the North African Theater of Operations, you appeared before thousands of American and Allied troops, both in rear areas and in the actual combat zone.

Records at this headquarters indicate that you have played to over 139,500 troups in the 140 performances you gave during your 21-week tour of NATOUSA. This is a record of which you may well be proud.

I know I express the gratitude and appreciation of all the thousands of Allied officers and enlisted men who attended your concerts.

Sincerely yours,
Leon T. David.
Colonel, F. A.,
Special Service Officer.

(Printed with the permission of Jean Darling.)

Another larger Jean Darling Doll Sewing Kit (plate 61) with the same 1949 date, doll, and clothing, but with added embroidery items, included a pamphlet, How to Embroider with The History of Embroidery. The pamphlet stated:

Embroidery is the oldest form of handicraft in the world. Almost 4,000 years ago the Egyptians were practicing this fascinating art. Embroidery at one time was considered as essential to a lady's education as reading or writing. In Grandmother's day every little girl embroidered. Girls still love to embroider and these Princess Sets are a real joy with their simple designs printed on materials which can be used and enjoyed.

Notice the Princess Sets mentioned in the above quote?

Sewing and Embroidery Sets for Composition Dolls

This pamphlet was used in Standard Toykraft Products' earlier Princess embroidery sets, as were the layout of the embroidery and the red panel that held the sewing supplies. It was quite common to see pamphlets and patterns and inserts from one company going from set to set through the years without changing.

The Jean Darling sewing set graphics changed after the war. The castle box tops, which had many changes to coloring, size, and windows through the years, were discontinued. The new box top echoed the new popular theme of the luggage-style sewing cases. In the late 1940s, it seems, there were many luggage-type sewing sets with travel stickers printed on the boxes.

The Little Traveler's Sewing Kits, manufactured by Transogram Company, were some of the more popular luggage-type sewing sets. Little Traveler's Sewing Kits span three chapters of this book, from composition to plastic to paper dolls. When trying to accurately date Little Traveler's sets, always look for the set number on the inside insert. The outside graphics and information usually were used longer than the inserts. The doll that was most used in the composition sewing sets resembles the doll in Little Ladies' Sewing Kit #260 (plate 59), the #19 doll from Kaye Novelty as mentioned earlier in this chapter. Dolls were just one of the items that seemed to be universal in many of the sets, the metal blunt-nose scissors all seem the same, pre-cut dresses, and even the layouts of some sets. Even though Miss Deb Sewing Kit #2206 (plate 53) by Pressman Toy

Corporation and Little Traveler's Sewing Kit #1579 (plate 62) by Transogram Company were by two different companies, the insides held the same doll, same felt hats, and same scissors. When collecting these sets you will find a lot of the same material used over and over again. It is refreshing to find unusual sets such as the Doll and Sewing Machine (plate 36). This is the only composition doll I have seen presented with a sewing machine in the set. I have also never seen this doll in another sewing set. The clothing is typical but in a scale for the larger doll. Another unusual set is Sewing Set (plate 37). Even though the set itself is very typical with pre-cut clothing and blunt-nose scissors, the doll is not typical. It is very unusual to find a bent-limb baby doll presented in a composition doll sewing set.

The composition doll sewing sets lasted only about 10 years, a short time frame for doll sewing sets. Lucky for us, the dolls were, for the most part, cheaply made and were not heavily painted. Most remain in fairly good condition with little cracking of paint or composition. Many composition doll sets were made during the war years when materials were scarce and, for the first time, American dolls were used instead of French, German, or Japanese. Even though the composition doll sewing sets only lasted a decade, these little girl toys are part of our history, the last era when sewing was still thought of as an important part of a girl's education. The composition doll sets would fade away, to be replaced by the new plastic doll sewing sets of the 1950s.

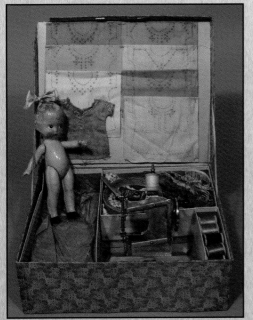

Plate 36. Doll and Sewing Machine gives not a clue to its maker — not on the box, doll, clothing, or the machine. The box measures 12½" x 10" x 4". The composition doll measures 8" up to her molded loop topknot, she is jointed at the shoulders and hips, and has molded, painted features, hair, and shoes. The socks are molded, but unpainted. There is a molded loop at the top of her head for a ribbon bow. Still attached to the lid are seven untouched stamped dresses and one that has been started; this one is all done except for the hem. There are four different cross-stitch patterns to embroider on the dresses. In the bottom of the box is a little 6½" x 6" polished metal sewing machine. At the side are five wooden spools of J & P Coats thread. Above the machine are sewing supplies, including an oilcloth tape measure, metal blunt-nose scissors, Peerless Elliptic large eye sharps, four hanks of embroidery rope, a felt apple needle holder, and a cardboard embroidery hoop. **Complete: $300.00 and up.**

Plate 37. Sewing Set is in a 14" x 9" x 2" cardboard box and is made by Victor Eckhardt Manufacturing Company, circa 1935. It is rather plain on the inside with no decoration. The contents consist of two skeins of embroidery floss, metal blunt-nose scissors, a strip of flannel for pins, thimble, three cardboard spools of cotton, and four pre-cut dresses. One dress has already been finished. The unmarked, all-composition, jointed, 6½" bent-limb baby doll rests in the center. This is a somewhat interesting presentation, as there are not many sewing sets that feature baby dolls; the dolls are usually straight-leg little girl dolls. **Complete: $100.00 and up.**

Plate 38. Jean Darling Sewing Outfit #150 comes in a 15" x 10" x 1½" box with a castle graphic. The set was copyrighted 1936 by Standard Toykraft Products. Included is a 6¼" unmarked all-composition doll with molded, painted features and hair, and molded shoes and socks. The doll is dressed in a pre-cut dress that has been sewn by the previous owner. Above the doll are three cardboard spools of sewing cotton, a small metal thimble, metal blunt-nose scissors, and a packet of needles. Along the sides, still stapled to the insert, are six pre-cut dresses. **Complete: $75.00 and up.**

Plate 39. Jean Darling Sewing Outfit #1100 is housed in a 17" x 13" x 2" cardboard box. Standard Toykraft Products copyrighted the set in 1936. The inside insert is undecorated. In the center recess is a 7½" all-composition doll with jointed arms. She has molded, painted features and hair. Her shoes and socks are also molded. In the box are seven pre-cut dresses, including the one she is wearing. There are also two pieces of flowered fabric and a pattern. "Standard Patterns for Doll's Wardrobe" is undated, printed on thin pink paper, and has the Standard Toykraft Products, Inc. name and logo printed at the bottom of the sheet. The patterns consist of a dress with collar, shorts with bib, and a coat, hat, and bag. To complete the set are metal blunt-nose scissors, two twists of assorted color thread, metal thimble, and a paper with two needles. **Complete: $75.00 and up.**

Note: See plate 60 for a Jean Darling Sewing Kit #1100.

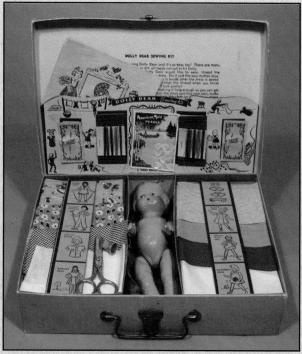

Plate 40. Dolly Dear Sewing Kit #5321 is in a luggage-type box with a metal handle and snap latch. It measures 12" x 9" x 3" and was made by Transogram Company, circa 1939. The inside lid is made with a cardboard pocket onto which is attached two cards of color thread, a card of American Maid Pearls (buttons), and two papers of needles. The pocket holds the printed "6 Dolly Dress Patterns," dated 1939. It contains four dresses, overalls, a blouse, and a playsuit. Each outfit has a girl's name with the drawing of the girl in the outfit to be made up. The instructions even include the color and type of material to use in the set. There are also instructions on how to use the set printed inside above the pocket. A very well thought out, informative sewing set. The fabric is laid out on each side of the doll. There are cardboard strips with drawings of the outfits holding the fabric in place. The unmarked, all-composition doll is 8½", jointed at the shoulders, and has painted features. The set also contains metal blunt-nose scissors and a small thimble. This set came to me with wax paper patterns traced from the original patterns and "child-made" overalls, however none of the fabric or thread from the set was used. **Complete: $100.00 and up.**

Plate 41. Modern Girls Sewing Set #400, circa 1940, was made by American Toys Works and is housed in a 16" x 12" x 2½" box. Inside in one of the four recesses is an unmarked, 7¾" all-composition doll with molded hair, features, shoes, and socks. The doll's eyes, hair, and mouth are painted. There are five pre-cut dresses still stapled along one side and on the other side are three rolls of fabric, a package of Dix and Rand needles, a hank of thread, metal thimble, and metal blunt-nose scissors. **Complete: $100.00 and up.**

Note: See Modern Girls Sewing Set #300 (plate 110) for the paper doll set.

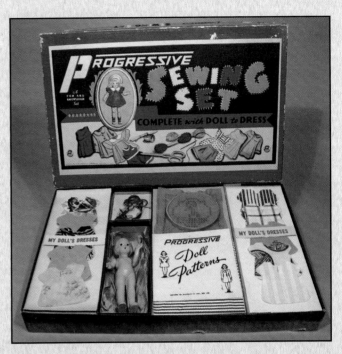

Plate 42. Progressive Sewing Set #1002 Complete with Doll to Dress was made by Progressive Toy Corporation and was copyrighted in 1941. The box is 20" x 1½" x 12½". Inside in a recess is an unmarked, 6¼" all-composition doll with molded, painted hair and features, molded shoes and socks, and jointed arms. Still stapled to the side papers are ten pre-cut dresses, a piece of fabric, stamped embroidery fabric in a hoop, metal blunt-nose scissors, needle, small metal thimble, and two hanks of thread. Also included in the set are "Progressive Doll Patterns," which include a dress with a belt, pocket, and collar and a coat with a belt and collar. **Complete: $75.00 and up.**

Plate 43. Little Traveler's Sewing Kit was copyrighted in 1941 by Transogram Company, Inc. The luggage-style case measures 14" x 8¼" x 3" and has a metal bail handle and latch. The inside lid is printed in blue and has two Transogram assorted color thread cards and a paper with two needles. The composition doll is 6¼", has molded, painted features, molded shoes and socks, and jointed arms. On the insert next to her are six pre-cut dresses, three pieces of fabric, a wooden thimble, and metal blunt-nose scissors. Under the doll are four Transogram "Gold Medal 4 Dolly Dress Patterns." The patterns include a party dress, play dress, overalls, and school dress. **Complete: $75.00 and up.**

Note: This same box was used for a paper doll sewing set, Little Traverler's Sewing Kit #1565 (plate 129).

Sewing and Embroidery Sets for Composition Dolls

Plate 44. I am calling this sewing set **Fairy Tin** as there is no name, but the tin is decorated with fairy like children. Transogram Company manufactured this lunch-box style tin circa 1942. It measures 8½" long x 5½" wide x 3½" deep and has two swing-up handles. The inside lid of the tin is fitted with two cards of colored thread, a card of snaps, and a paper with two needles. The tin has a tray that lifts out and holds three precut dresses and a thimble. Under the tray is a plain cardboard box that holds the 6¼" unmarked, all-composition doll. She is jointed at the shoulders with painted features, molded hair, shoes, and socks. The tin also holds four pieces of fabric and a paper pattern. The Transogram "Gold Medal 4 Dolly Dress Patterns," dated 1941, contains overalls, school dress, party dress, and play dress. The patterns are too large for this doll, although I have no doubt they came with this untouched set. **Complete: $100.00 and up.**

Note: This set was advertised in a Montgomery Ward Christmas Catalog in 1942. It was listed as "Good...Doll's Sewing Set in Case. 6¼" composition doll, movable arms. Set includes, 4 pcs. material, 4 dress patterns, play scissors (cut fairly well), lace, ribbon, buttons, needles, thread, thimble. In metal case, removable tray. Ship. Wt. 13 oz. 48 T 984-21 pc. Sewing Set..........98c."

Plate 45. Dolly's Dressmaker Set comes in a hinged, gray-blue, flower-embossed, paper-covered box. The outside has no name or manufacturer printed on it, however on the inside lid is the name and the maker, EffanBee Play Products. The box measures 10" x 8" x 2" and is circa 1942. The pink inside lid is printed in blue and reads:
Dolly's Dressmaker Set, an EffanBee Play Product. Sew her clothes yourself! All cut out — ready to be made by dolly's mama. This set includes: finished...rayon panties, lace trimmed with decorative rosette on hem. Unfinished...slip with contrasting colored edging...Flowered bathrobe with edging...Dress with white lace trim...Lovely pique coat. Needles, measuring stick, and sewing thread, and the EffanBee Durable Doll — The Doll with the Satin Smooth Skin. Over five inches tall, with movable arms and legs. Shoes and Stockings painted on. Beautifully painted features — a doll that is like a healthy, happy child.
The bottom of the box contains what doll collectors know as Wee Patsy. She is almost 6" tall with painted hair, features, shoes, and socks. All the above-mentioned items are stapled on the insert around the doll. Also still stapled in place is an EffanBee heart tag. A thimble isn't mentioned on the set lid, nor in the catalog write-up, however I found my set with a tiny thimble. **Complete: $700.00 and up.**

Note: This set was written up in a 1942 Montgomery Ward Christmas Catalog as "Better" Doll Sewing Set and had a price of $1.10. I have also seen the set with a Wee Patsy wearing a mohair wig. Another sewing set with a Wee Patsy was shown in a F.A.O. Schwarz 1938 Christmas catalog that offered her in a wooden sewing cabinet with an assortment of material: ribbon, lace, needles, thread, buttons, snaps, and scissors. And again in 1941, F.A.O. Schwarz offered another EFFANBEE doll Baby Tinyette in a similar wooden sewing cabinet along with the same list of materials.

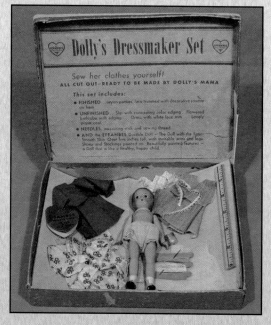

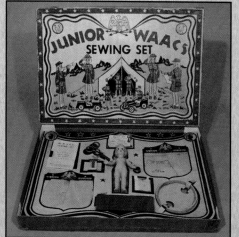

Plate 46. Junior WAACS Sewing Set #136, circa 1942, was made by New York Toy & Game Company. The box is 19" x 13" x 2". This is a very patriotic sewing set that was made during World War II. The inside is decorated in the colors of tan and blue with stars, stripes, and eagles. The little unmarked, 6¼" all-composition doll has jointed arms, painted features, and hair. Arranged around her are metal blunt-nose scissors, brown cord-like thread, metal thimble, a needle, wooden embroidery hoop, Jr. WAAC material, WAAC hat makings, cloth insignias, paper pattern, Jr. WAAC facts sheet, and certificate for the Jr. WAAC Association of America. The doll clothes pattern consists of a dickey, tie, skirt, and a jacket with a pocket. The Certificate reads:
Certificate Junior WAAC Assn. of America. This is to certify -------------------- has completed the required course of training satisfactorily and is hereby admitted to the Junior WAAC ASS'N. President
Complete: $100.00 and up.

Plate 47. Junior Nurse Sewing Set #133, circa 1942, was made by New York Toy & Game Company. The box measures 19" x 13" x 2". The box cover is a delight with small girls wearing nurse's armbands, hats, and aprons, all sewing for their dolls. A patriotic toy made during World War II, the inside of the box reflects the time. The contents of the box are untouched. In the center is the common 6¼" composition doll with painted features and hair, jointed arms, and molded shoes and socks. The nurse's supplies surround the doll. There is red, white, blue, and black cloth to make up the pattern shown that includes nurse's uniform, nurse's dress coat, nurse's aid uniform, ambulance drivers uniform, and a pattern for a child's nurse's hat. Printed in the pattern is a short course on first aid. There is also a note on war nurses: *Today America's Nurses are writing a glowing chapter in the history of our country. As actual members of our Armed Forces they stand side by side with soldiers on the battlefields always ready to lend an eager hand and to save an American life.* The child's nurse's hat is to be made from the strip of white material in the embroidery hoop after embroidering around the red stamped cross. Also included in the set are paper junior war nurse armbands, a card of red, white, and blue thread, a needle, blunt nose metal scissors, a plastic thimble, and a Junior War Nurse Association Certificate that states:
This is to certify that------------------has completed the required course of training satisfactorily, and is hereby admitted to the JUNIOR WAR NURSE ASSOCIATION.
The certificate is signed *The President.* In the instructions (pattern) it talks about a nurses first aid kit and bandages as part of the set. This is the only set I have ever seen, so I have no other reference. I don't know where the kit would have been placed, as there is no area in the insert that would accommodate it. Sometimes sets contents were changed and not reflected in the instructions, is this the case? **As seen: $100.00 and up.**

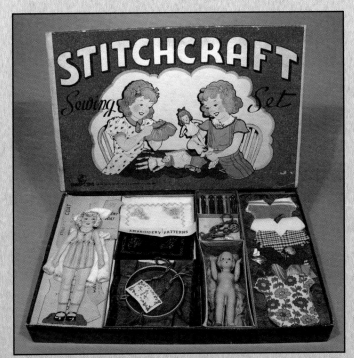

Plate 48. Stitchcraft Sewing Set #204 for work and play for every day was manufactured by Concord Toy Company, Inc. in 1942. The box is 20" x 12¾" x 2¼". Inside we find seven sections. One has a 10" heavy card paper doll called Nan with a pattern for a coat and hat. A previous owner sewed the coat and hat that rests underneath the doll, using the pattern that was included in the set. The next two compartments contain three embroidery pieces. Two look like hankies and have designs of flowers, birds, and children. The third is stamped with a flag and "God Bless America." The fourth compartment contains an unmarked, 6¼" all-composition doll with molded, painted features and hair, molded shoes and socks, and movable arms. Above the doll are metal blunt-nose scissors, a metal thimble, a paper with a needle, and eight colored clothespins. The last section has six pre-cut dresses. **Complete: $100.00 and up.**

Note: This set was advertised in September 1942 Playthings *magazine. See Stitchcraft Sewing Set #202 (plate 127) for this set with just a paper doll.*

Plate 49. Sewing for Every Girl #1235 was manufactured by J. Pressman and Company Inc., circa 1940. The box is 16" x 11" x 2¼". The inside is undecorated, and has four compartments. The center recess holds an 8" unmarked, all-composition doll with jointed arms and molded, painted features and hair. Above the doll are metal blunt-nose scissors, a hank of thread, needle, and a metal thimble. On one side of the doll are the "Patterns for Doll's Clothes," which includes two dresses and a coat and hat. On her other side are three pieces of 9½" x 6½" flowered fabric. **Complete: $100.00 and up.**

Plate 50. Stitch and Sew #1232 was made by J. Pressman and Company. The box measures 16½" x 10" x 1¾". The inside of the box is bright red, yellow, and blue with delightful graphics. The unmarked, all-composition 6¼" doll with jointed arms and painted hair and features rests in the center recess. On either side of the doll are two plates of dolls, each carrying a cardboard (muff) thread spools. There are six pre-cut dresses stapled into six separate compartments on the outer edges of the box, one dress holds a needle. There is no date on the circa 1940s box. **Complete: $75.00 and up.**

Note: The "Stitch and Sew" name was used by Pressman for other similar sets. Stitch and Sew #1212 (plate 119) on page 77, and Stitch and Sew #1205 (not pictured) both have different graphics and paper dolls.

Plate 51. Little Miss Seamstress Dress Outfit #3063 was manufactured by the American Toy Works, circa 1940s. The box is a large 20" x 12" x 2¼". It is a multi-use set, containing not only the doll and clothing but also a knitting dolly and supplies. The box has six inserts. On the far edges are eight pre-cut dresses to be sewn for the doll, one has already been sewn. The unmarked, composition doll is 7", with jointed arms and molded, painted features and hair. Below her are a pair of metal blunt-nose scissors, a metal thimble, and a skein of thread. In the compartment next to her are needles and the knitting dolly that looks more like a soldier than a dolly. The wood-and-metal pick along with wool yarn are also in this recess. Below are clothespins and the trappings for the clothesline still on the card, underneath the clothesline are the instructions for the knitting dolly. **Complete: $100.00 and up.**

Note: The same graphics and title were also used by American Toy Works on two earlier 1930s sets; Little Miss Seamstress Dress Outfit #3061 (plate 19) on page 19 with a 4¼" all-bisque doll, and #3063 with a 6½" bisque doll. For more information on the clothesline still on the card, see Sewing for Girls Stitchart #528 (plate 112) on page 72.

Plate 52. Little Miss Hollywood Sewing Set #600 was made by Minerva Toy Company, circa 1940. This is a totally untouched set with everything securely stapled in place. The box is 19¾" x 12" x 2". The inside platform is printed in blue and tan. The tan areas show placement where the clothing and fabric should be stapled. The unmarked, 6¼" composition doll has molded, painted features and hair, jointed plastic arms, and molded shoes and socks. The articles include nine pre-cut dresses, a dolly blanket and pillow, a stamped sailboat in a cardboard hoop to embroider, a pair of metal blunt-nose scissors, a needle, and a bit of thread and cord. **Complete: $75.00 and up.**

Note: The hard plastic arms on this doll are correct, it is a transition doll. At this time, both hard plastic and composition were interchanged. Little Miss Hollywood Sewing Set #400 (plate 121) on page 77 was sold in a box with the same name and graphics and contained two paper dolls instead of a composition doll.

Plate 53. Miss Deb Sewing Kit #2206 was manufactured by Pressman Toy Corporation, circa 1940s. The box is 14½" x 10¼" x 2¼" and the cover is signed "Lynn Rambach creation, design: Milton Herder." The box has a metal latch on the front. The inside lid has the same graphics as the outside. The insert is pink with a blue outline. The unmarked, 9½" all-composition doll has molded, painted features and hair, molded shoes and socks, and jointed arms. Attached to the insert are six pre-cut dresses along with three hats, feathers, ribbon, net, a card of thread, a package of needles, a paper measuring tape, metal blunt-nose scissors, thimble, and three cardboard hangers. **Complete: $75.00 and up.**

Plate 54. Sewing Set #26, circa 1940s, is a product of Toy Creations, Inc. The box measures 20" x 13" x 2¼". Inside is a raised platform divided into five compartments. In the recess is an unmarked, 7" composition doll with jointed arms, molded, painted features and hair, and molded shoes. The section next to her has a paper pattern for a party dress, coat, and three-piece playsuit. Below the doll are metal blunt-nose scissors, a wooden embroidery hoop, a needle, thread, brads for the needlepoint frame, and a metal thimble. The remaining sections hold a needlepoint canvas with a cardboard frame, three pieces of fabric, and five pre-cut dresses to be sewn. There is also a tapestry instruction sheet. **Complete: $100.00 and up.**

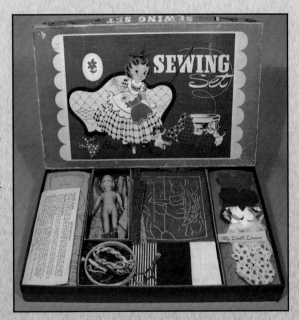

Sewing and Embroidery Sets for Composition Dolls

Plate 55. Little Traveler's Sewing Kit #1567 was copyrighted in 1947 by Transogram Company, Inc. This luggage-style case measures 14" x 8¼" x 2½" and has a metal bail handle and a metal latch. The inside lid graphics are the same as the outside cover. The insert is brown and orange with darker brown outlining the articles. The unmarked, 6¼" composition doll, has jointed arms, molded, painted features, and molded shoes and socks. Still stapled to the insert are eight pre-cut dresses and a card of thread. There are also two spools of thread, a small metal thimble, metal blunt-nose scissors, and a card with two needles. Resting under the doll is a paper pattern dated 1948 named "Gold Medal 4 Doll Dress Patterns" that includes a party dress, play dress, overalls, and school dress. **Complete: $75.00 and up.**

Note: See plates 62 through 64 for more Little Traveler's Sewing Kits by Transogram Company, Inc.

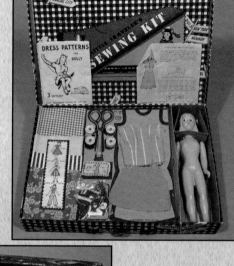

Plate 56. Little Traveler's Sewing Kit #1580 is in a 14½" x 10¼" x 2¼" luggage-style box with a metal bail handle and latch. The inside lid has the same graphics as the outside cover and is copyrighted 1947 by Transogram Company, Inc. In the recessed area is an unmarked, 10" composition doll with molded, painted hair and features, molded shoes and socks, and jointed arms. The two-tone blue insert is dated 1948. The insert has dark blue outlines for the articles that include, four pieces of fabric, four spools of thread, metal blunt-nose scissors, a metal thimble, a card with a needle, a package of trimmings, and a pre-cut blouse and skirt. The blouse and skirt have separate instruction sheets on how to assemble them. There is an illustrated card stapled to the fabrics that shows the made-up outfits from the separate paper pattern included in the set. The pattern is called "Dress Patterns for Dolly" and has a 1947 copyright. The pattern contains a party dress and panties, blouse, skirt and panties, and a pants set. **Complete: $75.00 and up.**

Note: See plates 62 through 64 for more Little Traveler's Sewing Kits by Transogram Company, Inc.

Plate 57. Designer's Wardrobe Trunk Sewing Set was made by Transogram Company, Inc. and is copyrighted 1947. The outside of the trunk measures 10¾" x 6½" x 5½" and is decorated with travel stickers. It has a metal bail handle and latch. Opening the trunk, you see two sides, one has the unmarked, 7" composition doll with molded, painted features and hair, molded shoes, and hard plastic jointed arms. Next to the doll are drawers for lingerie, blouses, and a closet with four hangers holding dresses. Two of the dresses are waiting to be stitched and the other two are finished. Along the bottom is a drawer for sewing supplies; in it are a pair of metal blunt-nose scissors and "Gold Medal 4 Dolly Dress Patterns," copyrighted 1948. The pattern includes a party dress, school dress, play dress, and overalls. The other side of the case contains two cards of assorted colored thread, a bag of trimmings, two needles on papers, a hank of fabric, and an illustration of three of the outfits in the pattern. **Complete: $200.00 and up.**

Note: This set has a copyright date of 1947 and the pattern in the set is copyright 1948; it is obvious that the set was on the market in 1948, and probably even later. I have also seen this set with an extra pattern and plastic material for a raincoat but I'm not sure if it was included in every set. In every Designer's Wardrobe Trunk Sewing Set that I have seen, to date, the arms on the composition doll have been hard plastic, never composition.

Plate 58. Small Fry Trousseau #2206. J. Pressman Toy Corporation manufactured this set in the late 1940s. The trunk measures 12" x 8" x 5½". The outside is decorated with stickers and photographs of a honeymoon trip including the bride in New York. It has a metal bale handle and a snap-latch. Inside the trunk is a 7" composition doll with painted hair and features and plastic arms. Above the doll is the drawer where the hat and head trimmings are stored that include net, veiling, feathers, flower, and ribbons. To the side of the doll is her closet. It holds four dresses on hangers including her wedding gown and above is her felt hat to decorate. The bottom drawer holds a paper with a needle, a card marked "Small Fry Sewing Thread," a plastic thimble, blunt nose metal scissors, and a booklet that has instructions for trousseau bonnet and dresses, apron, knitted a scarf, and bridal costume. The other side of the trunk holds three hanks of knitting wool, two metal double pointed knitting needles, a pattern of an apron printed right on the box to trace and the fabric to use. **Complete: $200.00 and up.**

Note: This set is very much like the Transogram Set (plate 57). However, this set differs from the Transogram set in that it offers knitting and hat decorating and the pattern for an apron to trace. The plastic arms on the doll are correct, as it was a transition time from composition to plastic dolls. I have only seen this set once, so I would consider it very hard to find.

Plate 59. Little Ladies' Sewing Kit #260 comes in a 9" tall, 3½" diameter canister with a rope handle. Rosebud Art Company manufactured the set circa late 1940s. The canister advertises: "a portable kit containing complete sewing supplies." Inside there is a rolled, 8" square of cardboard to which is attached an unmarked, 6¼" composition doll with molded, painted features and hair and jointed hard plastic arms. Also included are three pre-cut dresses, a needle, card of thread, metal blunt-nose scissors, and a plastic thimble. **Complete: $50.00 and up.**

Note: Little Ladies' Sewing Kit #260 also came with an all plastic doll, the kit was made in the same manner except there were four pre-cut dresses instead of three.

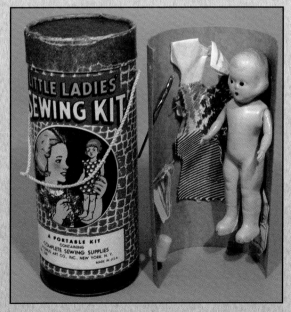

Plate 60. Jean Darling Doll Sewing Kit #1100 was copyrighted in 1949 by Standard Toykraft Products, Inc. The luggage-style case is decorated with travel stickers. It has a metal bail handle and latch and measures 13½" x 9½" x 2¼". On the inside lid is a plate of "Jean Darling Sewing For Her Doll." The message reads:
Jean Darling Tells You How To Sew Her Doll's Clothes. In this sewing set you have a lovely doll and dresses for it that are already cut out. All you have to do is select an outfit, then fold it in half on the reverse side of the fabric so that the parts fit together. Next, stitch the side seams up neatly. For a more finished look, turn under small hems around neck, sleeves, and skirt or jacket bottoms. You can use ribbons to trim the clothes.
The bottom insert has a recessed area for the unmarked 6" composition doll with molded, painted features and hair, molded shoes and socks, and jointed hard plastic arms. The doll is wearing a pre-cut dress to be sewn. Arranged around the doll on a raised red platform are six pre-cut dresses, a card of assorted colored thread, a needle, a small metal thimble, and a pair of metal blunt-nose scissors. **Complete: $75.00 and up.**

Note: See plate 39 on page 31 for a Jean Darling Doll Sewing Outfit #1100.

Plate 61. Jean Darling Doll Sewing Kit was copyrighted in 1949 by Standard Toykraft Products, Inc. The luggage-style box is 15¼" x 12" x 2½" and has a metal bail handle and latch. The inside lid has six squares to embroider and a wooden embroidery hoop. Included is an information sheet on the history of embroidery and how to embroider. There are also instructions for the running stitch, cross-stitch, and edging (buttonhole) stitch. The unmarked, 7½" all-composition doll, has molded, painted features and hair, molded shoes and socks, and jointed arms. At the top of the insert is a red strip holding a metal thimble, embroidery floss, thread, needle, and metal blunt-nose scissors. Surrounding the doll are four pre-cut dresses, one robe, and a pant-set ready to be stitched. **Complete: $75.00 and up.**

Plate 62. Little Traveler's Sewing Kit #1579 is in a circa 1950 luggage-style case with a metal bail handle and snap latch. The case measures 14½" x 11" x 2¼" and was manufactured by Transogram Company. Inc. The inside lid graphics are the same as the outside and are dated 1942. The pink and blue insert is dated 1950 and the blue outlines show where articles are to be placed. The unmarked, 10" composition doll has jointed arms, molded, painted features, and molded hair, shoes, and socks. To one side of her are three felt hats and on the other side are metal blunt-nose scissors, two spools of thread, a metal thimble, plastic purse, pre-cut blouse, pre-cut skirt, and two pieces of fabric. There is an instruction sheet for the pre-cut blouse and skirt on how to assemble them, and the previous owner has completed these. There is a paper pattern sheet titled "Susie's Wardrobe" that contains two patterns, one is an evening or afternoon dress, the other a "diaper" playsuit. **Complete: $75.00 and up.**

Note: See plates 43, 55, 56, 63, and 64 for more Little Traveler's Sewing Kits by Transogram Company, Inc.

Plate 63. Little Traveler's Sewing Kit #3577 is a Transogram Company Product and is copyright 1952. The luggage-type case has a metal bail handle and a latch that is marked "Transogram Patent Pend." The case measures 12½" x 8" x 2½". The composition doll with jointed, hard plastic arms, is 6¼", has molded, painted hair and features, and molded shoes and socks. The doll is secured behind a scalloped insert that is printed "Betty Dress-up Doll with Movable Arms" across the center. The insert next to her holds eight pre-cut dresses, a Transogram card of assorted colored thread, two plastic hangers, a cardboard needle holder with a needle, metal blunt-nose scissors, and a plastic thimble. **Complete: $75.00 and up.**

Note: See plates 43, 55, 56, 62, and 64 for more Little Traveler's Sewing Kits by Transogram Company.

Plate 64. Little Traveler's Sewing Kit #3579 was manufactured by Transogram Company. The insert is dated 1951, there is also an earlier 1947 copyright on the inside of the lid. The 14½" x 10½" x 2¼" luggage-type case comes with a metal bail handle and latch. The inside of the lid is the same design as on the outside of the case. The insert is pink with blue shadows for placement of articles. The unmarked, 6¼" composition doll has jointed plastic arms, molded, painted hair and features, and molded shoes and socks. The kit comes with 12 pre-cut dresses, a green plastic pretend sewing machine, two cards of thread, three plastic hangers, metal blunt-nose scissors, a metal thimble, two spools of thread, and a paper with a needle. **Complete: $75.00 and up.**

Note: See plates 43, 55, 56, 62, and 63 for more Little Traveler's Sewing Kit by Transogram Company.

Sewing and Embroidery Sets for Hard Plastic Dolls

The Second World War changed the attitudes of women towards sewing; after the war it was considered strictly utilitarian. During the war there was a shortage of fabric and patterns. The government asked American women to makeover clothing using articles that were already in their closet. Sewing pamphlets were printed with titles such as "Make and Mend for Victory." These gave instructions on making over garments, alterations, mending, darning, turning collars and cuffs, and using only what one already had rather than buying new patterns and fabric. These practices were hard to break for the young women after the war ended. Many American housewives were still holding on to the "war years economy" and only used their sewing machines to mend or do alterations.

New magazines were coming onto the market targeting teens. *Seventeen, Calling All Girls,* and *American Girl* were all filled with fashions, self-help, girl talk, and advertising. They were well received by the teenage consumers and proved to be very successful. The sewing industry knowing their need to create a new demand for sewing had turned to teenage girls.

The Singer Sewing Company, America's largest retail sewing machine company at the time, began advertising the Singer Teen-Age Sewing Course in the teen magazines in the late 1940s and continued until the middle 1960s. The advertising was, for the most part, the "girl gets boy" approach. In a typical ad, Betty might need a new prom dress, but dad said no unless Betty pays for it herself. Betty doesn't have enough money to buy the dress she wants. Betty sees an ad for the Singer Teen-Age Sewing Course. Betty decides to take the course and sews the dress herself. Dad thinks Betty is a genius, Mom looks on approvingly. Betty wears the dress to the prom and Betty's friends are all impressed. Betty's boyfriend is impressed also and the date is a success.

The pattern for future Singer sewing machine ads was set, playing to the teenage girl's imagination by making the girl the star, not the advertised product. Most teenage girls had money in the 1950s either from parents or odd jobs like baby-sitting. Better yet, if the teenagers didn't have a lot of money, Singer ads gave teenagers hope that they could still be well dressed by taking Singer's sewing courses and learning to sew their own wardrobes.

The 1950s saw a large increase in the sewing books put on the market for children and teenagers. Not since the early 1900s, were so many sewing books written for the under-twenty population. The difference between the sewing books written in the early 1900s and the 1950s was the reader's age. The early 1900s books were written for grade-school children, and while some of the 1950s books were still written for grade-school children, there were now also sewing books written just for the teenager. Not only were the teenage books selling the idea of sewing beautiful gowns of shirred taffeta and gay, full petticoats with layers of ruffles, but they had teenagers also dreaming of the bedroom they could make their own. *Sewing Magic for Teen-Ager* written by the Greist Manufacturing Company asked the teenager:

Why don't you stop dreaming and make those dreams become a reality? Make the bedroom you are dreaming of the one with crisp organdy curtains, ruffled and full, the dressing table with its bouffant skirt bound in delicate pink, and the bedspread with its rows of cording which gives a sweeping effect as it dips to the floor.

Sewing Magic for Teen-Agers gave instruction on how this could be achieved by using Greist sewing machine attachments. The 1950s was the first time the teenager was singled out as a consumer in the sewing industry. These teenage girls were the sewers of the future, the wives and homemakers of tomorrow, and the sewing industry knew it.

The popular press wrote that women were happiest when marriage was their chosen life option. The housewives portrayed on new popular television shows were always shown with smiles on their faces, doing their every day chores in a clean, starched, fashionable dress, fancy apron, pearls, and high heels. "Domestic life is bliss" was surely the message. With the emphasis on wife, home, and family, home economics was widely taught to girls in junior and senior high schools, with at least one semester dedicated to sewing. It was reported in *Time* magazine in 1958 that the home sewing boom was as strong as ever. It was estimated that women sewed an average of four to six garments for their family in a year, and that 20% of women's and children's clothes were made at home.

The Singer campaign in the 1950s reinforced the message that American girls accept the only future open to them after World War II; to be a loving wife. Taking Singer sewing lessons and producing their own stylish dresses was the surest way to attract their prince charming, allowing them to live happily ever after by capturing a husband and ultimate happiness with their talents shown on the Singer sewing machine. Popular women's magazines encouraged this thinking by advertising women's products in connection with men.

On one of the most popular television shows of the 1950s, *Leave It To Beaver*, the father, Ward Cleaver, asked his wife June, "What type of girl would you have Wally (Beaver's older brother) marry?" "Oh," answered June. "Some very sensible girl from a nice family, one with both feet on the ground, who's a good cook and can keep a nice house, and see that he is happy." Mothers were encouraged to prepare their daughters for their role as wives to keep house and take care of their man.

The children of World War II, now becoming parents themselves, remembered the leaner times and wanted to give their kids all the things they had missed out on during the war. The new television in many homes was a constant reminder of what could be purchased in consumer land. The dream for many American families was a home in the newly built suburbs. The GI bill and the Federal Housing Administration with easy down payments and low interest rates made it possible to achieve these dreams. In the 1950s consumer purchases became even easier with the new easy credit, "Buy Now, Pay Later," and the new "Diner's Club" credit card.

The toy industry understood the new parents' wish to create a happy home after the unrest of war and looked to the home for playthings that reflected home life and harmony. The catalog pages were full of little girl homemaking toys including new sewing sets with the new hard plastic dolls. It was suggested that these miniature tools of play would teach and mold the child for her future, and thus assure her of a happy home.

The American toy business had grown and was taking advantage of the new advertising medium — television. In the early 1950s, before toy supermarkets such as Toys R Us, most toys were sold through department and novelty stores. *Playthings*, a magazine dedicated to toy retailers, for years had been encouraging the promotion and advertising of toys year round and not just for the holidays. In the 1950s the magazine encouraged promoters to use television as an advertising media, giving examples of prosperous merchants whose toys were walking off the shelves. Many retailers heeded this advice and the toy boom was on. In past years toys were considered special gifts for achievements, birthdays, and holidays. The 1950s changed that concept forever and suburbia soon became a vast wonderland of toys.

Toy manufacturers were embracing the new plastics. Still a fairly new material for toys, it was the new kid on the block. Plastic featured built-in color, fine surface finish, was lightweight, and had reduced production costs. Maurice Block, a patent attorney, wrote in the February 1950 *Playthings* magazine quoting from a then-recent company publication:

Molding material production for the industry (plastics) has more than doubled. Since 1941...an estimated one quarter of a billion dollars has been spent by the industry for new buildings, molding facilities, molding presses, high-frequency preheating equipment, and tool equipment for economical mold-building.

The new plastic dolls were cheaper to make had their flesh color mixed in the plastic so paint never flaked off. Mohair wigs and sleeping eyes added to their popularity. The new plastic also made it possible to add attractive, inexpensive, children's toy plastic sewing machines to the sewing sets. Hassenfeld Brothers advertised the first sewing machine in their sewing sets in 1955, Jr. Miss Sewing Kit #1541 (plate 82). By 1958, they were advertising four different sewing sets with sewing machines.

The plastic doll sewing sets were fun, most of the sewing sets were made with a carry case that had a handle to tote them about, almost all were easy to use with pre-cut clothing. Toy sewing sets were familiar and brought back memories to mothers because they played with sets similar to them when they were children. The clothing was still pre-cut in the old familiar shapes and the metal blunt-nose scissors were still there, only the dolls and fabrics had changed.

One toymaker that capitalized on this familiar toy was Hassenfeld Brothers. Two brothers, Henry and Helal, began the company in 1923 in Providence, Rhode Island. The brothers began selling textile remnants and later began manufacturing pencil boxes and school supplies. Henry's son, Merrill, was named president of Hassenfeld Brothers in 1943 and shortly after, the company expanded its products to include boxed toys such as painting sets and doctor and nurse kits. On October 10, 1968, Hassenfeld Brothers became a public company and changed its name to Hasbro Industries, Inc.

It is not clear when Hassenfeld Brothers manufactured their first sewing kit but it could have been as early as 1952. A 1955 catalog shows eight different sewing sets. Hassenfeld Brothers 1955 trade catalogs stated:

Sewing and embroidery sets are recognized by leading educators as being enjoyable, practical, and entertaining methods of developing creative exressions plus coordination and dexterity in girls from 6 to 12.

Hassenfeld Brothers even entered the paper doll field with their Jr. Miss Sewing Kit #1520 (plate 133). In December of 1956, Hasbro had a full-page color ad in *Parents* magazine, "America's Top Toys," among them was the Little Miss Seamstress Sewing Kit, featuring Toy Necchi #1542 (plate 83).

Hasbro's motto was "A Hasbro toy is a toy with a purpose." True to their word, Hasbro was the largest manufacturer of children's sewing sets in the 1950s. Hassenfeld Brothers were giving the parents a goal for the future, while granting children the ability to express them selves in creative play.

The biggest toy-selling tool in the 50s was the television. By 1950, over four million families were watching black-and-white television in their living rooms. By 1960, 90 percent of Americans owned a television. The *Howdy Doody Show* was one of the first kid's shows, making an appearance in 1947, even before most American homes had a tv. Other shows soon followed: *Ding Dong School*; *Kukla, Fran, and Ollie;* and *The Pinky Lee Show*. Saturday morning cartoon shows were introduced in 1955, the same year as *The Mickey Mouse Club* and *Captain Kangaroo*.

All children's programming carried toy advertising. Many companies, especially Milton Bradley and Transogram, began to produce box games around the television shows and their heroes, sometimes using the identical game for different programs, changing only the cover of the games when one show or character was replaced by another. Still, there were only a few children's sewing sets that cashed in on familiar celebrities or television shows.

Sewing and Embroidery Sets for Hard Plastic Dolls

Walt Disney gave licensing to both J. Pressman Toy Corp. and Transogram Co. to make sewing sets using his name. The Alice in Wonderland Sewing Kit #1545 manufactured by Hassenfeld Brothers sometime around 1955, is a good example (plate 68). The sewing set has only the name and graphics of Alice in Wonderland. There isn't any item in the set that would indicate it was different from any other Hassenfeld Brothers sewing set. The 5" plastic doll, Sew Rite sewing machine, and the paper pattern had all been used before in other Hassenfeld Brothers sewing sets.

The Sleeping Beauty's Sewing Set #3595 that Transogram Co. manufactured in 1959 was a special sewing set (plate 93). Transogram Co. advertised the set as:

Walt Disney Sleeping Beauty Sewing Outfit based on the beloved popular movie, offers little girls of 5 to 10 two forms of stimulating play — dolls and sewing — plus the thrill of dressing up and playing with the adorable Prince and Princess Dolls. Both have charming features, eyes that open and close, and movable arms for easy dressing, plus 2 complete court costumes ready-cut for simple sewing. Sewing and doll play are two activities most recommended by child psychologists for little girls in this age group, as it stimulates their imaginations and gives them a sense of achievement.

Pressman Company manufactured another sewing set from the 1950s that featured a television star, the Annie Oakley Sewing Set #2256 (plate 74). The cover of the set carried a photograph of Gail Davis from the series *Annie Oakley*. Gail Davis was on television from April 1953 to December 1954. A little lady of five-foot-two, 95 pounds, and pigtails, she played Annie Oakley. It was the only western in the 50s that starred a cowgirl.

Annie was a crack shot, and rounded up the bad guys every week to the delight of little girls all over America. The show was set in Diablo, her hometown, where she lived with her brother Tagg; the rest of her family was never mentioned. Gail Davis was discovered by Gene Autry, Gene Autry was a popular western star in the 1950s. He featured her not only in his television series, but also in his movies, finally spinning her off into a series of her own.

Annie Oakley, both on television and in real life, was an excellent marksman. The real Annie, born in 1860 in Ohio as Phoebe Anne Oakley Mozee, was known for her sensational trick-shots with pistol, rifle, and shotgun. She was the sixth of nine children and began shooting small game when she was nine. She became so good a shot that she contributed to paying off the family's farm mortgage with the game she shot and sold. In the 1870s she challenged Frank Butler, a vaudeville marksman, to a shooting match and beat him winning by only one shot. They later married and Annie became a star in his act.

The Butlers joined Buffalo Bill's Wild West Show in 1885, and it was there that she gained her greatest fame. She toured with Buffalo Bill for 17 years. In 1901 she suffered injuries from a train wreck and was left partially paralyzed. Though she never completely recovered, she continued to tour for another 20 years. Annie died in the place of her birth, Ohio, on November 3, 1926, never knowing the impact she would have on little girls in the 1950s.

The Annie Oakley Sewing Set #2256 is an interesting sewing set. It gives only one costume to make for Annie, but when you are done, you really have a western Annie Oakley doll, complete with hat, holster, rope, and gun. I thought it was also appropriate that the inserts were printed with a western theme and the embroidery piece was "Home Sweet Home," showing some special thought went into this set.

With marriage and a happy home as a girl's goal, it's hardly surprising the most prevalent theme of the 1950s sewing set was the bride. However it is surprising that it seems only Hassenfeld Brothers manufactured the bride sewing sets. Hassenfeld Brothers Bridal Party Sewing Kit #1559 was made with two different box tops and contents, see plates 79 and 92. This was also the case with Bridal Trousseau Sewing Kit #1539 (plate 80). In each case they scaled down the sets as time went on. Hassenfeld Brothers also manufactured the Bridal Wardrobe Sewing Trunk #1537 (plate 91) and Bridal Set #4005 (plate 81).

The plastic doll sewing and embroidery sets were most prevalent in the 1950s. A few were made into the middle 1960s, but for the most part it is here that children's doll sewing sets disappeared. We find a few specialized sets today with dolls, but no large manufacturer has added sewing sets to their regular line. The catalogs in the early 1960s started to show more craft sets and fewer and fewer sewing sets. In glancing through a 1963 *Plaything* magazine, I found not one plastic doll sewing set however I did find activity sets such as bead craft, glitter craft, fun with flowers craft, tile craft, jewelry craft, and sea shell craft. The children's sewing sets, which used dolls as a sewing incentive, were fading away.

Plate 65. Embroidery Set was made in the 1950s in Czechoslovakia. The 6" x 4½" x 2¾" red papered-covered box has the title paper applied to the top. Inside there is a pink paper that reads: *Embroidery Set, "Sewing Set" Working procedure: Decoration of the skirt and dress is to be embroidered first with the respective thread, which is enclosed. Then cut with scissors all kinds of dressing as indicated by dotted line, stitch together as per interrupted line and hem. Sew in the collar attached to finish the nightdress. The same procedure is to be taken when making pillow and feather-bed, except embroidering.* The little jointed, pink plastic doll is about 3½" tall with molded, painted hair and painted eyes. She is wearing little pink panties even though she is placed securely under her blanket. The doll and outfits are all sewn to accordion folded cardboard, with each outfit shown in a colored line drawing next to the clothing and thread. The first panel shows the doll, bedding, thread, needle, and thimble. The other outfits are a sundress, party dress, red cape with hood, and a patterned nightgown, all with thread and trimmings. Some outfits are stamped for embroidery, all need to be cut out and stitched together. There is a little red ribbon loop on the first panel to lift the doll and her outfits up. This is a very nice set; the clothes are nicely printed and well displayed. **Complete: $50.00 and up.**

Plate 66. Little Miss Sew It #114 sewing kit comes in a 14½" x 8" x 4½" cardboard carry case with a cellophane window. Manufactured by Empire Plastic Corp. circa 1950s, it was advertised as "A complete dressmaker's outfit in a handsome traveling case." Inside the case are a square doily to embroider and a 7½" unmarked hard plastic doll with moving eyes, jointed arms and head, and a mohair wig. There are also a plastic doll stand, three pre-cut dresses, buttons, plastic thimble, metal blunt-nose scissors, and a little red plastic rocking chair. The rocking chair is also a sewing box. It has three wooden spools of thread beside each arm, the scissors fit into a loop on the back of the chair and the little drawer under the pincushion seat is for pins and needles. This is a cute, well thought out sewing piece. **Complete: $75.00 and up.**

Note: The original retail price in 1950s for this set is $1.98, written in pencil on the box side.

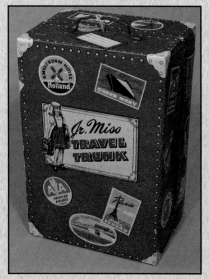 

Plate 67. Jr. Miss Travel Trunk #1560 is made like a steamer trunk with a metal bail handle and lock. It measures 12" x 8" x 6". Hassenfeld Brothers made this sewing set circa 1950s. The outside of the trunk is decorated with travel stickers. The case opens up into two sections, one holding two 5" unmarked plastic dolls. They are jointed at the shoulders and have molded hair and painted, molded features. The dolls are wrapped in pre-cut dresses and next to them, hanging on cardboard hangers, are four more dresses. Below the hanging dresses is a printed faux shoetree. At the top of the case is a shelf with a plastic hatbox and the drawer beside it holds a hank of white trim. Under the dolls are four wooden spools of thread and below, in another drawer, the "Junior Miss Dolly Dress Patterns" that include a pattern for a school dress and party dress. The other side holds four lengths of fabric, a paper tape measure, two papers with needles, a pair of metal blunt-nose scissors, and a small metal thimble. **Complete: $100.00 and up.**

Note: This particular set was old store stock from the W. J. Borcher's General Store in Fort Loramie, Ohio, and still has its retail tag of $1.98. Jr. Miss Travel Trunk #1550 is similar to the above trunk, but only has one doll and is slightly different on the inside.

Plate 68. Walt Disney's **Alice In Wonderland Sewing Kit #1545** is housed in a 13" x 8" x 3" luggage-style case with a metal handle and latch. Hassenfeld Brothers manufactured it circa 1950s. The inside lid has the same graphics as the outside lid. The most important feature in this set is the Sew Rite sewing machine #1500. Under the machine are the instructions for the machine and "Junior Miss Doll Dress Patterns" that include a pattern for a school dress and party dress. The set also holds a 5" hard plastic unmarked doll, jointed only at the shoulders. The doll has molded hair, molded, painted features, and is dressed in a pre-cut dress to sew. Above the doll are four wooden spools of thread and a small metal thimble. Below the doll is a paper with a needle. On the other side, the four pre-cut dresses, metal blunt-nose scissors, and a length of cloth complete the set. **Complete: $100.00 and up.**

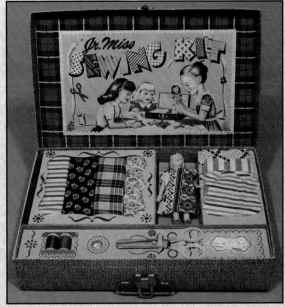

Plate 69. Jr. Miss Sewing Kit #1535 is in a 12" x 8" x 2" luggage-style box with a metal bail handle and lock. Hassenfeld Brothers manufactured this set circa 1950s. The inserts are gaily decorated in green flowers. The 6" unmarked plastic doll in the recess is jointed at the arms, has molded hair, molded and painted features, and is wrapped in a pre-cut dress to sew. To one side of her are three pre-cut dresses and on the other side are four lengths of fabric. Below are two wooden spools of thread, a small metal thimble, metal and plastic blunt-nose scissors, and a paper with needles. **Complete: $50.00 and up.**

Note: Jr. Miss Sewing Kit #1535 has a red woven type print on the outside of the case. On the inside lid is a number 1530 with the plaid print. I believe the inside print and number 1530 was left over graphics from an earlier set. There is uncut fabric in this set but I have never seen a printed paper pattern included.

Plate 70. Jr. Miss Sewing Kit #1535 was produced by Hassenfeld Brothers, circa 1950s. The luggage-style case has a metal bail handle and latch and is 16" x 12" x 3". The inside lid shows the same graphics as the outside lid of the case. The case has five sections. The center section holds a 7½" hard plastic doll jointed at the shoulders, with molded, painted features and a mohair wig. The doll is embossed "Hasbro" and is wrapped in a pre-cut dress, ready to sew. The set also holds six more pre-cut dresses, a metal thimble, wooden spool of thread, metal blunt-nose scissors, a card with two needles, three skeins of embroidery floss and a needle threader. This set also includes an embroidery set with four, 7" squares stamped with a teddy bear pattern, a cardboard hoop, and embroidery instructions. **Complete: $75.00 and up.**

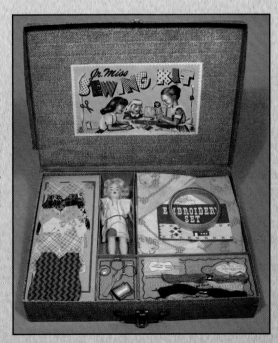

Plate 71. The Little Dressmaker #1731 comes in a 15½" x 9" x 2" luggage-style case with a metal bail handle and latch. The set was made by De Luxe Game Corp., circa 1950. The inside lid has the same graphics as the outside lid. The 6" unmarked doll is plastic with movable arms. She has molded painted hair and features with a blue molded bow in her hair and is wearing a voile dress. Unlike most of the plastic dolls in the 50s sets, this well modeled doll looks to be made from a mold used for the earlier composition sewing dolls. The insert in the box has cute graphics of little girls sewing and doing laundry for their dollies. Stapled to the insert are six pre-cut dresses, a card of sewing thread, and a paper with a needle. To complete the set are a plastic thimble and a pair of metal blunt-nose scissors. **Complete: $25.00 and up.**

Note: This is the smaller of two The Little Dressmaker sets made by De Luxe Game Corp. The larger The Little Dressmaker set has patterns and fabric.

Plate 72. Sewing Bag and 8" Doll #3306 is a plaid vinyl sewing case in a cardboard box. The outside box measures 12½" x 10" x 3½"; the inside case measures 9" in diameter. J. Pressman Toy Corp. made this set circa 1950s. The inside lid of the zippered round case shows a little girl sewing with her doll and the words "Sit Up Straight and Sew Pretty." A thin plastic insert has molded recesses to hold the sewing tools which include a small tomato pincushion with emery, two wooden spools of thread, plastic thimble, paper measuring tape, packet of needles, small darning egg, metal blunt-nose scissors, and a card of six small snaps. The unmarked, plastic 7½" doll is jointed only at the arms and has molded, painted hair and features. She is wearing a pre-cut dress to be sewn. Under the doll are two lengths of cloth, a cotton print and a piece of white satin to be used with the patterns enclosed that include a wedding gown and a going away outfit. **Complete: $50.00 and up.**

Note: The inside vinyl zippered sewing kit is not marked Pressman in any way. The outside box of Sewing Bag and 8" Doll #3306 shows the picture of a sewing set with the plastic tray insert like Pressman's Sewing Bag set #3356 (not pictured). The paper pattern with the above set #3306 set is the same pattern as Pressman's set #3356.

Plate 73. Happy Time Sewing Kit #1535SR was manufactured by Hassenfeld Brothers for Sears, Roebuck and Co. circa 1950s. The luggage-style box is 14½" x 10½" x 3" with a metal bail handle and latch. Written on the box top is "Sears, Roebuck and Co. made in U.S.A." This set has the 7½" doll embossed "Hasbro," with jointed arms and head, sleep eyes, and mohair wig. She is wrapped in a skirt and blouse to be sewn. Underneath the doll is the "Jr. Miss Sewing Kit" pattern that includes a skirt, blouse, dress, panties, and hat. The set has five lengths of fabric, two pre-cut dresses, three pre-cut blouses, and one pre-cut skirt. The accessories include two wooden spools of thread, a small plastic thimble, needle, snaps, and metal blunt-nose scissors. **Complete: $50.00 and up.**

Note: I have seen Happy Time Sewing Set #1535SR with the "Happy Time" graphic repeated on the inside lid, instead of the Jr. Miss. The "Jr. Miss" graphic on the inside of the lid pictured has #1530 printed on it, indicating that possibly it was left over from an earlier set.

Plate 74. Annie Oakley Sewing Set #2256 is in a box that measures 18" x 13" x 2½". It has the Annie Oakley trademark and the top corner of the box has a picture of Gail Davis who played Annie Oakley on television. J. Pressman manufactured this set in the 1950s. The box insert is decorated with ropes and western gear. Inside we find an unmarked, 7½" hard plastic doll with molded and painted hair and features, jointed at the neck and arms. In a decorated cellophane bag are the clothing supplies to dress Annie. The bag lists the contents: skirt, vest, blouse, gauntlets, holster, belt, and gun. Also included are two cords, a small card of snaps, metal blunt-nose scissors, two felt cowboy hats, paper with needle, metal blunt-nose scissors, Small Fry Pressman sewing thread, three Pressman marked wrapped skeins of embroidery floss, a cardboard hoop, a Home Sweet Home motto to embroidery, and "Sewing Set Instructions." **Complete: $100.00 and up.**

Note: Annie Oakley Sewing Set #2256 box top carries three stamps, The Educator Approved Prestige Toy Award for 1955, Toy Guidance Council Inc., and the Commended by Parents Magazine seal.

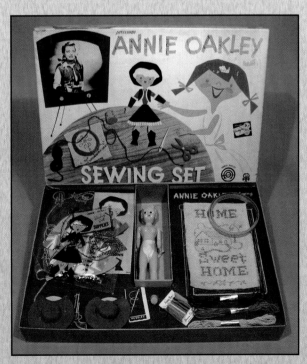

Plate 75. Little Miss Model Sewing Kit #5383 was manufactured by Transogram Company in 1954. The plastic hatbox shaped case is about 6½" in diameter with a colored sticker on the front depicting a child carrying a hatbox. Upon opening it we find an insert with a mirror and a cellophane packet stapled to the insert which contains sewing instructions, embroidery floss, blunt-nose medal scissors, needle, and a plastic thimble. The 6" unmarked plastic doll has molded, painted features and hair, is jointed at the arms, and is wearing a dress to sew. The name Betty is printed in script on her box. On both sides of her are clothing and fabric that consists of two pre-cut dresses and four lengths of fabric all rolled over cardboard. The sewing instructions are very simple, instructing the child to cut out the fabric to fit the doll. **Complete: $25.00 and up.**

Note: The cost of this sewing kit in 1954 was $1.98. Transogram Company also used this plastic box for a beauty kit. In a December 1954 Parents *magazine ad both the beauty kit and the sewing kit were advertised.*

Plate 76. Priscilla Doll Sewing Set #561 is a product of Standard Toykraft Products, circa 1955. The box is 12½" x 8" x 1¼". In a center recess under a decorated cut out frame with the name Priscilla printed on it is the 5" plastic doll. She is jointed at the arms, has molded hair and molded, painted features, and is wrapped in a pre-cut dress to be sewn. On the sides stapled to the insert, are the doll's pre-cut clothing that consists of five short dresses, one long dress, and two pantsuits. Arranged above the clothing is a thimble, a paper with a needle, a Standard Quality card of thread, and a pair of metal blunt-nose scissors. **Complete: $25.00 and up.**

Note: The above Priscilla Doll Sewing Set #561 box still has the Woolworth's price sticker of 59 cents. The Priscilla set also came in a larger size luggage-style case with the same graphics. It contained a doll sewing tools and pre-cut clothing with an added embroidery set, complete with instructions and hoop in the lid.

Plate 77. Junior Miss Sewing Kit #1532 was manufactured by Hassenfield Brothers and shown in their trade catalog in 1955. It was advertised as:
A sewing set that is truly an outstanding value. Beautifully designed and priced to literally walk off your counters.
The box measures 15½" x 11½" x 1½". The contents are artfully laid out with swatches of fabric framed at the top and pre-cut skirt and pants outfits along the sides. Sewing supplies including cards of ribbons, thread, a metal thimble, metal blunt-nose scissors, and a paper with a needle are arranged along the bottom. The 7" hard plastic doll embossed "Hasbro" is jointed at the arms, has molded painted hair and features, and wears a pre cut dress to be sewn. Under the doll is a "Junior Miss Dolly Dress Patterns" that includes a school dress and party dress. This box top, carries the Toy Manufacturers of America stamp. **Complete: $50.00 and up.**

Note: This set retailed for $1.00 in 1955.

Plate 78. Junior Miss Sewing Kit #1535 manufactured by Hassenfeld Brothers is really both a sewing and embroidery kit. The luggage-style case measures 15½" x 11½" x 2½". In a 1955 Hassenfeld Brothers catalog, the retail price was $2.00. Stapled into the lid are five fabric squares stamped with patterns to embroider. Tucked in the center is the instruction sheet for embroidery stitches. The 7½" hard plastic doll in the recess below has jointed arms, molded, painted hair and features, and is embossed "Hasbro." Stapled to a platform on one side of the set are pre-cut fashions: two blouses, one circular skirt, and a pair of slacks. On the other side are two lengths of fabric and pink and blue ribbons. The tools included are metal blunt-nose scissors, small metal thimble, card of assorted thread, needle threader, a paper with two needles, three skeins of embroidery floss with the Hasbro label, and a cardboard embroidery hoop. Underneath the doll are the instructions and "Junior Miss Dolly Dress Patterns" that includes a play dress and party dress. The box top carries the Toy Manufacturers of America stamp. **Complete: $50.00 and up.**

Sewing and Embroidery Sets for Hard Plastic Dolls

Plate 79. Bridal Party Sewing Kit #1559 is housed in a large 18" x 14½" x 2" box. Hassenfeld Brothers made this set circa 1955. The box has a lavender background decorated with bells and lilies of the valley. The inside graphics of the hinged lid feature a bride, two bridesmaids, and a flower girl. The same graphics are on the outside lid of the box. There are four dolls fitted in the recesses. The three larger hard plastic dolls, a bride and two bridesmaids, are 7½" tall, have sleep eyes, molded painted features, mohair wigs, and are jointed at the arms only. They are marked "Hasbro." The smaller unmarked doll is 5", has molded, painted hair and features, and is also jointed at the arms. The two bridesmaid dolls have their gowns already finished by a previous owner. The bride is still wrapped in her unfinished white satin gown with ribbon, flowers, net, and lace, as is the flower girl in yellow; these two dolls still have to be dressed. There are two inserts on either side at the bottom of the box, one has four wooden spools of thread and a thimble; the other has a card with two needles, a needle threader, and three vinyl purses, one already finished. **Complete: $50.00 and up.**

Note: This is the first Bridal Party Sewing Kit #1559 issued by Hasbro. In a 1957 Hassenfeld Brothers trade catalog, the same title and numbered set was issued shown with different colors and graphics and scaled-down contents. See plate 92 for the smaller, later kit.

Plate 80. Bridal Trousseau Sewing Kit #1539 is in a box that measures 18" x 12" x 1½". Hassenfeld Brothers manufactured the set circa 1955. The background of the box lid is pink striped and featuring a bride with five pictures of her trousseau along the bottom. Inside, in the center top recession, is an unmarked plastic bride doll. The doll is 5" tall with jointed arms molded hair, and molded, painted features. She is wrapped in a pre-cut wedding gown with ribbon, net, and a flower. Surrounding the doll is her pre-cut trousseau, four dresses with either braid or ruffle trim, felt jacket, hat, purse, needle, two wooden spools of thread, and a small metal thimble.
Complete: $50.00 and up.

Note: The bride in this set is the same doll that is the flower girl in the four-doll Bridal Party Sewing Kit #1559 by Hasbro (plate 79). This set #1539 was also shown in a 1957 Hassenfeld Brothers trade catalog with confetti print box top, insert with blue decorations, and the pictures of the trousseau had been eliminated. It contained a larger doll but only four pre-cut dresses, including her wedding gown, and a pair of metal blunt-nose scissors were added. There was also a transition period in which the pink striped box top was used with the new contents.

Plate 81. Bridal Set #4005 came in a hanging package to display on a rack. The cardboard-backed package is 12" x 7", circa 1950s, and is manufactured by Hassenfeld Brothers. The set comes with the 5" unmarked plastic doll that is in many of the Hasbro sets. Also included are satin for the gown, net for the veil and skirt, fabric and trim for a housecoat, needle, thread, metal thimble, and a sprig of lily of the valley. Printed on the cardboard backing of the set are the instructions:
FOLLOW THESE SIMPLE INSTRUCTIONS FOR SEWING BRIDAL SET. THESE OUTFITS ARE ALREADY CUT AND READY FOR SEWING. 1. Remove outfits from bride doll and housecoat from card. Start with the white bridal outfit. 2. Tack down "V" shaped cloth at the neckline of the blouse. 3. Reverse cloth and roll edges of sleeves and neckline, then sew. 4. While the cloth is still reversed, sew down sides from sleeve to bottom of blouse. 5. Now take the bridal skirt and net. Place the net over the satin cloth and ruffle together at the long end. You are now ready to sew the long end. 6. Take the blouse and the ruffled skirt. Sew together at the waist. Follow the above instructions when sewing the housecoat, except adding the lace trim, as shown in the plate.
This set, along with plates 79 and 80 shows how some companies used one set in several different ways to appeal to every pocketbook. **Complete: $25.00 and up.**

Plate 82. Jr. Miss Sewing Kit #1541 was shown in Hassenfeld Brothers 1955 trade catalog. It was advertised as: "A completely equipped, beautiful portable style sewing kit, featuring the famous Sew-Rite sewing machine, made of durable, colorful plastic. Each machine factory tested to assure satisfaction." The case is cardboard covered in a brown plaid printed paper. It is shaped in a satchel style with a metal bail handle and latch. Opening it reveals six pre-cut dresses lined up along the top on cardboard hangers. Below the dresses are eight lengths of fabric stapled to the cardboard. The plastic Sew-Rite sewing machine is embossed "Hasbro U.S.A. No. 1500." Standing next to the machine is a 5" unmarked hard plastic doll with molded hair and molded, painted features and jointed arms. The doll is wrapped in a pre-cut dress ready to be sewn. The tools in this set are a paper tape measure, four wooden spools of thread, small metal thimble, a paper with two needles, needle threader, and a pair of metal blunt-nose scissors. Included in the set are instructions for the machine and "Junior Miss Dolly Dress Patterns" with a school dress and party dress. **Complete: $100.00 and up.**

Note: To my knowledge this was the very first sewing kit with a sewing machine to be presented by Hassenfeld Brothers. The box of this set is hard to find in good condition.

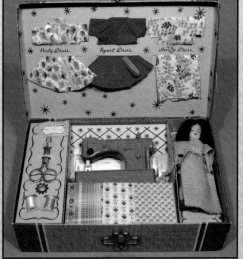

Plate 83. Little Miss Seamstress Set featuring Toy Necchi Sewing Machine #1542 is in a luggage-style case measuring 15½" x 12" x 2¾". The 7½" plastic doll is jointed only at the arms, has a mohair wig glued over molded hair, molded, painted features, and is embossed "Hasbro" on the back. In the center recess is a plastic Necchi Supernova sewing machine complete with instructions. Under the machine are "Junior Miss Dolly Dress Patterns" with instructions featuring a play dress and party dress. Below the machine are three lengths of cloth to be used with the patterns. On the other side of the case are two wooden spools of thread, a small metal thimble, a paper with a needle, and a pair of metal blunt-nose scissors. Attached to the lid are three pre-cut outfits to be sewn, party dress with ribbon trim, sports dress with a plastic belt, and a housedress with rickrack. This set was advertised in a December 1955 *Parents* magazine for $4.00. **Complete: $75.00 and up.**

Note: This set #1542 has also been found more than once with two different style patterns; a "Jr. Miss Sewing Kit" pattern with two blouses, two skirts, panties, and a hat or "Junior Miss Doll Dress Patterns" with a school dress and a party dress. I feel either is correct and think the company interchanged the patterns when making this set.

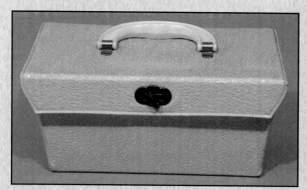

Plate 84. Delux Sewing Basket #1555 was advertised in a Hassenfeld Brothers 1956 trade catalog as: "A good looking practical sewing basket." Manufactured by Hassenfeld Brothers, it is a 9" x 5" x 4" unmarked padded vinyl case with a hard plastic handle and metal latch. Inside on the lid is a cardboard insert that holds three wooden spools of thread, a card with trim, a paper with a needle, metal thimble, and metal blunt-nose scissors. The 8" doll with this set is embossed "Hasbro" with molded painted features, mohair wig, moving arms, and wrapped in a pre-cut dress to be sewn. The bottom of the basket has three hanks of fabric, two pre-cut blouses, slacks, circular skirt, and a cellophane packet with buttons, snaps, and needle threader. To complete the set are a small tomato pincushion with emery and "Junior Miss Dolly Dress Patterns" containing a play dress and party dress. **Complete: $50.00 and up.**

Note: This sewing set was sold in a pink cardboard box advertising it as Delux Sewing Basket #1555. There is no identification on the sewing case after it leaves its box. The only clue is the doll marked "Hasbro" and the number 1555 on the cardboard insert.

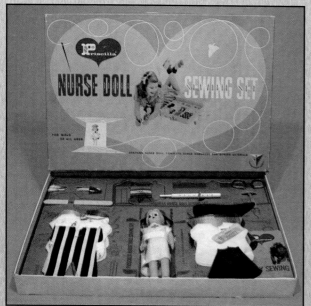

Plate 85. Priscilla Nurse Doll Sewing Set #562 manufactured by Standard Toykraft Products in 1956 is in a 15" x 10" x 1½" box. The inside of the box has great graphics; all types of medical accessories are printed over the surface. Printed on the insert to punch out and use are a medical chart, hot water bottle, and a watch. Inserted into tabs and recessions are a tongue depressor, two cotton swabs, wooden thermometer, and a pair of metal blunt-nose scissors. The unmarked 6" plastic doll is jointed only at the arms; she has molded, painted hair and painted features. The doll is dressed in a pre-cut nurse's uniform to be sewn. On either side of her, stapled to the insert, are a cape, five dresses, scarf, pants suit, and a Curad bandage. A Standard Quality card of thread with a needle is over her head. Included in the set are "Priscilla Easy Sewing Instructions." **Complete: $50.00 and up.**

Note: Priscilla Nurse Doll Sewing Set #562 sold in 1956 for $1.00. A Priscilla Cowgirl Doll Sewing Set #564 with added embroidery inside the lid sold for $2.00, and a Priscilla Bride Doll Sewing Set #567 sold for $4.00. All were manufactured by Standard Toykraft Products.

Plate 86. My First Nursery copyrighted by Samuel Gabriel Sons and Co. in 1957. The box measures 14½" x 12" x 1½". It is a play set as well as a sewing set. Printed in pink and blue on the cardboard insertion are a dresser, lamp, baby powder and lotion, cradle with rockers, four hangers, rattle, and baby bottle to be punched out. Also included are a metal washbasin, pillow, and felt blanket. The 4½" little baby doll was made in Hong Kong and is fully jointed with moveable arms, legs, head, and eyes. She has molded painted hair and is still wrapped in cellophane along with the stuffing for her pillow. Centered in the set are two strips of patterns and instructions with pre-cut fabric stapled to the outline of each pattern. The patterns include jacket, bonnet, coat, bib, and panties. At the bottom of the box are the instructions for assembling the cradle. **Complete: $75.00 and up.**

Plate 87. Junior Miss Sewing Case #1516 was advertised as a new item in the 1957 Hassenfeld Brothers trade catalog. Stating that: "Every little girl will want to own one of these beautiful luggage-style kits." The kit measures 9" in diameter and 4" high. The box is done in a bright, red plaid hatbox style with a lock and handle, with no advertising or title on either the outside or inside of the case. The inside lid holds the 7½" "Hasbro" embossed plastic doll jointed at the arms and head, with a mohair wig and sleep eyes. A pre-cut circular skirt and blouse is tied on her ready to be sewn. On either side of her are the needle threader and the paper with the needle. Stapled to the raised platform in the bottom of the box are two blouses and a circular skirt. Inserted into various flaps and recessions are metal blunt-nose scissors, plastic thimble, a card of sewing thread, and a length of fabric to use with the "Jr. Miss Sewing Kit" pattern and instructions. The pattern consists of a skirt, blouse, panties, dress, and hat. **Complete: $50.00 and up.**

Note: Junior Miss Sewing Case #1516 was sold in a yellow cardboard box with "Jr. Miss Sewing Case" written on the front and a picture of the red plaid case shown both open and closed. The above case has no identification once the box is missing except for the name "Hasbro" which is embossed on both the doll and the handle of the plaid case. I have also seen the same plaid case with a large stick-on label on the front that shows a picture of a girl sewing and the printed title "Junior Miss Sewing Case." This case is marked "pat//Pending."

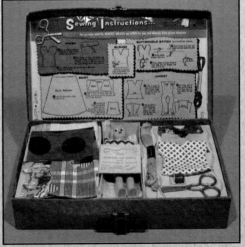

Plate 88. Little Traveler's Sewing Kit #3575 was manufactured by Transogram Company in 1957. The 12" x 7½" x 2½" luggage-style case has a metal bail handle and latch. Inside, in the lid, are the sewing instructions. Children could make jackets, blouses, dresses, and skirts for their doll following the picture directions. The instructions showed you how sew the clothing and make a blouse or jacket from the pre-cut dresses. There was also a skirt pattern to trace. The 6" unmarked doll is under a cardboard sign that states: "Betty dress-up doll with Movable Arms." Betty has molded hair and molded, painted features. The doll is wrapped in a pre-cut dress to be sewn. On one side of Betty are two lengths of fabric for the skirts and two pre-cut dresses. The other side contains three more pre-cut dresses, a plastic thimble, embroidery floss, needle, and a pair of metal blunt-nose scissors. **Complete: $25.00 and up.**

Sewing and Embroidery Sets for Hard Plastic Dolls

Plate 89. Jr. Miss Sewing Kit #1522 was manufactured by Hassenfeld Brothers, circa 1958. It is in a 13" x 9 ½" x 1" box. The 6" tall plastic doll is ⅟₁₆" thick. The doll is white with red embossed features and clothing. Arranged around her in a decorated insert are six pre-cut dresses, a paper with a needle, card of thread, small metal thimble, and metal blunt-nose scissors. The graphics on this box top were used for many different sewing sets in the 1950s. **Complete: $25.00 and up.**

Note: Two other 1950s Hassenfeld Brothers sewing sets offered the flat plastic doll. Junior Miss Sewing and Embroidery Set #4015 was a hanging card with four pre-cut dresses, thread, needle, metal thimble, cardboard hoop, stamped embroidery square, and embroidery instructions. Wardrobe Sewing Set #1531 was in a wardrobe trunk with a see-through front, pre-cut clothing, needle, and thread and sold for $1.00.

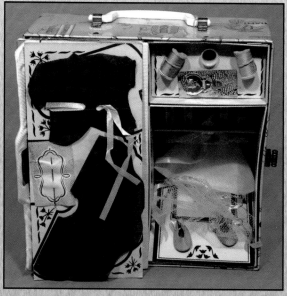

Plate 90. Ballerina Wardrobe Sewing Trunk #1527 was manufactured by Hassenfeld Brothers. The set was shown in their 1958 trade catalog as a new product. It retailed at $4.00. They advertised it as: *A graceful ballerina, moving eye-doll, with real hair, complete with her dancing costume ready to be sewn. Plus a fashionable real velvet costume, plastic clothing hangers, thread, needle, thimble, etc. Beautifully packaged in a sturdy washable vinyl colorful wardrobe trunk. Size 9¼" x 9¼" x 4" Complete with lock and handle...Ages 6 to 12.* **Complete: $75.00 and up.**

Note: The only identification that this set was made by Hassenfeld Brothers is the star-shaped tie-on tag and "Hasbro" embossed on the plastic handle and doll. It is interesting to note the picture of the set in the catalog has the doors to the wardrobe both opening from the center out to the sides to get a better photograph of the contents of the set. It is important to note that the catalogs are not always correct in the true representation of these sets.

Plate 91. The double-bell-shaped hang tag reads "**Bridal Wardrobe Sewing Trunk #1537**." Hassenfeld Brothers manufactured the set in 1958. The pink trunk is 9¼" x 9¼" x 4" and opens at each side. The opening with the window holds the 7½" hard plastic doll. The doll is jointed at the neck and arms, has sleep eyes and a mohair wig, and is embossed "Hasbro." She is wrapped in a pre-cut satin gown with net and ribbon. Tucked beside her is more net and lily of the valley. The other side of the case opens to reveal the rest of her wardrobe. Stapled onto the door are a pre-cut velvet blouse and skirt, some ribbon, and a paper with a needle. Inside the closet is a cotton pre-cut blouse and skirt with cotton trim and two plastic hangers. A wooden rod is secured across the closet to hold her dresses when finished. Above the closet are the sewing supplies, two wooden spools of thread, plastic thimble, and needle threader. **Complete: $75.00 and up.**

Note: There were a series of these sewing wardrobe trunks put out in the late 1950s and they were only marked with the hang tag and "Hasbro" embossed on the handle and doll.

Plate 92. Bridal Party Sewing Kit #1559 was made by Hassenfeld Brothers, circa 1957. This 18" x 12" x 1½" set has a white background with color confetti print. The hinged lid has a picture of a bride and two bridesmaids, the exact same graphics that are shown on the outside of the box. Inside are three 7½" dolls jointed at the head and shoulders. They have sleep eyes, molded features, and mohair wigs. The dolls are all embossed "Hasbro," The bride in the center of the box is wrapped in a pre-cut white satin gown with flowers, ribbon lace, and net. The two bridesmaids at her sides are wrapped in pre-cut pink satin gowns with flowers, ribbons, and net. There are three raised platforms that hold voile circular half-slips, lace, three wooden spools of thread, three hanks of ribbon, plastic thimble, needle threader, and a paper with two needles. **Complete: $25.00 and up.**

Note: This set is the second, smaller Bridal Party Sewing Kit #1559 by Hassenfeld Brothers. The inside of this box is much more lavishly decorated than the larger set. This set doesn't have the flower girl, however the three 7" dolls are upgraded with swivel necks and the purses in the earlier kit are replaced with half-slips. See plate 79 for the larger, earlier kit.

Sewing and Embroidery Sets for Hard Plastic Dolls

Plate 93. Walt Disney's Sleeping Beauty Sewing Set #3595 was presented by Transogram Co. circa 1959. The box is 17" x 12" x 2". This fantasy sewing set has both Princess Aurora and Prince Phillip. The 7½" plastic dolls both have sleep eyes and swivel heads. The prince has a matte finish, molded painted hair and features, and is unmarked. He is wrapped in a pre-cut plastic tunic with a black felt belt, and his legs and shoes are painted back. This doll is definitely a boy doll with a thinner sculptured face and larger nose. Under his tunic he has molded briefs. The prince's pre-cut clothing consists of a cap, shirt, cloak, sword, and shield. The princess has a gloss finish with mohair hair, painted features, and is marked "Transogram." The princess is wrapped in a blouse and a circular skirt, which has been sewn by the first owner. She has another pre-cut blouse, skirt, bodice, and crown. The set also contains a hank of ribbon, rickrack, needle threader, three wooden spools of thread, plastic thimble, needle, blunt nose medal scissors, and "Sleeping Beauty Sewing Instructions" that show running, hemming, and buttonhole stitches. The quality inspection slip is still in this set. **Complete: $100.00 and up.**

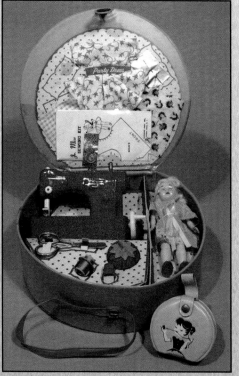

Plate 94. Deb-U-Teen Sewing Kit #1546 was manufactured by Hassenfeld Brothers, circa 1960. It is vinyl and measures about 11" diameter with a squared-off bottom and a carry strap to which is attached a smaller version of the case, 3" in diameter. The inside lid has a plastic pocket and slots that hold a pre-cut party dress, needle threader, needle, two lengths of fabric, and a "Jr. Miss Sewing Kit" pattern. The pattern contains a circular skirt, panties, dress, blouse, and hat. The main compartment holds a Necchi sewing machine with instructions and warranty. The 7½" plastic doll marked "Hasbro" is jointed at the arms and neck, has sleep eyes, and a mohair wig. The doll is wrapped in a pre-cut dress with a hank of ribbon tucked in the waist. To complete the set is a tomato pincushion, plastic thimble, wooden spool of thread, and a pair of metal blunt-nose scissors. **Complete: $75.00 and up.**

Note: This set is rather confusing. It was advertised in a Hassenfeld Brothers trade catalog in 1959 with an Elna sewing machine and in a Rockwell's 1959 Toyland catalog with a Necchi sewing machine. The set was also advertised in a 1960 Hassenfeld Brothers trade catalog with the Necchi machine. I have never found an Elna machine in any of the sets. My feeling is they switched to Necchi before any sets were on the market. I have seen the Necchi machines presented in this sewing set in two colors, red or blue. I have also found the case itself in two colors, aqua or light blue.

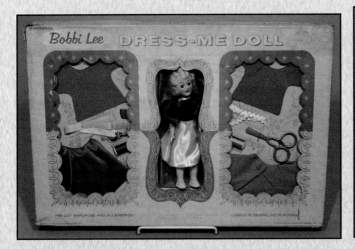 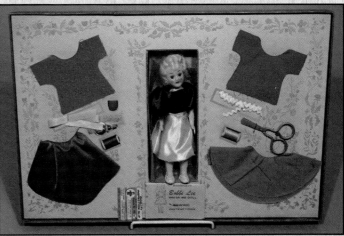

Plate 95. Bobbie Lee Dress Me Doll #3576 is in an 18" x 12" x 1½" box with a window lid. Transogram Company produced this set in 1960. Slipped into the slots in a flowered cardboard insert are two pre-cut blouses, a skirt, and a hooded cloak to sew for the 7½" hard plastic doll. The doll is marked "Transogram" and has a mohair wig, jointed arms and head, and sleep eyes. The doll is wrapped in a pre-cut blouse and skirt ready to sew. The accessories include metal blunt-nose scissors, two wooden spools of thread, small plastic thimble, needle threader, and hank of ribbon and rickrack. Stapled to the cardboard just below the doll is the "Bobbie Lee Dress-Me Doll Sewing Instructions." It shows running, hemming, and buttonhole stitches with detailed instructions on sewing the articles in the set. The set still retains its quality inspection slip. **Complete: $50.00 and up.**

Note: The original retail price of the Bobbie Lee Dress Me Doll set in 1960 was $1.98.

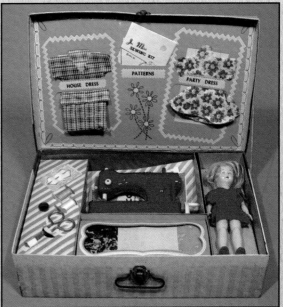

Plate 96. Little Miss Seamstress Sewing Kit #1542 is in a yellow striped luggage-style case, 14" x 9½" x 3½" with a metal bail handle and latch. Hassenfeld Brothers manufactured it circa 1960. The inside lid is decorated with flowers and rickrack and holds a house dress, party dress, and a "Jr. Miss Sewing Kit" pattern. The main compartment holds a Necchi Supernova sewing machine with instructions and manual. Three lengths of fabric are below the machine. The 7½" hard plastic doll is embossed "Hasbro," has molded painted features, mohair wig, and is jointed at the neck and shoulders. Two wooden spools of thread, a paper with a needle, a small plastic thimble, and metal blunt-nose scissors complete the set. **Complete: $75.00 and up.**

Note: The above set #1542 was also offered in a Hasbro trade catalog in 1960 with the machine, clothing, and a red tomato pincushion, but no doll.

Sewing and Embroidery Sets for Hard Plastic Dolls

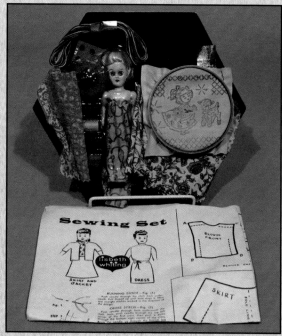

Plate 97. Princess Sewing Set #270 was manufactured by Lisbeth Whiting Co. in 1963. The box is a 9" cardboard hexagon with a carry handle. It has wonderful graphics on the sides of the box of little girls playing with sewing sets. The 6" plastic doll is jointed at the neck and shoulders, has sleep eyes, and a mohair wig. A red tomato pincushion, four wooden spools of thread, card of snaps, needle threader, and a skein of embroidery thread are nestled around the doll. There is a pasteboard hoop holding a square of stamped cloth to be embroidered. There are also eight lengths of fabric to be used with the paper pattern provided in the bottom of the box. The pattern is titled "Sewing Set Lisbeth Whiting." It contains embroidery instructions, a three-piece suit (blouse, jacket, and skirt), and a dress. **Complete: $25.00 and up.**

Plate 98. Model Miss Fashion Sew 'N Show Set #4201 is presented by Transogram Company and is dated 1964. The luggage-style box measures 11" x 7" x 2". The inside lid has the same graphics as the outside lid. On a raised platform are five pre-cut dresses; the last dress holding the needle. Stapled to the bottom of the box is a skein of red embroidery thread with the Transogram Company label. Above the thread, in a recess, is a 6" hard plastic doll with jointed arms and head, molded, painted hair, sleep eyes, and molded, painted red high heels. The doll is marked "Made in Hong Kong" and is dressed in a soft vinyl bra and panties that are removable. A small red plastic thimble and the quality inspection slip complete the set. **Complete: $25.00 and up.**

Note: Still attached to one side of the box is the original Montgomery Ward price sticker of 79 cents.

Plate 99. Little Genius Sewing Basket was made by the Alexander Doll Co., Inc. and was an exclusive from FAO Schwarz in a 1965 Christmas catalog. The wicker basket is 9" x 6½" x 5½" and has a wooden FAO Schwarz hang tag. The doll in this set Madame Alexander's 8" Little Genius with a hard plastic swivel head, sleep eyes, open mouth, synthetic wig, and a fully jointed vinyl body. She is dressed in a Madame Alexander tagged sunsuit and holds a vinyl baby bottle. There are five pre-cut outfits and white bias tape tied with ribbons and arranged around the doll in the bottom of the basket. The lid of the basket holds two wooden spools of thread, a plastic thimble, tomato pincushion, metal scissors, and packet of needles. The calico bag holds five little papers of instructions for the pre-cut outfits that include a nightgown, robe, coat and hood, diaper set, and a two-piece dress. **Complete: $1,000.00 and up.**

Note: In the Little Genius Sewing Basket in the 1961 FAO Schwarz Christmas catalog the doll wore only panties. The 1961 set was advertised for $7.98. The above 1965 Little Genius Sewing Basket was offered for $9.95.

Plate 100. Wendy Loves to Sew was manufactured by Alexander Doll Co., Inc. in 1994. It came in a varnished wicker basket 9" x 5½" x 4" with handles and slide closures. Wendy, the doll, is part of a Wendy Loves series. The doll is 7", all hard plastic, jointed at neck, arms, and legs, with sleep eyes, synthetic wig and molded, painted features. She is dressed in a tagged Wendy Loves to Sew sunsuit and a matching hat. A Wendy Loves to Sew pink hang tag is tied on her wrist. The bottom of the basket is lined with a quilted pad printed with miniature sewing implements, to which is tied a vinyl tape measure and a pair of blunt-nose Fiskars scissors. There are four little loose packets. One packet contains a metal thimble and sheer pink tights. The others are pre-cut fabrics and trims for outfits, including a ballerina tutu, pajamas, and a sundress. Also included are instructions for making the pre-cut outfits. A really nice learning set. **Complete: $100.00 and up.**

Note: FAO Schwarz marketed a number of exclusive sewing sets using Madame Alexander dolls through the years, but this is not one of them. The above set was made and sold by Madame Alexander and available in most retail outlets that carried the Madame Alexander doll line.

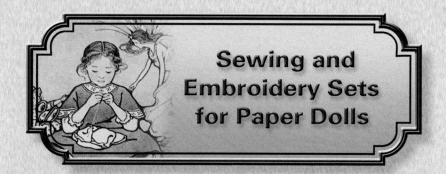

Sewing and Embroidery Sets for Paper Dolls

According to Clara Fawcett in *Collector's Guide to Antique Paper Dolls*, the first paper dolls appeared in Europe in 1791 and were advertised in *Journal der Moden*. The advertisement read:

A new and very pretty invention is the so-called English doll which we have lately received from London. It is properly a toy for little girls, but is so pleasing and tasteful that mothers and grown women will likely also want to play with it, the more since good and bad taste in dress or coiffure can be observed and, so to speak, studied. The doll is a young female figure cut out of stout cardboard. It is about eight inches high, has simply curled hair, and is dressed in underclothing and corset. With it go six complete sets of tastefully designed dresses and head-dresses which are cut out of paper…The whole thing comes in a neat paper envelope which can be easily carried in a hand-bag or work-box to give amusement at parties or to children.

In about 1850 paper dolls began to find their way into the American market. Around 1857 in the United States McLoughlin Brothers began to supply the market with printed paper dolls, paper furniture, and paper toy soldiers.

As early as the 1870s patents were granted for action paper dolls (paper dolls jointed at the shoulders and hips so that the arms and legs could be moved). These dolls were lady dolls, famous actresses, and operetta stars. Many of the dolls were printed in Germany by the firm of Littauer & Bauer, however almost all the actresses depicted were English or American. They were sold in Germany as decorations; in the United States they were usually sold undressed to be dressed in paper or cloth costumes.

Dennison was founded in 1844 and started as a manufacturer of artistic paper boxes for jeweler's use, and later distributing many paper products including crepe paper and paper dolls. Dennison became the largest distributor of jointed dolls in the United States and they included the jointed dolls in their catalogs of crepe paper supplies. The first dolls were the lady dolls which were not sold in sets, but offered individually to be dressed as one pleased with Dennison's crepe paper, gummed gold and silver stars, and "flitters" (glitter). There were suggestions in the catalogs on how one might dress the dolls with Dennison supplies.

Collectors find these dolls in their early crepe and tissue paper confections and marvel at the ingenuity shown in the making of the intricate costumes. The dresses are plaited, gathered, flounced, and trimmed to exhaustion. In Clara Fawcett's book *Collector's Guide to Antique Paper Dolls*, she tells of a

booklet by Mr. Wilbur Macy Stone and how he talks of homemade paper dolls and their costumes.

They are built up of plaited paper and overlays of great ingenuity, while the evening gown, with a train, is made of blue tissue paper with an underskirt of white chiffon and lace. The skirt is garnished with white embossed flowers from an old valentine. While all of these dresses are fronts only, they surely come pretty near to being three-dimensional creations. They would serve as excellent models for a dressmaker.

Dennison also put together craft boxes for children. One such box shown in an early catalog was Dennison's Complete Outfit. It was advertised as follows: "*Put up in an attractive illuminated box.*"

It contained 36 sheets of (15" x 20") assorted imported tissue, eight pieces of crepe paper, one piece tubing each, small and large, one dozen each cutouts, cut sprays, natural moss, one spool hair and cotton covered wire, one dozen each poppy centers, poppy buds, rose centers, daisy centers, one dozen daisy petals, four dolls heads, four pairs legs, four body forms, four dress forms, and a book of instructions.

Because records of the earlier years of Dennison Manufacturing Company are sketchy, it is not certain when the first Dennison sets were dedicated just to dolls. I have found two early catalogs with doll sets offered at the turn of the nineteenth century.

Dennison's Nursery Outfit was described in an undated catalog as such:

We have made a complete outfit for paper doll making, which we call our "nursery outfit." It includes one doll's dress, complete, a number of heads, also stiff paper bodies for new dresses, lace paper for edging and trimming, and an ample supply of tissue paper in selected colors for making dresses. It may be said of the paper dolls in this outfit, with the tissue paper dresses, that they are far ahead of the old style of paper dolls in beauty and variety. Where the nursery is supplied with these the child's artistic instincts will be cultivated and its ingenuity stimulated. The softened, beautiful tints and colors of the tissue paper material are in themselves an education to the eye and the taste.

The set contained materials for four complete stationary limbed dolls, six sheets of tissue paper, paper lace, star ornaments, silver embossed paper, and a booklet of instructions, and sold for thirty-five cents.

The Little Mothers' Outfit came in an 11" x 6" box. It contained five 15" x 10" sheets of tissue, two pieces of crepe paper, two jointed dolls, four dress forms, gold and silver stars, one piece of paper lace, three sheets of lace paper. Included was "Little Mothers' Fashion Book" showing designs and directions for making doll's dresses, and a copy of "Art and Decoration in Crepe and Tissue Paper," an instructional catalog with 144 pages and 130 samples of tissue and crepe papers. Little Mothers' Outfit sold for 35 cents.

Dolls were also sold separately, or in envelopes. In a 1905 Dennison catalog under Crepe and Tissue Paper for the Children are advertised Dennison's doll's heads and legs in envelopes.

We put up in attractive envelopes, one dozen each, assorted Dolls' Heads and Legs, Body Forms and Dress Forms. Per Envelope, 20 cents. Postpaid 25 cents. The envelopes of heads, and legs supplied a demand for a variety of extra dolls different from those in the doll outfits.

In a 1906 Dennison catalog under Jointed-Doll Forms was the advertisement of:

Lithographed dolls, a new patented style complete in all parts; that is, with head and limbs attached to a body form. The arms and legs are movable, being jointed with eyelets, as shown in the cut. These dolls are very handsome and can be artistically gowned by using Dennison's Crepe Paper.

The list had a 6½" and an 8½" baby, each with four designs; a ballet dancer 5¾" in four designs, 9¾" in three designs, and a 13¾" in three designs; the prima donna came in sizes 9¾" and 16¾", both with three designs; a child was offered in sizes 7" and 9¼" each with six designs; also included were an American Indian, 10" with two designs; and an African baby size 9" with three designs.

The first set catalog set I have actually seen is Dennison's Crepe and Tissue Paper Doll Outfit (plate 101). It doesn't have a number as the later sets do. It was advertised in a Dennison's 1907 catalog as follows:

Dennison's Doll Outfits. This outfit is a new combination of dolls, and materials for dressing. Every little mother will be delighted with it. The dolls have pretty faces and jointed arms and legs. The material will make all sorts of pretty dresses, hats, etc., and there are patterns and directions to tell how. The outfit is complete, put up in a handsome box with transparent cover.

The contents were listed as follows: *Assorted Colors Crepe Paper. Assorted Colors Tissue Paper. Gold and Silver Stars. Paper Lace. Crepe Paper Ribbon. Two Jointed Dolls. Patterns and Directions for Making Hats and Dresses.*

I found Dennison's Crepe & Tissue Paper Doll Outfit #31 (plate 102) in a 1912 – 1913 Dennison catalog. The advertisement read:

This is an outfit containing two dolls and all materials necessary to make dresses, hats, etc. The forms are ready-cut, so that even little people can enjoy the dressmaking. While the older ones may, of course, elaborate with the material ready to cut. An enclosed circular gives illustrated directions for making the wardrobe.

The contents are listed as:

Two Paper Dolls, movable arms and legs. Small rolls of

Crepe Paper, assorted colors. Colored Tissue-Gold and Silver paper. Gold and Silver Stars. Crepe Paper Ribbon. Paper Lace. Strips of Decorated Paper. Dress and Hat Forms. Fashion Sheet with Dressmaking instruction. The price was still thirty-five cents.

It is interesting to note that in the 1913 catalog there were only two sizes of dolls listed separately, a 7" and 9½" each with six designs, pretty faces, and movable arms and legs.

In a 1916 Dennison's catalog I found Dennison Doll Outfit #34 and Dennison Doll Outfit #33, the write-ups were small. Under the heading of Dennison's Paper Doll Outfits, it read:

No. 34. Dennison's Dolls and Dresses Just the outfit for the littlest girl. Contains three paper dolls, crepe paper printed with dresses, hats and coats to fit them, white paper for cutting slips and a circular of patterns. 25 cents.

The dolls in this outfit were also sold separately at five cents for No. 1, the small baby doll; six cents for No. 2, the next largest doll; seven cents each for the largest, No. 3.

Set No. 33 Dennison's Crepe and Tissue Paper Doll Outfit (plate 105) was a larger outfit containing not only three dolls and crepe paper printed with dresses, hats, and coats, but dress forms, tissue paper, crepe paper, dress trimmings, a tube of paste, and a fashion book. It sold for 50 cents. The two larger girls in this set were different from the two larger girls in set #34; the baby was the same. Both sets #33 and #34 have underwear printed on the front of the body. In the previous sets the body sections were plain white; with colors being used only on the head, arms, and legs.

Little Tot's Crepe Paper Doll Outfit #36 (plate 113) has the same dolls and supplies as Crepe Paper Doll Outfit #36. In a 1931 catalog there were three sets advertised, the advertising stated:

Doll Outfits. Lots of fun for the children. The dolls are life-like, with movable arms and legs. The dresses are printed on crepe paper, ready to be cut out. Material for making extra clothes is included in each outfit. Boxed set #36 is a very gay box containing three dolls, a printed sheet of dresses, plain and decorated crepe papers, dress and hat forms, paper lace and trimmings, wooden stands for the dolls, and an instruction leaflet. Each $1.00.

The other two sets were envelopes: Dennison Dolls and Dresses #37, with three dolls for fifty cents, and Nancy Crepe Paper Doll Outfit #38, with only one doll for twenty-five cents (plate 114). The middle girl in Little Tot's Crepe Paper Doll Outfit #36 and Crepe Paper Doll Outfit #36 is the same doll as in Nancy Crepe Paper Doll Outfit #38. Dennison seemed to be adding more printed clothing as time went on and less and less crepe and tissue paper and trimmings for decorating. The sets became simpler, and seemed to be aimed at the younger child. The three sets above seem to be the last of the creative crepe paper dressed dolls from Dennison; the sets after this date only came with printed dresses to be cut out.

Milton Bradley, the name we associate with board games, was another company that put out a splendid boxed set of paper dolls. In September of 1914 *Little Folks* periodical ran an advertisement for Bradley's Tru-Life Paper Dolls. The ad stated:

Bradley's Tru-Life Paper Dolls The most up-to-date Paper Dolls made, with dresses such as every little girl wears herself and made from patterns just like her own little dresses are made. Contains three dolls, a 'girl of fourteen,' 'one of six years,' and a 'baby doll,' outline patterns, lithographed plates, showing dresses in colors, colored paper 'dress goods.' trimming, cardboard buttons, patterns for foundation of dresses, and complete book of instructions, showing how to make up the dresses for all sizes of dolls. Put up in an attractive box size 11⅔" x 7½". Send 35¢ in stamps for a set of these Paper Dolls. Also made in two larger editions, 50¢ and $1.00. Milton Bradley Co.

There were three doll sets that I know of, set #4319, set #4320, and set #4321. Bradley's Tru-Life Paper Dolls Set #4321 (plate 103) was the largest of the three sets, and had 12 dolls. There were three styles of dolls, a big sister, little sister and baby sister, with two blondes and two brunettes in each style. This provided four sets of the same paper dolls in each box. Bradley's Tru-Life Paper Dolls Set #4320 had six dolls, a blonde and brunette in each size; and Bradley's Tru-Life Paper Dolls Set #4319 came with three dolls, in either blonde or brunette. Sometime later Milton Bradley also made Bradley's Cutie Dolls #4716 and #4717. They were along the same line as the Tru-Life, but much smaller. Milton Bradley's paper dolls sets were used as toys, yet they taught dressmaking and design, they are wonderful creative sets.

Samuel Gabriel & Sons was established in 1907 and started making paper dolls around 1911. Through the years the company has made many unusual paper dolls, dolls with moving eyes, changing heads, Velcro dolls, dolls with "real" hair, and a number of dolls with real cloth clothing to sew. Sew Easy Doll #D-119 (plate 107) came with pre-cut dresses to sew, along with ribbons to use for trim and sashes. The doll was very heavy cardboard with arms jointed at the shoulder and elbow so they would bend easily when dressing. My Complete Sew-Dress Doll #D-114 (plate 109) had two cardboard dolls that had double-jointed arms. The outfits for these dolls were quite a bit more involved; they had to be cut out and came with belts, pockets, and various trimmings to be added when sewing. The little booklet that came with the dolls was called "Modes and Fashions for Sewdress Dolls" and gave instructions on how to make the outfits. The general instructions stated:

The little dressmaker will then note that the muslin sheets of dresses and the muslin sheets of hats are correspondingly named and numbered. Each box does not contain the full range of dresses shown in this fashion magazine. The larger boxes have a more elaborate assortment than the smaller ones, but in the magazine you will surely find illustrated the particular dresses contained in your box. The patterns will then indicate to you how each dress should look, back and front. Match up the dresses and hats and cut out on the outermost outline all the various pieces printed on the muslin sheets. Since the dresses and hats are printed both back and front, fold the dresses accurately on the shoulder lines, and hats on the top lines, so that the front and back match perfectly before sewing. Remember to sew on the back or plain side of material, allowing about a quarter inch margin as indicated by the dotted lines, for a seam. Turn the dress or hat when sewn on the right side. For buttons, the little brass pins enclosed in each box answer admirably. These can be readily slipped in to place and bent back to hold, and can be used over and over again.

There were also individual directions for each separate outfit. The outfits were very stylish and reflected the fashions of the time. The box top advertised:

Cardboard dolls. Real cloth dresses and hats to cut out with all necessary materials. Easy work for nimble little fingers. To keep busy the little hands and little head.

Other sets of paper dolls with sewing manufactured by Samuel Gabriel & Sons Company that are not shown in this book are:

D-104 Cloth Dresses to Sew for Polly Pet
D-106 Dresses to Sew for Mary Ann
D-108 Cloth Dresses to Sew for My Twin
D-119 Sew-Easy Doll Dainty Dot
D-120 Sew-Easy Dolls

Emmylou Specialties by Charles Bloom Inc. (plate 108) advertised their dolls sometime around the 1920s, but not much is known about this company. The first dolls were not named and could be bought in either blonde or brunette hairstyles. The dolls are very well made of a heavy board and wouldn't bend or break when dressing. When you purchased an outfit for your doll it came in a brown craft envelope with everything needed to complete it, including a paper draft of the pattern that was already printed on the fabric, and complete instructions for sewing the garment. On the reverse side of the instructions were the wonderful illustrations of the other Emmylou clothing kits you could buy.

The first set showed all dresses, many with matching bloomers, and all had matching hats with large brims. The advertising sheet was marked in the two upper corners with the initials CB entwined in a diamond. The blonde doll that was shown was portrayed a little differently than the actual doll sold, in the illustration she had black shoes and a ribbon across her forehead, the purchased doll had white shoes and no ribbon. The dolls were priced at thirty cents and the clothing kits were 60¢.

Sometime later, a second series of clothing and a new doll named Brother was offered. In the second set the same blonde doll was called Emmylou, but the dark-haired doll wasn't mentioned. The prices for the dolls and clothing kits were still the same. This advertising sheet not only had the initials CB, they had added Inc. underneath the initials and Charles Bloom Inc., New York was printed in a lower corner. The outfits shown for Emmylou were a party dress, pajamas, automobile coat, garden apron, gymnasium suit, and school frock. Brother's costumes were a morning suit, pajamas, sport coat, afternoon suit, play and undersuits, and a sailor suit. In the second set the dresses didn't show bloomers, and some were without hats. In all, there were 18 outfits for Emmylou, and six for Brother.

The cloth used in the costumes were quality fabrics; the first set had most outfits out of organdy and gingham, only one was colored crash, the second set included net, organdy, crepe, crash, sateen, cretone, percale, Indian head, gingham, linen, and Palm Beach cloth. These dolls and the outfits are hard to find. What a thrill it would be to find an Emmylou with a whole wardrobe!

American Toy Works was founded in the 1920s by two brothers Adolph and Max Wein. They advertised sewing and embroidery sets and kindergarten toys in *Playthings* magazine from the late 1920s well into the 1940s. In a February 1929 issue of *Playthings* magazine they offered several new numbers in sewing and embroidery sets, featuring a special Children's Day number in the form of a combination paper doll and sewing outfit to retail at $1.00.

There were a number of paper doll sewing sets presented by this company. Modern Girls Sewing Set #300 (plate 110) was one of the simplest with only one doll and four dresses to be sewn. Sewing for Girls Stitchart #528 (plate 112) was more typical of their sets with many things and activities to do most of their sets had a lot of play value.

Other sets offered by American Toy Works that are not shown in this book are:

#102 Paper Doll Outfit
#417 Modern Sewing for Little Girls
#901 Little Folks Crepe Paper Doll Outfit
#903 Little Folks Crepe Paper Doll Outfit (larger set)
#1000 Every Day Play Set
#3081 Dolly's Kut-Out Klothes
#3083 Make Dolly's Wardrobe

John McLoughlin founded his business in 1828 in New York City, as a publisher of children's books. Sometime after 1857, he and his brother Edmund formed a partnership and the first paper dolls were produced under the name of McLoughlin Brothers. McLoughlin Brothers became the largest manufacturers of paper dolls in the United States. When the last of the McLoughlin Brothers sold out their interest to Milton Bradley in 1920, the business was then relocated to Springfield, Massachusetts. Milton Bradley retained the McLoughlin name and during the 1930s produced many paper dolls under it including The Sewing Book of the Round About Girls (plate 115). After 1944, Grosset & Dunlap Inc. absorbed McLoughlin. The name McLoughlin Brothers was still retained under Grosset & Dunlap, however they published only certain types of books under the McLoughlin name. The name was reserved for board books for very young children, pop-ups, and other toy and activity books. As far as I've been able to find out, the name of McLoughlin went out of publication sometime in 1978.

Transogram Company was making bisque doll sewing sets in the 1930s, composition doll sewing sets in the 1940s, and plastic doll sewing sets in the 1950s, so it is no surprise they made paper doll sewing sets, too. The paper dolls sets were not as impressive as their other sewing sets; the paper dolls were made with the thinnest of cardboard, and were interchanged in different sets, all dolls looking about the same. Often the dolls had to be punched out of a decorated cardboard insert. The clothing was always a bit too large and very simple.

There are four Transogram paper doll sewing sets in this chapter. The Style Show Sewing Set #1531 (plate 117) is one of the nicest, containing five cardboard dolls and 12 dresses that look like they might actually fit the dolls. The box is nicely arranged and has ample supplies. Doll House Dress Shop #1515 (plate 116) is a cheaper set, again with five dolls, but this time to be punched out of the insert. The clothing looks too large even if a generous seam allowance was allowed in the sewing. The last two, Little Travlers Sewing Kit #1565 (plate 129) and Little Travelers Sewing Kit #3574/5 (plate 130) are very much the same. Each is a luggage-type with different graphics and closures, but the insides reflect essentially the same dolls and clothing. The Transogram Company paper doll sewing sets were offered during the 1930s and 1940s along with the company's bisque and composition dolls sewing sets.

Concord Toy Co. Inc. of New York produced paint, crayon, and sewing sets during the 1940s. Concord's most popular sewing sets were the Stitchcraft sewing line. Stitchcraft Sewing Set #202 (plate 127) was one of their paper dolls sewing sets. There were at least three different box top graphics that used the Stitchcraft title. Inside were either one or two paper dolls, depending on the size of the set. Concord also carried Stitchcraft Sewing Set #204 (plate 48) in chapter 2 that was larger and carried both a composition and paper dolls. Concord Toy Company, Inc. also made the Mayflower Sewing Set #200 (plate 124). Most of the paper dolls that came with the sets were blonde with jointed arms, but occasionally there was a dark-haired girl with stationary arms. The patterns that came with the sets never varied.

Whitman Publishing Company is best known for its books, especially the Little Golden Books. It was in 1907 when E. H. Wadewitz founded the Western Publishing Company in Racine, Wisconsin. It changed its name to Whitman in 1915. Samuel Lowe, who worked for Whitman, discovered Queen Holden in the 1920s, and was largely responsible for Whitman entering into the paper doll trade. Queen Holden drew paper doll books for Whitman for 20 years. Samuel Lowe left Whitman Publishing Co. in the 1940s to form a company under his own name. There are three paper doll sewing sets from Whitman in this chapter. Two are boxed sets that are quite inventive. Make Marys Clothes #5338 (plate 131) is a well thought-out set. The instructions lists the things needed to make the clothing: needle, scissors, clean cloth, and paste. Each outfit has detailed instructions, along with the general instructions.

The general instructions are:

1. Lay the dress material on the table with the bright side facing down. Cover it with a thin layer of paste and lay the tissue pattern on it with the printed side up. Be sure the printed border of the pattern is even with the edges of the material.

2. Pat carefully with a clean cloth so the pattern will stick smoothly and neatly to the material.

3. Cut along the heavy lines of the pattern. Be careful in cutting the edges from the tissue pattern. These strips will be used later. "Special Helps." While the paste is still damp on the material, the pieces can be molded so they will fit Mary perfectly. If the edges are not smooth, touch them lightly with colorless nail polish. Remember that the pattern is pasted on the back of each dress, and all trimming is pasted or sewed to the other side on the material. By holding the dress up to the light you can see the lines on the pattern plainly enough to follow them.

There were a couple of outfits done in the set by the previous owner and they worked out quite well.

The other boxed Whitman set, Trim Dotty's Dresses #5336 (plate 132) is for the younger child and teaches embroidery. The set came with all the necessary items to trim Dotty's dresses. Each outfit was pre-punched and color-coded to match up with the thread, although this didn't give the child a chance of coordinating their own color choices, it did assure the child an attractive outfit when done, and most children love the matching game.

Saalfield Publishing Company was founded in 1900 when Arthur J. Saalfield purchased the publishing division of Werner Co. In 1902, Saalfield published his first children's book *Billy Whiskers* written by Mrs. Frances Montgomery. This endeavor launched Saalfield into becoming one of the United States most successful publishers of children's books. Saalfield was impressed with England's rag book line, and wanted to add a line of cloth books to his company.

In 1906, he purchased the Globe Sign Co., a manufacturer of advertising signs lithographed in color on muslin. Not only did he print the muslin books with pictures for babies, Saalfield went on to print *Babies of All Nations*. It was the first doll-book that the company printed, and it had 12 dolls to cut out, stuff, and sew. He also printed muslin dolls on single sheets to be cut out and sewn.

He published as many as 40 different sheets of dolls. Some of his single dolls were the Greenaway Muslin Doll, Muslin Teddy Bear, Dolly Dear, Topsy-Turvy Doll, Mammy Doll, Little Mary, Golden Locks, The Rag Family, Fritz, Baby Blue Eyes, and Priscilla. Saalfield muslin dolls were printed from 1908 until the late 1930s.

Saalfield's biggest break came from the movies and Shirley Temple. In 1933, they were given the exclusive rights to publish Shirley Temple products. A true sewing doll published by Saalfield was Corrine #5181 (plate 134) along with Jeannette #5180 (not pictured). They both came in a sturdy box with real cloth dresses to sew.

Saalfield also published Paper Dolls with Lace-on Costumes #6068 (plate 135). This set was the first of three sets with the same name and number, however the paper dolls were different. The above set was published in 1955 and had dolls named Janie, Sue, and Nancy; the second set was published circa 1960s and had dolls Carol, Bunny, and Linda, and the last set was published in the late 1960s and had dolls named Michele, Carolyn, and Elaine. All three sets continued to be printed with only the box covers changing for a number of years.

Saalfield made other sewing dolls but mostly with lace-on costumes. Sets not shown in this book are:

#735 Bonnie Lassie
#735 Indian Paper Dolls with Papoose
#6189 6 Standing Dolls with Lace-On Costumes
#9859 Shirley Temple Play Kit with Lace-On Costumes
#9868 Shirley Temple Play Kit

Standard Toykraft Products produced children's boxed sewing sets from the 1920s into the 1960s. The dolls in their sewing sets ranged from bisque to composition to plastic, and in the 1950s and 1960s, the company entered the paper doll field. The sets I have found are paper dolls made in the likeness of vinyl dolls of that time period. Betsy McCall's Fashion Shop Embroidery Set #401 (plate 137) was one of the paper doll sewing sets this company manufactured. The booklet, copyrighted by Standard Toykraft Products and McCall, states:

You'll enjoy embroidering pretty clothes for Betsy McCall. It's fun to choose a lovely party dress or smart playsuit and the prettiest color thread for it. Then, thread your needle. Knot the ends of your thread. Push needle up from underneath side of cloth to start your design. Stitch away. Soon your nimble fingers will fly.

At the same time the above #401 set was put on the market, Betsy McCall's Fashion Shop Embroidery Set #402 (plate 138) was also advertised. It was a larger set with two dolls, Betsy and Linda McCall. Some of Betsy's clothing was duplicated, with only a color change, between the two sets. The booklet was the same except for color. Written on the back of both booklets is:

The Betsy McCall Fashion Shop Embroidery Set is just one of the many educational play products that Standard Toykraft manufacturers. Have you tried some of the others? Priscilla Charm Jewelry — Embroidery, Tapestry, and Doll Sewing Sets. Sampler Tapestry Weaving Set and Terry Towel Applique Set. Tom Sawyer Paints — Finger Paints, Slate & Chalk sets. Petal Craft, the creative design set and many more.

Barbie & Ken Fashion Embroidery Set #502 (plate 141), advertised in the early 1960s, was another Standard Toykraft Products set that was taken from the likeness of a vinyl doll. In all three sets the clothing was to be embroidered before it was cut out.

Paper dolls have an enormous appeal and have been entertaining children for centuries. Paper dolls have been made with houses to live in, carriages to ride, beds to sleep in, have been made to walk, to be dimensional, and have real hair and moving eyes.

But most important, paper dolls have been our link to fashion through the years, and have been instrumental in teaching little girls about fashion and sewing.

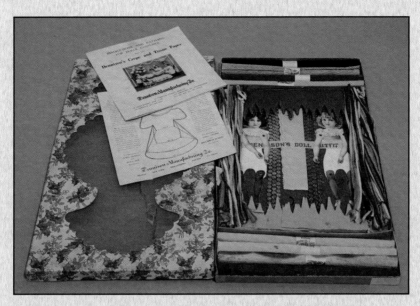

Plate 101. Dennison's Crepe and Tissue Paper Doll Outfit manufactured by Dennison Manufacturing Company, circa 1905. This set is complete and shown as sold in 1907. The box is 14½" x 8" x ½" and is covered in holly. Inside still sewn in place under the Dennison's Doll Outfit banner are the two 7" grommet jointed dolls, a brunette and a blonde. Between the dolls is crepe paper imitation lace and gold and silver gummed stars. Under the dolls are five pieces of tissue paper, and at their sides are ⅛" x 9" crepe paper ribbons. Above and below the dolls are strips of crepe paper flutings for "fancy-work" and eight rolls of crepe paper in assorted colors. Completing the set are instructions and patterns for doll costumes which also contain four pages of advertisements for Dennison products. In addition, there are three patterns for the dolls' dresses superimposed on one page: the baby dress, little girl's dress, little girl's blouse suit and hat. **Complete: $100.00 and up.**

Note: Dennisons' Crepe and Tissue Paper Doll Outfit doesn't have a number. The white box version was listed in a 1905 Dennison catalog for twenty-five cents or thirty-five cents postpaid. It was offered again in a 1907 catalog as: "The outfit is complete, put up in a handsome box with transparent cover, plain white or holly covered. A beautiful gift for any child, and one which never fails to please. Price, 25¢." There are no printed sheets (forms) for backing the tissue dresses, just the superimposed patterns in the instructions. You used your own paper, however there are instructions on how to cut the patterns: "to be cut double with seam on top." I have found ledger paper, old letters, and envelopes used for forms on the backs of the crepe and tissue dresses of these early Dennison paper dolls.

Plate 102. Dennison's Crepe & Tissue Paper Doll Outfit #31 was manufactured by Dennison Manufacturing Company circa 1913. The box is 14" x 8" x 1". There are two 7" dolls, one blonde and one brunette, jointed at the arms and legs with grommets, slightly different from the 1905 Dennison set. Also in the box are four small rolls of assorted color crepe paper, colored tissue, gold and silver paper, crepe paper ribbon, paper lace, parasol wire, strips of decorated paper, dress and hat forms, and a fashion sheet with dressmaking instructions. This set has two sets of instructions, both are titled "Dennison's Fashions for Dolls Vol. 1." They are exactly the same in printed content, and have instructions for a variety of costumes, however the Plates vary, one booklet having much finer drawings than the other. The instructions are very clear and give excellent directions for making up the costumes. There are directions and Plates for 11 outfits: middy dress, party dress, fancy star costume, laced dress, semi dressy style walking suit, afternoon toilet, morning dress, tub dress, dress with yoke, high-waist frock, a bathing suit and parasol, two hats, and two pages of advertisements. **Complete: $100.00 and up.**

Note: Dennison's Crepe & Tissue Paper Doll Outfit #31 was offered in a 1913 Dennison's catalog for the price of thirty five cents. This is the first Dennison set I have found with the dressmaking forms pre-cut.

Plate 103. Bradley's Tru-Life Paper Dolls #4321 manufactured by Milton Bradley Company, circa 1914. The box top measures approximately 15" x 12". Found with the set are 12 lithographed paper dolls, two blonde and two brunette 9½" big sisters, two blonde and two brunette 8" little sisters, and two blonde and two brunette 6" baby sisters. It has been written that an American artist painted the dolls using real life models hence, the name Tru-Life. The set comes with four color-printed dresses for each doll all ready to cut out and use. There are also two foundation forms to trace and eight sheets of brown paper patterns for each size doll, 24 in all. The box contains a variety of dress goods (printed and plain papers), trimmings, and buttons from which extra dresses can be made. Even though there is no actual sewing, the patterns provide the means of practical experience in the fundamental principles of dressmaking, including cutting, plaiting, gathering, trimming, and general construction. The papers are amazing in this set; some are tissue and other heavier papers have different textures to look like calicos, leather, linen, tweed, polished cotton, suiting, wool, etc. The buttons are tiny circles punched from thick paper and have a domed look. The patterns are wonderfully creative and easy to follow with ideas on trims and style. Each pattern has a completed garment to show how it should look when done. The color-printed dresses in the set give the child an idea of colors and trims. The instruction booklet for Bradley's Tru-Life Paper Dolls says it is: "presenting modern and artistic dress designing by means of fashion plates and actual patterns." There is an extra pattern in the instruction booklet for the little sister dolls and instructions on how to put it together. **Complete: $100.00 and up.**

Note: Bradley also sold two smaller sets in 1914, set #4319 with three dolls and #4320 with six dolls.

Plate 104. Embroidery Dolls Sister Helen manufactured by Kaufmann & Strauss, circa 1915. The box is missing from the plate but, it is approximately 10" x 6". Sister Helen is 9" and made of thin-weight card stock. She has tiny pin pricked holes in a design on her underclothes to be embroidered. Sister Helen came with four dresses with matching hats. The hats are missing from this set. The set comes with embroidery silk and a needle. All her dresses have tiny pin pricked holes to be embroidered with the embroidery silk, the previous owner has done some of the embroidery. Sister Helen is holding a different toy with each of her costumes. **Complete: $75.00 and up.**

Note: Embroidery Dolls came in four different sets: Sister Ruth, Sister Helen, Sister Mary, and Brother Jack, each with four costumes and hats.

Plate 105. Dennison Crepe and Tissue Paper Doll Outfit #33 was manufactured by Dennison Manufacturing Company, circa 1916. The box is 14" x 8" x 1". Included in this set are two 7½" little girl dolls, one blonde and one brunette, and a 6¼" baby doll. All dolls are jointed with grommets at the arms and legs. There is a 17" x 20" piece of crepe paper printed with dresses, hats, and coats for each doll. This is the first Dennison set I have found with the pre-printed costumes. They were to be cut out and pasted to the pre-cut forms. Included in the set are 20 dress forms, 12 hat forms, six legging forms, six sheets of 8" x 10" tissue and crepe paper in assorted colors, white paper lace, gold and silver stars, paper buttons, flower petals, wide and narrow crepe paper ribbon, a tube of paste, and an instruction book. The instruction book, "Dennison's Fashion for Dolls" has directions and plates for nine outfits; a cape and hat, little white suit, white apron, negligee, sleeper, jumper dress, fine crepe dress, middy suit, and checked dress. There is also one page of advertisements. **Complete: $100.00 and up.**

Note: I have found this set advertised in a 1916 and a 1922 Dennison catalog. The price of the 1916 set was fifty cents, by 1922 it had reached one dollar. It is the only Dennison set I have found with the Dennison art paste included.

Plate 106. Dollie's Sewing Box, circa 1917, doesn't have a maker's name on the 7½" x 6" x ¾" box, however it says it is instructive and amusing for children. There is also a little poem on the front of the box that reads: "I love to sew for Dolly Dear, She is so cute and sweet; and so I'll make my stitches very small and neat." The doll is a 7¼" hand-tinted photographic paper little girl. Also included in the set are squares of cotton fabric and a gathered piece of red crepe paper, to which are attached four needles and white thread. **Complete: $50.00 and up.**

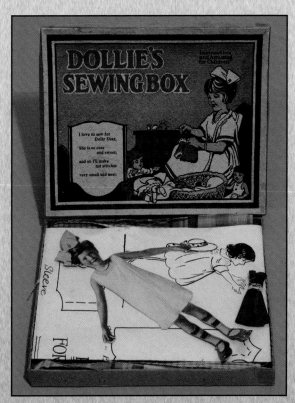

Plate 107. Sew Easy Doll Real Cloth Dresses To Make #D-119 by Sam'l Gabriel Sons & Company, circa 1920. The box is 12" x 7" x 1". Inside the box is an 11" stand-up cardboard doll with grommets at her shoulders and elbows. In the box are four pre-cut dresses with matching cloche hats. With each outfit there is embroidery rope and ribbon for trimming and binding. Inside the lid are pictures and directions:

Suggestion for the little dressmaker. The cloth dresses provided in this set are already cut, making very simple work for the beginner. They should be sewn together on the reverse side, then turned, and the trimming and embroidery applied. The hats should also be made this way. The trimmings and finishing of the dresses and hats will give the little dressmaker opportunity to use her own originality and taste, and the completed articles can be as simple or elaborate as desired. **Complete: $50.00 and up.**

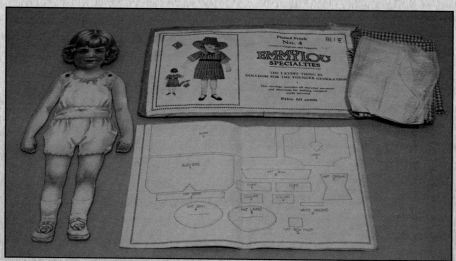

Plate 108. Emmylou and Emmylou Specialties Plaited Frock #4 was produced under the name of Emmylou Specialties by Charles Bloom Inc., circa 1920. Emmylou is 13¾" tall and beautifully lithographed on both front and back, she is ⅛" thick and her arms are inserted between the front and back layers and secured with grommets. Emmylou came in blonde and brunette hairstyles and could be purchased at the price of thirty cents. Her clothing was purchased separately for fifty or sixty cents an outfit. The clothing came in a plain brown 12" x 7½" craft envelope with an applied 11" x 6¾" front label with a front and back plate of the outfit, the content, and color. The outfit pictured is plaited frock #4 checked gingham and organdy. The pattern is stamped right onto the fabric, so you just had to cut it out and assemble it. There were 12 outfits available, lazy daisy frock #1, lazy daisy frock #2, morning frock, #3, plaited frock #4, guimpe frock #5, surplice frock #6, Russian slip on #7, coat frock #8, smocked frock #9, white organdy frock #10, sport set #11, and colored organdy frock #12. Each clothing envelope had a sheet of instructions for assembling the chosen frock and a draft of the pattern printed on the fabric. On the other side of the instruction sheet was a complete listing with plates of all the dress outfits including the name, number, and fabric. **Doll and one outfit: $100.00 and up.**

Note: Emmylou Specialties added a second series of new outfits and a new doll named Brother. There were six new costumes for Emmylou and six for Brother.

Plate 109. My Complete Sew-Dress Box #D-114 by Samuel Gabriel & Sons Co., circa 1928. I don't have the box to this set, but decided to list it anyway. I know it has a box because it is mentioned in the booklet. Each box set contained varied amounts of clothing, as stated in the booklet, depending upon size and price. In this set there are two dolls and eight outfits, each with a hat. The outfits are all numbered and named as follows: 1. morning frock and hat, 3. play frock and hat, 4. afternoon frock and hat, 5. party frock and hat, 6. garden frock and hat, 7. tea frock and hat, 8. sports coat and hat, 9. dress coat and hat. Number 2, school frock and hat are not shown. The booklet states: *Each box does not contain the full range of dresses shown in this fashion magazine. The larger boxes have a more elaborate assortment than the smaller ones, but in the magazine you will surely find illustrated the particular dresses contained in your box. The patterns will then indicate to you how each dress should look, back and front.* The booklet is printed in color and has instructions for sewing each of the nine outfits shown. **Complete in box: $100.00 and up.**

Note: Samuel Gabriel Sons & Company advertised My Complete Sew-Dress Box #D-114 in the January 1929 issue of Play- things *magazine. The box is also pictured in Mary Young's* A Collector's Guide to Paper Doll's II *on page 69.*

Plate 110. Modern Girl's Sewing Set #300 was manufactured by the American Toy Works, circa 1930. The box measures 14½" x 11" x 1". Inside in three sections are the 10" posterboard-weight paper doll with jointed arms and four dresses to sew. To complete the set are blunt-nose scissors, two hanks of colored thread, and a needle. **Complete: $25.00 and up.**

Note: The exact same paper doll was also used in Sewing for Girls Stitchart #528 (plate 112) and also in Dolly's Kut-Out Klothes #3081 (not pictured) however in #3081 her arms have grommets both at the shoulder and elbow. See also Modern Girls' Sewing Set #400 with a composition doll in on page 32 (plate 41).

Plate 111. A Dress A Day Makes Dolly Gay #466 was manufactured by Advance Games Co., circa 1930. The box is 16" x 12" x 1½" and the graphics are signed Elizabeth R. as are the paper dolls. Inside, still in untouched original condition are three 7½" paper dolls named Lynn, Greta, and Bette and all their clothing. The dolls, all their clothing and accessories are made of heavy pasteboard. There are small holes punched in the costumes to sew beads or designs with the embroidery floss. Included in the set are rayon and cotton embroidery floss, cotton thread on a wooden spool, glass seed and bugle beads, plastic thimble, paper tape measure, metal blunt-nose scissors, and a needle. The original instruction sheet reads: *A Dress A Day 'Lots of Fun for Any Little Girlie' Cut out the dollies and the dresses. Insert the stands in the cut slits on the dolls before dressing the dollies in their varied costumes. The wardrobe is complete — outfits for every occasion. Little mother can add pretty trimmings by embroidering dolly's dresses with the yarns or beads.* **Complete: $50.00 and up.**

Note: The box advertises "With Real Wool Embroidery," however the yarns in the set are rayon and cotton. The contents of this set are totally untouched with the original glue all in place. My thought is that this particular set never had wool embroidery and perhaps it was offered in earlier sets. I have seen a second set with the same number and graphics with the same contents but arranged differently.

Plate 112. Sewing For Girls Stitchart #528 was manufactured by American Toy Works, circa 1930. The box is 20" x 13" x 2". Inside are seven sections. In one section are three 10" pasteboard dolls with stands. They are jointed at the shoulders with grommets. There are eight pre-cut fabric dresses to sew for the dollies, complete with needle, scissors, and four hanks of assorted thread. To wash and dry dolly's clothes are clothesline and pegs. The clothesline card reads: *Dolly's clothesline no outfit complete without one. Will be essential for many purposes. This is the day we wash dolly's clothes and when they are finished we have no more woes her clothis are then so nice and sweet to look at her is quite a treat.* Also included in the set are two tapestries; on one is a drawing of a girl's head with a large bow on top and the other a ship in full sail, a wooden frame, tapestry needle, wooden hoop, four skeins of wool, and instructions for the tapestry. **Complete: $50.00 and up.**

Note: One of the paper dolls in this set is also seen in Modern Sewing Girls' Set #300 (plate 110) and two of the paper dolls are seen in Dolly's Kut-out Clothes #3081. Both of these sets are by American Toy Works.

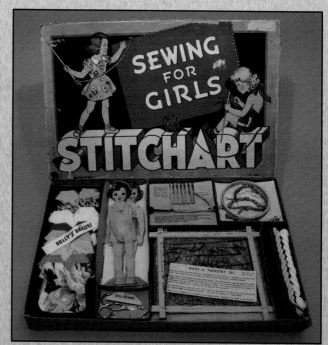

Plate 113. Little Tot's Crepe Paper Doll Outfit #36 manufactured by Dennison Manufacturing Company, circa 1931. The box measures 14" x 9" x 1". Dennison actually named the paper dolls in this set, Eleanor 10", Betty 8½", and Bobbie 7½". Notice the spelling of "Bobbie" even though he is a boy. The rest of the set includes a pre-printed sheet of dresses, suits, coats and hats, plain and decorated crepe papers, plain dress and hat forms, paper lace, paper ribbon, gold, silver, and lace paper, paper buttons, flower and animal stickers, small round lace doilies, fringed crepe paper strips, pink paper cord, three wooden stands, and an instruction leaflet. The leaflet is a three-section fold out and there are instructions for making Betty's pink crepe paper dress and bonnet, Eleanor's Bo-Peep costume, and Bobbie's clown suit. Besides the leaflet, there is a loose sheet of instructions in eight different languages. **Complete: $100.00 and up.**

Note: Little Tot's Crepe Paper Doll Outfit #36 has the same content as Crepe Paper Doll Outfit #36 (not pictured). Both box tops are signed by the artist Mary Hays Huber. The only difference being the background color of the box and the title. "Little Tot's Crepe Paper Doll Outfit #36" was advertised in a 1931 Dennison's catalog and was priced at $1.00. I think the idea of the title change was to advertise a set for the younger child and the name Little Tots would certainly address the younger set.

Plate 114. Nancy Crepe Paper Doll Outfit #38 circa 1931, was manufactured by the Dennison Manufacturing Company. The set comes in an 11" x 6" envelope. The paper doll, Nancy, measures 8½" and is printed both on the front and back. The set also contains a sheet of printed dresses, colored crepe paper, plain white paper, and instruction sheet. The instruction sheet is made especially for the Nancy set, using her name in the title. It has a pattern for a dress and hat and instructions to make crepe paper outfits. **Complete: $75.00 and up.**

Note: Nancy is the same doll as the middle-sized doll in the Little Tot's Crepe Paper Doll Outfit #36 plate 113.

Sewing and Embroidery Sets for Paper Dolls

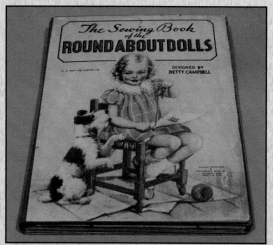

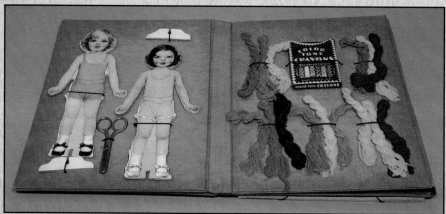

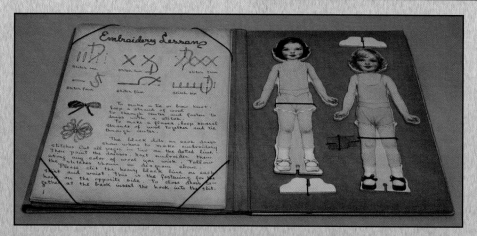

Plate 115. The Sewing Book of the Round About Dolls was designed by Betty Campbell and copyrighted by McLoughlin Brothers Inc. in 1937. The lithographed cover is applied to the top. The set has four sections that fold into a rectangular 13½" x 10" x 1½" case. Opening the cover exposes two pages, the first containing two heavy board 10½" dolls, one a blonde, the other a brunette, their stands, and a pair of scissors. The second page has the yarn and crayons to decorate the clothing. Folding the next section out reveals the embroidery lesson directions that show straight stitch, cross-stitch, connected cross-stitch, running stitch, backstitch, and blanket stitch; each stitch has a number. There are also directions on how to use the wool and how to color and cut the clothing that is on sheets under the instructions. The last fold shows two more dolls identical to the first set of dolls with stands and a needle. There are 28 sheets of costumes under the instructions. Each outfit has an embroidery number, corresponding with the stitch number in the instructions, so the child would know what stitch should be used on each costume. **Complete: $100.00 and up.**

Note:The Sewing Book of the Round About Dolls was published in two sizes, one with three fold-out pages and only two dolls, and the other (above) with four fold-out pages and four dolls. I have also seen another sewing book of the Round About Dolls with the instructions glued on the backside of the fourth page, and the clothing on a page all by itself. It had the same cover and four dolls. There were many paper doll sets of The Round About Dolls that had no sewing involved.

Plate 116. Doll House Dress Shop #1515 was manufactured by Transogram Company, Inc., circa 1938. It is a small box with wonderful lithographs measuring 9½" x 6¼" x 1". Inside there are five 4½" cardboard dolls waiting to be punched out, each has her own little stand. Written above the dolls are the only instructions: "Remove these lovely cut-out dolls and dress them in the pretty new dresses that you will sew for them." Still stapled to the dolls are their pre-cut cotton dresses. The thread-card marked "Transogram" says there is approximately 500" of colored thread. There is a needle stuck through the thread and a pair of metal blunt-nose scissors lying loose in the box. The worker assembling this set must have been in a hurry as the last flowered dress is stapled with the fabric inside out. **Complete: $25.00 and up.**

Note: The paper dolls in this set are the same as the paper dolls in Little Traveler's Sewing Kit #1515 (not pictured). Little Traveler's Sewing Kit #1565 also has the same dolls but they are a little larger with different coloring (plate 129). See Doll House Dress Shop #555 with a bisque doll, (plate 14) on page 17.

Plate 117. Style Show Sewing Set #1531 by Transogram Company, Inc., circa 1936. The box is 13½" x 10½" x 2". Inside we find five little 5¾" cardboard girls and their stands. On either side of them are two Transogram cards with 500" of assorted colored thread. Just below the dolls are metal blunt-nose scissors, a small metal thimble, and two cards, each with one needle. There are 12 dresses pre-cut from a variety of fabrics, six on each side. This is an untouched set in original presentation. **Complete: $50.00 and up.**

Note: There is a circa 1939 Style Show Sewing Set #1531 showing the same cover. However the inside arrangement is different as are the five larger 6½" paper dolls. I have also seen this box top used for a 6½" bisque doll sewing set also manufactured by Transoram.

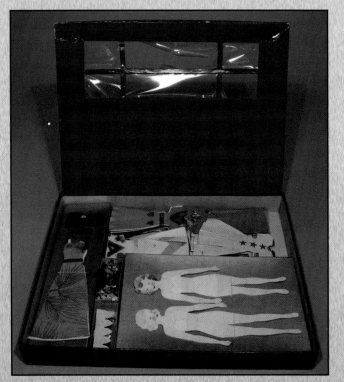

Plate 118. Ruth's Hand Painted Front and Back Dolls comes in a bright red box that measures 17" x 13" x 2". The set is copyrighted 1941 by Ruth Greider McCandless. The two 10" hand-painted dolls are done in watercolor. The set has been used and many of the materials are made into clothing. Luckily there is still an instruction sheet included in the box that tells us what the set was like when new. The instructions read:

Here are two basic patterns for Margie and Dot and a lining pattern, which is used for both. A one-piece dress with circular skirt is the easiest, so we will start with Dress 1. First cut out a double lining from plain white paper, placing the lining pattern with the shoulder seam at the fold of the paper. Unfold the lining and lay it out flat on the table. Cut a piece of dress material slightly larger than the lining. Now put a little paste around the neck opening, lower edges of the sleeves and waistline of your white paper lining. Lay the dress material over the lining and press into place, holding firmly until paste is dry. Trim off excess dress material and make circular skirt effect by stretching the crepe between your fingers at the hemline. Add a belt, turning the ends under and pasting them to the under side of the lining. Decorate dress with flowers from your seals, or other trimmings. When dress is thoroughly dry, fold at the shoulder seam and make a cut down the middle of the back, from the neck opening to well below the waist. Slip the doll's head into this opening first, then gently ease the dress into place.

Dress 2, a dance frock, is a little more difficult, so I have drawn you a pattern for it. Cut the blouse double and paste to paper lining, pressing in gathers at the waist with your fingers. Then paste on back and front pieces of skirt, using paste only at the top. Make a sash of two colors of crepe paper ribbon or cellophane ribbon. Crepe paper ribbon will tie nicely if it is first well stretched—or you may make a separate bow and paste it on. Decorate neck and sleeves with bands and bows of the same ribbon.

Dress 3 is a school dress with inverted pleats in the skirt. Cut the skirt pieces first, press the pleats into shape and paste to front and back of lining (street length of course). Cut blouse double and paste to lining, overlapping skirt. Add belt, buckle, collar, cuffs, and buttons.

I have included a simple hat pattern which may give ideas for other designs. Paste the front and back together with a very narrow line of paste around the upper edge and sides. These patterns are, of course, only suggestive — you can think of dozens of variations. With a little practice you will no longer need patterns, but can design all sorts of original costumes yourself. Just lay the doll down with its shoulders at the fold of a double piece of lining paper and draw a lining around it. Paste on a piece of dress material, pressing in pleats or gathers if desired, trim off excess material, and decorate as you choose.

There are the patterns mentioned above, still in the set with only dress 3 and the lining cut out. There are 16 dresses made up including a long gown with a jacket. The crepe and tissue paper has been used up except for the crepe paper ribbon, of which we still have a whole box including silver and gold. The other small box has a few pieces of Dresden lace and trims in it. Trims found on the dresses include gold Dresden lace and bands, flower, flag, and star stickers. This set is in played-with condition, but since it is so unusual I wanted to list it. Helene Marlowe collection. **Complete: $100.00 and up.**

Plate 119. Stitch and Sew #1212 is by J. Pressman & Co., circa 1940. The box is 12" x 9" x 1½". Inside are two cardboard paper dolls. The 8" dolls are to be punched out of the insert in the box. On each side of the dolls are their dresses and stands. There are six dresses in all. The set also contains a cardboard spool of lavender sewing thread and a needle. **Complete: $25.00 and up.**

Note: Pressman used the Stitch and Sew name for other similar sets. Stitch and Sew #1205 had similar graphics (more of a side view of the little girl), different dolls, and a cardboard bobbin of thread. Another Stitch and Sew #1212 had the exact same dolls, but only two dresses and a cardboard bobbin of thread. Its cover had a girl sewing in a window with her cat looking on and the box was of much thinner cardboard. There is also a Stitch and Sew #1232 by Pressman & Company with a composition doll (plate 50) on page 36.

Plate 120. Sewing Set Sewing for Little Girls #500 was manufactured by Cardinal Games Division of Deluxe Game Corp., circa 1940. The box is 12" x 8" x 1" and the graphics are signed Eisner. The 10" pasteboard doll inside is stapled to a raised insert; to the side of her are two dresses and the needle all still stapled to the box. Lying loose in the box are two hanks of sewing thread and the paper-doll stand. **Complete: $25.00 and up.**

Plate 121. Little Miss Hollywood Sewing Set #400 was manufactured by Minerva Toy Company circa 1940. The box is 19" x 10" x 2". Inside in the center inserts are two 9¼" cardboard paper dolls named Joy. On one side of the box are six pre-cut dresses with the original "Doll's Cut-Out Dresses" label and on the other side with their labels are "Doll's Cut-out Jacket" and "Dolly's Blanket." Also included in the set are a cardboard hoop with a cross-stitch piece ready to stitch, two hanks of thread, a needle, and a pair of metal blunt-nose scissors. **Complete: $50.00 and up.**

Note: Little Miss Hollywood Sewing Set #400 always has two paper dolls. I have seen this set with either two paper dolls named Joy, or two paper dolls named Sue, or with one of each. There is also a Little Miss Hollywood Sewing Set #600 with the same name and graphics that contains a composition doll (plate 52) on page 37.

Sewing and Embroidery Sets for Paper Dolls

Plate 122. My Favourite Sewing Kit #79 was made by Ontex, circa 1940. The box is 13" x 9½" x 1". There is a flat piece of cardboard lining the bottom of the box and stapled to it are the contents. Included are a "Modes de Paris" pattern #5113 for a dress, apron, and cape and a "Modes de Paris" pattern #5301 for an evening dress. Also included are a card of thread, blunt-end metal scissors, a needle, and a 5¼" cardboard doll and stand. **Complete: $25.00 and up.**

Plate 123. Little Miss Sewing Kit #28 was manufactured by Peter Austin in Canada, circa 1940. The luggage-type box with a metal latch and bail handle measures 9½" x 6" x 2½". Upon opening the case, we find five 5½" little paste-board dolls secured inside the lid. One doll is wearing a nurse's cap and holds a bandage in her hand. In the bottom of the box, arranged on the insert, are ten pre-cut dresses, two in white for the nurse. To complete the set, are five doll stands, wooden thimble, two tubes of thread, metal blunt-nose scissors, and a needle. **Complete: $25.00 and up.**

Plate 124. Mayflower Sewing Set #200 was manufactured by Concord Toy Company, Inc., circa 1940. The box measures 9" x 6" x 1". The doll inside is just a little over 8". She has grommet-jointed arms at the shoulders. The set comes with three pre-cut dresses, a needle, and a twist of green floss. Everything is still stapled onto the insert. **Complete: $25.00 and up.**

Note: The same paper doll was also used in Concord Toys' Stitchcraft Sewing Set #202 (plate 127). See Mayflower Sewing Set #S50 (plate 17) and Mayflower Sewing Set #S100 (plate 18) on pages 18 and 19 for sets with bisque dolls.

Plate 125. Pretty Things for Baby #68 was manufactured by Ontex, circa 1945. The box measures 9" x 9" x 1". On two of the sides is written "Complete Sewing Set With Doll" and on the other two "Made in Ontex Canada." Inside, still stapled to the bottom of the box, is the baby, a 7" pasteboard toddler with a stand. Underneath the baby are the "Instruction Chart of Popular Embroidery Stitches" and a piece of white cotton fabric that is stamped with a dress and cape. On each side are two pink squares folded in triangles, one has a dress, the other a dress and a bib. To complete the set are two skeins of cotton embroidery floss and a needle. The clothing is all stamped to be sewn and trimmed with embroidery. **Complete: $75.00 and up.**

Plate 126. Sister Susie Sewing Kit #28 was manufactured by Peter Austin, Canada, circa 1940. The luggage-type box measures 9½" x 6" x 2¼" and has a metal bail-type handle with "Peter Austin" engraved on it. The inside lid has four 5¾" pasteboard dolls, one doll has Peg printed on her swimsuit. Arranged on the insert are 10 pre-cut dresses, metal blunt-nose scissors, a tube of thread, a needle, and a wooden thimble. **Complete: $25.00 and up.**

Plate 127. Stitchcraft Sewing Set #202 is a Concord Toy Company, Inc., product, circa 1940. The set comes in a 14½" x 11¼" x 1¼" box. The edge of the box cover says, "learn to sew like mommy." Inside, stapled to a raised side platform is a 10¼" pasteboard doll with blonde hair and jointed grommet arms and a paper pattern for a style-number-nine dress underneath her. In the center, still stapled, is a printed dress to embroider and cut out, along with the embroidery hoop, two hanks of thread, needle, and metal blunt-nose scissors. At the other side are four pre-cut cloth dresses with the "dolly dresses" banner still stapled to them. **Complete: $25.00 and up.**

Note: The same paper doll was also in Concord Toy's Co., Inc. Mayflower Sewing Set #200 (plate 124). I have seen Stitchcraft Sewing Set #202 with a dark haired girl named Judy with stationary arms and only three pre-cut cloth dresses. I have also seen three different box graphics using the name Stitchcraft Sewing Set, with similar content and either one or two dolls. Stitchcraft Sewing Set #204 (plate 48) on page 35 and Stitchcraft sewing set #205 (not pictured) came with different contents and two dolls, a composition and a paper doll.

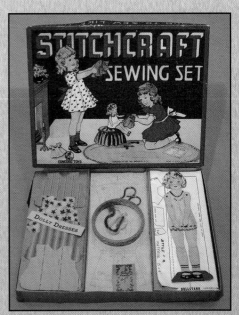

Sewing and Embroidery Sets for Paper Dolls

Plate 128. Progressive Sewing Set with Doll to Dress #252 copyrighted by Progressive Toy Corporation in 1941. The box is 14" x 9½" x 1¼". Inside, still stapled to the insert, is an 8¼" pasteboard doll with a stand. There are three dresses stapled to the far side of the box, and directly in the middle is a 5½" x 9½" piece of open-weave fabric, metal blunt-nose scissors, needle, thread, and metal thimble. **Complete: $25.00 and up.**

Plate 129. Little Traveler's Sewing Kit #1565 by Transogram Company, Inc., circa 1941. The set comes in a luggage-type box with a faux-leather handle and latch. It measures 12" x 7½" x 2½". Lined up on the inside lid are five 5½" paper dolls waiting to be punched out. Written above the dolls are the only instructions: "remove these lovely cut-out dolls and dress them in the pretty new dresses that you will sew for them." Still stapled to an insert in the bottom of the box, and lined up five on each side, are 10 pre-cut dresses. In the center of the box are two skeins of thread, a needle, wooden thimble, and a pair of metal blunt-nose scissors. **Complete: $25.00 and up.**

Note: The paper dolls in this set are almost identical to the paper dolls in Little Traveler's Sewing Kit #3574/5 (plate 130) and Doll House Dress Shop #1515 (plate 116) with the exception that these are a bit larger and different in color. The graphics and title Little Traveler's Sewing Kit without a number were also used for a composition doll sewing set (plate 43) on page 33.

Plate 130. Little Traveler's Sewing Kit #3574/5 manufactured by Transogram Company, Inc., circa 1947. This luggage-type box has a metal bail handle and latch, and measures 10" x 6¼" x 2¼". Inside on the lid are five 4½" cardboard dolls with their stands waiting to be punched out. Written above the dolls are the only instructions: "remove these lovely cut-out dolls and dress them in the pretty new dresses that you will sew for them." The pink insert holds eight pre-cut dresses still stapled in place at the sides. The center has a place for a needle, a small plastic thimble, card marked "Transogram" with 400" of assorted colored thread, and a pair of metal blunt-nose scissors. **Complete: $25.00 and up.**

Note: The paper dolls in this set are the same as the paper dolls in Doll House Dress Shop #1515 (plate 116). Little Traveler's Sewing Kit #1565 (plate 129) also has the same dolls but a little larger with different coloring.

Plate 131. Make Mary's Clothes #5338 was manufactured by Whitman Publishing Company, circa 1949. The box size is 12½" x 9" x 1¼". Inside are two compartments, one for Mary and one for her fabric, patterns, and trimmings. Mary is 8½", and is made of heavy board with a round plastic stand. Her clothes consist of a Sunday dress, pajamas, party dress, school dress, peasant dress, and sunsuit. There are six different pieces of fabric and six different patterns, bias tape, small rickrack, and a plastic thimble. There is a color instruction sheet with directions for each outfit. The instructions tell you to paste the fabric and tissue patterns together before cutting out, working with the pattern while the fabric is still damp so it can be molded, pleated, and gathered. **Complete: $25.00 and up.**

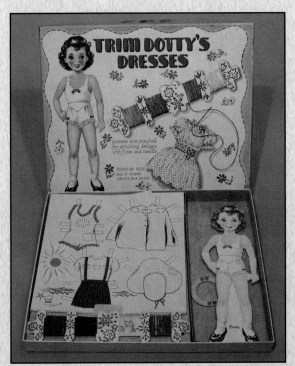

Plate 132. Trim Dotty's Dresses #5336 was made by Whitman Publishing Company, circa 1950. The box is 13" x 11" x 1". Inside is a recessed section holding Dotty and her round plastic circle stand. Dotty is 10" and is made of teakwood. On a raised platform next to Dotty are six sheets of clothing punched for stitching designs with floss. Completing the set are four colors of floss on a decorated card along with a needle. **Complete: $25.00 and up.**

Plate 133. Jr. Miss Sewing Kit #1520 was manufactured by Hassenfeld Brothers, circa 1950. The plaid luggage-type box with its metal bail handle and snap closure is 11" x 7" x 2½". I believe this is the cheapest set that Hassenfeld Brothers made; the inside of the box and the paper dolls are all printed on plain cardboard in blue with no other colors. There are four paper dolls, all girls, ranging in size from 4½" to 5½", and they each have a cardboard stand and a dress to be sewn up the sides. Included in the set are metal blunt-nose scissors, a metal thimble, a card with multicolor thread, and a needle. **Complete: $25.00 and up.**

Note: Hassenfeld Brothers later changed their name to Hasbro.

Sewing and Embroidery Sets for Paper Dolls

Plate 134. Corinne #5181 was manufactured by Saalfield Publishing Company, circa 1954. Printed on the box is: "Corinne a Darling Doll with Wavy Hair, Real Cloth Dresses, and Ribbon Sashes." The box is 13" x 5" x 1¼". The heavy 10" cardboard stand-up doll has four pre-cut printed cotton dresses to be sewn up the sides and four ribbons for sashes. **Complete: $25.00 and up.**

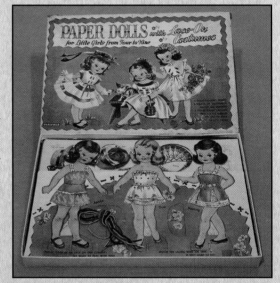

Plate 135. Paper Dolls with Lace on Costumes #6068 was manufactured by The Saalfield Publishing Co. in 1955 for little girls ages four to nine. The box measures 15" x 10½" x 1¼" and has the listing of the contents on the cover. Inside the box are Janie, Sue, and Nancy, three 9½" dolls of heavy pasteboard. "Please stand us up; lace on our clothes — we want to play with you. Match the lacing with the trim — It isn't hard to do." Under the dolls are six sheets of posterboard weight clothing punched at the bodice and waist to be laced on to the dolls. The sheets are named: Off to Dreamland, Our Sunday Best, At the Beach, School Days, We're having Company, and A Costume Party. Each doll has one costume from each sheet. To complete the set are five different colored lacing ropes. **Complete: $25.00 and up.**

Plate 136. Betsy McCall Biggest Paper Doll #D90:200 is housed in a box that measures 17" x 13½" x 1¼". The paper doll set was copyrighted in 1955 by Samuel Gabriel Sons & Company and McCall Corporation. The box top is signed Alton S Toley and shows a little girl dressing a large paper doll in the same outfit she is wearing, on the floor are crepe paper, trimmings, doily's, etc. The Betsy paper doll measures a big 35" when put together. Both the doll and her clothing is made of cardstock-weight paper. The doll has a finished back as well as the front and the skirt is three-dimensional that comes in three parts with tabs to construct it. All the extra clothing is made from crepe paper. There are matching outfits for the child and paper doll that include a Native American costume, party dress, flower wreath and apron. There are also instructions for making a handkerchief, corsage, hat, button jewelry and fan. The box top lists some of the contents of the set such as: "Wonderful Ribbon by Burlington Mills, 1508 Square Inches and Verybest Crepe Paper in 6 Fashionable Colors by Dennison." Also listed are "Assorted Antique lace Paper Doilies, Gold Lace Paper Doily by Roylies, Hundreds of Glistening Glittering Appliques, Colorful Yarn and Fancy Trimmings." The clothing is made by cutting, pasting, and sewing crepe paper in sizes given for both the child and the doll. The instruction's state: "You can make wonderful crepe paper dresses for yourself and your Biggest Paper doll. Crepe paper is easy to work with; it has a grain, which must be considered when cutting. Crepe paper can be pasted, sewed by hand or machine; it can be pressed with a warm iron. Mother will show you how." This set is hard to find. **Complete: $50.00 and up.**

Plate 137. Betsy McCall's Fashion Shop Embroidery Set #401 was manufactured by Standard Toykraft Products, circa 1959. The box has a see-through top covered with cellophane and is 15" x 10" x 1¼". The box top states: "embroider your own dress 'n play wardrobe featuring magic stay-on costumes for stand-up doll." Betsy is an 8½" heavy cardboard flocked doll. Under Betsy are a yellow plastic thimble and her stand. Betsy's clothing is printed on flannel in four colors, red, yellow, blue, and black and it consists of three dresses, five blouses, two pairs of shorts, one pair of pants, a skirt, and a coat. Included with the set are a needle, a skein of assorted color embroidery floss secured with a Standard Toykraft band, a packet of assorted sequins, and the "Betsy McCall Embroidery Instructions" that show how to do a running stitch, cross-stitch, and how to sew on sequins. **Complete: $50.00 and up.**

Note: The Betsy McCall's Fashion Shop Embroidery Set #401 sold for ninety-eight cents in 1959.

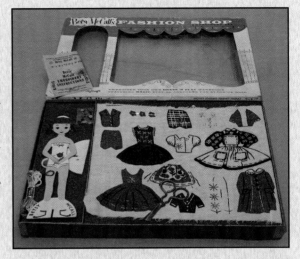

Plate 138. Betsy McCall's Fashion Shop Embroidery Set #402 was manufactured by Standard Toykraft Products, circa 1959. The box has a see-through top covered with cellophane and is 18" x 12½" x 1½". The box top states: "embroider your own dress 'n play wardrobe featuring magic stay-on costumes for stand-up doll." Betsy and Linda McCall are both made of flocked heavy cardboard. Betsy is 8½" and Linda is 6" tall. The clothing is flannel and printed in blue, black, red, and yellow. The clothing in my set has been cut so I am not sure it is all here, but for Betsy it consists of four dresses, nightgown, a skirt, two pairs of shorts, four blouses, and a pair of pants. For Linda there are seven dresses, a nightgown, and a short set. Also included are metal blunt-nose scissors, a packet of sequins, needle, embroidery hoop, yellow plastic thimble, two skeins of assorted color embroidery floss with a Standard Toykraft band, and a "Betsy McCall Embroidery Instructions." The booklet shows how to do a running stitch, cross-stitch, and how to sew on sequins. **Complete: $75.00 and up.**

Note: Betsy McCall's Fashion Shop Embroidery Set #402 sold for $1.98 in 1959.

Plate 139. Cut and Sew Handicraft Set was manufactured by Sosaku Toys, circa 1960. The box was covered with a see-through plastic covering and measures 15" x 11" x ½". The recessed box holds two 7" cardstock dolls and their stands, one blonde doll and one brunette. Still secured to the box are four heavy card dresses, three pre-cut cloth dresses to be sewn with one ready-made cloth dress on one of the paper dolls, three hanks of fabric, a card of thread, blunt-nose-scissors, two paper patterns, and lace and braid trims. The patterns are for a dress and blouse. **Complete: $25.00 and up.**

Plate 140. Shirley Temple Play Kit #9869 was copyrighted in 1961 by Saalfield Publishing Co. The three-section folder measures 11¼" x 8¼" when folded all together and when spread out it is 27" long. The set shown has been really played with. It originally came with a box of crayons, a coloring book, two round picture frames, two rayon laces, a standing Shirley doll, lace-on clothing, and a daisy-chain necklace to punch out. The coloring book, daisies, and the cord to make the necklace are missing. Printed on the first foldout section are a color-matching game, maze, and a follow-the-dots picture. Glued to this section are a 2" x 3" pad and a box of "Cra-o-tec" crayons. The second center section must have held the sheets of clothing and the coloring book, but the child that previously owned this set has made and taped pockets to hold the clothing. The clothes included are pajamas with kitty slippers, black dancing suit, seven dresses, one with a jacket, a sundress, and a coat. There is also a teddy bear, stuffed cat, and a handbag. One rayon cord remains to lace the clothing on Shirley. Since this set has been used I'm not sure if all the clothing is present, however I am sure that some lucky young girl truly enjoyed this set. **Complete: $75.00 and up.**

Plate 141. Barbie & Ken Fashion Embroidery Set #502 was manufactured by Standard Toykraft Products and copyrighted by Mattel, Inc. in 1962. The 18" x 12½" x 1½" box has a clear plastic covered window opening in the shape of a hand mirror to view the dolls and clothing. Inside the box on a platform are 9½" Barbie and 10¼" Ken, both are of flocked heavy cardboard. The clothing for Barbie consists of three dresses, three casual wear outfits, a short nightgown, barbecue apron, three hats, and a purse. Ken has a suit coat, two casual shirts, one pair of slacks, one pair of shorts, school sweater, loafers with knee socks, tennis racket, two hats, and a school flag. Also included in the set are two stands, a pair of metal blunt-nose scissors, needle, embroidery thread, and an instruction sheet. **Complete: $50.00 and up.**

Note: There are three other embroidery sets with the same window-box top as the one above with different teen figures to dress. There was just Barbie with her clothing in a 15" x 10" box (the same clothing as above). A harder to find set in the same size box was just Midge with the same clothing as the Barbie set. The largest is another set that is hard to find. It included all three dolls, Barbie, Midge, and Ken. The same clothing is also in this box, with matching outfits for Barbie and Midge. The larger sets had safety scissors.

Plate 142. Sassie A Paper Doll #1972 was published by Whitman Publishing Co., Inc., in 1972 with the permission of Mattel Inc. The 15½" x 7" book has eight pages including the cover. The paper doll is on the back cover and measures 11¼". She has a stand and is marked "1972 Mattel." The doll has paper punch out clothing. The sewing part of this paper doll set is in the back of the book; Sassie a Stuff'n Sew Doll. The instructions state: "find a string 30" long and knot at Bow 1. Sew to Bow 2 and knot. Stuff with scraps of paper and finish sewing doll." Sassie the Stuff'n'Sew Doll is 9" high. **Complete: $5.00 and up.**

Plate 143. Bride Original Designer Set #6000 was manufactured in 1991 by Western Publishing Co., Inc. The box is 15½" x 10½" x 1½". The set includes a 14" flat plastic doll, three sheets of tissue paper, paper patterns, press-out paper fashions, paper fashions to color and cut out, a glue stick, over 30 stickers, and an idea starter sheet. The idea starter sheet shows how to wrap, bunch and scrunch, pleat, ruffle, fluff, add on rows, and make bows and braids as well as giving other hints and ideas. This set has a lot of creative play value and could encourage a child to learn more about sewing. **Complete: $25.00 and up.**

Note: There were at least three and maybe four Original Designer Sets, Bride #6000, Fashion Model #6003, Set #6002, and possibility Set #6001 that I haven't been able to find.

Sewing and Embroidery Sets for Mannequin Dolls

Note: The word mannequin was spelled differently by different companies when advertising their dolls. I have used the spelling that each company used when referring to their dolls.

In the 1940s sewing was a way for the modern woman to have a smart wardrobe, with clothing that fit well, in the styles and fabrics she loved. Pattern companies were each promising their patterns as the short cut to Paris styles. There were sewing books on the market that promised a feeling of pride and accomplishment, as well as the pleasure of feeling well dressed, with the added benefit of real savings in dollars and cents.

By the 1940s, the printed pattern dominated the American market. The new printed pattern was being advertised with the cutting and stitching lines along with notches and symbols printed right onto the tissue pattern. Butterick, McCall's, and Vogue produced 600 or more patterns per year during the 1930s and early 1940s. The Simplicity Pattern Service (including their patterns and the *Simplicity Sewing Book*) was being promoted as the smartest and easiest way to good dressing. It promised women a smart, up-to-date appearance which, at the same time, signified good taste.

There were four major pattern companies vying for the consumer's approval: Simplicity, Vogue, McCall's, and Butterick. There were also cheaper patterns, such as Advance and Hollywood, as well as newspaper patterns such as Anne Adams, Sue Brunett, and Marion Martin.

Many sewing books were on the market, all with the latest sewing secrets. One such book, published in 1941, was *Easy Ways to Sew and Save* by The Spool Cotton Company. The very first page tells the consumer the value of a smart, well-groomed appearance. Stating:

The modern woman is demanding...she wants her clothes to fit well...she loves fine fabrics...but she is resourceful and practical. Because the modern woman must budget her time as well as her income, short simple explanations with detailed illustrations have been used to amplify each step.

There were chapters on choosing the pattern; fabric and notions; sewing tools; fitting the pattern to one's figure; and, of course, sewing the garment. A small chapter at the back of the book included mending, patching, and darning. Fashion and looking one's best was the goal.

But in just a few short months, sewing wasn't just a pastime or hobby anymore; it was a duty. On December 7, 1941, the Japanese attacked Pearl Harbor and declared war on the United States. In an instant our world changed, and so did our habits. By 1942 we were fully engaged in war, and there was an all-out attempt to help America with the war effort. Books were now suggesting that the women who stayed home become part of the war effort by "Sewing for Victory."

In 1942 the Spool Cotton Company published a new book, *Make and Mend for Victory*. The first page began with the Consumer's Victory Pledge:

As a consumer, in the total defense of democracy, I will do my part to make my home, my community, my country ready, efficient, strong.

I will buy carefully — and I will not buy anything above the ceiling price, no matter how much I may want it.

I will take good care of the things I have — and I will not buy anything made from vital war materials which I can get along without.

I will waste nothing — and I will take care to salvage everything needed to win the war.

Consumer Division,

Office of Price Administration

The book went on to say:

It's up to you to keep the home fires burning, to see that you and your family stay easy-on-the-eyes. Fortunately, you can be patriotic and pretty both. It's easy to teach an old wardrobe new tricks, to resurrect the skeletons in your closet and bring them up to date. Come on, take those old knockabouts and turn them into knockouts, keep that glint in Uncle Sam's eye and still do your stint towards Victory!

Make and Mend for Victory was full of hints, such as the saving of all zippers, buttons, and snaps on discarded clothing. The importance of caring for your needles and pins, how to make needle books and wrist pincushions, and picking up all dropped pins and saving them to help the war effort (all metal was needed for the war effort). There were chapters on how to mend, patch, and darn; turning collars; alterations; restyling dickeys and collars to change a neckline; remaking hats; accessories from scraps of yarn, cotton, and fabric; and how to reclaim used knitting wool. Nothing was to be wasted.

But I find most interesting the chapters on making women and children's clothing from men's old shirts and suits. The book gives instructions on how to sew the garment, the name and number of the commercial pattern used, the layout of the pattern on the old garment, and the cutting. One has to wonder what the men away at war thought when they came home to empty closets all, having been pilfered by wives at home.

In a May 1942 "McCall Style News," McCall's Pattern Company was asking their sewers to "enlist":

To serve your country on the home front. By signing: The United States Governments's Cosumer's Pledge for Total Defense. Sewers signed the pledge in the back of their "Style News" flyer, and were promised:

McCall's will send you a certificate of honor testifying that your name is on file in our national capital. Also, as long as the supply lasts McCall's will send each signer a red, white, and blue button — the symbol of the Home Defenders.

Also in 1942, the War Production Board began seriously restricting the amount of yardage used in garments. The War Production Board felt it was the designer's duty to design clothing that would use less fabric and remain stylish through more than one season. On March 8, 1942, the War Production Board issued Regulation L-85, which regulated every piece of clothing. American designers complied and skirts were shorter and straighter, jackets became shorter, sheath evening dresses became popular, all patterns were made to use less fabric.

Large department stores enlarged their sewing departments and many offered sewing classes. Some even included evening classes for working women. In 1942, Bloomingdales department store sponsored the McCall's Sewing Corp., a sewing class over the radio once a week for six weeks. There was also a supplement booklet, which outlined the main points of each lesson that could be purchased in their store. Sears offered "semimade dresses," which included all the material, trimmings, and instructions cut to size. Sears also gave complimentary 32 page booklets, "Sewing with Cotton Bags." The first page offers this explanation:

Not all empty cotton bags, such as are used for flour, feed, meal, salt, sugar, etc., end their lives as humble dish towels. Many of them find their way to the sewing room to hobnob democratically with silks and satins and laces. From there they emerge in a variety of forms so practical in use and attractive in appearance that their lowly origins would never be suspected. This book is a catalog of articles for household and personal use that can be made out of various cotton bags. These articles have all been actually made, and directions for making them have been carefully worked out. Where patterns and embroidery designs for articles shown here are necessary, they may be purchased for the small cost of 10c each. An order blank appears on page 28. Where the articles are so simple that no pattern is required, and full directions for making are given.

The booklet showed all types of household goods, stuffed toys, dolls, children's clothing, ladies' summer dresses, and sportswear.

Singer advertised sewing classes for teenagers, offering membership in their National Junior Sewing Club. Singer placed these ads in teen magazines like *Seventeen* and *Calling All Girls*. Pattern companies including Butterick, McCall's, and Simplicity all supplied patterns for the mannequin doll sets. Singer partnered with Butterick to produce at least two sets. Singer Sewhandy Mannikin Set, (plate 161) and Singer Mannikin Doll Set (plate 162). The patterns were actually real Butterick patterns made for adults and teenagers but scaled down to mannequin size.

Latexture Products Incorporated manufactured the Fashiondol mannequin and copyrighted the name Fashiondol. Simplicity supplied exclusive patterns and books for Latexture Products just for their mannequin dolls. See Miniature Fashions #102 (plate 149) and Fashiondol #705 (plate 150). Simplicity also used actual adult and teenage patterns scaled down to fit the Fashiondol; the same pattern was available in your size at your local stores. The idea was to make the fashion of your choice for your mannequin doll in order to learn the construction method and see how nice it looked when finished, then go and buy the pattern for yourself. Any problems or mistakes have already been worked out on the doll's pattern and there would be very little wasted fabric. The most prevalent book, in mannequin sets *Simplicity Sewing Book for Fashiondol Miniature Fashions* (the one with the green cover) states on the cover: "for Girls from Six to Sixty." On the back page of the book it states:

It's Fun to Sew On A Fashiondol Here's Why — It's fun to make something yourself. It's thrilling to have your friends admire something you have created. You will happily pass many otherwise dull hours. You are proving to yourself that you have a good imagination. You are preparing yourself for useful womanhood. You become more fashionwise as time goes by. You are likely to become a better dressed woman because of your knowledge of styles and materials.

Inside the front cover there were eight sets of patterns which could be ordered separately, with three patterns in each set. Among the patterns were a war nurse's uniform, woman's navy uniform, and a woman's army uniform. The price was 25¢ a set. There was also a 15" Fashiondol pattern set listed with eight sets of patterns, at 30¢ a set. These were not the Simplicity patterns, but the Fashiondol patterns.

Simplicity Miniature Fashions Set (plate 147) has a blue Simplicity book *Hints for the Young Designer*. Page one offers the following suggestion:

Begin by making your wardrobe complete — In Miniature. Plan the fabric and colors! Work out your complete wardrobe in miniature and make your changes of line and detail as you go. When it's completed to your satisfaction, then start on a duplicate wardrobe for yourself. It's a sure way of making clothes that look as if they are for you and you alone!

One of the most interesting and hard to find sets is the Simplicity Fashiondol (plate 151) with the drawing on the cover by James Montgomery Flagg. Mr. Flagg was an illustrator and author. He sold his first plate to *St. Nicholas* magazine in 1890. From 1917 to 1919 he designed 46 World War I posters, but he is best known for his "I Want You" Uncle Sam posters. The drawing on the cover of the Simplicity Fashiondol set depicts a young lady holding a Fashiondol wearing a nurse's uniform. All the patterns in the set are nurse's uniforms, Nurses were highly respected, especially during the war. The young lady holding the doll looks remarkably like Ilse Hoffman, the great love of Flagg's life. Ilse committed suicide in 1937, and it was said that Flagg never fully recovered from the loss.

Latexture Products also produced the same doll, under other names such as Marianne's Fashion Designing Set #100

Sewing and Embroidery Sets for Mannequin Dolls

(plate 144) and Susanne's Fashion Show (plates 146 and 148). Latexture Products used their own patterns with either the name of the doll in the box such as Susanne, or with just the name Fashiondol. It is interesting to note that Susanne's Fashion Show sets were not consistent with the names on the patterns. In Susanne's Fashion Show (small box), the patterns were all marked "Fashiondol" and Susanne's name wasn't mentioned anyplace on the pattern, however, there was a yellow paper pasted to the inside lid with a list of patterns to complete Susanne's wardrobe. These patterns were available in sets of three at 25¢ a set.

Set A Pinafore, Slip, Panties, and Play Dress
Set B Nurse's Uniform, Nurse's Cape, and Evening Dress

In Susanne's Fashion Show (large box) the patterns were all marked "Susanne." Marianne's Fashion Designing Set #100 also has her name on the patterns, and printed on the liner in her box were three pattern sets to order to complete her wardrobe. These patterns were:

Set A Pinafore, Slip, Panties, and Nurse's Cape
Set B Play Dress, Evening Dress, and Pajamas
Set C Housecoat, Skirt, Blouse, and Bathing Suit
The three sets were 25¢ each, postpaid.

Dritz-Traum Company and McCall's Pattern Company teamed up to make the Peggy McCall sewing sets. Peggy McCall (small box) (plate 154), Peggy McCall (double door box) (plate 155), and Peggy McCall (hat box) (plate 156). The Peggy McCall sets had only three patterns that were supplied with the dolls.

Number 6600-1, a Nurse's Uniform and Apron
Number 6600-2, Princess Dress
Number 6600-3, Daytime or Date Dress

They were made just for Peggy. An ad in *Toys and Novelties* magazine in August of 1942 said there are three sizes of Peggy McCall sewing boxes to retail at two, three, and five dollars. They described the five-dollar set:

Peggy is 13 inches high, and each set contains two McCall patterns designed and made especially to fit Peggy. All boxes are carried out in red, white, and blue — patriotic design. In the $5.00 box also are 3 pieces of fabric, wool, knitting needles, package of sewing needles, tape measure, thimble, thread and needle threader, as well as a descriptive booklet carrying a message to Young Americans who are just learning to Sew. Because of the great interest in home sewing which is now apparent, this new line of sewing boxes put out by the Dritz Traum Company, Inc., will be of special interest to toy buyers.

As mentioned previously, McCalls only made three patterns for their 13" Peggy McCall that was included in the sewing sets. I have never seen a Peggy McCall doll in any size other than 13". However, McCall's also made a pattern that was sold over the counter containing a wardrobe for Manikin Fashion Models, in sizes 12½", 15", and 20". The doll shown on the pattern envelope modeling the wardrobe is a 13" Peggy McCall.

Butterick supplied patterns and sewing books for Singer, George Borgfeldt, Educational Crafts Company, and Ideal Toy Company. Butterick, like Simplicity, made patterns of adult and teenage styles and scaled them down to fit the mannequin. Ideal Butterick Sew Easy Designing Set (plate 160) promised on the inside lid of their set, that you could make a dress for the mannequin and then make the same dress for yourself. The doll in this set is the same doll that Singer used in their sets. It is not marked and there is no mention of who made the doll in any of the sets. However, an October 1949 *Playthings* magazine ran this ad:

Educational Crafts Company are the originators and manufacturers of the Butterick Fashion Designing Set. This popular Craft item for girls has been completely restyled, and in the opinion of the manufacturers its sales appeal has been enhanced with the addition of several important innovations. The Manniken, which comes with every set, is now manufactured of molded rubber and is equipped with a metal base. The Manniken is 14" high and is realistically sculptured to represent a modish teen age girl. It has removable arms, the purpose of which is to make for easier dressmaking. Young dressmakers will be delighted with the six miniature Butterick patterns and the assortment of practical accessories such as needle, thread, tape measure, spool of cotton, etc.

The other two sets Butterick supplied patterns for were earlier 1943 sets with composition dolls. Deluxe Fashion Craft (plate 159) and Junior Miss Fashion Designing Sets (plates 157 and 158). It was advertised on the boxes that Educational Crafts Company manufactured the dolls. On a pink paper pasted on the inside of Junior Miss Fashion Designing Set (plate 157) was a list of additional patterns:

Additional Patterns are obtainable in sets of three to complete your "Junior Miss" Fashion Manikin's Wardrobe.
Set #1 Dirndl, Party Dress, Bridal Gown
Set #2 One Piece Pajamas, Camisole Slip, Bra-Top Culotte Slip
Set #3 Princess Frock, Evening Gown, Tailored Robe
Set #4 Wacs' Uniform, Waves' Uniform, Nurses Uniform
These sets may be obtained from the store where set was purchased, or by sending 25 cents for each set to- Educational Crafts Company.

Two interesting hard-to-find sewing set were designed by Helen Huntington Jones — The Debutante Doll Sewing Kit (plate 163) and The Young Dress Designer Visits the Attic (plate 164). Both sets have hand-drawn patterns, but the dolls are very different. The Debutante Doll Sewing Kit doll has floss hair and removable arms. There are instructions to cover the dolls' hair with a net when dressing her. The Debutante Doll Sewing Kit doll is named Belinda and has molded, painted hair, and her arms are not removable. On Belinda's patterns there is a note about Belinda:

Belinda is not an ordinary doll, she requires care just like your best party dress. She is washable, but do not scrub her or use any cold cream. Luke warm water and a soft cloth are all you need to clean her well. Her arms are flexible to a certain point. Only move them close to her body and slightly toward the back to enable you to put her clothes on. Do not try to bend her arms and legs or her wrists. Also, do not move her arms away from her body. With good care, Belinda will last a long time. To make a platform for Belinda to stand up, use a round disc which you can find in the 5 & 10 cent store at the hardware counter. It is made of different materials such as rubber, glass, or metal and is used for resting the legs of furniture in. Buy a small amount of clay and fill the opening until it is level with the edges, if possible use a bright color clay. Press the doll's feet into the clay and she will stand by herself.

When I first found The Debutante Doll Sewing Kit there were no markings anyplace on the set as to the maker and the doll looked so much like a Margit Milsen minikin, I was sure I had found one of her doll sets. However, shortly after, I found another set with a full label and have since found one more labeled set to assure me Helen Huntington Jones did indeed design these sets. My research so far seems to indicate Margit Nilsen did not design any of the mini-mannequins that are found in the children's sewing sets.

Margit Nilsen was a name well known in the mannequin world. Margit Nilsen sculpted many of the 1940s store display mannequins. She was originally a dancer in vaudeville who decided she wanted to study art. She studied during the day and danced at night to pay for the classes. While in school she sculpted a small mannequin from soap and took it to a store on Fifth Avenue. The store ordered four immediately.

Margit Nilsen filed for organization as a corporation in the state of New York in October of 1940. On the same day, she also filed for a patent for her Deb-U-Doll (plate 166). The doll, similar to a mannequin, was admired by both children and adults and sold for $7.95. In a short time another doll, Deb-U-Doll's Kid Sister (plate 167) was put on the market. The two dolls had numerous outfits made for them and some were matching sister outfits.

During World War II latex was classified as a strategic war material. Since Deb-U-Doll was made of latex, Margit had to reduce her staff of 150 people down to six. This is when she began designing her composition Minikins for McCall's.

McCall's Pattern Company hired Margit Nilsen to make 30" Minikins to help support pattern sales. The Minikins were dressed in a finished garments from McCall's patterns, and displayed with a card that showed the amount of yardage needed, notions, and the final cost of the garment. These figures proved to be very popular, especially during the war when fabric was scarce, and they boosted the sales of McCall's patterns. Soon, schools, home economics classes, and other pattern companies such as Simplicity ordered mannequins, such as the Simplicity Display Mannequin (plate 168) and had their patterns made up

and displayed on their own models. McCall's, Simplicity, and Butterick all supplied mannequin patterns for 30" display mannequins.

Margit gave up the Minikin business in the early 1960s, and devoted her time to sculpting. She passed on at the age of 80 in 1989. Her dolls and Minikins are very collectable today. With age, both have become very fragile, particularly the dolls, so very few remain in good condition.

Another way to save money and promote sewing was the half-scale model form. It was used in a lot of sewing classrooms. The half size dress Form (plate 172) was used in a classroom from the 1960s to the 1980s in San Francisco. The technique was flat pattern making, and the book *Pattern Making by the Flat-Pattern Method* by Hollen and Kundel was the textbook used. The form is a half scale dress form size 14 that stands 26" tall. The forms had patterns made just for them in the half scale. This allowed the teacher and students to save money on fabric when trying out new patterns and styles. A student made the skirt and vest you see on the dress form. Both McCall's and Simplicity made half scale dress form patterns.

Marie Osmond, who loved sewing as a young child and young adult, teamed up with Mattel in 1976 to present the Marie Osmond Modeling Doll (plate 165). Marie designed it and Mattel manufactured it. In 1981 in *Doll Reader* magazine, it was advertised as a "buy out" product from Mattel at a large discount. It was being offered for $15.95 down from the original price of $29.95. The Marie Osmond Modeling Doll is an amazing sewing doll! It is made from vinyl and is an excellent size for a child to work with. The patterns can all be interchanged and the style ideas are endless. The patterns teach you how to be creative in sewing. It is evident that a lot of thought went into designing this sewing set.

Most of the mannequin dolls were made only in the 1940s, a few held over into the early 1950s, and Marie Osmond into the 1980s, but for the most part, the end of the 1940s signaled the end of the era of sewing mannequin dolls.

You might say mannequin type sewing dolls are back. The larger vinyl fashion dolls now on the market including Gene, Alex, and Tyler are wonderful to dress, design, and sew for. Pattern companies are offering patterns featuring period clothing just for these beautiful dolls. But these new dolls are really for adults and are made mainly to collect. I am sure there are very few little girls or teen-agers that will learn to sew using them. I wish there were a doll made for our children today to learn to sew. I'm afraid we are cheating our children by not passing on to them the art of sewing.

Plate 144. Marianne's Fashion Designing Set #100 was manufactured by Latexture Products, Inc., circa 1940. The box for this set is very thin cardboard, so it is difficult to find in good condition. The box is 12¾" x 8" x 2¼". The mannequin Marianne is 12½" tall and is marked "Pat. Pend. Latexture N.Y." on her back above the waist. She has painted features and shoes, and her arms are pegged and removable. The three patterns that come in her box are #101 Marianne's Easy-to-Make Dress, #102 Marianne's Nurse's Uniform, and #103 Marianne's Day-Time Dress. The book in this set is *Latexture Simplicity Sewing Book for Young Fashion Designers* with 88 pages and many plates. There is a printed liner inside the box offering three additional patterns: Sets A, B, and C for Marianne. **Complete: $300.00 and up.**

Plate 145. Vivianne's Fashion Designing Set is made by Latexture Products, Inc., circa 1940s. The composition 11½" mannequin is marked on the back just above the waist "Pat. Pend. Latexture N.Y." She has painted features, hair, and shoes, a red-painted square stand, and three Simplicity patterns. The patterns are #4359 Drop-Waist Dress with Square Collar, #4401 Button-Front Dress, #4387 Two-Piece Dress with Bows. **Complete: $100.00 and up.**

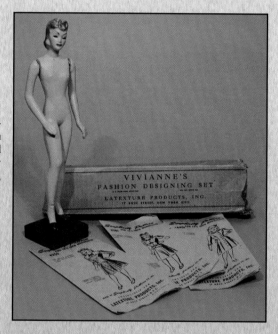

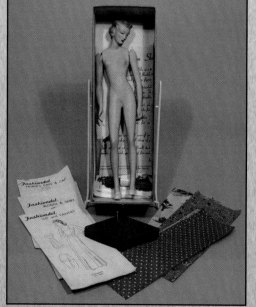

Plate 146. Susanne's Fashion Show (small box) was manufactured by Latexture Products, Inc., circa 1940s. Susanne comes in an unmarked, pink and blue paper-covered box. The box measures 12" x 4" x 3". Susanne is 11½" tall without her stand and she has painted features, hair, and shoes. Her arms are removable, and she is marked "Copyrighted Latexture" on the back of one of her legs. The set comes with three lengths of fabric, a red-painted stand, a hank of baby rickrack, a hank of seam binding, and three patterns. The patterns are #109 Fashiondol Nurse's Cape and Cap, #111 Fashiondol Blouse and Skirt, and #306 Slip and Panties. Glued to the inside lid is a yellow slip of paper advertising additional pattern sets A and B to complete Susanne's wardrobe. **Complete: $200.00 and up.**

Note: See Susanne's Fashion Show plate 148 for a larger set.

Plate 147. Simplicity Miniature Fashions Set, circa 1940s, is in a flap-front box printed with red bows. The box measures 19½" x 13" x 2". Printed in blue on the end of the box is "Miniature Fashions, Latexture Products, Inc., N.Y.C. price $1.29." The lid of the box has three Simplicity patterns made exclusively for the Latexture Products Company. The patterns are #4387 Two-Piece Suit, #4401 Front-Button Dress, and #4710 Sunday Dress. The doll is a 12½" mannequin with painted features, hair, and shoes and detachable pegged arms. Also contained in the box are two booklets, "Miniature Fashions" and "Simplicity Hints for the Young Designer," and a wooden stand. **Complete: $100.00 and up.**

Plate 148. Susanne's Fashion Show (large box) was manufactured by Latexture Products, Inc., circa 1940s. The box measures 17" x 13½" x 3¾". The mannequin, Susanne, is 11½" tall without her stand. She has painted features, hair, and shoes and detachable pegged arms. Included in the box are a plastic thimble, cloth tape measure, two wooden spools of thread, a length of material, assorted rickrack, scissors, Susanne's wooden stand, a dress form, a needle book, snaps, a paper of pins, and six patterns. The patterns are Susanne's Play Dress, Susanne's Nurse's Uniform, Susanne's Nurse's Cape, Susanne's Daytime Dress, Susanne's Pinafore, and Susanne's Slip and Panties. **Complete: $300.00 and up.**

Note: I found this set in complete disarray. I tried to replace the items where I thought they belong, but I have not seen another set like this for comparison. So if something is shown out of place or is missing, please, don't adjust your own set, as likely mine is wrong. I chose to include it so collectors would know it was available. See plate 146 for Susanne's Fashion Show in a smaller set.

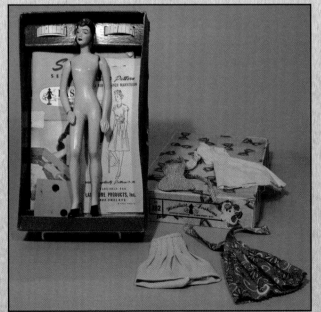

Plate 149. Miniature Fashions #102 comes in a box printed with blue bows that measures 13" x 8" x 2½" and was manufactured circa 1945 by Latexture Products, Inc. The doll inside is 12½" tall and made of composition with detachable pegged arms and painted hair, features, and shoes. A cloth tape measure is threaded through the platform her head rests in. Underneath the doll is the "Simplicity Sewing Book for Fashiondol" and three Simplicity patterns: #4359 a Drop-Waist Dress with Collar, #4401 a Button-Front Dress, and #4710 Cap-Sleeve Dress with Set-in Waistband. This set usually has a length of fabric, but I think it was used by the previous owner because there are a pink skirt, a red print apron, and a pink and blue print jumper already made up, and dress #4359 is started. **Complete, as shown: $100.00 and up.**

Plate 150. Fashiondol #705 was manufactured by Latexture Products, Inc., circa 1945. The window box is 16" x 10¼" x 2". The doll in this set is 15½" and is stamped just above her waist "Copyright Fashiondol." The features and hair are painted, as well as the shoes. Her pegged arms come off for dressing. To one side is her blue flocked dress form. Just below that is the stand that will support the dress form or the doll if you insert the dowel sticks provided into her legs. On the other side of the box are the "Simplicity Sewing Book for Fashiondol," fabric, and three Simplicity patterns. The patterns are, #4938 Over Dress, #4980 a Square-Neck Dress, and #4984 a Dress with Cap Sleeves. In the compartments above are a cloth tape measure, tomato pincushion, needles, a plastic thimble, two spools of thread, and assorted trimmings. This set is also available with a 12½" size doll. **Complete: $200.00 and up.**

Plate 151. Simplicity Fashiondol comes in a box covered in blue bow paper with a black and white drawing applied to the top. Signed James Montgomery Flagg, it shows a teenage girl holding the Fashiondol dressed in a nurse's uniform and cape. This picture adds to my delight in this set. Latexture Products, Inc., made the set, circa 1943. Inside the box is a recess to hold the 12" Fashiondol and accessories. The doll is made of latex composition with painted features, hair, and shoes. Above her is a spool of thread and assorted baby rickrack. On the far side is a dress form and the center holds the stand for the doll and dress form, a plastic thimble, oilcloth tape measure, and Simplicity patterns. The patterns are made by Simplicity exclusively for the Fashiondol. They include a Student Nurse's Uniform, Graduate Nurse's Uniform, Graduate Nurse's Cape, Public Health Nurse's Uniform, and Nurse's Aprons. The upper corner carries a "Simplicity Sewing Book for Fashiondol." Inside, it states that the doll is not just an ordinary doll, but a miniature of a teenage girl. **Complete: $500.00 and up.**

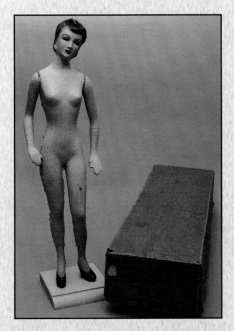

Plate 152. Joanne's Fashion Designing Set #400 was manufactured by Latexture Products, Inc., circa 1940s. Joanne is 20" tall, and comes in a plain brown 22½" x 6½" x 4" box. She has painted features, hair, and shoes and detachable pegged arms. It is printed on the end of her box that she comes with a basic pattern and a sewing book. I have seen this doll and the box three times and it didn't have a pattern or sewing book. I am beginning to wonder if it was really was included. **Complete: $300.00 and up.**

Plate 153. Fashiondol #503 with the new flexible and unbreakable rubber, was manufactured by Latexture Products, Inc., circa 1940s. The mannequin is 12" tall and is incised on her back at her waist, "C Fashiondol." She had painted features, hair, and shoes. The box measures 15½" x 12" x 2¼" and has the word "Fashiondol" and a silhouette of a fashion doll printed all over the box top. My first reaction to this set when I saw it was that the doll doesn't belong. I had only previously seen this set with the standard composition doll as in Simplicity Miniature Fashions Set (plate 147). However, I now believe this doll is original to this set. She is marked "Fashiondol" and the dress form is different from the standard form; it is flatter at the hip area and the shoulders are much broader. The cincher was the die-cut areas holding the items in the box. They are exactly the same as the other sets, except for the cutouts where the doll and her dress form rest. The recess where the doll goes is different, particularly the head shape, and the recess for the dress form is cut larger for the shoulder area. The doll and the stand fit perfectly in their recesses. The stand is interesting too; the two larger holes do not fit into the standard composition doll, nor do they fit this doll. However the smaller holes line up with her feet, and there is a blue painted thin dowel included in the set that fits into these small holes. The larger center hole fits the dress form. Also included in this set are cloth tape measure, plastic thimble, wooden spool of thread, pieces of rickrack, and four Simplicity patterns. The patterns are #4359 Drop-Waist Dress with Square-Collar, #4401 Button-Front Dress, #4710 Dress with Cap Sleeves and Set-in Waistband, and #4977 Dress with Puffed Sleeves and Round Neckline. Also included is the "Simplicity Sewing Book for Fashiondol." **Complete: $300.00 and up.**

Note: I have seen this doll in this set twice, with the "adjusted holes" stand.

Plate 154. Peggy McCall (small box), circa 1940s, has a long narrow box that measures 13" x 3" x 2½". Peggy McCall the fashion model is a 13" mannequin complete with a wooden stand. Dritz-Traum Company manufactured Peggy McCall. Peggy is painted composition with pegged arms that detach for easy dressing. She is unmarked. Included are instructions on how to remove Peggy's arms and place her on her stand. She has painted features, hair, and shoes and there is a hole in her foot to accommodate the stand. The pattern that comes with her is a miniature McCall's #6600-2, a Princess Dress made especially for Peggy. The glassine envelope that held the nails for Peggy's stand was still in the box. The pattern has a copyright date of 1942. **Complete: $100.00 and up.**

Sewing and Embroidery Sets for Mannequin Dolls

Plate 155. Peggy McCall Fashion Model (double-door box) was manufactured by Dritz-Traum Co., Inc. in 1943. This set was advertised as a new product in the March 1943 issue of *Toys and Novelties* as one of the patriotic boxes. The box measures 13½" x 10½" x 3¼". When the red and blue double doors open, we see Peggy McCall tied in the center recess. Peggy is painted composition and is 13" tall with painted hair, features, and shoes, her pegged arms are removable. Underneath her is the pamphlet telling how to remove Peggy's arms safely. In the box itself are two wooden spools of thread, a plaster dress form, a plastic thimble, cloth tape measure, talon zipper, and a felt piece with needles. On the inside of the lids are "McCall Tricks in Sewing" booklet, three pieces of fabric, and three McCall's patterns. The patterns are #6600-1 Nurse's Uniform and Apron, #6600-2 Princess Dress, #6600-3 Daytime or Date Dress. **Complete: $300.00 and up.**

Plate 156. Peggy McCall (hat box) is actually half a hatbox shape that measures 17½" along the straight edge when closed, opens to a 17½" diameter and is 4" deep. This is probably the most difficult Peggy sewing set to find. Dritz-Traum Company, Inc. offered this set in 1942 in patriotic colors. The set features a 13" painted composition Peggy McCall with painted features, hair, and shoes. She is dressed in the Nurse's Uniform, made by her previous owner. Arranged around her are two wooden spools of thread, a metal thimble, plaster dress form, and three lengths of cloth. Secured on the inside of the lid are a package of needles, a pair of knitting needles with a red sweater knitted by the previous owner (using the enclosed pattern), a cloth tape measure, two miniature McCall's patterns, and a needle threader. The patterns are #6600-1 Nurse's Uniform, and #6600-2 Princess Dress. Included in the box are the instruction sheet on how to remove Peggy's arms, "McCall Tricks in Sewing" booklet, and "Peggy The Modern Fashion Model" booklet that tells all about Peggy. The last page shows a sweater to knit, just for Peggy. **Complete: $500.00 and up.**

Plate 157. Junior Miss Fashion Designing Set comes in a plain brown box that is 15" x 6" x 3½" and is circa 1943. Printed in black on the end of the box is "Junior Miss Fashion Designing Set with Butterick Manikin, Educational Crafts Co., New York, 51, N .Y." The composition doll is 13½" including her stand. She has detachable, pegged arms, a suggestion of painted features, hair, and painted shoes. Included in the set are her stand and a small pink paper advertising additional patterns. Glued to the lid of the box are two Butterick patterns for Junior Miss. Pattern Set #1 is for a Dirndl Dress, Party Dress, and Bridal Gown. Set #4 has a Wac's Uniform, Wave's Uniform, and Nurse's Uniform. All the patterns are printed on the stiffer paper usually reserved for the instruction sheet. **Complete: $100.00 and up.**

Note: The additional patterns that could be ordered were patterns Set #2, One-Piece Pajamas, Camisole Slip, and Bra-Top Colotte Slip, and Set #3, Princess Frock, Evening Gown, and Tailored Robe.

Plate 158. Junior Miss Fashion Designing Set #10 was manufactured by Educational Crafts Co., circa 1940s. The box is 14½" x 5¼" x 3¼" and reads: "Junior Miss Fashion Designing Set with Mannequin. Three Butterick patterns and material for Making Dress. Teaches girls to design and make their own clothes. No.10 Butterick Designing Set." The mannequin is made of painted composition and is 13" without her stand. She is presented as she was originally sold, with her arms detached. She has painted features, hair, and shoes. The pattern was glued to the inside lid of the box, and is pattern set #1 Dirndl Dress, Party Dress, and Bridal Gown. The piece of fabric that was in the box is now made into the Dirndl dress. **Complete: $100.00 and up.**

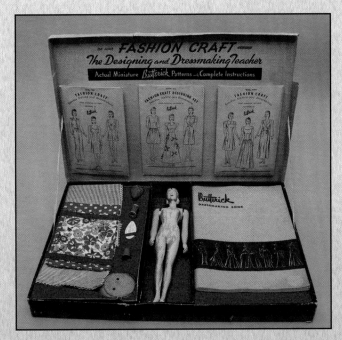

Plate 159. De Luxe Fashion Craft Butterick sewing set was distributed by George Borgfeldt Co., N. Y., circa 1943. The plain orange and blue box measures 19" x 13" x 2". The lid opens to show three full-size pattern envelopes, and printing in blue on the inside lid: "De Luxe Fashion Craft-The Designing and Dressmaking Teacher. Actual Miniature Butterick Patterns with complete Instructions." Each pattern envelope holds three patterns. Envelope #1 in the center has a Dirndl Dress, Nurse's Uniform and Party Dress. Envelope #2 contains One-Piece Pajamas, Camisole Slip, and Bra-Top Culotte Slip. Envelope #3 has a Princess Frock, Evening Gown, and Tailored Robe. The box bottom has three compartments. The first holds fabric, pincushion, thread, needle threader, plastic thimble, and the doll stand. The center compartment holds the doll, a 12½" unmarked, painted composition mannequin, with detachable pegged arms. She has painted features, hair, and shoes. The remaining compartment holds the "Butterick Dressmaking Book." This is Butterick's general dressmaking book for amateur, business or high school girl, homemaker, teacher, dressmaker, or native genius. The book does not mention the doll or set anywhere in its contents and is copyrighted 1941. **Complete: $200.00 and up.**

Note: The doll in this set has flaking paint.

 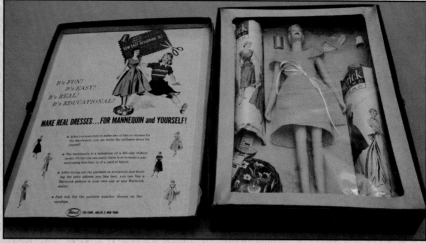

Plate 160. Ideal Butterick Sew Easy Designing Set measures 14" x 10½" x 2¾". The luggage-type set has a metal snap latch and handle and was manufactured in the 1940s by Ideal Toy Company. The front of the box shows a teenage girl in a sweater and skirt with her hand around the waist of a mannequin in a "walk away dress." The box opens to find the same picture that is on the front in miniature and a sales pitch that reads: *It's FUN! It's EASY! It's REAL! It's EDUCATIONAL! MAKE REAL DRESSES…FOR MANNEQUIN AND YOURSELF! *After you learn how to make any of the six dresses for the mannequin, you can make the selfsame dress for yourself. * The mannequin is a miniature of a life size fashion model. On her you can easily learn how to make a garment using less then ¼ of a yard of fabric. *After trying out the garment in miniature and deciding the color scheme you like best, you can buy a Butterick pattern in your own size at any Butterick dealer. *Just ask for the pattern number shown on the envelope.* In the bottom of the box is a tray with a cutout recess holding a 12¾" doll of very soft latex material. There are two dowels inside to support her legs to her waist, and then a single dowel from her waist to her head. The doll has painted features and shoes, removable arms, and is unmarked. She is dressed in an unfinished gauze wrap-around dress. Included in the set are plastic thimble, a wooden spool of thread, needle threader, cloth tape measure, a medal dome shaped stand, and a "Butterick says Fit's the Thing" alterations sheet. Also included are two Butterick standard-sized pattern envelopes each with three dresses. They are marked, Set number 8, which contains Set #979 Casual Dress, #6083 Evening Gown, #5917 Chemise Type Dress, and Set number 9 with #6057 Sundress, #5744 Coverall Apron, and #6015 Walk Away Dress. **Complete: $200.00 and up.**

Plate 161. Singer Sewhandy Mannikin Set comes in a 14½" x 11" x 4" heavy-duty luggage-type case with a plastic handle and metal latches. The Singer Manufacturing Company manufactured it circa 1953. The soft plastic, 12½" tall mannikin has removable arms, molded, painted features, hair, and shoes. A tan Singer Sewhandy child's sewing machine shares the space with her, along with two lengths of fabric and the mannikin's white painted stand. In the lid are a package of sewing machine needles, a spool of thread, thimble, scissors, the "Sewing Handbook for the Singer Mannikin Doll Set," a booklet "How to Use your Singer Sewhandy Model 20 Sewing Machine," and two Butterick pattern envelopes. In one envelope are #5366 Shoulder-Tie Dress, #5100 Pinafore, #5354 Dress with Sweetheart Neckline, in the other are #5460 Blouse, #5453 Button-Front Skirt, #5547 Over Blouse, and #5428 Double Breasted Dress. **Complete: $500.00 and up.**

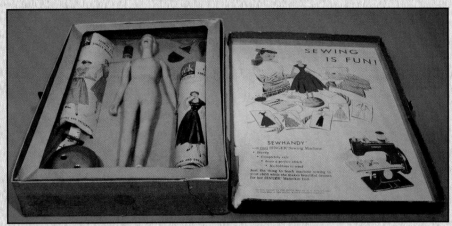

Plate 162. Singer Mannikin Doll Set manufactured by The Singer Manufacturing Company in 1949. The luggage-type box measures 14¼" x 10½" x 2½" and has a metal latch and handle. The front of the box states: "The Singer Mannikin Doll Set dress her up in these beautiful dresses you make yourself. Singer Mannikin Doll Set teaches sewing complete with Butterick patterns." The cover graphics are just like the inside, only the printing is different, the inside advertising the little toy Singer Sewhandy. Inside is the 12" soft latex doll, with removable arms, molded, painted features, hair, and shoes. Also included are a metal dome doll stand, cloth tape measure, plastic thimble, wooden spool of thread, and a needle threader. In the side recesses are two patterns. The first is Butterick pattern Group #1 that includes #5366 Shoulder Tie-Dress, #5100 Pinafore Apron, and #5354 Dress with a Sweetheart Neckline. Group #2 includes #5460 Blouse, #5453 Button-Front Skirt, #5428 Double Breasted Dress, and #5547 Over Blouse. To complete the set is a 16 page "Sewing Handbook for the Singer Mannikin Doll Set." **Complete: $200.00 and up.**

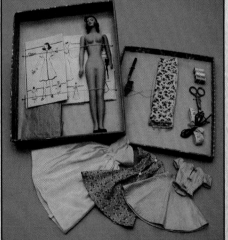

Plate 163. The Debutante Doll Sewing Kit was designed by Helen Huntington Jones, circa 1940. The box is covered inside and outside with treated cloth. Inside is a hard rubber mannequin 11½" high with painted features and shoes and stiffened floss hair very much in the style of the Margit Nilsen mannequin. She comes with three patterns, a daytime dress, slip, and panties, and after-skiing costume. There is a pattern list at the bottom of the pattern sheets, with a play suit, tennis dress, skirt and knitted sweater, hostess gown, skating outfit, and after-skiing costume. Secured in the lid are three wooden spools of thread, a pair of metal scissors, an oilcloth tape measure, trims, metal thimble, strawberry emery, marking pencil, and two lengths of fabric. In a paper bag are the tiniest little pink slip straps with metal adjusters and a 1" piece of elastic (for a girdle?). There are three outfits made up, a yellow gown, a two-piece dress, and a green print dress. **Complete: $200.00 and up.**

Note: On the bottom of this box is a sticker that says The Debutante Doll Sewing Kit Designed by Helen Huntington Jones. There is also a stamp that reads: "Undressed."

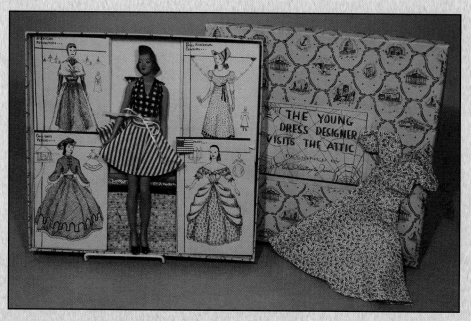

Plate 164. The Young Dress Designer Visits the Attic is designed by Helen Huntington Jones, circa 1943. The box measures 14" x 13" x 1½". On the bottom of the box is an F.A.O. Schwarz sticker with "11/43///Sewing K.///RX." The box is covered with a light blue paper with a red-and-blue patriotic print. The title of the set is printed on off-white paper with a spider web print background. The manikin's name is Belinda and she is unmarked and has stationary arms that do not detach. She has molded, painted features, hair, and shoes. Her eyes have molded lashes and blue eye shadow. Belinda comes with four patterns each with a front and back drawing and full size pattern pieces. They are all period dresses with their names written on the pattern, American Revolution, Civil War Period, 17th century, and Early 19th century. There are also four 34" x 9" of fabric for making the dresses. One piece of fabric was cut into to make the Early 19th Century dress. Printed on the bottom of the pattern sheets is information on obtaining modern patterns for Belinda by sending 25¢ in coin to Helen Huntington Jones in New York City. I am not sure if this set had any other sewing supplies, but I am sure that the patterns and fabric that are here are original to the set. **As shown: $200.00 and up.**

Note: Both The Debutante Doll Sewing Kit, (plate 163) and The Young Dress Designer Visits the Attic sewing sets have a handmade feeling about them. It seems likely that Helen Huntington Jones may have created sets exclusively for special stores like F.A.O. Swartz.

Plate 165. The **Marie Osmond Modeling Doll** was originally introduced in 1976 by Mattel. The doll stands 30" tall, has a very stable stand, and is jointed at the neck, arms, and waist. She has a hard plastic body, soft vinyl head, rooted hair, and painted features. She is modestly clad in a skin colored teddy embossed right onto the doll. Marie's untagged dress is pink satin with a silver-threaded knit bodice and sheer nylon flounces at the bottom of fitted sleeves. White plastic, chunky open-toe high heels complete her ensemble. The 30½" x 10" x 5" box is a delight to study. Printed on the front is "Learn to sew on the Marie mannequin! Share Marie's favorite hobby!" Also on the front of the box are a full-size color picture of the doll and a smaller insert of Marie sitting with a child and fitting patterns on the doll. One side of the box has a word from Marie: *I love sewing! It's a wonderful lifetime hobby. If you learn a few easy basics, you can make all kinds of things. This doll and the patterns and instructions will introduce you to the wonderful world of sewing. As you make each fashion, you can fit it on the modeling doll — like real designer's do! Have fun! And happy sewing!* There are also 10 color pictures of suggested fashions to make. On the other side are fifteen more line drawings of fashions, along with a listing of combinations of outfits: 12 different blouses, 28 different dresses, three lengths of skirts, three kinds of pants, 16 varieties of coats (from jacket to floor length), belts, and pockets. The variety is endless. **Complete: $100.00 and up.**

Plate 166. Deb-U-Doll a 22" fashion doll of the 1940s that was designed by Margit Nilsen. She has detachable pegged arms, painted features and shoes. The doll came with either black or blonde hair. Margit Nilsen was famous for her store mannequins. She sold her mannequins to better quality department stores such as Saks Fifth Avenue and Macy's in New York City. Deb-U-Doll was made to look like the miniature mannequins in the store windows and she had a complete wardrobe of ready-made clothing to buy. I have never seen any patterns for her, but I have a large box of clothing for her and some is obviously homemade, so I know she was used as a sewing doll. She was sold at a fairly high price in the 1940s. F.A.O. Schwarz was one of the stores that sold the Deb-U-Doll at $7.95. They later added Kid Sister, with a matching line of clothing. Both of these dolls were made of a flexible rubber that has hardened with age and they require careful handling. **With original clothing: $700.00 and up.**

Plate 167. Kid Sister by Margit Nilsen circa 1945. Made of latex is she is 16" tall has detachable pegged arms, molded painted features, and a real hair wig. Her socks are painted and her shoes are molded and painted. **With original clothing: $700.00 and up.**

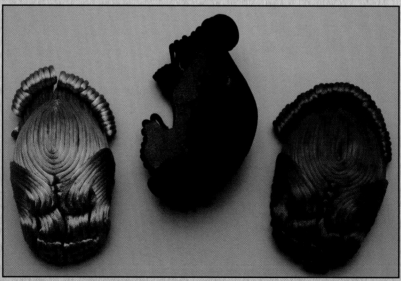

Plate 168. Simplicity Display Mannequin is a 30" composition display mannequin from Simplicity Pattern Co. She has removable arms to facilitate dressing. This mannequin has three fiber wigs, black, blonde, and red. This made it easy to dress her without messing her hair and the color of the wig could be changed to coordinate with the outfits. This mannequin stands on a base that has the name of the Simplicity Pattern Company and a place to put a card with the final cost of the garment. These mannequins continued to be popular into the 1960s for home economics teachers to use in the classrooms. **Complete: $300.00 and up.**

Plate 169. Mannequin, circa 1940s is from an unknown maker, possibly Margit Nilsen. This mannequin is 27" tall, made of composition and her arms detach for easy dressing. She has a stiffened-thread wig, molded, painted features, and has silver painted slippers. **$300.00 and up.**

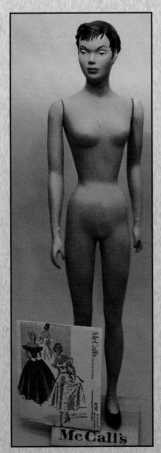

Plate 170. McCall's Mannequin, circa 1950s, is by an unknown maker. Made of composition, this lady stands about 30" tall. She has painted features, hair, and shoes, and is on her original McCall's stand. The stand holds a McCall's pattern from her time period. Her arms detach for easy dressing. This is one of the prettiest mannequins I have seen. It is reported that McCall's was the first to offer a new service to stores that included display mannequin dolls created by sculptor Margit Nilsen. These mannequins were used in schools and also supported pattern sales by showing the end product and helping women visualize how the pattern and fabric appear after finished. **With stand: $300.00 and up.**

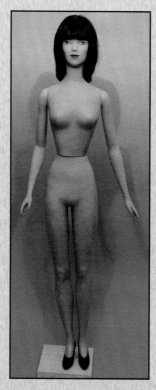

Plate 171. Mannequin, circa, 1960s was sold to me as a Margit Nilsen mannequin designed in the 1960s. She stands 29" tall and has jointed arms and a swivel waist. Her features are painted, as well as her shoes. Her shag hairstyle is a glued-on wig. **$100.00 and up.**

Plate 172. Half Size Dress Form for teaching young women to sew. This half size dress form was used in San Francisco in the 1960s in a high school sewing class. The text was *Pattern Making by the Flat Pattern Method*. Both Simplicity and McCall's pattern companies put out the half size patterns. The scaled down patterns saved the students and teachers both time and money. The students in the class made the clothing on this model. **Form, book, and patterns: $300.00 and up.**

Plate 173. McCall's Mannikin Pattern #1058 was put out by the McCall's Pattern Company and was copyrighted in 1943. The Wardrobe for Manikin Fashion Models pattern came in three sizes 12½", 15", and 20". It consisted of a dress, sport costume, party dress, coat combination, and petticoat. **Complete: $25.00 and up.**

Plate 174. **Butterick Minnekin Patterns** from the late 1930s, each has a Deltor (instruction sheet) but the patterns are still just plain tissue with no printing, just perforations. Shown are from left to right: Butterick Minnekin patterns #1444 Dress in Two Styles, #2084 Shirtwaist Dress in Two Styles, and #1459 Shirred Waist Dress in Two Styles. Two of the patterns carry the Fashion Fresh Seal, which says: "We hereby certify that this style is a current fashion. This seal gives positive assurance of authentic style." There isn't a size on these patterns just the word minnekin. **Complete, each: $50.00 and up.**

Plate 175. **McCall's Minikin Patterns**. Printed on the back of these patterns is: *This Is A 30 Inch McCall Display Doll Pattern. This McCall design was selected as one of the styles of the month for your 30 Inch McCall Display doll. Enclosed in this envelope is a special write-up, which suggests attractive accessories. If this costume requires a hat and bag, simple drawings are included which show you how to make them. Follow these accessory suggestions and your doll will be beautifully complete for display.* The patterns shown are, from top to bottom and left to right; McCall's Pattern #5259 Button-Front Dress with short or long sleeves, #4911 Shirred Front Dress, #8811 Two-Piece Suit, #5000 Open-Collar Dress, and #4334 Button-Front Dress in Two Styles. **Complete, each: $50.00 and up.**

Plate 176. **Simplicity Half Scale Patterns** from Simplicity Pattern Co. Half scale patterns were patterns some teachers used in home economic classes in the 1960s. Simplicity #4601 Simple to Sew skirts in three styles and Simplicity #7179 Simple to Sew blouse in five different styles. **Complete, each: $25.00 and up.**

Sewing and Embroidery Sets for Mannequin Dolls

Manufactured Patterns for 11½" – 15" Mannequin Dolls in Sets

Butterick Patterns for 12½" Mannequin Dolls

Set #1 13" Jr. Miss Manikin Set
    Dirndl, Party Dress, Bridal Gown

Set #1 Fashion Craft 12½" Set
    Dirndl, Party Dress, Nurse's Uniform

Set #2 Fashion Craft 12½" Set
    One-piece PJ, Camisole Slip, Cuelete Slip

Set #3 Fashion Craft 12½" Set
    Princess, Evening Gown, Tailored Robe

Set #8 Ideal Butterick 12½" Sew-Easy Designing Set
    #5979 Casual dress, full skirted with yoked bodice
    #6083 Wing backed evening gown
    #5917 Chemise type dress with pockets

Set #9 Ideal Butterick 12½" Sew-Easy Designing Set
    #6057 Button front sundress
    #5428 Coverall apron
    #5547 Wraparound "walk Aaway" dress

Group 1 Singer 12½" Mannikin Doll set
    #5366 Sleeveless shoulder tie, short dance dress
    #5100 Pinafore
    #5354 Sweetheart neck, cap sleeve afternoon dress

Group 2 Singer 12½" Mannikin Doll set
    #5460 & 5453 Dolman sleeve blouse and button front skirt
    #5428 Ballerina dress
    #5547 & #5453 Shortie jacket and button front skirt

Patterns for 15' Mannequin Dolls

Set #1 Junior Miss Manikin
    Dirndl
    Party Dress
    Bridal Gown

Patterns for 12½" Fashiondol

#101 — Easy to Make Dress
#103 — Day Time Dress
#104 — Play Dress
#105 — Evening Dress
#106 — Pajamas
#107 — Pinafore
#108 — Slip & Panties
#109 — Nurse's Cape & Cap

#110 — House Coat
#111 — Blouse & Skirt
#112 — Bathing Suit
#304 — Two Piece Suit
#305 — Date Dress
#306 — Slip and Panties

Jones, Helen Huntington Dolls

Debutante Doll Patterns for 11½" Debutante Doll
    Daytime Dress
    Hostess Gown
    Knitted Sweater
    Panties
    Play Suit
    Skating Outfit
    Skiing Costume
    Skirt
    Slip
    Tennis Dress

Young Dress Designer Visits the Attic
    American Revolution
    Early Nineteenth Century
    Civil War Period
    Seventeenth Century

Marianne's Patterns for 12½" Marianne (with Simplicity Book)

    #101—Easy To Make Dress
    #102—Nurse's Uniform
    #103—Day Time Dress

McCall's patterns for Manikin Fashion Models

Wardrobe for 12½" Manikin Fashion Models
    #1058 Wardrobe, Dress, Sport Costume, Party Dress, Coat, Combination, Long Petticoat

Peggy, 13" The Modern Fashion Model
    #6600-1   Nurse's Uniform
    #6600-2   Princess Dress
    #6600-3   Daytime, or Date Dress

Peggy McCall, 13½" The Fashion Model
    #6600-2 Princess Dress

Wardrobe for 15" Manikin Fashion Model
    #1058 Wardrobe, Dress, Sport Costume, Party Dress, Coat, Combination, Long Petticoat

Wardrobe for 20" Manikin Fashion Model
    #1058 Wardrobe, Dress, Sport Costume, Party Dress, Coat, Combination,

Minikin 29" Display Patterns
 #4334 Button-Front Dress in Two Styles
 #4911 Shirred front Dress
 #5000 Open-Collar Dress
 #5259 Button-Front Dress with short or long sleeves
 #8727 Junior Evening Dress
 #8811 Misses Two Piece Suit

Simplicity Patterns for Mannequin Doll

Vivianne's 12½" Fashion Designing Set
 #4359 Dropwasted Dress with Collar
 #4387 Two-piece Dress with Bows on Front *
 #4401 Front Button Dress with Long Sleeves *

Miniature Fashions 12½" (small box with red bow's)
 #4387 Two-piece Dress with Bows on Front *
 #4401 Front Button Dress with Long Sleeves *
 #4710 One-piece, Wasted, Cap Sleeve Dress

Fashiondol Set #05, 12½" (see through lid)
 #4496 Jumper & Blouse
 #4965 Square-neck dress, tailored sleeve
 #4977 Round neck dress, puffed sleeve

Fashiondol Set #103, 12½" (James Montgomery Flagg drawing)
 Public Health Nurse
 Graduate Nurse Cape

Graduate Nurse Uniform
Student Nurse Uniform
Nurse's Apron

Simplicity Patterns for 12½" Mannequin Doll
 #4553 Form Fitting Top & Full Skirt
 #4631 Jacket Style Top with Slacks
 #4774 Coat
 #4903 Dress with Rick-Rack trim and belt
 #4938 Dress with Pockets and belt

Simplicity Patterns for 15" Mannequin Doll
 #4065 Square-neck Long Gown
 #4390 Tailored Dress with Top Stitching
 #4402 Long Sleeve Blouse, Long Skirt
 #4938 Coverall Dress with Short Sleeves
 #4980 Square Neck, Cap Sleeve Dress
 #4981 Blouse & Shorts
 #4984 Dress with V-neck Style Opening
 #4995 Full Length Slip

Suzanne's 12½" Fashion Show Patterns for Suzanne
 #2001—Daytime Dress
 #2002—Nurse's Uniform
 #2004—Nurse's Cape
 #2005—Pinafore
 #2006—Play Dress
 #2007—Slip & Panties
 No #—Evening dress

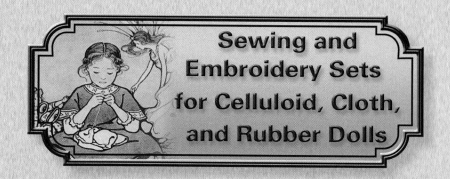

The earliest sets in this chapter have celluloid dolls from the Petitcollin factories in France. They are marked with the well-known "Tête L'Aigle" (eagle head). It is believed that the greatest era for celluloid dolls in France were the years between the 1930s and 1950s. There were three companies that were credited with these popular celluloid dolls, Nobel, Petitcollin, and G. Convert. It is theorized that the Petitcollin manufacturing company was founded in 1856 and their first products were jewelry and combs. Petitcollin registered the eagle mark on June 17, 1901. The company advertised their first dolls in 1909. In 1913, they were listed as a toy manufacturer, producing celluloid dolls, bathers, animals, and baby rattles, among other toys.

The Petitcollin dolls in the French celluloid 10" doll outfit (plate 177) and French celluloid 8" doll outfit (plate 178) have molded, painted features, mohair wigs, and are jointed at the shoulders and hips. Both have painted socks and one-strap black shoes. The sewing sets are very similar and look as if the same company might have made them to sell at different prices. I have also seen both the 8" and the 10" doll dressed in French provincial costumes without the sewing set. Poupeto, another French set, was made later, sometime around the 1950s (plate 182). The celluloid doll in this set is marked with the "diamond" mark belonging to Société Nobel Francaise. This is an interesting set that features a provincial costume to make for the doll.

One of the more fascinating doll sewing sets, in my opinion, is the snip 'n stitch (plate 181) by Dot & Peg Productions. This sewing set was made in the 1940s. The unusual doll is made of a rubber-type of composition that is the same as the fashion mannequin dolls of the period. That is where the resemblance ends; this doll is very "little girl like" with straight legs and a fat-cheeked face. The clothing is also very child-like and quite simple to construct. I am impressed by the completeness of this set, right down to the fabrics and trims for each outfit.

Dot & Peg Productions was the joining of two sisters. Mrs. Dorothy (Dot) Hedges and Mrs. Margaret (Peg) Lamb founded Dot & Peg Productions in 1941. Starting a company was Dot's idea, after creating homemade paper dolls for her two daughters. Dot & Peg advertised wonderful girls' toys. There first product was Young American Designer Paper Doll Kit, with costumes made from papers resembling fabrics such as tweeds, woolens, gingham, etc. It was so successful that Marshall Field and Company bought 10,000 sets the first year. *Good Housekeeping* magazine featured Young American Designer Paper Doll Kit in their December 1941 issue, giving it the Best American Toy of the Year Award, along with the Good Housekeeping Seal of Approval.

I have found advertisements in *Playthings* magazine from the early 1940s to the 1950s for their products. Besides paper dolls, they have advertised a baby in an egg, soft toys, musical toys and, of course, the lovely sewing set in this chapter. In the 1950s, the sisters started a line of ladies' accessories including sleepwear. This venture was so promising that they ended their toy line and put all their efforts into the new line. They sold their sleepwear and accessories to large department stores such as Marshall Field, Saks Fifth Avenue and I. Magnin. The sisters became so successful they decided to sell their business and retire in 1962.

Another unusual set is the Buttons and Bows #10630 (plate 184). It is unusual because it contains a bent-limb baby doll, and very few sewing sets were made featuring bent-limb baby dolls. The doll in this set is named Betty Bows and is unique because of the molded loop in her hair in which to tie a hair ribbon. She is one of the dolls in Sun Rubber Company's Sunbabe line. In a two-page article in a 1953 *Playthings* magazine about the Sun Rubber Company's new 1953 Sunbabe line was a paragraph about their new Buttons and Bows #10630 set:

The Sunbabe "Button and Bows" Sewing Set features the new 12-inch Sunbabe "Betty Bows" rubber doll with vinyl head. This remarkable lifelike Drink-Wet, sleeping-crying doll, designed by Sun, is ideal for the tiny seamstress who wants to make doll clothes, because the complete Sewing Set is neatly fitted in a handsome rectangular carrying case with handle. Included in this sewing set are a smartly-styled dress and bonnet of wrinkle-resistant material; die-cut sets of garments and accessories of quality materials in modern patterns; assorted buttons, ribbons, laces; generous supply of bows, ornaments and flowers; a complete sewing kit, with tape measure; and a complete pattern-and-instruction booklet.

The Sun Rubber Company was incorporated on April 4, 1923, in Barberton, Ohio. Mr. Thomas W. Smith, Jr. was the manager, secretary, and treasurer. Mr. Smith started his company selling toy hot-water bottles. They sold very well and within a short time the company expanded into the rubber doll line. Their first trade name was Sunruco. By 1928, the company had designed a squeeze doll and it became so popular it sold by the millions. Mr. Smith hired the best sculptors in the business, Mr. E. Peruggi and Mr. Bernard Lipfert. He worked closely with them to design appealing, life-like models.

The company was famous for their Sunbabe doll line that was designed by Ruth E. Newton. She was an author and illustrator of children's book from New York. We know she was with Sun Rubber in 1930, because she designed the animal line with molded clothing that included Bonnie Bear, Wiggy Wags, Susie-So-Soft, Bunny Buster, and Kitty-Be Mew.

It isn't clear to me when the first Sunbabe doll was produced, but it was sometime in or before 1947. The Barberton, Ohio *Magic City Review* ran an article about the Sunbabe doll line in 1948:

In order to fill the 1947 Christmas orders, the Sunbabe passed along the assembly line at the unbelievable rate of 20,000 each 24 hours. The genius that goes into the designing of these toys is a most interesting feature. Everything from the first pattern to the tinting that adds effective coloring to the toys is performed under delicate molding techniques and careful supervision.

The first Sunbabe was jointed and of flesh color. It had a hard rubber head, metal sleep eyes, and painted mouth and hair. It was 11" high in the sitting position, with a movable head, arms, and bent legs. She came with a flannelette diaper and safety pin. The doll was made with special Sunruco drinking-and-wetting feature and a glass bottle with a rubber nipple.

There are three cloth doll sewing sets listed in this chapter. The first is Little Princess embroidery Set #21 (plate 180). This set was sold through George Borgfeldt in New York City. This set has two Orphan Annie printed cloth dolls to sew and stuff, one is 5", the other 7". The 5" doll is the same cloth doll that

is included in the Little Orphan Annie Embroidery Set #1645 (plate 30) and Little Orphan Annie and Her Sewing Outfit #1680 (plate 31), so I assume Little Princess Embroidery Set #21 was made by J. Pressman and Company.

J. Pressman and Company also made the Sleeping Beauty Sewing Basket #2205 (plate 185) sometime in the 1960s. This basket has no identification as to its name except for the hang tag. It is embossed "Pressman Toy Corp." on the bottom of the basket. I believe the doll in this set is just a decoration; it is not a doll that you would normally dress and the pattern included in the set doesn't fit the doll. Hassenfeld Brothers offered Deluxe Sewing Set #1528 (plate 187) in 1967. The cloth doll in this set has a "Made in Japan" sticker on the foot and it is similar to the doll in the Sleeping Beauty Sewing Basket #2205. Neither of the dolls looks like they would be fun to sew for as the dresses when done, would be to large.

The last illustration in this chapter, Mini Magic Sew-O-Matic Sewing Center #780 (plate 188), is a set which includes an 11½" vinyl fashion doll. The F. J. Strauss Company in New York City made this set. There were a number of sewing sets made with the 11½" fashion doll in mind, but to my knowledge there have been no sets produced which included a genuine Mattel Barbie.

Plate 177. French Celluloid 10" Doll Outfit, circa 1920. This is a large box, it measures 15½" x 11" x 5½" and has no markings on the outside. The inner lid has a beveled mirror and numerous sewing implements attached. There are four lengths of fabric in two prints, nine spools and two cards of sewing thread, a box of pins, and a packet of needles. The sewing implements consist of a red wooden pin dish, a thimble, two red plastic thread holders, a threading tool, a crochet hook, and a pair of metal scissors. The bottom holds four skeins of pink knitting cotton and a pair of 3½" knitting needles. There is also a dress form of wood and paper maché wrapped in a centimeter-marked tape measure. In the center was tied an all celluloid doll (now shown sitting). It is marked with the French "eagles head" mark for Petitcollin. The doll measures 10" tall and has molded, painted features, a brown mohair wig, and is wearing her original chemise. The doll is jointed at the shoulders and hips and has painted white socks and black molded one-strap shoes. The bottom drawer of the box holds two stamped, white pieces to embroider a pillow and a collar-and-cuff set for a doll outfit. There are no markings on this set, except for the French printing on the thread, needles, and pin box. **Complete: $700.00 and up.**

Sewing and Embroidery Sets for Celluloid, Cloth, and Rubber Dolls

Plate 178. French Celluloid 8" Doll Outfit, circa 1920s, comes in a 12" x 10" x 2½" red paper-covered box. The 8" doll, still tied into this box, is all celluloid, with a mohair wig, molded, painted features, and is jointed at the shoulders and hips. Because she is still secured to the box, I can't see her mark but I am assuming she is Petitcollin, as the set is so much like the set in (plate 177). The doll has molded painted shoes and socks and is wrapped in a cut out dress that needs to be stitched up. The insert she rests on was once a vibrant pink; the original color can be seen under the implements. There is a paper tape measure marked in centimeters draped around her neck. Accompanying her in the box are two Paris thread cards, four paper spools of thread, two thread winders, a pair of metal scissors, a thimble, a mirror, a package of needles, a length of fabric, and a length of tarlatan. **Complete: $300.00 and up.**

Plate 179. Jouet De France (Toy of France) is written on the outside of this circa 1930s green paper-covered box that measures 10" x 8" x 2". In the center recess is a 7" celluloid doll that is jointed at the shoulders and hips. She has molded, painted features, a mohair wig, painted socks, and one-strap shoes. She is marked with the Petitcollin eagle. This box was once a sewing set, but the industrious owner has made up all the costumes. Completed and still in the box are a nightgown, a shift and panty, a printed dress with a collar, and a lined voile dress with a bit of smocking. The little owner did a beautiful job of sewing the clothing. All the outfits are French seamed, the lace is whip stitched on with very tiny stitches and she sewed the buttons on the back of each outfit and made thread loops to button them into. **Complete as shown: $200.00 and up.**

Plate 180. George Borgfeldt Corporation offered **Little Princess Embroidery Set #21** circa 1930. This embroidery set is in a plain brown 11" x 9½" folder. The only writing on the set is: "No.21 Little Princess Embroidery Set Toys that Keep the Little Fingers Busy. George Borgfeldt Corp., New York City, Made in U.S.A." Inside are two cloth Little Orphan Annie dolls to sew, one 5" and the other 7". The dolls are printed in red and yellow on a white background. This set also comes with a cardboard embroidery hoop, needle, and a skein of variegated cotton floss. **Complete: $50.00 and up.**

Note: The 5" doll is the same cloth doll that is included in the Little Orphan Annie Embroidery Set #1645 (plate 30) and Little Orphan Annie and Her Sewing Outfitt #1680 (plate 31) on page 24, so I assume it was made by J. Pressman and Company.

Plate 181. Snip n' Stitch was copyrighted by Dot & Peg Productions in 1947. The box measures 18" x 14" x 3¼". The doll is made from the same type of rubber composition the 1940s fashion mannequins were made from. The doll has molded, painted features, hair, and shoes. The socks are painted on. She is 12½" tall with a one-piece head, body, and legs, and pegged removable arms. The doll is signed on her back waist "Dot & Peg." There is a set of eight paper patterns and the fabrics to make up each of them. The patterns have the instructions written right on them. The patterns and fabrics consist of green gingham for the playsuit, blue pique with red heart print for the pajamas, white flannel for the bathrobe, pink polished cotton for the dress, pink felt for the bonnet, aqua-and-pink flower print for the pinafore, and blue pile fabric for the coat. There is a selection of trims, including cords and eyelet. To complete the set, a card of thread, metal blunt-nose scissors, metal thimble, and a folder that shows all the completed garments and their names are included. The previous owner cut out all the paper patterns, and made up the playsuit, pajamas, and the dress. There is no pattern for the panties she is wearing. They are the same fabric and trim as the slip, so I assume they were on her when the set was sold. The Snip n' Stitch sewing set is rare. **Complete as shown: $300.00 and up.**

Plate 182. Poppeto la couture en miniature Une collection de poupées que l'on fait soi-meme is in a very thin cardboard box that measures 14½" x 10¼" x 1½". Inside this circa 1950 set is a 7½" all celluloid doll, jointed at the shoulders and hips, she has a synthetic glued-on wig, molded, painted features, shoes, and socks. She is marked with the diamond mark of Société Nobel Française. Resting underneath her are the materials to make up the doll costume with the red wool skirt and black apron shown in the upper right corner of the box. The pieces contained in the set are for a red soft wool skirt, rayon blouse, tarlatan underskirt, black felt vest, black silk apron and bow, and all the trimmings to go with the outfit, down to the little gold cross worn around her neck. **Complete: $25.00 and up.**

Plate 183. Rubber Baby #103/31 with clothes to embroider is from the German Democratic Republic, circa 1950. A darling little 5" rubber baby dressed in a gathered dress, sacque, and bonnet is presented in a 14" x 10" x 1½" open display box. The baby has jointed arms and legs and is tied to a satin-bound blanket with an embroidered bib and a celluloid rattle tied next to her. Surrounding the baby are pre-sewn items to be embroidered including two matching blankets, a hooded cape, a cap, and a flannel dress. Decorating the box are tied bunches of silk embroidery floss, a little star-shaped silk winder, ribbons, and a circle of cloth with needles. **Complete: $100.00 and up.**

Sewing and Embroidery Sets for Celluloid, Cloth, and Rubber Dolls

Plate 184. Button and Bows #10630 sewing set is circa 1953. The luggage-style case is covered in a red alligator-print paper and has a plastic handle and metal clasp. It measures 15" x 12½" x 4". The inside of the lid holds a ready-made dress and bonnet in a blue pique, along with die-cut clothing to be sewn by the little seamstress. A bright yellow banner states "#10630 Sunbabe 'Buttons and Bows' Sewing Set. Sunbabe 'Betty Bows' doll *Drinks *Wets *Cries *Sleeps." The blue recessed insert in the bottom of the case holds Betty Bows a rubber doll with molded hair and a molded hair loop for tying her yellow ribbon. She is wearing a diaper and comes with a glass bottle with a rubber nipple. On raised platforms on either side of her are ribbons, rickrack, buttons, safety pins, tape measure, Betty's sewing kit, bows, flowers, and a paper pattern. The pattern sheet offers the same clothing that is found on the lid. **Complete: $200.00 and up.**

Plate 185. Sleeping Beauty Sewing Basket #2205 was manufactured by Pressman Toy Corporation, circa 1960s. The basket is soft plastic and has "Pressman Toy Corp." embossed on the bottom. There is also a tag on the handles that reads "Pressman Sleeping Beauty Sewing Basket #2205." The basket is 7¼" in circumference and 4½" high. Inside, attached to the lid, is a 7" bendable cloth doll. In the basket insert tray are two pieces of cloth, a tomato pincushion with emery, plastic thimble, metal blunt-nose scissors, paper of needles, a spool of thread, and a paper tape measure. Lifting the tray insert reveals a pattern that has a bra, panties, and skirt for an 8" doll. **Complete: $50.00 and up.**

Note: I believe the doll in this set is just a decoration; it is not a doll that you would normally dress and the pattern included in the set doesn't fit the doll.

Plate 186. Doll Basket. This little paper-woven sewing basket was made in Japan circa 1960. It measures 9½" x 6" x 4". The basket has a rayon-lined interior with a pincushion lid and a place to put your metal and plastic blunt-nose scissors, which are included. The little doll inside is 7" tall and made of a very soft vinyl. She has rooted synthetic hair, an open mouth, painted eyes, and is jointed at the hips and shoulders. She is dressed in a bra and panties. Waiting to be sewn for her are a skirt and blouse in a snappy plaid with lace trim and a red felt coat. The clothing is already cut out and included are buttons, snaps, and trims. There is a sewing sheet with easy instructions and pictures of all the finished garments. Also included in the set are two little spools of thread, a needle, and a plastic thimble. **Complete: $25.00 and up.**

Plate 187. This set is titled **Deluxe Sewing Set #1528** and is copyrighted 1967. The box is 14" x 11" x 1½" and is shrink-wrapped. After seeing some of Hasbro's earlier sets I hardly feel this is their Deluxe. The doll is made of a nylon stocking type material and measures 8". She has yarn hair painted features and can be bent in any position. The set contains two pre-cut dresses and four extra pieces of fabric, embroidery thread with the gold Hasbro wrapper, a needle, plastic thimble, and a plastic dress form that is bigger than the doll. This very same set was also sold as a Deluxe Stitch-a-Story set. Written in the catalog was *Colorful, exciting and diversified are these sewing assortments that provide the ultimate on sewing fun.* Once these sets were open, there was just be the tray to hold the contents and often they were scattered, making these sets hard to find complete. **Complete: $25.00 and up.**

Plate 188. Mini Magic Sew-O-Matic Sewing Center #780 was manufactured in 1979 by F. J. Strauss Company. It is contained in a see-through window box and measures 9½" x 7 ¼" x 4". Included in this set are a mini sewing machine, an 11½" vinyl fashion doll, instruction book, a paper tape measure, plastic scissors, two spools of thread, and "Fire Proof" material for two doll dresses. There are instructions for the machine and a pattern for a three-piece dress, a three-piece blouse, and a three-piece skirt. Unfortunately, the large-print fabric that comes with this set is a poor choice for the patterns and doll inside. **Complete: $25.00 and up.**

Clothing is, and always will be, an important part of our lives. At a very young age we are aware of what we are wearing and begin to evaluate it. As early as the age of two we begin to make choices in our clothing. What mother hasn't seen her daughter crying because she can't wear her favorite outfit that is in the laundry? Doll clothing is just as important in the realm of play. In order for a little mother to play properly with her "child," the doll must have a wardrobe.

The clothing for dolls has been just as important as, and often times more important than, the doll itself. Some dolls have had patterns and clothing created specifically for them. Toy makers, knowing that every parent cannot afford the more popular dolls and their wardrobes, have always come to the rescue with generic doll clothing and patterns. By selecting the most popular doll of the moment and making clothing, patterns, or clothing kits, toy makers have cashed in on the popularity of a product another company has produced. Not only was this good business for the toy maker, it was good for the parent who could make their child happy with a less costly generic product.

Through the years, children have always loved dressing their dolls and sewing for them was a special treat. In the June, 1895 issue of *The Ladies' Home Journal*, there was an ad for children to win prizes in a Fairy Wardrobe (plate 189) doll dressing contest. The magazine ad read:

$250.00 in Prizes to Children For the Best Doll Dresses Made from the Fairy Wardrobe.

We will give $250.00 in prizes for doll's garments, sewed by hand, made from the Fairy Wardrobe and sent us by Sept 15th, 1895. To give children of different ages opportunity to compete, we make two classes, dividing the prizes equally between the two: First—those over 11 years but not above 16 years; Second—those under 11 years.

PRIZES   *2 First Prizes of $10.00 each*
         10 Second Prizes of 5.00 each
         20 Third Prizes of 2.50 each
         40 Fourth Prizes of 1.50 each
         70 Fifth Prizes of 1.00 each

The judge of workmanship will be F. A. Foster & Co., the manufacturers, and as they best know how the garments should look, fairness to all is assured. All garments will be returned after the awards are made, if return postage is enclosed with the garments. The Fairy Wardrobe ready to cut and make, is printed in fast colors and dainty patterns on the finest cloths, *warranted to fit any 14" or 16" doll; so printed and outlined that a child can make a doll's outfit, consisting of a Nightgown, two Dresses, Red Riding Hood Cloak and Reefer with Tam O'Shanter. Full instructions on each pattern. Price 50 cents per full set. Single samples garments, 10 cents. Prizes given only for full assorted sets, consisting of above five garments. J. S. Tucker & Co., Boston. Mass.*

This is the earliest printed-by-the-yard doll clothing I have been able to find. The earliest printed cloth doll patent was granted to Edward Peck in 1886 for his Santa Claus. Edward Peck's Santa didn't have a back; he was presented with two fronts, so no matter which side was showing, it would be the front. Cocheco Manufacturing Co. printed the first doll designed by Celia and Charity Smith in late 1889. Cocheco also printed dolls patented by Ida Gutsell in 1893. All these printed toys on cloth for mothers and children to sew became a big business for many companies.

The H. E. Verran Company, Inc. manufactured Royal Society Embroidery Package Outfits. H. E. Verran Company, Inc. advertised stamped doll clothing kits, in the pages of ladies' magazines. In a 1914 magazine, their ad read as follows:

The mother who wishes her little daughter to be artistic and industrious will find a most pleasing means of cultivating these traits in the beautiful doll set included in the new line of Royal Society Package Embroidery Outfits just being displayed in Art Needlework Departments. The Outfit illustrated above consists of Blue Poplin Coat and Hat, fine White Lawn Dress, Knickers, Chemise and Petticoat Combination, all contained in one package ready for making. Simple embroidery designs and outlines for cutting are stamped on the materials, and with them is sufficient Royal Society Embroidery Floss to complete, also a diagram of stitches, simplified for children.

This ad was for Royal Society Doll's Outfit #369 (Dolly's "Day-Day" set) priced at 50 cents (plate 190). There was also a smaller set named Dolly's Lingerie Set #370 that consisted of a soft Nainsook nightgown, boudoir cap, chemise, knickers, and petticoat at the price of 25¢.

Of course there is always another company that can do it cheaper and the Ideal Company that manufactured Ideal Embroidery Packages did. They sold an Ideal Doll's Complete Dress Outfit #165 for only 10¢ (plate 191) packaged similar to Royal Society sets, they advertised:

Ideal Embroidery Packages Contain Articles Stamped on Materials of The Best Quality with Embroidery floss suffcent to complete the embroidery. Instruction sheet included. All For 10¢.

The package contained a dress, full slip, petticoat, drawers, and boudoir cap. These embroidery packages delight me (as they would any little girl). How I wish they were made today! I could find nothing about the Ideal Company. The logo is a circular sunburst, with Ideal Standard of Merit printed in red superimposed in the circle and Embroidery Packages printed in script across the center.

Finding a complete outfit made up, with all the pieces and still in pristine condition is a real treat. Completed Doll's Outfit (plate 192) is just such an outfit, beautifully embroidered, but it was not quite properly done. The maker, after going to all the work of doing the scalloped edges in a very fine blanket stitch, never cut the waste fabric from the scallops. She finished the edges straight across with a tiny hem. The proportions of the clothing are somewhat off also; the hat is way too small for the head of a doll that could wear the dress. And, even if the edge of the slip were done properly, it would still be too long to fit under the dress. Although I don't know the maker, the set is wonderful and I am delighted with it.

Most sets for sewing doll clothes in the 1920s were presented in boxes. Companies such as J. Pressman and Transogram packaged stamped materials including clothing and linens for dolls. Art Embroidery Outfit #920 (plate 193) manufactured by J. Pressman has three dresses, a nightgown, doilies, and a laundry bag. Gold Medal Art Embroidery Outfit (plate 194) manufactured by Transogram has two dresses, bedspread, pillow cover, laundry bag, cap, collar, bib, booties, bag, and two hankies. Neither set states what size doll might use the clothing, however after measuring, I would say most of the clothing was stamped for about an 8" doll. The dresses mostly were white, but occasionally there was a pastel color. The boxes were usually equipped with a wooden embroidery hoop, metal blunt-nose scissors, needle, small metal thimble and thread either in ropes or skeins loosely tied. Some of the sets didn't have a manufacturer's name on them such as Art Needlework Outfit #100S (plate 195). Some of the larger department stores, such as Sears and Roebuck and Montgomery Ward bought generic goods from a popular manufacturer and asked them to eliminate all advertising so they could sell under their own name. In a Montgomery Ward 1926 – 27 catalog there is advertised:

Embroidery Set. White close-weave broadcloth. Unstarched will wash and wear well. Three dresses, one carriage cover, one pillowcase, one bib, summer hat, and laundry bag, all for dolly. Pair of embroidery hoops, round pointed scissors, thimble, package of four large needles, and four skeins colored embroidery floss. $1.00.

It seems that the doll clothing sets of the 1920s went out of favor when the 1930s bisque doll sewing sets came on the market. If the child wanted to sew for dolly why not put it all in one package? For just a few pennies more, manufacturers could buy the cheap Japanese-made all-bisque dolls and put together a doll and clothing sewing set that was more appealing. This is exactly what they did. The market was flooded with bisque doll sewing sets and they did a bang-up business. Some of the stamped clothing that was once offered in the doll clothing sets was now found in the new bisque doll sewing sets. The new sets seemed to offer so much more; some had patterns for those who wanted to be a bit more challenged, others had pre-cut dresses for those who wanted instant gratification, and some had both. Doll sewing sets were popular in the 1930s and into the 1940s when little sewers went from bisque doll sewing sets to composition doll sewing sets.

In a 1950 February issue of *Playthings* magazine there was a photograph and article about the Nancy sets that were first introduced on October 15, 1949:

The accompanying photo shows how Gimbel's New York store featured the increasingly popular "Little Seamstress Nancy Sewing Kit" manufactured by the Ra-Gold Mfg. Co. Nancy, that mischievous little girl in the popular comic strip, is on the colorful box of the "Little Seamstress Nancy Sewing Kit" and is the first Nancy item to hit the market.

This unique sewing kit, which has been tested and commended by Parent's Magazine, *contains four pre-cut garments with instructions for assembling and a pattern with enough cloth to create an up-to-date dress. Also included are composition mannequin, thread, rick-rack, tape measure, and thimble. The clothes, upon completion, fit any standard 15" hard body doll. Girls from 7 to 14 can easily create a beautiful wardrobe from the contents of the kit.*

During the relative short time in which it has been on the market, "Little Seamstress Nancy" has lost little time in landing on best seller lists wherever it has been shown. A strong demand is currently being created through the medium of television, radio and magazines. The Ra-Gold firm feels that it presents an outstanding value at $1.98 retail. To stimulate sales the manufacturers have started "Nancy Sewing Clubs" throughout the country. Applications from the purchasers of the "Little Seamstress Nancy Sewing Kits" are already pouring in and attractive membership cards and bulletins will be going onward to them shortly. The members will be able to get the latest fashion hints and interesting ideas from the club bulletins. All this is given free with the purchase of each set. The "Little Seamstress Nancy Sewing Kit" line is on permanent display at the showroom of Brinkman & Tillman in New York.

The Little Seamstress Nancy Sewing Kit (plate 198) is the deluxe set and is twice as big as the set in the advertisement above. It is obviously a later set, made to continue the popularity by offering a bigger and better set. The Nancy Gram Message is included asking you to join her sewing club and buy more refills.

In the 1950s, sewing had become very popular and little girls all wanted to learn. The record player was also becoming an important part of young girls' lives. More and more record players were found in the children's department in stores and on toy pages in catalogs. In the Sears Wish Book catalog in 1950 there was one phonograph offered for children, by 1959 in the Sears Wish Book there were nine. Since sewing was becoming more and more of a popular pastime, it's no surprise to me that someone put the two together. Actually two "someones" did; they had the same idea and introduced sewing sets with records.

Sewing and Embroidery Sets Featuring Doll Clothing Only

Kathryn Kelley Recordcraft copyrighted Musical Sewing Kit #1 in 1950 (plate 200). Kathryn Kelley's idea was to add singing to the sewing lesson, a very old idea, but a good one. The articles to sew were printed on cloth with lines to cut out and sew. She wrote:

Dear Little Friends: Play the record before trying to sew. Choose which of the doll outfits you want to make first. Have your materials ready — pins, thread, needle and scissors. The record gave instructions with music and lyrics.

Grace-O-Leigh Talking Patterns (plate 201) had a slightly different approach. She packaged her set with a pattern, fabric, and a record with stories on how Susan sews for her doll. The story goes:

Susan folded the bright side of the material to the inside. She found the word FOLD on her pattern and placed it on the fold she had just made. "Oh Look! Pins on the Pattern?" She cried, "I'll put my pins here too," and she pinned all the way through the material.

Both record sewing sets are very hard to find. The ones I have found are in unused condition, which makes me believe they were not very successful.

The 1950s introduced the hard plastic doll, the new fashion dolls, the lady dolls with high heels. Even the little girl dolls wore more stylish clothing. It seemed like almost every doll that came on the market had a wardrobe that could be purchased separately. Some of the clothing cost as much, or more than, the doll. Manufacturers wanting to cash in on some of the action offered generic doll clothing for popular size dolls. Sally Seamstress (plate 204) created their dollie danties line, they offered packages for a least two different size dolls, 12" to 14" and 16" to 18" using a popular hard plastic doll as the model.

The 1950s were full of gender-type toys. Catalogs were full of miniature housekeeping toys for little girls and the sewing machine was one of them. J. Pressman Toy Corp. manufactured a miniature Pfaff sewing machine. It was sold in a sewing set titled Pfaff Sewing Machine Sew by Color #3360 (plate 208). The set consisted of the machine, accessories, and a sheet of color printed clothing for an 8½" to 10" doll. The seams were matched up by color. Inside was a pamphlet that explained about your new Pfaff sewing machine:

Congratulations! You are now the proud owner of Pfaff's junior model sewing machine, which will sew your dollies' dresses with pretty chain stitches. Your own machine resembles Mother's Pfaff 332 Automatic sewing machine which zigzags, appliques, makes flat and corded buttonholes, sews on buttons, hooks, eyes, monograms, darns, bastes, blind stitches, and sews an infinite number of embroidery stitches. Your junior sewing machine as well as Mother's Pfaff 332 Automatic were designed by G. M. Pfaff, A. G. which has nearly a century of experience in making and distributing household and industrial machines throughout the world.

Talk about getting your advertisement in for the Pfaff Automatic!

J. Pressman Toy Corporation also manufactured the Sew by Color #1142, combination outfits (plate 209). The interest-ing thing about the two sets is although they are both "Sew by Color" and are both manufactured by J. Pressman Toy Corporation, neither advertises the other, on the box or inside. The clothing in both sets are for an 8½" to 10½" doll.

Presson Pattern #116 (plate 207) was an interesting concept in the 1950s. The product was offered in a printed plastic bag and was manufactured by the J & J Novelty Company. The pattern was printed on a thin brown tissue-like paper with a wax coating. The child was to lay her material out on a padded surface with the print face down, and the pattern with the wax side down and press the paper to the cloth with a warm iron. The paper stayed on the cloth and you left the paper there until you had cut out the pattern and finished the sewing. The pattern was printed with black lines to cut and red lines to sew almost a foolproof system. I can't say much about their material choice though it looks more like fabric for men's pajamas than for a doll's dress.

Shortly after Barbie came on the market, the fabric stores started carrying panels by the yard of clothing to fit the 11½" fashion dolls. The outfits were printed in different colors, with easy-to-follow cutting and seam lines. Trim 'N Sew (plate 212) took it a step further and put the panels in an attractive envelope with the made-up clothing printed on the front. Four styles were listed, however there were really only two: Daytime and Sportswear. Each style was just printed in two different colors. Toy manufacturers always know a good thing when they see it, and Barbie was a good thing for Mattel, Inc. A lot of sales have been made using the shapely vinyl fashion doll.

Barbie was, and still is, responsible for many children learning to sew. There have been many Barbie look-a-like kits on the market since her very beginning in 1959. Quality Time Toys made a number of kits showing Barbie dolls on the cover such as Caribbean Cruise Kit (plate 222) and The Indian Princess Kit #6 (plate 224). The kits were presented in see-through plastic bags. The clothing is printed on non-frayable cotton knit fabric ready to cut out and sew. All the clothing is interchangeable, which makes for a very large wardrobe for Barbie.

Original Toys also came out with fashion doll clothing. There line was called Sew Simple. It was advertised in both the Montgomery Ward Christmas Catalogs and Sears Christmas Wish Books. In the Sears 1963 Christmas Wish Book, they listed mostly baby doll clothing like Sew Simple Newborn Baby Doll Layette #1454 (plate 217). There were three sizes 12" to 13", 14" to 15", and 18" to 20" to fit Thumbelina and Baby Dear. There was also a set to fit Tiny Tears and Betsy Wetsy in 12" to 13", 16" to 17", and 20" to 21". There was only one Sew Simple set for the new fashion doll. It was called the Sew Simple Fashion Doll Trousseau Wardrobe. This kit made a play dress, party dress, pajamas, panties, and bridal gown. In the 1965 Sears Christmas Wish Book they had dropped the Sew Simple name and advertised Ready to Sew Wardrobes for Barbie, Tammy, Ken, Skipper, Penny Brite, Tiny Tears, Susie Cute, etc. in sizes 7½" to 12". Montgomery Ward 1972 Christmas Catalog also carried Sew Simple kits. They advertised two sets in 1972, both for 11½" dolls like Barbie, Sew Simple

Here Comes the Bride and Sew Simple Merrily Mod fashions in zippy colors, zingy styles. Sew Simple Funtime Wardrobe and Sew Simple Groovy Threads Wardrobe (plate 218) were copyrighted in 1969 and 1971. I haven't been able to find either of these sets advertised. The last listing I could find for the Sew Simple clothing sets was in a 1973 Sears Christmas Wish Book. They advertised a Barbie-size Sew Simple Jet Set Trousseau, a Ken-size Sew Simple Campus Hero set, and a 15" to 17" Sew Simple Teen Dream set.

Wondering if there was any sewing kits with doll clothes in recent christmas catalogs, I thought I would flip through the pages of a few and see what I could find. In a 1999 Penney's Christmas Catalog, I found a Sew It Yourself Fashion Doll Clothing Bridal Kit, to be used with adult supervision. In the Penney's 2000 Christmas Catalog, there was a 18" Doll Sewing Kit, that had all the clothing sewn and you were to decorate it with flowers, sequins, and beads. And in the Penney's 2001 Christmas Catalog there was no doll clothing sewing sets offered at all.

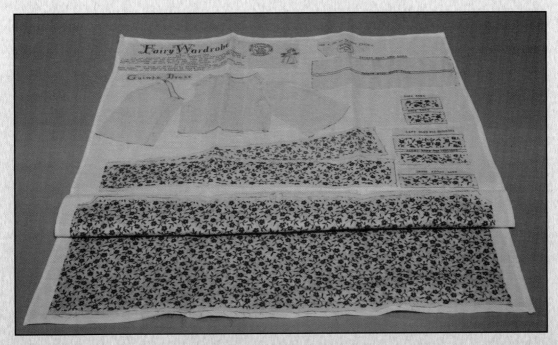

Plate 189. Fairy Wardrobe was patented by F. A. Foster & Co., in 1895. This company made only one size Fairy Wardrobe in 1895 and that size was for a 14" to 16" doll. It was printed on the finest of materials in fast colors and was sold in sheet form to cut out and sew. The cost was fifty-cents a set. The set consisted of a nightgown, two dresses, red riding hood cloak, and a reefer with tam o'shanter. If you didn't want the whole set you could just send ten cents for a sample dress. The example illustrated is the guimpe dress (the sample dress). This dress was found already cut out and started. All the pieces are present and basted onto a piece of muslin. The blouse of the dress is partially completed, the bodice has been seamed up the sides and one sleeve has been set in. The directions are printed on the fabric with the patterns. **Complete, as shown: $100.00 and up.**

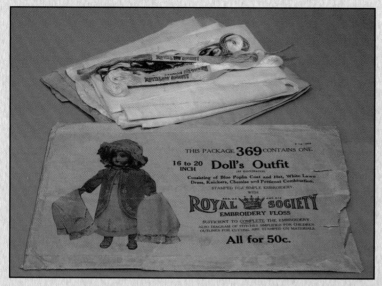

Plate 190. Royal Society Doll's Outfit #369 (Dolly's Day-Day Set) was manufactured by Royal Society, H. E. Verran Company, Inc., circa 1920s. The brown kraft-type envelope measures 12" x 7½". The envelope contains fabrics for a blue poplin coat and hat, white lawn dress, knickers, and a chemise-and-petticoat combination. All the pieces are stamped for embroidery. Also in the set were Royal Society embroidery floss and a diagram of stitches simplified for children. All the outlines were stamped on the material for cutting out. This set was for a 16" to 20" doll. **Complete: $100.00 and up.**

Plate 191. Ideal Doll's Complete Dress Outfit #165 was made by Ideal Embroidery Packages, circa 1920. The outfit comes in a brown craft envelope with three hanks of cotton embroidery floss and the instructions. The articles of clothing are stamped on fine quality Nainsook fabric for embroidery and cutting out. Included in the outfit are drawers, petticoat, full slip, dress, and boudoir cap. Included in the directions are instructions for washing: *Use warm suds made with Ivory soap or other pure neutral soap, rinse well in warm water, squeeze dry as possible between clean cloths, shake out then press face down on flannel. Do not fold or roll up the article while wet. Avoid cheap soap, boiling water and hard wringing.* **Complete: $100.00 and up.**

Plate 192. Completed Dolls Outfit by an unknown maker circa 1920s. This is typical of the doll outfits offered in the 1920s pre-printed on yard goods. This outfit is beautifully embroidered and finished with French seams. There are five pieces to this set, a dress with ribbon sash, full-slip, two bibs, and a hat (center top). The interesting thing about this set is the hat; it appears much too small to fit the doll that would wear the clothing. **Complete, as shown: $75.00 and up.**

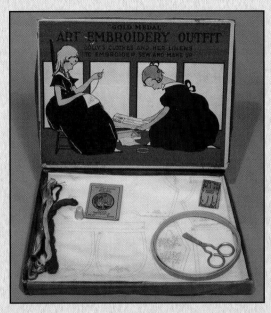

Plate 193. Art Embroidery Outfit #920 was manufactured by J. Pressman and Company, circa 1920s. The box is 11" x 8½" x 1". Printed on the top of the box is "Dolly's clothes and Linens to Embroider Instructive and Amusing for Little Folks." Inside the box, printed on cotton to be embroidered, cut out and sewn, are three different style dresses, a nightgown, laundry bag, and two dollies, a round one and a square one. Also in the set are metal blunt-nose scissors, wooden embroidery hoop, metal thimble, and a needle. **Complete: $50.00 and up.**

Plate 194. Gold Medal Art Embroidery Outfit manufactured by Transogram Conpany, Inc., circa 1920. The box measures 13" x 9½" x 1". The box top says Dolly's Clothes and Her Linens to Embroider, Sew and Make Up." Inside the box there are two 17½" square sheets stamped with dolly's things. The first sheet has a 5½" dress with a pocket, a bed spread that says "My Pet," a pillow cover that says "Dolly," laundry bag, and a dolly's hankies bag. The second sheet has an 8" baby doll dress, the collar for the baby dress, a matching cap, baby bib, booties, bag to carry, and two hankies. The sewing accessories in the set are a wooden embroidery hoop, metal blunt-nose scissors, a paper with two needles, metal thimble, four skeins of embroidery floss, and My First Lesson in the Art of Embroidery pamphlet. **Complete: $100.00 and up.**

Plate 195. Art Needle Work Outfit #100S is circa 1920s and doesn't have a manufacturer's name on the box. The only thing printed on the box is "Art Needle Work Outfit. Instructive and Attractive Designs in Embroidery. Useful Novelties Stamped on Fine Material." In the box are three doll-clothing items stamped for embroidery, a dress, a nightgown, and a romper. A previous owner started one dress. They are all stamped in the selvage of the cloth with "Solomco # 8." Also contained in the box are five skeins of embroidery floss, a wooden hoop, metal blunt-nose scissors, and a small metal thimble. **Complete: $75.00 and up.**

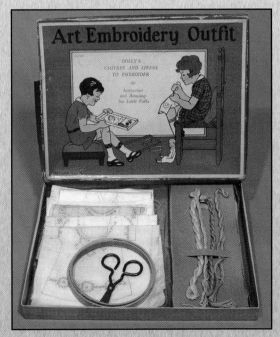

Sewing and Embroidery Sets Featuring Doll Clothing Only

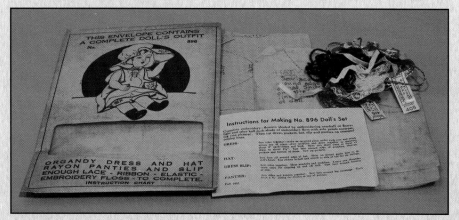

Plate 196. Complete Doll's Outfit #896. This little 10" x 7" envelope does not state a maker, but printed on the instruction sheet is Fall 1932. It looks like it might have been a "send away" from a magazine. Inside the envelope, printed on green organdy are the dress and hat, and printed on pink rayon are the slip and panties. Trimmings are off-white lace, a piece of ¼" elastic, ⅛" mint-green silk ribbon and burgundy, rose, and pink J. & P. Coats Sunsheen floss. Printed on a slip of paper are instructions on how to embroider the flowers stamped on the dress, slip, and panties and construct the garments. The instructions for sewing are also stamped on the fabric. **Complete: $75.00 and up.**

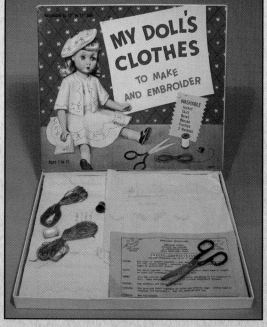

Plate 197. My Doll's Clothes to Make and Embroider #T177 was made by Sam'l Gabriel Sons and Company, circa 1940s. The box measures 14" x 13" x 1". The box top says the clothing is adjustable to fit a 12" to 17" doll and is washable. Inside, still attached to the insert, is the fabric stamped with the patterns for cutting and embroidery. To complete the set are metal scissors, pink and blue embroidery floss, a gray plastic thimble, a wooden spool of thread, and embroidery and sewing instructions. The clothing consists of a jacket, skirt, beret, blouse, panties, and two hankies. **Complete: $75.00 and up.**

Plate 198. Little Seamstress Nancy Sewing Kit is the deluxe version by United Features Syndicate, Inc., and manufactured by Ra-Gold Manufacturing Company, circa 1950. The box is 15" x 12" x 2½". The artist Ernie Bushmiller has signed his colorful cartoon drawing of Nancy on the box. Included in the box is a "Nancy gram message." Nancy writes, "The clothing in this kit is the same styles you might wear, and will fit a 13" – 15" doll." The inserts inside the box have openings to hold patterns and fabrics, a pincushion, scissors, a thimble, a measuring tape, a spool of thread, packages of tapes, buttons, rickrack, and a 10½" tall composition dress form with its round stand. Each pattern and fabric swatch is packaged in its own see-through bag and are for a dress, tea apron, panties, pinafore, circular skirt, peasant blouse, potholder, and a petticoat. **Complete set: $300.00 and up.**

Note: There is a smaller version of this set with four pre-cut garments, pattern and cloth for dress, dress form, spool of thread, thimble, tape measure, and rickrack. Nancy also offered refills with three items in each refill packet, two that are already cut out and the third has a pattern for the child to cut out herself. There are 12 refills, Party Girl, Beachwear, Skating, Sport Togs, Nurse's, Nightwear, Stormy Weather, Mother's Helper, Autumn Togs, Winter Wear, Bride, and Cowgirl.

Plate 199. Dolly Dressmaker was made by Kenner Products, circa 1950s. The package measures 9¼" x 6½". Dolly Dressmaker came in at least two sizes that I have found, 9" to 14" and 15" to 21". There were at least two styles. Style A has a jewel neckline with a sewn-down front scoop collar, short puffed sleeves, and a gathered skirt. Style B was a sleeveless dress with a square sewn-down front collar and gathered skirt. Inside each folder are the instructions, all the fabric required, and a packet of buttons. The fabrics varied in color and print and on the back of the folder there is a finished sketch of the dress and a cutout window so you can view the fabric choice. The package advertised that all pieces were accurately cut with generous seam allowances. You could adjust the size for your dolls by making seams and hems larger or smaller. **Complete, each: $25.00 and up.**

Plate 200. Musical Sewing Kit #1 by Kathryn Kelly was copyrighted in 1950. Musical Sewing Kit #1 comes in a 10" square envelope. It is a "listen and learn" kit. There is material included for three complete doll outfits. They are printed in pink on white muslin. There are three sizes of kimona-style dresses, hats, and panties to fit an 8" to 10" baby doll, 12" to 14" wetting doll, and a 16" to 18" mama doll. The instructions on the envelope say: *Dear Girls — Play the record before trying to sew. Choose which of the doll outfits you want to make first. It's easy and it's fun! Have your materials ready — pins, thread, needle, and scissors. Remember, you will always pin and sew on the wrong side of the cloth. Now, play the record and follow the directions. Sing while you sew! Heaps of Fun, Kathryn Kelly.* Inside the envelope is a 78 rpm record; on one side is how to make a dress, the other side, how to make a doll's hat and panties, with music and lyrics by Kathryn Kelly. There are plenty of directions for this set: directions printed on the fabric, directions on the record, and a pink page of directions included in the envelope. **Complete: $75.00 and up.**

Plate 201. Grace-O-Leigh Talking Patterns by Grace-O-Leigh Company is copyrighted 1952 and comes in a 16" x 11" x ¾" box. On the box top it says it's for ages 7 to 70. This pattern is for a street dress and comes with instructions on a phonograph disk and also in a pamphlet. The story is of how Susan sews for her doll without any help from mommy. The pamphlet goes on to say: listen to the phonograph disk and you can learn how. The 78 rpm record in the set is titled "How Susan Sews for her Doll" and is recorded on both sides. There is a full-size pattern for a dress and hat, and directions on how to pin it on the fabric. It says it will fit a 13" to 18" doll. Completing the kit is a pink plastic thimble, a card of ribbon, piece of elastic, card of white beading lace, needle, and a paper of pins. **Complete: $50.00 and up.**

Sewing and Embroidery Sets Featuring Doll Clothing Only

Plate 202. Child's Beginner Embroidery Set #1676 by H. E. Verran Company, Inc., circa 1950s. The Bucilla Embroidery Package measures 11" x 8½". Included in the set are a child's and dolly's apron, round table cover, and two napkins stamped in a cross-stitch design of teddy bears, ducks, and dolls. The design is stamped on unbleached sheeting and includes rayon edging for trim and Bucilla embroidery floss. The instructions for working the embroidery are on the inside of the package along with the embroidery color chart and instructions for finishing the items. **Complete: $25.00 and up.**

Plate 203. Doll's Baby Bunting and Carriage Set #1691 by H. E. Verran Company, Inc. The 11" x 8" Bucilla Embroidery Package doesn't have a date but my guess would be around 1950. It's one of Bucilla's Ready to Embroider Thrift Kit. It contains stamped rayon crepe for a carriage cover and pillow; flannel for hood, bunting, and booties; batiste for dress and panties; lace; ribbons, and Bucilla floss to complete the simple embroidery. On the back of the graphics are the instructions for working the embroidery and constructing the items. It will fit a 12" doll. The original price was $1.19. **Complete: $25.00 and up.**

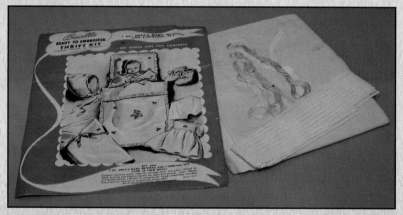

Plate 204. Sally Seamstress was manufactured by Ardee Company, creators of the dollie dainties line, circa 1950s. It comes in a 10" x 7" hanging package. Inside the package are all the materials to make a dress. They are pre-cut, ready to sew, and the trimmings are included. Printed on the inside of the package is a diagram with the outline of all the pattern pieces with written and illustrated instructions. There are four different styles of dresses. There are two different sizes that I have found 12" to 14" and 16" to 18". The doll modeling the dresses in the pictures is a 1950s hard plastic doll. **Complete, each: $25.00 and up.**

Plate 205. Angelcraft Doll Flannelettes #300 comes in a 16" x 30" x 1½" box. T. Buettner and Company manufactured it circa 1950s. The top of the box advertises: "Doll Flannelettes, ready-made fun to embroider. Fits 9" to 11" dolls. Designed for girls 6 years and older." Inside the box are two inserts, one holds a flannel sacque, wrapper, bib, six skeins of embroidery floss in three different colors, and a needle. The second insert has a doll bunting. The instruction sheet shows how to embroider the outline stitch, one-stitch French knot, and lazy daisy and includes a diagram for colors. **Complete: $75.00 and up.**

Note: The other children's sewing kits offered by Angelcraft were a Kitchen Set, Wash Day Set, Little Miss Bedroom Set, Doll Coverlet, Tea Party Set, Doll Blanket, Sheet, and Case, Ballerina Pictures, and Girl's Scarf and Handbag.

Plate 207. Presson Pattern #116 was manufactured by J & J Novelty Co., Inc. and was copyrighted in 1958. The package is 12" x 11". Written on the package is "Revolutionary New Type Pattern for making dress, cape and bonnet for 12" – 14" – 16" doll. No pinning press paper to cloth. No mistakes sew right through paper. No guesswork paper peels off when finished." It looks like the pattern is printed on freezer paper. In the kit is the press-on pattern with simple step-by-step instruction sheet for assembling Sanforized fabric into finished clothing, satin ribbon and rickrack for trimming. Included in the pattern are a dress with a collar and a cape with a matching hat. There is a large warning sign printed on the pattern not to use too hot of iron, if a hot iron is used the paper will be hard to remove. **Complete: $50.00 and up.**

Plate 206. Teri Doll Materials was marketed by Teri Doll Materials in 1956. The package measures 10¼" x 5½". In this set are fabrics precut and ready to sew for an 8" doll. It contains a complete wardrobe including a circle skirt and liner, double skirt (two layers) and liner, two blouses, three slips, three panties, and bridal hat. Trimmings, needle, elastic thread, and cloth flowers are also included. The instructions are on the back of the package. There is also a pattern sheet inside to identify the cut pieces, which are full size, so they could be used for a pattern. The instructions are repeated again on the pattern. **Complete: $25.00 and up.**

Plate 208. Pfaff Sewing Machine Sew by Color #3360 circa 1950 is in a 12" x 7½" x 3½" box. The contents include a Pfaff plastic sewing machine with a metal clamp, a wooden spool of thread, plastic thimble, a sheet of color printed clothing including a dress, hat, bra, panties, and half slip. There is also an instruction pamphlet on the Pfaff sewing machine and a pattern sheet with the patterns for each garment and instructions on how to cut and sew them. The patterns are for an 8½" to 10½" doll. The patterns are adjustable by using dotted or solid lines depending on which size doll you have. **Complete: $50.00 and up.**

Plate 209. Sew by Color #1142 was manufactured by Pressman Toy Corporation, circa 1950s. The box is 13½" x 8¼" x 1". The box states "Just Cut 'N Sew Ravel Proof Material." Inside is a panel of cloth with colored patterns already stamped to cut out and sew. This is pattern #1142, the Lingerie Ensemble. It consists of a bra, panties, girdle, baby doll pajama, robe, slip, and Oriental pajama. To complete this set are five pieces of ribbon, a wooden spool of thread, and a needle. The clothing fits an 8½" to 10½" high-heeled doll. The instructions are written on a pattern sheet with diagrams of each article. The pattern sheet has all the shapes in full size so you could use this as a pattern to make more doll clothes. **Complete: $25.00 and up.**

Sewing and Embroidery Sets Featuring Doll Clothing Only

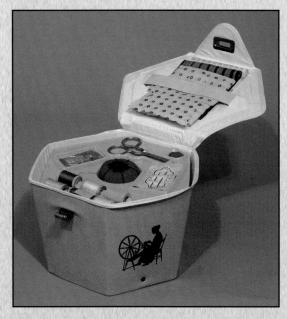

Plate 210. Jr. Miss Sewing Basket #1564 was manufactured by Hassenfeld Bros. in 1958. It is housed in a hexagon shaped box 8½" x 7½" x 4¾". It has a metal latch and soft plastic handle. Hasbro featured Jr. Miss Sewing Basket #1564 in their 1958 trade catalog as "A smart new practical sewing set made of durable, washable, colorful padded vinyl." Inside there is a plastic tray filled with sewing and embroidery needs, spools of thread, pincushion, emery, needles, scissors, thimble, and needle threader. The lid holds two hanks of fabric and a pre-cut doll outfit for an 8" doll. Under the tray are two napkins stamped for embroidery, embroidery instructions, hoop, and a "Jr. Miss Sewing Kit" pattern. **Complete: $50.00 and up.**

Note: There is nothing to identify this box except the Jr. Miss Sewing Kit pattern. The inside lid cardboard is missing from this set. I slid a strip of cardboard in the handle slits to hold the pre-cut outfit and extra fabric (this is how the inside lid was presented in a Hassenfeld Brothers trade catalog). The "Jr. Miss Sewing Kit" pattern is the same as in the Hassenfeld Bros. hard plastic doll sewing kits.

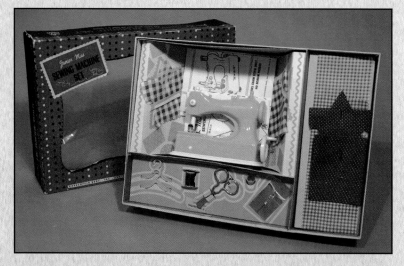

Plate 211. Junior Miss Sewing Machine Set #1540 is by Hassenfeld Brothers, Inc. The see-through window box measures 16" x 11½" x 3½". The set was written up as new in the 1959 Hasbro trade catalog: *A brand new colorful window display box. Contains a factory-tested Sew Rite sewing machine. Each machine is backed with a warranty. Complete with a beautiful apron to be sewn.* A year later in the 1960 catalog it was written up as *A colorful window display box. Contains a factory-tested Sew Rite sewing machine. Each machine is backed with a warranty. Complete with a beautiful outfit to be sewn.* That would date the above set at 1960. Indeed, it has two dresses pre-cut to be sewn, and two pieces of material. Also included are two plastic hangers, blunt metal scissors, paper with a needle, spool of thread, a paper that warns "do not operate machine without material," warranty paper, sewing machine directions, and a "Jr. Miss Sewing Kit" pattern. **Complete: $50.00 and up.**

Note: The Jr. Miss Sewing Kit pattern is the same pattern that is in the hard plastic doll sewing sets.

Plate 212. Trim 'N Sew was manufactured by Bac-A-Brand Products circa 1960s. The envelope package measures 9¼" x 6" and contains three outfits to fit all popular 11" and 12" dolls. The envelope says: *Complete-no pattern needed *Ready to Cut Out and Sew *No Extra Fabric Required *Colorfast-100% Cotton *Full, Easy-to-follow Directions Printed Right On the Fabric.* Inside the package is a fabric panel with the clothing printed in the colors shown on the front of the envelope. Although the envelope says there are four styles, there were really only two styles, sportswear and daytime, with two different color combinations in each style. The sportswear set with three different outfits, came in two different color combinations: style 1 came in cardinal red, apple green, and azure blue; style 2 came in beach tan, cherry red, and princess blue (not shown). Daytime, with three different outfits, came in two different color combinations: style 3 came in Cleopatra green, princess blue, and starlite print of blue and green; style 4 came in candy pink, scarlet red, and starlite print of red and pink. The original price was 98 cents each. **Complete, each package: $25.00 and up.**

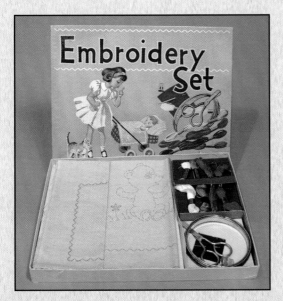

Plate 213. Embroidery Set was made by Pastime Products, a division of Parker Brothers. The box is 14" x 10½" x 1¼" and has a copyright date of 1960. Inside are a carriage cover and pillow cover, both stamped for embroidery. The carriage cover has a little bear holding a flower and the pillow has a zigzag design. The supplies include four skeins of Coats & Clark's embroidery floss, metal blunt-nose scissors, a felt pad with a needle, metal thimble, and adjustable metal embroidery hoop. There is still an original price sticker of $1.57 on the end of the box. **Complete: $25.00 and up.**

Note: I have seen this same set with a box top that shows a girl with a ponytail wearing a pink dress and tucking the carriage cover around a doll in the carriage. The sewing supplies are the same except there are six skeins of Coats & Clark's embroidery floss rather than four.

Plate 214. Sewing and Embroidery Basket #2205 was manufactured by J. Pressman Toy Corporation, circa 1960s. This basket is soft plastic with a window lid. "J. Pressman Toy Corp." is embossed on the bottom. It is 7¼" in circumference and 4½" high and there are two handles. Inside on the tray insert is a colored ballerina cloth in a cardboard embroidery hoop to embroider. On a wrap-around insert at the top of the basket are the sewing supplies that include a tomato pincushion with emery, plastic thimble, metal blunt-nose scissors, paper of needles, spool of thread, and two skeins of Pressman embroidery thread. When you lift the center insert there is an 8" J. Pressman Toy Corp. doll pattern for a bra, panties, and skirt, and two pieces of fabric. **Complete: $50.00 and up.**

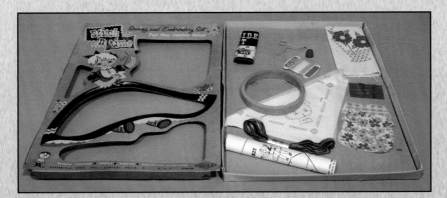

Plate 215. Stitch 'N Time Sewing and Embroidery Set #1530 was manufactured by Hassenfeld Brothers, Inc. in 1960. In the Hassenfeld Bros. 1960 trade catalog it was advertised as "A brand new sewing set designed for self service impulse buying. Will furnish the Jr. Miss with hours of constructive sewing, embroidery, and applique experience." The window box is 15" x 10½" x ¾". Inside, we find for embroidery a tea towel and two napkins, a skein of variegated embroidery floss, a needle, a cardboard hoop, and an embroidery instruction booklet. For sewing we find two 3¼" cut out dresses, needle, card of thread, plastic thimble, a plastic doll dress hanger, and a Jr. Miss Sewing Kit pattern. **Complete: $25.00 and up.**

Note: Stitch 'N Time Sewing and Embroidery Set #1536 was a larger set, 18" x 14" x 2". It had the same graphics and more items. The Jr. Miss Sewing Kit pattern is the same pattern that is found in the Hassenfeld Bros. hard plastic doll sets.

Sewing and Embroidery Sets Featuring Doll Clothing Only

Plate 216. Checks Sewing Set for the Junior Miss #1530 was manufactured by Hassenfeld Bros., Inc., in 1961. The box measures 15" x 10½" x 1". Inside are three pre-cut dresses for an 8" doll, two with skirts to be gathered and one with a circular skirt. There are three more pieces of fabric for the child to use with the "Jr. Miss Sewing Kit" pattern. There are also two plastic hangers, a plastic thimble, needle, card of thread, a blue plastic belt, and a piece of red satin ribbon. In the Hassenfeld Brothers trade catalog, the set is advertised in 1961 as a brand new set designed for self-service impulse buying. **Complete: $25.00 and up.**

Note: These Jr. Miss Sewing Sets were available in checks, plaids, and polka dots, with the names changing accordingly. The pattern in this set is the same Jr. Miss Sewing Kit pattern that is in the Hassenfeld Bros. hard plastic doll sewing sets.

Plate 217. Sew Simple Newborn Baby Doll Layette #1454 for a 18" to 20" baby doll comes in a 12" x 9" x 1½" box. The set is copyrighted 1963 by the Original Toy Corp. It has been tested and approved by the Educational Bureau of Coats & Clark Inc. Written on the box lid is: "To fit Thumbelina, baby dear and all other newborn baby dolls." Inside the box is pre-cut clothing including a nylon dress and bonnet, slip, kimono, coat, and matching bonnet. Also included are trimmings, snaps, needle, thread, Sew Simple instructions, knit cotton booties, and three doll clothes hangers. Each article of clothing is in its own plastic bag with all its trimmings. The instructions show the child the shapes of the fabrics and instructions with diagrams on how to sew them. **Complete: $50.00 and up.**

Note: Written on the side of the box lid is "Sew Simple For all popular types and sizes of dolls. See them all at your favorite quality store. °EconomicalL °Educational °American Made °American Materials °Fully Washable Fabrics °Developes Sewing Skills °Designed for Easy Sewing." This set was advertised in a 1962 Sears Christmas Wish Book for $3.33 before its 1963 copyright date.

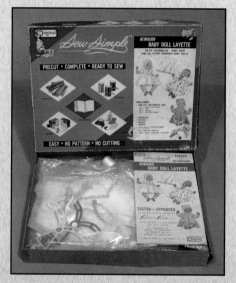

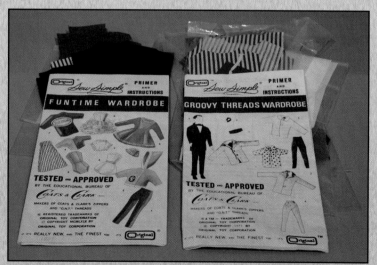

Plate 218. Sew Simple Funtime Wardrobe and **Sew Simple Groovy Threads Wardrobe** are by Original Toys Corporation and tested and approved by Coats & Clark's. Some of these sets were sold in Sears and Roebuck and Montgomery Ward Christmas catalogs. I have only seen these sets in plastic bags. The copyright on the pamphlets are Funtime, 1969 and Groovy Threads, 1971. There are no sizes listed on the patterns but in the catalogs they are advertised for the 11½" fashion dolls. Funtime includes ski pants, jacket, parka, bathing suit, tennis dress, street dress, skating dress and hat, panties, cheerleader skirt and top, and ballerina dress. Groovy Threads is for a Ken-type doll and includes sport shirt, slacks, sport jacket, dress shirt, tuxedo, cummerbund, bow tie, and pajamas. Each outfit is packaged in a separate plastic bag with trims if needed. The instructions are written and illustrated in the pamphlet. **Complete, each: $25.00 and up.**

Note: Other Sew Simple sets I have seen are Sew Simple London Look Wardrobe for fashion doll and a Sew Simple Miniature Doll Wardrobe with an unknown size.

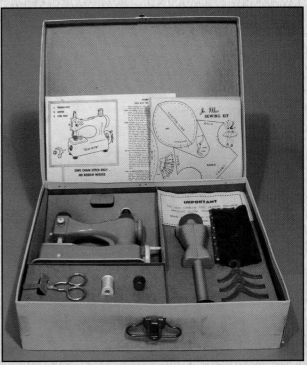

Plate 219. Hasbro Take Along Sewing Machine Set #1543. This 1969 set is housed in a luggage-type box with a metal latch and bail handle. It measures 14" x 11" x 3½" and is made by Hasbro Industries, Inc. The box top says "Beautiful take-along box with handy carrying handle that holds your Sew Rite Sewing Machine and Accessories." Inside is the Sew Rite sewing machine, a molded dress form, three plastic hangers, two pieces of cloth, plastic thimble, two plastic spools of thread, and metal blunt-nose scissors. Also included are a paper that warns "don't operate machine without material," warranty paper, sewing machine instructions, and "Jr. Miss Sewing Kit" pattern. **Complete: $50.00 and up.**

Note: On October 10, 1968, Hassenfeld Brothers became a public company and changed its name to Hasbro Industries, Inc. The Jr. Miss Sewing Kit pattern is the same pattern that is in the Hassenfeld Bros. hard plastic doll sewing sets.

Plate 220. Hasbro Sew-Rite Sewing Machine #1540 was manufactured by Hasbro Industries, Inc. in 1969. The box measures 11½" x 9½" x 2¼". The box top says it's for children 6 to 14. The box advertises "Create belts…headbands…and ties for Dad and Big Brother. Contains everything a little seamstress needs to sew just like Mommy." Inside is a Sew-Rite sewing machine all threaded with a small swatch of fabric under its needle. Also included in the set are instructions on using the machine, a warranty for the machine, a paper that warns "don't operate machine without material," and a "Jr. Miss Sewing Kit" pattern sheet. To complete the set are two pieces of fabric, a plastic spool of thread, metal blunt-nose scissors, a plastic thimble, and an advertisement for a child's book club. **Complete: $50.00 and up.**

Note: The Jr. Miss Sewing Kit pattern is the same pattern as in the Hassenfeld Brothers hard plastic doll sewing sets.

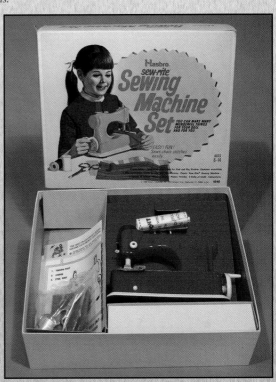

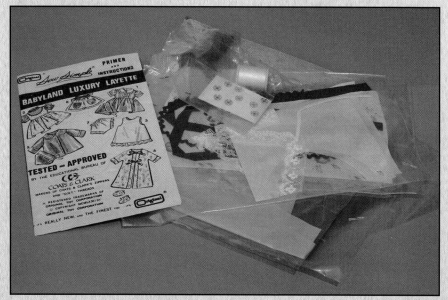

Plate 221. Sew Simple Babyland Luxury Layette is copyrighted 1972 by Original Toy Corporation and tested and approved by the Educational Bureau of Coats & Clark's. I am not sure if this set was sold in a package or box (probably a box). The size is for a 12" to 13" baby doll, such as Tiny Tears. There is no printed size on the instruction sheet (I measured the clothing to determine the size). The clothing in the set includes two different style dresses, one with a bonnet, a coat and hat, apron, slip and panties, and a sleeper with booties. All clothing is pre-cut in a separate plastic bag with all the ribbon, elastic, and trimmings included. Also included are plastic hangers, snaps, spool of thread, buttons, and an illustrated instruction sheet. **Complete: $50.00 and up.**

Plate 222. Caribbean Cruise Kit by Quality-Time Toys came in a 11" x 8½" package in 1991. The kit makes all nine outfits which mix n' match into many variations. The clothing is designed to fit 11½" dolls like Barbie, Maxi, etc. It is printed in color on non-frayable cotton-knit fabric ready to cut out and sew. Included are elastic and easy to follow instructions with plates. The clothing is made with no hooks and eyes, no snaps, no Velcro. The advertising says it is very easy to dress and undress the dolls in this clothing. **Complete: $10.00 and up.**

Note: These set were also called the Sew'n Play Doll Clothes. There were other kits available in this line, Beauty Queen, The Indian Princess Kit #6 (plate 224), Party Time, Fantasy Time, Mermaid and Glamour Gowns, and Bridal Outfit.

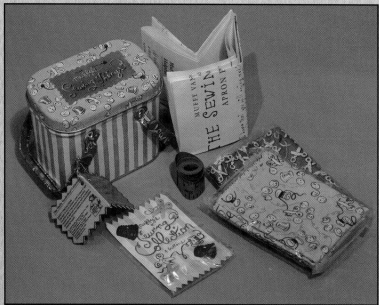

Plate 223. The Sewing Lesson Sewing Tin was manufactured by The North American Bear Co., Inc. in 1993. The tin measures 3½" x 2 ¼" x 3" and has "Muffy's Sewing Things" written on the top of the lid. Inside you will find a sewing pattern that will fit either Muffy or Hoppy, two pieces of fabric that coordinate with Muffy's and Hoppy's sewing lesson dresses, two thimble shaped buttons, and two scissors-shaped buttons. The pattern has a letter from Muffy about sewing and safety written for the child. **Complete: $25.00 and up.**

Plate 224. The Indian Princess Kit #6 was manufactured by Quality Time Toys, in 1995 and came in a 9" x 6" package. The Indian Princess Kit has 12 clothing items that mix and match. The clothing is printed in color on non-frayable cotton knit fabric ready to sew. There are easy to follow instructions with sketches and elastic included. On the package they say ages 4 – 6 needs adult sewing, and ages 7+ need adult supervision. **Complete: $10.00 and up.**

Note: These set were also called the Sew 'n Play Doll Clothes. There were other kits available in this line, Beauty Queen, Caribbean Cruise Kit (plate 222), Party Time, Fantasy Time, Mermaid and Glamour Gowns, and Bridal Outfit.

Plate 225. Fashion Doll Fun Bedroom Wardrobe Panel by DreamSpiners VIP. These panels were sold in fabric stores in 1998 for the 11½" dolls such as Barbie. It was sold in panels for rooms: bedroom, kitchen, and living room. There were corresponding panels for clothing to be used in each room. The panel in this plate is the clothing panel for the bedroom. The supply list of notions is printed on the panel, along with the instructions. This panel has a nightgown, robe, bubble suit, and hair tie. **Complete: $10.00 and up.**

Millinery Sets for Dolls

Hat — the dictionary defines it as head covering, a covering for the head usually having a shaped crown and brim. Hats have been around as long as history. The moment the first cave dwellers used a pelt or woven grass on their heads to protect them from cold or heat, the hat was born. For centuries, hats have identified religion, nationality, occupations, wealth, and authority, and for centuries little girls have been making hats for their dolls.

Hat-making sets are the hardest sets to find in the children's sewing set field. There were few made and many of those that are found today are incomplete. The first children's hat-making sets in America were presentation sets imported from France and Germany. We know very little about these early presentation sets they are not marked, as most were made by craftsmen and sold to large department stores. Collectors and historians have discovered wonderful French catalogs that show children's toys such as tea sets, sewing sets, doll sets, and hat sets in their original presentation boxes. In France they were very special toys, given to children at the New Year and known by French children as Etrennes. Among the late 1800s into the early 1900s Etrennes catalogs showed many children's hat-making sets in presentation boxes. There are five presentation sets listed, circa 1900 – 1915 (plates 226 through 230) in this chapter, these are the sets that were made at the turn of the century. They give us a peek into a time when Victorian splendor was overflowing.

At the turn of the century and the early 1900s skirts and blouses were shown on hourglass figures in all the new fashion magazines. The new style for women's clothing featured a wasp waist, leg-of-mutton sleeves, puffed at the top then fitted at the bottom, and a large wide-brimmed hat to top it all off. Hairstyles were growing larger and ladies purchased "rats" or hairpieces to extend their own hair to a higher topknot or pompadour. To accommodate these masses of hair, the hats had to be larger. Larger brims were in vogue and they held everything from complete birds to flower gardens. It seemed the more decoration, the more desirable the hat. Hatpins were a necessity to secure the precarious assemblages, and people had to beware when standing or sitting next to ladies with their oversized hatpins to avoid being stabbed.

In *Godey's Lady's Magazine* an article was written in March 1896 about "Millinery Monstrosities." The piece read:

The big hat nuisance at the theatre should be abolished by law, if women have not sufficient common-sense to subscribe to public sentiment. In several places, an attempt has been made to legislate in regard to the matter, but so far without success.

The managers of theatres, however, have the thing in their own hands, and certainly have the privilege of issuing a manifesto upon the subject. In London not even the tiniest hat is permitted in any but the cheaper parts of the house. American women, who claim to be progressive and sensible, should, of their own free will, abolish the big hat in the evening; for the street it is picturesque and becoming, but for the theatre and concert let us adopt the pretty little capote, which is so coquettish and flattering to most faces.

It wasn't until the 1920s that hats started growing smaller. By 1924, the traditional cloche was established and the war of the hat was over.

After World War I, the custom toys that were once imported from France and Germany were no longer favored and the enchanting children's presentation hat sets disappeared. Americans were encouraged to be patriotic and to buy American toys. There was a long, dry spell between the French presentation hat sets of the early 1900s and the American hat sets that came out in the 1940s. Dolls' hats were not forgotten; most dolls were advertised, displayed, and/or sold with a hat and dolls' hats could also be purchased ready-made from the stores. However, for some unknown reason, millinery sets were not considered to be a popular toy for little girls. If a child had a longing to make or trim a hat for their doll, they could buy a doll clothes pattern that included a hat or buy one of the children's sewing books that gave instructions for making doll clothes and hats. It wasn't until the 1940s that American toy manufacturers started advertising and selling millinery sets.

Around the same time Simplicity was making patterns for the mannequin doll sets of the 1940s, they came out with a hat set they named Simplicity Miniature Hat Maker Set #601 (plate 232). The box is wrapped in the same blue-bow printed paper as Miniature Fashion #102 (plate 149). Everything in the set is similar to the clothes mannequin sets done by Simplicity and Latexture Products, such as the patterns, tape measure, layout, etc. Simplicity Miniature Hat Maker Set #601 includes three Simplicity patterns that made a total of four hats and a designing cap. The mannequin head is made of painted composition and all the hats are designed to fit the form's head. I believe this hat-making set is quite unusual. I have seen only one set and I can find no additional information or ads.

Corona's Dolly's Bonnet Basket (plate 234) was advertised from 1949 until 1951 in *Playthings* magazine, many times with a full-page ad. They had a write-up on their hat baskets in *Playthings* magazine, in September of 1950 that stated:

Girls Like opular Corona "Bonnet Baskets"

A fantastic number of doll hats for separate sales are manufactured by Corona Hat Co., 13-19 University Place, New York 3. Doll hats are sold with dolls and still more with Doll Hat Kits. These Corona "Bonnet Baskets," hat boxes filled with untrimmed hats and fascinating Millinery "makings," have achieved a permanent, growing success in large and small stores alike. Girls who start with the small 79c size keep on asking for the larger $1.00 and $2.00 styles. Especially popular is the Cameo Kit, which permits girls to color the lid with watercolors or crayons, and leads to additional sales for the dealer. When emptied they are delightful sewing kits, lunch baskets, purses, and have 101 other uses. Educational as well as useful, Corona Bonnet Baskets are endorsed by educators and parents as well.

I have never seen an advertisement for La Mille Bonnet Box for a Small Miss (plate 233) circa 1940, however I have seen the same graphics on a square box advertised on eBay. The little booklet in La Mille Bonnet Box for a Small Miss is called "La Mille Millinery Designer" and was written by Sally Hector. Sally writes:

Is it to be a party hat to go with dolly's very best dress or perhaps a more tailored bonnet for school or morning wear? Whichever it is you'll find the trimmings for it in your La Mille hatbox. What fun you'll have trying first this pretty posy and then that fluff of a feather on the darling little felt shapes. And what a lucky doll to have so talented a milliner designing special hats. Be sure you look carefully at all the pictures in this little Magazine. Then show them to your doll and let her pick her favorites. You'll find hats a-plenty in your La Mille box and dolly can have a hat for every occasion. What's more, when you get tired of them one day, all you have to do is take them apart and retrim them. Presto, you have a brand new bonnet.

The Junior Miss Hat Shops #868 (plates 235 and 236) by Advance Games were made sometime around the 1940s. They are probably the easiest of all the hat sets to find. I have found two different box tops, similar, but with a number of changes. The Junior Miss Hat Shop #868 (plate 235) seems to be a snappier presentation on the inside. They have added a red interior in the center, brighter paper under the hats, and have painted the hat stand. I have found no advertising for these sets, but I do know that in *Playthings* magazine, Advanced Games only advertised sewing sets in the late 1940s.

A hat set that is hard to find in mint or even complete condition is The Campbell's Sew a Hat #4417 (plate 237). It was manufactured by Milton Bradley in 1954. I found The Campbell's Sew a Hat #4417 in a seven-page ad for Campbell's products at a bookseller's booth. The ad had been taken out of a 10" x 14" magazine without the source or date. The ad was a birthday celebration for the Campbell Kids. The Campbell Kids were "born" as a series of streetcar advertisements in 1904 when a Philadelphia illustrator by the name of Grace Drayton brought them to life. From this knowledge, I was able to date the advertising to about 1954. The ad had the Campbell Kids paired with many different items and manufacturers.

It was Milton Bradley that offered the Sew a Hat, along with a Campbell Kids Make It Box, for making finger puppets, mobiles, paper dolls, airplanes, boats, etc., and the Campbell Kids Eat-O-Mats, ready-to-color story-telling mats, with crayons and water colors. Each set was $1.00.

Campbell's Soup itself was born in 1869 when a fruit merchant Joseph Campbell and a tin ice box manufacturer Abraham Anderson formed a partnership to can vegetables, jelly, condiments, and minced meats in Camden, New Jersey. Eventually, in 1876 Anderson sold out to Campbell.

Have you ever noticed the gold medal on the Campbell's soup can? It reads "Paris International Exposition 1900." In 1900, Campbell's soups won the Gold Medallion for excellence. The medal has been on the can ever since, 103 years. As I mentioned before, the Campbell Kids were first drawn in 1904 and the first Campbell Kids dolls were offered as promotional items in 1910. Both the soup and the dolls have been going strong ever since.

There is one hat set that I have never been able to find, but have seen advertised over and over again in *Playthings* magazine. The Nancy Hat Kit made in the early 1950s. It came in a square box and sold at $2.00. It had a Nancy hat block (stand), felt and straw hats, a paper pattern, feathers, ribbons, flowers, tape measure, thimble, needle, and pins.

Books with Hat Patterns

In the Popular Children's Sewing Book chapter, I have listed the sewing projects in each book and a number of the books have bonnet and hat instructions. Children's Sewing Patterns, also has hats listed. I thought it might be of help if I elaborate on the hats a bit more in this chapter. Following is a list of doll hats in both the popular sewing books and patterns chapters.

The first sewing book for children that I have found that had a pattern or draft for a doll hat was written in 1860, *The Girl's Own Toymaker* (#3-P), page 290. In the section on how to dress a doll, it gives instructions on making a doll hat.

This little hat is typical of the hats worn in the first half of the 1860s. Hats had changed at that time from a round to an oval shape and came to a point in the front. The book suggests you make it from stiff black net and wire, and gives you step by step directions on fashioning it.

In *The Home Book of Pleasure and Instruction* 1868 (#5-P) page 291, there are directions on how to make a brown velvet bonnet trimmed with scarlet velvet ribbon. The book gives two drafts and directions:

Cut out the two pieces for the front and crown, in stiff paper or very thin cardboard. Cover them with the velvet, and sew the rounded part of the crown into the short side of the front piece. Line up the front of the bonnet with white ribbon or silk. Put a piece of scarlet velvet ribbon all round the neck for a curtain, and a narrower piece round the front and across the bonnet, a frill of lace inside for a cap, and a tiny sprig of flowers, or a bow or two of the narrow velvet ribbon, over the forehead.

Millinery Sets for Dolls

There is also an old woman's mobcap draft in this book.

The Doll's Dressmaker Magazine 1891 (#9-P) page 293 and plate 564, offered instructions for at least four hats in the year 1893. In April they had a pattern for a doll's Easter hat which could be made from any material, but needed a stiff piece of crinoline for the foundation. In September they offered a pattern for a doll's Quaker bonnet. It had five pieces and the interlining was to be cut from pasteboard. In August they had a boy doll's cap that was to be made up in blue flannel. The December issue had a Doll's Christmas Hat to be made up in black velvet and trimmed with pink rosettes and feathers.

How to Dress a Doll, 1908 (#18-P), page 296 and plate 568, has a doll's tam o' shanter cap, toboggan cap, and hood all made with a spool knitter and yarn. The book has complete instructions.

Sewing for Little Girls, 1911 (#22-P) page 298, has a draft and instructions for a hat and a coat. I have made it up using velvet plate 569.

A close bonnet is what *The Little Girl's Knitting and Crochet Book*, 1915 (#27-P), page 301 and plate 574, offers. It is a bonnet knitted by combining a plain and pearl stitch in a raised-rib-knitting pattern. It is a very easy knitting project.

Two wool bonnets and a tam o' shanter are in *The Little Girl's Fancy Work*, 1915 (#28-P) page 302 and plate 574. One bonnet is done in a pattern of plain and pearl stitch, the other is crocheted in blue and white, and the last is a crocheted tam o' shanter.

The Mary Frances Knitting and Crocheting Book, 1918 (#29-P) page 302, has three hats to make for Mary Marie, a crocheted cap with a pom-pon on each side, a crocheted turban, and a knitted hood.

Two darling hats from the 1920s are included in *Dolly and Her Dresses*, 1924 (#32-P) page 303 and plate 576. You make them the size of your doll's head with the book's instructions and diagrams.

The Piece Bag Book, 1927 (#36-P) page 305, shows you how to make a tam o' shanter using a round cardboard loom. All the instructions on weaving the hat, along with a matching muff done on a rectangle cardboard loom are in this book.

Belindas Bonnet on page 39 of *The Sew It Book*, 1929 (#39-P) on page 306, is an organdy sunbonnet. The bonnet is made by measuring the doll's head. Making a rectangle of paper, folding it, and then cutting off the folded piece. The book shows four different styles to make with this pattern.

A French beret is what *Sue Sew and Sew*, 1931 (#40-P) page 306 and plate 578 will teach you to make. The beret is made by measuring and folding paper to make a pattern.

My Needlework Book, 1947 (#43-P) on page 307, tells you how to make a doll's bonnet step by step, just as mother shows Hazel how to make one for her doll Winnie.

In *I Learn to Knit to Dress My Doll*, Primrose, 1950 (#45-P) page 308, Primrose gets three different knitted bonnets. Two have ties; one is more of a cap. They are very easy to knit.

Emily Dow, in a chapter in her book *How to Make Doll Clothes*, 1953 (#54-P) page 310, shows how to make patterns for a cap, a baby doll bonnet, a Scottie hat, and how to trim hats and bonnets. They all appear to be quite easy to make.

Sew Easy for the Young Beginner, 1956 (#59-P) page 312, has a very simple hat for an 8" doll. The hat is a part of a circle folded at the back, with a ribbon on each side and then trimmed.

A really easy hat to make for any size doll is created by drawing a circle and folding the hat in at the back and decorating it with ribbon or trim is found in *Sewing is Easy*, 1956 (#60-P) on page 312.

Dolls' Dressmaking, 1961 (#68-P) on page 314, has full-size patterns for a christening bonnet, cloche-type hat, beret, and a school cap.

A Ladybird Book Learning to Sew, 1972 (#80-P) on page 317, features a cute little bonnet made out of felt with embroidery. The book gives you a diagram and has you measure your doll's head and duplicate the diagram with your measurements.

A book that was originally written in German and translated in 1991, *Dressmaking for Dolls*, 1909 (#19-P) page 297, gives step-by-step directions on making a winter bonnet to fit your doll perfectly.

Patterns Shown in Children's Sewing Patterns

Dolly's Dressmaker, 1860, plate 518 includes a pattern for a nightcap. The cap is made of Irish linen or cambric trimmed around the edge with a frill of either handmade tatting or crochet. The cap has a pleated bavolet (trimming on back of cap) and ribbon tie strings.

Young Ladies' Journal, 1882, plate 520, the hat patterns include a Capote, a crocheted nightcap, and a garden hat of piqué that has a double brim and is embroidered with a row of feather-stitching in blue silk; bows and strings of blue ribbon.

Harper's Bazar, 1883, plate 521, shows two hats. One is a bonnet style with ties and ruching around the face the other is a capote style with cording and feather trim.

Puppenmütterchens Hähschule, 1900, plate 522, has a sheer tulle bonnet with pattern 1. There is a sailor hat and a Dutch cap with pattern 3, a tulle hat with pattern 5, and a cap with a ruffle around face and neck in pattern 6. Pattern 7 has a hat with fur around the face and ties under the chin.

Schnittmuster Zu Puppenmütterchens Nähschule, 1900, plate 523, has a woolen bonnet with ruching in front and ribbon ties, a sailor cap, and a mob cap.

Dolly's Dress Patterns to Dolly's Wardrobe, 1900, plate 526, has five hats with instructions including a baby cap, sailor cap, dress hat, sunbonnet, and fur cap. The baby cap is lace with white or colored silk lining, rosettes of small silk ribbons and little flowers sewn on the side where the ruching finishes. The sailor cap is of the same fabric as its suit and trimmed with a bow and ribbon of silk. A dress hat is of stiff gauze and covered in silk ruching around the inner brim and lace trim on the side. A sunbonnet is made of white cloth and a tuft of feathers for trimming. The fur cap has the band of the cap stiffened with gauze.

Butterick Pattern #314, 1899, plate 530, has a cap. The directions are:

Gather back along straight edge until coming to notches, join back to front with double notches matched, and draw gatherings at bottom as required. Roll front over at perforations forming revers. (Lapel) Tack ribbon ties to lower corners of cap, and finish with lace or a binding of fur or ribbon.

Butterick Girl's Doll Set, #375, 1899, plate 537, has a bonnet of four pieces. The instructions are "gather and baste, stay to center back edge, sew side to back, tack on ties, roll brim back."

In the Home pattern Girls Doll Set #5791, 1911, plate 540, there is an automobile bonnet. The pattern had only three pieces, back, side, and front band. The sides are to be gathered into both the back and the front band. The front band is long enough to also be the ties.

Pictorial Review Pattern #5938, 1914, plate 543, has a Mob-type cap with one piece of fabric to be gathered around with a 1" ruffle.

McCall's pattern Doll Special 16" long, circa 1915, plate 538, has a tall hat with a one-piece pattern with the instructions: "Turn lower edge over on outside at small circles."

Character Doll's Set #2823, circa 1915, plate 545 has a baby cap with a round back piece, straight sides, and a turned-back brim with ties.

Das Fleissige Puppenmütterchen, 1915 style, plate 548, has six hats to make: a baby's bonnet, sailor hat, tobogganing hat, Tyrolian hat, fancy hat, and a swimming cap.

The baby's bonnets peak is to be lined with silk fabric. On the bonnet itself, one makes first the back seam and the lower hem. Then one sews on the lined peak at the indicated point and decorates it with ribbon.

The sailor has the side seams of the lower parts sewn together and basted to the upper parts in such a way that one of the brims joins on one side and the other one on the other side and they must be placed wrong side on wrong side. Now its stitched, then turned over, and the headband is attached.

To make the tobogganing hat the cap is crocheted with a thin crochet hook and only half stitches.

Tyrolian Hats: *Both made from crepe paper. For this, cut even straps, 1 cm. wide. Braided 7 times, this will make a braid, width of 2 cm. If the braid has a length of 80 cm. it will do to make the complete Tyrolian hat. If you wish to make a larger brim, it will take at least 1 meter, or more! Start in the middle of the head part to roll up the braid and set it one row to the other. When necessary width of the head has been reached you stop to increase the diameter and go on normally until the necessary height has been reached. To make the brim, you must again increase the diameter as you go on. When you have finished, sew the end neatly underneath. To decorate the hat, use a red cord and a small feather and, we assure you, the hat will look very nice.*

The Fancy hat is also made with crepe paper: It is made as the Tyrolian hat but one needs a braid of at least 1 meter because of the rim, which is larger for this model. The embroidered hat consists of lining the head part and eyelet it is trimmed with ribbons and flowers. The swimming cap: Cut out following the pattern, the head part is gathered twice and the edge inserted into the headband. Elastic has to be pulled through the latter in order to fit it tightly to the head.

Butterick Pattern including Deltor #427, circa 1923, plate 551, shows a cap with a small brim to which a large frill is attached going towards the back of the head away from the face with a tie under the chin.

New Butterick Pattern including Deltor #431, circa 1923, plate 552, has a cute little hat with a ruffled front brim to be made of lawn or organdy that ties under the chin.

McCall's Doll Set, hat, dress, and bloomer, circa 1926, plate 553, has a bonnet in three pieces with instructions: "Join center back seam, gather back edge of cap to crown. Gather along lines in front and sew to stay."

Children's Vogue Pattern #20010, circa 1930s, plate 554, has both a hat and bonnet.

Advance Learn to Sew #6570 and #6919, circa 1950s, plate 556, has a simple baby bonnet and a bridal veil.

Millinery Sets for Dolls

Plate 266. La Mode (The Fashion) was made in Paris, France, circa 1900. This is the smaller of the two sets I have found titled La Mode. The wooden box measures 12½" x 8½" x 4", and is covered with a stenciled type paper. The cover has a 10" x 6" recessed area surrounded by a 1½" apple blossom band. In the center of the recessed area is a 6" x 4½" applied lithograph of vines and flowers, and in the center of the flowers is a round gold frame with a portrait of a lady with long flowing hair and a large brimmed hat. The box closes with a small brass latch engraved "Paris." When opening the box the front wall folds down to expose white silk flowers, leaves, and stamens tied in with gold ribbons. The main compartment has seven sections, they hold two wooden spools of cotton thread, bits of ribbon, dotted netting, three styles of straw, heavy lace, veiling, tarlatan, three cardboard spools of silk cord, and folded strips of silk organza all tied in with crisscross ribbons. The recessed lid has a 5½" x 3½" mirror applied to its hot-pink interior with a scalloped gold-and-blue Dresden band, and above it is a silk flower spray. Along the sides of the lid are four little hats, three of straw and one of felt. Below the hats on each side are papers of pins and cards of cotton cord labeled "Paris." Between the hats and mirror are green and red wooden spindles and the bases to construct doll hat stands. On both sides of the mirror at the bottom are two gold paper tubes of thread. To complete the set are a pair of metal scissors, a small metal thimble, and the paper "Bébé Mode Journal Des Filletes" (The Doll Fashion Paper For Little Girls). The instruction sheet tells about fashions and hats, and how to use the presentation set. **Complete: $1,000.00 and up.**

Plate 227. La Mode (The Fashion) was made in Paris, France, circa 1900. This is the larger of the two sets that I have found titled La Mode. The wooden box measures 18" x 13" x 4" and is covered with a floral print paper. The cover has a 15" x 10½" recessed area surrounded by a 1½" apple blossom band. In the center of the recessed area is a 8¼" x 6" applied lithograph of vines and flowers, and in the center of the flowers is a round gold frame with a portrait of a lady with long flowing hair and a large brimmed hat. The box closes with two small brass latches that are engraved "Paris." As the box opens the front wall folds down to show six cards of assorted thread and on the board above are five different types of netting. The lid has a celluloid doll hand mirror in the center and secured around it are five different hats nestled among millinery flowers made of silk and feathers. The main compartment of the set holds more flowers, assorted straw braids, feathers, lace, net, ribbons, thread, and millinery wire. At the very center of the compartment is a raised area containing a small mob type hat, rose decoration, needle holder, package of needles, bone bobbin, bone crochet hook, bone and metal button hook, card of thread, and a small medal thimble. Along each side of this area are two wooden hat stands, one painted red and the other green. Not shown are the instructions "Bébé Mode Journal Des Filletes" (The Doll Fashion Paper For Little Girls). The instruction sheet tells about fashions and hats, and how to use this wonderful presentation set. **Complete: $1,000.00 and up.**

Plate 228. Modiste (Milliner) was made in France, circa 1900. The wooden box, 11" x 7" x 3", is covered with green shamrock paper and closes with a tiny brass latch. Applied to the lid of the box is a gold-framed paper square with a basket of flowers on the lower right hand corner and swag of flowers on the left upper corner. Written in black and gold script is "Modiste." Upon opening the lid, we find nestled inside five little hats, four of felt and one of stiffened buckram. The "Bébé Mode Journal Des Fillettes" (The Doll Fashion Paper For Little Girls) tells about fashions and hats and how to use this little set. The box itself has three sections, one holds blue plaited straw, and another pink plaited straw and white cloth flowers. The center section holds two colors of net, two types of lace, and two rolls of ribbon. A dainty little set for the young milliner. **Complete: $700.00 and up.**

Plate 229. Doll Millinery Shop circa 1910 is most assuredly French. This unnamed and unmarked 15" x 10" x 7" plain blue, paper-covered box has two metal latches in front and opens out into three sections. The inside lid includes five straw hats with additional feathers and trims. The main section houses a miniature millinery shop interior with three counters and a shelf area in the center back. The shelves contain various types and colors of straw braid along with a feather "bird." The counters display feathers, ribbons, berries, and assorted trimmings. Three miniature doll hat stands are tied to the box, each displaying a hat. The fold out section in the front has an assortment of spools of thread and flower trimmings. Lying loose in the box are two cards of hatpins. The clues to the origins of this set are the three "Made in France" labels that are attached to trimmings. **Complete: $1,000.00 and up.**

Millinery Sets for Dolls

Plate 230. Although this red-paper-covered cardboard **Doll Millinery Set with Tray** has no name or maker, we do know the date. Written in pencil on the lid is, "Given to me by Dan Fraser, 1914." The box measures 16½" x 11½" x 3¼". Applied to the cover is a softly colored lithograph of two angelic children dressed in their finery. A small metal clasp opens the box to reveal a lace-edged cardboard in the inside lid with hat trimmings, flowers, chenille, silk ribbon, spools of thread, and netting all artfully arranged and tied in with ribbon trim. In the bottom of the box are two layers. The first is a tray holding additional flowers, sequined and braid trimmings, silver and gold stamens, spools of thread, pieces of velvet, silk, lace, and two hats ready to trim. The final bottom layer displays three felt and four straw bonnets. **Complete: $1,000.00 and up.**

Plate 231. La Velle Millinery #30 was made by La Velle Mfg. Co. and copyrighted in 1924. The box top says: "This outfit for girls between ages of 6 and 12 years." There is also a picture of Miss La Velle with a poem:

"My what a charming Dolly's hat!"
"I made it myself."
"Did you really do that?"
"Yes—and it's surely loads of fun,
Get your own set, and see how it's done."

The box measures 18" x 10" x 1¼". Arranged on a green platform are two paper hats, a card of pins, cloth flower, metal thimble, wooden hat stand, two lengths of colored straw, three pieces of colored tarlatan, one piece of printed cotton, and feathers and ribbons. I am not sure all the contents still remain in this set, but hat sets are very hard to find and I felt it necessary to include this one. **Complete: $75.00 and up.**
Helene Marlowe collection.

Plate 232. Simplicity Miniature Hat Maker Set #601 was manufactured by Latexture Products, circa 1940s. The box top is covered in a white paper with a red bow pattern and the bottom of the box is in a plain blue paper. The box measures 11" square and 3" high. Inside, resting on a blue insert is a 7" tall, composition mannequin head. The unmarked head has molded, painted hair and features. Below the head, threaded through slots, is an 18" cloth-backed tape measure. Above the tape measure on each side are two hat-shape cut outs in the insert, each with two hanks of fabric underneath, showing the top piece of fabric in the cut out. Also, under the raised insert are muslin, ribbons, and felt. There are three Simplicity hat patterns, one on each side of the head and one above. These are Pattern #3651 Sectioned Beret with Ribbon Binding; pattern #4089 Bow Hat and Beret, and pattern #4700 Small Hat and Designing Cap. The designing cap is to be made of muslin and the instructions stated: *The purpose of this cap is for marking the line where the hat sets on the head. This is done*

with chalk, pins or tape. For example, the drawing to the right shows how the Simplicity hats were marked on the cap. The solid line (—) shows the beret of number 4089 and number 3651. The dotted line (..........) shows the bow hat of 4089. The dot and dash line (.-.-.-.-.-.-) is for hat number 4700. The hats are to be made of fabric or felt with ribbon or felt trim to fit the mannequin head. The hat patterns were also available at pattern counters in leading stores to fit teenagers and women in the same styles. **Complete, as shown: $300.00 and up.**

Plate 233. La Mille Bonnet Box for a Small Miss is a Regent Product, New York, circa 1940. The box is 8" in diameter and 4¾" tall. Inside the bonnet box is a pamphlet titled "La Mille Millinery Designer." The pamphlet shows how to make doll hats that fit, and even a wedding veil. It also tells you the parts of the hat, and how to measure your dolly's head. The box itself contains four different shaped hats, three of felt and one of heavy molded lace. There are four tape bands, cloth-covered wire, three bunches of flower petals, a cellophane packet of feathers, three spools of thread, measuring tape, pair of metal blunt-nose scissors, needle, and a cellophane packet with a plastic thimble, pins, and three gold studs. **Complete: $75.00 and up.**

Note: I have seen these same graphics and title in a square box, as well as the round.

Plate 234. Dolly's Bonnet Basket #130 was manufactured by Corona Hat Company, circa 1949. The raffia woven basket measures 7" in diameter and is 3" high. Inside, we find three felt hats in three different styles, three different colored ribbons, three feathers, three felt flowers, a cardboard spool of thread, a packet of needles, and a plastic thimble. **Complete: $50.00 and up.**

Note: This basket is #130, and retailed at 89¢ in 1949. There were six sizes of Dolly's Bonnet Baskets and they sold from 59¢ to $2.00.

Plate 235. Junior Miss Hat Shop #868 was manufactured by Advance Games Inc., circa 1945. The box measures 17½" x 2" and is signed by the artist Lichty. There is a little blue paper inside that reads: *Junior Miss Hat Shop a wonderful game for all little girls who like to play "Shop." The game contains little hats and lovely accessories to trim them with. Use all the items to decorate Dolly's hats, and you can always change them according to the newest fashion.* The set is divided into seven sections; four have molded felt hats in different colors. Between the hats are a card with colored feathers and the instructions. In the center section are needles, a cellophane packet with shaped plastic buttons, ribbons, scissors, a spool of thread, hank of net, a bunch of flowers, mirror, and a painted wooden hat stand with a round base. **Complete: $75.00 and up.**

Note. See Junior Miss Hat Shop #868 (plate 236) for another hat shop with the same and number. Notice the difference in the box tops graphics, hat stands, mirrors and button arrangement. Neither the box nor the content has a date, so your guess is as good as mine as to which set was manufactured first. In Playthings *magazine, Advance Games were only listed as making sewing sets in the late 1940s.*

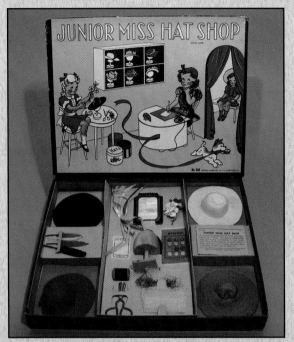

Plate 236. This version of **Junior Miss Hat Shop #868** was also manufactured by Advance Games Inc., circa 1945. The box measures 17½" x 2". There is a little blue paper inside that reads the same as Junior Miss Hat Shop #868 in (plate 235). This set is divided into seven sections; four of the sections hold molded felt hats in different colors. Between the hats are a card with colored feathers and the instructions. In the center section are needles, a card with plastic dome-shaped buttons, ribbons, scissors, a spool of thread, hank of net, a bunch of flowers, mirror, and an unpainted wooden hat stand with a square base. **Complete: $75.00 and up.**

Note: See Junior Miss Hat Shop #868, (plate 235) for another hat shop with the same and number. Notice the difference in the box tops graphics, hat stands, mirrors and button arrangement. Neither the box nor the content has a date, so your guess is as good as mine as to which set was manufactured first. In Playthings *magazine, Advance Games were only listed as making sewing sets in the late 1940s.*

Plate 237. The Campbell Kids Sew a Hat #4417 by Milton Bradley, circa 1954. The box measures 16½" x 11½". Inside on an elevated tray are two full-color hats of thin cardboard to be punched out and stitched together with yarn. Under the tray are more hats. These hats are printed on construction-weight paper in black and white to be colored, cut out, and stitched together with the yarn. There are 12 hats in all, a flower hat, space hat, kitty hat, teddy bear hat, Indian hat, bunny rabbit hat, clown's hat, chef's hat, circus hat, feather hat, king's crown, and pirate hat. The set comes with four crayons with MB printed on the papers and a hank of yarn with a plastic needle. **Complete: $100.00 and up.**

Note: The Campbell Soup Company advertised a 50th birthday celebration for the Campbell Kid's in 1954. There were seven pages of toys and merchandise advertising the Campbell Kid's in popular magazines, showing everything from dolls to trucks. This set was one of the toys advertised and it retailed at $1.00.

Children's Plain Sewing Sets

Living in the twenty-first century, with all our modern conveniences, it is difficult for us to imagine the importance of needlework in women's lives in the eighteenth and nineteenth centuries. No woman, regardless of age or position, was allowed to grow up without learning how to sew. It was taught to all female (and some male) children as soon as they could safely handle a needle.

I have titled this chapter "Children's Plain Sewing Sets" but I believe an explanation is in order here as to what "plain" sewing is. Plain sewing is the stitches used to assemble and repair garments, linens, and household items. The plain stitches included running, seam, overhand, gathering, buttonhole, hem, and such. These were always learned before "fancy work." The following advice was given to young girls in, *The Young Ladies Friend*:

A girl should learn needlework to perfection, put principally the useful parts, and though the ornamental be highly commendable, yet it must not be encouraged to the prejudice or neglect of the useful.

Thérèrse de Dillmont wrote the *Complete Encyclopedia of Needlework* in 1884. In the first chapter, which was titled "Plain Sewing," she writes:

Many people, upon opening the Complete "Encyclopedia of Needlework," will be disposed to exclaim as they read the title of this chapter: What is the use of all this information about hand sewing now that machine-stitching has so nearly superseded work done by hand?

We hasten to reply that, among the many accomplishments of women, there is none in which it is of such importance to be thoroughly grounded as in plain sewing properly so called, which is, indeed, the foundation of all other needlecraft. A hand well trained to the execution of various kinds of plain sewing will easily surmount the difficulties encountered in any sort of fancy-work.

Furthermore, whatever may be the present gifts of fortune, the fact of being able to sew well will always be found useful; for as, on one hand, a practical knowledge of plain sewing enables one to appreciate the other peoples' work at its true value. so, on the other hand, it renders one personally capable of turning out strong and durable work should the necessity arise.

A plain sewing set is a set that has tools or articles that would use only the plain stitches with a needle and thread. This would exclude needlepoint, lace making, weaving, etc. Quilting would be considered plain sewing, as it uses a needle and thread, is utilitarian, and is done in a running stitch. The sets in this chapter all have plain sewing as their main purpose. Some may also include embroidery for decoration.

I have taken the liberty of including a few plain sewing "model notebooks" at the beginning of this chapter. So many American girls made these plain sewing notebooks in school while learning their sewing lessons. These books have an important place in plain sewing history. Unlike the ABC samplers in the early 1800s, the plain sampler in America was introduced about 1890. Few careers were open to women at that time and those that were, such as teaching and domestic services, required the use of a needle. Educators recognized this and introduced the plain sewing samplers into the curriculum of ladies' schools and academies. They were to be used as a sample of their work when applying for employment or, in the case of a housewife, a reference book for refreshing the memory. Some plain sewing samplers are a long, continuous piece of cloth with each type of construction or stitch worked within its boundaries. More often in America, the samples or "models" were mounted in a blank exercise book, as in the Plain Sewing Book of Lucy Holt's (plate 238). Sometimes students were asked to make miniature garments to assure the teacher that the student not only knew the stitches, but could also properly construct a garment as in the Plain Sewing Book of Lucy Riechel (plate 239).

When looking back at letters and diaries of middle class women of the late 1700s and 1800s, plain sewing was their most frequently recorded domestic task. In *The Light of the Home* written by Harvey Green, he quotes letters written by the Huntington sisters in the late 1800s:

Was so excited with the thought of the amount of sewing I had to do that I was awake at daylight…Mrs. Corkill working with me all week. Julia Gritten [a neighbor] is helping with her machine.

I thought if Sue is to do the housekeeping, I would assist her in making her clothes so this week I have fixed her cloth dress and spotted merino and now we shall endeavor to do Kate's dress…and finish Carrie's black dress. I suppose Frank's clothes all will need some call and your Father must have some shirts made as soon as we can get to them.

I became interested in making Beart's clothes and have kept on. Fanny Hooker [a relative] helps me baste and Fannie Gay [a friend] stitches so I have cut out over thirty garments this week.

The women of the house had the primary responsibility of the entire household's linens and the clothing for every member in her family. As you can see in the Huntington sisters' letters, it was such a large task that friends, neighbors, and relatives stepped in to help with the sewing. Many times it was done in an assembly line fashion: one person cutting, another basting, and another stitching. If needed, most women could hire a dressmaker to assist them for about a dollar a day.

Children's Plain Sewing Sets

Lucky was the woman who had daughters to help her with this overwhelming chore. Young children could help with the stitching and hemming of pillowcases, bed sheets, towels, undergarments, and clothing for infants. They also assisted in "marking," the stitching of initials and numbers on bed linen, blankets, and personal undergarments such as petticoats, drawers, and handkerchiefs. It was important to be able to identify your articles if you sent them to a laundry, or even if drying them outside at home and they should be blown about.

Before the widespread use of sewing machines there was a constant supply of "white work" to keep middle class women occupied. Usually next to a chair in the parlor was a basket of endless mending: shirts, socks, underclothing, etc. It would wait until the lady of the house had time to sit and mend. I imagine it was also one of the few times a woman could actually sit down and still feel she was being productive. Mending was also one of the ways the less fortunate could make a living; it was taken in much the same as washing, to earn a few dollars. As the sewing machine took over more and more mending in ladies' homes, *Godey's Lady's Book* complained that much of the sewing had been banished from the parlor.

The letters of Anna Green Winslow, a Boston schoolgirl twelve years of age in 1771 are full of her sewing tasks. It is written of Anna:

Anna was an industrious little wight, active in all house-wifely labors and domestic accomplishments, and attentive to her lessons. She could make purses and embroider pocket books and weave watch strings and piece patchwork.

Anna was sent to stay with her aunt so that she might attend school in Boston. Anna herself writes (I have used her spelling):

Dec. 6. I began a shift at home yesterday for myself, it is pretty forward.

Dec. 28. Last evening a little after 5 o'clock I finished my shift. I spent the evening at Mr. Soley's. I began my shift at 12 o'clock last Monday, have read my bible every day this week and wrote everyday save one.

Feb 28. My needlework at school and knitting at home, went on as usual.

Feb 22. I have spun 30 knots of linning yarn and (partly) new footed a pair of stockings for Lucinda.

Wednesday. Very cold, but this morning I was at sewing and writing school, this afternoon all sewing, for Master Halbrook does not in the winter keep school of afternoons.

March 9. I think this day's work may be called a piece meal, for in the first place I sew'd on the bosom of Unkle's shirt, mended two pair of gloves, mended for the wash two handkerchiefs (one cambrick), sewed on half a border of a lawn apron of aunts.

March 10. 5 o'clock P.M. I have finished my stint of sewing work for this day.

March 17. My Aunt gives her love to you and directs me to tell you that she tho't my piece of linnin would make me a dozen of shifts, but she could cut no more than ten out of it. There is

some left, but not enough for another. Nine of them are finish'd, wash'd and Iron'd, the other would have been long since done if my fingers had not been sore. My cousin Sally made three of them for me, but then I made two shirts, and part of another for Unkle to help her.

April 18. Some time since I exchang'd a piece of patchwork, which had been wrought in my leisure intervals, with Miss Peggy Phillips my schoolmate, for a pair of curious lace mitts with blue flaps.

April 20. This is a very stormy day — no going to school. I am learning to knit lace.

April 25. I learn't three stitches upon network to day.

The duties pertaining to sewing school were, in Anna's days, no light matter. In America children were usually fitted with their own sewing baskets. In some of the text books there are suggestions to teachers on how to outfit the beginner.

In the book *Manual of Exercise in Handsewing* (#6-S) Margaret Blair writes:

The sewing basket, which in itself will be a delight to the child, should be well equipped with scissors, needles, thread, thimble, tape-line, and emery.

In the textbook, *School Needlework* (#2-S) in the author advises:

A convenient outfit for your school sewing consists of a bag large enough to hold certain necessary materials and the garment to be made. The bag should be made of dark or medium-colored cloth, so that it may not soil easily, and should have a strong gathering tape.

Some books were more precise about what was needed. *Elementary Home Economics* (#24-S) page 343 stated:

A Sewing-Basket in which to place the implements used for sewing is needed by every seamstress if she is to do her sewing easily and well. A basket or box can be kept in better order than a bag, and sewing materials when kept in a box or basket are less rumpled than when put in a bag.

In the popular sewing books such as the *Mary Frances Sewing Book* (#25-P) Mary Frances is given a sewing basket by her grandmother. It is pictured as an open-weave reed basket. In the *One-Eyed Faries* (#33-P) Margaret Allen was given a pretty new workbasket from her auntie. It too, was a woven reed basket with a pink satin lining. In the *Little Girl's Sewing Book* (#26-P) the first project to make is a sewing apron, with large, deep pockets to keep sewing supplies in. Looking through old mail order catalogs, the first sewing basket I found for little girls was in a 1926 Sears, Roebuck and Company catalog. It is described as:

Here's an outfit every girl will enjoy. Made of bright red raffia interwoven with fancy straw braid. Hinged cover and inside padded and covered with colored sateen. Six spools and two balls of colored thread, bodkin, thimble, celluloid tatting shuttle and three needles. Fancy snap for fastening. 98c.

In France the tradition of giving New Year gifts, "étrennes" is said to go back as far as the Roman days. Over the centuries, "étrennes" evolved from food gifts in the eighteenth century to more expensive objects, which led to the wonderful decorated presentation boxes made by French craftsmen. Eventually, after World War I, the giving of "étrennes" switched to Christmas day. "Étrennes" for children became a large business venture, and the "étrennes" catalogs published by French department stores were full of wonderful presentation sets. Among them was presentation sewing sets for children. Many of them held a doll such as the sets in Children's Sewing and Embroidery Sets Bisque Dolls and some held many types of fancy work, as in, Children's Assorted Needlework Sets. A few held just plain sewing supplies, but were arranged in such a way that the boxes were works of art. There were small scissors and thimbles made just for children, one thimble that seemed to be popular had "For a Good Girl" printed on the band.

I don't think America women really considered their sewing baskets as needing to be a work of art. I am sure there were some ladies that were equipped with the latest sewing implements from France, and had silk-lined fitted sewing boxes. But for most, sewing was a utilitarian task, and any decent basket or bag that could be brought out among guests was all that was needed.

I have found in the early mail-order catalogs that covered baskets were a favorite, and I have seen many in antique stores or household sales still filled with scissors, tapes, thimbles, etc.

I imagine husbands and fathers' handmade sewing boxes and stands for their wives and daughters. Sometime in the 1930s there was a pattern published for a ladies' fold-up sewing stand made of wood and fabric. It was made in two parts that were hinged together. There was a handle on top and a latch on the side so it could be folded away without disturbing the contents. It was a good size maybe 30" high, and 20" wide and could stand on the floor right next to a chair or sewing machine where it would be handy. I have found one that was made for a child in exactly the same way only in miniature, plate 243, outfitted with miniature scissors, thimble, pincushion and the patterns. The patterns are both by McCall's one looks like a Shirley Temple doll pattern, for a 22" doll and has 14 pieces and one embroidery transfer. The other is for a 20" doll like Dye-Dee Baby and has nine pieces and an embroidery transfer.

There were many sewing kits on the market in the 1930s, but most of them held a little all bisque doll and are discussed in Sewing and Embroidery Sets for Bisque Dolls. Sewing for dolly seemed to be the sewing of choice of children in the 1930s and into the 1950s.

In the 1940s, H. Davis and company manufactured the Davis Novelty Sewing Set #404 using the yo-yo (plate 244). The box has a number of 4" pre-cut circles to make yo-yos and a square of fabric to make a mat. The instructions are well written with good plates.

According to Virginia Gunn in an article she wrote for *Piecework* magazine, yo-yos have been around since the 1840s or 1850s. Yo-yo quilts were a great fad in the 1920s. They were easy to make, bright and cheerful, and were made by the hundreds. Some true quilt makers were insulted that they should

even be called quilts and considered them simply novelties. There really was no quilting involved, just the gathering of circles, and sewing of circles together, which made a very colorful bed cover. However, with all the holes between the circles there was not much warmth. But yo-yo's caught on and were very popular. The yo-yo later went on to be made into dolls, animals, mats, and even clothing.

Felt has always been a favorite in sewing kits. It is colorful, easy to handle and doesn't ravel. It was very popular in the 1950s. A look through needlework catalogs of the 1950s shows just how popular it was. In *Aunt Ellen's Needlework Catalog 1950 – 51* there was a two-page spread showing felt jackets in kits to make and embroider or applique with felt shapes. There was also a page of felt circle skirts and scattered throughout all the catalog were felt baby shoes, boots, beanies, slippers, pictures, appliques, and a hobby felt pack.

There are three felt sewing kits in this chapter. I have two favorites. The first is Susie's Sewing Set #919 (plate 247). It was manufactured in the 1950s by Birdean Industries and is a very simple set. There are three pieces of felt all cut the same. These three pieces are first decorated with pre-cut flowers by making a design with the yarn, sewing over the flower and leaves and then decorating each flower with beads and sequins. The three felt pieces are then sewed together making a three-sided felt bag. After stringing the cord through a few slits in the top for a handle, you have a cute little purse. I think a little girl would love this. It is so simple, yet so cute!

The other felt kit that impressed me was Little Girl's Sewing Kit #7000 (plate 255) made by S. B. Toy Company. I was impressed with the fine materials and the thought that went into making it. The felt in this kit is very thick, the pieces were all beautifully cut and punched for sewing with the yarn, and the fasteners are top-notch gripper snaps. The instructions are very well written with a lot of arrows and diagrams for the child to follow. This set has two purposes: the child learns to assemble and sew, and when finished has a very nice outfit to be used in play.

J. Pressman Toy Company has made quite a number of sewing sets, with and without dolls. The company has been in business since 1922 when founded by Jack Pressman. Jack Pressman's first big break came in 1928 when his company acquired the rights to Chinese checkers, a product they still sell today.

In the 1930s Pressman broadened their line to include role-playing activities including building and sewing sets. They were also the first company to manufacture a doctor's kit. It was designed because one of Pressman's children was afraid to go to the doctor, and they felt the kit would help the child overcome his fear. It proved to be such a successful seller that they later added a nurse's kit.

One of the first companies to begin licensing, J. Pressman Toy Company manufactured toys under the names of Little Orphan Annie, Dick Tracy, Snow White and the Seven Dwarfs, and many other Disney characters.

Children's Plain Sewing Sets

In the 1950s there was a child's television program called "Grandpa's Place" for the Dumont Network produced by WDAB TV in Washington D.C. Lee Reynolds hosted the show in the role of Grandpa, who conversed with various toys and other magical characters, including a puppet named Jingle Dingle. Jingle Dingle lived in a tree when he wasn't working. But when he was working he was everywhere. You could find him in a doorbell, telephone bell, cow bell or school bell. In fact, anytime you heard a bell you can bet Jingle Dingle was there. Pressman Toy Company and the Jingle Dingle enterprises got together and manufactured the Jingle Dingle Sewing and Embroidedry Apron Kit #1167 (plate 248). The kit contains a pre-cut apron to embroider, assemble, and sew. The apron comes with two pockets each with a picture of Jingle Dingle to be embroidered. There are four jingle bells; two are sewn on Jingle Dingle, the others on the ends of the apron ties.

In 1959 Pressman came out with a rather sophisticated sewing set, Oriental Sew-Ji Fabric Wall Panel #2206 (plate 252). It looks more like a kit for an adult than for a child. The design is printed on a silk-like material and you are to do embroidery to accent the design. Then the panel must be hemmed on both sides and sleeves made that fit the wooden rods provided, for hanging on the wall.

Pressman also joined with the *American Heritage* magazine editors in 1961 to make The American Heritage Betsy Ross Flag Making Kit #2249 (plate 253) and The American Heritage Quilt Making Kit #1150 (plate 254). The flag making kit is very nice. There are three flags to be made and all the materials to make them. It comes with a booklet with stories about the flags and even poles on which to mount the flags. It is a well put together set. I am disappointed in the quilt making kit however. It seems with the *American Heritage* name on the box, it would have been more thought out. The booklet in the kit tells a nice story about quilting bees but when you get to the instructions in the kit it becomes disappointing. There is no quilting to be done on the project, which is a potholder. The instructions are to place the two pieces of machine-quilted fabric face up, with the batting in the middle, and secure with the bias tape all around, leaving a loop at the top for hanging. A child certainly

didn't learn to quilt with this kit.

Most pieced quilts date from about 1830 on, when the domestic textile industry made colorful inexpensive cotton prints more readily available. Patchwork was a family thing. Most nineteenth century women made all the quilts for their household. Both boys and girls were taught patchwork. Some children had to finish their stint of patchwork before they were allowed to play. Every woman waited for her invitation to a quilting bee. Quilting bees were a very social occasion sometimes called frolics. Women and children would all assemble in one house and finish a quilt that had already been pieced by one of them. The pieced quilt would be put on a large frame with the batting and backing and each person would gather around and quilt a section. There was gossip, and stories, and a lot of visiting among the women, and after the quilt was finished, and the men came home, there was often eating, music, and dancing.

Quilting Bee #QB883 (plate 258) is an interesting quilting kit. It was made by Creativity For Kids in the 1990s. The instruction sheet starts out with the four basic steps, Cut, piece, sew, and quilt, then how to turn things into completed projects, starting with the easiest to the most challenging. From a doll's quilt to a drawstring bag. After the real quilting projects, the kit even shows how to make yo-yos and the fun things you can do with them. The last sewing set in this chapter involves a bear, Sew Fun Dress Up Bear #68 (plate 259) is manufactured by Alex and looks to be is a fun and rewarding sewing project, I would think any child would love to sew for this bear. I was very impressed with the instructions. They were very complete starting with threading a needle and tying a knot; each step was completely explained even to sewing on the buttons. Looking back over the plain sewing sets in this chapter, I see the majority of the sewing sets being made in the 1950s, giving way to the craft sets as time marched by. But even though there are not as many sewing sets offered in the last ten years or so, those that are, seem much more sophisticated and child friendly. The projects offered in the sets made in the 1990s and later, could be purchased and enjoyed by an adult as well as a child.

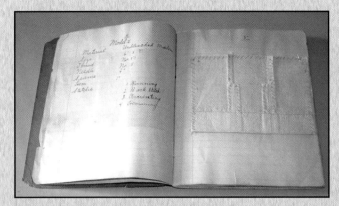
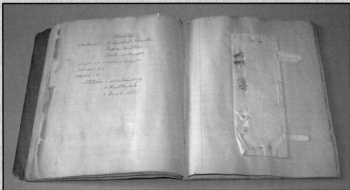

Plate 238. Plain Sewing Book of Lucy Holt, work done by Lucy Holt in 6th grade at Grant School, circa 1904. Above are two pages from Lucy's book; Model I has samples of running, over-cast, hem, and back stitches. Model IV has samples of the sewing of tapes, buttons, hooks, and eyes. The book is a simple school composition notebook. The text is written in pen and ink and there are 14 models. The models not pictured are mending on gingham, buttonholes, eyelets, hemming on damask, hemstitching, catch stitching, feather stitching, darning, gathering, basting, tucks, and the blanket stitch. **Complete: $100.00 and up.**

Plate 239. Plain Sewing Book of Lucy Riechel, work done by Lucy Riechel in 7th grade at Peter Cooper School in 1905. This is Lucy's notebook and some of the miniature garments she completed including a flannel sacque trimmed with blanket stitching, corset cover with bound armholes and trimmed in lace, nightgown with lace trim, and a gored gingham skirt with flounce at hem. In her notebook there was one other completed garment, a wool petticoat with an attached bodice. Lucy also had 12 pages of sample sewing models including patching, hemming and a variety of different stitches. **Complete: $200.00 and up.**

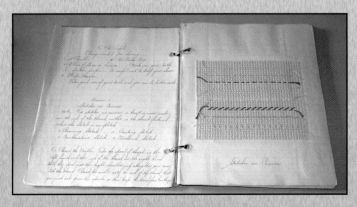
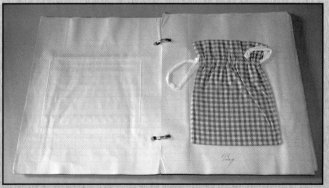

Plate 240. Plain Sewing Book of Irene Hunter, work done by Irene Hunter, St. Benedict Academy, circa 1911. What is interesting about Irene's model book is that it follows the instructions of the school text of *Sewing Tablet #1 A New and Practical Course of Graded Sewing Text* (#12-S). The plates above are the Stitches on Canvas Model and Lesson IV Making a Bag. There are 14 models in Irene's book, and many pages of text. Irene's overhand patch is so perfect I had to feel with my fingers to tell where the patch was! **Complete: $100.00 and up.**

Plate 241. Child's Square Wicker Sewing Basket is a sewing basket on legs with attached lid, circa 1910. This little woven wicker sewing basket measures 8" x 8" and is 15" high. How delighted the child that owned it must have been! It is filled with numerous little child-size sewing things. Among these are two small McCall's doll patterns for a 16" doll, thread wheels, needles, a straight pin block with die-cut angels decorating two sides, thread on small wooden spools, scissors, thimble, small wooden oval embroidery hoop, tiny tomato pin cushion, ribbons, fabric, and lace. Hanging off the side is a needle keeper and on the shelf below is a revolving thread holder with six small wooden spools of thread and a tiny velvet pincushion in the center. **Complete with sewing items: $500.00 and up.**

Note: The items in this sewing basket are all antique or vintage and were placed there by me. I have seen this basket in catalogs as a presentation set. Sometimes the contents were sewing items other times it held toys, such as dishes or a doll with a wardrobe.

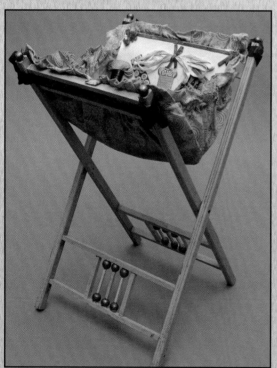

Plate 242. Standing Sewing Basket is a folding wood and cloth sewing basket on legs from Germany, circa 1900. Overall it measures 17" x 9" and opens to 8" wide. The stand is wood painted cream with gilded wooden ball decoration at the bottom spindles and top edges. The cloth basket is a white background with black squiggle dot lines and little pink open roses. Inside is a white folding cardboard with sewing necessaries still tied in with the original red silk ribbons. It includes tapes, thread, floss, buttons, rickrack, straight pins, hooks and eyes, and a tape measure marked in centimeters. The top and edges of the cardboard are trimmed in red silk ribbon as are the four finials on the stand. **Complete: $400.00 and up.**

Plate 243. Folding Hinged Sewing Stand is homemade by an unknown maker. Stand measures 14" x 10" x 4". This is a homemade case just like mommy used in the 1930s. It opens up to reveal two standing storage areas. One side has a shelf with dowels to hold spools of thread, just below are three pockets to hold laces, buttons, ribbons, and patterns. The other side has a shelf, for ribbons braids, buttons, pincushion, scissors, thimble, snaps, and a measuring tape. In the bottom pockets are lengths of fabric. When finished sewing, the child could just fold it together and put it away. **Complete with sewing items: $400.00 and up.**

Plate 244. Davis Novelty Sewing Set #404 was manufactured by H. Davis Company, circa 1940. The box measures 15" x 12" x 1½", and states: "Make*Doilies*Scarves*Arm and Head Rests*Patch Quilts *Needle Holders*Doll Carriage Covers." Inside there are three inserts; the two outer ones have pre-cut 4" circles and a 6½" square of fabric. The center insert has two hanks of cotton yarn, a sample rosette yo-yo, instruction book, plastic thimble, and a needle. The instruction book has a yo-yo pattern; it shows how to make yo-yo's and sew them together to make mats, doilies, quilts, etc. **Complete: $25.00 and up.**

Plate 245. Nancy's Sew-A-Toy was copyrighted in 1943 by Nancy's Sew-A-Toy Doll and Animal Series. The thin cardboard box is 18¼" x 13½" x 1½". The box contains a layer of kapok about 1" thick in batting form, four sheets of fabric, eight small gray buttons, a spool of thread, and six toy patterns. The patterns are for a horse, cat, rabbit, swan, kangaroo, and doe. All have detailed instruction sheets with diagrams. **Complete: $25.00 and up.**

Plate 246. Felt Kit #12 manufactured by The Funcrafter Company, circa 1950s. The kit comes in a 14½" x 9½" x 1¼" box. The box top advertises: "For girls 7 to 8 an educational kit filled with things to make and use." Inside are a beanie cap, purse, and a Scottie-dog pin to make from felt. All the pieces are pre-cut and ready to sew together. All the stitching is to be done in an overcast stitch. There are instructions for each item included, along with the thread, pre-cut flowers for trimming, and a cord for the purse. On the bottom of the box is an original $1.40 price sticker from Hess Brothers. Complete: $25.00 and up.

Note: In the above set there was an advertisement for a Fun-Crafter Kit #14 with a gingham apron to be made for yourself and dolly.

Plate 247. Suzie's Sewing Set #919, circa 1950s, by Birdean Industries is in a 14" x 10" x 1" box. Recessed in the middle of the box are three bright red pieces of pre-cut wool felt, ready to sew into a three-sided drawstring bag. Included in the set are a needle, yarn, thread, pre-cut felt flowers and leaves, beads, sequins, thimble, drawstring cord, and the instructions for making the bag. The bag is decorated with the felt leaves and flowers using the beads, sequins, and yarn to attach them. Complete: $25.00 and up.

Plate 248. Jingle Dingle Sewing-N-Embroidery Apron Kit #1167 was made by Pressman Toy Company, circa 1955. The colorful box measures 14½" x 12" x 1" and the box graphics are copyrighted by Leon Jason. The inside of the box has a scalloped frame around the edge. Inside the frame are the pre-cut apron and waistband, also two pockets stamped with "Jingle Dingle." There are three skeins of Pressman marked wrapped floss, a needle, cardboard embroidery hoop, metal blunt-nose scissors, four silver jingle bells, a plastic thimble, instructions for making the apron, and "The Jingle Dingle Story." The instruction sheet gives embroidery directions for the running stitch, cross-stitch, and French knots. Complete: $25.00 and up.

Plate 249. Betsy Ross Magnetic Pot Holders #6100 is presented in a box that measures 15" x 10" x 1½" and was manufactured in 1956 by Avalon Manufacturing Corporation. The contents include three squares of cloth stamped on both sides for embroidery, one a kitten, one an elephant, and one a puppy. Also included are batting, plastic thimble, cardboard embroidery hoop, card of thread, needle, three magnets, and instruction book. The instruction book shows three stitches: running, cross-stitch, and buttonhole stitch, and gives directions for assembling the potholders. **Complete: $25.00 and up.**

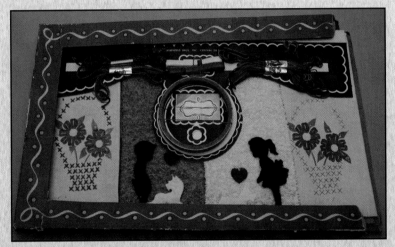

Plate 250. Guest Towel #1576, circa 1950, is housed in an 18" x 11" x 1" window front box and was manufactured by Hassenfeld Brothers. The contents include two terry towels with felt applique to be sewn on, two cotton towels to be embroidered, three skeins of Coats and Clark's embroidery thread, a cardboard hoop, needle, and binding for the edge of the towels. The instructions are on the back of the box and the embroidery stitches shown include running stitch, outline stitch, cross-stitch, daisy stitch, French knot, and a new stitch called an "After a Finish Stitch" (similar to the French knot). **Complete: $25.00 and up.**

Plate 251. Terry Towel Applique Sewing Set #306 was manufactured by Standard Toykraft circa 1950s. The box is a window display and measures 15" x 10" x 1¼". It contains four hand towels, two terry and two cotton. Each towel has a pre-cut felt design to be appliqued to it. Included in the set are three skeins of Coats and Clark's embroidery floss and "Terry Towel Applique Sewing Instructions." The stitch they use to applique is the running stitch. **Complete: $25.00 and up.**

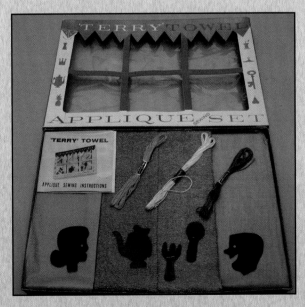

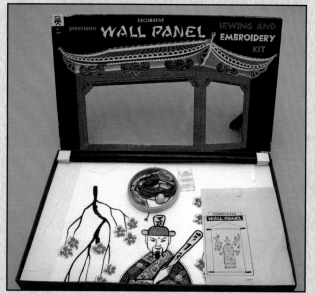

Plate 252. Oriental Sew-Ji-Fabric Wall Panel #2206 was manufactured in 1959 by Pressman Toy Company. The box has a window lid and measures 18½" x 11¾" x 2". The panel is 16" x 24" and is printed on a silk-like material in bright colors that is accented with gold. Included in the kit are two black rods, a hanging cord, cardboard embroidery hoop, plastic thimble, a package of needles, three skeins Pressman marked wrapped embroidery floss, and instructions. The instruction sheet shows the basting stitch, cross-stitch, chain stitch, and buttonhole stitch. **Complete: $25.00 and up.**

Plate 253. The American Heritage Betsy Ross Flag Making Kit #2249 was manufactured by Pressman Toy Corporation and prepared in cooperation with the editors of *American Heritage* magazine. It is dated 1961. The kit makes three famous flags, "Bunker Hill Flag," "Stars and Stripes," and the "Gadsden Flag." The box is 17½" x 13" x 2". Inside, still stapled to the box, are three flags with backgrounds of navy blue, yellow, and red-and-white stripe. Also included are smaller red and blue squares, four skeins of Pressman marked wrapped embroidery floss, three flag poles, cardboard embroidery hoop, plastic thimble, wooden spool of thread, needle, embroidery transfers, and the instructions. In the instruction sheet are facts and stories of the flags. **Complete: $25.00 and up.**

Note: There were other American Heritage/Pressman sets, The American Heritage Quilt Kit, the American Heritage Knit Set, American Heritage Sampler Kit, and American Heritage Tapestry Kit.

Plate 254. The American Heritage Quilt Kit #1150 comes in an 11" x 8½" x 1" box with a cutout window lid. It was prepared in cooperation with the editors of *American Heritage* magazine and manufactured by Pressman Toy Corporation in 1961. The box contains materials to make two quilted pot-holders that includes two pre-quilted 6" squares, four 6" squares of fabric in two prints, a roll of bias tape for the edges, a wooden spool of thread, a small plastic thimble and the instructions. The instruction booklet includes a story about quilting bees. **Complete: $25.00 and up.**

Plate 255. The Little Girls Sewing Kit #7000, is circa 1960s by Jean-style, and manufactured by S. B. Toy Company. The box is 16" x 9¼" x 1". Inside the box is a child's pre-cut nurse's outfit including a blue cape and a white hat and skirt. The pieces are all of heavy felt and have holes punched around the edges to whip stitch together with the red yarn included in the kit. The skirt has three snap fasteners so that it can be adjusted to the child's waist. The hat has extra holes so that it too may be adjusted. The kit comes with a needle, yarn, and nurse insignia for cap and cape. **Complete: $25.00 and up.**

Note: There were two other Little Girl's Sewing Kits: a Majorette with pre-cut felt for a hat, skirt and bolero jacket, and a Stewardess with pre-cut felt for a cap, skirt, and bolero jacket.

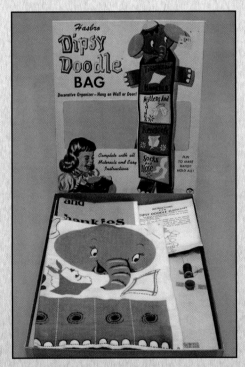

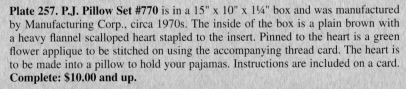

Plate 256. Dipsy Doodle Bag #586, circa 1950s, was manufactured by Hassenfeld Brothers. The box is 15" x 12" x 2" and has a see-through window. The contents of the set include a "fabfelt" sheet with backing and pockets, a flannel sheet with the elephant and pocket appliques, a tube of glue, wooden spool of thread, needle, thimble, and instructions. The tube of glue is to hold all pieces in place while you sew. The Dipsy Doodle Bag #1586 should measure about 37" when finished. **Complete: $25.00 and up.**

Plate 257. P.J. Pillow Set #770 is in a 15" x 10" x 1¼" box and was manufactured by Manufacturing Corp., circa 1970s. The inside of the box is a plain brown with a heavy flannel scalloped heart stapled to the insert. Pinned to the heart is a green flower applique to be stitched on using the accompanying thread card. The heart is to be made into a pillow to hold your pajamas. Instructions are included on a card. **Complete: $10.00 and up.**

Plate 258. Quilting Bee #QB 883. Creativity for Kids manufactured it circa 1990s. Advertised as "An easy, Fun Patchwork and Quilting Kit," the box measures 14½" x 10½" x 2¼". The box contains patterned 6½" fabric squares, muslin, quilt batting, pillow stuffing, braid, pin back, thread, pins, needle, and complete illustrated instructions and quilt pattern. The pattern sheet gives instructions for cutting, patterns for piecing, hints on sewing, directions on quilting, and patterns for complete projects such as a doll quilt, pillow, soft heart necklace, drawstring bag, soft baby block, and a number of yo-yo projects. **Complete: $25.00 and up.**

Plate 259. Sew Fun Dress Up Bear #68 manufactured by Alex and dated 1997. Sew Fun Dress Up Bear #68 comes in a 10¼" x 5¼" rectangle box. The bear is 10" plush with movable joints. He has pre-cut felt shirt and overalls to whip stitch together. The kit also has craft needles, needle threader, straight pins, pincushion, rickrack trim, embroidery floss, ribbon, colored buttons, and instructions. The instructions are easy to read and have large diagrams. They start by showing how to thread a needle, and ends with decorative stitches. **Complete: $25.00 and up.**

Children's Embroidery Sets

When I think of early embroidery, I imagine a scene of young ladies in the parlor with full-skirted dresses bending over wooden embroidery hoops, working deftly with their fingers while discussing the latest news or fashion.

Early needlework was indeed an acceptable pastime. While young ladies were visiting, their workbags were always at hand, ready to grab at any opportunity. In the needlework books published in the 1800s, there were two kinds of needlework: practical or plain sewing and fancy work. Plain sewing was the mending and construction of clothing and household linens, an essential part of a young lady's upbringing. Fancy work involved stitching artistic and decorative items, such as fire screens, pictures, patchwork, pillows, or any other decorative item used in the home or for one's self. It was proper to work on any type of needlework including plain sewing while visiting except underclothing in mixed company.

Not all people thought young ladies should fritter away their hours on fancy work. There seemed to be an on-going battle between plain sewing and fancy work sewing in the ladies' publications. Eleanor Hunter wrote in 1891 in her book, *Talks to Girls*:

A girl ought to exercise her conscience in her fancy-work as well as in anything else. Sometimes a girl spends too much time in making pretty things, and it is a most fascinating occupation — the beautiful colors and fabrics of the materials are a great temptation to any woman; but remember, my girls, that fancy-work comes after lessons and housework and plain sewing and practicing. Fancy-work should not be considered as a "work" at all, excepting by those who earn their living by it, but to the ordinary girl it should be a recreation.

Even *Godey's Lady's Book*, which was one of the first magazines to print embroidery patterns for its readers, warned those readers against:

Only expanding beyond a narrow female routine of gossip, fancy needlework, and novel reading.

Reminding young women that they must not shirk their womanly duties and leave the household mending while they indulged in hours doing useless embroidery.

On the other side of the coin, Emma Churchman Hewitt wrote in her book, *Queen of Home* in 1884:

I would strongly urge upon mothers the value of teaching their little ones all the arts of "Fancy-work" that lie within their grasp, for it has a decided mission in women's lives. Some doubtless, think that there is no such thing — that so-called 'fancy-work' is placed upon a too elevated plane when one attributes to it anything so exalted as a "mission." Certainly

it can be carried to excess, and then its mission is ended. But the stronger minded sisters, the ones who look upon all fancy-work as the refuge of weak brains, cannot for one moment imagine what an element of beauty, what delightful possibilities the much despised "fancy-work" brings into some lives, even though the work be of the commonest and coarsest kind. It is hard for the more aesthetic to comprehend a life so barren of all but drudgery, that the piecing of a calico bed-spread, in some cherished design, is the only element of beauty that ever enters it. And who shall say, that that which adds an innocent pleasure to a barren life, has not mission. "But why not make something which is really beautiful in itself?"

Even the ABC samplers of the 1800s were in the fancy work category. Plain sewing samplers were a long narrow piece of cloth upon which the young lady would do her new stitches for remembrance; she would then refer to it when sewing. The plain sampler was usually rolled up and put out of sight in a workbox or basket until needed.

The ABC samplers had evolved into a shorter and wider shape, using the alphabet and numbers with the addition of borders, decorative trees, houses, animals, etc. They now were framed pieces to proudly be hung on walls, as visible evidence of the deftness of one's abilities with the needle.

Transograms Sampler Sewing Set #1527 (plate 274) is an example of a simple sampler of the 1800s. A booklet in the set "How to Embroider an Oldfashioned Sampler" tells the story of Alice:

One day, Alice and her mother were rummaging through an old dusty trunk that stood in a corner of the attic. They found many pretty things that Mother had had for a very long time. They were having a wonderful time laughing and joking when mother said, "Oh, look what I have here." She held up a beautifully embroidered piece of cloth. "What is it?" asked Alice. "This is an old-fashioned sampler your grandmother made and gave to me when I was a little girl like you. You can see by the date on it, grandmother must have embroidered it when she was about your age."

The story goes on to tell how mother has bought Alice a Transogram Sampler Sewing Set. The story follows Alice through the making of the sampler, showing the stitches and the pride Alice felt when her project was finished.

Most young ladies were taught the plain sewing stitches either at a school or by a member of their family, as it was a must in a girl's education in keeping a happy home. Fancy needlework on the other hand was considered only a leisure activity. Only the families who could afford the extra expense could send their daughters to school to learn fancy stitches. Some families perceived fancy work as a way of proving her well-rounded education thus elevating her status in society.

Regardless of what was written, fancy needlework was indeed the pastime of many ladies in the late 1800s, and I imagine that there were baskets of common household sewing tucked away, while the needle plied colorful threads upon an article of whimsy.

The Victorians, lovers of adornment, embraced embroidery with a passion, and carried it into the turn of the twentieth century. Although woman's magazines such as *Godey's Lady's Book*, and *Peterson's Magazine* had been on the market since the middle of the 1800s and included fancy work patterns, it wasn't until the late 1800s that you could send away for full-size embroidery patterns. An advertisement in *The Youth's Companion*, December 26, 1889 reads:

A Wonderful Tool is the needle. When loaded with silk and guided with skill it can be likened to the brush in the hand of an artist. Art Needle Work and Stamping in the United States began in the office of "The Youth's Companion" in 1878. "The Companion" has been the pioneer in developing the popular ART and Mechanical Home Industries of the United States for the past fifteen years. Its purpose is to lead in the future as it has in the past.

The advertisement also offered a gold watch to a girl that could make the greatest proficiency:

A Special Stamping Offer good for 90 days. Any young lady who learns Stamping and Embroidery during the next 90 days, and makes the greatest proficiency, will be presented with a beautiful gold watch. Specimens of your work must be sent us within 90 days from date. Price of outfit is only $1.00, and 15 cents postage.

In an 1887 *The Ladies' Home Journal* magazine there was an advertisement for perforated stamping patterns, for ten cents you could order a catalog of 3,000 choice patterns for embroidery, painting, etc. A perforated stamping pattern was a paper pattern with small holes. This was laid on the fabric and then rubbed with a pad filled with stamping powder that would fall through the holes, and thus make a printed pattern.

In 1913 The Ladies' Home Journal Home Pattern Company offered transfer patterns that could be ironed on. These patterns filled an 86 page catalog with over 800 designs. Transfers were printed in blue, for use on light color material, and in yellow for dark material. There were patterns for waists, dresses, children's clothes, infants' garments, underwear, and accessories. There were designs for initials in many styles; they could be used on borders, and centerpieces, pillows, or anything you wanted to decorate. The iron-on patterns made embroidery so easy it became even more popular. Magazines offered many catalogs and patterns and there wasn't anything that was not adorned with embroidery of some type. In just one catalog we find shoes, stockings, hats, parasols, handbags, lampshades, pillows, laundry bags, newspaper bags, slipper bags, silverware holders — I could go on and on. It was an embroidery explosion and it continued as

a popular hobby for women all over America into the 1950s.

In chapter one of *Queen of Home* written in 1888, Emma Churchman Hewitt wrote:

Parents should select for their children their amusements, just as carefully as they select their food, clothing or studies; for, so will the child herself be.

I imagine this was on the minds of the mothers when they bought the first children's embroidery outfits. Unlike the early doll sewing sets, which were imported from France and Germany, the boxed embroidery sets seem to be an American toy, at least this seems true of the sets that were devoted exclusively to embroidery. The early sets in this chapter have the same type of stamping as seen advertised in the embroidery pattern catalogs from 1913 into the 1920s. The doilies in the Bradley's Needle Work Embroidery for Nimble Fingers #4712 (plate 260) are the same type of dotted transfer as in the *Ladies' Home Journal* 1913 Transfer Pattern Catalog.

Transfers played an integral part in the making of children's embroidery sets, and Transogram's Gold Medal Needlework Set (plate 262) with its own transfers is a perfect example. Transogram Company was founded as the Friction Transfer Pattern Company. The company manufactured embroidery patterns that were transferred to fabrics with a hot iron. Charles S. Raizen landed a summer job at the company and while he was there, he invented a process by which he could transfer a pattern with friction. This simple process involved laying the paper pattern face down on the fabric, then rubbing a blunt stick across the paper to transfer the pattern to the fabric. In 1915 the companies transfer patterns were being printed in Sunday papers. The patterns won a gold medal at the Panama Pacific Exposition. Raizen became sales manager, and a few years later he bought the company, became president and in 1917 changed the name to Transogram.

The friction patterns seemed to be better suited for fun toys than serious embroidery, so the company started manufacturing toys. His toys were advertised as Gold Medal toys, wisely using the medal they won at the Exposition in their advertising. In a 1925 *Playthings* magazine, Louis Wolf & Co. (Importers and Commission Merchants) advertised Gold Medal toys, saying they had been featuring them for more than ten successful years. That year among other toys they were offering:

"Gold Medal" Embroidery and Sewing Sets The largest and most complete line of Toy Sewing Sets made in America. Complete outfits that delight the little Needlewoman attractively put up in novelty paper boxes, decorated metal boxes, sweet grass baskets, etc., etc. To Sell at popular prices from 25c and up.

Pictured in the ad was a set with rub-on transfer patterns. Charles S. Raizen ran Transogram as a successful business specializing in boxed toys and games, until he died in 1967. Two years later the company was sold and liquidated.

The Princess Real Embroidery Set #618 (plate 261) by Ullman Manufacturing Company has a stamped rabbit toy, vanity case, and sewing bag. They are the same types of stamped articles offered in the 1920s McCall's Embroidery Patterns Catalogs. Ullman Manufacturing Company, a fairly short-lived toy company, advertised in 1926 *Playthings* magazine:

It's An Ullman Product... Paint Boxes, Priscilla Crayon Outfits with Picture Books to Paint and Color.

An article in *Playthings* magazine in 1928 stated:

The Ullman Mfg. Co. brought out quite a few new things, in fact went on record as having 28 new numbers for '28. The "Princess" embroidery and quilting sets for little girls had been considerably augmented, toy samplers to embroider, and fresh additions of their crayon and painting outfits were just a few of the latest creations to bid for popular approval.

Ullman Manufacturing Company advertised in the back of *Playthings* in "The Market Place." They eventually changed their headings to "Toy Ullman-AC" and advertised sewing sets until the early 1930s. Later in 1938, we see the same graphics and name Princess Real Embroidery Set #206 on an embroidery set put out by Standard Toykraft (plate 275). The January 1936 issue of *Playthings* magazine announced that:

On January 1ˢᵗ 1936, Standard Toykraft Products and the Ullman Manufacturing Company combined their resources into one large company to be devoted exclusively to the manufacture of toys and novelties under one roof, under the name of Standard Toykraft Products Inc. The modern Ullman factory at 319 – 327 McKibbin Street, Brooklyn N. Y., built in 1930, will house the merged firms. With up-to-date machinery all boxes, colors, crayons and other toy parts will be produced in this plant. Sol Luber will continue as president, treasurer and general manager of the enlarged company. Jerome M. Ullman will be vice president and secretary. The Printing Division of the Ullman Manufacturing Company, which was established in 1888, will be continued as a separate company under the firm name The Ullman Company, Inc.

Stamped goods were the sole items in the early embroidery sets. Most of the transfers were stamped on white or pastel fabric, suitable for quilt blocks, napkins, or hankies. In some sets there were popular icons of the time, such as the Campbell Kids, and Peter Rabbit, but for the most part, there were blocks with flags, boats, flowers, or children with names like Soldier Boy, or Little Housekeeper. The blocks were usually about 6" x 6", although most of the squares were not carefully cut and ended up with as much as an inch difference in size. There were some embroidery sets with stamped doll clothing to be embroidered and sewn, and other clothing sets with finished items to be embellished with embroidery. These doll-clothing sets will not be addressed in this chapter, but rather in Doll Clothing Sewing and Embroidery Sets.

Parker Brothers were well-known boxed-toy makers, however they were better known for their games. George S. Parker started his company in 1883 in Salem, Massachusetts. In 1885, his catalog had only eight items, but in only two years his listings went up to 125 items. His sewing sets were produced circa 1920. There doesn't seem to be any advertising for these sets, so I suspect they didn't do as well as the games. It's really a shame, because of all the early stamped pieces in the embroi-

dery sets, I think the items in Parker Brothers Embroidery Set (plate 263) are the most interesting and delightful of all.

Unlike Parker Brothers, Standard Toykraft was in the toy sewing set business in a big way. They were one of the first toy makers to use celebrities to endorse their toys and their Mitizi Green and especially their Jean Darling sets were widely advertised. One of the squares to be embroidered in the Jean Darling and Her Embroidery Outfit #200-10 (plate 269) has a transfer of Jean herself, sitting and stitching with her own embroidery set. It is taken from the same photograph that Jean sat for in 1931 to endorse the first sets. The picture was published in a 1931 *Playthings* magazine as a press release, and was printed on the covers of Jean Darling's first sewing and embroidery sets. This same photograph was also used on advertising card put into other Standard Toykraft sets. That's a lot of mileage from one little girl's picture.

In 1926, Walt Disney formed a company he named Walt Disney Studios. In 1928, Walt Disney Studios introduced Minnie Mouse in their first Mickey Mouse cartoon, *Plane Crazy*. In 1930, they released the cartoon, *Chain Gang* and introduced Pluto the dog. *Mickey's Review* came out in 1932, and introduced Goofy who starred in *Dippy Dawg*, and Donald Duck was introduced in 1934, in the cartoon, *The Wise Little Hen*. These cartoon stars made up the Disney characters, and started the largest character-merchandising trend known in toy history.

An article in a September 1938 issue of *Playthings*, congratulated Kay Kamen of Kay Kamen Ltd. on the occasion of a contract renewal of with Walt Disney Enterprises. The article stated:

Kay Kamen of Kay Kamen LTD., who congratulates R. H. McCready of Playthings *on the thirty-fifth anniversary of the publication, is himself due congratulations on the occasion of a renewal of contract with Walt Disney Enterprises. A regular advertiser in* Playthings, *Kay Kamen, Ltd., has become one of the most important factors in the toy industry in the six short years since the business was founded, and makes grateful acknowledgment to* Playthings *magazine in his congratulatory letter.*

Kay Kamen, Ltd., exclusive representative of Walt Disney Enterprises, is engaged in the business of licensing manufacturers and advertisers to use names and designs of Walt Disney characters. So sensationally successful has been operation of Kay Kamen, Ltd., over a period of years, that announcement of renewal of contract with Walt Disney Enterprises comes as no surprise. This success is eloquently demonstrated in the recently issued 1938 – 1939 Walt Disney Character Merchandise Catalogue. Over a hundred manufacturers producing more than a thousand new items are represented.

The licensing of Disney characters was not exclusive to the United States. One of the first manufacturers to jump on the bandwagon of Disney character merchandising was the Ontex Company of Canada. They manufactured Disney Stars Sewing Circle #541, circa 1930s (plate 270). The box doesn't have a date but we know it couldn't be before 1930, because the George Borgfeldt Company reported the first Mickey and Minnie Mouse merchandising, a deal signed between Roy

Children's Embroidery Sets

Disney and George Bourgfeldt Company, to sell figurines of Mickey and Minnie Mouse on February 3, 1930. The Disney character contract with Ontex Company included *Snow White and the Seven Dwarfs*, the first full-length animated feature. Nearly one million drawings were made, of which 250,000 were used in the final film. It was a smashing success, children all over America waited in long lines to see it. It seems the Canadians fell in love with Disney, as we Americans did, as Ontex Company also manufactured the Snow White Sewing Set #537, circa 1940 (plate 272) and another Canadian Company Make Believe Playsuits manufactured Walt Disney's Sleeping Beauty Embroidery Set #130 in 1959 (plate 296).

However Ontex wasn't the only embroidery set manufacturer that was licensed with Walt Disney. Standard Toykraft manufactured Walt Disney Characters Embroidery Set #43-25 in 1939 (plate 271). Hassenfeld Brothers, who manufactured a long list of doll sewing sets, got into the Disney picture rather late. The first Hasbro Disney embroidery sets I could find were the Mary Poppins sets in there Stitch a Story line in 1966. They continued using Disney licensing until at least 1969, when they manufactured the Mickey Mouse Sewing Set #1526.

During World War II, there was a decline in children's embroidery sets. It was a time when utilitarian sewing once again emerged and few sets were offered. However one set that surely reflected the times was the Little Miss America Embroidery Set #1075 (plate 278). The box top had been used before in a set #1050 with the same name and graphics, except it contained hankies, instead of flags and on the box top where the flags are seen on set #1075, set #1050 had prints of hankies.

Just as the plastic doll sewing sets, the embroidery sets once again rallied in the 1950s. Oscar Hammerstein's musical *Oklahoma* from the 1940s became a movie in 1955, featuring Gordon MacRae and Shirley Jones. It was a great success both children and adults stood in long lines to see it. Shortly after the movie, Golden Needle Corporation came out with The Surrey with the Fringe on Top Embroidery Set #2804 (plate 288).

In 1957, Shirley Temple and her adorable head of curls once again emerged. Ideal Toy Co. reissued the Shirley Temple doll in vinyl. It had been over 20 years since the composition Shirley Temple doll had been issued, and the children who once played with the doll in the 1930s, were now delighted to buy them for their own children to play with in the 1950s. This started a whole new Shirley Temple generation. On January 12, 1958, NBC introduced *Shirley Temple's Story Book* on television with the a grown-up Shirley Temple as the hostess and narrator. Two years later September 18, 1960, ABC aired *Shirley Temple Theater*, again with Shirley Temple the hostess and narrator. Shirley Temple items once again started appearing on the toy shelves.

I have found two Shirley Temple sets manufactured by Samuel Gabriel Sons and Company. The first Shirley Temple Movie Favorite Embroidery Set #310 was manufactured in 1959 (plate 294); the second, Shirley Temple Luncheon Embroidery Set #311, was manufactured circa 1960 (plate 295).

Luncheon sets were a very popular embroidery item and almost every boxed toy manufacturer offered them. With these sets a child could produce an item that was useful as well as beautiful when finished. Luncheon sets were offered in all the art needlework catalogs for adults at the time and what child doesn't like to have things like mommy? The Junior Miss Embroidery Case #1586 (plate 293) was advertised in a Hasbro 1957 catalog, as:

"Just Like Mother's." A big, good looking, circular luggage style case, complete with lock and handle, and everything necessary to embroider a smart tea napkin set.

I have found a lot of untouched embroidery luncheon sets still on the secondary market. I imagine parents and relatives found the sets nostalgic and were more interested in them than the children. The following note was found written on the inside box top of an untouched Small Fry Embroidery Set #1136 (plate 287).

August 25, 1955

Colleen dear, This will teach you to embroider if you follow directions. I imagine your aunts can assist you in getting started. I thought you would like this as you could frame and hang your first embroidery piece for your Daddy as a present you had made all by yourself. Honey, be sure you sit and embroider near a lamp where there is good, bright light. Some people weaken their eyes by trying to embroider away from direct light of the lamp. You could even learn to embroider your name on your blouse pocket or your initials. Please write and tell me how you're coming along with sewing. It's wonderful to learn to sew I hope you have lots of fun getting started. Lovingly, Aunt Noreen.

As this set was untouched, I wonder how long Aunt Noreen waited for Colleen to write. We all want our children to enjoy the same interests we do, I hope Colleen did learn to sew later, as her aunt was right. It is, indeed, a wonderful thing to learn to sew.

In looking back through this chapter we find the 1930s and 1950s seem to be the decades that produced the largest quantity of children's embroidery sets. The three companies who were the leaders in manufacturing embroidery sets are Transogram Company, Standard Toykraft, and Hassenfeld Brothers. Both Transogram Company and Standard Toykraft Company started making embroidery sets in the 1920s and continued into the 1950s. Hassenfeld Brothers began manufacturing embroidery sets in the 1940s and continued into the 1970s. We might find a few specialized children's embroidery sets on the market today, but by 1970, the embroidery set as a toy was no longer a staple in toy stores.

There are a lot of craft sets on the market today for children, but very few children's embroidery sets. I hope the art of embroidery is not lost to the child, as it has been a wonderful way to show creativity with a needle and thread, and make something not only pretty, but many times useful, that a child can share.

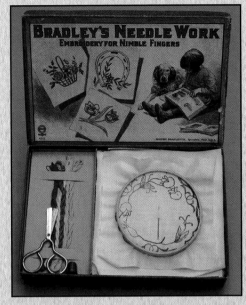

Plate 260. Bradleys Needle Work Embroidery for Nimble Fingers #4712 was manufactured by Milton Bradley Co., circa 1910. The box measures 10" x 6" x 2". The set has a delightful lithograph of a little girl with high button shoes and long stockings sitting looking at a picture book with her faithful dog at her side. Inside, on a cardboard insert are three printed doilies on heavy, sized cotton, one is still in a wooden embroidery hoop with its needle. There are also five twists of embroidery floss tucked into another insert on the side, along with a small metal thimble and metal blunt-nose scissors. **Complete: $50.00 and up.**

Plate 261. Princess Real Embroidery Set #618 was manufactured by Ullman Manufacturing Company, circa 1920s. The box measures 13½" x 10½" x 1½". The printed cross-stitch box top is signed Dorothy Morhan. The contents are a stamped rabbit to be sewn and stuffed, stamped vanity case, stamped sewing bag, six skeins Royal Society mercerized embroidery cotton, wooden hoop, needles, thimble, and instructions. The graphics and the name is the exactly same as the Princess Real Embroidery Set #206 produced later by Standard Toykraft. The instructions also have the same "The History of Embroidery," word for word as the Princess and Priscilla sets by Standard Toykraft. **Complete: $50.00 and up.**

Note: Ullman Manufacturing Company was known for its paper products, postcards, prints, and puzzles in the early 1900s. They printed the well-known Sunbonnet Babies postcards.

Plate 262. Gold Medal Needlework Set was presented by Transogram Company circa 1920. The box is 10½" x 7" x 1". Printed on the top of the box is "A New Embroidery and Stamping Outfit. For the Industrious Little Needlewoman." The graphics are signed HP. The content of the Transogram booklet "My First Lesson in the Art of Embroidery" is stamped on the inside of the lid. In the box are three white squares of cloth, one with a stamped outline of a Campbell Kid, the other two are unstamped to be used with the transfers included. The transfers consist of a sailboat, American flag, bird, and butterfly. To complete the set are three skeins of embroidery cotton, a decorated card with a needle, metal thimble, metal blunt-nose scissors and a wooden transferer. The instructions on the lid for stamping are: *First cut or tear out carefully the design you wish to embroider and place it face down on the material. Hold both firmly to prevent shifting — pinning the design to the material will help to keep it in one position. Then RUB the back of the design with the wooden "Transferer" making sure to go over every line. The design will then immediately transfer to the material and is ready to be embroidered.* The embroidery stitches that are shown are outline, satin, buttonhole, and eyelet work stitches. **Complete: $50.00 and up.**

Plate 263. Parker Brothers' Embroidery Set manufactured by Parker Brothers, Inc., circa 1920. The box measures 8" x 8" x 1". The graphics are of a little girl sewing for her dolly, below her is a sewing set and the dolly is sitting on a table next to her. Inside the box is a diverse assortment of fabric squares, 12 in all. There are three miniature table covers, two larger 3" doilies, six 1½" doilies on one square, a shoe bag, pillowcase, baby bib, stamped drawing of an under bodice, and two quilt squares. The rest of the set consists of a wooden hoop, five hanks of embroidery floss, needle, metal thimble, metal blunt-nose scissors and an advertising card for the Parker Brothers games, Rook, Pollyanna, and Pit. **Complete: $75.00 and up.**

Note: The value of this set really depends on the things offered to embroider the miniature linens are delightful. If the same set were found with only quilt squares, the value would go down.

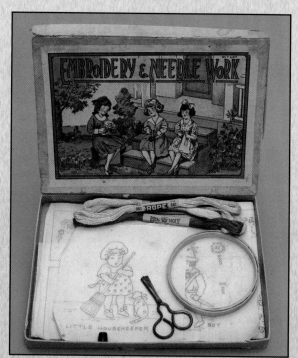

Plate 264. Embroidery & Needle Work #7 Art was manufactured by the American Toy Works, circa 1920. The box is 10½" x 7½" x 1". In the lithograph on the lid three little girls are pictured, each doing a different needle art. One is embroidering, one is spool knitting and the other is plain sewing. Inside are two white stamped squares, Little Housekeeper and Soldier Boy, a 10" table runner, a luncheon set with an 11" cloth, and four 2½" napkins. Four skeins of Royal Society cotton floss, a tiny metal thimble, needle, and a wooden embroidery hoop complete the set. **Complete: $50.00 and up.**

Note: Embroidery & Needlework #1 was offered in a smaller box with the same graphics. Also Sewing Set #3 (plate 338) has the same graphics.

Plate 265. Gold Medal Needlework Set #720 is a Transogram Company product, circa 1920. The small box is 7" x 7" x ¾". The graphics are a stylized drawing of two young ladies admiring the contents of the sewing set while a kitten plays with the thread. It is signed Isabelle Mago. The contents are simple; eight cotton squares in different colors. Out of the eight, four are titled, Peter Rabbit, Little Japanese Girl, Little Dutch Boy, and Duckies. Some of the squares are marked with a superimposed TC. The set also holds a wooden embroidery hoop, needle, four Belding Bros. skeins of silk floss, a metal thimble, metal blunt-nose scissors, and a booklet "My First Lesson in the Art of Embroidery" with the outline, satin, buttonhole, and eyelet stitches shown. **Complete: $50.00 and up.**

Plate 266. Tapestry Picture embroidery set is presented in an 11" x 7½" x 1" pasteboard box. The lithograph is signed but is illegible. Transogram Company made this set circa 1920. This is a "Gold Medal" set and is "The Latest Vogue Simplified for the Young Child." There are three sections, the first holding a gold-painted picture frame, matted and ready to use. The center section holds two skeins of silk floss with plain wrappers. The third and last section has a card with a needle, wood-grained cardboard hoop, and three pieces to embroider. There are two stamped cotton squares, one titled Little Sister, the other Spring Time. The third piece is a three-color stamped print as shown on the lid of the box. **Complete: $25.00 and up.**

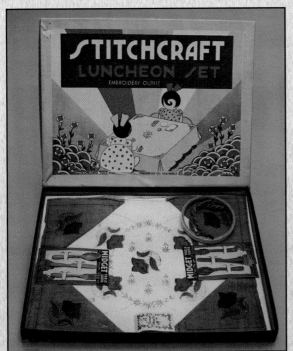

Plate 267. Stitchcraft Luncheon Set Embroidery Outfit #501 was manufactured by Concord Toys circa 1930. The box with its art deco design is 16" x 12" x 1½". Still stapled to the insert is the tulip luncheon cloth and four table napkins printed in three colors. There are two cards of "Midget" tableware, each holding a knife, fork, and spoon. To complete the set are two skeins of embroidery rope, a wood-grain cardboard embroidery hoop and a card with a Conco needle. **Complete: $25.00 and up.**

Note: Stitchcraft Luncheon Set Embroidery Outfit #501 also came with a butterfly stamped cloth and napkins and plastic Junior Cutlery made by Ideal. There was also a larger set with the same graphics and red, white, and blue stripes added to the sides. This larger set contained four sets of cutlery.

Plate 268. Mitzi Green's Art Needlework #1M was copyrighted in 1931 by Standard Solophone Manufacturing Company (later Standard Toykraft). The box is 11½" x 7½" x 1¼". The cover of the box has a lithograph of Mitzi Green, Paramount's child star. Mitzi appeared in both *Tom Sawyer* and *Skippy* movies. Mitzi Green and Jean Darling were both asked to endorse not only bisque doll sewing sets, but also embroidery sets for Standard Solophone Co. The box tops for the Mitzi Green and the Jean Darling sets are exactly alike except for the center picture, and the child star's name. The two that I have seen both had the same contents. Inside the box are three skeins of cotton floss, needle, metal blunt-nose scissors, metal thimble, a wooden embroidery hoop, and a "Little Mother's Bridge Set" to embroider. The cloth is about 9" square with the suits of playing cards; hearts, spades, clubs, and diamonds, at each corner with a horseshoe, leaves, and berries surrounding them. The napkins are about 6" square and each has a playing card suit in one corner. There is an advertising card inside this set that promotes Jean Darling embroidery and sewing sets; it has a picture of Jean, a story of her rise to stardom and her sewing sets. **Complete: $100.00 and up.**

Note: See plate 21 for the Jean Darling Art Needlework Outfit #2D.

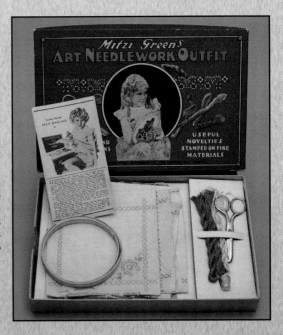

Children's Embroidery Sets

Plate 269. Jean Darling and Her Embroidery Outfit #200-10 manufactured by Standard Toykraft in 1933. The box measures 7" x 6" x 1¾". It has a cut out window and door backed with cellophane. Inside are four cotton squares stamped with blue outlines to be embroidered. They include a boy with a sword, little girl with a broom, and a little girl with a watering can, titled Spring Time. Also included is a square of cloth with a picture of Jean Darling sitting in a chair working with a Jean Darling Sewing Set. Four twists of cotton thread, a metal thimble, metal blunt-nose scissors, and an embroidery hoop complete this set. **Complete: $50.00 and up.**

Note: On the bottom of this box is a J. C. Penney Company original price sticker of ten cents. The print of Jean Darling on the cotton square in this set is the same picture of Jean that was used on the boxes of the first Jean Darling Art Needlework Outfit #2D (plate 21). The picture was also used for an advertising card that was placed in Standard Toykrafts boxed toys.

Plate 270. Disney Stars Sewing Circle Complete Embroidery Set #541 was manufactured by Ontex Company, circa 1930. Walt Disney Productions copyrighted the graphics, featuring Daisy Duck, Minnie Mouse, Donald Duck, and Pluto. The box measures 12" x 8½" x 1". Inside arranged on an insert are a stamped tablemat and four napkins. The tablemat shows Donald Duck on his way to school. The napkins are different color pastels, each with a different Disney character; Donald, Mickey, Minnie, and Pluto stamped in a corner. The tablemat and napkins are to be bound around the edges in a blanket stitch. The accessories for the set are five hanks of floss, a cardboard embroidery hoop, a plastic thimble, a needle on a gold paper, metal blunt-nose scissors, and an instruction sheet of popular embroidery stitches. **Complete: $75.00 and up.**

Plate 271. Walt Disney Characters Embroidery Set #43-25 was manufactured by Standard Toykraft Products in 1939. The graphics on the box include Snow White and the Seven Dwarfs, Donald Duck, Baby Mickey, Pluto, Ferdinand the Bull, Three Little Pigs, Big Bad Wolf, Minnie, and Mickey Mouse, and is copyrighted by Walt Disney Productions. The box is 13" x 9½" x 1½". Inside is a white cotton luncheon cloth and four napkins stamped with blue outlines. Snow White is in the center of the cloth with the Seven Dwarfs around the edges, the napkins each have a different Disney Character, Minnie and Mickey, Ferdinand and the Matador, Pluto, and Donald Duck. Included in the set are blunt-nose scissors, a Standard Quality card of thread, needle, metal thimble, and a wooden embroidery hoop. **Complete: $75.00 and up.**

Plate 272. Snow White's Sewing Set #537 was manufactured by Ontex Company with the permission of Walt Disney, circa 1940. The box measures 14" x 10" x 1½". Walt Disney Productions copyrighted the graphics, a delightful scene of Snow White and the Seven Dwarfs. Inside, still stapled to the center of the insert is a scalloped tablemat stamped with Snow White in the center and flowers and leaves at each corner. Stapled at the corners of the set are napkins, each stamped with a print of one of the Seven Dwarfs. Included in the set are two skeins of Beldings rayon embroidery floss, wood-grained cardboard embroidery hoop, metal blunt-nose scissors, plastic thimble, a paper with a needle, and an instruction chart of popular embroidery stitches. **Complete: $75.00 and up.**

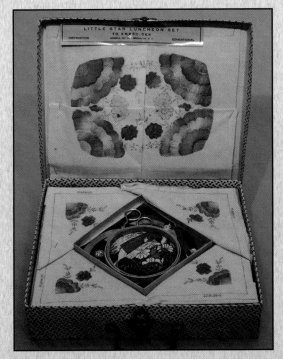

Plate 273. Little Star Luncheon Set to Embroider manufactured by Minerva Toy Company, circa 1930s. The luggage-style carry case has a metal handle and latch. The case measures 12" x 10" x 2½". Inside the case we find, still stapled to the lid insert, a color-printed luncheon cloth decorated with fans and flowers. The bottom insert has a diamond shape in the center featuring an Art Deco print of a lady with a shawl. Artfully arranged in the corners are the color-printed napkins. The remaining contents are a wooden embroidery hoop, metal thimble, metal blunt-nose scissors, needle, and a hank of cotton embroidery floss. **Complete: $75.00 and up.**

Plate 274. Sampler Sewing Set #1527 was manufactured in 1938 by Transogram Company. Its bright red 14" x 10" x 1" box top shows cross-stitch designs surrounding an alphabet sampler. Printed across the bottom edge in cross-stitch is: "An Old Fashioned Sewing Set for the Modern Little Girl." Inside there are three samplers, one a house as shown on the cover, the others are a large ship, and a sunbonnet girl, which is encased in a cardboard frame. All are stamped in cross-stitch with a space for a name and date. In the side insert are three skeins of rayon floss, a pair of metal blunt-nose scissors, metal thimble, needle, and the instructions. "How to Embroider an Old-Fashioned Sampler." It gives a charming story of Alice finding her grandmothers' sampler." Alice wishes she could make one. Alice's mother just happens to have purchased a Gold Medal Sampler Sewing Set the day before. The story takes Alice through the embroidering of the sampler and how pleased she is with her finished work. **Complete: $50.00 and up.**

Plate 275. Standard Toycraft Products Inc. offered the **Princess Real Embroidery Set #206** circa 1939. Dorothy Morhan signed the graphics on the box. The box is 17" x 13" x ¾". The cover of the box has the contents listed as: "Guest Towels and wash cloth with Embroidery Materials." The contents of the box are still untouched (stapled in place) and there seems to be more items than advertised. I count four 12" x 8½" towels, (they are marked towels), two smaller 7" x 8" cloths, and a 9" x 8" sampler of a Dutch girl. The embroidery accessories are all lined up at the top of the box in a slotted insert, and consist of a packet of Standard Highgrade sharps, metal thimble, six balls of cotton, and metal blunt-nose scissors. In a 1938 issue of *Playthings* magazine there is a picture of the contents of this set #206 and it shows the exact same contents as above. **Complete: $50.00 and up.**

Note: The Princess Real Embroidery Set #205, a smaller set with the same graphics, was offered with hankies to be embroidered. Some of the box tops were brightly colored, others more subdued, but always they had the cross-stitch motif with the little girl in her chair with her cat. The Ullman Manufacturing Company was the first to produce the Princess Real Embroidery Set #618 (plate 261). It had the same graphics and title, but a different content.

Plate 276. Luncheon Cloth and Napkins to Embroider #3 is circa 1940. American Toy Works was the manufacturer of this embroidery set. The box measures 11½" x 9¼" x ¾". On the side of the box is printed: "Fascinating Work for Nimble Little Fingers." Inside are a luncheon cloth and four little napkins to be hemmed and embroidered. They are printed in pink, yellow, and green with black outlines. To complete the set are metal blunt-nose scissors, a wooden hoop, thread, floss, and a needle. **Complete: $25.00 and up.**

Note: The stamped patterns on the pieces to be embroidered are shown on two corners of the box top.

Plate 277. Hankerchief Set to Embroider #5 is in an 11½" x 9½" x ¾" box. It is circa 1940, and was presented by American Toy Works. Inside are five napkins stamped for embroidery, a pair of metal blunt-nose scissors, needle, thread, embroidery floss, and a wooden hoop. **Complete: $25.00 and up.**

Note: The stamped patterns on the pieces to be embroidered are shown on two corners of the box top.

Plate 278. Little Miss America Embroidery Set #1075 was manufactured by Concord Toy Company, circa 1940. Dimensions of the box are 12½" x 9" x 1½". Inside the box, on a plain cardboard insert is a cotton sampler stamped with a 48-star American Flag with "God Bless America" printed underneath. Included in the set are a wooden embroidery hoop, needle, metal thimble, and red, white, and blue embroidery floss. This very patriotic embroidery set is from World War II era. **Complete: $25.00 and up.**

Note: There is another Little Miss America Embroidery Set #1050 manufactured by Concord Toy Co. with hankies. The graphics are the same except the handkerchiefs take the place of the flags, both on the box top and inside.

Plate 279. Little Lady Luncheon Set #1550 circa 1945, was introduced by the Transogram Company. The box top states it is "in the latest Mexican Motif," and shows some of the stitches on the box top. The box measures 19" x 12½" x 1½". There is a luncheon cloth and eight napkins in a rust and green Mexican motif to hem and embroider. Still stapled to cards are 12 skeins of embroidery floss in two colors and two cards of colored sewing thread. Also included are blunt-nose scissors, needle, and a cardboard embroidery hoop. The hoop in this set is very interesting; it is a square cardboard with a round hole in the center and slits at each corner. The instructions state: *Place cloth flat over circle and draw ends of cloth into slits in each corner. Then embroider cloth over cut out circle.* **Complete: $50.00 and up.**

Note: The same graphics were used on the Colonial Luncheon Set also manufactured by Transogram, but with a colonial motif instead of Mexican.

Plate 280. Little Miss Practical Luncheon #131 was copyrighted in 1950 by the New York Toy and Game Manufacturing Co. It came in an octagon tote with a rope handle. The tote measures 6½" x 5" x 7½". Inside is a foldout cardboard with a luncheon-cloth and four napkins still stapled in place. The luncheon cloth is stamped in red and blue with a Mary had a Little Lamb print. The flowered napkins are also stamped in red and blue. Included in the set are metal blunt-nose scissors, black embroidery floss, needle, wooden embroidery hoop, and a plastic thimble. **Complete: $25.00 and up.**

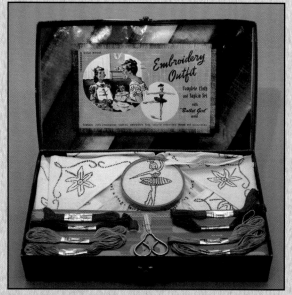

Plate 281. Embroidery Outfit Complete Cloth and Napkin Set with Ballet Girl #3496 was copyrighted in 1950 by Transogram Company. It comes in a 14" x 8½" x 2" luggage-type box with a metal handle and latch. The inside lid has the same graphics as the outside of the case. The 12" square tablecloth in the cardboard hoop has a ballerina stamped in a blue cross-stitch pattern. The four 6" napkins have flowers stamped in red cross-stitch pattern. The sewing accessories are stapled to a red cardboard insert at the bottom, which includes metal blunt-nose scissors, a plastic thimble, eight skeins of embroidery floss, and a needle. **Complete: $25.00 and up.**

Note: Embroidery Outfit Complete Cloth and Napkin Set with Ballet Girl #3496 seems to have a variation of the amount of embroidery floss given to complete the projects. I have seen this set with inserts that allowed only one skein of floss, another with four skeins, and the above with eight. It has also been offered with the ballerina cloth and six smaller ballerina napkins.

Plate 282. Stamp and Stitch Embroidery Set #713 was made in Italy by MultiPrint. The graphics are signed Gil. The box measures 13" x 11" x 1" and is circa 1950s. The box still has the $4.00 price sticker from Lord and Taylor in New York. Inside the set is arranged with elastic and recessed areas to hold 12 rubber stamps, four cardboard spools of embroidery thread, scissors (marked "Multiprint"), needle holder, stamp pad (marked "Multiprint"), and a wooden hoop with fabric for stamping. The booklet with instructions and patterns states: "The patterns shown in this booklet give an idea of a few of the combinations that can be made with these finely cut rubber stamps. They will stimulate the youngster not only to develop finger dexterity but originality in thought and good taste as well. These patterns are also well suited to be stamped and embroidered on dresses, collars, handkerchiefs, belts, bibs, napkins, and many other items." **Complete: $50.00 and up.**

Note: Stamp and Stitch Embroidery Set #713 was made in a smaller size set, Stamp and Stitch Embroidery Set #723 with different graphics signed Gil. Set #723 contained six stamps, three spools of thread, a smaller wooden hoop, scissors, needle holder, fabric, stamp pad, and instructions, and patterns.

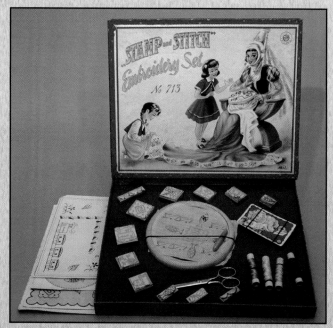

Plate 283. Personalized Bag and Hankie Embroidery Set #203 was the name H. Davis Company gave this circa 1950 sewing set. The box measures 15" x 10" x 1½". It states on the lid that the sewing set is "For girls of all ages Embroider your own initialed Bag and Hankies." It consists of a loose-weave cotton bag and two surged-edged hankies stamped for embroidery. Also included are two skeins of cotton embroidery floss, a needle, plastic thimble, instructions, and an initial transfer sheet to personalize your items. The instructions show you how to do running, cross-stitch, chain stitch, daisy stitch, and buttonhole stitch. **Complete: $25.00 and up.**

Plate 284. Bag 'N' Hankie Embroidery Set for Girls of All Ages #406 manufactured by H. Davis Company, circa 1950. The box is 18" x 12" x 1½". Stapled to an insert, along the sides, are four cotton animal-print hankies that are stamped in one corner with a cross-stitch pattern. The center holds a hand bag and change purse stamped for embroidery in two colors. Completing the set are two hanks of Royal Society cotton yarn, Star brand cotton floss, a needle, and Davis Embroidery instructions, illustrating the running stitch, cross-stitch, chain-stitch, daisy stitch, and buttonhole stitch. Tom Yams signed all the hankies. There are two prints, one with a rabbit and chick playing baseball, and the other is a Scottie dog with a tam and plaid bow. I would guess the hankies were also sold alone without the cross-stitch stamp. It is obvious that they were stamped with the cross-stitch pattern just for this set. **Complete: $25.00 and up.**

Note: This box has an original $1.89 sticker tag on its side from National Stores.

Plate 285. Make Your Own Luncheon Set #5652 designed by Anne Orr was manufactured by Whitman Publishing Company in 1953. The box is 12½" x 9½" x 1". Inside is a luncheon set made completely of paper. The contents are printed on the lid of the box so we know this set is complete. The set contains four heavy paper place mats and eight paper napkins. All are printed with color cross-stitch patterns. Still in the cellophane are the seven hanks of J&P Coats cotton embroidery floss and a tapestry needle on a checked paper. Completing the set is a booklet "Make you own Luncheon Set" with detailed instruction on doing a cross-stitch and instructions on completing the luncheon set. **Complete: $10.00 and up.**

Plate 286. J.W. Spears & Sons, Ltd. (Spear's Games) offered **My Hankies Embroidery Set**, circa 1953. The box is 15½" x 11½" x 1". Inside, still stapled to the insert are five surged hankies, each stamped in a cross-stitch pattern in one corner. The accessories contained in the set are four balls of cotton thread, a cardboard embroidery hoop, and needle. There is also a color chart and embroidery stitch chart illustrating the outline stitch, back stitch, darning stitch, raised stitch, rose stitch, block stitch, cross-stitch, lightning stitch, French knot, feather stitch, buttonhole stitch, couching stitch, Mexican stitch, and long and short satin stitches. This set is better quality than most of the handkerchief embroidery sets. The hankies are of fine cotton and are neatly surged around the edges. A child would have a lovely piece to be proud of when finished. **Complete: $25.00 and up.**

Note: My Hankies Embroidery Set was offered in the FAO Schwarz catalog in 1953 and 1954 with a retail price of $2.00.

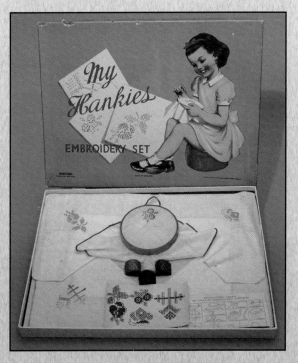

Plate 287. Small Fry Embroidery Set #1136 is a Pressman Product and was offered in 1955. The box measures 14½" x 12" x 1" and the contents are displayed within a scalloped cardboard frame. Inside the frame rest a luncheon cloth, four napkins, and a sampler still in a wooden embroidery hoop. All are stamped in cross-stitch and lazy daisy stitch. Included in the set are three skeins of cotton embroidery floss, needle, pink plastic thimble, metal blunt-nose scissors, and "Small Fry Embroidery" instructions. The instructions include the running stitch, leaf stitch, daisy stitch, bow stitch, cross-stitch, and buttonhole stitch. **Complete: $25.00 and up.**

Note: The instructions in Small Fry Embroidery Set #1136 indicate the contents include a tablecloth with four napkins and two handkerchiefs. I have personally seen three of these sets, and all have had a tablecloth, four napkins, and a sampler. I know from other sets that sometimes the instructions get passed down from one set to another without being changed. Despite the instructions, I am certain the above contents are correct.

Plate 288. The Surrey with the Fringe on Top Oklahoma Embroidery Set #2084 was manufactured by Golden Needle Corporation, circa 1955. The movie *Oklahoma* is the theme for the box top and contents. The box is 18" x 13" x 1½". Inside is a full-color wallhanging of a surrey, still stapled to the insert. There is a peach-colored, scalloped pasteboard frame around the wall hanging to which sewing accessories are attached. These accessories include metal blunt-nose scissors, four skeins of Lily embroidery floss, two plastic boxes, one of studs, the other contains sequins, a package of Dix and Rands sharps, plastic thimble, and a cardboard embroidery hoop. "Golden Needle Oklahoma Embroidery Set General Instructions" completes this set. **Complete: $50.00 and up.**

Plate 289. Jolly Hobby Embroidery Set #1585. Hassenfeld Brothers made this set circa 1950s. The box measures 17½" x 12" x 1½". The set contains four napkins and a luncheon cloth to be hemmed and embroidered. The Hasbro Embroidery Set banner is stapled in the center, a loose cardboard holds a pair of metal blunt-nose scissors and a metal thimble. There are two cardboard hoops each holding a napkin and a needle, three skeins of embroidery floss and the directions for chain stitch and cross-stitch. **Complete: $50.00 and up.**

Note: Three skeins of floss are securely stapled to the cardboard and two have the Hasbro label but the third is finer thread and has a J&P Coats label.

Plate 290. Girl Sewing and Embroidery Set was produced by Chad Valley with permission to use "Girl" from Hulton Press LTD. The box measures 12" x 7" x 2" and is probably circa early 1950s. The sewing set shown on the table of the box lid mirrors exactly what is inside this set, three cards of thread, a red plastic thimble, and a polished-cotton embroidery piece in a wooden hoop. **Complete: $25.00 and up.**

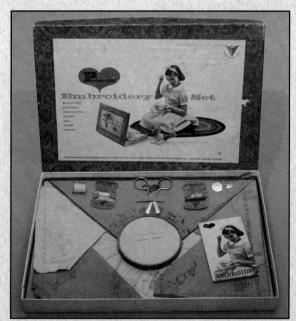

Plate 291. Priscilla Embroidery Set #206 was manufactured by Standard Toykraft Products in 1956. The case measures 15" x 10" x 1¼". The box top advertises: "Embroider your own hand towels, doilies and centerpieces." Inside the content does not match the advertising. There are five colorful cotton squares stamped with designs, the four around the edges are 7" and the center-square in the cardboard hoop is 9". The squares are still stapled onto the insert so we know they are original. The accessories card at the top holds a plastic thimble, two Standard Quality thread cards, metal blunt-nose scissors, and a needle theader. Also included in the set is a "Priscilla How to Embroider" pamphlet that gives the history of embroidery and shows the running stitch, cross-stitch, and buttonhole stitch. **Complete: $25.00 and up.**

Note: Two Priscilla Embroidery Sets with the same graphics as above were advertised in Toys & Novelties *magazine in 1956. Standard Toykraft advertised set #207 which was in a slightly smaller box. The content was the same except it didn't have a needle threader. Priscilla Embroidery Set #208 was a combination embroidery and tapestry set in a larger box. The retail prices of these sets in 1956 were $1.00 to $3.00.*

Plate 292. Stitch a Story #1595 is a Hassenfeld Brothers product. The box is 18" x 14" x 2". Hassenfeld Brothers advertised this set in their 1956 trade catalog. It was advertised as the "Deluxe Stitch a Story" with a nursery rhyme theme. The set contains four stamped nursery rhyme cloth pictures in plastic frames. This set has Jack and Jill (separate), Little Miss Muffet, and the Three Little Kittens. The center platform holds the metal blunt-nose scissors, five hanks of Hasbro embroidery thread, small plastic thimble, a paper with two needles, and directions for the cross-stitch, running stitch, satin stitch, outline stitch, daisy stitch, and French knot. The retail price in 1956 was $2.00. On the same page in their catalog was a smaller version with only two framed pictures with a $1.00 retail price. **Complete: $25.00 and up.**

Note: Stitch a Story #1595 is the first Stitch a Story embroidery set that I have found offered in the Hasbro trade catalog. The Stitch a Story items were a long running item for Hasbro; the advertisements ran from the mid-1950s to 1970s. Single framed pictures to embroider were also included in sewing sets in the late 1960s, with other items (place mats, napkins, and sewing cards) especially when it was based on a movie or television show. The line came in many box styles and retailed from 49 cents to two dollars.

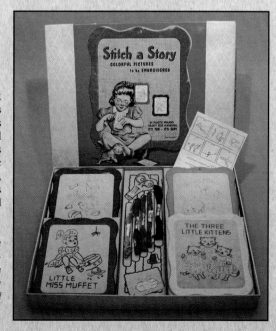

Children's Embroidery Sets

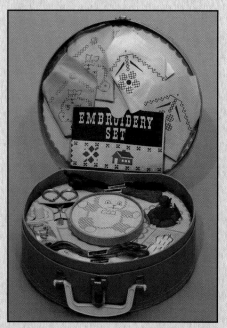

Plate 293. Junior Miss Embroidery Case #1586 was shown in a 1957 Hassenfeld Brothers trade catalog. Hasbro advertised it as: *Just Like Mother's. A big, good looking, circular, luggage style case, complete with lock and handle, and everything necessary to embroider a smart tea napkin set. Height is 10½", diameter 9¾"*. Retail in 1957 was $2.00. Inside there are five napkins to embroider, four are attached to the lid along with the embroidery instructions. The bottom insert has a fifth napkin in a cardboard embroidery hoop, four skeins of Coats & Clark's embroidery floss, plastic thimble, metal blunt-nose scissors, needle threader, a paper with two needles, and a small tomato pin cushion with an emery. **Complete: $50.00 and up.**

Note: Junior Miss Embroidery Case #1586 has no identification except for the embroidery instructions and "Hasbro" embossed on the plastic handle. Hasbro put some of these hatbox-type cases in decorated cardboard boxes with the name of the set only on the box and still others were sold with just hang tags and no box.

Plate 294. Shirley Temple Movie Favorites Embroidery Set #310 was manufactured by Samuel Gabriel Sons and Company in 1959. The box is 13" x 10" x 2". A picture of Shirley Temple is printed in the upper corner and cross-stitch patterns decorate the sides. Inside a see-through window are two towels 12" x 10" to be hemmed and embroidered. They are printed in red, yellow, and blue depicting Shirley in two of her memorable movies, *Captain January* and *Heidi*. Stapled at the top of the box and secured in a plastic bag are red, yellow, and blue embroidery floss, a yellow plastic thimble, needle, and a cardboard embroidery hoop. The instructions for embroidery are on the back of the box. We find that these instructions were used for yet another set, as it reads: "Your Shirley Temple 'Movie Favorites' dish towels and pot holders are designed with simple embroidery stitches." I have seen this set more than once and it always contained only two towels. The embroidery stitches given on the back of the box are trimming stitch, chain stitch, daisy stitch, cross-stitch, and running stitch. The retail price in 1959 was $1.00. **Complete: $75.00 and up.**

Note: The box on Shirley Temple Movie Favorites Embroidery Set #310 is very hard to find in good condition. The Shirley Temple Movie Favorites with two towels and two potholders was set #301 and was in a larger box. The directions with the two towels set #310 were obviously written previously for set #301, as it also has the instructions for the potholders.

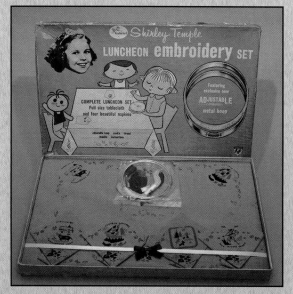

Plate 295. Shirley Temple Luncheon Embroidery Set #311 was copyrighted by Samuel Gabriel Sons and Company, circa 1960. The box is 18" x 11" x 1¼". Printed inside the lid are the instructions for embroidery, which include trimming stitch (or blanket stitch), chain stitch, daisy stitch, cross-stitch, and running stitch. Inside carefully arranged on a raised insert is a 23" square tablecloth (the largest I have found in a children's luncheon set) and four napkins. The tablecloth is stamped in three colors, pink, yellow, and black with the Gabriel Angel trademark in the center and Shirley Temple movie titles at each corner. The 5½" napkins each have a different Shirley movie title including *Rebecca of Sunnybrook Farm, Captain January, Heidi,* and *Wee Willie Winkie.* The tablecloth and napkins are blue with pinked edges. Still stapled in a plastic bag to the insert are three skeins of embroidery floss, all with Gabriel sleeves, and the new adjustable metal embroidery hoop. The needle is in the cloth behind the napkins. The box top advertising includes a thimble in the contents but this set does not have one and I believe it never did, as the contents were sealed. **Complete: $75.00 and up.**

Plate 296. Walt Disney's Sleeping Beauty Embroidery Set #130 was put out by Make-Believe Playsuits Inc. in Canada. The box is 18" x 12" x 1¼", circa 1959. This set features characters from *Sleeping Beauty* and has never been out of its wrappings. The dishtowels are stamped with the fairies Flora and Fauna ready to be embroidered and hemmed. The potholders are finished around the edges and are stamped with Owl and Squirrel. In the center enclosed in a plastic bag are three skeins of Coats and Clark embroidery thread, needle, cardboard hoop, and a red plastic thimble. The instructions for the embroidery stitches are printed on a separate sheet and encased in the plastic on the back. **Complete: $75.00 and up.**

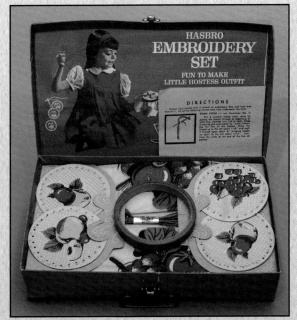

Plate 297. Hasbro Embroidery Set #1518 was manufactured by Hassenfeld Brothers (Hasbro) in 1964. The luggage type case with a metal latch and handle is 12" x 7" x 2½". The outside graphics are the same as seen on the inside lid. This is a very attractive presentation containing two gaily fruit and vegetable decorated cloth napkins and four round cardboard coasters, one skein of variegated floss with the Hasbro label, a paper with a needle, cardboard embroidery hoop, and a stitch and directions sheet. **Complete: $25.00 and up.**

Note: Hasbro Embroidery Set #1518 was part of a Sewing Assortment presented to toy dealers in a 1964 Hasbro Co. catalog. Hasbro advertised: "Sewing Assortment #1518. Three styles: Sewing Set has doll, dresses, and materials, Embroidery set has napkins and coasters, Stitch-A-Story has printed patterns, yarn plus plastic frame. Each in luggage case with metal handle and snap. Sugg. Retail $1.00." There was also a larger set #1528 with the same name and graphics. Set #1528 had four fruit and vegetable cloth napkins, four cardboard coasters, and four place mats to color and stitch around. The sewing supplies were the same with a box of Cray-o-Tone crayons added.

Plate 298. Take-Along Embroidery Set #1515, circa 1965, was offered by Hassenfeld Brothers. (Hasbro). This set is presented in a large format but the upper part is only the contents to put in the lower suitcase type box. The carrying box is 9¾" x 6½" x 2" and has a metal latch and handle. For the child to embroidery are cardboard pre-punched coasters and crepe paper like napkins. The set also includes a red cardboard hoop, a skein of variegated floss, needle, and a plastic thimble. **Complete: $25.00 and up.**

Note: In a Hasbro 1965 catalog this set and two others were advertised to toy dealers as part of a "Luggage Sewing Assortment #1515. This lovely visible pack, featuring an assortment of Embroidery, Sewing, and Stitch-A-Story themes is a fine way to develop a little girl's needlecraft skills. Each unit comes complete with yarn, thread, cloth, colorful ribbons and more."

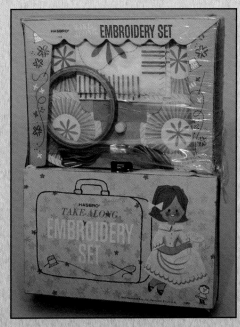

Children's Embroidery Sets

Plate 299. Mickey Mouse Sewing Set #1526 was a product of Hasbro licensed by Walt Disney in 1969. The box measures 18" x 11" x 1¾". Inside are one pre-colored framed Mickey Mouse picture, two sewing cards, one of Mickey and one of Minnie. Also two cardboard coasters, one cardboard round mat, two cardboard place mats, two color printed cloth napkins, plastic thimble, Hasbro variegated embroidery floss, cardboard hoop, needle, and directions for chain, cross, and running stitch. **Complete: $25.00 and up.**

Note: Mickey Mouse Sewing Set #1526 sewing set was shown in the Hasbro catalogs with many popular television and movie personalities, in 1967 Snow White, in 1968 Doctor Dolittle, in 1969 Chitty Chitty Bang Bang, Mickey Mouse, and Bozo the Clown, and in 1973 Charlotte's Web.

Plate 300. Muffy's Embroidery Basket was made by North American Bear Co. circa 1997. The little reed basket measures 2" tall and 3" across, it is lined with red fabric with white stars. Inside is a pre-printed cushion with Muffy on one side and Hoppy on the other. It is to be embroidered and sewn together for Muffy's ladder back chair (not included). Included in the kit are three tiny skeins of thread, navy blue ribbon, a 3" wooden embroidery hoop, and a piece of foam for the inside. **Complete: $10.00 and up.**

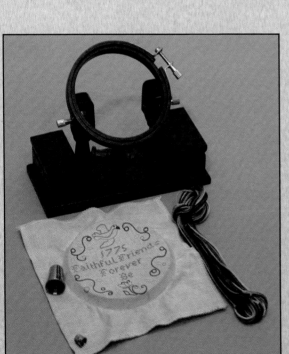

Plate 301. Felicity's Needlework & Frame was made by the Pleasant Company, circa 1998. Felicity is one of the historical dolls put out by American Girl. In a 1998 American Girl catalog an ad states: *Felicity's stitching certainly improved once she got her own "needlework frame." The "sampler kit" contains "needle" and "thread" to stitch a colorful bird, vines, flowers, and the words "Faithful Friends Forever Be." There are even two "thimbles" a tiny one for Felicity and one for you, too! Open the storage boxes on the base of the frame and tuck the supplies inside when her lesson is through.* The frame measures 4" high and 5¼" wide, the hoop is 3" across. The frame and hoop are all made of stained and varnished wood. **Complete: $25.00 and up.**

Note: The needlework frame in this plate made for Felicity's embroidery is actually an eighteenth century copy of a tambour frame with thread reel beneath.

Children's Assorted Needlework Sets

The nineteenth century was the most prolific period for manufacturing sewing tools. It was during this time that needlework was elevated from a pure necessity to an art and social grace. Ladies in society believed needlework, knotting, and tatting were important social accomplishments. They felt that not only skill, but also good taste and ingenuity were executed when conceiving various needlework projects.

The first children's needlework sets in this chapter were manufactured at the end of the Victorian era. This was the age of opulence, decoration, and splendor, and this was very evident on children's furnishings and toys. The children's sewing sets were made to resemble the beautiful sets that were available for the ladies. We will probably never see again the craftsmanship that went into the needlework sets made especially for children. Needlework sets with tapestry make up the majority of this chapter. In fact there are only three needlework sets shown that don't have some type of tapestry or at least a charted pattern in them.

Young girls were encouraged to learn needlework. The *Ladies' Needlework Instructor* by Mrs Bradbee written in 1884 stated:

There are few recreations more pleasing than fancy needlework, which, while it affords ladies great opportunities of displaying their taste, makes them no less sociable to those around them. It is a graceful occupation, and an inexhaustible source of innocent and laudable employment.

Therese de Dillmont in 1884 wrote in the *Encyclopedia of Needlework* about tapestry:

Tapestry is of very ancient origin, and has always been a favorite feminine occupation. Now-a-days we include under the name of tapestry every kind of embroidery worked upon counted threads, and in which the stitches entirely cover the material on which the work is done. Of these there is a great variety, namely all embroidery upon canvas in cross-stitch, tent stitch, gobelin stitch and straight stitch, besides knotted stitch and knitting stitch work, etc.

Tapestry patterns began in Germany in the early 1800s. In Berlin, Germany, in 1805, a print seller by the name of Philipson began producing patterns on graph paper that could be followed block by block and used as a pattern for embroidery canvas. To add to the desirability of these new patterns, they could be hand colored. These were the first Berlin patterns. Berlin patterns before 1850 were engraved on white paper; after that date, blue paper was also used. Even though they originated in Berlin and were called Berlin patterns, they later came from France, Holland, and Vienna.

Unlike the other larger Berlin patterns, the French patterns are usually of separate little objects, several to a page. At the Great Exhibition of 1851 in England, the first needlework canvases with the pattern actually painted on the canvas were shown. However the pattern charts continued to be printed and valued. You will find the small French patterns in abundance in the children's needlework sets.

By the 1830s, the Victorians considered the needlework canvas that was made by the French was the best, although the wool and patterns from Germany were still the favorite choice. England and Germany made a cotton canvas too, but the German canvas was not very strong. The German canvas had every tenth thread in yellow to help in the counting of stitches. Later in the century the yellow thread became blue and the canvas threads changed from single-thread (mono) to double-thread (penelope). By 1877, German cotton, penelope canvas was known as Berlin canvas and became the popular choice.

Victorians adored the Berlin wool work. Berlin work became so popular that many of the other needle arts were put aside in favor of the bright colors and soft yarns of the Berlin wool. As the industrial age progressed, many families became more affluent and more and more households could hire maids and servants. There was more leisure time for the Victorian lady and Berlin work often filled many of her idle hours.

Many of the children's needlework sets contain little glass-topped boxes of beads and some sets are predominantly beads. Beadwork started in the eighteenth century, but in the nineteenth century with the popularity of Berlin work, it was revived. The beads were stitched on the canvas with a half cross-stitch using a strong silk thread. In the periodicals of the late 1800s, there were many ads for beads. They were sold by the bunch and were made of glass or metal, the German beads being the most popular. See plates 302 and 305 for children's tapestry bead sets.

During the Victorian era there were many fancy work books on the market, such as *The Ladies' Handbook of Fancy Needlework and Embroidery* (in six volumes), *The Lady's Manual of Fancy Work*, *The Ladies' Handbook of Fancy and Ornamental Work*. There were books dedicated just to patterns, *Book of Cross-Stitch*, *Priscilla's Colored Cross Stitch Books 1* and *2*.

There were also the ladies' periodicals: *Peterson's*, *Arthur's*, and the most prolific of periodicals, the *Godey's Lady's Book*. These books and periodicals all carried patterns for lace making, Berlin work, bead work, embroidery, etc. The periodicals encouraged women to think of their homes as temples where everything should be beautiful and serene, and it was the

Children's Assorted Needlework Sets

homemaker's job to accomplish it. The periodicals were full of lambrequins, wall pockets, footstools, fire screens, and cushions, all to be stitched in tapestry.

Since the invention of the sewing machine, more and more mending and plain sewing was done on the machine. Fancy work took over as the preferred work to do in the parlor in the evening or when visiting. Ladies could swap patterns, just as they did with dressmaking. There were some that thought such useless work was wasteful, that it was criminal for any person to waste so many hours on work of such folly. Others would justify it, by saying that it was better to do fancy work than sit with idle hands.

However, in the end, most women abandoned plain sewing to the sewing machine and embraced "fancy work as a new art, not the drudgery and duty that was felt with plain sewing. There was an excitement in garnishing their homes and displaying their handiwork for all to appreciate. In fact, there were very few surfaces that escaped the needle in a Victorian household. It was a sign of prosperity that the woman of the house had the leisure time and talent to do fancy work.

Everyone agreed that fancy work was an occupation for leisure hours. It was written in 1875 not to set a deadline for fancy work because if done:

Is to make labor out of what should be recreation.

With the new affluence in the Victorian era, Christmas became not only a religious day in celebration of the birth of Christ, but it also led to a new commercial development of gift giving, especially for the children. The abundance of toys coming out of France and Germany was staggering. France published catalogs with toys such as *Grands Magasins Du Louvre Des Étrennes* and *Petit St. Thomas Étrennes*.

According to Francois Theimer in his book *Les Catalogues d' Étrennes des Grand Magasins*, the tradition of étrennes goes back as far as the Roman days when branches from the verbena plant were cut in the woods and dedicated to the goddess Strena (who symbolized strength). The branches were given for good luck.

The Romans had given the first day of the year to the god Janus and gave his name to the month of January. It is believed that Janus, the god of doorways and of beginnings, has two heads and is depicted looking both forward to the future and backward to the past. On January first, wishes for a Happy New Year and optimism were exchanged along with the gift of branches. It was a day to show only thankfulness and good deeds so that the god Janus would grant you favor in the coming year. The presents were called "strenoe" which led to the French word étrennes that dates to 1636 and means gift.

Over the centuries, the gifts of branches and food étrennes evolved into more sophisticated items. In the latter part of the 1800s, "the time of the child" in France, French craftsmen concentrated on these remarkable children's assemblages. Large department stores published catalogs of étrennes where pages and pages of toys in presentation boxes were shown in detail. The first étrennes catalogs were published in 1875.

The children's fancy work sets of the Victorian era are bolder, brightly colored, often beribboned, mirrored, and beaded. The imported presentation needlework sets from France were the cream of the crop. France always has been the leader in fashion, and they most assuredly were the leaders in presentation needlework sets as the 1800s drew to a close. In France, the catalogs of children's étrennes (gifts) were devoted to children's presentation boxes of every sort. They contained toy dishes, games, animals, dolls with wardrobes, and many different types and styles of needlework sets.

Some of the early children's needlework sets had wooden frames. In the eighteenth century in France, it was the style to do one's needlework in a wooden frame. Many frames were made as a piece of furniture, very decorative and highly carved with brass or gold ornaments. There were also more common frames with just turned pieces and little or no decoration. The more common needlework frames seem to have been miniaturized for some of the larger needlework sets for the children (plates 303, 308, 314, 315, and 316).

In this chapter, there are 14 needlework presentation sets from the turn of the century until the 1920s (plates 302 through 316). It is interesting to note what the most popular tools were in these children's early sets. Of course, every set had a plethora of thread of every conceivable weight, style, and color, and in so many varied presentations. Thread was found on wooden spools, cardboard spools, thread wheels, thread cards, skeins, braided, and on silk winders. Most of the needlework sets have scissors with sharp points, a "no-no" in today's world. Twelve of the 13 sets have a Berlin chart and nine have tapestry canvas. Eleven of the sets have small glass beads in boxes, 10 of them glass-top boxes. Five of them have a doll's printed collars and cuffs for embroidery. Nine have needle holders. Only two have lace bobbins, but of course there were children's sets that were dedicated only to lace making (plate 306). The Great Exhibition of 1851 displayed the first entirely machine-manufactured lace pattern. Lace making hand skills died shortly after the 1800s. Teaching tools, such as children's needlework sets, attempted to revive the art again in children.

After World War I, America stopped importing large amounts of toys from France and Germany, and started manufacturing American-made toys including children's sewing and needlework sets. By the 1920s, tapestry had lost some of its momentum. There were children's tapestry sets, but tapestry didn't seem to be as popular as it once was. The four big children's sewing set manufacturers, Pressman, Standard Toykraft, Hasbro, and Transogram, seem to have concentrated more on sewing and embroidery sets than needlework sets.

Tapestry wasn't completely forgotten however. Pressman Toy Corporation manufactured Wool Tapestry Outfit #1850 (plate 317) in the 1930s. It had pre-printed canvases and easy-to-follow patterns, but not enough yarn or the right colors to finish even one picture. Even if some of the yarn has been lost from this set, you can see there is no way the amount of yarn that was needed for four pictures could have even fit into the box. Another set Pressman Toy Corporation put out in the 1950s, Needlepoint Samplers #1148 (plate 322) was more realistic; you didn't need to fill in the background, so less yarn was needed. They also supplied the correct colors to match the colors on the cards.

Standard Toykraft Products offered Priscilla embroidery Set #208 (plate 321) in the 1950s. It came in a nice luggage-type box with a handle and three tapestries in the lid, but again there doesn't seem to be enough yarn included to finish all three pieces. This seemed to be a problem in many of the later tapestry sets regardless of the manufacturer.

Kay Stanley's Young Designer's Set C-21 (plate 320) is a good example of salesmanship and advertising through toys. Upon seeing the name Kay Stanley, I immediately thought this must be an important person to have a set named after her. In the instruction book, Kay Stanley writes a letter on the back page:

Dear Young Designer, When you run out of worsted, yarn or thread such as I have placed in your Young Designer's Set, go to your dealer and ask for Red Heart yarn or any of the Coats & Clark's products I have shown you in the little catalog sheets enclosed with this set. If you cannot obtain what you need, write to me. I do hope you have enjoyed this set and if you would like to go further with Designing, let me know and I shall tell you about all the other interesting sets I have in my factory. Yours for Useful Fun. Kay Stanley.

The Kay Stanley kit was manufactured by Model-Craft, Inc., but the Coat's & Clark's labels are all over it, and of course it is outfitted with only Coat's & Clark's products. Inside are three advertising cards for Coats & Clark's sewing thread, Red Heart knitting worsted (a product of Coat's & Clark's), and Coats & Clark's embroidery floss. Even the little plastic thimble has Coat's & Clark's advertising on it. There have been other sets with advertising especially the mannequin doll sets, but since this set is for a younger child, it struck me as unusually commercial. Kay Stanley's Young Designer's Set C-21 set is an excellent example of advertising through toys. I admire the set; I think the box top is colorful and informative and the inside presentation for a set of the 1950s is wonderful. The projects in the set are fairly easy to do, well thought out and interesting. I certainly would have purchased this set for a child in the 1950s, had I come across it.

Kay Stanley's Young Designer's Set C-21 brought back a bit of nostalgia, with all the items so nicely presented. I can remember when I was a child and was all prepared for first day of school. I had my new dress and shoes. But more important, a shiny new pencil box with all the pencils newly sharpened and lined up in inserts made especially for them. The gum eraser was in its place at the end of the pencils and the little plastic ruler even had its own space. How delighted I was to own that arranged pencil box. I didn't know it then but that was *presentation!*

Presentation is what is missing in the children's needlework sets today. The delightfully arranged assemblages of yesteryear are all but gone. As late as the 1960s, there were attractively arranged inserts inside some of the needlework boxes. Needlepoint (plate 324) manufactured by Transogram Co., Inc. is one example. Today's needlework boxes, more commonly called crafts, are all jammed together inside the box in separate little plastic bags, often packed so tightly you cannot get all the pieces back in the box without an instruction sheet. Most of the boxes today are just a wrap to keep the contents together until sold, today's boxes are not made to be used again to store the items. It is a shame, as I am sure the arrangements of the needlework items, to many children, myself included, were almost as important as the needlework itself. Being able to lay your work nicely into a well arranged box when you were finished for the day, somehow made you feel your work was special and you looked forward to returning to it another day.

Children's Assorted Needlework Sets

Plate 302. French Sewing Ménage is circa 1890. Beautifully arranged under a covering of glass in a sectioned wooden box are charted designs, boxes of beads, and tiny flower-covered boxes. The main paper-covered wooden box has eight compartments and measures 11" x 8" x 1½". The set contains seven round and four rectangular glass-covered boxes of glass beads in assorted sizes. All the glass-covered boxes are trimmed in gold Dresden. Also trimmed in gold Dresden are two charted designs of birds and flowers applied to center panels in the box. Along the top of the set are two 3½" x 1½" boxes, each with two flower prints applied to the lids. One contains cards of French silk thread; the other holds more charted designs to use with the beads. Along the bottom of the box are four 1¾" x 1¼" boxes that hold snaps, hooks, buttons, and a package of #9 French Bohin Demi-Longues needles. This is an early set and in remarkably good condition. **Complete: $500.00 and up.**

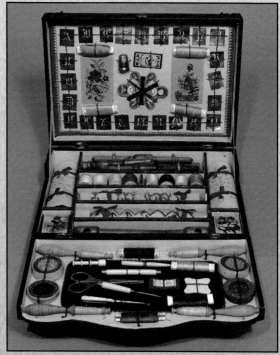

Plate 303. Alphabet Presentation Case, circa 1890. A French presentation case in all its glory. The outside of the case is covered with faux burgundy leather with silver metal filigree corners and filigree center plate and handle. The little silver latch on the front has the initials H. R, (perhaps the manufacturer). I have named this case myself in honor of the lovely copper alphabet stencils lining the lid. The case itself measures 11" x 7½" x 3½" closed. It is in three sections; inside lid, main box, and a hinged tray that lifts up and out to display more implements. The inside lid holds 24 little copper stencils, four spools of silk thread, a package of #5 needles, a brass thimble, two needlework charts (one a rose, the other a little maiden), and a wheel of black thread. In the center body of the case there are a tapestry frame, eight spools of thread, two presentation tapestries, two stamped table mats, and two little gilt boxes with scenes of children sledding and skating that are filled with glass-head straight pins and also fasteners. The fold out hinged tray contains all the wonderful little French implements, which are all still tied down. They include four wooden lace bobbins, two bone thread winders, a bone stiletto, bone and metal stiletto, small metal scissors, bone needle holder, bone and metal button hook, and packet of #9 needles all artfully arraigned on a black velvet pad trimmed with red silk braid. Along each side are boxes of mauve and ruby glass-beads and pearls. **Complete: $1,000.00 and up.**

Plate 304. Au Bon Marché Mercerie, circa 1900, comes in a paper-covered wooden 13" x 9½" x 3" box. Written across the lid in a banner is "Mercerie" (notions). Inside the case there is a vast array of needlepoint items. Packed in the lid are three samples of needlepoint, one has beads and four have colored pattern charts, a crocheted doily, and a beveled mirror. The bottom section holds four glass topped boxes of glass beads, four spools of silk thread, white and colored cotton, a sample needlework pattern on canvas, and a roll of blank canvas with a paper pattern on top. There is a velvet-covered tool section that holds metal tools consisting of a ribbon threader, a crochet handle with four different hooks to screw in, a bodkin, a pair of scissors, a thimble, a tatting shuttle, and two packages of needles. Found in this set was an Au Bon Marché advertisement. So I assume that the set was purchased there. **Complete: $500.00 and up.**

Plate 305. Austria Beading Set, circa 1900, has a darling chromolithograph applied to its lid of two children tending their dolls. The flower-papered box is 11¾" x 9" x 1½" and is stamped on the bottom "Made in Austria." Inside the box amongst paper lace and still secured to a piece of penelope canvas are two beaded strips on canvas for patterns, two hanks of floss, two hanks of yarn, a stamped felt piece, pattern stitches worked on a canvas, a tiny basket pincushion and a mirror in a perforated frame made for beading. Along the top of the box are five cardboard boxes of beads each has a colored cellophane windows. On both sides of the box are recesses with penelope canvases, one takes up the whole recess and is rolled up in a pattern chart showing children, the other has been cut into a strip and worked with beads and red yarn; more wool rests underneath it. **Complete: $200.00 and up.**

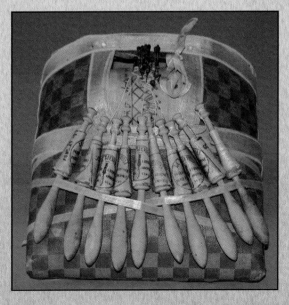

Plate 306. Child-size French Lace Making. This petite lace making pillow is unmarked except for its lace bobbins, all but one of the bobbins are wrapped in a paper that gives a number and has "Le Tjevoli //Fuseau A Bobine//Porte Ful Amovible// Bréveté C D C." written in French. The 6½" x 6" x 3" ca. 1900 pillow is a firm-sided lacquered checkerboard with a cloth wheel in the center. The wheel in the center has a paper lace pattern into which pins are placed. The child would make the lace by following the pattern winding the thread around over and under the pins using the thread on the 10 wooden bobbins. As the lace progressed the pins would be pulled, the wheel would be turned and the finished lace would rest inside until the amount needed was obtained. **Complete: $800.00 and up.**

Children's Assorted Needlework Sets

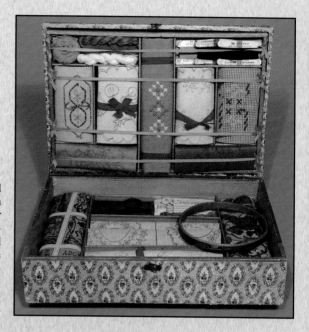

Plate 307. Mercerie. This attractive set has an allover oval flower print in gold and blue. On the lid is a separate applied blue piece trimmed in gold with the French word "Mercerie," which in English means haberdashery. A haberdasher is a dealer in small wares or notions. When you open the lid you find all manners of needlework. In the lid are pieces on which to practice net darning, embroidery counted cross-stitch, and needlepoint, along with threads and wool. In the bottom of the case are patterns for counted cross-stitch and needlepoint. Printed on cloth are four patterns for doll's collars and a flowered square to embroider. There are also metal scissors, needle case and needles, thimble, bodkin, and threading needle. To one side is a metal and wooden hoop. The case measures 13½" x 9" x 4" and dates to around 1900. **Complete: $500.00 and up.**

Plate 308. Tapisserie is another circa 1900 French product. This beautiful wooden 13" x 9½" x 5½" box has three layers of tools and supplies just as the Alphabet Presentation Case (plate 279) and in fact it resembles it in more than one way. Tapisserie is also covered in burgundy faux leather and has filigree corners and a decorative center plate. It also has copper alphabet stencils arranged around the inside of the lid; they are framed with a paper print band. The center of the lid has a scalloped piece covered in maroon velvet that is decorated with tiny embossed die cut of children and flowers on each corner. Attached to the scalloped center piece in the lid with narrow blue cord are the sewing tools, including two silk winders, bodkin, ribbon threader, crochet hook, thimble, needle holder, and silver metal stork scissors. There is also a package of #7 sharps and a bone and metal buttonhook. The second level has 10 sections trimmed with gold Dresden strips. The sections hold two rolls of crochet cotton, two gold boxes decorated with lithographs of children containing glass beads, two pieces of canvas with wool patterns worked in, along with two stamped patterns of fans on red polished cotton. There is also a doll's tablecloth stamped in cross-stitch, eight wooden spools of thread, and a paper with a graph pattern. A lower drawer pulls out to expose a crocheted doily, a Kate Greenaway stamping of children on polished cotton, a canvas worked in a pattern, and a wooden needlework frame. **Complete: $1,000.00 and up.**

Note: The Kate Greenaway-type children print in this set helps to date it. Kate Greenaway published her first book in 1878, so we at least know that the set dates after 1878.

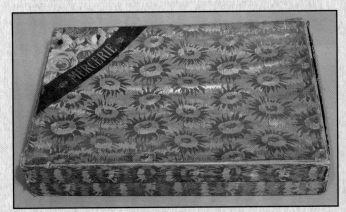

Plate 309. Mercerie. The wooden box of this circa 1900 set is covered in an allover blue-and-gold, sunflower-patterned paper, there is a banner with "Mercerie" written across one corner. The box is 14" x 9" x 2½". In the center of the inside lid is a mirror edged in the same paper as the outside of the box. Surrounding the mirror are eight cards of thread and three metal silver-colored sewing implements, which include a pair of scissors, a needle case, and a thimble. The main section of the set has two loose-weave mesh pieces tied with ribbons, a paper crochet pattern, two braided thread bunches, ten spools of silk, and a doll's collar and cuffs to embroider. The final piece is a rolled-up needlepoint sampler with letters. **Complete: $300.00 and up.**

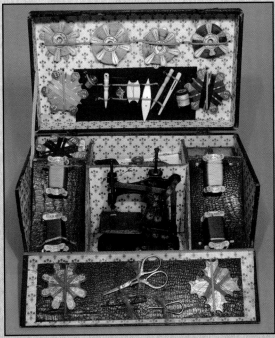

Plate 310. La Petite Couturiére is written in gold script on this French red faux-alligator-print case, circa 1905. The case measures 12½" x 7" x 6" and has two brass fasteners on the lid. It opens to reveal a decorative paper and red faux alligator print interior. Secured in the set's lid are six thread wheels, a thimble, a bodkin, needles, a thread winder, a tatting shuttle, a stiletto, a bone needle, and a spool of thread. A Muller model sewing machine made in Berlin and its table clamp are seated in the center area, along with the machine directions in French. Reels of thread and two glass-covered boxes of white and gold glass beads rest along each side. The front drop section holds two thread reels, scissors, a penknife, and a buttonhook. **Complete: $1,000.00 and up.**

Children's Assorted Needlework Sets

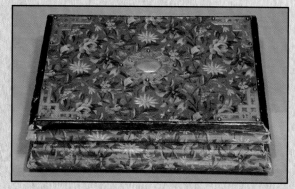

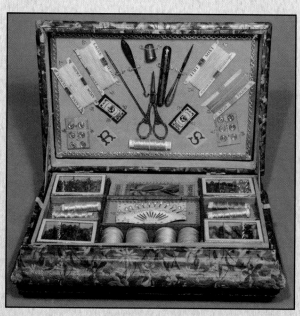

Plate 311. French Pink-Flowered Needlework Box is circa 1910 and abundant with sewing supplies. The box measures 12" x 8½" x 3½". The outside is covered with an allover flower print paper; there are metal corner decorations and a metal plate in the center. It has three sections, the inside lid, a tray, and a place to keep your work under the tray. The lid inside is decorated with gilt Dresden trim and two letter charts. Still secured in the lid are a metal bodkin, buttonhook, scissors, thimble, needle holder, stiletto, four cards of darning thread, one reel of silk, two packages of #7 needles, and two cards of snaps. In the tray below are four glass-topped boxes of beads, four paper reels of silk, four wooden spools of silk, a needlepoint chart, and a card of pins. **Complete: $500.00 and up.**

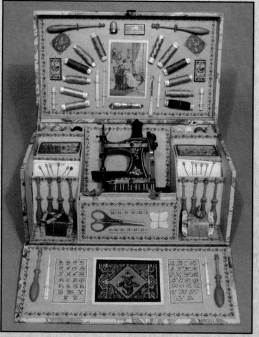

Plate 312. La Machine A Coudre. This wonderfully detailed set, circa 1910, seems to have every manner of miniature sewing equipage. The hardboard case measures 13½" x 8" x 6½" and is covered in a large allover flower-print paper. It has no name or manufacturer, but it is decidedly French. The top has, still tied in place, two wooden lace bobbins, a metal thimble, #9 needles, 12 paper tubes of silk thread, two cards of snaps, two packs of #5 needles and a metal needle case. Bone implements include two thread wheels, a screw top cylinder, a fine crochet hook, a buttonhook, and a stiletto. The picture of a young lady sewing a pink frock on a treadle sewing machine has the caption "La Machine a Coudre" (sewing machine) written on the bottom. The main section has in the center an unmarked decorated metal sewing machine and clamp. In the set's side sections are eight wooden spools of thread, two glass-covered boxes of beads, two cards of glass-head straight pins, eight wooden lace bobbins, and two square cardboard spools of floss. Below the machine there are a doll's stamped linen collar and cuffs set to embroider, silver scissors, bone thread winder, and 2 charted border patterns. The fold-down flap has two wooden lace bobbins, two charted letter patterns, a Berlin chart, a bodkin, and a large crochet hook. **Complete: $1,000.00 and up.**

Plate 313. French Mercerie Printing Set circa 1910 is packed in a valise-styled wooden box with a silver-plated latch and handle. Brass nail-heads decorate the strips of faux leather along the edges and secure the plaque that says "Mercerie" to the lid. Upon opening the box, we find a printing wheel still with its blue ribbon on the handle lying in the center recess. Under the tapestry charts on either side are 12 more pattern rollers, each with a different design for the printing wheel. Both below and above the tapestry charts are wooden spools of silk thread, along one side is a square of fabric with little blue sprigs, on the other side are a doll's collar and cuffs to be embroidered. The lid holds four cards of wool and linen yarn, two cards of tiny black snaps, a button hook, crochet hook, thread spool, bodkin, needle case, tiny thimble, package of needles, and a tapestry chart. The inside lid corners are decorated with corner charts. This little pattern wheel is used to stamp borders on the edges of collars, cuffs, linens, hankies, hats, etc. You could change the design by changing the pattern roller. The ink was applied to the felt pad at the top of the printing wheel and when the rolling stamp turned, the ink would go on to the roller design. As you rolled the printing wheel the design would transfer to the fabric. When the ink was dry the pattern would be ready to be embroidered. This set is very rare. **Complete: $1,000.00 and up.**

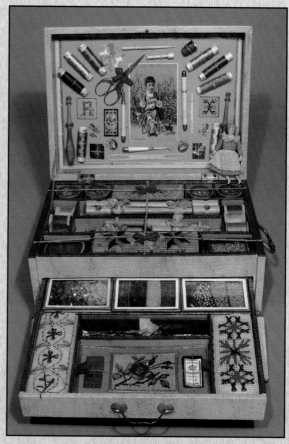

Plate 314. La Tapisserie, circa 1910, is a French presentation box in its original layout that measures 12" x 9" x 4½". The outside is covered in faux alligator skin with brass filigree on the corners; brass handles on the sides and a brass lock in front. Found in the set was a card from the store Au Bonheur Des Enfants (Children's Happiness). There are three sections to the box. The inside lid contains eight paper spools of silk thread, a thread winder, thread wheel, crochet hook, stiletto, buttonhook, weaving needle, bodkin, needle keeper, package of needles, two wooden lace bobbins, two brass stencils, two small flower scraps, and two printed letter charts. In the center of the lid is a picture of a girl working on a tapestry with her doll sitting in a miniature chair beside her, the caption underneath it reads "La Tapisserie." In the body of the box, still tied in with straps and pink bows, are six glass-covered boxes of glass beads, a wooden tapestry frame, two decorated tapestries, one on net, the other on canvas, and eight wooden spools of thread. The drawer underneath holds three more boxes of beads, a roll of oilcloth, and two decorated tapestries. There is a removable lid which conceals a hidden compartment at center front that includes a charted rose pattern and two packages of needles #5/9 and #4 sharps still attached. Tucked into the hidden compartment is a charted alphabet, a border pattern, extra lace bobbin, scissors, and a paper spool of thread. Also found was a 3½" stone bisque doll with a cloth body and bisque lower arms and legs. The doll is marked on the shoulder plate with a "2." It is questionable that the doll belongs with the set, but since the child owner might have put her into the set, and she was in the set when I purchased it, she shall stay. **Complete: $1,000.00 and up.**

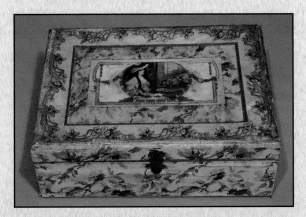

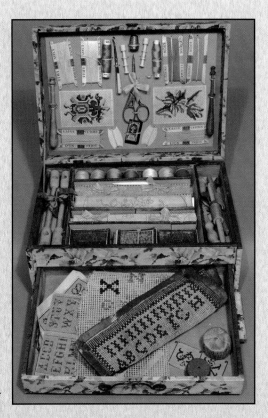

Plate 315. French Lavender-Flowered Needlework Box. This lovely box has a recessed top with a print of a young lady sitting at a table with a book in her hands, around the print is a frame of pink and lavender flowers in a swag. On the remainder of the box are lavender flowers done in a paper with a needlepoint-look. The box measures 11" x 8" x 4". The inside lid is lined in lavender and attached to it are six cards, two spools of colored thread, four bone thread holders, button hook, bone crochet hook, stork scissors, two needlepoint patterns, two wood thread bobbins, a packet of needles, and a thimble. The bottom has seven compartments. The sides hold the pieces to construct a wooden needlework frame. The center holds seven spools of colored thread, a roll of fabric, two printed pieces to embroider, one a round doily, and three sets of collars and cuffs for doll's outfits. The last section holds three glass-top boxes with pink, lavender, and green glass beads. The front of the box folds down to access a small drawer which reveals two alphabet pattern sheets, an unfinished sampler, a practice piece of canvas, two round finished doilies, two cards of thread, and two spools of cotton. **Complete: $1,000.00 and up.**

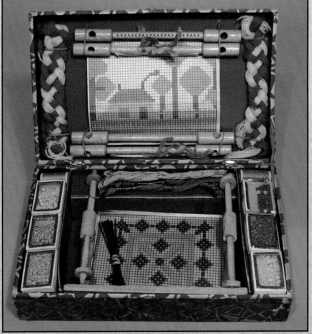

Plate 316. Tapestry Set. A photograph of two beguiling little girls having breakfast with their dolls is what was chosen to decorate the lid of this little German tapestry set circa 1920s. The box measures 13" x 8" x 3½". Upon opening the box, we find tied to the top inside lid the wooden stretchers to a tapestry frame, yarn braids are at each side, and in the center are two needlepoint charts. In the main section is the rest of the needlepoint frame, including the pins. On each side of the frame are glass-top boxes of glass beads, six in all, and above them are two wooden spools of thread. Also included are four skeins of embroidery cotton, and under the frame are pieces of needlepoint canvas, three more pattern sheets and a metal tapestry needle. **Complete: $300.00 and up.**

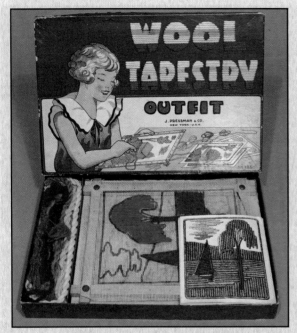

Plate 317. Wool Tapestry Outfit #1850 was manufactured by J. Pressman and Company, circa 1930s. The box measures 14" x 9½" x 1½". Inside are four tapestries, including a house with trees, a bridge, a parrot, and a sailboat. There is a color chart to match each tapestry (the sky is left undone). Along the side are colors of wool yarn to match the color charts. There is a wooden frame that is held together with paper fasteners. The previous owner has started the sailboat picture and has used all of the blue yarn and all but one strand of the green. In many of these early sets, there obviously isn't enough yarn to finish all the tapestries. **Complete: $25.00 and up.**

Plate 318. Picture Art #1840 has a patent pending stamp and a 1949 copyright by Playstar. The set was manufactured by Union Novelty Company, Inc. The box is 14" x 10" x 1½". Picture Art #1840 is nicely presented; arranged on the bottom insert are two metal picture frames with heavy paper inserts of two well costumed little girls. At the top, in cellophane envelopes, are seed beads and sequins, and down the middle are a needle and a spool of thread. The instructions with plates are printed inside the lid. The child's instructions are to take the pictures out of the frames and sew the sequins and beads on the girls' costumes sewing through the paper. The frames open at the bottom for easy access. **Complete: $25.00 and up.**

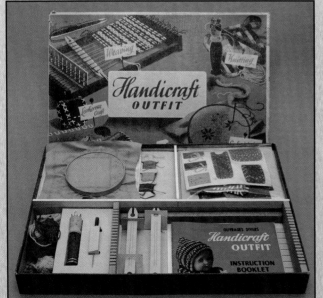

Plate 319. Handicraft Outfit was made in England by J.W. Spears & Sons, Ltd. (Spears Games) in 1953. The box measures 17" x 11¾" x 1¾". The inside of the box has sections for each craft. The embroidery section has two pieces to embroider, a wooden hoop, a card of assorted thread, and a needle. The leatherette craft section has a purse, scissors case, stamp case, sewing roll up, and a picture frame. The knitting section has a knitting spool, yarn and a pick. The weaving section has a wooden weaving frame, a metal heddle, two metal shuttles, and the instruction booklet. The booklet gives you detailed directions with plates on every craft in the box. **Complete: $25.00 and up.**

Note: Handicraft Outfit was advertised in FAO Schwarz in their 1953 Christmas catalog as four easy yet fascinating occupations for girls. The set sold for $3.75. There also was a smaller set with similar graphics without the leatherette work that was called the Junior Handicraft Outfit.

Plate 320. Kay Stanley's Young Designer's Set #C-21 was manufactured by Model-Craft Inc., in 1954 with materials from Coats & Clark's. This multipurpose kit comes in a 20" x 12 ¼" x 1½" box. The set has a very nice presentation; the box has a flip-up extension that holds two lengths of rayon-type fabric behind cutout areas that show a scarf and a beanie. This designing set comes with two skeins of Red Heart knitting worsted, six skeins of Coats & Clark's embroidery floss, and a spool of Coats & Clark's sewing thread. Also included are two cork squares, package of needles, thimble, three mobile heart shapes, pack of sequins, knitting spool, package of pins, knitting pick, metal blunt-nose scissors, package of butterfly cutouts, package of earring clips and safety pins, three color charts. Also included is "Kay Stanley's Young Designers Instruction Book." **Complete: $25.00 and up.**

Note: Key Stanley's Young Designer's Set C-21 was advertised in the FAO Schwarz Christmas catalog in 1954 as a new set that was "Designed to encourage a youngster's sense of pattern and design." The price in 1954 was $3.00.

Plate 321. Priscilla Embroidery Set #208 comes in a luggage-type box with a metal snap latch and bail handle that measures 18¼" x 12¼" x 2½". Standard Toycraft manufactured this multipurpose set in 1956, which offers both tapestry and embroidery. The articles are very nicely arranged. Secured in the lid are three pieces of single-weave canvas, each with its own pattern, a needle, four skeins of yarn with a "Hobby Kraft" label, and a tapestry instruction pamphlet. The pink bottom insert holds a plastic thimble, a card of thread with "Standard Quality" written on it, metal blunt-nose scissors, a triple spool of thread, and a needle threader. Under the pink insert are five printed napkins and two handkerchiefs, one with a cardboard embroidery hoop and two needles. There are also three skeins of embroidery floss and a pamphlet on how to embroider. **Complete: $25.00 and up.**

Note: Priscilla Embroidery Set #208 and another set with the same graphics were both advertised in Toys & Novelties magazine in 1956. The other Priscilla set was #207, which was in a smaller box. The retail prices for the sets in 1956 were $1.00 – 3.00.

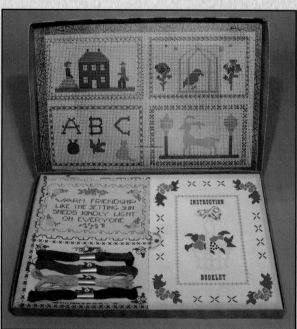

Plate 322. Needlepoint Samplers #1148 is in a 15½" x 10½" x 1" box. Pressman Toy Corporation manufactured the set in the 1950s. The hinged lid opens up to reveal four perforated paper samplers. In the main section secured to an insert are four skeins of floss in the colors of the samplers, a metal needle, and a very large instruction booklet. The instruction booklet is written especially for the needlepoint samplers #1148 kit and shows how to make the tent stitch, backstitch, cross-stitch, running stitch, and blanket stitch. The instructions also address each sampler and tells the proper stitches that should, be used. At the end of the lessons they state: "You may use other stitches than those prescribed in this instruction sheet. Be as original as you wish." **Complete: $25.00 and up.**

Plate 323. Twin Set Needlepoint #1572 is displayed in an 18" x 14" x 1¾" box and is manufactured by Hassenfeld Bros., Inc. It shows a mother and daughter on the cover. The set gave me the impression that it was meant to be a shared craft with mother. That isn't the case; it is simply two coordinating pictures. The preprinted canvas pictures are in black plastic 9½" x 9¾" frames with colored cardboard backing and plastic clips to keep everything together. The yarn is along the side, and a needle is in one of the canvas pieces. The instruction sheet gives instructions for a tent stitch and says it is not necessary to fill in the background; if you do, you will require extra yarn. **Complete: $25.00 and up.**

Note: This set was advertised in Rockwell's Toyland catalog from Corning, New York, for the retail price of $1.98 in 1959.

Plate 324. Needlepoint comes in a 20½" x 13¾" x 1¼" pasteboard box. Transogram Company copyrighted this set in 1959. The box advertises: "Framed needlepoint pictures ready to hang. Just match the yarn to the picture — Easy needlepoint stitch will do your entire picture." Inside tucked in the inserts, are two 9" x 7", and two 7" x 5½" perforated plastic pictures with frames. Also included are hanks of nylon yarn in the colors needed, a needle threader, and needle. There are no instructions; however on the front of the box, there is an plate of the one stitch you need to do for the entire picture. The set says it is for young girls 6 to 12 years old. **Complete: $25.00 and up.**

Plate 325 Sampler Tapestry Weaving Set #507 is presented in a 18" x 12½" x 1¼" widow box. The set is manufactured by Standard Toycraft circa 1960s. Displayed inside are two tapestries and their patterns with gold cardboard frames, and two more in the center with their patterns. The frames are made so that you can change the tapestry by just pulling out a tab. There are two skeins of yarn Hobby Craft labels in the four colors needed to complete the pictures. In the instructions it advises: *Your color guide pattern is framed ready for weaving. Sew right through tapestry material and color guide.* They show a cross-stitch design, and tell you to use your frame over again for weaving the other tapestry patterns. **Complete: $25.00 and up.**

Plate 325. Deluxe Needlecraft Chest #994 was manufactured by Avalon in 1980. The suitcase type box measures 15½" x 12" x 2¼" and has a plastic handle. This chest has a little bit of everything; it contains 10 complete projects. The contents are coronet knitter, weaving loom and hook, two pre-printed guest towels, two pre-printed handkerchiefs, preprinted stuffed doll pattern, knitting spool, embroidery hoop, two knitting needles, needlepoint, assorted embroidery thread, starter supply of yarn and loopers, thimble, scissors, tape measure, and instruction booklet with project ideas. **Complete: $25.00 and up.**

Plate 327. Beginners' Running Stitch #703P was manufactured by Pastime Industries in 1980. The box is 10" square and 1¼" thick. Inside there are yarn of different colors, plastic needle, plastic canvas, stiffen burlap frame, a color diagram of the design, and an instruction book. The instruction book is very complete with a lot of diagrams and instructions. **Complete: $10.00 and up.**

Plate 328. Needlepoint Box #5791 comes in an 8" x 6" x 3" box and was made by Fisher Price in 1994. As usual Fisher Price has a very nice product. The contents in the box include a two-piece heavy plastic box that has a lid with pre-printed rigid plastic grid, a lid insert with a place to write your name, a metal tapestry needle, yarn, ribbon, silver cord, and a instruction sheet. It is a nice little package and makes up into a lovely durable little box. The instructions are illustrated, and are eight pages long. This is a project even an adult might make for a gift. **Complete: $10.00 and up.**

Note: These box sets also came in a unicorn and star design.

Plate 329. Battat Funart #AC3149 was made by Asica Pongo Inc. in 1996. The box is 9½" x 7" x 2½". A lot of crafts are stuffed into this small box. It contains an adjustable loom for loopers or yarn, four-peg spool knitter, six-peg spool knitter, flower loom, fashion knitter (Coronet), two crochet hooks, looper hook, needle, thimble, loopers, yarn, two sewing cards, knitting needles, and an instruction sheet in English and French. The instruction sheet tells you how to make a potholder with the loopers, a scarf for a doll and a bracelet with the loom, a doll dress with the fashion knitter, a cord with the spools, a yarn flower with the flower loom, and how to knit and crochet. **Complete: $25.00 and up.**

Children's Sewing Card Sets

In the book, *Queen of the Home* published in 1888, Emma Churchman Hewitt wrote:

The question of home amusements is one of much more serious import than is presented upon the surface. There are amusements "and" amusements, and parents should select for their children their amusements, just as carefully as they select their food, clothing or studies; for, as before said, as the child's amusements are, so will the child herself be.

Throughout time, there has been an ongoing battle in child raising over the useful toy versus the whimsy. In the middle 1800s many parents thought building blocks were the most useful toy that they could buy their sons. It was believed that building blocks prepared children for rational thinking. In the middle-class American Victorian nursery it was a must. Little girls occasionally played with blocks, but they were mostly reserved for boys.

Where boys mostly played with wood toys, the girls' favorite materials for toys were cloth, paper, reed, raffia, cord, and yarn. Where boys liked to build things that moved, girls liked to make things that had usefulness and could be given as gifts. Girls' playthings tended to be small, fragile objects that often required quiet, careful handling and encouraged solitary play indoors. In fact, many toys discouraged play altogether; they were so delicate and displayed in such as way that their allure might be ruined if disturbed. While boys were urged to play outside and compete, most families offered less encouragement for girls to play at all. Most of their toys weren't toys at all, but miniature tools to train them to become useful wives and mothers. Parents bought blocks and wagons for boys and bought dolls and sewing toys for girls. The purpose of most girls' toys was to prepare them for their role in life and sewing was one of their duties. Sewing cards were intended to teach this practical lesson. Some early cards had double benefits such as the moral cards that not only taught the child her stitching, but could also remind her of her duties. Once such example is Transogram Company's Gold Medal Sewing Cards (plate 335). The inside lid gives these instructions for the set:

A Pleasant and Useful Playtime Occupation. Follow these suggestions and you will find the use of Gold Medal Sewing Cards one of your happiest playtime occupations. You will like this set immensely, for it will afford you many hours of pleasant, amusement and will help you, like Mother and Big Sister, to make pretty decorative little things for your Home. To use the "Gold Medal Sewing Cards" you must first "perforate" the cards. Perforate means to make a hole through. Take the Sewing Card Perforator which you will find in this Set, pick out the card you wish to sew first and perforate each little dot that

forms the letters or design of the Card. Be sure to get the point of the Perforator right on the dot and do not perforate any dots that are very close together. Be careful not to keep your fingers underneath the line you are perforating.

The instructions go on with step-by-step directions on how to sew the cards and what colors to use, of course always using Transotoy crayons or Gold Medal water colors. The instructions include directions on making secondary colors by mixing the primary colors. The instructions also suggest obtaining a suitable frame, or to hang the card with a ribbon when finished, stating:

Use this set with care and the time you spend with "Gold Medal Sewing Cards" will prove pleasant, useful and gratifying.

Transograms Gold Medal Sewing Cards is the first sewing card set in this chapter that has a printed background. Most of the sets up to this date had plain cards with only pinpricks or dots to be pricked. The child was supposed to be surprised with the subject as it was taking form, by going from dot to dot with the thread. Transogram's president Charles Raizen formed the Toy Research Institute and was one of the first companies to test his toys with the help of a child psychologist. Transogram's stamp not only stated "Gold Medal" but also "Playthings that Serve a Purpose." Later on, in the 1920s, Transogram Company also advertised that their toys were "Kid Tested."

Milton Bradley was another toy manufacturer that had an interest in children's education. Milton Bradley was born in Vienna, Maine, in 1836. As a teenager he became interested in lithography and by 1860, had founded the Milton Bradley Company and the first color lithography shop in Springfield, Massachusetts.

His first moneymaking venture was a lithograph of the clean-shaven face of Abraham Lincoln who had just been nominated for President of the United States. Shortly after the picture, Lincoln decided to grow a beard and that was the end of Milton Bradley's Lincoln sales.

His business was going downhill and he needed a new idea, so he came up with a game called The Checkered Game of Life. The object of the game was to live to a happy, comfortable old age instead of financial ruin. There were 64 squares in his game and the player had to spin a spinner and try to land on a colored square that would bring him good fortune. It is said that Bradley printed the game, assembled it, boxed it, and personally took it to New York. There he sold several hundred to sales managers and news merchants. The game was a success and by 1861 he had sold 45,000 copies of his game.

When the Civil War broke out, Bradley stopped production

on his game and put all his effort into drafting plans for the new percussion-lock Springfield rifle. After spending time with the soldiers, he noticed they needed a diversion to keep their minds off the living conditions and fighting. He went back to the game business and produced a game that was a combination of nine different games; including his checkered game of life, chess, checkers, backgammon, and five variations of dominoes. He packaged it in a small, flat kit and called it Games for Soldiers.

But games weren't Bradley's only interest. In 1869, he went to a lecture given by the founder of the kindergarten movement in the United States, Elizabeth Peabody. Elizabeth Peabody was inspired by the ideas of a German gentleman, Friedrich Froebel. Froebel stressed the socialization of learning through play. He divided the process of early education between birth and age six, into distinct stages of mental and physical development. He had worked with very young children and formulated an idea based on the use of the hands and senses. In *Education of Man*, he states:

The mind grows by self revelation. In play the child ascertains what he can do, discovers his possibilities of will and thought by exerting his power spontaneously. In work he follows a task prescribed for him by another, and does not reveal his own proclivities and Inclinations—but another's in play he reveals his own original power.

Froebel formulated the Kindergarten System, with its emphasis on play and the use of "gifts" (play materials, balls and blocks, etc.) and "occupations" (activities, lacing, coloring, etc.)

Bradley agreed to publish a book on kindergarten education. He became so interested in the movement that he wrote a series of kindergarten manuals and supplementary materials. Milton Bradley Company was given the first award ever created for the teaching of children through play, the Medal of Excellence award at the Centennial Exposition in 1876. It was after this date that the ideas of Froebel became popular. The idea was not always welcome in middle-class homes for their own children.

Most middle-class families believed that rearing a child at home, while also imprinting the morals of the family, was a better way to raise a child. However Froebel's ideas were widely accepted as a means of training immigrant children and children of the slums. The advocates of kindergarten believed the proper training of these children might lead to the elimination of urban poverty. Milton Bradley continued to manufacture the materials needed for kindergarten classes, even though they were not a profitable part of his business. Bradley also put many sewing card sets on the market for middle- and upper-class children to enjoy at home such as Embroidery Cards #4370 (plate 330) and Animal Sewing Cards (plate 331). Realizing the growing acceptance of Froebel's theory, many of the toy companies such as American Toy Works, Samuel Gabriel Sons & Co., and Standard Toykraft Products advertised their activity box toys as Kindergarten Toys.

Indeed, the sewing card was considered an educational tool. In the book *A Sewing Course* written in 1893, Mary Woolman, the author stated:

In early years the child should not be allowed to do fine sewing. Primitive nations used the needle in many ways adapted to the use of children, in coarse weaving; in basketry, in which more or less rigid material was sewed together with softer fibers, such as wool and twisted bark; in mats, hats and baskets of the raffia palm fiber; in braiding; knotting; twining and netting. All of these early steps in household art make an excellent foundation for sewing, and may be used to great advantage in the primary grades, where the awakening power of the child demands work in rapid construction and large adjustments. The articles should be simple in construction and of a character to appeal to their interests. They should be worth doing. Pricked cards are sometimes used, but they are often injurious to the eyes. If they are felt to be a good link between kindergarten and primary the simplest designs should be chosen.

Even though some thought that the cards might be injurious to the eyes, sewing cards have always been good sellers. Educational supply companies always kept them on hand. Peter Rabit and Brother Bruin Series #2 (plate 339), Ideal Sewing Card Set #1 (plate 340), and Ideal Pricked Sewing Cards Set B (plate 343) were all made for kindergarten and grade schools.

In the back of some of the early schoolbooks were designs for sewing cards. School Needlework (#2-S) has 26 cards in the back to be copied for students. Practical Methods, Aids, and Devices for Teachers Vol. II (#17-S) shows spring designs all done in dots and dashes for the teacher to copy off. The subjects are an egg, chick, rabbit, lily, bird, and a kite.

Just before World War II Bradley put out a delightful set, titled Button Pictures #4745 (plate 350). On the inside of the box top is written: *After coloring the design, select the buttons best suited for the composition. Consider the buttons for size and color. If there are not enough buttons of a special kind, divide those you have so they will balance the design. Be sure to sew large buttons upon the large spaces, although small buttons may be used if desired. A small x marks the places on which to sew the buttons. When the buttons are sewn on, write your name upon the second line under the design. Think of some name you would like to call the design. And write it upon the first line. Many of these buttons can be strung to make beautiful necklaces or bracelets. They can also be combined with beads to make many attractive designs.*

The instructions go on to tell you how to make a button flower headband, necklace, and bracelet.

The same year, Samuel Gabriel Sons and Company came out with Button Button Sewing Cards and they advertised:

Entirely different! Consists of six cards with cute full color plates with a large assortment of plastic buttons in beautiful solid tones of green, blue, red, orange, etc., a needle and generous quantity of yarn, and complete directions for sewing the colored buttons onto the plates.

As early as 1920, picture books with pages of sewing cards were offered. Charles E. Graham Company published Picture

Sewing (plate 342). The cover looks much earlier but the pictures indicate the 1920s date. Sewing card books were very popular during World War II when we were trying to conserve paper. They were a lot less costly than the cardboard card sets that were put up in boxes.

After World War II Samuel Gabriel Sons & Company came out with their Picture Weaving Pleasant Pastime #T 180 (plate 356) and National Games with their new set Weave 'N' Sew # 5003 not really a sewing card, but in the sewing category of weaving. Both companies put their sets up in large colorful boxes, and the cards were as bright as the boxes, it seemed like the plain old sewing card had been expanded into a brighter more appealing boxed toy.

Parker Brothers Big Animal Sewing Cards #399 (plate 348) have a direction sheet in their set that is very interesting. It states:

The set is supplied with a sufficient quantity of colored strings to finish two or possibly three cards. There are also three extra Animal Cards (the set has 6 cards altogether) which can be worked by removing the strings from the First Cards finished. The animals are much more interesting by using an assortment of colors rather than to finish one animal in one color. For example, the Cow might be finished with a combination of blue, green and red strings. The plate below shoes how to work the cards so that the strings may be easily removed to finish the other cards.

The instructions go on to show how to sew for easy removal and how to do the removing and says if you desire extra strings, they will be mailed postpaid on receipt of 15 cents for six. This set is totally untouched, and I can see why, what child is going to enjoy sewing a card only having to tear it apart to do another. Where is the pride in doing a good job if you have to take it all out again?

As the sewing cards progressed, they became more interesting, using new and inventive ideas to captivate their young audience. Gig-Sew Series #15 (plate 355) is a perfect example. Small separate pieces were punched out and then sewn onto a larger board to make a complete picture.

One card that was fun to lace over and over were the doll dressing cards. There are eight doll-sewing sets in this chapter. The sets I have found were first made in the 1950s, a square card with the doll printed on, with punch out clothing to add to the doll such as Sew-on Cards (plate 359). Later in the 1960s they became shaped cards with the clothing also shaped to be sewn on such as Sew-on Sally's Clothes #2990 (plate 371) and Holly Hobbie Sew Ons #910D (plate 375).

A set I was captivated with was Dolly Sewing Box #6043 (plate 360). Saalfield Publishing Company published it in 1952.

It has a doll, a bed with bedding and a kitten, the mattress, pillow, doll, and kitten all have to be stuffed with pre-shaped stuffing before sewing all around with yarn. The bottom of the box makes into a bed with the help of a headboard included with the set, you add the mattress, pillow, and a top blanket (all included) and you have a bed to use for your dolly.

In the 1950s the sewing cards became very creative. The manufactures started adding extra pieces to the sets such as bells, pre-shaped stuffing, and often you didn't just stitch around a card, you made a paper toy. There are four sets in this chapter that make a toy such as Tinkle Toy Stuffies to Make #6176 (plate 365). The child sewed the front and back pieces together with preformed stuffing in between and added a jingle bell with a bow at the end. Sew Many Animals (plate 372) has ten animals all with multiple parts to punch out and assemble with yarn ties.

Dress Me Up Professions by Battat Games (plate 376) has the inside of the lid reserved for a note to the parents. It states:

This combination game has been specially designed for entertaining the little ones, at the same time it develops their capacity to handle things and their imagination. By tying and uniting bows, the child acquires skill and manual ability, which is not only recommendable, but is also one of the indispensable factors for aiding the child's correct development. The game consists of suitably dressing the two dolls, whose clothes, shoes and accessories must be chosen by the child from among all those included in the game. There are many possible combinations, but an attempt must be made to dress the doll logically, unless funny results are wanted, which is also and entertaining way of playing. An attempt should be made with the smaller children to get them to overcome the difficulties in handling the woolen strings on passing them through the different holes and they must also be helped to tie the final bow holding them tight. At the same they may be encouraged to name the different items while they are dressing the doll: the shoes, the bow, etc. The slightly older children should be required to give an overall view of the clothing and its function: for winter, for summer, etc. and they should give the fullest possible details of each garment: I am putting a very thick, green woolen jersey on Charles because it is very cold, etc. Finally when all the dolls have been dressed and have been placed on their respective stands, the child may be asked to make up and tell a story: On a very cold day in January, they went out... This set was well thought out.

From the beginning, sewing cards were made to teach children dexterity and hand/eye coordination. Children have used them for at least 100 years and they are still being sold as an educational product.

Plate 330. Embroidery Cards #4370 were manufactured by the Milton Bradley Company, circa 1900. It is a large box, 13" x 10" x 1¼" with a wonderful lithograph of children skating on ice. There are five sections in the box. The largest section holds 7½" x 5½" pinpricked cards of an egg and chick, boys and snowman, blacksmith, windmill, and cardinal. The two trays above, each hold six 5½" x 4" cards including a moose, anchor, sheep, puss in boots, star, owl, vase, shield, beehive, swan, sickle, and Cinderella and the Prince. The small section below holds six 5½" x 3½" cards that are evenly pricked in rows and columns, to make your own designs. Completing the set are assorted colors of cotton floss to use in sewing the cards and a color sample sheet with drawings of the cards completed. **Complete: $50.00 and up.**

Plate 331. Animal Sewing Cards, circa 1900, are in a 7½" x 5½" x 1" box that is not numbered. The box is covered with a paisley-print paper with a lithographed animal picture applied to the top. Printed inside the box lid is this message to adults: *This box, besides the cards, contains a variety of colored threads for working the designs. These cards are made by a patented process and are ready for working, the holes being already perforated at the proper points. The lines to be sewed are represented by the printed dots. After a design is completed tell the child what it represents, its history, etc. Milton Bradley Co.* The cards are 5½" x 4", and included are a moose, penguin, cardinal, sitting rabbit, rat, a kitten reading, bear, sitting dog, sitting cat, horse, running dog, and a bird in a nest. Some of the cards are finished. This set has the thread wrapped around cardboard thread spools, which are printed "Milton Bradley Co. Springfield Mass. Educational Home Amusements." **Complete: $25.00 and up.**

Plate 332. Animal Sewing Cards #4223 are by Milton Bradley Company, circa 1905. The box measures 7½" x 5½" x 1". The cards are 5½" x 4", this is a pinpricked set of animal cards with some already sewn. The animals are a rabbit, both sitting and running; dog, both sitting and running; sheep; moose; bear; kittens; and a piggy going to market. Included in the set are sewing floss and a sewing needle. The sewing floss was presented in a loop with a loose knot and I believe this is correct for this set. **Complete: $25.00 and up.**

Plate 333. Flower Sewing Cards #4227 is in a 7½" x 5½" x 1" box, circa 1905. The Milton Bradley Company manufactured this set. The cards are 5½" x 4" and are pinpricked for a needle and sewing thread. There are ten cards, all are flowers, among them are a tulip, a daisy, a lily, and a water lily. A few of the cards are completed and the floss in this box is looped and secured with a loose knot. **Complete: $25.00 and up.**

Plate 334. Sewing Cards Animals was manufactured by Parker Brothers, circa 1910. The paper-covered box measures 7½" x 5½" x 1", and applied to the top is a lithograph of a sweet little girl sitting in a wicker rocker and sewing. The ten pinpricked cards are the same size as the box. Each card has been finished with colored sewing thread by a previous owner. The cards are all of animals and include a horse, horse's head, deer, buffalo, elephant, bear, rabbit, fox and hounds, kangaroo, and a big horn goat. **Complete: $25.00 and up.**

Plate 335. Gold Medal Sewing Cars, To Sew, Color and Frame was manufactured by the Transogram Company, circa 1920. The box measures 13" x 9½" x 1½". The front of the box has the Gold Medal seal, which says "Playthings That Serve a Purpose." The box is paper covered with an applied print to the top. The five cards inside are 9" x 7" and each one is to be colored and stitched. In the set is a perforator for punching the holes in the cards yourself. Each card has a well-known motto such as "Never Find Yourself Idle," "Forgive and Forget," "Practice Makes Perfect," "Mother Dear" (with a place for a picture), and "Live and Let Live." Every card has been worked and finished. Two are signed on the back: "Olive Katharine Jameson age 8 1914." To complete this set, are six (used) Transotoy crayons, a perforator, a needle, and some green and white floss. **Complete: $50.00 and up.**

Note: A larger Gold Medal Sewing Cards set with the same graphics had a watercolor set included.

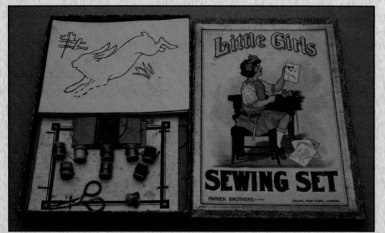

Plate 336. Little Girls Sewing Set, manufactured circa 1920 by Parker Brothers Company, is in a 10" x 7" x 1¼" paper-covered box wit h a lithographed picture applied to the top. The cards inside are 7" x 5" and are pinpricked for sewing thread. There are four cards, as depicted on the front of the box. Two have been finished and two have been started. There is a decorated insert with two cards and eight tiny wooden spools of cotton thread attached, but I believe originally there may have been 12 spools. Also attached to the card is a tiny 2¼" metal scissors and a small metal thimble. **Complete: $50.00 and up.**

Plate 337. Animal Sewing Cards manufactured by J.W. Spears & Sons, Ltd. (Spears Games), circa 1920. The box measures 14¼" x 9" x 1". The box top states it is an "improved editon." The cards are 7½" x 6", each is beautifully colored, and signed "Spears." Every card in this set has been finished with a backstitch using twisted floss. The subjects are a camel, dog, sheep, horse, cat and kitten, and ostrich. There is one hank of floss that was not used. **Complete: $50.00 and up.**

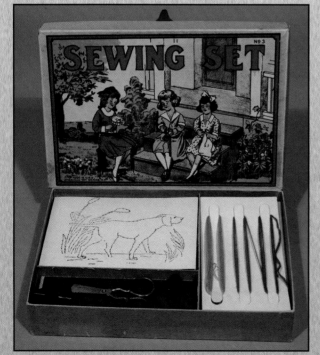

Plate 338. Sewing Set #3 was manufactured by American Toy Works, circa 1920. The box measures 10" x 6½" x 1¾". Inside are three sections, one with four 6" x 4" pinpricked cards of a dog, steer, pears and a painting easel. Another section has thread, and the last has metal blunt-nose scissors, a needle, and a tiny thimble. **Complete: $50.00 and up.**

Note: The graphics on this box were also shown on embroidery set Embroidery & Needleworkd #7 ART. See plate 264.

Plate 339. Peter Rabbit and Brother Bruin Series #2 are presented in a 7½" x 5½" brown envelope. The set was manufactured by Hall & McCreary Company and was copyrighted in 1920. There are six cards with Peter Rabbit (no clothing) and six cards of Brother Bear. These cards are not pricked; there are light dots where the needle goes in but the cards are all solid. They are to be pricked, sewn, and colored. There are four extra cards that are samples of other Hall & McCreary sets. The sample cards are Tom the Piper's Son from the Mother Goose Series #1, an elephant from the Circus Friends Series #3, a turkey from the Familiar Birds Series #4, and a horse from Familiar Animals Series #5. **Complete: $25.00 and up.**

Plate 340. Ideal Sewing Cards Set #1 comes in a 9½" x 6½" orange envelope. The Ideal School Supply Company made the set, circa 1920. The cards are to be pricked, sewn with yarn, and colored by the child. There are two subjects on each card, and there are 25 cards. Some of the cards are seasonal; others are flowers, fruits, animals, children, birds, etc. **Complete: $25.00 and up.**

Plate 341. Spear's Perforated Sewing Cards are from circa 1920. The box measures 8¾" x 4¾" x ¾", and was manufactured by J.W. Spears & Sons, Ltd. (Spears Games). On the outside of the box the flowers are named; on the cards inside of the box they aren't. There are six 3¾" x 3" pinpricked flower cards. The flowers are a daffodil, tulip, crocus, daisy, carnation, and rose. The cards are pre-colored with lines showing where the stitches should go and the colors that should be used. Most of the cards have been started and some are completely finished. **Complete: $25.00 and up.**

Plate 342. Picture Sewing is a delightful little 9¾" x 7" book, circa 1920s. It has seven pages of pictures, all with a little rhyme to go with each picture. Charles E. Graham & Company published it. There are instructions on the first page: *Provide yourself with needle and colored worsted and when ready to start, punch a small hole in the dot on which you intend to start. Knot the end of your yarn, and draw it through first hole from the back of picture and from then on always punch the second dot ahead so that you will know just where the next stitch from the wrong side is to come. Always cross from one dot to another on reverse side and then you will have a continuous picture in Yarn. Select colors that match the natural colors of the subjects. Do not draw the yarns too tight or the cards will bend. When you have finished, paste a piece of plain white paper on the back of each subject to cover knots and rough work.* **Complete: $75.00 and up.**

Plate 343. Ideal Pricked Sewing Cards Set B was made by Ideal School Supply Company, circa 1930. The box measures 7¼" x 3¾" x 1¾". Inside are 100 pinpricked sewing cards, some are 3½" square, others are 3¼" round. Obviously these cards are for a school, as the subjects are repeated more than once. Some of the subjects are fruits, vegetables, household items, shapes, and designs. **Complete: $25.00 and up.**

Plate 344. Easy to Do Large Hole Sewing Cards, circa 1930, are from the Milton Bradley Company. The box measures 12" x 7" x 1½". The cards are 6½" x 5". There are 10 cards, including two clocks, two bubble pipes, horseshoe, milk pail, milk can, heart, balloon, and pear. Thin wool yarn and a blunt needle complete this set. **Complete: $25.00 and up.**

Plate 345. Sewing Cards is a 12½" x 10½" book with four pages to sew and was published by Saalfield Publishing Company in 1935. The cover art is signed Corinne Bailey and every page has her initials. The pictures cover the whole page and consist of a boy fishing, Puss in Boots, Mary-Mary Quite Contrary, and a Sailboat. **Complete: $10.00 and up.**

Plate 346. Princess Elizabeth Wool Sewing Set #501 comes in a 6¾" square box 1" thick. Standard Toycraft Products copyrighted the set in 1937. The cards are 6½" x 5¼". On the outside of the box it says it is "without needles," and has educational subjects. The educational subjects are a parrot, castle, and Princess Elizabeth. Included in the box was three metal-tipped pieces of wool. **Complete: $25.00 and up.**

Note: I have seen this set in a larger rectangular box still with just three cards. Different picture cards I've seen in these sets are a flower (shown on the box) and a sailor.

Plate 347. More Work with Yarn #2147 is a 12½" x 10½" eight-page book copyrighted in 1937 by Saalfield Publishing Company. The cover is signed, "The Bailey's." The inside cover states: *This book contains 8 patterns, 4 crayons, 4 colors of yarn, 1 needle. It is made for children who like to color and sew. Sew along the outlines with the colored yarns and then color in with the crayons. The back cover suggests the colors to use. The pictures you make will be pretty enough to hang on the wall. Corinne Ruigrl Bailey.* The pictures in the book are a fish, rooster, soldier, ship, castle, toys and blocks, Little Miss Muffet, and a vase of flowers. **Complete: $25.00 and up.**

Plate 348. Big Animal Sewing Cards #399, circa 1940, was manufactured by Parker Brothers Inc. The box is 10½" x 8¾" x 1". Inside is an instruction sheet on sewing the cards with plates. The six realistic sewing cards are 10" x 6¾", and include a cat, cow, elephant, rhino, mountain goat, and collie dog. There are six colored rayon cords with cellophane tips that complete the set. **Complete: $25.00 and up.**

Plate 349. Glitter Straws, circa 1940, is another clever idea from Samuel Gabriel Sons & Company. The box is 13½" x 10¼" x 1". The six cards are 8" x 6½" and are to be laced with colored cellophane straws. The subject's are a boat, lamp, basket of flowers, house, chair, and a bird in a cage. **Complete: $25.00 and up.**

Plate 350. Button Pictures #4745 is in a 9¾" x 7¾" x 1¼" box. Milton Bradley Company made this set in 1940. Printed on the front of the box is "Button Pictures to Sew…and so to make Designs. An educational and pleasurable activity for little children." There was a lot of provenance that came with this set. Inscribed on the lid is "Eleanor Ruth Bullock from Grandpa & Aunt Nora." All of the cards are finished. Eleanor Ruth Bullock signed two of the cards and she shared with her friends, Amelia and Melissa, as they each signed their finished card. The remaining three cards, I assume, were also done by Eleanor. **Complete: $50.00 and up.**

Plate 351. Jolly Dolly Sewing Cards #T184 was manufactured by Samuel Gabriel Sons & Company circa 1940. The box is 15" x 9" x 1". There are six 9" x 6½" cards of adorable children, three girls and three boys. Included in the set are six metal-tipped cotton laces. **Complete: $25.00 and up.**

Plate 352. Darlings Sewing Cards #T111 were manufactured by Samuel Gabriel Sons & Company, circa 1940. The box measures 9¼" x 9" x 1". There are four 8½" x 6" cards, three girls and a boy. There are also four metal-tipped laces. **Complete: $25.00 and up.**

Plate 353. Pictures to Sew is a 7¾" x 6¾" book and was copyrighted in 1942 by The Saalfield Publishing Company. The graphics are signed D+D Downs. There are eight pages in the book and one line of instruction: "Sew from dot to dot with colored yarn. Color with your crayons." **Complete: $10.00 and up.**

Plate 354. Sewing Pictures is an eight-page book that measures 10½" x 8½", and is copyrighted 1944 by Samuel Lowe Company. Inside, on the back of the first page, are the directions that state: *In Mother's knitting bag or work basket are many short pieces of bright colored yarn. Ask mother for the yarn and for a needle with a big eye. First puncture holes in the sewing sheet at the points indicated by little black dots on the printed side of the sheet. Then thread the needle with a piece of bright colored yarn and start to sew from the blank side of the sheet. Follow the dots by always covering the black lines connecting the dots. Fasten the yarn on the reverse side and start again whenever a separate object is indicated. Different colors often make the yarn pictures more interesting. When the sewing sheet is complete, color the pictures with crayon or watercolors.* The book is of thin tan paper all printed in black; the cover is just a tad bit heavier. It is obvious the book was printed during World War II when paper was being conserved. **Complete: $10.00 and up.**

Plate 355. Gig-Sew Kit Series #15 was manufactured by AJA in Chicago. It came in an 8½" x 7" envelope and was copyrighted in 1945. It is a clever idea for sewing cards; there are small pieces on separate cards to be punched out and matched to the pictures on the 8" x 6½" cards and then stitched in place with yarn. The pictures included in this set are a clown, house, sailboat, and a girl in the rain. **Complete: $25.00 and up.**

Plate 356. Picture Weaving Pleasant Pastime #T180 was manufactured by Samuel Gabriel Sons & Co. circa 1945. The box is 14" x 11½" x 1". On the bottom of the box top is a banner that reads "To Keep Busy The Little Hands And Little Head," a statement that was used in Samuel Gabriel Sons & Company advertising for at least a decade. Inside this set there are three compartments. Two, contain seven 8½" x 6½" colored cards with slits to weave ½" paper strips through. The third compartment contains colorful paper strips. **Complete: $25.00 and up.**

Plate 357. Du-Tu Weave 'N' Sew #5003 was manufactured by National Games, circa 1945. The box is 12½" x 11" x 1½". The contents are six 9" x 6" cards, three dolls of France, Greece, and Poland for weaving, and three sewing cards, a fish, a kitten, and a picture of the sun and flowers. Also included are paper strips, various colored-yarn, and a metal needle. A completely untouched set, the holes are not even punched out. There is a little paper from National Games saying: *This activity set is designed to teach colors and coordination of little girls busy minds and fingers. The dolls of different nations can be given multi-colored dresses by weaving the colored paper strands through their skirts. The sewing cards are perforated so that the colored threads can be sewn right into the various patterns.* **Complete: $25.00 and up.**

Plate 358. Furry Sewing Cards #305 are manufactured by Built Rite. The box measures 11" x 7" x 1" and is circa 1950. There are two compartments inside, one holds five rolls of yarn with plastic tips, the other holds five 8¾" x 6¾" flocked cards to sew, the subjects are cowboy, girl on a swing, mice and a boot, ball and whistle, and a teddy bear. **Complete: $10.00 and up.**

Plate 359. Sew-On Cards were manufactured by Ed-U-Cards in 1951. The box is 13" x 8¼" x 1¼". The cards are 8" x 5½". There are three girls and two boys to dress. Each doll has an outfit, there are a few hints, as to which outfit goes with which doll, such as, one boy has a cowboy hat, and there is a cowboy suit available. There are seven metal-tipped laces. **Complete: $25.00 and up.**

Plate 360. Dolly Sewing Box #6043 comes in a 14½" x 11½" x 1½" box. The box top graphics are signed by Ben Greenberg. Saalfield Publishing Company copyrighted the set in 1952. The set comes with a 10" cardstock doll, kitten, bed, mattress, pillow, and bedspread. There is an instruction sheet that comes with the set and it states: *There is a shaped piece of padding for the doll, the kitty, the pillow and the mattress. Put the padding between the front and back pieces of each toy and sew together with the colored yarn, using a running stitch. Assemble the dolly's bed as it is shown on the box top. Then you can put dolly to bed and cover her with the pink bedspread.* **Complete: $25.00 and up.**

Plate 361. Easy Sewing Cards #310A was manufactured by The Platt & Munk Company, Inc., circa 1950s. The box measures 10¾" x 9" x 1". There are five cards in the box. They have been all laced by the previous owner. The cards are 10" x 7" and include girl with flower, girl with house, girl on elephant, kitten, and bird figure. **Complete: $10.00 and up.**

Plate 362. Toymakers Sewing Cards #6037 was manufactured by the Saalfield Publishing Co. in 1953. The box top graphics are signed Mager. The box measures 15½" x 8¾" x 1½". The sewing cards in this set are shaped with two sides, that get folded together and then whip stitched around and the ends tied into a bow. Most make about a 5½" x 4" toy when completed. The 14 cards in the set include a penguin, tulip, train, "Kaliko" Kat, cup, piggy bank, puppy, butterfly, stuffed horse, apple, doll, clown, teddy bear, and gingerbread boy. Also included are plastic tipped laces. **Complete: $25.00 and up.**

Plate 363. Sewing Card Book and Sew-On Clothes #2556 was published by the Samuel Lowe Company in 1953. The original price was 25 cents. The book is 13" x 10" and has five pages of cards and dolls with clothing to be sewn. There are six sewing cards 8" x 6" and five paper dolls ranging in sizes of 11½" to 4¼" taken from previously published books, #1045 Playtime Pals, #1284 Toni, and #1252 Rockabye. Stapled to the book are two cellophane tipped laces for sewing. **Complete: $25.00 and up.**

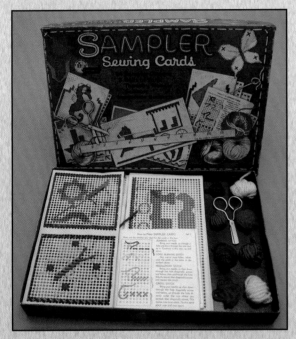

Plate 364. Sampler Sewing Cards #6175 is in a 16" x11" x 1¾" box. The graphics are signed Mager. Saalfield Publishing Company made this set in 1954. It contains ten 10½" x 5¾" cards with pictures of a pagoda, bull, surrey and horse, fire engine, lion, duck, house, and train. There are sixteen 5¼" x 5¾" cards with pictures of tugboat, whale, tulip, rooster, cherries, pineapple, dog, cat, owl, squirrel, flower, butterfly, schoolhouse, apple tree, seahorse, and fish. There are two instruction sheets that show the stitches, with a color chart that tells how much yarn to cut for each card. To complete the set are eight balls of yarn, a needle, and a pair of blunt-nose metal scissors. There is also a ruler to measure the yarn printed on the cover of the box. **Complete: $25.00 and up.**

Plate 365. Tinkle Toy Stuffies to Make #6176 was manufactured by The Saalfield Publishing company in 1954. The box measures 16" x 11" x 1¾". Ben Greenberg signed the cartoon type graphics. Inside are 15 double-sided cards to stitch together, each with a matching shape of filling, a rayon cord, and a jingle bell. The toys to make are doll, lion, blue bird, bear, kitten, puppy, skunk, chipmunk, owl, cowboy, elephant, penguin, pig, ducky, and bunny. Six are already made up. **Complete: $25.00 and up.**

Plate 366. Jingle Dingle Sewing Card Kit with buttons and bells was manufactured by Pressman Toy Corporation, circa 1955. The box measures 14" x 10" x 1½" and is copyrighted by Leon Jason. Inside are four 10" x 8¼" cards, Jingle Dingle at the Circus, Jingle Dingle at the Park, Jingle Dingle playing outside, and Jingle Dingle on the Farm. Jingle Dingle was a clown on a 1950s television show. Included in the kit are yarn, bells, and buttons to sew on the cards. **Complete: $25.00 and up.**

Note: Pressman Toy Corporation also came out with a Jingle Dingle Sewing-N-Embroidery Apron Kit (plate 248).

Plate 367. Six Sewing Cards #4600, circa 1950s, was manufactured by Whitman Publishing Company. The attractive box measures 8½" square and is 1" thick. The cards inside are 8¼" x 6¼" and the subjects are nursery rhymes including Humpty Dumpty, Jack be nimble, Rock a bye Baby, Old Woman in a Shoe, Little Bo Peep and Polly put the kettle on. Six cellophane-tipped yarn pieces complete the set. **Complete: $10.00 and up.**

Plate 368. Six Sewing Cards #4600, circa 1950s, was manufactured by Whitman Publishing Company. The box measures 8½" square and is 1" thick. The eight cards inside measure 8¼" x 6¼" and are all pictures of toys. Included are a duck on wheels, toy airplane, doll, teddy bear, jack in the box, and a clown marionette. Completing the set are six cellophane-tipped yarn laces. **Complete: $10.00 and up.**

Plate 369. Six Sewing Cards #4600, circa 1950s, was manufactured by Whitman Publishing Company. The box is 8½" square and is 1" thick. The eight cards inside are 8¼" x 6¼" and are of animals, insects, or birds including a rooster, tiger, lamb, squirrel, bees, and a duck. Included in the set are six cellophane-tipped yarn laces. **Complete: $10.00 and up.**

Plate 370. Sewing Card Carnival #6879 comes in a 8½" x 6½" x 2½" box. Saalfield Publishing Co. manufactured the set in 1963. It states on the outside of the box "14 tickets to fun," and inside are 14 sewing cards. The subjects are a cow, rooster, bunny, mountain goat, calf, puppy, chick, collie dog, kitten, pig, lamb, sheep, donkey, and pony. There are also 14 yarn laces with plastic tips. **Complete: $10.00 and up.**

Plate 371. Sew-On Sally's Clothes #2990 was manufactured by Samuel Lowe Publishing Company, circa 1960. Sally is 13½" high and 6" wide with the cards still stapled to her body. There are four cardboard outfits to punch out and lace to Sally. Included with the doll are three plastic-tipped laces. **Complete: $5.00 and up.**

Note: There was also a Sew-on Sherry Ann's clothes #2904 made the same way.

Plate 372. Sew Many Animals #4798 was manufactured in 1967 by Whitman Publishing Company. The box measures 14¾" x 5" x 2". The set comes with ten animals to punch out and assemble using the ten plastic-tipped yarn laces. This set was obviously enjoyed, as all but one animal was assembled. The animals are alligator, bear, hippopotamus, camel, penguin, tiger, kangaroo, elephant, giraffe, and lion. **Complete: $25.00 and up.**

Children's Sewing Card Sets

Plate 373. Sew By Number #1309 was manufactured by Platt & Munk Company, Inc. in 1969. The box is 11" x 8½" x 1¼". The box has the Child Guidance Educational Activity Seal. The six cards are 10½" x 6½" and each hole is numbered so you can follow the numbers when doing the sewing. The subjects are children picking apples, children playing with a kitten, pink elephant, puppy, train, and Dutch boy. Six plastic-tipped laces complete the set. **Complete: $10.00 and up.**

Plate 374. Let's Walk in the Park Sewing Cards #4669 was made by Whitman under Western Publishing Company in 1973. There are six 14½" x 8¼" cards to be punched out into shapes then sewed together to be made into a park, complete with benches, jungle gyms, picnic benches, and a popcorn stand. To complete the set are nine pieces of yarn with plastic-tips, four finger-puppets to play in the park and a policeman to watch over them. **Complete: $10.00 and up.**

Plate 375. Holly Hobbie Sew Ons #910 D is a Colorforms Inc. product. It comes in a 12½" x 8" x 1" box, and was copyrighted in 1975. There are four thick pasteboard cards to punch out including a Holly Hobbie doll, a friend, and a cat. There are six dresses, all with hats to be laced onto the dolls. Two synthetic yarn pieces with plastic-tips complete the set. **Complete: $10.00 and up.**

Plate 376. Dress Me Up LaCage Professions #3002 Battat Games, was manufactured and copyrighted by Sallent Hermanos in 1987. It comes in a 13" x 9" x 1¼" box. You get two genetically correct 10¼" pasteboard dolls, a girl and boy, to dress up in clothing representing different professions, such as Chef, Ballet Dancer, etc. The set includes, shoes, hair ornaments, things to hold in hands, and etc. **Complete: $10.00 and up.**

Plate 377. Sesame Street Sewing Box #230 was manufactured by Sandberg Manufacturing Company, circa 1988. The box measures 11¼" x 8¾" x 11". The set comes with a wooden sewing box, Bert & Ernie hardboard figures, and six sets of clothing, including farmer, pajamas, fireman uniform, baseball uniform, police uniform, and doctor, they all include hats. There are also five colored wooden spools, and three plastic-tipped laces. **Complete: $25.00 and up.**

Plate 378. Lacing Bears LR-2521 was made by Lauri, Inc. and copyrighted in 1988. The box measures 8½" square by 1" thick. The box top reads: *Lace the 3 bears, their house and Goldilocks. After the pieces are laced, they will stand using the rubber bases. Suggested lacing creations are shown, but the real fun is for kids to be the designers.* The set contains three bears, a house, and Goldilocks, made from chipboard, ten laces and five foam rubber bases. **Complete: $10.00 and up.**

Plate 379. Bear Lacing Box #530 is 9½" x 7¼" x 2¼". Made of all wood it is crafted by hand and copyrighted by Lights, Camera, Interaction, circa 2000. The bear is painted on the sliding lid of the box. In the box are 35 wooden pieces, clothing, shoes, and accessories to lace onto the bear. It also has four colored laces and is all contained in the box. **Complete: $10.00 and up.**

Plate 380. Fun-n-Learn Learning Sewing comes in a plastic carry box and is manufactured by The Eagle School, circa 2000. The box is 8¼" x 6" x 2½". Inside are four plastic shapes of a teddy bear, bunny rabbit, kitten, and duck. There are also two plastic spools and four plastic-tipped laces. **Complete: $10.00 and up.**

Plate 381. Lace-Up Dress-Up comes from Creative Toys Ltd., circa 2000. It comes in an 11¾" x 8" x 1¾" box. There are two dolls a boy and girl, six lacing cords, and 11 complete outfits, some even including hats, 42 pieces in all. There is an instruction sheet included with directions on lacing on the dolls clothing, and also for playing a game with another player. **Complete: $10.00 and up.**

Children's Knitting, Crochet, and Weaving Sets

Weaving is one of our ancestor's first efforts at becoming civilized we used it for shelter, tools, and clothing. Whenever primitive man began to use his hand for creating, he began to make articles for his convenience. The weaving of grasses, bark, twigs, and reeds to make baskets, hats, and mats was some of the first done by man. The earliest records of weaving have been found as far apart as Egypt, Peru, China, and Mexico. There is a painting on the walls of Ben Hassan's Egyptian tomb 2500 B. C. that shows an upright loom and weavers. Account books have been found in the Chaldean City of Ur that give the records of weavers working as early as 2200 B. C.

American weaving dates back to the pre-Inca, along with other South American civilizations, proven by woven fabric found in excavations. The Native Americans wove flax, hemp, grasses, and animal hair. Starting with simple weaving, they progressed to creative complex designs, and wove them into their fabrics. Their looms were similar to those found in Egypt. The weaving of Native Americans is well documented in American history. The Algonquin tribes have proof of early woven fabric, as their ancient earthenware vessels bear the impressions of fabric or cord used during their construction. In the ancient rock shelters of the Ozark Mountains, fishnets, woven bags, sandals, and overshoes of woven grass have been found.

The earliest settlers also brought weaving to America. Most women either married or single were spinners; linen was the first American-made cloth in the colonies.

There were few sheep, and most families only had a flax wheel with which to spin. As more sheep were imported and bred more families invested in, and found room for the much larger walking spinning wheel. Because wool was so scarce and its warmth so sought after, a new kind of cloth called linsey-woolsey was invented by the early Americans. The warp was of linen thread, and the weft was of the scarce wool, it was used for most everything from clothing to household use.

Most villages had professional weavers who wove for their living, supplying the colonies with the needed cloth. At the turn of the eighteenth century itinerant weavers carried their looms in wagons from farm to farm, stopping at each to gather the threads the women had spun that year and turn them into cloth. Not every woman had a weaver, indeed some made their cloth entirely from scratch, securing the fibers, preparing them, spinning, and finally weaving them into cloth.

In many colonial homes little girls learned their first weaving on a lap loom, held between the legs. These were also called tape looms, and they made simple white linen tape. As the child became more experienced at weaving they advanced to making shoe laces, suspenders, and hatbands. Some children learned to use a lucet (a tool in the shape of a wishbone) to make strong cords and drawstrings to use for fastening corset stays. For most children the weaving of cords and tapes was the only weaving they were expected to do.

The Child's Welfare Co. in Chicago advertised in 1920 that you could make your child a master weaver by buying and using their looms. They made a loom for a doll rug, a loom for a doll beaded necklace, and the Welfare loom that was 10¼" x 8¼" x 6½" with treadles and shifters like the industrial loom that weaves dolls rugs, carpets, and scarves, teaching the industrial principle of weaving. Pastime Occupations Tam O Shanter (plate 382) is one of their products. It is a wooden circular weaving frame that has already been started to insure the loom would be threaded and started in the proper manner. The directions are: *To finish Tam O'Shanter which is started on the frame weave as begun until you get to the edge of the frame, pushing wool toward the center as you weave. This makes the cap firm and strong. When the yarn gets short, tie on another strand alternating in colors to give stripes shown in figure 3. When you have woven to edge of frame push loops off with needle. Draw the last thread a little tighter until the tam is properly shaped. A piece of elastic should be sewed all around the edge on the under side.* Even though no dolls are present in the Child Welfare sets, dolls are certainly used as a vehicle in which to sell the sets, knowing every little mother wants her baby to be in style.

Spears Games had a wooden loom that came out in 1940 and was aimed at the little girl to make useful things, such as a needle case, sectioned cushions, egg cosys, serviette rings, dusters, and washing flannels. Spear's loom gave you directions to do two types of fabrics, a ribbed fabric, and a linen fabric. The directions for the ribbed fabric are thus: *The long strands are stretched singly. Weave one over and one under. To obtain a nice firm edge double the outside long strands and draw the weaving needle between them.* The directions for the linen fabric are *The long strands are stretched double and the weaving needle is drawn through the double strand, one over and one under.* What I find interesting about most children's weaving sets and the directions is the simple lack of the proper terminology for the threads, why they could not have explained the proper language and used "warp" and "weft" is a mystery to me.

The Concord Waving Loom #860 (plate 386) made in 1943 trys to give the correct terminology for one of the threads, but misspells it. The directions state *To start weaving wind as much wool on the shuttle as it will hold, taking into consideration that the shuttle must pass through the threads. Then cut the wool. When all the wool on the shuttle has been used, repeat this process. Take care to tie the wool neatly so that all knots will be on the down side. This loom is already strung and is ready for weaving by tipping the bar backwards and forwards. This changes the position of the thread so that the threads are lifted alternately. The shuttle is slipped between the threads over and under. By straightening the lifting bar, the woven material can be pushed into place. Stop the weaving about two inches from the end of the loom. Remove the tilting bar and then cut the wrap[sic] threads at the bottom of the loom tying them together in pairs and, then lift the entire mat from the other end of the loom.*

K L Weaving Loom (plate 398) was sold through FAO Schwartz and is a real table loom not just a toy. It could hold a 10" width of warp threads and has a roller on one end so that the length of the weaving could be rolled up as it is woven, allowing the weaving to be longer than the length of the frame. The directions are very detailed and give you the parts of the loom, as well as how to string it and weave. It is pre-strung and has the work started, like most of the wooden looms shown in this chapter. It is unfortunate the maker didn't do more advertising than the KW logo, as this is a very nice loom for a child, obviously FAO Schwartz also thought so, they carried it for at least 14 years in their catalog.

It's hard to believe today with our plethora of toys on the market and the toy department stores front and center in every mall, that once toys were only bought for Christmas, Easter, and birthdays. For years the toy manufactures and retailers had been trying to figure out how to sell toys to the public the whole year through, even to the point of launching a Children's Day.

In 1927 Children's Day was established as the third Saturday in June. Endorsed by the Better Play for Children League, staunchly supported by the American Doll Manufactures' Association and leading toy manufactures and buyers. There even became a Children's Day promotion committee, and every year there would be prizes for the best advertisements in newspapers, best window displays, and sales promotions featuring Children's Day. Even with Children's Day, the toy industry wasn't increasing the sales and profits and most stores needed to stay open all year.

In the January 1945 issue of *Playthings* magazine there was a large article about handicrafts and hobbycrafts. The article, written by Paul Auer, was about increasing sales not just at the holidays, but all year through with merchandise that has no season "hobbycrafts." Paul Auer wrote: *The increased interest manifested in craft pursuits may be attributed, in part to the schools where courses in domestic science now supplement the familiar three R's. Boy's and girl's camps, too, have been responsible for the growing popularity of crafts. The toy manufactures, who ever since the beginning of the American toy industry have strived to produce playthings embodying "do with" properties, have done their part to popularize crafts. Outside agencies have also lent their support to the craft move-ment. In the final analysis, however, it is the retailer who must carry crafts to the heights, which they are capable of attaining. Among the handicraft items which should be featured during the next few months are bead weaving sets, leather working set, metal tapping, knitting, embroidery outfits, basket weaving set, soap sculpturing and all manner of construction kits.*

It was about this time that H. Davis came out with the Davis Loom #600 (plate 392) it is shown with both a boy and girl on the cover. "Pat. Pending" was on the box and booklet inside. It advertised on the box that it would make potholders, afghans, mats, ties, and purses. In the pamphlet it illustrated potholders, mats, scarfs, sweaters, afghans, bedspreads, and bags. The metal loom was adjustable to make four to seven inch squares, and their relative rectangles. The instructions showed how to loop the loom and weave, and how to take the weaving off the loom and finish it off or join it to others.

There were also directions on using baby, sport, worsted, or rug yarn for the squares, which could be made into bedspreads, bags, afghans, scarves, and sweaters. In the 1950s Davis came out with the Davis New Adjustable Loom for Boys and Girls #602 (plate 397). The set was in a bigger box and came with more jersey loopers and Davis yarn, but the loom wasn't as nice. It was still made of metal and adjustable but the teeth were farther apart and you could only use four ply and worsted weight yarn. The looper pads would be made thinner also. The instruction sheet was the same but using only the heavier yarns.

The looper sets I remember as a child were more like the Nelly Bee Metal Weaving Loom 102 (plate 399) — a small box, a stationary painted metal loom, jersey loopers, and a metal hook to pull the loopers through. There are instructions in the pamphlet of this set on using the loom with yarn on the back, but the weave is so loose because of the large spaces between the teeth you couldn't make anything except a doily. I don't remember using yarn but I do remember everyone in my family having more than one jersey loop potholder made by me. Weaving has always been more of a game than work for most children. Knitting is altogether another subject, in colonial America one of the first needle arts children learned was knitting, it was a necessity.

When knitting was first originated, no one really knows. According to Mary Thomas in her book *Mary Thomas Knitting Book*, historians place the date about A. D. 200. However, there is the legend that Christ's knitted garment was seamless and Roman soldiers cast lots for it because it could not be divided without destroying it. This places knitting at an earlier date. Mary Thomas goes on to write that Arabs and Mediterranean sailors were the first knitters.

The master knitters were members of the guilds. A boy served as an apprentice for three years, working and studying in his master's shop and another three years traveling to learn new methods, styles, and designs from foreign shop keepers. To earn his place in a guild he had to complete a knitted beret, woolen shirt, a pair of hose with Spanish clocks (designs), and a carpet with a design of flowers, foliage, birds, and animals in natural colors.

To begin the process, the apprentice had to submit his design in color, swearing under oath, that it was his own original work. Once this was accepted, he was then informed of the workshop in which he was to perform his work. The four items were to be finished in thirteen weeks. If all these items were completed satisfactorily, he then earned the title of Master and member of the guild.

In the fifteenth and sixteenth centuries knitting and hosiery guilds were formed throughout Europe and England. These Guilds bought the art of knitting to perfection. Brocade knitting was practiced after the introduction of silk to Europe. It involved knitting with several colors and often adding gold or silver threads in outstanding patterns of intricate floral designs. The use of silk completely changed the appearance of knitting. The master knitters were in awe of it and used it profusely, but it was reserved only for royalty or the very rich. A celebrated silk knitted garment worn by King Charles is in the collection of the London Museum. The King wore this garment when his subjects beheaded him in London in 1649.

Women, no matter what their station, were never inducted into the master knitters guild, but women have always been known to knit. Possibly the earliest tribute to women knitters is the painting done by Master Bertram between the years 1390 and 1400. The painting, *The Visit of the Angels*, also known as *The Knitting Madonna*, was part of the inside right wing of the Altar in the Buxtehuder Abbey. It is an historical picture of great interest to knitters as it depicts not only knitting, but also the process of forming the neck of a garment by "picking-up" stitches.

One thing that almost every child learned in colonial America was how to knit. For first attempts, children often knit garters: long narrow strips, which wound around the legs to keep up the cotton stockings they wore. If the knitted garter wasn't perfect it wouldn't matter, as it would be concealed. By the age of four colonial children had already mastered plain knitting and by six they were taught to narrow or widen.

It was the fireside occupation of most women and children. Children were needed to replenish the family woolens such as mittens, scarves, caps, and plain stockings. Young girls, and often boys, also were expected to knit for the family as part of their daily chores.

In *Labors of Love* by Judith Reiter Weissman and Wendy Lavitt, they quote diary of a pioneer girl.

I had to knit my own stockings and the stockings for all the children younger than myself. Each day mother would give me a stint of thirty rounds and then I could play. Some days it would take me all day to knit, and on other days I would hurry and do it in a few hours. . . .

By the turn of the nineteenth century, knitting was no longer a necessity, it became more of a ladies' pastime, an art for leisure hours. Ladies' periodicals such as *Godey's Lady's Book* and *Peterson's Magazine* were full of patterns for doilies, antimacassars, afghans, tidies, mats, reticules, and pillows. Ladies many times carried their knitting workbags for something to do while visiting with friends, comparing their work and trading patterns.

When I was a child, a favorite activity I remember was spool knitting. This type of knitting originated from rake or frame knitting, and has had many names: French knitting, ring knitting, Knitting Nancy, spool knitting, corking, knitting knob, knitting dolly, and horse-reins knitting. The knitting spools have also been made in many shapes such as animals, toadstools, tree branches, dolls, and soldiers. They can have as few as two knitting pegs to as many as the piece will hold, however most have four or six pegs. The cord produced from the knitter has been used for mats, rugs, belts, hats, dress trimmings, doilies, child's horse reins pincushions, balls, baskets, egg cozies, dolls, bags, slippers, cushions, doll clothes, etc. The origin is unknown, yet there is evidence of peg frames in Germany dating back to 1535.

The instruction booklet for the Early American Ring Knitter (plate 412) says:

The Ring Knitter is a simple craft tool that dates back to the days of Colonial America and has been popular ever since. In the early days of ring knitting, small wooden curtain rings, hand-turned on manual lathes, were used. These rings were well suited for small hands. Later, during the Industrial Revolution of the 19th century, ring knitting became more widespread, largely due to the capability of machine lathes to mass-produce the wooden rings.

In 1888, the advertising for the toy knitter promised:
It charms the girls, and calms and quiets the noisy boys.

A book written in 1909 by Mary McCormak, *Spool Knitting* (#20-P) and (plate 569), lists 31 spool knitting projects including doll clothing.

One of the most popular twentieth century spool knitters was made by Spears Games of England, the Knitting Nancy. I haven't been able to determine when Spears first introduced Knitting Nancy, but in the February 1929 issue of *Playthings* magazine, Spears Games took out a full-page ad with half the page devoted to Knitting Nancy. Spears advertised a large variety of novelties, games, kindergarten pastimes, educational embroidery, and figural ten pins.

The 1929 illustration of the Knitting Nancy has a pair of knitting needles and a swatch of knitting in her hands and she is much more detailed (with a hat, dress, legs, and a round spool-like base) than the later Nancy. Nancy is also shown like this three years later in a 1931 ad. By the 1940s, Knitting Nancy #6001 (plate 390) was very different. She had lost her hat, was no longer wearing a dress, and her arms were folded in front of her, almost as if she just couldn't, or wouldn't, take another stitch. By the 1950s, the box was bigger but Nancy was still standing with her arms folded. The pick in the box had turned from wood and metal to plastic and the instructions were printed in a pamphlet instead of the inside lid of the box, Knitting Nancy #6001 (plate 395).

Probably one of the most interesting spool sets I have seen is the German-made Strickpilz Handarbeitsgerät (plate 401) it is

Children's Knitting, Crochet, and Weaving Sets

all wood with four pegs and shaped like a toadstool. The spool is nice, but really interesting is the booklet that comes with it, which shows 24 items to make with the cord. I have listed 17 spool knitters in this chapter, some are in sets along with knitting needles and they are all different in some way.

Knitting sets including dolls have a double appeal. Manufacturers knew that if they produced a toy that could not only be played with, but also was teaching the child a meaningful craft, they could appeal to both the child and the adult. What child wouldn't want to add to her favorite doll's wardrobe and what mother wouldn't want her daughter to learn a new craft that she would surely use in later years. Bear Brand Baby Doll Kit #7540 (plate 394) not only gave the child a new doll to play with, but all the materials to either knit or crochet the doll a complete outfit. The doll was not only sold in complete kits featuring a company's brand of yarn, but was also know as the Thrift Kit Doll (plate 449) and sold separately, dressed only in panties. There were also a number of separate sewing kits to be purchased with assorted styles of clothing made especially to fit the doll.

Kwiknit #48-4612 (plate 405) manufactured by Spears Games pictured a doll on the cover of their pattern booklet. There were patterns for seven doll garments in 16" to 17" sizes, for both girl and boy dolls. However, the outfit on the cover of the pattern booklet isn't one of the patterns in the booklet. The introduction states:

You surely have seen the big knitting machines which the grown-ups use for making garments. Well here is a little machine of your own. You can knit dolls' dresses on it, and all sorts of small articles for presents, and — what is most important — much more evenly, and much quicker than by hand. Let us start!

The Kwiknit is very interesting; it can make up to seven different knitting patterns just by winding the thread differently on the loom. Of course, all the patterns in the booklet can *only* be used with the Kwiknit.

Kekkertoys produced Knitting Pretty #1053, (plate 406) and put their own doll in the set, a little 8½" vinyl doll with sleeping eyes and rooted hair. There is a complete wardrobe shown on the box cover that includes a dress, vest, poncho, jacket, hat, boots, bag, and scarf. This set teaches knitting with plain old knitting needles only, no gimmicks. The knitting instructions on how to knit are shown in large print and are quite simple and easy to understand. The doll clothing patterns are a bit more difficult and the child would probably need help from an adult.

Pastime's Knitting Fun Dolly & Me Knitting Set #2923 (plate 410) is designed by Suzanne McNeal who is known for her many clever craft books. The idea of this set is very appealing, first the child knits a sweater, skirt, and headband for their 13" doll, and then they knit the same three items for themselves to match. The knitting machine that comes with the kit is along the same line as the knitting spool only rectangle in shape. The yarn comes out flat but very thick and the widest piece would only be about 11". It would have to be a thin child or the clothing would have to have many seams.

Barbie was a big seller and other companies got in on the profits by selling sets for 11½" fashion dolls. Simplicity and Pastime Activities got together and came out with Simplicity Delux Knitting & Weaving Activity Set #2927 (plate 409). There is a Barbie doll shown on the box cover, and in the doll clothing directions Barbie is named along with Tammy and Tracey. Other dolls to knit for in this set are Heidi, Jan, Spunky, Scooter, Skipper, and Dodi. The set actually has seven different looms, three different sizes of spool, or round looms, two sizes of teeth on the square loom, and two sizes of teeth on the rectangle loom. Beside the doll clothing there are purses, hats, sweaters, potholders, mats, belts, suspenders, and afghans. All the doll clothing is made on the ring knitter. The dolls clothing list is impressive — dresses, shorts, blouse, handbags, scarves, muffs, and bathing suits. To see exclusive Barbie sets see plates 475, 481, and 483.

In colonial America, a child would sit quietly by the fire for hours with her homemade ring knitter and knit a cord. It is amazing that a simple little circle of wood, a few brads and a few scraps of yarn have entertained children for over 300 years! The art of manipulating threads into a garment or other useful items by pulling loops through other loops is one of the oldest forms of needle arts known to man. Today, with machines to make all the knitted and woven fabric we need, fine hand knitting has become, again, a fine art, like it was centuries ago. It has also become a prized pastime activity. With a pair of needles and some yarn one can make a garment that can be as detailed, or as simple, as one desires.

Plate 382. Pastime Occupations Tam O Shanter to be woven in wool, manufactured by the Child's Welfare Co. circa 1920. The box is covered in brown patterned paper and measures 9½" x 7" x ½". Inside are a wooden loom with a hat already started, a needle, and three skeins of yarn. There are instructions on how to finish the tam, and the directions on how to wind the frame for another cap if you wish to make it. There is an advertising paper stating: "Children Become Masters In Play Thru Using The Child's Welfare Playthings." A list of Welfare Playthings was added. Also offered for dolly from the Child's Welfare Co. was a rug and necklace. This set sold for twenty-five cents. **Complete: $50.00 and up.**

Note: This set has a G. A. Schwarz 1006 Chestnut St. Philadelphia sticker on the bottom of the box.

Plate 383. Polly Ann Knitting Knob #3935 manufactured by Whitman Publishing Co., in 1939. The box measures 5" x 5" x 1¼". The box is divided into two sections; one side holds the 4" long wooden knitting knob with four loops and a 3½" pick, the other side has four hanks of string and the Polly Ann Knitting Knob instructions which show a hot-pad, gloves, hat, scarf, teddy bear, and purse. **Complete: $25.00 and up.**

Plate 384. Knitting Spool Set #1082 was manufactured by Lido Toy Company, circa 1930. The set is contained in a 6½" x 5" x 1½" red cardboard box with a cellophane see-through top. The box has the contents listed on the front. On the back are the instructions and a paper doll to cut out. The contents include a 2½" long plastic spool with four straight pegs, two hanks of cotton yarn with Lido labels, and a plastic needle. **Complete: $25.00 and up.**

Children's Knitting, Crochet, and Weaving Sets

Plate 385. Spears Wool Weaving was manufactured by J.W. Spears & Sons LTD., circa 1940. The sturdy box is paper covered with the graphics glued to the lid. The box measures 11½" x 6½" x 1½". Inside we find a 10" wooden loom, 6" long metal needle, and balls of various colors of wool yarn. The instructions are written on the inside of the lid. The articles to be made are a potholder, egg cosy, a needle case, nine-sectioned cushion, serviette ring, duster, and washing flannels. **Complete: $25.00 and up.**

Plate 386. Weaving Loom #860 was manufactured by Concord Toy Co. The box top is delightful with an older lady sitting at a spinning wheel and a child sitting at a loom, both working at their craft. Inside in a snakeskin paper decorated insert is a small 8" x 4" wooden loop already strung with the warp threads. This set also includes a wooden shuttle, three small hanks of yarn, and the directions. The yarn and directions are still stapled to the insert. The directions are only on how to use the loom, no further information on how the weaving could be used. Concord Toys only advertised weaving looms in *Playthings* magazine for one year in 1943. **Complete: $25.00 and up.**

Note: A lot of the value in this set is the graphics, and the total untouched mint condition.

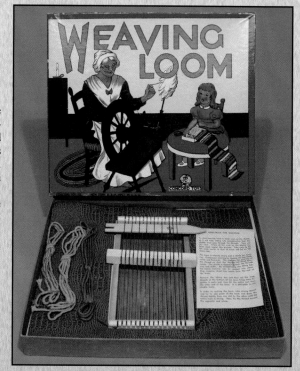

Plate 387. Davis Knitting Kit with Knitting Bag #306 was manufactured by H. Davis Company, circa 1940s. The box is 15" x 12" x 1½". The graphics show two little girls, one knitting and one holding a knitting bag. A doll sits on the table sporting a newly knit tam and vest. Inside we find the knitting bag the girl is holding along with two wooden knitting needles, four hanks of wool yarn, and How To Knit instructions with H. Davis Co. printed at the bottom of the sheet. **Complete: $25.00 and up.**

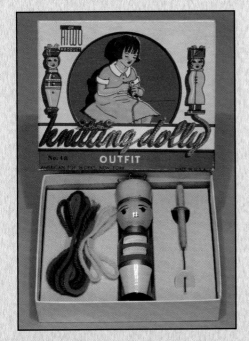

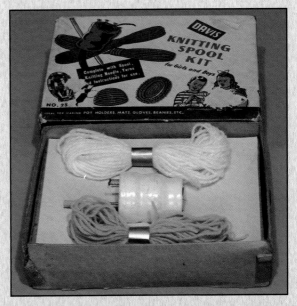

Plate 388. Knitting Dolly Outfit #48 was manufactured by American Toy Works, circa 1940. The box is 6" x 5" x 1½". The graphics on the box top show a little girl knitting with the dolly. The knitting rope spells out the name of the set. Inside, still untouched, are a knitting soldier, a hank of variegated yarn, and the wood-and-metal needle. Around the outside edges of the box top are the directions on using the knitter and what can be made with the rope. The items to make are a skipping rope, rug, scarf, potholder, belt, lariat, hammock, sweater, and blanket. **Complete: $25.00 and up.**

Plate 389. Davis Knitting Spool Kit #25 was manufactured by H. Davis Company, circa 1940. The box is 6½" x 5" x 1½". Inside the box is a 2" long wooden knitting spool, a wooden needle, and two hanks of yarn. Printed on the inside of the lid are the directions for using the spool. It is suggested you use the reins to make potholders, round mat, circles for afghans, hats, belts, and suspenders by sewing together the desired number of rope strands. **Complete: $25.00 and up.**

Plate 390. Knitting Nancy #6001 with Improved Staples was manufactured by J. W. Spears & Sons, LTD., circa 1940. The box is 7½" x 5" x 1". In the cover graphics is an interesting handkerchief holder in the shape of a ball. Inside is a 4½" long wooden Nancy with four bent metal loops, assorted wool yarn, a wood-and-metal needle, and a fold-out color picture brochure showing a hot mat, potholder, handkerchief holder, hat, scarf, and a doll. The instructions for using the knitting spool are on the inside box lid. On the box top, there is an original $1.35 price sticker printed with a Girl Scouts insignia. **Complete: $25.00 and up.**

Note: See Knitting Nancy #6001 (plate 395) for a later knitting set.

Children's Knitting, Crochet, and Weaving Sets

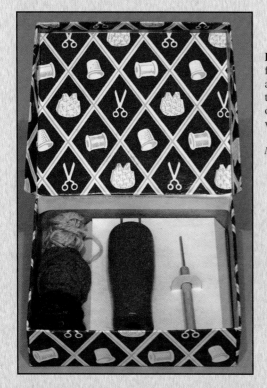

Plate 391. Peter Austin Spool Set #36 was manufactured by Peter Austin, circa 1940. The flip-lid box is covered in a sewing-theme paper printed with scissors, thimbles, dresses, and spools of thread. The box measures 5" x 3½" x 1½". Printed on the hinge paper are the set's number and the maker. This set does not have an instruction sheet, but I am sure it once did. The contents are a 3" long wooden knitting spool with four brads, three balls of wool, and a wooden-and-metal needle. **Complete: $25.00 and up.**

Note: There is still a 25¢ Woolworth's Department Store sticker on the bottom of the box.

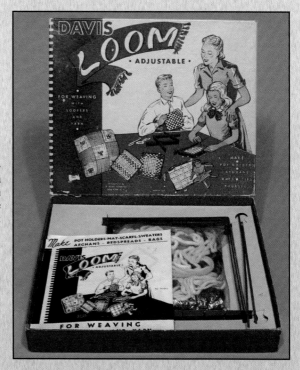

Plate 392. Davis Loom #600 for weaving with loopers and yarn was manufactured by the H. Davis Co., circa 1940. The box is 12" x 10" x 1¾". Inside in a platform rests a 7½" metal loom, looper tool, long metal needle, bag of cotton jersey loopers, and an instruction sheet for weaving loopers or yarn to make squares. The metal loom is adjustable to make 5", 6", or 7" squares. **Complete: $25.00 and up.**

Note: See plate 397 for Davis New Adjustable Loom for Boy's and Girl's # 602.

Plate 393. Big Knitting Spool Outfit was manufactured by Parker Brothers Inc. in 1948. The box measures 10½" x 5½" x 1¾". The outfit includes two wooden knitting spools, both with a yarn guide spring on the side. The larger spool is 1¾" and has eight ½" wire loops, the smaller spool measures 1" and has four ⅜" wire loops. Also included in the set are a 3¼" wood-and-wire pick, a hank of variegated yarn, and a Parker Brothers Directions for Knitting Spool showing how to use both spools and make a flower, mat, beanie, and belt. **Complete: $25.00 and up.**

Note: The yarn guide spring on the spools was to aid in securing an even stitch, and was moved in place as you made each stitch. I have found these springs only on the Parker Brothers sets. By the 1950s Parker Brothers had discontinued the spring. See Big Knitting Set, plate 402.

Plate 394. Bear Brand Baby Doll Kit #7540 was manufactured by Bernhard Ulmann Company, Inc., circa 1951. The box is covered with pink paper printed with blue stars and babies playing on blue moons. The top of the lid has a picture of a doll with a pink crocheted bonnet, sacque, and booties. The box measures 11½" x 7½" x 3½". Inside the box there are three compartments. The doll rests in the largest compartment with her glass bottle. The hard plastic doll is marked "Ideal Doll" and has side-glancing sleep eyes, molded painted hair, and a closed mouth. She is jointed at the shoulders and hips and is 11½" tall. Underneath the doll are a triangle of flannel for a diaper and a piece of fine white cotton stamped with a yoked dress to cut out and sew. Along with the fabric are the instructions for the cloth dress and both crochet and knitting patterns for the sacque, bonnet, and booties. In the smaller compartment are the trimmings for the dress, bonnet, and booties. The last compartment holds the pink and white baby yarn to complete the outfit. **Complete: $25.00 and up.**

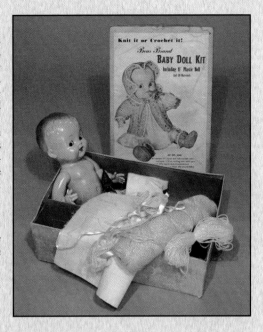

Note: I have seen this kit #7540 also sold with the Fleisher's name on the box in place of Bear Brand. The doll in these knitting sets is the same mold as Ideal Toy Company's Baby Mine, also known as the Thrift Kit Doll sold in the early 1950s. The Thrift Kit Doll (plate 449) plastic dolls came in a see-through box wearing only panties. You could buy sewing kits for the dolls and dress it as a child, nurse, cowboy, etc

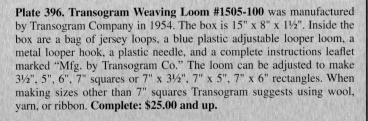

Plate 395. Knitting Nancy #6001 was manufactured by J. W. Spears & Sons, LTD. in 1953. The box measures 9" x 6" x 1". This updated box has a plastic insert with four sections. Nestled in these sections are Nancy, the 4½" long wooden knitting spool with four bent loops, a plastic needle, yarn, and a booklet. The booklet contains instructions and five different plates of items to make including a turtle, doll, sunflower, bouquet of flowers, and a flower design. **Complete: $25.00 and up.**

Note: See Knitting Nancy #6001 (plate 390) for an earlier knitting set.

Plate 396. Transogram Weaving Loom #1505-100 was manufactured by Transogram Company in 1954. The box is 15" x 8" x 1½". Inside the box are a bag of jersey loops, a blue plastic adjustable looper loom, a metal looper hook, a plastic needle, and a complete instructions leaflet marked "Mfg. by Transogram Co." The loom can be adjusted to make 3½", 5", 6", 7" squares or 7" x 3½", 7" x 5", 7" x 6" rectangles. When making sizes other than 7" squares Transogram suggests using wool, yarn, or ribbon. **Complete: $25.00 and up.**

Children's Knitting, Crochet, and Weaving Sets

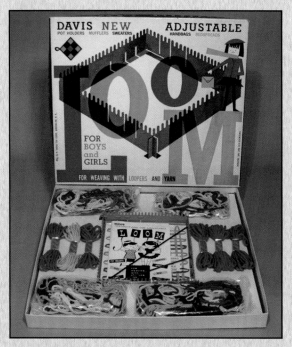

Plate 397. Davis New Adjustable Loom for Boy's and Girl's #602 was manufactured by H. Davis Corp., circa 1950. The box is 17" x 14" x 1½". Inside we find a metal loom that will adjust to 7", 6", 5", 4" squares and rectangles of various sizes. Placed around the perimeter of the box are six hanks of yarn with Davis labels, four bags of jersey loops, a metal needle, a looper hook, and the Davis Instructions for weaving with loopers and yarn. The instruction book says you can make potholders, mufflers, sweaters, handbags, hats, scarfs, and afghans. This set still has its $1.33 sticker on the side. **Complete: $25.00 and up.**

Note: Davis New Adjustable Loom for Boy's and Girl's #602 was advertised in a 1959 Rockwell's Toyland catalog, the exact same content, but the box top was different. It showed two children, a boy and girl.

Plate 398. K W Weaving Loom. Except for the instructions on the inside lid identifying the loom as a K W loom, this set doesn't have any type of identification as to its maker. This set was advertised in FAO Schwarz catalogs as imported, it was shown in a 1955 catalog, and was still being shown in their catalogs in 1969. FAO Schwarz advertised it as a "hardwood loom with no machinery to get out of order or to make weaving difficult." The box measures 17" x 14" x 3". The set includes a 16" x 12" wood loom consisting of the following parts: warp beam, yarn beam, (turner) fabric beam, and three shuttles. There is also a clamp to secure it to a table. The instructions state: "You will naturally want to begin by completing the work already started for you on the loom." Instructions on how to string the loom and a color pamphlet with pictures of a wool scarf, purse, belt, and a doll dress and hat are also included. **Complete: $50.00 and up.**

Note: The price for K W Weaving Loom in the 1955 FAO Schwartz Catalog was $6.95 and in 1969 it was $7.50, not much of a change in fourteen years.

Plate 399. Nelly Bee Metal Weaving Loom #Art 102 was manufactured by Nelly Bee Products, circa 1950. The box is 7" x 7" x 1". Printed on the box top is: "This weaving loom and the method of weaving thereon protected by U. S. Pat. No. 2,186,692." In the box are a rather standard 7" square metal loom, loopers, and a metal looper hook. The Nelly Bee instruction book shows same way of weaving the loopers as does all the other instruction books for loom sets. The book also shows how to use yarn to make wool squares, and the method of joining together to make larger items. There is a Gimbel's Department Store price sticker of sixty-nine cents on the box. **Complete: $10.00 and up.**

Plate 400. Campus Knit #333 was manufactured by H. Davis Company, circa 1950s. The knitting kit comes in a cardboard 6½" x 4" hexagon shaped box decorated with stylized girls with ponytails and various knitted items. Upon lifting the lid, we find six balls of colored yarn, two wooden 6" knitting needles, 2" long wooden knitting spool with six brads, and Davis Knitting Instructions. The instruction sheet gives directions on how to knit, bind off, and use the knitting spool. **Complete: $25.00 and up.**

Plate 401. Strickpilz Handarbeitsgerät (Knitting Mushroom Needlework Set) is in a 6" x 4½" x 2½" box. R. L. manufactured this set in Western Germany, circa 1950. Inside the box are a 4" long wooden mushroom-shaped knitting spool with four bent loops, two hanks of yarn, a wooden needle, and a Strick-Trick instruction book. The 32-page book looks older than the set itself. On page 4 there is a message to the reader. *The use of "Strick-Trick" (Knitting-Trick) awakens the senses to colour, trains the eye in mixing the shades, and makes the children ambitious in finding other patterns than those shown in the catalogue. Thus "Strick-Trick" (Knitting-Trick) is of ideal educational value besides finding interesting work for idle hands.* The book contains directions on using the knitting spool. There are plates of four different hot pads, children's toy-horse reins, two pincushions, ball, egg basket, two egg cozies, a doll, child's bag, child's slippers, balls on a string, three different borders, two designs for flowers, four tea cozies, a cushion with a tassel, and a slumber roll. **Complete: $25.00 and up.**

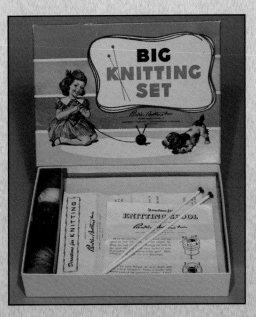

Plate 402. Big Knitting Set was manufactured by Parker Brothers Inc. in 1956. It came in a 10" x 7" x 2" box. It contains six balls of yarn, a 1½" long wooden knitting spool with four straight loops, two plastic Susan Bates size 5 knitting needles, a Parker Brothers Directions for Knitting Spool, and Parker Brothers Directions for Knitting. **Complete: $25.00 and up.**

Note: The yarn guide spring on the spools was to aid in securing an even stitch, and was moved in place as you made each stitch. I have found these springs only on the Parker Brothers sets. By the 1950s, Parker Brothers had discontinued the spring. See Big Knitting Spool Outfit (plate 393).

Children's Knitting, Crochet, and Weaving Sets

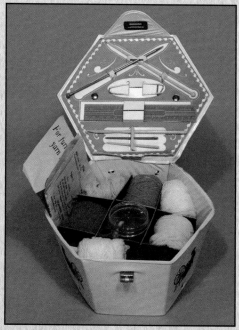

Plate 403. Hassenfeld Brothers introduced the **Junior Miss Knitting Set #1566** in their trade catalog in 1958. *Now in a new! Practical attractive useful case #1566 Junior Miss Knitting Set. A very practical introduction to knitting for ages 6 to 16. A durable two-tone vinyl case, with turn lock and handle, containing an ample supply of colorful wool yarn, knitting needles, plastic yarn holders, etc. Easy to follow illustrated instructions for knitting a complete doll's outfit. Size 8½" x 4¾" x 7½". Retail at $3.00.* The "etc." in the content is a 6" plastic ruler, a crochet hook, two plastic knitting needles, and a stitch holder. The instructions came in two sheets, Hasbro knitting instructions, and instructions for making a doll's outfit. The outfit can be made for a 7½", 12", 15", or 18" doll. The doll's outfit consists of a blouse, skirt, panties, and stole. The pattern is marked Hassenfeld Bros., Inc. There is no identification on the case, but there are four panels decorated with silhouettes of a lady at a spinning wheel; other than that, it is plain. I don't know if it had a box or a hang tag. I have seen neither. **Complete: $50.00 and up.**

Note: The Junior Miss Knitting Set was offered in at least two other variations with the same contents. Hassenfeld Brothers Set #1565 was offered in an oblong vinyl case with a turn lock in 1956. In 1959, Set #1566 was offered with the same hexagon shape and content, but it had different graphics of little girls knitting and Jr. Miss Knitting Basket written on the front.

Plate 404. My Knitting Set was manufactured by Parker Brothers, under their Pastime Products division in 1961. The box measures 8½" x 7" x 2". Listed on the side of the box are the contents: "Kit contains attractive knitting tool, a pair of knitting needles, and 6 balls of bright-colored yarn." The kit also included "Parker Brothers Directions for Knitting." The attractive knitting tool is plastic in the shape of a 4" long toadstool and has four bent loops. The plastic knitting needles are #5 Susan Bates. Everything is just as it was sold, still under the cellophane. **Complete: $25.00 and up.**

Note: The knitting directions have a 1956 date on them and are the same directions that came with the Big Knitting Set (plate 402) by Parker Brothers, however the two instruction sheets have been combined into one for this set and the "toadstool" name has been substituted for knitting spool.

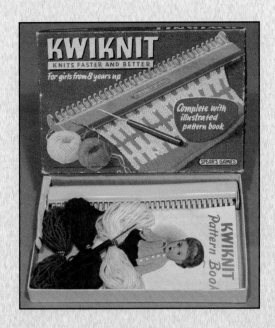

Plate 405. Kwiknit #48-4612 was manufactured by J.W. Spears & Sons, LTD., circa 1960. The box is 9" x 6" x 1". The Kwiknit is 9" long and has two parts with different size teeth that are riveted together. The two parts are joined so that they can be moved back and forth. The Kwiknit pattern book has detailed instructions on how to use the Kwiknit using various windings and knitting patterns. The articles to make for dolls are a dress, hat, knickers, scarf, shorts, jacket, beret, sports pullover sweater, skirt and a twin sweater set. There are also patterns for a child's hood, scarf, mittens, baby bottle warmer, coat hangers, potholder, pincushion, baby's sweater, bonnet and booties. To complete the set are three hanks of wool yarn and a wood-and-metal pick. This set is quite impressive with its Kwiknit and the many things you can do with it. **Complete: $25.00 and up.**

Note: Kwiknit #48-4612 was found advertised in a Montgomery Ward 1967 Catalog and priced at $1.89.

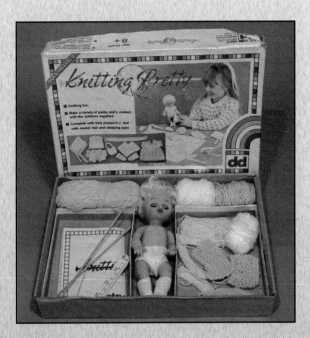

Plate 406. Knitting Pretty #1053 was manufactured by Kekkertoys, circa 1960s. The box is 13½" x 9½" x 2½". There is a listing of the contents on the side of the box and a picture on the top that shows the clothing to knit for the doll inside. Inside the box we find a 9" soft plastic doll with rooted hair and sleep eyes. She is unmarked. All the contents listed on the box are here: three balls of colored wool, knitting needles, tape measure, sewing needle, and the pattern sheet along with some extra baby blue yarn. The pattern sheet contains the directions and the patterns for a doll's jacket, dress, vest, poncho, hat, boots, bag, and scarf. **Complete: $25.00 and up.**

Note: A child used this kit and some of their knitting is still in the set. However I can't quite figure out what the child was trying to knit. I am sure the child added the blue yarn as it is a slightly different weight.

Plate 407. It's Easy to Knit, It's Fun to Knit #261A was manufactured by Lisbeth Whiting in 1962. This set is housed in a cardboard hexagon-shaped carrying case with a cellophane front. Inside, in a bubble pack there are ten balls of colored yarn and a 3¼" plastic knitting spool. Underneath the bubble pack, are plastic knitting needles and very well written directions with diagrams for knitting and how to use the knitting spool. The stitches include casting on, knitting, purling, garter stitch, purling increasing, knitting increasing, decreasing, binding off, and how to pick up dropped stitches. **Complete: $25.00 and up.**

Children's Knitting, Crochet, and Weaving Sets

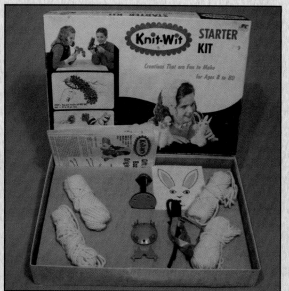

Plate 408. Knit Wit #65 Starter Kit was manufactured by Yankee Homecraft Corp. in 1965. The box measures 16" x 11" x 2½". The kit contains three winding tools, the Knit Wit with metal prongs, the adapter that is used with the Knit Wit, and a pom-pon maker. The supplies include four small skeins of Knit Wit Bulky Orlon, two chenille wires, felt bunny cutouts, and pink ribbon, these are to make the three items shown on the cover of the box, a pink poodle, bunny rabbit, and ear warmer. Two sets of directions come with the kit, the "Basic Instructions" and "The Knit Wit Gift and Bazaar Originals." The Knit Wit Gift and Bazaar Book gives instructions to make all three items on the cover plus bunny slippers, colonial afghan, sweater, kooky birds, pink baby bird, blue bird, mother bird, baby birds in nest, and a lorikeet. The price of this set was $2.79 in 1965. **Complete: $25.00 and up.**

Note: There were over 40 Knit Wit kits with different items to make. A 1961 FAO Schwarz catalog offered Kit #803-65 that made animals, dolls, and clothing for the dolls.

Plate 409. Simplicity Deluxe Knitting & Weaving Activity Set #2927 is in a 15½" x 12" x 3" box. Pastime Industries Inc. manufactured it in 1992. The contents are listed on the side of the box and include two sided knitting machine, two sided weaving loom, two sided large mushroom knitter, four-prong knitting spool, knitting needles, crochet hook, assorted yarns, and silicone backing for potholders. There is also Simplicity "Knitting & Weaving Deluxe Set Instructions" that show how to use the various weaving and knitting looms, and how to make doll clothes, a small and large handbag, hat, belt, sweater, and round and square potholders. **Complete: $25.00 and up.**

Plate 410. Knitting Fun Dolly & Me Knitting Set #2923 was manufactured by Pastime Industries in 1996. The box measures 15½" x 11" x 2" and was designed by Suzanne McNeill. The box contains a knitting machine, plastic sewing needle, plastic crochet hook, 250-yards of assorted yarns. "The Dolly & Me Knitting Set" directions show how to use the knitting machine and patterns for a sweater, skirt, and headband for a 13" doll and a sweater vest, skirt, and headband for a seven year old child to match. The instructions are in English, Spanish, and French. **Complete: $25.00 and up.**

Plate 411. Knitting Nancy for French Knitting was manufactured by Flights of Fancy in 1997. Written on the 6" long brown cardboard tube is "Anyone bought up pre 1950s will remember French Knitting, included is a rustic Knitting Nancy complete with wool and full instructions. It's so simple anyone can do it!" The knitter is made from the branch of a tree, and four copper brads, the needle is a pointed dowel. The instructions also have the history of peg knitting. **Complete: $10.00 and up.**

Plate 412. Early American Ring Knitter was made circa 2002 by American Folk Toys, Games and Crafts. This set comes in a plastic bag and includes a 3" wooden ring with five brass nails, a wooden stick needle, sample yarn, and instructions. Included in the instructions is the history of ring knitting and how to make a belt, skipping rope, hot mat, and a rug. **Complete: $10.00 and up.**

Dolls and Their Patterns

This chapter includes the dolls with their own exclusive patterns that have encouraged children to sew. A lot of doll patterns have been marketed by pattern companies for the popular "doll of the moment" and the numerous clones of these dolls. These are generic patterns that list the dolls that are on the market at that time, hoping to sell the patterns because of the dolls' popularity. These are not the dolls I have included in this chapter. The dolls listed here are those for which children have lovingly sewed for, while improving their sewing skills. There are dolls that were made to sew for recently, but not intended for children. These include the new fashion dolls like Gene or Tyler Wentworth. Since these dolls were not made for children they are not included.

Bleuette Doll

Bleuette was introduced in France in 1905 as a premium for subscribing to *La Semaine de Suzette*, (Suzette's Week). This publication cost the equivalent of $1.20 a year for 52 issues. It was a weekly paper conceived to entertain and instruct little girls from ages eight to fourteen and was the creation of the publishing house of Henri Gautier. There was some concern at the time that the little girls of France needed guidance in becoming good wives and mothers. There were magazines for little boys, but other than children's pages in the ladies' magazines, there were none especially for little girls. Monsieur Gauiter decided to launch a paper that would fill this need and, to ensure the success of the magazine he offered a "bonus" doll with each new one-year subscription purchased before publication. In 1905 Monsieur Gautier ordered 20,000 Bleuette dolls. The dolls were gone in a very short while.

After the initial bonus doll giveaway to launch the magazine, Monsieur Gautier quickly ordered more so that children who didn't get one of his dolls could purchase one through the publishing house. The new shipment of dolls was offered for the purchase of one issue of *La Semaine de Suzette*, plus 2.50 francs. Bleuette was popular from the start and was included in articles and stories written by Tante (Aunt) Jacqueline. There was at least one activities page in every issue of *La Semaine de Suzette*, and a good many were dedicated to Bleuette. However one of the most significant features in the magazine was Nous Habillons Bleuette with wonderful patterns and accessories to make for Bleuette.

In 1917 Gautier partnered with his nephew, Maurice Languereau. Gautier Languereau owned the name Bleuette and was the only firm licensed to sell the doll and her wardrobe.

She was sold either through the magazine or at the Gautier-Languereau shop in Paris. Almost from the beginning, there were two ways to dress Bleuette. Outfits could be hand sewn at home using patterns published in *La Semaine de Suzette* or, starting in 1906, ready-made garments created by Gautier Languereau were available. In the first years, these were much like the clothing patterns offered in the magazine, since the seamstresses employed by the publishing house used the same patterns. It was a very successful endeavor and by 1908 we find there are also hair combs, jewelry, purses, vanity items, closets, beds, washstands etc. to buy for Bleuette. Each year the patterns and costumes were updated, so she was never out of style. There were also other dolls added to the Bleuette family through the years.

Benjamine, baby sister, 1926
Bambino, baby brother, 1928
Bamboula, black baby friend, 1931
Rosette, older sister, 1955

However none of them was as popular as the original Bleuette. She lasted for three generations and taught the little girls of France how to sew and love doing it.

Throughout the years there were many dolls offered as Bleuette by the Galtier-Languereau publishing house and sometimes it can be difficult to identify a real Bleuette. Bleuette was manufactured to Gautier-Languereau's specifications by La Société Français de Bébés Jouets, a conglomerate formed in 1899 and better-known today as S.F.B.J. The first 20,000 used an Emile Jumeau head mold marked only with a "1" or "2" or "2" over "1" on the back of the head.

I find all the sizes and marks of Bleuette very confusing and have consulted an expert in this field, Agnes J Sura. I have great confidence in Agnes, the editor of the quarterly magazine titled *Bluettes's World* and she has graciously allowed me to copy her latest list of marks and sizes:

Bleuette Identified (revised 5/2005) (A Gift from Bluette's World).

| Size: 1905 – 1933 | 27cm or 10⅝" |
| Size: 1933 – 1960 | 29cm or 11 ⅜" |

All bodies: composition and wood, fully jointed, including wrist, incised 2 on back 1 on sole of each foot.

All Bleuette dolls have open mouths except those marked with an asterisk.

1905 — 27cm, bisque head, marked: 2 over1, or 1 or 2

1905 – 1915 — 27cm, bisque head, marked: 6/0

1916 – 1933 — 27cm, bisque head, marked: SFBJ 60 8/0 or 71 Unis France 149 60 8/0 or SFBJ 301 1

*1930 – 1933 — 27cm. composition head, two teeth marked: SFBJ 252-2

*1933 – 1937? — 29cm composition or bisque head, two teeth marked: SFBJ or Unis France 251-2

1933 – 1960 — 29cm, all-bisque head, composition after

WWII, marked: 71 Unis France 149, 301, 1¼ (neck), composition same 1½ (neck)

*1951 – 1954 — composition head, SFBJ-301-1, late in the period: SFBJ 301-1

1958 – 1960 — 33cm, plastic, five-piece jointed body, head marked: Gégé, body: Made in France//Gégé//8A Déposé

Plate 413. **Bleuette and Her Trunk.** This Bleuette is incised on the back of her head SFBJ//60//Paris//8/0. She is 10⅝" tall has stationary blue glass eyes, open mouth with teeth, human hair wig, and is fully jointed. Her trunk is filled with homemade clothing created long ago by an admirer. The dark wool outfit hanging in the trunk is Bleuette's skating costume from *La Semaine de Suzette*. The first pattern was in the November 15, 1917, issue and it was Son Manchon (Her Muff). The second part was the jacket and the skirt from the January 24, 1918, issue. There was a third part to this outfit, which is the toque (hat) published in the January 31, 1918, issue (not shown). **Dressed doll only: $1,000.00 and up.**

Plate 414. **Four Issues of** *La Semaine De Suzette* magazine. This is a full run of the October 1913 issues, dated October 9, 16, 23, and 30. Each issue has a pattern for Bleuette. These patterns include a fan, bonnet, shoes, and robe. Each magazine, in newspaper format, measures 9" x 13", has eight pages printed on front and back with stories, amusements, plays, comics, poems, and best of all patterns for Bleuette. **Each: $10.00 and up.**

Plate 415. **Bleuette's Catalog of Clothing 1916 – 1917.** This little copy of the first Bleuette catalog contains all manner of clothing for Bleuette. The reprinted is by Carter Craft Doll House. Pictured are dresses, skirts, blouses, play clothes, coats, jackets, capes, shoes, slippers, hats, slips, stockings, chemises, drawers, sleepwear, and numerous other costumes. All these, as well as Bleuette herself, could be ordered from the catalog. **Reprint: $10.00 and up.**

Dolls and Their Patterns

Daisy the Doll Who Came to Life

Daisy started as a paper doll for a paper doll named Lettie Lane in the October 1, 1908, issue of the *Ladies' Home Journal*. The Lettie Lane paper dolls were drawn by Sheila Young and ran from 1908 until 1915. In September 1909, the *Ladies' Home Journal* published the *Lettie Lane Paper Family. Presenting Lettie's Doll's Party of Little People Dressed in Fancy Costumes* (plate 416). On this page are paper dolls representing the bisque dolls of the era, some with extra clothing and hats.

The first mention of a doll coming to life was in the December 15, 1910, issue of the *Ladies' Home Journal*. This announcement appeared on the very first page above the contents:

The Children Will Have a Treat in 1911. During 1911 they will also have some special features all their own. Flossie Fisher's Funnies, which begins in this number, will run through the year, and so will the popular Lettie Lane Doll pages — and, what will please the children most of all and will cause a sensation with them, is that a Lettie Lane Doll will Really Come to Life. How? Just wait and see. Ask your mother to subscribe to the Ladies' Home Journal *now so that you will be sure not to Miss it.*

The January 1, 1911 issue stated:

The Lettie Lane Doll that Will Come to Life. We shouldn't, perhaps, have said anything about it beforehand, for the children are already waiting and watching and writing. But is isn't an easy matter to bring a doll to life, and it takes a little time to do it as we are going to do it. For it is going to be done in a way that no child will ever dream of its being done. So let every child be patient, and just as-soon as we can bring it about 'The Doll Will Come to Life'.

In the February 1, 1911 issue was another message.

We are sorry, in a way, that we wrote anything about the Lettie Lane Doll that is going to come to life, for the little readers of the Journal *have fairly jumped at our words and 'want to know all about,' or they 'want the doll right away'. They shall know, and they shall have the doll: no doubt about it. "And* <u>what</u> *a doll it is. But it takes time and thought to bring a doll to life, and when we have done it we do not want to disappoint. All we can say to the children now is — have a little patience. The doll is coming to life surely if slowly, and very soon we shall be able to say: Look for it next month.*

There were two messages in the February 15, 1911, issue. The first promised:

The next Journal will have a definite announcement about this wonderful doll, and every child that is on tiptoe of expectation will, we think, be pleased. Be sure to read what Miss Young says on her next Lettie Lane Doll Page.

The other message was:

We are now busy with Miss Young on The Lettie Lane Doll that will come to life and it will come to life, too, in a way that no child will suspect — not in a way that you may think, but in a better way than even the best guesser among the children would ever think of. That alone will be a surprise, but there will be a second surprise about it too. We shall soon be ready.

And sure enough, the first issue in March promised the doll would come to life in the very next issue:

The Lettie Lane Doll comes to Life In the Next Journal. After months of waiting the Lettie Lane doll that we have promised should 'come to life' will appear in the very next Journal. And so important and successful do we think it is, that we have made it a frontispiece to the number, radiant in full and brilliant colors. We shall wonder what the Journal *children have to say about this wonderful doll. And the best of it is what we have not said before; that every little girl will have a chance to take this doll, the real doll, to her heart and arms.*

There was one more message to the young viewers in this issue. This message appears on the paper doll page and reads:

A special word to Lettie Lane's friends. The children will be delighted to hear I am going to be in the middle of the month Journal as well as in the first–of-the-month number, and in the next Journal, *that dated March 15, I am going to give every Lettie Lane girl a tremendous surprise. 'The Lettie Lane Doll That Has Come To Life' will be in that number. It will be out March 10, so DO watch for it and get a copy, and you will be oh, so pleased, and oh, so surprised! Sheila Young.*

And as promised there appeared in the March 10 issue a full-page ad about Daisy, with her picture, her patterns, and how every little *Journal* girl could have her for her very own (plate 417).

Then how can you have Daisy? Easily. You cannot buy her from us or from any one else, because she comes from across the sea, three thousand miles away, and we do not want little girls to send us their own pennies, nor to have them tease Father or Mother to give them enough to pay for her. Now listen very carefully and I will tell you how little you will have to do. Send to us three yearly subscriptions for the Ladie's Home Journal, *accompanied by a remittance of $4.50, and the doll and patterns for all the clothes illustrated on this page will be sent to you, all shipping expenses prepaid.*

Reading the advertisement that reveals how to obtain Daisy leads me to believe Daisy was always sent with the patterns that were shown in her ad. So when a child sent for her, she would receive the latest patterns from the latest ad. All the patterns were also offered for sale in the magazine or available from a pattern dealer for 10 cents.

Lettie Lane's Sewing Box in the February 15, 1911, issue announced a sewing contest.

A prize offer of $100 for little Journal *girls. This is something very new for all the little girl readers of the* Journal, *who are going to make the pretty clothes for Daisy, the Lettie Lane doll that has come to life, shown on page 4. You all love her, don't you? Yes. Well, when the dresses are finished we want to see them, and to show the best-made ones on a page in the* Journal.

There are $100 in the Sewing Box ready to be awarded in prizes for the best-made outfits — this means the three dresses and the coat shown on the page, but not the hats nor the muslin slip — so please try hard and let us see how well you can sew.

The Prizes will be:

One Prize of $25: for the very best-made outfit.

One Prize of $15: for the next best-outfit.

Sixty Prizes of $1 each: for the best examples of good sewing on the outfit.

But all of these things must be really made at home by the little girls themselves. Anything bought in a shop should not be sent. The name of the sender, with her age and full address, must be on the outside of the package, and she must be able to say to us truthfully that she has made the clothes herself. Do not write us about the clothes, as all the directions you need are in the magazine and in the paper patterns. Enclose postage for the return of dresses.

All contributions must be received by April 25.

If one stops to think about it, the doll wasn't even offered until March 15. A child had to sell three subscriptions and send them in to obtain the doll. The doll had to be delivered and she had to make three dresses and a coat and send them all in "before" April 15. Not a lot of time!

Another sewing contest was offered again the next month this time it was the bridal trousseau. Lettie Lane's Sewing Box stated: *Once again we offer prize money for our little girl friends who make dresses for Lettie Lane's Doll. We have already heard from so many who read last month's announcement that we are going to repeat the same kind of a prize offer this month. So get out your scissors, needle, and thread, and go at your pleasant task.* All the rules were the same.

In the August 1, 1911, issue the first sewing contest winners were announced.

More than four hundred little girls made the first Lettie Lane doll outfit which we asked for in the March 15 Journal. We are so pleased with the response to this offer that we are sending to many of those who could not win prizes a little card showing our appreciation of what they have done, placing them

on the Roll of Honor in this competition.

The winners of the contest were:

First Prize of $25. Marion Lake, New Jersey

Second Prize of $15. Lena Dunlap, Ohio

There was a note about the second prize winner:

The workmanship of the second prize winner is especially worthy of recognition, as this little girl has only one arm — the left — and every stitch in the outfit was done with her one hand.

The sixty "one dollar" winners were also listed.

The winners of the second contest were announced in the October issue.

In the March 15 issue of the *Ladies' Home Journal* Lettie Lane introduced Betty Bonnet to the paper doll page. Betty Bonnet, her family, and friends took over the paper doll page and continued to delight children until September of 1918.

The Lettie Lane Daisy doll is 18" tall, has blue or brown glass sleep eyes, a blonde mohair wig, open mouth with two teeth, and a fully jointed body including wrists, elbows, and knees. Research to date indicates the dolls were ordered from two German factories, J.D.Kestner, Jr. and Heinrich Handwerck. The Kestner marks are "Made in // Germany // 171." The Heinrich Handwerck heads are marked: "Germany // Heinrich Handwerck // Simon & Halbig." Frequently among new doll collectors, there is confusion about the Daisy doll. Kestner produced mold number 171, the same mold used for Daisy, in several different sizes. It is important to realize that the *Ladies' Home Journal* Daisy doll was made in only one size: 18". She was advertised as 18" and all the Daisy patterns that were sold with her are for an 18" size doll. A Kestner mold number doll in any size other than 18" is **not** a Daisy. To find out more about the *Ladies' Home Journal* Daisy doll, I recommend the book *Daisy's Album, Lettie Lane's Daisy, The Doll That Really Came to Life* by Atha Kahler. Atha has thoroughly researched Daisy and her book is very informative.

Plate 416. The Lettie Lane Paper Family. The Lettie Lane paper dolls were drawn by Sheila Young and ran from 1908 until 1915. The September 1909 issue of the *Ladies' Home Journal* published the Lettie Lane Paper Family. Presenting Lettie's Doll's Party of Little People Dressed in Fancy Costumes. This page from the magazine shows paper dolls representing the bisque dolls of the era. **Page: $25.00 and up.**

Plate 417. The Doll that Has Come to Life. Lettie Lane presents Her Most Beautiful Doll to Every Little Journal Girl. This was the page that every little Journal girl was waiting for; finally information on how to send for Daisy. Daisy is shown, surrounded by her pattern wardrobe, #5954: *The Green Gingham is Daisy's Morning Dress. It May, However be Made of Any Color. With a Guimpe of Striped Lawn. For Afternoon Wear it was Thought a Light Blue Lawn Dress Would Please Daisy. Nearly All Little Girls Can Sew This Simple Embroidery of Eyelets and Scallops. Daisy's New Coat is One of the Latest Fashions. There are No Patterns for the Hats, Which are About the Same as Those in the Shops. For a Very Best Dress for "Parties" Here is a Lovely Pink silk. The Hat May Be Trimmed With Different Colored Ribbons to Match Any Dress Daisy May Wish to Wear With It*. Daisy could be yours postpaid with her patterns for sending in three, one-year subscriptions of the *Ladies' Home Journal* and remittance of $4.50. **Page: $25.00 and up.**

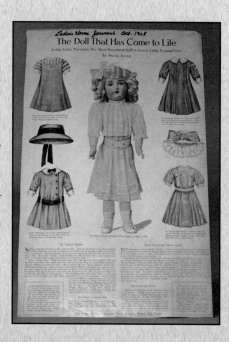

Plate 418. The Lettie Lane's Daisy doll shown here is marked 171 on the back of her head. The J. D. Kestner Jr. doll firm of Germany produced the doll for the *Ladies' Home Journal*. She is 18" tall and has a bisque head with blue sleep eyes, open mouth with teeth and a blonde mohair wig. Her body is ball jointed at the elbows, shoulders, hips, and knees. She is wearing a dress made from pattern #6012. Next to Daisy is the *Ladies' Home Journal* page Lettie Lane's most beautiful doll as a bride. The dress is the Best Sunday blue dress seen at the lower corner closest to the doll. **Daisy Doll: $1,000.00 and up.**

Plate 419. Lettie Lane's Most Beautiful Doll as a Bride pattern #6012 was printed in the April 15, 1911, issue of the *Ladies' Home Journal*. The descriptions of the costumes are as follows: *This month Daisy is a bride. Her bridal gown is white satin, with the veil of chiffon fastened to the hair with artificial flowers. The handkerchief and slipper bows have edges of lace. There is a gown for evening wear made of white Swiss over pink silk, and a band of pink ribbon with rosettes for her hair. The blue and white foulard and the hat to match are for calling. The pretty striped dress and hat are for morning wear. The apron is to wear she serves tea. For Daisy's wedding trip a tan-colored light-weight cloth gown would be very becoming trimmed with brown silk. For a hat to wear with this gown you might make one of cloth to match. A little straw suitcase can be bought, and the fancy hand-bag can be easily made of raffia*. The offer to receive Daisy was the same. **Page: $25.00 and up.**

Note. The note box at the bottom page stated: "The next time you see this doll (in The Journal for June 15) she will have a complete outfit for vacation: with pretty things to wear on all occasions — even to a bathing suit. Won't that be nice? If you do not have time to do all the sewing before starting away you can finish it afterward some rainy day on the porch."

Plate 420. Lettie Lane's Doll in her Vacation Clothes was in the July 1911 issue of the *Ladies' Home Journal* and offers pattern #6137. The listing of Daisy's vacation clothes states: *Her best dress may be worn with or without the white guimpe. The blue shoes may be purchased in any toy shop, and you may buy or make the stockings to match. The yellow dimity would be pretty to wear at an afternoon garden-party, with a white lawn hat with a frill of embroidery, trimmed with ribbon and artificial rose. For afternoon wear use the pink plaid gingham trimmed with bands of embroidery. This may also be worn with or without a guimpe. The apron is made of blue-and-white check, with collar, pockets and cuffs of white cotton-poplin. The sunbonnet, worn with this apron, should be made of chambray of a plain color to harmonize with the apron. If Daisy is going to the seashore for a part of the summer she will need a bathing suit; so here is one made of blue serge trimmed with red and blue braid. A red handkerchief or square of red material will answer for a bathing cap. A white straw hat may be bought, or the hat may be made of soft straw-braid trimmed with a ribbon band. Daisy will not want to wear her blue hair-ribbon with all her dresses, so it would be well to have other ribbons to match the different frocks.* There was a note under the bathing suit saying: *If Daisy Has No Need of a Bathing suit Why Not Use This Garment as a "Gym" Suit or as a Play Suit, Lengthening the Blouse to Cover the Bloomers?* It seems like Daisy really did take a summer vacation, the note at the top of the page states: *Owing to the popularity of this offer in earlier journals our stock of dolls has been exhausted, but orders placed in Germany, where Daisy is made in the quaint villages, will bring a fresh supply soon. We think this will be by September 1, perhaps sooner. So no orders can be filled, we fear, earlier than that date. Every effort is being made to get the dolls here.* There was no mention of more patterns for Daisy. **Page: $25.00 and up.**

Note. The note in the box at the bottom of the page states: "Did you ever go shopping to the attic or the sewing scrap-bag? It's splendid fun and just the nicest way to procure the material for Daisy's clothes. Ask Mother's permission to shop in this way, and you will surely find just as pretty and becoming materials and colors for you doll's clothes as are shown here."

Plate 421. Lettie Lane's Doll in her School Clothes pattern #6436 was offered in the October 1911 issue of the *Ladies' Home Journal*. The top of the page announced: *Any Little Girl May Now Have the Real Daisy for Her Very Own. Thousands of the Dolls, Fresh From the German Villages Where They are Made, are Now in the Journal's offices ready for immediate shipment.* The pattern clothing was listed as such: *Now that the summer vacation days are over and Daisy is back again, sunburnt and happy, and eager to begin school, she will need some suitable clothes for this extraordinary occasion. First of all there is the serviceable every-day dress to consider, and for this nothing could be better than a blue serge or challis made in a jolly sailor style, with a big collar fastened with a knotted red silk ribbon. If Mother gives you a piece of material sufficiently large perhaps there will be enough for not only a cap, but a school bag as well, in which to carry the books and other thing a doll needs for this business of going to school. Daisy should have a second-best dress, and surely the pretty one on the right of the page next to the luncheon-basket, with the hat above to wear with it, would be just about right for high days and holidays. If you want her to be particularly neat make her a dainty white apron like the one in the upper right-hand part of the page to slip on over her pretty dresses while she is playing about the house. A piece of barred muslin or a sprigged lawn would be dainty, and if you can find a piece of narrow lace to sew around the neck and armholes, so much the better, or turn a narrow hem and trim with featherstitching. For school concerts and afternoon teas she can wear the little Kate Greenaway frock illustrated above, with a green ribbon tied about her waist. Then there is the coat, which may be made of any light-weight cloth, or a heavy duck, linen or piqué Mother may have put aside in her bundle-drawer, and which is not too thick for little fingers to cut and stick the needle through.* At the bottom of the page there is the doll Daisy dressed in the blue and white outfit shown on The Doll That Has Come To Life page, (plate 417). And we are informed that this is the costume she is dressed in when she arrives. This leads me to believe that what we think of as a dress, is what was then called as a "muslin Slip." **Page: $25.00 and up.**

Note. The little box at the bottom of the page gave instructions on how to obtain all of Daisy's patterns.

Plate 422. A Merry Christmas for the Children Lettie Lane's Most Beautiful Doll In Her Party Clothes, December 1911 was the last offer of the doll and her patterns from the *Ladies' Home Journal*. The pattern offered was #6511 and it was for making Daisy's "New-Year Frolic" clothes: *Like all little-girl dolls Daisy is in a great flutter of excitement over her first party, wondering what it will be like and whether she will enjoy herself or not. There will be lots and lots of cakes and candies, a tall Christmas tree lighted with candles, and best of all, no one is expected to wear her regular party dress trimmed with lace and fussy bows-which makes one's mother say, "Now please don't tear or soil your dress, Daisy darling" — but to wear a real play dress, such as is worn by the little girl in the story book, in which one can jump and run. As Daisy loves little Red Riding Hood, one dress is to be made like the dress Red Ridding Hood wore on the day she visited her grandmother and met the wolf. This dress is to be of green cambric, with a pinafore of printed calico and a red satin cape and cap, and Daisy will have a tiny basket in which to put the dainties for Grandmother. For another day there is the Indian girl's dress made of brown cambric and trimmed with bias strips of plaid. A white muslin belt, decorated with patches of embroidery, and a band for the hair with two funny little feathers on the side make this a very joyful dress. For trimming the cambric is slashed to look like fringe. As only a tiny bit of flowered lawn is needed Daisy could also have a "Dolly Varden" dress trimmed with pretty white ruffles, and she would look "just too sweet" with a little hat, like the one above the bag, tied around with a wide ribbon band and bow. She will need a dinner dress of pale green challis with lace collar and cuffs. Last of all is the coat of plaid woolen goods, with red collar and cuffs trimmed with black braid. There was also a hat to go with the coat that is not mentioned.* **Page: $25.00 and up.**

Note. The note in the box at the bottom of the page gives information on obtaining the other four patterns for Daisy. Each for 10¢.

Plate 423. Lettie Lane 18" Doll-Set #5954 was the first pattern offered along with the Lettie Lane doll. The *Ladies' Home Journal* Daisy patterns were made exclusively by the Home Pattern Company. Pattern #5954 offers patterns for a hat, coat, tucked-dress, dress with plaited-skirt, pinafore dress, petticoat, under waist, and drawers. Even though it wasn't advertised every Lettie Lane pattern included an underwear pattern. **Complete: $75.00 and up.**

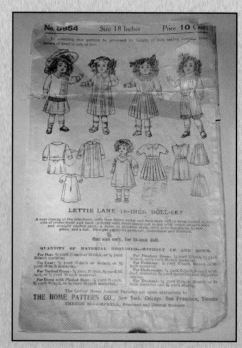

Plates 424. Reprinted Patterns from Carter Craft Doll House. Pattern #37, afternoon or going away dress, #38 evening or party dress and #39 empire or Sunday dress. They are reprinted patterns with no date except the *Ladies' Home Journal* 1911 date. **Each: $10.00 and up.**

Marilú Doll

Alicia Larguia of Buenos Aires, Argentina, read *La Semaine de Suzette*, the children's magazine from France featuring a doll named Bleuette, and thought that it would be a good idea to have a similar doll for *Billiken*, Argentina's own children's magazine. She contacted the German firm of Kammer & Reinhardt in 1932 to ask them to make a special doll for *Billiken*. Marilú was first advertised in the *Billiken* magazine in November 1932. The magazine announced that Marilú was made especially for *Billiken* and imported from Germany. The doll was sold through *Billiken's* publisher and was an enticement to subscribe to the magazine for their weekly patterns for children to sew for Marilú. She was marketed as a high fashion doll for Argentina's upper class and soon became so successful that within a short time it was decided to produce a new magazine. *Marilú* magazine was launched in 1933 and soon became as popular to Argentina children as *La Semaine de Suzette* was with the little French girls. The magazine carried stories, poems, games, puzzles, recipes, and, of course clothing and accessory patterns for Marilú.

The first heads for the Marilú doll were made by Kammer & Reinhardt and are marked "K*R // 917 // Germany." This was the composition version of the K*R open-mouth bisque head marked "117." In 1936 the supplier of heads changed to the German firm of Konig and Wernicke. These heads were marked "K & W Germany" and were much like the K*R heads. Later, during World War II when the German doll heads were no longer available, the dolls were made in Argentina by a firm named Bebilandia.

In May of 1933 *Billiken* moved from Lavaell 720 Street to Florida Street which was a very exclusive shopping area, much like our Fifth Avenue in New York City. It was at this time that Alicia Larguia launched the *Marilú* periodical and also opened her own children's clothing shop. Marilú was also sold at the shop as well as through the *Marilú* magazine. The shop sold well-made, stylish clothing and matching doll clothing for Marilú. All were marked Marilú with the Floridia Street address on a tag sewn securely into each garment. There was also Marilú doll furniture and many accessories, including trunks, shoes, bags, toys, etc. The furniture, like the clothing was always marked with Marilú. Marilú was indeed supplied with everything a little mother could wish for. Bebilandia manufactured a baby brother for Marilú called Bubilay sometime after 1940. He also had an extensive wardrobe and furniture and his clothes as well as all other items were also tagged Marilú. Marilú and her magazine continued to delight little Argentinian girls until sometime in the late 1950s at which time both the publication of the magazine and the manufacturing of the dolls came to a halt.

Plate 425. The **composition Marliú** doll stands 16" high and is made by Kammer and Reinhardt. The back of her head is incised "917." She has glass sleep eyes with painted lashes, an open mouth, and a dark blonde mohair wig. The body is a wood and composition ball jointed, flapper type body with the leg joints above the knee. She is wearing a dress and hat made from Marilú magazine patterns. See plate 428 for pattern. **With clothing: $500.00 and up.**

Plate 426. This later hard plastic Marilú was made by the Bebilandia Doll Company of Argentina. The doll's body is stamped in blue "Made in Argentina" in an oval with "Marilú" across the center. There are no markings on her head. The doll stands 16" tall and has an all plastic jointed body. She has black mohair braids, sleep eyes with both painted and synthetic lashes, and an open mouth with teeth and tongue. Her costume seems to be homemade and underneath the costume the doll wears a full set of underwear with what appears to be a corset made of white flannel. **Complete, with clothing: $200.00 and up.**

Agnes J. Sura Collection.

Plate 427. *Marilú* **Magazines** shown above are all from 1934. The *Marilú* magazine was first published in 1933. The magazine carried stories, puzzles, comic strips, crafts, and best of all, patterns for little mothers to sew for their Marilú dolls. Just like *La Semaine de Suzette* magazine for Bleuette this magazine also had a Bécassine type character with her own comic strip. Her name was Chorlita and she mirrored Bécassine both in looks and personality. *Marilú* magazine was in production until the 1950s. **Each: $10.00 and up.**

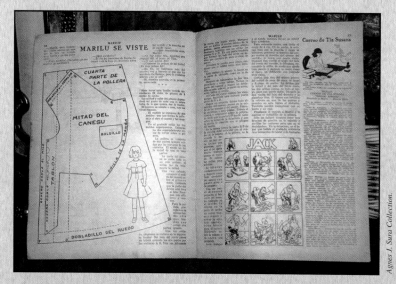

Agnes J. Sura Collection.

Plate 428. A Marilú pattern is shown inside this *Marilú* magazine see plate 425 for a composition Marilú wearing the dress made from this pattern. **Magazine: $5.00 and up.**

Agnes J. Sura Collection.

Plate 429. Marilú ad in *Marilú* magazine is advertising the Marilú dolls and also fashions, furniture, and the magazine subscriptions. **Magazine: $10.00 and up.**

Agnes J. Sura Collection.

Plate 430. Marilú Fashions. The skirt and blouse with the flower print is made from a pattern found in the *Marilú* magazine. The blue checked dress with the white voile collar and cuffs is a commercially made dress believed to be a Marilú dress but is not tagged. **Each: $50.00 and up.**

Mary Hoyer Doll

Mary Hoyer began her needlework study at an early age. Her older sister Alice was accomplished in sewing as well as knitting and crocheting. When Mary was eight years old she had appendicitis and after the operation she went to live with her big sister to recuperate. During this time Alice taught Mary to knit and crochet and even taught her a bit of sewing. Big sister Alice moved to Reading, Pennsylvania, and opened a needlework store. She was quite successful and expanded the business. When Mary was 18 and attending McCanns Business School, she went to work for Alice and learned to design and write knitting instructions.

Mary Hoyer began her designing career with knit and crochet fashions for infants and children. She was putting together a juvenile knitting and crochet book when she decided to add a pattern for a doll's hat and coat to match the little girl's. This pattern started Mary's career in knitting and designing for dolls. After a few patterns, Mary decided that she needed a doll with a slim body that would be easy for a child to handle. The Ideal Novelty and Toy Company produced Mary's first doll in 1937. They manufactured a 13" composition jointed doll with sleep eyes with lashes, and a mohair wig that could be ordered in three colors, blonde, dark brown, and auburn. About 2,000 of these dolls were sold by Mary Hoyer until Ideal halted production.

Mary then decided to have her own doll designed. She commissioned the well-known Bernard Lipfert to sculpt a doll to her specifications. She then hired the Fiberoid Doll Company in New York City to produce her doll in composition. The doll was 14" tall, jointed at the neck, hips, and shoulders. It had painted features and a mohair wig that could be ordered in four colors. The first 1,500 of the 14" dolls were unmarked. Mary sometime later decided to add her trademark. The earlier Mary Hoyer 14" dolls featured painted eyes and later they were changed to sleep eyes. The composition Mary Hoyer dolls were discontinued in 1946. Mary Hoyer estimates that there were approximately 6,500 dolls made in composition.

After the composition dolls were discontinued the newer material plastic was the choice for Mary Hoyer dolls. The mark was changed from "THE//MARY HOYER//DOLL" to "ORIGINAL//Mary Hoyer//DOLL" embossed in a circle. In the early 1950s Mary Hoyer produced an 18" doll she named Gigi. To date, no patterns for Gigi have surfaced. She wasn't as popular as the 14" doll and only about 2,000 were made. Another doll was introduced in the middle 1950s. She was 20" with rooted hair in a ponytail, but again, she didn't have patterns and wasn't as popular as the 14" doll. She was discontinued after just one shipment.

There were, however, other Mary Hoyer dolls with patterns. In 1957 a Vicki, was marketed. Vicki had feet molded for high heels and originally came in three sizes 10½", 12", and 14". The 10½" size was the only one that was made for any length of time. In 1958, there was a 10" toddler Margie and in 1961, 10" infant Cathy and 8" baby Janie. There were instructions for knitting and crocheting garments as well as sewing kits for all of the 1958 dolls. Ready-made clothing was also available for purchase.

In 1960 the 14" hard plastic Mary Hoyer doll was discontinued and a new vinyl 14" Becky doll was introduced. Becky was discontinued in 1968 and that was the last of Mary's dolls.

Mary Hoyer's granddaughter resurrected the Mary Hoyer Doll Company and in 1989, Mary Lynn Saunders produced the new 13½" Mary Hoyer doll. When I purchased my new vinyl Mary Hoyer doll in 1994 at a luncheon, I received a four-page Mary Hoyer Play Doll Patter which reads: *Welcome to the magical world of Mary Hoyer and our new addition of dolls "Let's play Mary Hoyer." Your new Mary Hoyer pattern is a universal pattern designed to mix and match pattern pieces to create many different fashions. You will find four sleeve styles, three bodice styles, two different skirt styles, a sport shirt, slacks, and shorts. Additional pieces will be available as our playline expands. Many of our styles are currently available as ready wear.*

So far, my research seems to indicate there were no more patterns.

The new Mary Hoyer dolls are still available on the Internet from the Mary Hoyer Company, but there is no mention of patterns or kits. However, ready-made clothing is still available as well as a new line of collectable dolls.

Plate 431. Composition Mary Hoyer Doll with her trunk. This 14" doll is all composition and jointed at the neck, shoulders, and hips. She has an auburn mohair wig, sleep eyes with lashes, and a closed mouth. The clothing in the trunk is a mix of ready-made or knitted and sewn from patterns. On the floor in front of the trunk are ready-made items with Mary Hoyer tags, a blue playsuit and a white fur cape. The yellow garment in the front is Annabelle Sport Suit from volume 5 of *Mary's Dollies*. Inside the trunk are shoes, roller skates, slippers, a fur muff, and hairnets. Hung over the top of the case is Anita skiing costume from volume 11 of *Mary's Dollies*. Mary Hoyer is wearing Julianna Skiing Costume from volume 5 of *Mary's Dollies* and carrying her skis. **Doll only dressed in Mary Hoyer costume: $300.00 and up.**

Plate 432. Mary's Dollies Volume No. 5 was the first booklet dedicated exclusively to the Mary Hoyer doll. Volumes one through four are the *Juvenile Styles* booklets. Mary started a publishing company to print *Juvenile Styles* and *Mary's Dollies* the booklet were numbered, in order, as they were written, regardless of the title. There were nine booklets of *Mary's Dollies*. Volumes 5, 6, 9, 10, 11, 12, 13, 14, and 15. **Each booklet: $25.00 and up.**

Plate 433. *Mary's Dollies* **Booklets 6, 9, 10, and 11.**

Plate 434. *Mary's Dollies* **Booklets 12, 13, 14, and 15.**

Mary's Dollies Booklet #5

> **Goldilocks** — Princess Dress and Beret: dress, panties, and beret (knit)
>
> **Julianna** — Ski Suit: ski pants, jacket, and hood (knit)
>
> **Arlene** — Bathing Ensemble: panties, bra, cape, and hood (knit)
>
> **Annabelle** — Sport Suit: blouse, skirt, and pants (knit)
>
> **Olga** — Skating Outfit: dress, panties, hat, and muff (crochet)
>
> **Mayree** — Party Frock: jacket, skirt, panties, and bonnet (crochet)

Mary's Dollies Booklet #6

> **Judy** — Lace Party Dress: dress (crochet)
>
> **Mary-Belle** — The Majorette: jacket, skirt, panties, and hat (crochet)
>
> **Nadine** — Red Cross Nurse: dress, panties, cape, and kit (knit)
>
> **Sonja** — Skiing Costume: jacket, hood, and ski pants (knit)
>
> **Lucretta** — Skating Costume: dress, muff, panties, and hat (crochet)
>
> **No proper name** — The Wavette: jacket, pants, skirt, vestie, hat, and bag (knit)

Mary's Dollies Booklet #9

> **Terry** — Little Miss Victory: dress and Dutch cap (crochet)
>
> **Sunny** — Queen of the Courts: tennis dress, panties, and hat (knit)
>
> **Janie** — Modern Cinderella: evening jacket, fascinator, skirt, and panties (knit and crochet, skirt, and panties sewing)
>
> **Kathleen** — Another Dance…Another Date…Another Gown: dress, angora jacket, and snood (knit and sewing)
>
> **Susanna** — V mail to her V male: skirt, panties, and hat (knit)
>
> **Zorina** — Miss Victory Dressed as a Charming Ally: coat, hat muff, and robe (crochet)

Mary's Dollies Booklet #10

> **Corine** — Queen of the Jungles: long dress, panties, and cap (knit)
>
> **Paula** — Bathing Ensemble: bra, panties, and cape (crochet)
>
> **Billie** — Riding Habit: vest, jodhpurs, and hat (knit and crochet)
>
> **Jackie** — Bare Back Rider: dress, panties, and flowers (crochet)
>
> **Patsy** — Coat Hat and Bag: coat, panties, hat, and bag (crochet)

Mary's Dollies Booklet #11

> **Anita** — Skiing Costume: jacket, pants, tassel, and cap (knit)
>
> **Dolores** — Skating Costume: dress panties, cap, and mitts (crochet)
>
> **Lucille** — Roller Skating Outfit: jumper, panties, blouse, mitts, and hat (knit)

Mary's Dollies Booklet #12

> **Peggy** — Travel Costume: coat, hat, panties, and bag (crochet)
>
> **Greta** — A Dutch Treat: dress, vest, panties, and cap (crochet)
>
> **Jo-Ann** — Swimming Suit: bathing suit (knit)
>
> **No proper name** — The Westerner: pants, blouse, bolero, and hat (knit and crochet)

Mary's Dollies Booklet #13

> **Nancy and Dick** — The Cow Boy and Girl: pants or skirt and panties and jacket (knit)
>
> **Hans and Tina** — The Pond's Sweethearts: jacket, jacket bib, pants or skirt, hat, scarf, cap, ties, and panties (knit)
>
> **Carol** — Suit and Hat: jacket, skirt, muff, and bonnet (crochet)
>
> **Betty and Bobby** — Mary Hoyer Twins: slipover, cardigan, pants, beanie, panties, and skirt (knit)

Mary's Dollies Booklet #14

> **Connie** — Short and Sweet: coat, beret, and panties (knit)
>
> **Nan and Jack** — The Ship's In: coat, panties, hat, jacket, and pants (crochet and knit)
>
> **Janette** — In the Spotlight: skirt, turtle-neck sweater, panties, and cap (knit)
>
> **Louise** — Travel in the Best Circles: dress, panties, and hat (crochet)

Mary's Dollies Booklet #15

> **Reneé** — Crocheted Sun Dress and Cape: dress, cape, and panties (crochet)
>
> **Isabelle** — Knitted Skating Costume: dress, cap, and panties (knit)

All knit and crochet patterns were also available as kits with all the necessary materials to complete each outfit.

Dolls and Their Patterns

Plate 435. Slacks and Shirt Sewing Kit by Mary Hoyer. This kit's identification and directions were written to be used for any of three different sets. The front of the header shows three different outfits, slacks and shirt, halter and shorts, and beach robe. On the back of the header are the instructions for each of the three outfits. To identify what is in the package, the correct name of the garment is underlined on the front. This package for the slacks and shirt has the garments cut out and ready to sew. There are six pieces to the shirt and three for the pants. **Complete: $50.00 and up.**

Kits to Sew

Kits include all necessary materials to make the ensembles.

Alice Blue Pinafore: pre-cut dress, pinafore, with shoes
Ballet Costume, short: pre-cut ballet dress and panties
Ballet Costume, long: pre-cut ballet dress and panties
Bridal Gown: pre-cut gown, panties, and veil
Bridesmaid Gown: pre-cut dress hat, and panties
Corduroy Jumper: pre-cut jumper and blouse
Dolly Madison: pre-cut dress and cover for parasol frame, with slippers
Evening Gown of Sparkle Net: pre-cut gown
Felt Coat and Hat: pre-cut coat and hat
Lawn Party Dress with Parasol: pre-cut dress and cover for parasol frame
Maxicoat: pre-cut coat, buttons, and yarn
Party Taffeta Dress: pre-cut dress and cover for parasol frame
Polly Prim: pre-cut patent leather coat, belt, and hat
Scotch Plaid Jumper: pre-cut jumper, blouse, and beret
Woolen Coat with Dress: pre-cut dress and hat
Shorts and Halter: pre-cut cotton halter and shorts
Slacks with Belt and Shirt: pre-cut shirt, pants, and belt
Southern Belle: pre-cut dress, cover for parasol frame, with shoes
Sun Bonnet Sue: pre-cut dress, bonnet, and panties
Terry Cloth Beach Robe with Sun Glasses: pre-cut robe
Twin Sets: sweater (knit) pre-cut skirt or slacks

In the fifteenth volume of Mary's Dollies Mary Hoyer introduces her Child's Sewing Kit.

First in a series of patterns designed by Mary Hoyer.

Children just love to use their little hands, whether to model in clay, dabble in finger paints, or one hundred and one other pastime pleasures.

They're forever asking mother "What can I do now?" It's been many years since we mothers were youngsters and we too often forget that little hands must be kept busy in order to keep them out of trouble. Yes, normal children have active little bodies and minds — they want to be kept occupied.

Mary Hoyer, internationally-known designer of hand-knits for children, has a daughter, too, one who is no different than your child, who has often asked the same question you mothers are confronted with — "What can I do now?"

So long as children are willing to do something, we mothers might just as well have them work on a worthwhile project…one that will entertain as well as educate them.

Mary Hoyer now presents the first in a series of such projects — Sun Bonnet Sue a Child's Sewing Kit! Just think of the fun your child will get dressing her Mary Hoyer Doll in a costume, which she herself has made!

Plate 436. This hard plastic **Mary Hoyer Doll** is 14" tall and has "ORIGINAL//Mary Hoyer// DOLL" embossed in a circle on her back. The doll is all hard plastic with green plastic sleep eyes, a closed mouth, saran wig, and is jointed at the shoulders, hips, and neck. She is wearing a hand-knit outfit titled Queen of the Courts shown in *Mary's Dollies Volume No. 9* on page 5. **Doll and costume: $300.00 and up**

Plate 437. McCall's Pattern #1564 for Mary Hoyer was copyrighted in 1950. This pattern was made after the composition dolls were discontinued. It was made for the 14" hard plastic Mary Hoyer dolls. Included in the pattern are a ballet costume and hatband, evening dress and cap, sun-suit and bonnet, slip and panties, cape and a crochet pattern for a skating costume. The pattern for the skating costume is the same as the Dolores Skating Costume in *Mary's Dollies Volume 11*. **Complete: $25.00 and up.**

Plate 438. McCall's Pattern #1891 for Mary Hoyer has a copyright date of 1954. This pattern was made four years after the first Mary Hoyer McCall's pattern. It is unusual for a doll clothes pattern to be issued four years after the doll was introduced and it shows how popular this little doll was. Included in the pattern are a street dress, gown and parasol cover, peignoir with nightgown, long or short petticoat, panties and a pattern for knitted cape, headband, and muff. **Complete: $25.00 and up.**

Plate 439. My Mary Hoyer Play Doll was purchased in 1994 at a luncheon. She has the long ringlet hairstyle. Three other hairstyles were available: long and wavy with wispy bangs, braids, and bob with bangs. The doll could be ordered with choice of three hair colors, blonde, brunette, or auburn and two eye colors, blue or brown. She stands 13" tall is made of hard vinyl and is entirely pose-able, has glass eyes, and painted lashes and mouth. She came in with a universal pattern that features interchangeable pieces for mix-and-match fashions designing. She is wearing a jumpsuit made from the pattern. **Complete with pattern: $75.00 and up.**

Dolls and Their Patterns

Godey's Lady Book Doll

The Godey's Lady Book Dolls of Ruth Gibbs were made both for children to sew for and to collect. On December 21, 1948, Ruth Gibbs of Flemington, New Jersey, was issued patent number 3 524 702 for Ruth Gibbs Godey's Lady Book Dolls. The 12" size china Godey's Lady Book Doll was the first doll she produced (plate 440). These dolls had a white china head, painted features, and white china limbs with a hard stuffed white cotton body. Their molded flattop hairstyle of the 1860s was painted black and each doll had a painted 22K gold necklace and bracelet. It is said that they were fashioned from a china doll in Ruth Gibbs own antique doll collection. The dolls had been made for some time before the patent, as Ruth Gibbs had made the 12" dolls a year earlier in 1947 when she dressed and sold the 12" dolls to G. Fox and Company for their 100th anniversary celebration.

The G. Fox and Company of Hartford, Connecticut, dealt in fancy goods especially for the ladies to use with the fashions of the day. The store carried all manors of trims, ribbons, lace, fringes, and special fabrics. It was a discriminating store where only the most fashioned minded shopped.

In 1948 G. Fox and Company was celebration 100 years in business and as a special promotion, Ruth Gibbs was asked to supply their company with seven special dressed dolls representing seven specific women of Hartford, Connecticut, in the year 1847. The seven dolls were each dressed differently in the fashions of that era. Each doll and their costume was identified as follows:

Mrs. Charles Hosmer in her street dress
Mrs. Julius Catlin in her calling costume
Mrs. David Watkinson in her winter afternoon gown
Mrs. Lydia Huntley Sigourney in her ball gown
Mrs. Sarah McClellan in her morning walking dress
Mrs. John Warburton in her walking dress
Mrs. Henrietta Porter in her bridal gown

The dolls were put in G. Fox and Company's standard everyday boxes, which were very exquisite with white embossed net and flowers over a soft aqua blue base.

The G. Fox and Company also sponsored a Godey's Lady Book Doll Dressing Contest. G. Fox and Company partnered with McCall's to tie in a doll and pattern offer to celebrate G. Fox and Company's centennial anniversary. McCall's printed pattern #1292 with transfer, was for costumes for the 12" Godey's Lady Book Dolls (plate 440). The envelope also included patterns for making six stuffed cloth Godey Lady's Book Dolls. Information on the back of the pattern envelope stated: *Patterns and complete directions are given for making all the costumes and underwear illustrated. These costumes with fit the 12" commercial Godey Lady Book doll, with china head. However, we are including a pattern and transfers, which can be used for making six Godey Lady Book Dolls, 12" high. Doll collectors will be pleased with these authentic costumes (circa 1860) for such noteworthies as Mrs. Cartright (A); Mrs. Cabot (B); Mrs. Carter (C); Miss Jennifer Boyles (D); Mrs. Enright (E); and Mrs. Eustis (F), pictured on the front of the envelope.*

Notice the ladies named on the McCall's pattern were different that the ladies dressed by Ruth Gibbs for G. Fox and Company. Also that the pattern spells the name of the dolls Godey Lady Book Doll and Ruth Gibbs' pamphlets are titled Godey's Lady Book Dolls and so were the boxes that contained the dolls from G. Fox and Company.

The intent of the contest was to inspire young people of Connecticut to use the McCall's pattern #1292 or to even create their own costume representing fashions worn a century ago. The contest was to run from September 2 through October 23, 1947, and the entrant had to be at least five years old to enter. There was no maximum age limit. There were seven classifications of costumes including: coat and bonnet, dinner dress, walking dress, morning dress, bridal gown, tea gown, and ball gown. All of the costumes had to be submitted on a Ruth Gibbs Godey's Lady Book Doll, which was available for purchase from the toy department at G. Fox and Company. Each individual could enter the contest as many times as they liked, but each entry had to be entered on a Godey's Lady Book Doll. The dolls ranged in price from $4.98 undressed to $7.98 dressed. In each doll box was a booklet containing the information about the doll-dressing contest, line drawing of fashions and accessories from 1847, and a little history about G. Fox and Company.

Just how and when the idea of the Godey's Lady Book Doll was conceived is somewhat a mystery. Discovered in a notebook filled with past issues of *Doll Talk* from Kimport Dolls was a single page advertising Godey Lady Dolls and printed next to a line drawing of two china dolls was:

This charming china dolly is an American, and quite the little aristocat amongst a collection of foreign dolls. The lady herself is an exact replica of (an) early day china-headed doll with milk-white complexion delicately tinted cheeks, ridiculously small booted china feet, and hands, while the body is authentically shaped and really sawdust stuffed. The Godey dolls are individually dressed, never two exactly alike, but each is copied from the exquisite old prints in the bound volumes of "Godey's Ladies Book" belonging to the Kimport library. A piece of antique lace or swatch of really old fabric is used whenever possible in copying the pictured costume. The period will be between 1850 and 1858, as these are the bound volumes used for reference. These are the aristocrats of American doll, and they grace any group and add beauty wherever shown.

There is no date on the page, but on the back of the page is pasted a cut out advertisement for the first book published by the Doll Collectors of Americas Inc., *American Made Dolls and Figurines.* Research shows this book was written in 1940, which is seven years before G. Fox and Company's anniversary. After the stores centennial, Ruth Gibbs continued to advertise her 12" doll along with McCall's pattern #1219 as a Little Lady Doll to Dress Yourself. Another patent was granted to Ruth Gibbs on September 12, 1950, patent number 560,692 was for

Godey's March family, representing the characters in the book, *Little Women*, written by Louisa May Alcott. The set of dolls was comprised of Mrs. March, 12" tall, and daughters Jo, Amy, Meg and Beth, all 7" tall. By 1951 the advertising pamphlets were showing the 7" "Little Lady Dolls for which you can sew." These were advertised as:

Pliable play dolls, with firmly stuffed percale bodies, wired to hold any position. The heads, arms and legs are of Practically unbreakable china. All Pink Luster. Hand-painted with the colors fired on. All have 22K gold slippers.

Little Lady Dolls for which you can sew

#51-105 Little Dressmaker — 7" doll packed in the "Village Deb Shop" Toy Town box. Contains a miniature pattern (just like the full size one's Mother buys) and all the materials for two complete outfits ready to cut and sew. Hats, muffs, parasols, aprons, dresses, etc.

#51-205 The Original Godey Lady 12" tall. McCall Pattern #1292 was made for this doll it contains six patterns for dresses, bonnets, coats and lingerie. May be purchased at any McCall Pattern counter for 50c.

#51-205M 7" Undressed Doll — Has printed patterns on the box for two complete outfits (plate 441).

Dolls #51-105 and #51-205M had the same pattern. In the 1951 booklet there was also a new size china doll a 10" with a real hair wig that could be shampooed and clipped. In later catalogs the last doll to be shown was Miss Moppet, an 11" hard plastic doll with a wig and unpainted molded shoes and socks. Ruth Gibbs did not make patterns for these dolls; they were purchased and dressed by her with extra outfits available. As far as I know there were no patterns for the 10" or 11" dolls. As time went on, the doll business became too competitive and Ruth Gibbs was showing fewer and fewer doll in her shop. She turned to small giftware as the main inventory. In 1963 fire clamed the factory building and Ruth Gibbs's health had declined. She closed the store and sold off the remaining inventory. Ruth Gibbs died on December 22, 1970, but her little dolls will live on to continue to delight doll collectors and seamstresses for years.

Plate 441. Little Play Friend doll was advertised as your Practical Little Play Friend. She was shown in a 1951 advertising pamphlet as a 7" Little Lady Doll for which you can sew. The advertisement stated: *Pliable play dolls, with firmly stuffed percale bodies, wired to hold any position. The heads, arms, and legs are of practically unbreakable china. All pink lustre. Hand-painted with the colors fired on. All have 22K gold slippers.* She came tied in a box that flattened out so you could cut or copy the patterns that were printed on the inside. There was a blouse, two different skirts, hat, apron, parasol, and muff. These are the same patterns that came with the Village Deb Shop toy town box. **Doll in pattern box: $100.00 and up.**

Plate 440. 12" Godey's Lady Book Doll and McCall's pattern #1292. Godey's Lady Book doll in her original underclothing has black molded hair, and painted features, she also has a painted 22K gold necklace and bracelet and black painted shoes. She is shown with the McCall's pattern #1292 that was advertised by J. Fox and company in their doll-dressing contest. The pattern consists of a dinner dress, tea gown, walking dress, bridal gown, morning dress, ball gown, coat with bonnet, and long panties and petticoat. Also included was a pattern for a 12" cloth doll that included six face transfers. **Doll: $150.00 and up; pattern $10.00 and up.**

Plate 442. 7" Godey's Little Lady with painted red hair is dressed in a blouse, skirt, apron, parasol, hat, and muff made from view number one in Godey's Little lady Patterns for the 7" little lady dolls. In the background is the cut pattern that was used for her costume, and in the bottom corner is the 3½" x 2¼" envelope that contained the pattern. **Doll and pattern: $100.00 and up.**

Sweet Sue Doll

In 1948 Sweet Sue was introduced to the market. American Character did not manufacture Sweet Sue; Model Plastics Company in White Plains, New York, in fact, produced her to American Character's specifications. At the same time Model Plastics Company was also manufacturing dolls for the Arranbee and Madame Alexander doll companies. Each company supplied the wigs and dressed the dolls in their own clothing and then sold the dolls under their own company name.

Even though Sweet Sue had a teenage body, she is not considered to be a fashion doll because she doesn't have a large ready made wardrobe that could be purchased separately. She was always offered dressed in one of a selection of outfits each year, but extra clothing was offered only in 1955 and in 1956. A small booklet was issued in the winter of 1955/1956 that contained four outfits that were available for purchase only by mail from the company. The four outfits were Easter Parade, Fun in the Sun, Indian Summer, and Ballerina. They were priced at $6.00 each and were available in sizes 15", 18", 22", 25", and 31". Sweet Sue remained on the market, with various changes, from 1948 until 1966

Sweet Sue was one of the first dolls that utilized children's television programming to target children with advertising. One of the television programs that was used to advertise Sweet Sue was *Ding Dong School*. with Miss Frances. A 1954 American Character catalog shows a picture of Miss Frances on the front cover with a Tiny Tears and a Sweet Sue doll. Inside is a full-page ad with clothes and pattern outfits for Sweet Sue. It reads: *Sweet Sut Outfits — featured on NBC-TV's Ding Dong School. Lots of fun for mother and daughter, a gift package of extra clothes and patterns for Sweet Sue. In it is a complete dress outfit — taffeta dress and matching panties, shoes, socks and as an extra dividend; a package of McCall's Patterns, for three additional outfits — lots of thrills for little girls and mothers, too.*

Plate 443. Sweet Sue #1025 Bride is 18" and was introduced in 1956. She has a hard plastic head, body, and legs, and soft vinyl arms with extra joints at elbows and knees. Her synthetic dark blonde hair is rooted into a soft plastic skullcap. She has green plastic sleep eyes and a closed mouth. Her synthetic tulle and lace over satin wedding gown has a v-neck and is trimmed both at the neck and sleeves with lace. She also wears satin panties, nylon stockings, and white shoes. Her tulle veil is centered under a circle of lace and is edged in lace. She is missing her bride's bouquet. **Complete: $200.00 and up.**

Plate 444. Simplicity and McCall's Sweet Sue Patterns #1336 and 1720 were both made exclusively for Sweet Sue. Simplicity's undated pattern is number #1336 and it was for doll sizes 15", 18", 22", and 25". The pattern is for an all-occasion wardrobe that includes a dress, hat, and coat, party gown, negligee, baby-doll pajamas, slip, and panties. McCall's 1952 pattern #1720, Doll Clothes to fit the Sweet Sue Dolls, with electric blue transfer included overalls, blouse, kerchief, dress, jacket, skirt, beret, snow suit and cap, panties, and petticoat. **Complete, each: $10.00 and up.**

 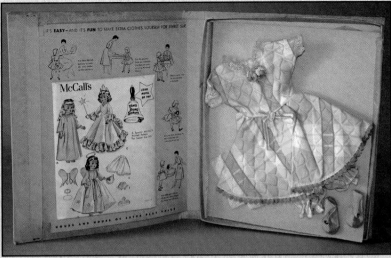

Plate 445. Extra Clothing for Your American Character Doll is printed on the spine of the 13" x 11" x 1" book style box. The front of the box reads: *complete outfit for your Sweet Sue doll with a special McCall's pattern of 3 designs for extra clothes that you can make yourself. Buy One outfit — make Three more.* On the inside box cover is a McCall's pattern that makes three fairy type outfits, the pattern for one gown is used twice. Still in the box recess is an aqua, pink and white striped cotton pique dress, trimmed in lace and flowers with matching panties. Also included are rayon socks and pink center-snap oilcloth shoes. The pattern glued on to the inside lid is a regular McCall's pattern #1823, however the number does not appear on the envelope. Printed in it's place is: "Star pupil of the Ding Dong School. A Special McCall's Printed Pattern For Sweet Sue Doll." The pattern number 1823 is printed on the instructions and pattern pieces. I have seen three different styles of the ready-made dresses in this set, but only one pattern. The pattern is for fairy-type clothing that consists of two gowns (one used twice), net over skirt, slip, panties, crown, wings, halo, harp, and wand. There is no date on the box or pattern, however this set was advertised in a 1954 American Character catalog. **Complete: $100.00 and up.**

Lingerie Lou

In the August 1949 issue of *Playthings* magazine, Doll Bodies, Inc. announced a new Dress-Me doll. The article stated:

Doll Bodies, Inc., Fifth Avenue, New York 10, N.Y. are now offering a series of eye-appealing "Dress-Me" dolls. Their first number, "Lingerie Lou" is a 7½" doll with movable head and arms and a charming face. The doll is dressed in a new type of plastic bra and panties. An interesting play feature of these garments resides in the fact that they can be buttoned and unbuttoned, thus enabling the youngster to dress and undress the doll at will. This doll dressed in blue, black and white panties, packed in an attractive open-window box is reported to be receiving an excellent reception from the trade. The Company states that a complete line of plastic dolls will soon be put on the market. It is interesting to note that this Company supplies doll manufacturers with doll parts. There was also a full-page ad showing the dolls actual size with the following information:

"Lingerie Lou," our cute little Sew 'N Sew
*Removable plastic panties and bra (white, blue, and black)
*Washable unbreakable plastic body
*Genuine mohair wig (blonde, brunette, redhead)
*Movable head and arms
*Hand-painted features and shoes
*Individually packaged in sales-appealing window box

The 7½" doll was priced at 49¢. Notice there is no mention of a sewing pattern in this advertisement. In the January 1950 *Playthings* magazine, an article stated:

Doll Bodies, Inc., is a new concern specializing in the manufacturing of plastic doll bodies for the trade. Although this Company has been in business only since October 15th, it is interesting to note that they shipped over 37,000 dozen before the first of December. The firm members state that production has now been increased to 1,400 dozen per day. Their 7½" doll has three different heads from which to choose. The company further adds that they were among the first to turn out an 11½" all plastic doll with movable arms, head and legs.

Doll Bodies Inc. also offered a 10" x 6½" magazine in 1952 titled *Make Your Own Dresses for Your Doll Collection* featuring "Lingerie Lou." Inside was written: *Out of these pages step dolls from far-away lands to win your heart...start your collection today, a collection completely different from any other. It's easy and fun to make these lovely costumes with Lingerie Lou Patterns. Although you follow the patterns for style, you choose your own fabrics and colors. And so you wind up with a National Dolls Collection nobody else can copy, which becomes a beautiful decoration for your room.*

The 32 costumes offered from Doll Bodies Inc. were numbered 101 to 132 and are listed below.

#101 Colonial Doll　　#103 Italian Doll
#102 Spanish Doll　　#104 German Doll

Dolls and Their Patterns

#105 Scotch Doll
#106 Irish Doll
#107 American Bridesmaids
#108 American Bride
#109 American Maid of Honor
#110 Norway Doll
#111 Sweden Doll
#112 French Doll
#113 Dutch Doll
#114 Poland Doll
#115 Argentina Doll
#116 Swiss Doll
#117 Denmark Doll
#118 Russian Doll

#119 Gypsy Doll
#120 South American Doll
#121 Welsh Doll
#122 Puritan Doll
#123 Slavonic Doll
#124 Austrian Doll
#125 Queen Elizabeth
#126 Israeli Doll
#127 Hindu doll
#128 Japanese Doll
#129 Greek Doll
#130 Turkish Doll
#131 American Playsuit
#132 American Blue Jeans

1. Any Famous American Fashion, modern or historic.
2. World Famous Character, historic or modern.
3. National Costumes.
4. Fun and Fantasy Themes.

Each contestant was allowed no more than three entries. Every doll entered was donated, in the constants name, to the March of Dimes to be used for their benefit. The entrants each received a handsome parchment certificate from the March of Dimes acknowledging their contribution of dolls.

Lingerie Lou was sold first in a box with a cellophane window, but by 1952 she was found without the plastic underclothing and packaged in a cellophane wrapper with red and yellow printing on the front which reads: *An original "Lingerie Lou" product includes Ready-To-Dress Doll and 2 Real Dress Patterns*. In a larger 1952 set Make your own Dresses with two 7½" dolls, heart-shaped stands and the booklet "Make your own dresses for your doll collecting featuring 'Lingerie Lou.'" was offered. By 1957 the dolls were offered in cellophane packaging with red and yellow lettering that read "an original 'Lingerie Lou' product includes 2 costume patterns with sewing instructions." The dolls were still priced at 49¢.

Throughout the 1950s the 7½" Lingerie Lou face changed; her eyes went from painted to sleep set, and she lost the plastic underwear, but her size and body stayed the same. She was a popular doll that was sold in dime stores and yarn shops and she was marketed both dressed and undressed, but the company sold many more of the undressed dolls. Both children and adults would crochet, knit, or sew her outfits. McCall's Pattern Company offered patterns for a 7½" doll such as Lingerie Lou, and her name was used along with others on the pattern envelopes. The patterns were McCall's #1898, #1965, #2057, #2150, #2270, #2323. My research indicates that only the 7½" doll had patterns made exclusively for Lingerie Lou.

In 1956 Doll Bodies Inc. offered a sewing contest for their Lingerie Lou dolls, "Dress a doll Today// In A Costume Of Your Choice//Grand Prize $2,500." There were also 122 additional cash prizes. All the information was printed on the paper header folded and stapled at the top of the cellophane bag containing the Lingerie Lou doll. A year later, in 1957, it was the National Doll Dressing Institute, Inc. in New York City sponsored the doll-dressing contest. All the information was again printed on the paper header at the top of the bag. It was advertised as the Second Annual Dress-A-Doll Contest and was aimed at the ladies, encouraging them to put their leisure time to creative fun and profit. The doll sizes that were eligible were from 7½" to 11½" only. Use of the Lingerie Lou doll was not required, but the following was printed in red ink beneath the rules:

"Lingerie Lou" contest dolls are nationally distributed. On sale in all variety stores in the toy and art Needlework sections.

There was a grand prize of $2,500 and 127 additional prizes that totaled $15,000. The entry blank was in the folded paper that was stapled to the doll's cellophane packaging at the top (plate 447). There were four categories:

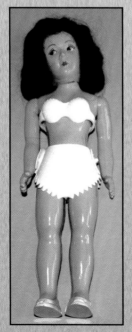

Plate 446. The 7½" **Painted Eye Lingerie Lou Doll** was advertised in the August 1949 *Playthings* magazine as a new "Dress-Me" doll by Doll Bodies, Inc. It came with molded plastic underwear. The underwear was a selling point for the doll because little fingers could snap and unsnap the garments when dressing and undressing the doll. The first dolls were sold in a pink and blue window box with dressmaking suggestions and priced at .49¢. **Complete: $10.00 and up.**

Plate 447. The **Sleep-eye Lingerie Lou Doll** was offered in 1952 in a pink window box, which included two dolls, four patterns and a doll collector's book showing Lingerie Lou modeling all the patterns made up. The patterns in the set were #101, #103, #104, and #108. The same doll was also sold in a single cellophane package in 1957 with an offer to enter a doll-dressing contest. Along with each doll came two patterns, the same book only smaller, and the rules of the contest with an entry blank. The pattern choices were from #101 through #132 and could be viewed through the back of the cellophane package for ease of selection. **Two doll box complete: $50.00 and up, one doll package complete: $10.00 and up.**

Note: I have seen the Lingerie Lou dolls in the two-box set with and without the plastic clothing but I have only seen two sets. Some, but not all, of the cellophane packages contained a heart shaped doll stand.

Plate 448. Dress Them Yourself Lingerie Lou patterns. Research to date indicates the first 16 patterns were sold in one of three ways: either packaged with the doll (two in a package) or in a standard pattern envelopes showing all of the first 16 patterns on the front. At first the envelope contained all 16 patterns and was printed on the front: *16 complete doll dress patterns and illustrated book*, and indeed there were 16 patterns, but sometime later the wording was changed to: *Dress them yourself!* The number 16 was crossed out on the back of the envelope and the number 8 was added. There were now eight patterns in each envelope. Pattern A envelope held patterns #101 – #108 and Pattern B envelope held #109 – #116. It seems the last series with numbers 117 through 132 were sold only by twos packaged with the dolls. All the patterns were at some time, sold in twos with the dolls. And all the patterns regardless of how they were sold were printed on a folded 14" x 18" tan, craft-type paper, with instructions. **Complete, eight patterns: $10.00 and up.**

Bucilla Thrift Kit Doll

Plate 449. Ideal Toy and Novelty made the **Bucilla Thrift Kit Doll**, also sold as Baby Mine, from 1951 to 1954. The doll is all hard plastic and 11" tall, with side-glancing sleep eyes, molded painted hair, and jointed at the shoulders and hips. "Ideal Doll" is embossed on the back. It could be ordered from the Bucilla Company using Bucilla Doll Form #8901. **Complete: $25.00 and up.**

Plate 450. Bucilla Thrift Kit #1679 is for a 12-piece Cowboy and Cowgirl outfits. The kit contains stamped materials to make two complete wardrobes including skirt, jacket, trousers, two blouses, two pair boots, scarf, and two hats. Gun belt with two guns and holsters, also Bucilla flosses sufficient to complete the simple embroidery included. The kit was advertised for a 12" doll. **Complete: $25.00 and up.**

Plate 451. Bucilla Thrift Kit #1881 is a Boy Skater Wardrobe Kit. Contains cap, sweater, trousers stamped for simple embroidery and sewing. Also socks, shoes, rollerskates, buttons, and Bucilla flosses sufficient to complete the simple embroidery. There was a matching Girl Skater Outfit #1880. The kit was advertised for a 12" doll. **Complete: $25.00 and up.**

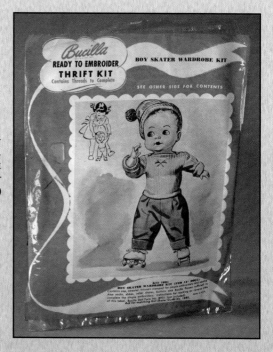

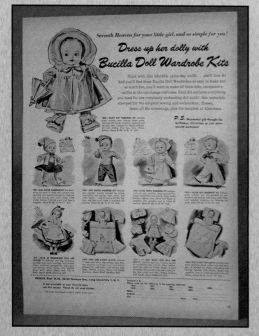

Plate 452. Bucilla Doll Wardrobe Kits ad from the 1952/53 *McCall's Needlework* magazine. Shown in this ad are the boy and girl skaters outfits shown in plates 450 and 451. Three other Thrift Kits are also shown: A Rainy Day Wardrobe Kit #1884 that includes dress, panties, coat, bonnet, shoes, socks, raincape with hood, rain boots, umbrella, and carrying case, Little Nurse Wardrobe Kit #1882 that contains uniform, cap, panties, bag stamped for simple embroidery and sewing, shoes, and socks; and Sailor Boy Wardrobe Kit #1883 containing sailor uniform, hat, tie, shoes, and socks. **Ad: $10.00 and up.**

Betsy McCall Doll

Betsy McCall was officially born in print in the May 1951 issue of *McCall's* magazine (plate 453) with her picture on the cover. Betsy started out as a little girl of five years old, going on six. Introducing Betsy McCall is on the last page of the magazine. There is a picture of mother, father, Betsy, and Nosy McCall. The introduction reads: *This is a design for Betsy McCall. Betsy is five, going on six and she lives in a little white house with a porch and a yard to play in. Her mother and daddy and Nosy, her puppy, live in the white house too.* Nosy is six months old. *Betsy and Nosy and Betsy's friends play together all the time. And every month from now on they'll come to play with you too.*

Betsy's creator was Kay Morrissey, but in 1958 the Betsy McCall feature passed to Ginnie Hofmann. Betsy was a typical little girl in the '50s who traveled extensively and for each destination, she modeled the appropriate clothing for *McCall's* magazine.

Betsy was a fun paper doll but she was also created to advertise children's clothing. She helped sell actual Betsy McCall style dresses made by Cinderella, Kate Greenaway, Young Land, Mary Jane, Nanette and White Stag Sports among many others. She also promoted Betsy McCall toys and *McCall's* dress patterns for little girls. In the beginning Betsy was simply a *McCall's* magazine paper doll for children to cut out and play with, however in the June 1952 issue of *McCall's* magazine there was a story about Betsy at the beach that changed Betsy's and little girls lives forever (plate 454).

Plate 453. McCall's Magazine Introduces Betsy in May of 1951. "Your children will love to play with Betsy McCall" is printed on the front cover of the magazine. Inside is the first paper doll and an article about the little girl shown on the cover meeting Betsy, the paper doll. The cover girl is four year old Peggy McGregor of Westfield, New Jersey. **Complete: $5.00 and up.**

Note: See Betsy McCall paper doll sets (plates 136. 137 and 138) in the chapter on Sewing and Embroidery Sets Featuring Paper Dolls.

Plate 454. Betsy McCall Goes to the Beach the June 1952, paper doll page was titled "Betsy McCall Goes to the Beach." Along the left side are four pictures with captions telling the story of Betsy's day at the beach. *"Now Nosy,"* said Betsy, *"You've had your lunch so sit down and rest a while with Fluffy and me."* Then a big wave rolled up the beach and washed Fluffy, the duck, out to sea. Nosy swam to the rescue! He brought Fluffy back. *"Oh, Mummy, he's ruined." "Don't' cry,"* said Mummy, *"we'll get a new toy." "I want a doll that looks like me." "Well maybe that's what it will be,"* promised Mummy. *"Wait and See."* **Complete: $10.00 and up.**

Plate 455. Betsy McCall Gets a Doll. Finally in the September 1952 issue Betsy gets her wish, but not, without advertising three new dresses. The title of the paper doll page was *Betsy McCall Gets a Doll*: Betsy and her mother were buying a new dress. *"Eeny, meeny, miney, mo."* said Betsy. *"Oh, Mummy,"* she broke off, *"they're so pretty! Can't I have all three?" "All right."* Mummy relented, *"and you may wear the red dress home, but let's save the others for school." "Now,"* she said, *"shall we see about that new doll?"* They took the escalator to the toy department. *"I want a doll"* Betsy told the clerk. *"Now this is a 'lovely doll,'"* said the salesgirl. *"No,"* said Betsy, *"she's too big. Besides, I want a doll that looks just like me!" "Why I have 'just' the doll!"* — and the clerk led Betsy to a counter where there was a row of dolls — and they all looked *"just like Betsy."* And they wore dresses exactly like Betsy's. *"Oh my,"* she said. *"Let me have the one in red so right away everyone will see she's mine."* In the same issue there is a photo story about the new doll. The doll was made by the Ideal Toy Corporation and was sculpted by Bernard Lipfert to McCall's specifications. **Page: $10.00 and up.**

Plate 456. Betsy McCall doll and apron pattern. The first Betsy doll, made by Ideal was 14" with dark brown saran hair. Betsy was dressed in one of the three different style dresses shown on the September 1952 paper doll page. She wore a wrist tag with hair curlers on it and came with a pattern for an apron. The apron pattern was included as a bonus with Betsy McCall as an enticement to buy McCall's patterns for Betsy's wardrobe. The back of the pattern-envelope states: *Make an entire Wardrobe for your Betsy McCall doll...with McCall's Patterns! McCall's has created a whole wardrobe for you to make for your Betsy doll...every thing she needs just like a real little girl! All Easy-as-pie to make. McCall's pattern 1729 has a cute raincape and hat; a pantie-blouse that goes with a little bolero and wrap-around skirt; a sun suit and a cover-all! In McCall's pattern 1728 there are undies for Betsy: panties and a petticoat; and a robe and pajamas, a sun-dress and two coats and a little hat! All have special Talon zippers. Ask for them today in your favorite pattern department.* The pattern instructions are written very simply with lots of diagrams, obviously made for a child. The second doll had more pronounced bangs and retained the apron pattern. The Betsy shown here is wearing a two-piece outfit; the dress and apron are made from McCall's pattern #1812, view C (plate 459). **Doll: $200.00 and up, apron pattern: $10.00 and up.**

Plate 457. The Betsy McCall doll gets a wonderful wardrobe was the title of a page from the October 1952 *McCall's* magazine. Two easily made patterns from *McCall's* were offered for Betsy — McCall's patterns #1728 and #1729. The patterns were created by the Talon Department of Design and copyrighted by McCall's. The caption beneath the little girl at the top with the Betsy doll states: *This little girl has a new dress (McCall's children's pattern #9092) just like the one the Betsy McCall doll wore when she came from the store.* The pattern for it even includes an apron that's a duplicate of the doll apron pattern that comes in the box with Betsy. **Page: $10.00 and up.**

Plate 458. Betsy McCall's 1952, patterns #1728 and #1729. These patterns for the 14" doll were issued in 1952. Pattern #1728 includes pajamas, quilted robe, sundress, two coats, a hat, panties, and a petticoat. Pattern #1729 includes a pantie-blouse, cape, hat, sun-suit, coveralls, and cap. The patterns were advertised as easily made and most were only one piece. **Complete, each: $10.00 and up.**

Plate 459. Betsy McCall's #1812 was issued a year later with four new outfits for Betsy. "Doll Clothes Designed for Betsy McCall Doll" is printed on the front of the envelope, however it was in sizes 14" and 16". The 16" size is for the Ideal Toni doll. The envelope contains patterns for two styles of dresses, crocheted stole, fabric hat, straw hat, apron, nightgown, petticoat, and panties. **Complete: $10.00 and up.**

Plate 460. Betsy McCall's 1954 pattern #1894. McCall's pattern #1894 is titled "4-H Club and Red-Cross Nurse Doll Uniforms Designed for Betsy McCall Doll." It also includes the 16" size to fit the Toni doll. There are four outfits a Red Cross nurse's dress and cap, nurse's cape, 4-H Club dress, cape, cap, slip, panties, and 4-H Club crocheted cap. **Complete: $10.00 and up.**

Plate 461. Tiny Betsy McCall. In 1957 McCall's issued another license, this time to American Character and the 8" all hard plastic version of Betsy McCall was born. She was very different from the first Betsy not only was she smaller, but her fashions had more of a teenage look than the little girl Betsy dresses to which we were accustomed. She was also jointed at the knees, which allowed her to kneel and sit properly. The first year, the dolls were dressed in a sheer nylon chemise with a chevron design and white lace trim. A large and lavish wardrobe was available for Betsy and some of her outfit's cost more than Betsy herself. This Betsy is wearing a costume made from McCall's "instant" Pattern #2239, view D. **All original: $200.00 and up.**

Note: The 8" Betsy also came in a Designer's Studio #B498. The box is 10½" x 16" x 1¾" with a window front. The backboard inside is printed to look like a dress studio. In the center is Betsy dressed in a red seersucker housecoat with the edges trimmed in white bias binding and a large white pocket on the front. She wears white shoes and socks, a chemise, and a white tam on her head. To one side of the box, hanging on a hanger, is a pre-cut white dress with a red flower at the waist. Above is a sewing kit with thread, needles, and a thimble, and below are two cellophane packages of ribbon, lace, and trim. On the other side of Betsy is a pre-cut pair of pajamas tied with a ribbon to a plastic dress form marked American Character. Behind the dress form is McCall's pattern #2239 for Betsy. This is a very rare piece.

Plate 462. 8" Betsy McCall patterns #2239 and #2457. McCall's pattern #2239 "instant" Doll Clothes paper pattern is all one piece; pin to fabric according to cutting layout and cut instantly. The 1958 pattern contains pinafore with attached petticoat, pajamas, robe, leotard, skirt, collar, bonnet, chemise, and ball gown. McCall's pattern #2457 copyrighted in 1961, contains a bridal outfit, pajamas, robe, jacket dress, hat, tights, top, shorts, panties, skirt, petticoat, and pantalets. This pattern came in 8½" and 30". **Complete, each pattern: $10.00 and up.**

Plate 463. Betsy McCall's Dog "Nosy's" Pattern #1810. Nosy was immortalized in a pattern in 1953. McCall's pattern #1810 had a pattern for Nosy and a kitten. Nosy was 15" high and the kitten was 11". The patterns were very simple with only four pattern pieces for Nosy. **Complete: $5.00 and up.**

Plate 464. 16" Cloth Betsy McCall Pattern #2097 and #3423 was first issued in 1956. McCall's #2097 was advertised as an "instant" pattern. It contains patterns for the 16" cloth doll, her chemise, petticoat, dress, and jacket, and three different styles of dresses. McCall's Pattern #3423 in 2001 was a repeat of #2097. It is the same doll with the same, chemise, petticoat, dress, and jacket, but only one style dress and a pattern for a pair of shoes. It is interesting to note the prices; in 1956 it was 35¢, in 2001 it was $13.95 with fewer pieces. **Complete, each: $10.00 and up.**

Plate 465. Victorian Betsy McCall #7933, #7934 and 8139. These patterns were first offered in 1995 and 1996. This cloth doll is 18" tall and is dressed in a Victorian dress, bloomers, and tights. The same year, McCall's pattern #7934 Winter Holiday Wardrobe was offered for Betsy McCall. There is a Christmas dress, a dress for tea, a winter coat with muff and hat, and a nightgown for bedtime. Also included are ice skates, boots, shoes, and slippers. A year later in 1996, McCall's published pattern #8139 with four more dresses for the 18" cloth doll along with apron, two styles of pantaloons, socks, and two different styles of shoes. **Complete, each: $5.00 and up.**

Plate 466. Fabric Paper Doll Betsy McCall's Pattern #8207 is copyrighted 1996. The set includes a flat house-shaped carrying case, a flat fabric doll, ballet dress, recital dress, party dress, school dress, tights, hair bows, crown, hat, boots, and slippers. **Complete: $5.00 and up.**

Note: See plate 136 for Betsy McCall Biggest Paper Doll.

Plate 467. 14" Tonner Betsy and her 2003 and 2004 patterns #M4334 and #M4743 are what you will find on the shelves in 2005. The Tonner Doll Company McCall's Crafts pattern #M4334 was issued in 2003 and was for both 8" and 14" dolls. It includes baby doll pajamas, play dress with rick rack trim and headband, raincoat, capri pants, and top. McCall's Crafts pattern #M4743 was issued in 2004, also for both the 8" and 14" dolls. It contains patterns for a dress and sash, coat and dress and ballet outfit. This Toner Doll Company Betsy is wearing the dress made from McCall's Crafts pattern M4743. **Complete: pattern, $5.00 and up; doll, dressed, $75.00 and up.**

Elizabeth the Dressmaking Doll

Elizabeth the Dressmaking Doll was produced by Pedigree Soft Toys Ltd. Originally named G & J Lines Ltd., this company was founded in the mid-nineteenth century by two brothers George and Joseph Lines to make baby carriages and wooden toys. Joseph Lines had three sons who took over and in 1919 incorporated Lines Brothers Ltd. In 1924, Lines Brothers Ltd. moved to a new location in Merton London and registered the name Triang Toys, using a triangle as a symbol to represent the three brothers. The Pedigree name was registered in 1931 and was used as a trademark for baby carriages. It wasn't until 1937 that the Pedigree Soft Toys, Ltd. name was used for soft toys in their line of dolls and Pedigree Pets. Although the company branched out in other toys, Lines kept the name Pedigree Company of Soft Toys for its dolls and animals until its demise in 1988.

Elizabeth the Dressmaking Doll debuted in 1953 (plate 468). Her sole purpose was to be a dressmaking doll for *Woman* magazine, a weekly, which was published every Thursday. Elizabeth could be purchased in Britain at good toyshops everywhere, but her patterns could only be obtained by mail from *Woman* magazine. A *Junior Woman* magazine (plate 469) was free with the doll, along with one Veronica Scott pattern for an afternoon dress to sew for Elizabeth (plate 470). The first pages in *Woman Junior* introduced you to Elizabeth. On the third page

in the magazine is a message from Veronica: *You can make lovely clothes for Elizabeth says Veronica Scott of Woman. Here they are...the patterns I've designed specially to fit Britain's prettiest doll! I so fell in love with Elizabeth when I met her, that designing her a wardrobe has been as much fun as designing clothes for the grown readers of WOMAN! And just think what fitting real, professional patterns to your own doll means...with teenage Elizabeth as a guide, you'll soon be able to carry right on and make up patterns yourself!*

There are three series of patterns to choose from, all in the very latest teenage fashions — the ones you'll be wearing soon yourself. They're smart, but not a bit difficult — read on and study my sewing tips on pages 9 – 12!

Start with the free pattern that comes with Elizabeth; it's an easy beginning — then send off for your favourite series — A, B, or C — or all three with the Pattern Order Form on page 13.

The three sets contain patterns for a total of 12. Series A contains patterns for a three-piece beach outfit, a duster coat, a suit and blouse, and a nightdress. With Series B you can create an evening dress, an evening slip, cami-knickers (teddy), and a housecoat. Series C is for a winter coat, a winter dress, a party dress, and a slip and knickers (panties). The rest of the little magazine contains girl-toy ads from Pedigree Soft Toy Company.

Dolls and Their Patterns

Plate 468. Elizabeth the Dressmaking Doll was introduced in 1953 by the Pedigree Company Soft Toys Limited of Britain. She has the same face as the Pedigree Pin-Up series of dolls. Elizabeth is a 19" hard plastic doll with a teen-type body. She has a very soft saran wig, blue plastic flirty sleep eyes with synthetic upper lashes and painted lower lashes. She has very rosy cheeks and knees. Elizabeth comes dressed in the frock that was designed for her by Veronica Scott who at the time was a fashion expert for *Woman* magazine. She came with a *Woman Junior* mini magazine and a pattern D for an afternoon dress. **Doll, pattern and magazine: $300.00 and up.**

Plate 469. A page, in the **Woman Junior magazine** that came with her asks: *Who is Elizabeth? She's Britain's most beautiful doll "and" the girl with the brightest idea for years — to make "you" a real-life dressmaker. How is she dressed? She wears a frock designed by Veronica Scott, fashion expert of WOMAN. In her box is a FREE paper pattern for another charming Veronica Scott style, and you can get in addition proper paper patterns for twelve other delightful garments, all designed by Veronica Scott. And you make her pretty clothes yourself, WOMAN JUNIOR gives you the first hints on sewing and the patterns contain full instruction for making the loveliest outfits for Elizabeth. They will fit beautifully too, for Elizabeth is the first doll ever made to have a true teenage figure — tiny waist and beautifully shaped arms and legs. Elizabeth herself is sweetest of all. You're sure to love her bright blue eyes and beautiful face, especially when she wears the cute clothes you will be able to make for her. Look out for Elizabeth, she's not only lovely, she's longing to meet her life-long friends. You must make sure it's You!* **Good condition: $25.00 and up.**

Plate 470. Elizabeth's Patterns Pattern D in color was the pattern that came with Elizabeth. It was suggested that the dress be made in a gay, colorful silk. I made mine with a pretty 1950s polished cotton. Elizabeth the Dressmaking Doll is printed on both the front and back of this pattern envelope. Inside is a printed pattern with a sheet of complete instructions. There are nine pieces to the dress pattern. Pattern B and C are done in black and white. Pattern B contains: evening dress, housecoat, petticoat, and cami-knicker (teddy). Pattern C contains: winter coat, winter dress, party dress slip, and knicker (panties). **Complete: each $25.00 and up.**

Luster Creme Starlet Doll

Plate 471. Lustre Creme Starlet is a 7½" unmarked all hard plastic doll, with glued on synthetic blonde wig, sleep eyes with molded lashes, and a closed mouth. Her jointed body is strung with rubber bands and she has molded T-strap shoes painted white. She is dressed in a silky, pink rosebud print gown trimmed with ribbon. The Starlet doll was offered in 1953 as a mail-away premium for Lustre Creme products. Each Starlet doll ordered required $1.00 plus one label or carton from Lustre Cream, or tab from the $1.00 or 60 cent size Lustre Creme shampoo. The offer expired February 28, 1954. The doll came with a booklet titled "Lustre Creme Starlet" by Inez Holland House on: *how to keep "Starlette's" hair…and yours, too…soft and shinning, so easy to curl and wave.* Also included with her were three miniature replicas of children's Vogue patterns. **Doll, $50.00; doll, booklet and patterns: $75.00 and up.**

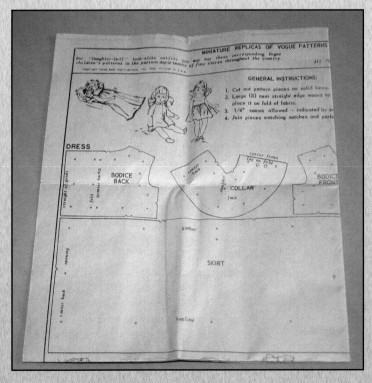

Plate 472. Starlet Patterns were available only for the Starlet doll and were miniature replicas of Vogue patterns. The easy-to-make, one-page pattern is copyrighted 1953. The following advertising was printed across the top of the pattern: *For "Daughter-Doll" look-alike outfits you may buy these corresponding Vogue children's pattern in the pattern departments of fine stores throughout the country.* The children's patterns used were Vogue #2541 coat in sizes 1 – 6, Vogue #2665 dress in sizes 1 – 8, and Vogue #2652 nightgown in sizes 3 – 12. Each of the three patterns was sized down to fit the Starlet doll.

Note: I have seen advertisements for Starlet that had a different booklet advertising a "Forever Fresh" wardrobe that could be wiped clean with a damp cloth. There was also a Lustre Creme Movie Star doll offered by the company. She was 9", had a synthetic glued-on wig, sleep eyes, closed mouth, and was fully jointed. Movie Star was a hard plastic walker with a head that turned when she walked. She came in a pink dress with blue trim, and a 10-piece accessory set was available with her. As far as I know there were no patterns included for these dolls.

Dolls and Their Patterns

Barbie Doll

Barbie was the brainchild of Ruth Handler. While Ruth was shopping in Switzerland, she came across a doll unlike any other she had seen before. It was an adult curvaceous doll named Lili with high heel shoes. For years, Ruth had toyed with an idea for a female adult doll after watching her daughter play with adult paper dolls preferring them to the three-dimensional baby dolls available at the time. This Bild Lili doll was exactly what she wanted. After much discussion and justification, she finally convinced the engineers at Mattel to produce a doll like Bild Lili. When Barbie was shown at the Toy Fair in 1959 in New York City, the reception wasn't very good and only a few orders were placed. However when the doll hit the market the little girls loved Barbie the grown-up doll and mothers went out to hunt for her. As other retailers heard about the demand they too ordered the new Barbie doll and it was several years before Mattel could keep up with the orders.

Barbie was always a clotheshorse. Her fashions were as important as she was. This was indeed her appeal. Little girls could dress her in grown-up clothes and pretend they too were older.

From the beginning Barbie was all about the clothes. What better way to increase sales? Clothing is, of course, made using patterns and involves sewing, so naturally patterns were one of the first sewing items to be advertised for Barbie. Early patterns made exclusively for Barbie are shown in plates 474, 476, 477, and 478. The number of patterns on the market for Barbie is vast and would be quite an undertaking to list them all, I have listed a number of them at the end of this chapter in the Dolls with Patterns section.

In 1973, Mattel Inc. came out with the Sew Magic Barbie Fashion Set #8670 (plate 479). It was featured in the J. C. Penny Christmas Catalog in 1973. They advertised:

No needle — just a little magic makes pattern pieces stick together. Just pop in the special cartridge, and you are ready — liquid formula in cartridge joins fabric fast.

It came with patterns, fabric, and accessories to make Barbie four outfits. You could also buy more kits for the machine. Barbie's Sweet 16 Fur Fashions Sew Magic Add-ons #7850 (plate 480) for making "Fur Fashions" also came out in 1973 and was made to use with the Sew Magic machine. It has a "fur" making mandrel. In the kit was the mandrel and loose weave nylon yarn. The instructions were to wrap the yarn in and out of the mandrel in a figure eight wrap until it is full. Lay the mandrel on flat fabric where you want the fur to be and sew down the middle of the mandrel, remove the mandrel, wrap again, sew etc. until you have made the amount you need. Cut the yarn loops and brush into "fur." The set also came with a plastic waistband guide that allowed you to sew a rubber band in the skirt casing for elastic. Sew Magic was a big success and was offered in the J.C. Penny Christmas Catalog for three years.

Mattel, Inc. and Simplicity got together and made Begin to Sew with Barbie and Simplicity #107 (plate 482). This set wasn't anything new, it was the same 11½" type of clothing that you could purchase by the panel in most yard good stores.

I guess it was good advertising, as mom knew the Simplicity name and the child wanted anything with Barbie doll's name on it, so it made both mother and child happy. Barbie embroidery sets were also offered. Barbie & Ken Fashion Embroidery Set #502 (plate 141) shows just one variation of these sets.

Most assuredly, the most "knitted for" doll in the last generation is Barbie. There have been a number of sets on the market made exclusively for Barbie and other generic sets for 11½" fashion dolls which would include Barbie. One of the earliest Barbie knitting sets was offered in 1962, The Deluxe Knitting For Barbie set. The set was housed in a box that opens up to show two windows. Inside was a purple and pink knitting-canister with pink and blue butterfly graphics and Knitting for Barbie printed on the front. Knitting needles, five balls of wool yarn, thimble, ruler, and pencil as well as three knitting patterns were included. These are for a sleeveless dress and stole, two-piece skating outfit, and blouse and skirt. I believe this may have been the first of these sets produced. Another set offered in 1962 is Knitting for Barbie #8012, a pink, white and blue canister with graphics including the ubiquitous "ponytail Barbie profile" and four numbered outfits (plate 475). Knitting for Barbie #8012 actually has only one pattern, #8012, the same number as the set. The set number on each canister is the same number as the pattern contained within. Mattel must have reasoned that if each set contained only one pattern, consumers might buy more than one set to obtain the other patterns. There were five Knitting for Barbie canisters offered in the year 1962. Knitting for Barbie #8012, Knitting for Barbie #8013, Knitting for Barbie #8014, Knitting for Barbie #8015, and the purple and pink Deluxe Knitting For Barbie set, that as far as I know, had no number, at least not on the canister.

Barbie Glitter Knitting Kit #50523 (plate 481) was offered in 1986. It recommended adult supervision in the instructions. The step-by-step instructions promised elegant and unusual fashions for your Barbie dolls. The looms in this set are spool-knitting looms that produce round tubes. The larger 3½" curricular-loom is called a coronet loom in this set. The real selling point of this set I believe, is the glitter yarn, every little girl loves a bit of glitz. Barbie Super Knit Magic #12588 (plate 483), made eight years later in 1994, is a glorified version of the spool knitter. A handle is turned to activate the knitting needles to create either a knit tube or a knit panel, depending on how the machine is strung. Knitted tubes can become a dress with long fringe, a hat, sleeveless top, tube dress, or handbag. With the panels Barbie can have a sleeveless jacket. There are also patterns for a handbag and hair bow the child can make for herself, and a stuffed kitten. It is interesting to note that the first Barbie knitting sets were made in part by other companies such as Miner Industries, Standard Toykraft, and Avalon, a division of Craft House Corp. Barbie Super Knit Magic #12588 was done entirely by Mattel.

Other Barbie knitting sets (not pictured in this book) are:
#891 Barbie Knitting Set early 60's in a hexagon-shaped cardboard tote by Standard Toykraft (rare)
#50540 Barbie Mini-Brights Knitting Kit 1988/89
Barbie Fashion Knitting Kit (unknown number)

Plate 473. Bubble Cut Barbie dolls were first introduced in the 1961, before that date all Barbie dolls had ponytails. Barbie is 11½" tall all vinyl and jointed at neck, arms, and hips. She was made with feet to fit high-heel shoes. Barbie has rooted synthetic hair, molded features and lashes. These dolls are marked on their backside "Midge TM 1962 // c Barbie r 1958 // by Mattel, Inc. // patented." The blonde doll is dressed in the Career Girl #954 ensemble. It consists of a two-piece tweed suit and matching hat, red sleeveless pullover with long black gloves, and black shoes. The gloves are missing. The brunette doll is wearing the Garden Party #931 fashion. It consists of a pink print dress with white eyelet ruffles, white gloves, and white shoes. The gloves, are missing. **Doll and costume: $75.00 and up.**

Plate 474. Official Barbie Pattern #9939 by Advance is also known as Group B. Copyrighted 1961, it carries the Official Mattel Inc. Toymakers seal. The instructions inside were written for a child. It is titled: Barbie's Sewing Book and goes on to say: *"Barbie's Sewing Book" is a fun book! It will show you that sewing is so easy...and so much fun. It is a "Know-How" book too. After you follow its simple instructions, do as the pictures tell you to do, you will know how to make clothes, not only for Barbie, but for yourself as well! Wouldn't it be fun to make matching outfits for Barbie and you? The advance Pattern Catalogue is sure to have designs in your size which look almost alike and are just as easy to make.* The pattern contains a suit, blouse and culottes, sheath, skating separates, two-piece shirtwaist dress, cape, and panties. **Complete: $10.00 and up.**

Plate 475. Knitting for Barbie #8012, two-piece Skating Outfit was manufactured by Miner Industries, Inc. and copyrighted by Mattel in 1962. The set comes in a cardboard cylinder 4½" in diameter and 10½" high. It is decorated with Barbie in four different knitted outfits. Each of the outfits has a number: #8012, two-piece Skating Outfit; #8013, Hat, Skirt, and Sleeveless Blouse; #8014, Fitted Coat and Pillbox Hat; and #8015, Sleeveless Dress and Stole. The number of the set designates the outfit pattern you receive. The contents of this illustrated container are two skeins of yarn, two knitting needles, and two printed pages: *Directions for knitting Barbie's 2 pc. skating outfit and knitting for Barbie basic instructions.* **Complete: $25.00 and up.**

Note: The deluxe knitting for Barbie was also offered in 1962 in a purple and pink canister. This set contains the basic knitting instructions and three of the four patterns; Sleeveless Dress and Stole, 2-piece Skating Outfit, and Hat, Skirt, and Sleeveless Blouse. The patterns for this set were on pink, green, or blue papers and the instructions were printed on yellow paper.

Plate 476. Sew-Easy Advance Barbie Pattern #2895 was copyrighted in 1962. It carries the Official Mattel Inc. Toymakers seal. This pattern definitely was made for a child to sew. Included with the instructions is the Sew-Easy Sewing Booklet which advises: *How to sew for your doll start with these seven sewing steps 1 Fingertip Tools, 2 Fabric Facts, 3 Fabric and Pattern Layout, 4 Your Printed Pattern Speaks, 5 On Your Mark, 6 Stitch It, 7 Pressing Pointers. Making clothes is Sew-Easy! This little sewing booklet will start you on your sewing adventure with the first seven steps.* Pattern #2895 is a trousseau wardrobe and includes a bridal gown and crown, dress and jacket, afternoon dress, engagement dress, nightgown, peignoir. **Complete: $10.00 and up.**
Note: This pattern was first advertised in a 1962 catalog as one of four Easy-Sew patterns sold in a display unit. There were four different patterns each containing six individual costumes. They are marked Group A, B, C, or D.

Plate 477. Official McCall's #7137 Barbie Instant Wardrobe was copyrighted in 1963. It carries the Official Mattel Inc. Toymakers Seal. The instructions "Easy Sewing Guide" in this envelope are the same as in any adult McCall's pattern. The pattern includes a western shirt, pants and boots, square dance dress, leotard, jacket and skirt, bathing suit, bolero and bag, wrap-around sheath dress, drawstring sheath dress, hat, sarong dress, coat, ball gown and stole. **Complete: $10.00 and up.**

Plate 478. This Official Barbie Pattern #7840 by McCall's was copyrighted 1965. It carries the Official Mattel Inc. Toymakers seal. The envelope states that it also fits Miss Barbie and Midge. The pattern includes a knitted coat and hat, knitted sweater and cap and matching sweater and cap for 12" boyfriend. It also includes a cloth coat, two-piece dress, slacks, negligee, nightgown, panties, gown, mantilla, and comb. **Complete: $10.00 and up.**

Plate 479. Sew Magic Barbie Fashion Set #8670 was copyrighted in 1973 by Mattel, Inc. In 1973 this was the new way to sew: *So easy even a five year old can do it! The new way to sew! Safe-no needles! No thread!* The box measures 12" x 10" x 5½". Included in the set are a dressmaker's form, Sew Magic machine, Miracle Stitch cartridge, instructions, eight templates/patterns, four pieces of fabric, plastic waistband guide, two buckles, and two ribbons. The patterns include a dress, two blouses, two skirts, shortie pajamas, and a purse. **Complete: $10.00 and up.**

Plate 480. Barbie's Sweet 16 Fur Fashions Sew Magic Add-Ons #7850 was manufactured by Mattel Inc. in 1973. It comes in a 12" x 10" x 1" box and is made to be used with the Sew Magic Barbie Fashion Set #8670. The kit comes with four templates/patterns, "Sew Magic add-ons instruction book," marking pencil, fur maker, one piece of red flannel, waistband guide, marking pencil, two bundles of yarn, and two rubber bands. The articles are a short and a long dress, and a skirt and jacket with "fur" trim. **Complete: $10.00 and up.**

Plate 481. Barbie Glitter Knitting Kit #50523 was manufactured by Avalon Division of Craft House Corp. in 1986. The box measures 11" x 10" x 2½". Included in the set are two knitters, a 3½" coronet knitter, and a 2½" long, six peg knitting spool. There are also two hanks of glitter yarn and four balls of four-ply yarn. Adult supervision is recommended in the instructions, which also claimed that with "the step-by-step instructions and your Barbie knitting kit, elegant and unusual fashions can be created for your Barbie dolls." The Barbie Step-by-Step instruction sheet shows how to use the knitters. The larger loom makes hats, evening gowns, shawls, fringed collars, and dresses. The smaller knitting spool makes gloves, mittens, scarves, and leg warmers. All the garments are just tubes that slip over parts of Barbie doll's body, but they look nice and are simple to make. **Complete: $10.00 and up.**

Plate 482. Begin to Sew with Barbie and Simplicity #107 was manufactured by Wesco Reltex a subsidiary of Reliable Textile Company, in 1987. The package is 11" x 8½". Inside are two outfits for Barbie printed on polyester/cotton fabric, a two-piece suit and a coat with a scarf. The patterns are printed on the fabric with easy-to-see darts and seam allowances and there are printed directions included. **Complete: $10.00 and up.**

Note: Other available kits include #100 pin Dot Tropical, #101 Peasant Casual, #102 Dress Gown, #103 Nautical Play, #104 Jumper Jumpsuit, #105 Western Karate, #106 Tuxedo Sport. Kits #1005 and #106 were for Ken.

Plate 483. Barbie Super Knit Magic #12588 was manufactured by Mattel Inc. in 1994. The box measures 11" x 10" x 7". The kit consists of a Super Knit Magic machine that knits in the round. The Super Knit Magic has a carrying handle and two drawers on the bottom for supplies. In the drawers are plastic scissors, ruler, thimble, crochet hook, needles, beads, and charms. There is a "Barbie Knit Magic Instruction Book" with instructions on how to use the machine and how to knit Barbie a sleeveless jacket, tube dress, handbag, long dress with fringe, hat, tube top, and a kitten. To complete the set, there are four balls of three-ply yarn. **Complete: $10.00 and up.**

Chatty Cathy Doll

Mattel's Chatty Cathy was the new talking doll of the 1960s. She was another brainstorm of Ruth Handler. Ruth wanted a talking doll that could say a number of different phrases. The idea was handed over to Mattel's engineer Jack Ryan and designer Tony Haller and they created this freckle-face little girl. Ruth Handler and her husband Elliot named her Chatty Cathy.

Chatty Cathy was introduced at the February 1960 American Toy Fair in New York City. She was a success at the Toy Fair and later on the toy shelves. Many little girls found her that year under their Christmas tree. The first Chatty Cathy stood 20" tall with a hard plastic body and limbs. She had a soft vinyl face, sleep eyes, and two prominent front teeth. Her hair was blonde with bangs and a softly curled bob. But best of all, she spoke 11 different phrases at the pull of a string. In 1960 she was available in only two costumes, either a red cotton sun-suit with a white voile pinafore lined in red cotton or a blue cotton dress with a white eyelet short over-blouse. Throughout

the five years Chatty Cathy was sold by Matter, her hairstyles, face materials, and hands were changed many times. But the one thing that always stayed the same was the body size, so the many extra outfits that were offered always fit her well no matter when she was purchased. After 1960 Mattel also made other Chatty dolls such as Chatty Baby, Tiny Chatty Baby, Tiny Chatty Brother, Charmin' Chatty, and Singing Chatty.

Most people wouldn't think of 20" Chatty Cathy as a doll that promoted sewing for children, however in 1962 Mattel and Advanced Pattern Company joined ranks and offered two Sew-Easy patterns for Chatty Cathy. The two patterns were presented in a large counter display box with a picture of Chatty Cathy being a fitting for an outfit. The Advanced Pattern Company made the official licensed patterns for Mattel. The first patterns had no number but were instead called Group F and Group G (plate 485). On second issue, Group F changed to #2897 and Group G to #2898. The price had changed from 60¢ to 75¢. The patterns inside remained the same.

Plate 484. This 20" Chatty Cathy is the fifth and final issue. The back is embossed "CHATTY CATHY // 1960 // CHATTY BABY // 1961//BY MATTEL INC. //U.S. PAT'D 3,017,187 // OTHER U.S. & // FOREIGN PATS. PEND. // PAT'D IN CANADA 1962." She has a hard plastic head, blue sleep eyes, open/closed mouth with two teeth. She is wearing her original shoes and a dress made from pattern #2897, Group F, view 3. Her original dress is a red velvet top with a white lace skirt over taffeta and a red ribbon tie at the waist. Chatty Cathy says 18 different things: "What can we do now?" "Tell me a story," "May I have a cookie?" "Give me a kiss," "Please brush my hair," "Let's play house," "Let's have a party," "Please take me with you," "Will you play with me?" "I love you," "Please carry me," "Let's play school," "Please change my dress," "I'm so tired," "I hurt myself," "Do you love me?" "I'm hungry," and "Where are we going?" **Original condition: $100.00 and up.**

Plate 485. Sew-Easy Chatty Cathy Patterns #2897, and Group G. Printed on the back of each envelope is: *Chatty Cathy will be the best-dressed doll in the clothes you will make, and Sew-Easy too!* Tucked in the envelope are patterns for four different outfits. Each is printed on a separate tissue with its own step-by-step instruction chart. There is also a little sewing book titled *Sew-Easy Sewing Booklet, How To Sew For Your Doll* that shows you, in simple words and drawings, the steps you take to make Chatty Cathy's clothes. *It doesn't matter which outfit you make first — one is as easy as the other. Pin a tissue to the fabric and cut...do what the little book and chart tell you...and you're on your way.* Group F or #2897 contains a pleated skirt and blouse, sports set (trousers and overblouse), dress, and nightgown. Group G or #2898 pattern contains a coat and hat, dress trimmed in rickrack, pajamas, and robe. **Complete, each: $10.00 and up.**

Plate 487. Official Chatty Cathy Pattern #7181 was made in 1964 by McCall's Patterns with permission from Mattel. The pattern sold for 75¢ and had 36 pattern pieces. It contained a coat and hat that could be made of cloth or knitted, smock, tights, dress, blouse and kerchief, robe, nightgown, and panties. **Complete: $25.00 and up.**

Note. McCall's also made an official pattern #7269 the same year for 24" Charmin' Chatty. It contains a nightie, robe, panties, jumper, turtleneck blouse, matching tights, cape and beret, A-line dress, felt high boots, and knitted sweater, and knee socks. Chatty Cathy and Charmin Chatty are the only Chatty dolls that have their own exclusive patterns, but don't be dismayed there are always generic patterns that fit Chatty Cathy and her family of other Chatty dolls.

Plate 486. Chatty Cathy Simplicity Pattern #4652 was issued circa 1962. This was a wardrobe pattern designed exclusively for Chatty Cathy. The pattern shows a coat with a hood, dress, weskit, pinafore, kerchief, slip, panties, pajamas, and cap. The back of the envelope stated: "wardrobe for Chatty Cathy" but there was no official Mattel stamp on this pattern. **Complete: $10.00 and up.**

Golden Princess Doll

Plate 488. Golden Princess. Sometime in the late 1960s in France the Singer Company offered a new doll for which little girls could sew. Her name was Golden Princess. She was marketed with the Golden Panoramic Singer children's sewing machine. The doll is 19½" tall and made of vinyl. She has light blue sleep eyes with synthetic lashes, softly colored lips, and rooted synthetic hair in a reddish-blonde shoulder-length bob. Her head, arms and legs are strung with a heavy rubber band. She is wonderfully balanced and can stand alone. Kits titled "The Golden Princess Collection" were offered for little seamstresses to sew. This doll is wearing a short sleeved dress with a front placket and side flap pockets from a kit called Corinne. The kit includes pre-cut pink fabric, thread to match on a spool marked "Padler," two bobbins to fit the Golden Panoramic Singer sewing machine, a zipper, and instructions. Golden Princess originally sold in a red dress with white trim and white panties. The white socks and black loafers on this doll are original. The shoes are marked Padler on the bottom. There was booklet titled "Golden Princess de Singer" that was included with the doll that shows a child holding both the Golden Princess and the Golden Panoramic Singer. Inside are advertisements for the doll, all the sewing kits, and the Golden Panoramic Singer. **Dressed doll: $100.00 and up.**

Plate 489. Nathalie Ensemble. This outfit, which has been assembled, is from one of the five kits, all with pre-cut pieces that were offered for the Golden Princess doll. The Nathalie kit contains pre-cut red felt for a coat, a spool of thread marked Padler, six snaps, six gilt buttons, two bobbins to fit the Golden Panoramic Singer machine, a strip of faux fur, and the instructions for putting it all together. Other kits available for purchase in the Golden Princess Collection doll were Aline, a pre-cut pink gingham blouse and a rose jumper; Valerié, a blue flowered dress with a belt; Sophie, a short sleeved blue A-line dress with a zipper down the front; Isabelle, a short sleeved yellow-blouse with buttons and a matching gathered skirt with a border. **Each kit: $50.00 and up.**

Plate 490. Golden Panoramic Singer Sewing Machine was made by The Singer Company. The sewing machine and case measure 9½" tall, x 10" wide x 4½" deep. The Golden Panoramic Singer was promoted with the Golden Princess doll and her outfits. The machine's booklet shows all about, and how to operate the Golden Panoramic Singer. In the back of the booklet are instructions on how to make a doggie coat, purse, apron, and a dress and shawl for a doll. **With box: $50.00 and up.**

My Friend Dolls

Plate 491. My Friend Mandy #210 was issued in 1977 and produced through 1978 by the Fisher Price Toy Company, Inc. and was marketed as Your Very Best Friend. She is 16" tall has a pink rosebud-print cloth torso, vinyl head and limbs, painted features, rooted synthetic hair, and a cloth Fisher-Price tag sewn in a back seam of her body. The pink rosebud-print was used only for the first issue #210; after this doll, all other girl dolls had yellow rosebud-print bodies. Mandy was first issued in a pink dotted-Swiss dress with lace trim and tiny buttons, light pink tights, off-white hat with a pink ribbon, and white vinyl slip-on shoes. She also came with her own pink flower-sprigged nightgown. Every doll came with a booklet detailing how to care for your best friend. This included instructions on how to wash her in the washing machine, how to style and set her hair, and of course, a list of the clothing available purchase. Many ready-made outfits were offered for My Friend dolls, however, patterns for making additional clothing were an important part of the series concept. Mother and child were encouraged to sew for Mandy and some advertising showed a mother and child laying out and cutting the pattern supplied. The first issue Mandy came with pattern #210 a hooded cape. **Doll in original clothes: $25.00 and up.**

Plate 492. The Second Issue Mandy #211 and Third Issue Mandy #215. The second Mandy #211 was issued in 1979 and produced through 1980. She has a yellow rosebud-print body and was dressed in a pink flower sprigged dress with tucks down the front and a pink ribbon at the neck, off-white hat, pink tights, and white slip-on shoes. This Mandy came with pattern #211 a Gaucho outfit. The third issue Mandy #215, issued in 1982 and made through 1983, was wearing a white polka dotted navy dress with a white yoke and red bow at the neck, red hat, and red slip-on shoes. This third issue Mandy was not packaged with a pattern, but instead included a mail-in offer of a free pattern for shorts and pants. There were no more free patterns after the third Mandy. **Dolls in original clothing: $25.00 and up.**

Note. The fourth issue Mandy #216, issued in 1984, was made for one year only. She was dressed as a cheerleader, in a blue and white knit top with a Mandy monogrammed megaphone on the front, matching skirt, white ankle-length socks, sneakers, headband, and two pompons. Fisher-Price produced one additional Mandy with a completely different face, Special Birthday Mandy #4009. She was issued in 1985 and produced through 1986 and came in a lavender, pink, and cream striped party dress, lace tights, white slip-on shoes, and a silver party hat. Measuring 18", she was taller than the others and came with a gift box, which contained a pink plastic bracelet for the child. Special Birthday Mandy was the final issue of Mandy.

Plate 493. My Friend Dolls with Patterns. Mandy had a large family of friends, all the same size and with the yellow rosebud-print bodies except for the only boy, Mikey, who has a plain white-cloth body. Each has a tag with their number sewn somewhere in the back of the body. The numbering system gets confusing in the later dolls since as they were reissued, the company gave each one a new identification number sometimes reusing the old numbers. All Fisher Price dolls are incised on the back of their neck with "Fisher Price," a date and various numbers, but the easiest way to identify the dolls is with the sewn in tag on the back of their bodies. Another My Friend doll that came with a pattern way My Friend Jenny #212, 1979 – 1981. Jenny has brown rooted hair with straight bangs and is dressed in a brown print cotton jumper, white blouse, brown tights, brown slip-on shoes, and tan straw hat with brown ribbon. She came with pattern #212 My Friend Jenny Nightgown pattern, ID 231470, (no date). A second issue My Friend Jenny #217, 1982 – 1983 had brown rooted hair, yellow checked dress with white yoke and sleeves, white straw hat with yellow ribbon, and white slip on-shoes. This Jenny featured the mail-away offer for pattern #217, My Friend Mandy's Poncho pattern, ID 207960, copyright 1977. **Dolls in original clothing: $25.00 and up.**

Dolls and Their Patterns

Plate 494. More My Friend Dolls with Patterns. The final doll with an offer for a pattern was My Friend Becky #218, 1982 – 1984. She has rooted red hair, green eyes, and freckles. Dressed in a blue-green dress with an organdy pinafore type overlay, white shoes, and a white straw hat with a green ribbon. Becky featured the mail away offer for pattern #218 My Friend Mandy's Short Jacket and Purse pattern, ID 339340 (no date). My Friend Mikey #205, 1982 – 1984 was a boy doll with rooted red-brown hair, plain white-cloth body, blue jeans, red and white striped shirt, baseball jacket, and blue shoes. Mikey was included in the group with mail-away offer for patterns. Mikey was included in the group with mail-away offer for patterns. I have found only one pattern made exclusively for him — #205 My Friend Mikey Pajamas. **Dolls in original clothing: $25.00 and up.**

In the Fisher-Price catalog the following dolls did not have any mention of patterns included with them or free pattern mail-away offers.

#206-My Friend Nicky African American, 1985 – 1985, short curly black rooted hair and dark skin. Nicky was dressed as a cheerleader in a blue and white knit top with a mono-grammed Nicky megaphone on the front, a matching skirt, white ankle socks, sneakers, headband and two pompons.

#0209 My Friend Jenny 1984 – 1985, brown rooted hair with straight bangs. She wears an aerobics outfit with magenta and turquoise sweatshirt, mini skirt, braided headband, striped tights, leg warmers, striped sneakers, and gold purse.

1985 was the last year My Friend 16" dolls were shown in the Fisher-Price catalog and there was no offer of free patterns in either the clothing packages or with the dolls.

The September 20, 1977, issue of *Woman's Day* magazines includes a full-page ad for Mandy showing four ready-made outfits available for purchase. They were Country Fair Bib-Jeans, Sleighride Ensemble, Patio Party Denim, and Town & Country Pantsuit. These were the first outfits offered for My Friend Mandy. There were new outfits each year until 1985 when outfits previously worn by My Friend dolls in 1982, 1983, and 1984 were reissued.

In 1982 Fisher-Price changed the packaging for My Friend Fashions from the early 12" x 12" box to a new flatter style. Patterns were no longer given with the outfits and instead there was a free mail-away offer stated:

Collect all the fashions for "your" my Friend Dolls. Even make your own with a free pattern from Fisher-Price. Free Sewing Pattern Offer. To receive your Free Pattern, just send the proof of purchase label from this package with your name and address to: Fisher-Price Toys, Consumer Affairs, Pattern Offer, East Aurora, NY 14052.

In a Fisher-Price pamphlet that was dated 1983 there was a special card insert that read:

The response to our free sewing pattern offer has been overwhelming. This has caused us a delay in processing requests. We sincerely apologize for any inconvenience that this may have caused you and hope that you enjoy using your free sewing pattern for your Fisher-Price doll. Fisher-Price

Following is a list of patterns for Fisher-Price dolls and the dolls or fashions with which they were found. They are listed with the pattern first and partnered with the doll or fashion in which the pattern was found.

#210 My Friend Mandy's Hooded Cape pattern, 1977
#210 first-issue My Friend Mandy, 1977
#211 My Friend Mandy's Gaucho Outfit pattern, 1980
#211 second-issue My Friend Mandy, 1979
#212 My Friend Jenny's Nightgown pattern, 1979
#212 first-issue My Friend Jenny, 1979
#215 My Friend Mandy's Pants or Shorts pattern, 1977
#215 Patio Party Denim Outfit, 1977
#216 My Friend Mandy's Robe pattern (caftan), 1977
#216 My Friend Mandy's Dress, 1977
#217 My Friend Mandy's Poncho pattern, 1977
#217 My Friend Jenny, 1982
#218 My Friend Mandy's Wrap Around Skirt pattern, 1977
#218 Town I Country Pantsuit, 1977
#218 My Friend Mandy's Short Jacket & Purse pattern (no date)
#218 My Friend Becky, 1982 (reissued number)
#219 My Friend Mandy's Tote Bag and Yours pattern, 1977
#219 Rainy Day Slicker, 1977
#220 My Friend Mandy's Sun Dress pattern, 1977
#220 My Friend Mandy's Springtime Tennis Outfit, 1978
#221 My Friend Mandy's Slip pattern (no date)
#221 Party Time Dress, 1977
#222 My Friend Mandy's Sleeping Bag pattern, 1977
#222 My Friend Mandy's Lets Go Camping Outfit, 1977

#223 My Friend Mandy's Baby Doll Pajamas pattern (no date)

#223 My Friend Mandy's Jumper and Blouse Outfit, 1979

#224 My Friend Mandy's Robe pattern (bathrobe) (no date)

#224 My Friend Mandy's Jogging Outfit, 1979

#225 My Friend Dolls Blouse pattern (no date)

#225 My Friend Dolls Coat Set, 1979

#226 My Friend Dolls Pinafore pattern (no date)

#226 Footwear & Tights, 1979

#227 There was not a number 227.

#228 My Friend Dolls Reversible Wrap Jumper pattern, 1980

#228 My Friends Dolls Ballerina Outfit, 1980

#229 My Friends Reversible Vest pattern, #229

#229 Knickers Outfit, 1982 (mail order)

#230 My Friend Dolls Stocking Cap & Knitted Sweater pattern (no date)

#230 Winter Wear, 1979

#231 My Friend Dolls T-shirt Dress or Tunic pattern (no date)

#231 Roller Skating Outfit, 1978, 1980

#232 Unknown pattern

#232 Bedtime Outfit

#233 My Friend Dolls Athletic Bag pattern (no date)

#233 My Friend Dolls Baseball Outfit, 1982

#205 My Friend Mikey Pajamas, 1982

#205 First issue of My Friend Mikey, 1982

There are no known patterns offered with the last outfits listed below.

#0238 Valentine Party Dress, 1985. This is the original blue dress with white dots (plate 492) that the third issue

#215 My Friend Mandy was sold in.

#4108 Sunshine Party Dress, 1985. This is the original light blue dress with the pinafore overlay (plate 494) that #218 My Friend Becky was sold in. As a separate outfit the Fisher-Price catalog titled it Springtime Party Dress.

#4109 Cheerleader Outfit, 1984. This is the original outfit #206 that My Friend Nicky and #216 My Friend Mandy was sold in.

#4110 Aerobics Outfit, 1985. This is the original outfit, third issue #0209 My Friend Jenny was sold in.

One of the hard-to-find items for Mandy is #234 Overnight Case and Nightgown. This was a mail-away item and contained a pink plastic case, print nightgown, and dark blue hairbrush. It was priced at $3.95 and had no pattern.

Fisher-Price also offered baby dolls at the same time as My Friend Dolls and four of these dolls included patterns. However the babies were never as popular as My Friend Dolls and no other clothing or patterns followed. The patterns and their dolls are listed below.

#209 My Baby Beth Baby Sleeper and Hooded Jacket

#209 My Baby Beth, 1978.

#207 My Sleepy Baby Jumpsuit

#207 My Sleepy Baby, 1979

#213 Coat Outfit for Fisher-Price Soft Sounds

#213 Baby Soft Sounds, 1980

#249 Baby Ann and her Care Set, Dress & Leggings

#249 Baby Ann and her Care Set, 1981

Plate 495. Four Seasons Fashion Book #234 was advertised in 1978 as: *My Friend dolls very own 16-page fashion book includes an easy-to-sew pattern, tips on making accessories, plus a story of best friends for each of the four seasons. Price: $3.95.* The 11" x 8½" book has four full-size patterns, each in its own envelope in a pocket at the back of the book. The first pattern set is "Spring Happenings" V-791, ID 272001, with a pantsuit, belted jacket, shirt, belted jeans, shorts, and a scarf. "Summer Fun," V-792, ID 272002 is the second set. It has two outfits: a peasant costume including a floppy hat and the other is a long dressy gown. The pattern for both is the same skirt and blouse; it is the fabrics and trims that make the change in style. The third set is "Fall Adventures" V-793, ID 272003, with just two patterns, a long-sleeve blouse and a jumper. However it can be made three different ways: a long jumper with a tucked-in blouse, a short jumper with a tucked in blouse, or a short skirt with an overblouse. "Winter Wrap-Ups" V-794, ID 272004 is the final set of patterns. This set contains three patterns: a coat hat, and muff. The coat can be made either short or long with different trim. The hat is reversible and is shown both ways in the drawing. Throughout the book are color drawings and cute stories of My Friends outings and how they wore the clothing offered in the patterns. At the end of the book each pattern is shown and suggested fabrics, yardage requirements and notions are listed. The last page is Fun Things To Make. These are accessories to add to the fashions in the book, a tailored belt, tie-belt, shawl, and fuffy muff. **Complete book: $5.00 and up.**

Plate 496. McCall's My Friend Dolls, Pattern #705. In 1983 McCall's Pattern Company issued a pattern for Fisher-Price My Friend Dolls. Pattern #705 was advertised as "Clothes for your Fisher Price Friends Jenny, Becky, Mandy and Mikey." All the dolls are shown in full color on the pattern envelope. The pattern envelope contains 33 pattern pieces that make up a coat and hat, long dress and bonnet, apron, coveralls, polo shirt, short dress, shirt, and handkerchief. Some of the outfits were very similar to the patterns offered in the Fisher-Price book, *Four Seasons Fashions*. **Complete: $5.00 and up.**

Plate 497. Dress made from McCall's pattern #705. Mandy is shown here modeling a pink dress with pastel ribbon trim made from McCall's Craft Pattern #705. The dress printed on the pattern cover is shown on a doll sitting towards the front she is modeling a blue dress with red, white, and blue ribbon trim and a red straw hat. **Dress: $25.00 and up.**

Plate 498. McCall's My Friends Dolls Pattern #737. The following year, 1984, McCall's Pattern Company offered a second pattern. Pictured on the cover is a group of My Friends Dolls and the caption reads: "Doll clothes galore for Jenny, Becky, Mandy, Mikey from Fisher-Price." Pattern #737 contains 38 pattern pieces to make lots of clothing including girl and boy tennis outfits, majorette outfit, exercise outfit, jogging suit, and sweat-suit. Some of the outfits in this pattern are to ready-made fashions offered for My Friend Dolls. This same pattern was also issued with the number 9167 at a later date. **Complete: $5.00 and up.**

Katie Dolls

The American School of Needlework offered Katie to the public in 1992 as part of the Craft Doll Collection. Katie was packaged in a 15" x 5½" x 3" lavender window box decorated with eight of her 12 fashion instruction books. A 1992 brochure ad from the American School of Needlework reads: *Create Your Own Katie Doll for only $19.95. Katie is an all-vinyl, 14" doll that looks as lovely as an expensive porcelain collector doll. She comes wearing pretty undies, lace-trimmed socks, and black Mary Jane shoes.*

Katie came in eight different styles.
#2101 Blue eyes with short light blonde curly hair
#2102 Blue eyes with long light blonde curly hair
#2103 Blue eyes with long strawberry blonde curly hair
#2104 Blue eyes with long strawberry blonde wavy hair
#2105 Brown eyes with short brown curly hair
#2106 Brown eyes with long brown curly hair
#2107 Green eyes with auburn braided pigtails
#2108 Green eyes with long auburn wavy hair
Inside the pattern books is a special note stating:
These dolls are intended for children from eight to ninety-eight. There was also an invitation to join Katie's Fan Club:
If you love Katie and want to become a member of her fan club, send your name and address to the address listed below. You'll receive your membership card, a free pattern, available to club members only, and a subscription to Katie's Newsletter which will bring you information about new patterns and accessories for Katie.

By 1997, the club had been discontinued but some of the dolls, booklets, and accessories were still available for purchase.

There were 12 different pattern books for Katie some sewing patters and others crochet patterns (plates 500, 501, and 502).

Crochet Patterns:
#8401 Summer Days
#8402 School Days
#8404 Fantasy Princesses
#8405 Wedding Day
#8406 Little Girls of Yesterday – Vol. 1 (1930)
#8407 Little Girls of Yesterday – Vol. 2 (1900)
#8408 Little Girls of Yesterday – Vol. 3 (1890)
#8409 Merrie Christmas
Sewing Patterns:
#8403 Important Days
#8410 Ruffles and Lace
#8411 Little Ballerina
#8412 Velveteen Princess

Whether you sew or crochet, a wardrobe could be created for Katie that was perfect for any occasion. Some booklets contain a single pattern and others are collections of patterns. The original prices were $2.50 and $4.50.

Katie also had accessories that could be purchased from the Craft Doll Collection at local craft stores and through mail order. The shoes were $2.99 and the hats $1.99.
#2203 Red Mary Janes
#2204 Pink Mary Janes
#2205 White Satin Slippers
#2206 Pink Satin Slippers
#2207 Blue Satin Slippers
#2208 Gold Rimmed Glasses
#2209 Sandals
#2210 Saddle Shoes
#2211 White Boots
#2212 Cowboy Hat
#2213 Sailor Hat
#2214 Bonnet

Plate 499. Katie Dolls #2101 and #2103 are marked both on the head and body. On the back of the head is incised "C 1991 ASN," and on the back of the body is incised "The Craft Doll // Collection // C 1991 ASN." The American School of Needlework sold Katie in the yarn department in various stores. She is 14" tall with a flange swivel head, a glued on synthetic wig, painted features, and a dimple in her chin. She is made of a light colored vinyl that looks like porcelain, is jointed at shoulders and hips, and comes in lace trimmed undies and socks and black patent shoes. She is an easy doll to dress with a delightful wardrobe. **Complete: $10.00 and up.**

Plate 500. Sewing Pattern Books for Katie. Starting at the top and going left to right are *Little Ballerina*, *Ruffles and Lace*, *Important Days*, and *Velveteen Princess*. *Little Ballerina* #8411 gives the sewing pattern for a leotard, skirt, and headpiece trimmed with sequins and silver rick rack. *Ruffles and Lace* #8410 is a sewing pattern containing Christmas Cookie dress and pinafore, Mint Parfait dress and pinafore, Peach Cobbler with an overskirt, Blueberries and Cream with hair ornaments, and Strawberry Sundae with headpiece. *Important Days* #8403 has patterns for Flower Girl, First Day of School dress and pinafore, First Communion, Easter Parade, and Birthday Girl. *Velveteen Princess* #4812 sewing pattern shows a long gown with a silver crown and beaded necklace. **Each booklet: $5.00 and up.**

Plate 501. Crochet Pattern Books for Katie starting at the top and going left to right are *Wedding Day*; *Little Girls of Yesterday*, Volume 2; *Little Girls of Yesterday*, Volume 3; and *Little Girls of Yesterday*, Volume 4. *Wedding Day* #8405 contains instruction for a crocheted wedding gown and veil trimmed in lace. *Little Girls of Yesterday*, Volume 1, #8406 shows a crocheted Shirley Temple type dress from the 1930s. *Little Girls of Yesterday*, Volume 2 #8407, offers instructions to crochet a calf-length dress and hat from the early 1900s. *Little Girls of Yesterday*, Volume 3 #8408, contains a long ruffled gown and bonnet to crochet and trim with ribbon in the 1890s style. **Each booklet: $5.00 and up.**

Plate 502. More **Crochet Pattern Books for Katie**. Starting at the top and going left to right are, *Fantasy Princesses*, *Merrie Christmas*, *Summer Days* and *School Days*. *Fantasy Princesses*, #8404 Crocheted Gowns, contains patterns for Snow Princess, Emerald Princess, Rainbow Princess, Rose Princess, and Heavenly Princess. They are trimmed with ribbons, flowers, or lace. *Merrie Christmas*, #8409, shows a white crocheted dress trimmed with white lace and a red ribbon belt. *Summer Days*, #8401, has crochet patterns for a swimsuit, swimsuit topper, western dress, Off to Grandma's Dress, purse and hat, and a playtime top and bloomers. *School Days*, #8402 offers crochet patterns for a sailor dress, frilly white dress, pink dropped waist dress, raspberry sherbet dress, and a perky polka dot dress. **Each booklet: $5.00 and up.**

Sew Adorable Doll

Sew Adorable was found in the craft department at Michael's stores in 1993. She was marketed under the Just for Keeps line by Wang International Inc. in Memphis, Tennessee. This all cloth doll is 13" high and is not tagged or marked but her chemise has a small tag sewn into the back seam that informs us she is made of 65% polyester and 35% cotton with registration number "PA-4684 (RC)." Sew Adorable has printed features and shoes, a synthetic wig, and is swing jointed at the shoulders and hips. She is dressed in white pantaloons and a chemise with lace and ribbon trim.

Sold separately, in hanging packages, was the clothing for Sew Adorable. This was very special clothing, all pre-printed in heavy ink or paint. Each of the hanging tags reads: *Just for Keeps // Sew Adorable Doll Clothes Pattern // Easy to Make Just Cut and Sew Together // No Fraying Pre-Printed Pattern // Instructions included // Easy Enough For Beginner Level Sewing Skills // Especially Designed For the Sew Adorable Doll // *Sewing Notions Not Included (See back for items needed).*

Listed on the back of the tag were the notions required, such as needle, thread, elastic and snaps.

Plate 503. Sew Adorable Doll. This cute little 13" cloth doll was made by Wang International, Inc. She is swing jointed at shoulders and hips, has a synthetic wig, and painted features and shoes. The doll is dressed as she was sold in the stores in her original polyester/cotton chemise and pantaloons. **Complete: $5.00 and up.**

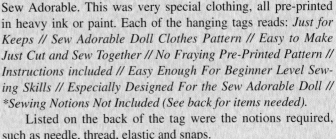

Plate 504. Sew Adorable Outfits are very interesting. They are printed with heavy ink that leaves the edges fused when cut so there is no fraying and thus no hemming. This makes them very simple to make and sew up. Each panel comes with related accessories to cut out. The instructions for the accessories are *for flat accessories, glue the cut pieces to cardboard or for three-dimensional accessories, cut out, back with scrap fabric, sew and stuff.* The six outfits that were available are from top left: HBP001 Molly Sunshine Tulip & Butterfly, HBP002 Miss Madeline Stripes & Flowers, HBP003 Melanie's Picnic Watermelon, HBP004 Sweet Dreams Maggie Nightgown, HBP005 Morning Glory's Garden Jumpsuit, and HBP006 Monique's Party Dress Pink Stripes & Bow. **Each outfit: $5.00 and up.**

Plate 505. Sweet Dreams Maggie Nightgown HBP004 is shown all finished. The pattern includes nightgown, nightcap, slippers, teddy bear, doll, stars, and a cloud trimmed pillow. **Complete: $5.00 and up.**

Plate 506. Sew Adorable in Presentation Case. I made this presentation case myself using the six packaged costumes available for the doll. Listed on the back of each package are the items needed to complete each costume such as thread, snaps, lace, and such. I lined a basket large enough to hold the doll and all the printed clothing. I then added the notions, tying them in with elastic and ribbons. Next, I rolled up each unfinished costume and tied it with a ribbon and finally I put in the instructions and placed the doll on top. I think any little girl who was learning to sew would love to receive a sewing set such as this. Value: Many Hugs and Kisses

Daisy Dolly Doll

Daisy Dolly got a slow start in the sewing world. She was first shown on the cover of Simplicity's children's dress patterns from Daisy Kingdom featuring little girl's dresses. Daisy Kingdom, a brand from Springs Creative Products Group, is well known for their colorful and appealing border fabrics and their line of dress patterns in the Simplicity catalog. The 17" matching doll dress pattern was offered as a bonus and included in the envelope when you bought the children's pattern. The first Simplicity Daisy Kingdom patterns with the bonus doll patterns that I saw were dated 1996. They were patterns #7076 and #7084 (plate 507). Both patterns were for sailor type dresses. I was immediately taken and even though I didn't have a child to sew for, I purchased both of the patterns, the Sailor Collars Kit, and the printed fabric to make the dresses. The printed fabric not only had the border print on one salvage side for the child's dress but it also had a doll size border print on the other salvage. The instructions showed where to lay the child and doll patterns to take advantage of the border prints.

The Daisy Dolly was what I really wanted and I found how to obtain her on the sewing instruction sheet provided in the pattern envelope. The coupon at the bottom of the page that had the instructions for the doll's dress stated that Daisy Dolly was a limited edition, available only through special order from Daisy Kingdom. The coupon stated:

Made of vinyl with molded hand-painted face, blonde hair and movable arms and legs; Daisy stands approx. 17" tall. She will arrive wearing a lace and ribbon trimmed teddy, and leather-like white shoes with matching socks. Free bonus dress patterns are included in selected Daisy Kingdom styles for Simplicity. You'll want to collect them all. Just look for Daisy's picture on the envelopes.

Daisy was $19.99 plus the $5.00 shipping and handling and would be delivered to your doorstep.

The doll arrived and was everything I expected. Daisy Dolly was a vinyl light skinned blonde straight-legged doll that looked-a-lot like the Effanbee Patsy doll. She was well made and balanced so she could stand alone. I was very pleased with

my purchase, and planned to buy more Daisy Kingdom children's patterns just to get the doll dress pattern.

Just a short time later in 1997 a Simplicity craft pattern for Daisy Dolly was issued. Simplicity's Craft Pattern #7497 was especially for 17" Daisy Dolly and pattern showed a variety of outfits. two party dresses, a floppy hat, two pinafore dresses, and a romper (plate 510). About the same time the first cut-and-sew panel for Daisy Dolly, Patty's Attic, showed up in fabric and craft stores. They were found right along with the Daisy Kingdom border fabrics on bolts (plate 511). A new doll had also been issued, Daisy Baby, and she was making her appearance on the covers of some Daisy Kingdom's Simplicity children's patterns. It wasn't too long before Daisy Dolly and Daisy Baby started appearing for sale in clear plastic bags in fabric and craft stores.

Daisy Baby was a 13½" vinyl light skinned blonde toddler doll that looked remarkably like Rose O'Neill's Scootles. Both of the dolls had a soft translucent peach colored skin and were soft to the touch with a little give if squeezed. The dark-skinned Daisy Dolly and Daisy Baby were issued in October of 1997. At this time new light-skinned dolls were also issued, they were made from the same mold but with a much harder vinyl which could not be squeezed (plate 512). The skin was a light tan with a matte finish that looked like bisque and the hair was a much darker golden-blonde. Daisy Dolly was a little larger, and an inch taller. A second Daisy pattern was offered in 1998. It showed the new dolls the darker haired Daisy and the dark skin dolls with black hair.

The size of the Daisy Doll pattern listed on the back of the pattern changed from 17" to 18". Patterns that had the copyright date before 1998 listed a doll dress pattern for a 17" doll — all after and including that date were for an 18" doll. The Daisy Baby patterns went the other direction. Patterns copyrighted before 1998 were for a 13½" doll and after and including that date were for an 13" doll. To confuse matters more Daisy Baby's packaging listed a 12" vinyl doll. With all this confusion on sizes, I am happy to say all the patterns seem to fit all sizes of the dolls they were made for.

Pansy Doll was copyrighted in 1998 (plate 513) and soon took her place among the Daisy Dolls. She has the same body-mold so clothing patterns for both dolls could be interchanged. Pansy was made both in light and dark skin, with three different hair/eye colors offered with the light-skin version. Also in this year a new pattern was on the market for Daisy Dolly from Simplicity Crafts. Pattern #8245 had the new 18" size on the back and showed the new darker-haired, light-skinned Daisy Dolly along with the dark-skinned Daisy Dolly (plate 510). The dolls modeled a romper and hat, dress with a pinafore, dress with an apron, dress and hat, and a full slip with lace. This was the last of the patterns that used Daisy Dolly as models on the cover.

Daisy Kingdom dolls were made completely of vinyl and had molded painted hair and features. They are incised on the back "C 1991//Daisy Kingdom, Inc." All the dolls came dressed in a white lace and ribbon trimmed undergarments (teddy) with white nylon anklets and white side-snap leatherette shoes. The earlier dolls have undergarments (teddy) tagged in the back with "Daisy Kingdom // China // style #." The later dolls' undergarments are marked "Daisy Kingdom // Style# // age recommendation // content of materials // China."

Rosie was the last of the Daisy Kingdom dolls and she debuted in 1999. Rosie has the same body-mold as Daisy Baby and was made in both dark and light skin. Rosie was the only doll to have a molded hat. Rosie's hat had molded flowers, lace, and a loop on each side with pink ribbons (plate 514).

The cut-and-sew panels were made only in the Daisy Dolly 17" – 18" size. The first panels had a full view of Daisy wearing the dress offered in the panel along with a message from Daisy on how to order her. Later after the dolls were sold in fabric and craft stores, the panels had dropped Daisy Dolly and had just the completed dress and accessories shown. The first cut-and-sew panels stated the clothing was for 17" – 18" dolls. Later panels such as Bunny Hop Daisy Dolly Dress stated the clothing was for 17" – 19" and some such as Vintage Cherries stated fits dolls 18" – 20". Daisy Dolly cut-and-sew panels have borders that are the exact duplicates to the original children's border fabric, and some were made in more than one color combination.

Cut and sew panels in alphabetical order for Daisy Dolly.
Alphabears Daisy Dolly Dress
Animal Class Daisy Dolly Dress and Purse
Bear Hug Daisy Dolly Dress
Bears and Bees Daisy Dolly Dress
Bunny Hop Daisy Dolly Dress
Cherished Teddies Easter Daisy Dolly Dress, Slip, and Purse
Dogwood Daisy Dolly Dress
French Document Daisy Dolly Dress, Slip, and Purse
Garden Bears Daisy Dolly Dress, Hat, and Purse
Gingham Violets Daisy Dolly Dress, Purse, and Hat
Golden Angel Daisy Dolly Dress
Golden Ornaments Daisy Dolly Dress
Heaven and Nature Sing Dress

Homespun Violets Daisy Dolly Dress, Slip, and Purse
Indigo Vintage Gingham Dress
Morning Glory Daisy Dolly Dress and Purse
Noah Noel Daisy Dolly Dress
O Happy Day Pants, Shirt, and Backpack
Patty's Attic Daisy Dolly Dress
Patty's Paper Dolls Dress
Scottie Dog Daisy Dolly Dress, Headband, and Purse
Springtime Toile Daisy Dolly Dress, Slip, and Purse
Sweetheart Bears Daisy Dolly Dress
Teddy Angel Daisy Dolly Dress and Hair Bow
Tartan Terrier Daisy Dolly Dress, Dog, and Purse
Victorian Garden Daisy Dolly Dress and Purse
Vintage Cherries Daisy Dolly Dress
Yellow Vintage Gingham Dress

Daisy Dolly Accessories Panels
Cherished Teddies Christmas Apron Panel — matching Christmas aprons for a child and Daisy Dolly with Christmas teddies to appliqué and a Ginger Cookies recipe to frame.

Bunny Hop Accessories Panel — to make for a child and Daisy Dolly, a matching collar, hat, purse, plus bonus images for three-dimensional embellishment (pins). This panel has no instructions. You are to buy Simplicity Daisy Kingdom Simplicity pattern #7997.

Christmas Collar Panel — to make for a child and Daisy Dolly, a matching Christmas-collar with a bunny on ice skates and geese. Also on the panel are appliqués of Christmas bunnies and bunny Christmas ornaments.

Sailor Collars Kit #N20404N — packaged kit with four collars, two for a child and two for Daisy Dolly. This kit was to be used with Simplicity Daisy Kingdom Simplicity patterns #7084 and #7076 (plate 507).

All of the cut-and-sew panels except the Accessories Panels were also offered as a bonus doll paper pattern in Simplicity's Daisy Kingdoms children's patterns of the same design.

Daisy Baby never had cut-and-sew panels but there were many bonus patterns in the Simplicity Daisy Kingdom children's patterns for her. Unlike the 18" girl dolls that only had dresses with the exception of the play pants set in O Happy Day, the 13" baby dolls had mostly rompers but also dresses and some rompers with pinafores. "Doll clothing" was written on the back of the envelope if it wasn't a dress. There were hundreds of children's patterns sold with the bonus dresses for both Daisy Dolly and Daisy Baby. There were even a few that included in an adult size in addition to the child and doll pattern, such as bathrobes #9927 or overalls #9927. The styles of clothing were tremendous.

Daisy Kingdom also came out with ready-made outfits for the person who was sewing challenged, or just didn't have the time to sew for their child or their doll. You could order the dresses directly from Daisy Kingdom. In a November 1997 Daisy Kingdom flyer they offered ready-made dresses for girls in sizes 2T to 14. Sometime after 1997 they also added ready-made doll clothing in both the 18" and 13" sizes. These were

Dolls and Their Patterns

made as matching companion dresses to go with their ready-made children's dresses. Many of these ready-made doll dresses were the same as the cut and sew panels. All were offered in the children's patterns as a companion bonus pattern. Baby Daisy had ready-made dresses that were the same style as the child's pattern, however often a matching romper was offered instead of a dress. All the patterns had hats or bonnets. After the Rosey doll was added some of the bonnets were cut larger to fit over her hat. There were dozens of ready-made dresses for the Daisy Dolly and the Baby Daisy size dolls

All the ready-made dresses came on a white vinyl coated hanger in a plastic bag. All outfits had the large Daisy Kingdom hang tag. Some of the hang tags on the ready made dresses had the same name as the printed cut and sew panels, some only had the description of the dress such as Dress with Apron. The hang tags carried the item number, name or description of the garment, size of doll it fit, fabric content, and a warning not for children under the age of three. On the inside of the garment was a soft plastic tag sewn in a back seam listing its washing instructions, fiber content, where it was made, and the Daisy Kingdom trademark. There was also a ready-made white full slip with a double tulle ruffle at the hem.

A miniature 3½" Dolly's-Doll dressed in a crocheted cotton dress, panties, and bonnet was also available (plate 514). The dress has a cotton label but the doll has no markings. The doll is made of vinyl with painted features and hair. She has jointed arms and white painted stockings and black shoes. There is one outstanding feature to identify the doll; she has a large hole in the center back top of her head under her bonnet. As far as I know there were no patterns for Dolly's-Dolly.

Shady Lane Original Crochet Designs published four crochet booklets especially for Daisy Kingdom Dolls. Two booklets were published in 1998. One was "Daisy Baby & Dolly Sisters are Special Maritime Middy" with crochet designs by Carol Hegar the founder of the company. The second book was "Daisy Baby Crochet Winter Warmers" designed by Pam McGhee. The booklet stated it was designed specifically to fit the 12" Baby Daisy from Daisy Kingdom (plate 508). In 1999 "Daisy Baby Crochet Wardrobe Volume One" was published and was designed by Carol Hegar. In 2000 the last of the "Shady Lane Daisy Doll" books was written — "Rosie's Crochet Wardrobe." It was also designed by Carol Hegar. Inside it was written that the outfits were designed for Daisy Kingdom's 12" Rosie doll, but that they will also fit the 12" Daisy Baby (plate 509). The manufacturing of Daisy Kingdom Daisy Dolly cut-and-sew dress panels was discontinued 2001 and production of the dolls was discontinued in 2002.

There was one more Simplicity Craft doll pattern with Daisy Kingdom's name on it. Pattern #5266 Daisy Kingdom Sweet Memories (plate 515). The dolls shown wearing wedding party dresses are not the Daisy Kingdom dolls, but rather that of modern generic 18" dolls.

The days of the Daisy Kingdom dolls have come to an end except on the secondary market. Never before has a doll with her own patterns and sewing panels been so popular. We have many companies to thank for these wonderful dolls, patterns, panels, and ready-made clothing. Springs Creative Products Group, Daisy Kingdom, Simplicity, and Shady Lane Original Crochet Designs all had a part in making Daisy Dolls a success.

Plate 507. Simplicity Patterns #7076 and **#7084** were to be used with #N20404N Sailor Collars Kit. The kit was packaged with four collars, two for a child and two for Daisy Dolly. Both pattern collars were included in the kit. The rest of the dress was to be cut from the border print shown. All patterns and kits were dated 1996. **Complete with collar kit: $25.00 and up.**

Plate 508. Maritime Middy and Daisy Baby Winter Warmers were both issued in 1998. "Daisy Baby & Dolly Sisters Are Special Maritime Middy" with crochet outfits designed by Carol Hegar was issued in 1998 and contains two sailor-type matching outfits with dress, hat, and combination shoes and socks, one for Daisy Dolly and one for Daisy Baby. The second book, "Daisy Baby Crochet Winter Warmers" designed by Pam McGhee was designed specifically to fit the 12" Baby Daisy from Daisy Kingdom. It contains Skate Set with sweater, skirt, socks, boots, skates, hat, and scarf, Warm Up Suit with jacket, pants, headband, and slippers; Bunny Suit with hat; Pajamas with top, pants, headband, and slippers; and Coat Set including coat, hat, muff, leggings, and boots. **Each booklet: $10.00 and up.**

Plate 509. Daisy Baby Wardrobe and Rosie's Wardrobe were both designed by Carol Hegar. In 1999 "Daisy Baby Cochet Wardrobe Volume One" was published. It has four outfits designed for the 12" Daisy Baby; Shades Of Blue Velvet Baby that showed dress, headband, and shoes with socks attached; Romper Time Baby with top, bloomers, slippers, and hat; Gingham Baby with dress, hat, and shoes with attached socks; and Country Girl Baby with dress, bonnet, and boots with attached stockings. In 2000 the last of the Shady Lane Daisy Doll books was published "Rosie's Crochet Wardrobe." According to the book, the outfits were designed for Daisy Kingdom's 12" Rosie doll, but they will also fit the 12" Daisy Baby. The five outfits in this book are Scottie Appliqué with a dress, apron, hat, and shoes with attached socks; Nightgown with hat and slippers; Coat Set including coat, hat, and shoes with attached socks; Bubblesuit with a ruffled hat and sandals; and Sundress with hat and shoes with attached socks. **Each booklet: $10.00 and up.**

Plate 510. Daisy Patterns #7497 and #8245. Simplicity's Craft Pattern #7497 issued in 1997 was published especially for 17" Daisy Dolly and the pattern envelope showed a variety of outfits, including two party dresses, a floppy hat, two pinafore dresses, and a romper. The second Daisy pattern, Simplicity's Craft Pattern #8245 was shown in 1998 with the new darker blonde Daisy and the darker skinned Daisy with black hair. This pattern included a romper with two matching hats, pinafore, three styles of dresses, and a slip. **Each: $10.00 and up.**

Plate 511. Patty's Attic Daisy Dolly Dress was the first cut-and-sew Daisy doll-dress panel to show up in fabric and craft stores. They were found on bolts right along side of the Daisy Kingdom border fabrics. These panels were for 17" to 19" tall dolls. The first panels show Daisy Dolly wearing the dresses along with a message from Daisy.
Hi, my name is Daisy Dolly.

I was created from an antique doll found in the Daisy Kingdom archives. I have a vinyl body with head, arms and legs that you can pose. My molded blond hair and hand-painted face are classic features of dolls from the past.

I just know you will love the lace and ribbon trimmed teddy, leather-like white shoes and matching socks that I am wearing when I arrive. Then you can dress me in easy-to-sew Daisy Kingdom dresses like the one you see here.

If you would like to take me home or give me to someone special, look for me at your favorite fabric and crafts store. Or, you can order me for $24.99 including postage and handling.

Just send your name, address, phone number, and payment to Daisy Kingdom.

Look for my entire wardrobe of pretty Daisy Kingdom dresses printed in fabric panels or in the Simplicity Pattern Catalog.

Love, Daisy
Later panels only had a picture of the garments and no messages from Daisy. **Uncut: $10.00 and up.**

Dolls and Their Patterns

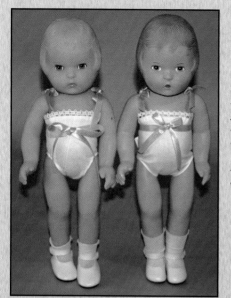

Plate 512. Daisy Dolls. The difference between the first Daisy and the later version is readily apparent. The first Daisy Doll has pink translucent skin, much lighter hair, and glossy lip color. She is also an inch shorter, and a bit smaller all over. The first Daisy's tag, sewn in the back of her teddy has "Daisy Kingdom Inc Made in China Style #0303-4001-002." The second Daisy has a more tan color skin with a mat finish. She is also taller and a bit chubbier all over. The tag sewn in the back of her teddy is printed in English and French. It reads: *c Daisy Kingdom Style #3075-32105 Daisy dolly is not a toy. For craft use only, not recommended for children under three years of age. Garment and lace trim 100% cotton; ribbon 100% polyester, stockings 100% nylon; shoes PVC (polyvinylchloride). Made in China. Both of the dolls are marked the same on there backs c 1991 Daisy Kingdom, Inc.* **Each: $10.00 and up.**

Note: The 3" shoes for my first Daisy Doll are too large; her toes had far too much room. The second doll had shoes that were smaller 2¾" and fit her perfectly.

Plate 514. The Babies. Daisy Baby, Rosie, and Dolly's Doll were all made in the later light vinyl, as well as the dark skin tones with black hair. Daisy Baby looks like the Rose O'Neill Scootles doll made in 1925 but without the side-glancing eyes. Rosie is what doll collectors refer to as a bonnet doll or hatted doll. The tag sewn in the teddy's back seam reads the same as the 18" dolls with a different style number. Daisy baby's number is 3074-32104 and Rosie's is 4100-10139. They stand 12" high and have the same body shape. My Baby Daisy seems to be a bit pigeon-toed, but I think that's is just how the legs came out of the mold, as I have also seen pigeon toed Rosie. Dolly's Dolly is 3½" tall and is dressed in a white crocheted dress and bonnet. Only her arms move and her shoes and socks are painted on. Research to date indicates Daisy Baby's sewing patterns were only found as a bonus pattern with the Daisy Kingdom children's patterns. Daisy Baby's patterns also fit Rosie. It seems that there are no patterns for Dolly's Doll. **Daisy Baby: $10.00 and up; Rosie: $50.00 and up; Dolly's Dolly: $25.00 and up.**

Plate 513. Pansy Dolls were made in light and dark skin tones, with three different eye/hair colors offered on the light-skinned version. They are blonde hair, blue eyes; brown hair brown eyes; and red hair, blue eyes. Pansy has a marcel wave hairstyle from the middle 1920s, a style that was in vogue the same time as Patsy's short bob. The dolls have the same body and skin tones as the later Daisy dolls. The only difference is the head mold. They carry the same tag sewn in the back of their teddys with the exception of the style numbers. The dark-skinned Pansy doll has style #4033-12222 and the light-skinned has #4032-12122. There weren't any patterns or cut-and-sew panels especially for Pansy, but of course she could borrowed Daisy's patterns and cut-and-sew panels. **Each: $10.00 and up.**

Plate 515. Sweet Memories Pattern #5266 is the last 18" Daisy Kingdom doll pattern I have been able to find. The envelope doesn't mention Daisy Dolly or any of the Daisy Kingdom dolls, but the pattern is for an 18" doll and the title can be construed two different ways. Sweet Memories does fit the pattern envelope image; the dolls are all drawn in wedding and bridesmaid gowns and indeed reminds one of the sweet memory of a wedding. However I am drawn to another Sweet Memory, of the time when the Daisy Kingdom dolls and the wonderful patterns and cut-and-sew garments lined the shelves of our local fabric stores. **Complete: $5.00 and up.**

Poupette Doll

Poupette (plate 516) was introduced to the market in 2002 by the Corolle Doll Company. Corolle, founded in 1978, is nestled in the Loire Valley, an area called the storybook region of France because of its scenic beauty and its impressive chateaux.

Corolle puts a lot of careful thought into dolls for young children, designing them to suit the child's age and size. There are seven collections, each tailored for a specific age range from 0 to 5+ years. Poupette is from the 18+ month collection and seems to be the only Corolle doll that has a dress sewing kit specifically produced for it (plate 517).

There are four dolls in the collection, Lulu with red hair in a pageboy style, Yoyo with black hair in long double ponytail style, Mimi with brown short double ponytail style, and Sosso with long blonde hair pulled up behind her ears at the sides. Lulu is considered to be the hardest to find of the series.

There was great play value in these dolls. All Poupette dolls came with a hairbrush and scrunchies, so the hair could be styled and restyled.

The easy dress and undress quality of the doll was also a big selling point. There were a number of fashions available for her all with easy openings and large Velcro closings. Some were reversible and all had good play value. Probably the best items available for Poupette are the My 1st Créations The Little Designer and The Little Dressmaker. The Little Designer is a craft set that included a vinyl type dress for the doll that has a color design on one side and a black outline design on the other. The color side gives the child an idea of what could be done, and the black-and-white side was designed to color with washable markers. The dress could be wiped off with water to design again and again. The Little Dressmakers set includes felt jumpers the child can cut out, lace, and decorate for her Poupette doll.

Poupeette and My 1re Créations won the 2002 Grand Prix Du Jousts Éveill Et Premier Äge award.

Plate 516. Poupette Lulu is 12", as are the rest of the series, Yoyo, Mimi, and Sosso. Lulu smells of vanilla, has a soft vinyl face, arms, and legs, and a soft cloth body with pellets in the bottom area for balance when sitting. Her face has painted features and her hair can be combed and styled. She even has her own hairbrush and scrunchie. Lulu is incised on the back of her neck "A-1-02 // Corolle." She is dressed in a reversible cotton jumper. Her body is made of green cloth, so her colorful body suit is with her always. The back of her box shows different hairstyles to try as well as some of her fashions. **Complete in box: $25.00 and up.**

Plate 517. Poupette's The Little Dressmaker was made for the Poupette line of dolls even though the dolls tested at the 18+ month age level and the My 1re Créations was tested for children 36 months and up. The set contains printed felt to make two dresses (jumpers) with Velcro fastening and four laces for sewing the dresses. Also included are die-cut felt shapes including three felt flowers, three stars, and three hearts, each with Velcro for placement. The instructions are:

1. *Cut out the pre-printed shapes (dresses) with scissors.*
2. *Put the laces through the eyelets to "sew" your dress.*
3. *Decorate your dress with the felt shapes.*
4. *There you go the dress is finished...and it looks great!*

The box states that the dresses are machine washable in the gentle cycle. **Complete: $25.00 and up.**

Children's Sewing Patterns

Before the commercial pattern, all clothing production was one of a kind, either made at home using guess-work or made by professional seamstresses or tailors. As early as the sixteenth century, methods of cutting up fabric to make it into garments was being illustrated and published, mostly by tailors with their own personal drafting systems within they're own observations. Plates were generally just the outlined shape of the garment with no size or scale. Tailors used narrow strips of fabric marked with their clients body points to measure for custom cutting. The cloth measuring tape we use today was derived from this early strip method of measuring.

Books on cutting out garments for the home sewer were published as early the late eighteenth century. Most books had instructions such as picking apart a favorite garment until flat and using the flat pieces as patterns; or fitting thin paper to one's body and marking folds, darts, and openings, or drafting a garment from instructions, the last being a real challenge.

The *Workwoman's Guide* published in London in 1838 contained:

Instructions to the inexperienced in cutting out and completing those article of wearing apparel & which are usually made at home; also explinations on upholstery, strawplatting, bonnet-making, and knitting, & C. by a Lady.

The Lady writes in her preface:

The Author of the following pages has been encouraged to hope, that, in placing them, after much deliberation, in the hand of a printer, she is tendering an important and acceptable, however humble, service to persons of her own sex, who, in any condition of life, are engaged, by duty, or inclination, in cutting out wearing apparel in a family, or for their poorer neighbours. She trusts, in particular, that Clergymen's Wives, Young Married Women, School-mistresses, and Ladies' Maids may find, in the "Workwoman's Guide," a fast and serviceable friend.

The *Workwoman's Guide* is a most comprehensive and instructional book with instructions on everything from mending to fashioning ladies' bonnets. In Chapter Three "General Rules for Cutting Out," a chart is given as thus:

Articles of clothing are measured by cloth measure.

2¼" make	1 nail
4 nails	1 quarter
4 quarters	1 yard
5 quarters	English ell
6 quarters	1 French ell

The *Workwoman's Guide* has many pages of small diagrams of finished pieces and pattern drafts of garments and instruction on completing them.

In the United States, the first full-scale foldout patterns were offered in *Frank Leslie's Gazette of Fashion* in 1854. Mme. Demorest drew the patterns. Demorest patterns were the first commercial patterns in the United States; these patterns used the Mme. Demorest's System of Dress Cutting. She had worked out a system of single patterns of either plain or trimmed bodices, sleeves, undergarments, nightgowns, children's clothing, etc. Patterns were available at dressmakers' shops, emporiums, or by mail.

Godey's Lady's Book, a fashion periodical on which all ladies relied, was first published in 1830. *Godey's Lady's Book* contained hand-colored fashion plates, novels, stories, poems, songs, and fancy work patterns. Occasionally, it would include a draft for a piece of clothing such as a bodice, but mostly it was for slippers, infants' clothing, niceties, etc.

In a July 1855 issue of *Godey's Lady's Book*, a pattern for an embroidered baby doll's cap was printed. In the same year in September, a doll's collar, in imitation Honiton Lace (bobbin lace) was offered. In a July 1856 issue of *Godey's Lady's Book*, under the title "For the Young Folks" there was a doll's embroidered collar. The collar is very much like the collars found in the 1900s presentation sewing cases. In Popular Sewing and Needlework Books. In 1860, Godey's also printed *How to Dress a Doll*, taken from a chapter in the earlier book *The Girl's Own Toymaker* #3-P. This was one of the chapters in *The Girl's Own Toymaker* that co-author E. Landels gives credit to his daughter for writing. Landels states the articles she wrote were entirely her own creation. There were no American periodicals for children in the 1860s that offered fancy work or doll dressing patterns. How pleased these little girls must have been to be occasionally included in mother's *Godey's Lady's Book*.

In *La Poupée Modèle*, François Theimer describes the first periodical on sewing written in France especially for little French girls. *Cendrillon, Journal des Petites Demoiselles* (Cinderella, the Journal for Young Misses) was intended for girls between the ages of 6 and 12. It was first published November 1861. It was short lived however, and only lasted two years. *Cendrillon Journal des Petites* published needlework and sewing patterns within its pages and paved the way for similar publications to follow. In November of 1863, the same time *Cendrillon, Journal des Petites* ended publication, *La Poupée Modèle* (not to be confused with Theimer's later book) published its first issue. It was competing with another children's sewing magazine, *La Gazette de la Poupée*, however, *La Poupée Modèle* (4-P) became the more popular magazine. *La Poupée Modèle* acquired the services of Mademoiselle Jeanne

Peronne to create patterns for their magazine. In the same year, Mademoiselle Peronne opened her own shop specializing in clothing and accessories for dolls. The first issue *La Poupée Modèle* featured a doll, which Mme. Peronne named Lily. Lily was a size 4 doll (45 cm) Parisienne. Lily had the most beautiful trousseau, all made exclusively from patterns published in *La Poupée Modèle*. François Theimer has reprinted Lily's wardrobe in a new book *La Poupée Modèle, Dresses and Accessories For the Fashion Doll "Lily"* by Mme. Lavallee-Peronne.

In 1863, the same year that *La Poupée Modèle* made its first appearance, a doll's pattern was printed in England and Berlin called the Dolly's Dressmaker. It was written by Frederike Lesser and translated into English by Mme de Chatelain. Published by Joseph, Myers & Company it was printed in two parts.

In the *Collector's Book of Dolls' Clothes* the Coleman's noted that the second edition of Dolly's Dressmaker portfolio #II showed in its advertising section that Joseph, Myers, and Company had won awards at the 1862 London Exhibition, for objects designed for the education and amusement of children.

Dolly's Dressmaker is possibly the earliest commercially printed pattern for doll clothing. The Dolly's Dressmaker, portfolio #I (plate 518) consisted of 12 sheets of patterns; a hand colored sheet showing finished items, and an instruction sheet with a description of each garment. There were no skirt patterns as most early clothing patterns didn't bother with simple skirt patterns; usually just a small diagram was all that was shown. The clothing was to be ankle length, and special attention was to be paid to the fitting of the waist, as it was noted in the instructions — *as it is in their waist sizes that dolls differ so very much.*

To those who made doll clothes patterns it was a serious business. Charlotte Slade lived in New York City in the 1870s and sold lady wax dolls in sizes 12", 16", and 20" and a 16" baby doll. On July 11, 1874, she took out a patent for a doll clothes pattern (plate 519). It read:

To all whom it may concern: Be it known that I, Charlotte L. Slade, of the city, county, and State of New York, have invented a new and useful Improvement in Patterns of Doll's Clothes, of which the following is a specification: This invention relates to that class of toys for children which combine amusement or entertainment and instruction. The invention consists in a set of miniature garment patterns for doll's clothes adapted for use by children, and to produce in the aggregate a trousseau or wardrobe, or two or more articles of the prevailing or any preferred style, as hereinafter set forth. In the accompanying drawing, Sheet 1 represents a lady-doll's trousseau as produced by an illustrative set of the patterns, which constitute the subject matter of this invention.

The patterns may be made of any prevailing or preferred style, and of tissue-paper or other suitable material, and of various sizes in different packages. The patterns in a set are of *one and the same scale or size, so as to require no adaptation, and the respective patterns, which might otherwise be confused, are unmistakably distinguished from each other. This has been accomplished by the use of distinguishing-colors, all the parts of one pattern being made alike in color, and different from others of similar or doubtful shape.*

Most of the doll clothes patterns children used in the late 1800s were obtained from pages of periodicals. Many times mother's favorite magazine would have a young people's page and occasionally a doll-clothing pattern would appear, or as in the case of a *Harper's Bazar* December 1882 issue, a whole supplement (Plate 521). The pull out pattern was typically 31" x 22" and printed on both sides with an overlay pattern. There were a number of different shaped patterns all having their own code-lines with dashes, dots, arrows, etc. and all superimposed on the sheet, each to be traced and marked according to its own code.

By the late 1800s there were also children's periodicals such as *The Young Ladies Journal*, in a December 1, 1882, issue there was a supplement containing doll clothing patterns (plate 520). This pattern was also done in the superimposed format. The practice of superimposed pattern sheets for supplements continued into the 1890s.

More "Girls Books" were coming on the market such as: *The Little Girl's Own Book* (#1-P) or *The Young Lady's Book* (#6-P). Most of these little books have chapters on sewing, doll dressing, making pincushions, pen wipes, etc; all with suggestions or pattern drafts.

Two little girls sewing pattern books were introduced to the market in Germany circa 1895. *Die Fleissige Puppenschneiderin* (The Busy Doll Seamstress) by Julie Lutz and Robert Lutz, Publisher (plate 525) and *Puppenmütterchens Nähschule* (Doll Mothers Sewing Room) by Agnes Lucas and Otto Maier, Ravensburg Publisher (plate 522). Despite being printed in German, both patterns are a delight and very well put together. I am sure an experienced seamstress could easily fit the patterns together without an English translation. In an 1897 page of advertising for Agnes Lucas doll sets and patterns, *Puppenmütterchens Nähschule* is shown as a boxed set with dolls, patterns, and implements. On the same page are just the *Puppenmütterchens Nähschule* patterns presented in their folder. This indicates the patterns were sold both ways with and without the doll.

Agnes Lucas also created a pattern book and doll set titled *Die kleine Puppenschneiderin* (The Little Doll Seamstress). In the introduction to *Die kleine Puppenschneiderin's* Agnes Lucas mentions *Puppenmütterchens Nähschule* saying:

This year again I would like to become a part of a play — and eager to learn group of girls, with a little book, patterns and doll. And I hope that the smaller doll will be as welcome as her larger sister in Puppenmütterchens Nähschule. I would be happy if I would succeed to place a seed in the susceptible hearts of growing young people for future productive work.

Children's Sewing Patterns

Agnes Lucas also made doll sewing sets for the French market. *Toilette De Ma Poupée* (plate 1) (My Doll's Attire) is written in French. I have been able to find three different pattern books by Agnes Lucas. *Toilette De Ma Poupée*, written in French, came with a doll, implements, and patterns. *Puppenmütterchens Nähschule*, written in German, came in a folder. And *Dolly's Dress Patterns to Dolly's Wardrobe* (plate 526), written in English, also came in a folder. All of the pattern sets have eight patterns. The underwear, nightgown, and baby items are the same in all of the three pattern sets. The outer clothing is different in each set except for the boy's sailor suit and the hanging dress which are the same in the German and French patterns. *Dolly's Dress Patterns to Dolly's Wardrobe* was done later than the other two, however the patterns are in the early 1900s style. The little booklet with the instructions: *Dolly's Wardrobe: Directions to enable children to make their own doll's clothes* states in the introduction:

Before my little friends begin work, I should like to give them some instructions, which must be remembered when cutting out either underclothing or dress. The patterns must not be cut out of the pattern sheet, but must be traced through with the help of the enclosed tracing paper. To do this tracing, lay a strong piece of white paper on a smooth surface, fasten the pattern sheet on it with drawing pins and slip the blue tracing paper between the blue side downwards and now follow the lines carefully with a pencil, using a ruler for the straight ones.

When all the patterns are traced through, both papers must be compared and all signs and letters inscribed on it. The dots in the pattern show where the fold is to be: Here the material is to be folded double, when the pattern shows only half of the garment, but if front and back are the same size and no seam at the side — the lower width is to be measured four times — the stuff folded and the pattern first laid against the fold and then against the straight line of the back and cut out.

The crosses show from where the stuff is to be gathered X gathers X.

If only half of the sleeve is shown — the inner-curved line is always meant for the undersleeve and you cut that according to it. To give the eye an exact idea of the pattern — they are drawn without turnings. For a seam you must allow 1cm for a hem 2 cm.

If this seems complicated for a child, let's look at a pattern written in the United States in 1889 with the name of Dolls's Dress Pattern Kindergarten Hour (plate 524) by Mrs. M. S. Schafor. Mrs. Schafor of Chicago writes:

First take large Chart from Pocket in Envelope and cut each pattern from the chart on the straight or outside line; be careful to cut even and smoothly on the line, as you must use the outside edge of each piece to draw your lines by. After you have the pieces cut out, then you are ready to draft a pattern. For example, to cut a waist for dollie: take dollie's bust measure around under the arms and suppose she measures ten inches around bust, then you would use the line marked thus + + Lay chart on paper and mark all the O's on the line marked

+ + and all the O's on the dart before you move your chart. Mark with your pencil from the + + line at the neck to the + + at the bottom of the Basque, then move chart up to where you stopped, and draw a line across to the dot you made at the bottom of Basque; Use the side of the chart from bottom of Basque to armhole, from armhole to shoulder, from shoulder to neck for your outside lines. Then place the pattern thus marked out on your cloth, and with your tracing wheel, trace all around the lines you have made.

Mind you, this child had only made the bodice "pattern shape" at this point. The complicated instructions go on. The early patterns were not easy child's play. A child had to really want to dress her dolly to have the patience to sew with early patterns.

At least the children's patterns had more information than the adult patterns. Adult patterns had little or no information on how to lay out the pattern or cut out the garment and usually had even less information for assembling. The pattern pieces consisted of tissue paper, usually white (sometimes colored) with large and small eyelets, triangles, squares, and notches. The holes were partially derived from tailor's markings. The notches were to indicate where a pattern was joined. Typical codes for the other perforations are:

1. *Small eyelets indicated take-ups such as tucks, pleats, hems and such.*
2. *Large single eyelets indicate pockets, center front, center back, and such.*
3. *Large double eyelets, often in a triangle, indicate no seam; place the edge on the fold of the fabric.*
4. *Large triple eyelets in a row indicated the lengthwise grain of the fabric.*
5. *Triangles indicate fullness as for gathers or shirring.*
6. *Squares indicated attachments such as buttons, trimmings and yokes.*
7. *Numbers punched in the tissue identify the pattern piece.*

The patterns were sold to retailers and dressmakers' shops and could be ordered by mail from women's fashion periodicals but in only one size. Patterns were usually placed in some type of folder or letter-type envelope. The pattern envelopes as we know them today didn't become standard until the 1890s.

If you wished to have a pattern in your size, you could send your measurements to Mme. Demorest (a pattern maker) for a custom pattern or you could take your pattern to a dressmaker and rely on her to alter it. It wasn't until the mid-1860s that patterns were individually sized.

It is said that Ebenezer Butterick, after watching his wife's struggle to cut out a child's pattern on the dining room table, came upon the idea of making children's patterns available in sizes by age. Mr. Butterick, a tailor by trade, published his first advertising, a Currier print of "Juvenile Fashions" in 1864. It was a print of men and boy's patterns. The patterns were a success and by 1866 he had added women's fashions to his line, sizing by the bust measurement. As his business grew, he added a publishing division. His first publication in 1865 was *Semi-Annual Report of Gents' Fashions*. It was followed in 1867 by the *Ladies' Report of New York Fashions* and in 1868, The *Metropolitan* and by 1872 it had evolved into *The Delineator*.

The *Delineator* was a favorite among the ladies in the late 1800s. As the sub-title confirmed, it was A Journal of Fashion, Culture and Fine Arts. The *Delineator* was full of fashion, advertisements, ladies' articles, and was of course, a courier for many of Butterick's patterns.

In a January 1891 issue there was a whole page of doll clothes patterns, the page was advertised:

Dolls' Patterns. This page illustrates an assortment of Dolls' Patterns which will be found very convenient in preparing lady dolls, girl dolls, boy dolls and baby dolls for the holiday festivals in which they take so prominent a part. The patterns can be had, in the sizes specified, from ourselves or any of our agents. In ordering, please specify the numbers and sizes desired.

With Butterick patterns of this period, the information on sizes, outline of pattern diagrams, directions for cutting, seam allowances, etc., are printed in small lettering on the front or back of the envelopes. The pattern pieces inside were tissue and marked with notches and eyelets of different sizes and shapes. Butterick Pattern #251 (plate 528) patented September 1899, is the earliest Butterick doll clothes pattern I have been able to find.

In 1916, Butterick began experimenting with a separate, more detailed, sheet of instructions, which went inside the envelope. The sheet was 11¼" x 8¼" and was printed on both sides with detailed information and plates, such as: *Turn under lower edge of body ¼" and baste over top of skirt with edges even*, with arrows pointing to the area to be done. It also left room on the outside of the envelope for instructions on the best placement of patterns on the fabric and a lesson in making tailor's tacks. It was a vast improvement over the scant information previously printed on the outside of the envelope.

In 1919, Butterick patented a larger revised sheet, 22½" x 8", and named it the Deltor, leaving out the middle four letters of his periodical, the *Delineator*. See New Butterick Pattern including Deltor #431 (plate 552). The envelope still had the pattern pieces outlined and numbered and the sizes of the pattern available with yardage needed. But now on the front, along with the drawings of completed garments from the pattern, was something new, a listing of fabrics that would best be suited for this design. Inside in the Deltor are the patent dates of August 1919 and later January 1923 was added. The layout of patterns that were once on the envelope, now were printed in the Deltor and in much more detail. Also included were instructions on embroidery stitches for this particular pattern.

In 1870, James McCall founded the McCall's Pattern Company. McCall was a tailor and had several copyrights on The Royal Chart, a pattern drafting system for grading garments to size. He began his advertising in *Harper's Bazar*. McCall showed patterns for ladies and children under ten calling them

Bazar Cut Paper Patterns. He later renamed the patterns Bazar Glove-Fitting Patterns.

By 1871, both Butterick and McCall's were offering patterns graded to size. McCall started his own magazine in 1873, it was named *The Queen*, for the first 18 years, then he changed it to *The Queen of Fashion* in 1891 and finally to *McCall's Magazine* in 1897.

The only early McCall's doll clothes patterns I have found are the little 3½" x 5" miniature patterns with no price markings. Each style was made in one doll's size only. McCall's Doll Special #5956 (plate 539) says it is "a fac-simile in Doll's size of Girl's Oliver Twist Dress #5956." These patterns were given out free as special incentives for the mother to buy the child's dresses in the same styles.

In 1919, McCall patented the first printed pattern. The instructions and plates were printed right on the tissue paper. There were no more punched holes or cut notches. The notches, along with seam allowances, were printed right on the pattern much the same as it is today. A miniature McCall's pattern for doll clothes The New McCall Pattern (plate 549) was one of these new printed patterns, it has "Free Sample" printed at the bottom of the envelope.

McCall's advertised their new pattern in the McCall's Quarterly Catalog as being the most accurate pattern on the market because:

It is the only pattern printed, one by one, from a metal plate, which, because it is metal, cannot vary a hair's breadth.

Other companies played up the value of hand crafted patterns, placing great emphasis on having everything hand done especially for you. In 1923, McCall's added yet another user-friendly feature, the "Printo Gravure," a detailed instruction sheet printed on tissue that was included in the envelope along with the printed pattern. In 1926, McCall's was first to enhance the appeal of their patterns by introducing color to the pattern envelope McCall's Doll Set, hat, dress, and bloomers (plate 553). In 1938, McCall's pattern printing patent expired and this method for printing patterns became public domain. All but one pattern company immediately began using the printing process. That one company was *Vogue*; they held out until 1956.

Albert McDowell of the Albert McDowell Dressmaking and Tailoring System held several patents for his system. He started publishing pattern drafts in *Pictorial Review* with the first issue in 1899. In a December 1914 issue there is a large ad for Designs to Meet Every Doll Need which shows fashions for every kind of doll, from a lady to an infant. Pictorial Review Pattern #5362 (plate 542), for a lady doll's coat was one of the patterns offered. The pattern is perforated tissue and all the instructions and illustrations are on the envelope.

Ladies' Home Journal was first published in 1883. When Condé Nast started the Home Pattern Company in 1905, The *Ladies' Home Journal* added a pattern division to its publication and used the Home Pattern Company as their sole provider. They printed doll clothes patterns including the Character Dolls set #2823 (plate 545). Written on the front of the envelope is:

Children's Sewing Patterns

Manufactured by the Home Pattern Company. Sole manufacturer of patterns for the Ladies' Home Journal the greatest family magazine in America.

They are probably best known among doll collectors for printing the *Ladies' Home Journal* Lettie Lane's Daisy. The Doll That Really Came to Life doll patterns in 1911. The Home Pattern Company went out of business in 1932 and that was the last of the *Ladies' Home Journal* patterns.

There were a number of smaller pattern companies that were also founded at the turn of the century. One of these, the May Manton Pattern Company, was founded in 1894 by Mr. and Mrs. George Bladworth, but had ceased production in 1926. The couple had once worked for McCall's Pattern Company. In 1890, Mr. Bladworth became president of McCall's Pattern Company and his wife, Mrs. Bladworth, was editor of the company's then current magazine, *The Queen of Fashion*. The couple left McCall's in 1893 and sometime in the next three years the May Manton Pattern Company was founded. A March issue of *Modes* magazine offered: "Dress designs originated and adapted by May Manton."

The Bladworth's never started they're own periodical but advertised in others such as *Mother's Magazine* and *Today's Magazine*. It is interesting to note that on their pattern envelopes they used McCall's old name, "Bazar Glove-Fitting Patterns," under their own May Manton's title, such as May Manton's Doll's Dress and Coat #6492 (plate 544). The Bladworth's used the back of their envelopes by selling advertising, there are five advertisements on the back of this envelope and a banner line stating: "Every line of Goods here advertised is recommended by May Manton."

By 1896 there were only four pattern companies that were considered primary companies, and those were Butterick, McCall's, Home Pattern, and Vogue.

Patterns were also being produced in other countries, as well as the United States. The *Australian Home and Fashion Journal* published an interesting doll pattern sometime in the 1950s, titled "The little dressmaker-dolls patterns set #1" (plate 555). The instructions read:

1. Now, lay out your sheet of paper, with the pattern guide on top and in the center of it. Fix a pin through the center of the cross and into the table. Fasten the pattern guide to the paper underneath.

2. Next, holding the tape measure straight, lay it out from the pin in the center of the cross and one of the dots at the edge of the diagram. It is easiest to choose first a point on the right hand side and work up and around to the left, i.e. move anti-clockwise. Lay the edge of your tape carefully along the line running from the dot. Measure along the tape always keeping it straight-the length shown beside the line. Measure always in inches and eighths-e.g. 6.3=6⅜".

Make a clear dot with a pen or a pencil at the edge of the tape. Be careful to mark your dot as close to the tape as possible. Work around the whole diagram, making sure that the tape is always kept in a straight line between the center of the

cross and the mark you make. If the pattern guide gets in the way, lift it up a little or stick a pin through and mark your dot in the proper place. Make sure that you measure through each dot on the diagram.

3. Now, join up all the dots marked in, checking with the diagram to make sure that your pattern is the same shape.

If any point is out of line, check again with the diagram. Do not remove the pattern guide until you are sure you have not missed out any point. Copy on to your patterns all the markings on the diagram, since this prevents different pieces of the pattern getting mixed up. Cut along the line you have drawn, or, if you like, add seam allowance to the pattern (⅝" for seams, or ¾" if you are using woollen or nylon material).

This sounds a bit like the early "Doll's Dress Pattern Kindergarten Hour," as it is a form of drafting, but it looks much easier and does sound like a fun thing to try.

Another pattern out of the 1950s that I think is interesting and would like to know more about is the Little Dress Designer (plate 557). Mollyé is probably best known for designing Shirley Temple doll clothing and producing the Raggedy Ann and Andy dolls. Molly Goldman of Philadelphia, Pennsylvania, is the founder of Mollyés. She was famous for designing doll clothing in the 1930s and supplied many companies in New York City. She also bought, dressed, and sold dolls using the title of Mollyés Creations. What I didn't know, until I found this set, was that she also designed at least one set of patterns. I found this set in a dress box along with other 8" doll clothing. The Little Dress Designer pattern sheet has her famous Mollyés logo and promises Creations #2, which I have not yet found. It's finds like this that keep the collector fires burning. If anyone has any information about these patterns that they would share I can be contacted through my publisher.

I remember Advance Patterns when I was first learning to sew. The company ceased production in 1964, but before they did, Advance came out with a Learn-to-Sew pattern line in the 1950s which used doll clothes to capture their young audience.

Advance patterns, Learn-to-Sew #6919 (plate 556) was sized for Toni and Harriett Hubbard Ayer dolls. The little girl doll patterns came in sizes 14", 16", 19", and 21", the infant sizes were 14", 16", 18", and 20". Advance pattern Learn-to-Sew #6919 included a Bridal Dress and was advertised as:

A "Learn-To-Sew" pattern with which a child can make three dresses for her doll. Designed for easy making, with instructions a child can follow. All dresses are completely open at back. Just one large pattern piece makes the skirt of the bridal or evening dress. Rows of large stitches, equally spaced, are pulled up, gathering skirt into tiers. Lace is applied flat on bridal version, then gathered. Both have attached petticoats, Ribbon sashes.

Do children still sew? I am sure some do, but on the whole, it is way down on the list of things they want to do. Even with their interest in clothing, it is so much easier to go to the mall and buy ready-made than it is to find a fabric store, hunt for a pattern, and then take the time to sew it.

I am sure I may have left out a lot of children's sewing patterns in this chapter that have been made over the years, especially doll clothing. After the 1920s, sewing became more of a pastime and hobby than a necessity and most doll clothes patterns were published at the adult level in sewing. Most children were no longer taught sewing at home at a young age, but instead learned it in school when they were older and much too sophisticated to make doll clothing.

Today in the pattern catalogs, there are numerous doll clothes patterns, all made for the adults to enjoy. Today, very few children could begin their sewing lessons (if, indeed, they even have sewing lessons) on the doll clothes patterns currently available. The doll clothes patterns of yesteryear are also complicated, in fact even more so. But sewing training came early, in the way of practice pieces, and sewing for a doll was the most rewarding type of sewing a child could do. In writing this chapter, I have found quite interesting the large role dolls have played in teaching children how to sew and use a pattern. I have not found even one early commercial printed pattern for a child that was not doll's clothes.

Plate 518. Dolly's Dressmaker #I was published in both London by Joseph Myers & Company and in Berlin by Winckelmann & Sons in the early 1860s. The patterns are presented in an 11½" x 9" portfolio with cotton tapes for tying. Inside the cover of the portfolio written in script, is "to Rose Smith from Auntie Cornish 1861." The first page, as well as the cover, is hand colored. The portfolio show ten articles: a white cap and chemise with pink ribbons, drawers with blue ribbon, nightgown with blue ribbons, rose-colored dress with bell sleeves, bertha (deep collar) of lace, dress with long sleeves and ribbon trim, and short cloak and long fichu (shawl) of tulle with lace. The patterns were for an 18" doll and are full size with instructions. **Complete: $300.00 and up.**

Note: Dolly's Dressmaker #1 was one of two parts. Dolly's Dressmaker #II offered a swaddling pillow and hat for a taufling (infant), four dresses, cloak, mantle (long coat with sleeves), casaque (fitted coat), chemisette, drawers, bag, stockings, and shoes.

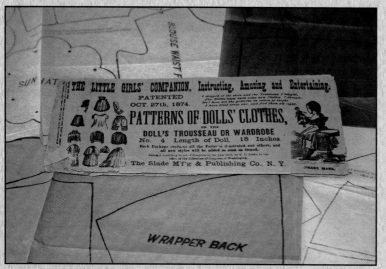

Plate 519. The Little Girl's Companion. The front of the envelope for this pattern set is printed with the following information: *The Little Girl's Companion, Instructing, Amusing and Entertaining. PATENTED OCT. 27th, 1874. I stopped at the store and the Trousseau I bought, For Dollie must have some new Clothes, I thought. See! Here are the patterns in colors so bright. I have tried every one and find them all right." Patterns of Dolls' Clothes, or the Doll's Trousseau or Wardrobe. No. 4 Length of Doll, 18".* Each package contains all the Patterns illustrated and others, and all new styles will be added as soon as issued. *Entered according to act of Congress in the year 1872, by C.L. Slade, in the office of the Librarian of Congress at Washington. The Slade M'f'g & Publishing Co. N.Y.* Also shown on the front of this 4½" x 9" envelope are 13 garment illustrations and an illustration of a small girl holding her doll and a Slade Trousseau doll pattern is printed on the front. All the pattern pieces for each garment are printed on one color. The garments included in this envelope are basque, 4 pieces; wrapper, 3 pieces; raincoat, waterproof with hood, 3 pieces; chemise, 1 piece; drawers, 1 piece; apron, 2 pieces; hood 1 piece, sun hat, 2 pieces; talma (short cape), 1 piece; walking jacket, 3 pieces; French sacque, 1 piece; skirt for dress, 3 pieces; over skirt, 3 pieces; and blouse waist 2 pieces. Some of the bodice patterns use the same sleeve pattern, and the waterproof also uses the talma pattern (short cape). These pattern sets were sold in different sizes and each size was presented in its own envelope with the size printed on the front. The directions for using the patterns are minimal: They state: *Double the cloth (as these are only half of the Patterns), and pin on the Pattern you wish to cut. Allow for all seams, hems, &c. The parts notched alike go together. The French Sacque is to be cut on exact bias on the back; and when cut a little longer than the Talma, with it makes the Russian Cloak. The Waterproof cut in white cloth makes a Sacque Night-dress, for a Cape to the Waterproof cut the Talma; it looks prettier if scalloped. The long seam of the sleeve is to be placed to the notch in the arm-hole, the dotted lines on the same are to cut the underside by, those on the Hoods are for the Shirr for the elastic cord, those on the Blouse show the bottom of the Waist, the ones on the Talma are for a seam. The Pockets, Sleeves and Collars can be used for any garment. The back breadth of the Skirts are to be gathered. Lay a small plait in the side gore and in the front breadth where they are notched. The Sun hat is to be joined front and Crown by buttons. Trim the Underclothes or not, as you please.* **Complete: $300.00 and up.**

Note: Charlotte Slades first patterns had C.L. Slade & Co. printed on the envelopes. Later this was changed to The Slade Manufacturing & Publishing Company as seen in the plate above. On the back flap of these later pattern envelopes was an advertisement for Toy Money with this little rhyme: "In playing store to buy or sell, To make up change and count it well, As good as genuine, let me tell, is Toy Money."

Plate 520. The Young Ladies Journal Doll Patterns were reprinted by Dorothy Cook in 1966. This is a reprint of a December 1, 1882, pattern. These patterns were a supplement in the weekly periodical *The Young Ladies Journal.* The patterns were for a doll approximately 18" to 22". The supplement has 17 pages of patterns and a picture from an 1882 *Harper's Bazar* showing children's fashions. The patterns consists of two walking dresses, dress for boy doll, dressing jacket, crochet nightcap, cambric nightcap, drawers, apron, collar and cuffs, knitted gaiter, capote (hat), garden hat, knitted petticoat, longcloth petticoat, knitted stockings, handkerchiefs, and hanging pincushion. The patterns are full size and there is information regarding the fabric and trim the garments should have: *The dress is of ruby cashmere with plastron of broché piped with satin; loop bows of satin ribbon. The capote is of satin, trimmed with narrow ribbon and an Ostrich feather tip.* There are no garment construction directions. **Complete pattern supplement, original: $75.00 and up; reprint: $5.00 and up.**

Plate 521. Harper's Bazar Supplement #52 Doll Patterns published by *Harper's Bazar* magazine. This is a copy of the supplement that came with *Harper's Bazar* in 1883. This pattern is an overlay of 60 pieces. The pattern pieces are defined by different line codes. The patterns are bonnet, crocheted bib, crocheted jacket, hat, knitted stockings, crocheted boot, knitted leggings, cloak, dress, and suit. The instruction has a list and descriptions of patterns written out for each article. You were to trace the patterns off the sheet using the code lines listed, cut them out, and construct the garment using the written instructions. Only two patterns had sizes listed: the cloak was for a 20" doll without head and the suit was for a 13" doll without head. It wasn't until later that the head was included in the size measurement for doll clothing patterns. **Complete pattern supplement, original: $75.00 and up; Reprint: $5.00 and up.**

Plate 522. Puppenmütterchens Nähschule (Doll Mother's Sewing School) patterns by Agnes Lucas, circa 1890s. Puppenmütterchens Nähschule is a hard board portfolio with tapes to secure it. The image on the cover is that of two larger girls sewing at a table, and two smaller girls in the foreground, one holding a partly dressed doll the other pulling hers in a wagon. The portfolio is 8¼" x 6¼" and inside are eight folders each with a colored plate applied to the cover to show the pattern inside. The patterns include 1. Hanging dress, shirt (slip), and nightgown. 2. Drawers, half-slip, dress, stockings, and shoes. 3. Boy's sailor suit, embroidered dress, and Dutch cap. 4. Full apron, "blousey" dress, apron, with straps. 5. Blouse, jacket, and skirt. 6. Raincoat and hat. 7. Long coat, hat. 8. Baby jacket, carrying dress, carrying pillow, flowing dress, and two bibs. The patterns are for a 29cm doll (about a 11½" doll. There is also a folder with carbon paper that is for tracing the patterns. **Original (all 8 patterns complete) in folder: $200.00 and up; Complete, reprint: $25.00 and up.**

Note: This pattern set was found in an 1897 advertisement for Agnes Doll Pattern and Doll Sewing Sets. It was offered both as a pattern set in a folder and a pattern set in a German sewing kit that also included a 12" doll. The folder with the patterns has also been reprinted and sold by Dollmasters.

Plate 523. Schnittmuster Zu Puppenmütterchens Nähschule (Patterns to Doll Mothers Sewing Room) by Agnes Lucas. This is a 1983 reprint of a children's German doll clothes pattern book first published in 1895 by Otto Maier Verlag Revensburg. The set comes in a pasteboard folder 8½" x 6" and has a separate instruction book. Each pattern is folded inside its own folder with the picture in color on the outside. It is written in German and some of the patterns are the same as the patterns in the German made set for the France trade Toilette De Ma Poupée. There are seven patterns to this set. There is no infant pattern as in the Toilette De Ma Poupée set. In both sets number 1, 2, 3, 4, and 7 patterns are exactly the same. Pattern 1 dress, chemise, bonnet, and nightgown; pattern 2 drawers, half-slip, full slip, dress, jacket, socks, and shoes; pattern 3 boy's sailor suit and a girl's gathered dress; 4, skirt with straps, pinafore, and full apron; pattern 7 short coat and bonnet; Patterns number 5 and 6 are different in both sets. Schnittmuster Zu Puppenmütterchens Nähschule pattern number 5 is a broderie anglaise (eyelet embroidered) dress with a dropped waist trimmed in pink ribbons in the right hand corner of the picture. Pattern number 6 is a puffed short sleeve dress with a skirt gathered high on the bodice and trimmed with a self ruffle at the bottom, it is shown on the bottom left. **Complete, reprint: $50.00 and up.**

Plate 524. Doll's Dress Patterns Kindergarten Pleasant Hour was copyrighted in 1889 by Mrs. M. S. Schafor and printed by the Doll Dress Pattern Company in Chicago. Doll's Dress Patterns Kindergarten Pleasant Hour set of patterns came in a 9½" x 8" envelope. Inside the envelope are seven pre-cut patterns of tissue, a waist chart, and a small envelope containing a tape measure, tracing wheel, and pencil. The tissue patterns are for a French dress, circular cape, skirt, hood, drawers, apron, and chemise. Each pattern is a different color tissue for identification. The instructions read: *The Chart printed on card-board makes sizes of waists from ten to twenty two inch busts, and the small one from six to nine inch busts, from which you can make larger or smaller ones by adding or taking off seams.* There are directions for using the chart and making up the garments. **Complete: $300.00 and up.**

Note: Doll's Dress Patterns Kindergarten Pleasant Hour put out a trade card as seen in the first photo. On the back of the trade card was printed: "Pleasant Hour" Kindergarten Instruction. Make the first lessons of life a pleasure to the little ones. This is attained by placing in their hands the "Pleasant Hour" Doll Dress Chart and Patterns, which appeal to the most potent feature in the Girl, this enables her to dress her doll neat and tasty and the result of play becomes Educational, impressing on her susceptible mind the most useful lesson of life, the art of Cutting, Fitting and Making wearing Apparel. The "Pleasant Hour" Outfit contains the chart embracing the system, with full instructions how to Cut and Fit Clothes of all kinds. Seven sets of Cut Patterns for Doll Clothes (that would cost in any Pattern Store 75¢), a Tape Measure, Tracing Wheel and Pencil, all contained in a beautiful Colored Lithographed Case. PRICE 25 CENTS. FOR SALE BY: Marshall field & Co.

Plate 525. Die Fleissige Puppenschneiderin (The Busy Doll Seamstress). This pattern book was first published in Germany by Robert Litz Publishers. It was a very popular little book. In 1902, Gustav Weise printed the fifth edition. Gustav Weise added Bertha Heyde after Julie Lutz's name, evidently Bertha added to the book. The outside folder measures 8" x 6" x 1" and shows two older children sitting at a table sewing and two younger girls in the foreground studying a doll. Inside are a book and another folder. The little book has a different picture of two girls at a table sewing with two younger girls standing, one carrying an undressed doll. This little book has the title "Die fleissige Puppenschneiderin" and has instructions for the patterns. The folder is holding the patterns sheets and has printed in gold "Schnittmuster Füt Die fleissige Puppenschneiderin." The patterns are all folded into the folder and are for a 27cm doll (about 10½"), the sheets are numbered 1 through 10. The pattern sheets have only the name of Bertha Heyde. The patterns are a full slip, two shifts, night gown, bathing suit with hat, two pair of pantaloons, two baby shirts, diaper, long christening slip, christening gown, three bibs or collars, lacy dress, two half slips, baby carrying pillow, party dress, cotton dress, pinafore, sailor outfit with hat, Russian costume, long sleeve dress, coat, bonnet, square yoke dress, cape with hood, sailor coat, play apron, silk dress, flannel baby dress with jacket, and shoes. There are also a number of knitted articles at the end of the book including bonnets, dresses, shirts, etc. This pattern was presented two different ways, one being just the folder as seen here and the other was with a doll in a sewing set. **Complete, pattern: $300.00 and up.**

Plate 526. Dolly's Dress Patterns to Dolly's Wardrobe was originally published circa early 1900s, by Agnes Lucas. The date is unknown on this illustrated reprinted set, but it was sometime after World War II because it is printed on the port-folio, imported by Coventry Associates from West Germany. Dolly's Dress Patterns to Dolly's Wardrobe comes in an 8¼" x 6½" portfolio. Inside are eight full size-pattern sheets and direc-tions: *To enable children to make their own doll clothes.* There is also tracing paper (carbon paper) to trace dolly's patterns. The patterns are not marked with sizes in this little set, however I measured one dress from shoulder to hem and it was 7¼". The patterns in the set include; I. chemise, nightshirt, stockings, strap-shoe, dress with yoke, lace cap; II. drawers, petticoat, petticoat with bodice, white muslin frock, button boots; III. boy's sailor suit and overall frock; IV. pleated skirt with shoul-der-strap, blouse, sailor cap, pinafore; V. empire dress, reform apron, combinations, hat for empire dress, low shoes; VI. blouse and skirt, sunbonnet, bag, lace gloves; VII. coat, hat, fur cap, fur collar, muff; VIII. chemise, baby jacket, bib, nursing pillow, and baby frock. **Reprint as shown: $50.00 and up.**

Note: See Puppenmütterchens Nähschule (plate 522) and Schnittmuster Zu Puppenmütterchens Nähschule (plate 523) for other pattern sets by Agnes Lucas. Also see Toilette De Ma Poupée (plate 1) for a doll and pattern set by Agnes Lucas made for the French trade.

Plate 527. Cosmopolitan Fashion Co. Model Paper Pattern #1810 Doll's set, circa 1899, comes in a 9½" x 4¼" envelope. There is no date however the styles are of the late 1800s. The pattern is for an 18" doll and calls for 36" material, ¾ yard for the dress and 1⅜ yard for the coat. The dress pattern consists of 14 pieces and the coat has eight pieces. The pattern is on white tis-sue paper with notches and perforations for darts, gathers, hems, etc. This doll's pattern was made in only two sizes 18" and 24". The original price was twenty-five cents. **Complete, original pattern: $50.00 and up.**

Note: This pattern was ordered from a spring and summer store catalog dated 1899. The store catalog had only three doll clothes patterns listed for that year. The other two were pattern #1019 Doll's Outfit (dress and jacket) and #1020 Doll's Set of Underwear (drawers, chemise, and night dress). My research has shown the pattern companies address was 244-246 West 23rd Street, New York and had no connection with Cosmopolitan magazine.

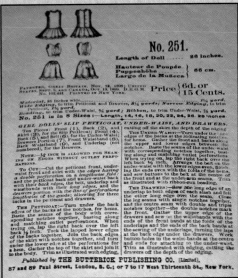

Plate 528. Butterick Pattern #251 was patented by the Butterick Pattern Company in Sep-tember 1899. The envelope measures 8½" x 5½". The pattern shown fits a 26", doll but it also came in sizes from 14" to 28" in two-inch increments. The pattern includes a girl doll's slip, petticoat, under-waist, and drawers. All the instructions and plates are on the front of the envelope. The pattern pieces are of white tissue paper with notches and perforation markings for matching tucks, hems, pockets, etc. There are 10 pieces to this pattern and the original price was fifteen cents. **Complete, original pattern: $50.00 and up.**

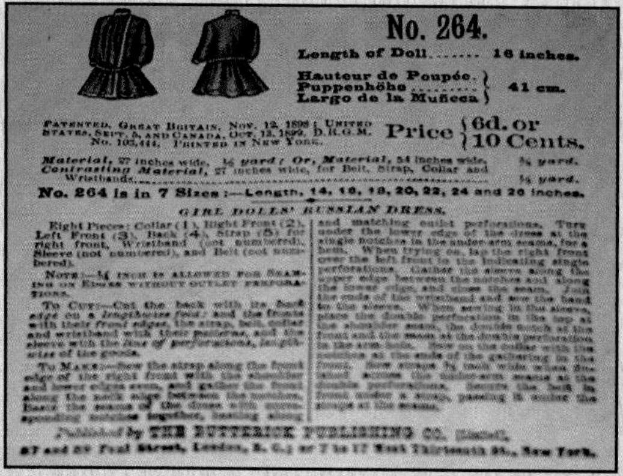

Children's Sewing Patterns

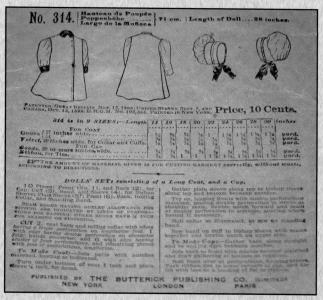

Plate 529. **Butterick Pattern #264** was patented by the Butterick Pattern Company in October 1899. The envelope measures 8½" x 5½". This pattern fits a 16" doll, however the pattern is made in seven sizes from 14" to 26" in two-inch increments. The pattern contains a girl doll's Russian dress there are eight pieces to the pattern. The pattern pieces are of white tissue paper with notches and perforation markings for matching, tucks, hems, pockets, etc. The instructions are on the front of the envelope along with illustrations of the front and back of the dress. **Complete: $50.00 and up.**

Plate 530. **Butterick Pattern #314** was patented by the Butterick Pattern Company in October 1899. The envelope measures 8½" x 5½". Butterick Pattern #314 is for a doll's set consisting of a long coat and a cap. This pattern is for a 28" doll, but it came in sizes 14" to 30" in increments of two. There are 10 pieces to this pattern. The pattern pieces are of white tissue paper with notches and perforation markings for matching, tucks, hems, pockets, etc. The instructions are on the front of the envelope and the back has advertising for Butterick patterns, and *The Delineator* magazine. **Complete: $50.00 and up.**

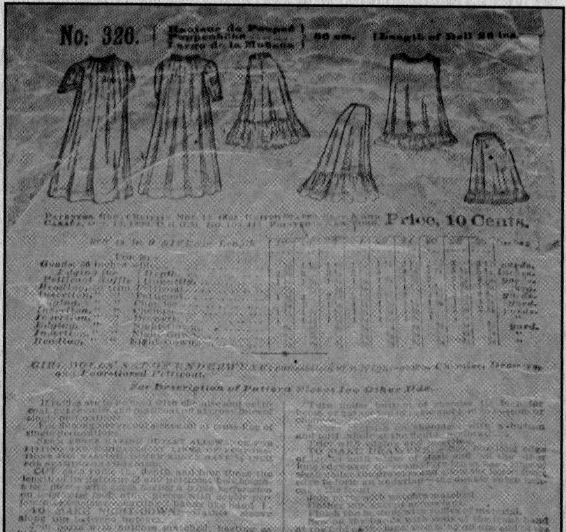

Plate 531. **Butterick Pattern #326** was published by the Butterick Publishing Company in October 1899. The envelope measures 8½" x 5½". Butterick Pattern #326 is for a girl doll's set of underwear consisting of a nightgown, chemise, drawers, and four gored petticoat. The pattern has 14 pieces and the original price was ten cents. The pattern pieces are of white tissue paper with notches and perforation markings for matching, tucks, hems, pockets, etc. The instructions are on the front and back of the envelope. **Complete: $50.00 and up.**

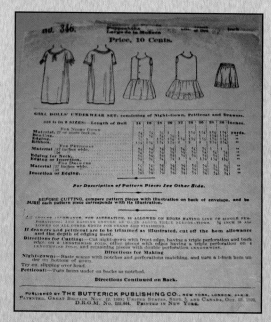

Plate 532. **Butterick Pattern #346** was published by the Butterick Publishing Company in October 1899. The envelope measures 8½" x 5½". It is for a 22" doll, the pattern also came in size 14" to 30" in two-inch increments and cost ten cents. This pattern is for a girl doll's underwear set consisting of nightgown, petticoat, and drawers. The pattern has eight pieces. The pattern pieces are of white tissue paper with notches and perforation markings for matching, tucks, hems, pockets, etc. The instructions and plates are on the front and back of the envelope. **Complete: $50.00 and up.**

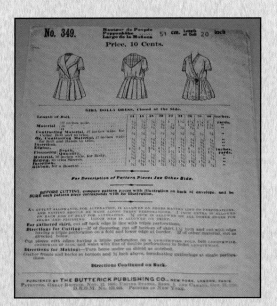

Plate 533. Butterick Pattern #349 was published by the Butterick Publishing Company in October 1899. The envelope measures 8½" x 5½". Butterick Pattern #349 consists of a girl's 20" doll dress the pattern came in size 14" to 30" in two-inch increments and cost ten cents. The pattern has only five pattern pieces, the dress can be made with or without a collar, both versions are shown on the pattern envelope. An outlet allowance, for alterations is allowed on edges having a line of perforations. The patterns are pre-cut of white tissue paper, with circle, perforations for hems, matching, pockets, etc. **Complete: $50.00 and up.**

Plate 534. Butterick Pattern #350 was published by the Butterick Publishing Company in October of 1899. The envelope measures 8½" x 5½". Butterick Pattern #350 consists of a girl doll's dress and sack and the original price was ten cents. There are nine pattern pieces of white tissue paper with perforation markings for darts, tucks, hems, etc. The instructions and illustrations are on the outside front and back of the envelope. This pattern is for a size 28" doll, however the pattern came in sizes 14" to 30" in 2" intervals. **Complete: $50.00 and up.**

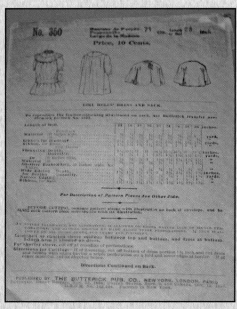

Plate 535. Butterick Pattern #352 was patented by the Butterick Pattern Company in September 1899. The envelope measures 8½" x 5½". This pattern is for a 18" doll, but it came in sizes 14" to 30" in two inch intervals. Butterick Pattern #352 is for a girl doll's dress with lining, which may be used as a guimpe. All the instructions and illustrations are on the front and back of the envelope. The pattern consists of nine pieces. The pattern pieces are of white tissue paper with notches and perforation markings for matching, tucks, hems, pockets, etc. The original price of this pattern was ten cents. **Complete: $50.00 and up.**

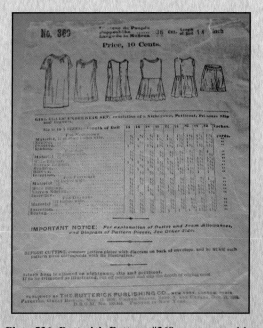

Plate 536. Butterick Pattern #369 was patented by the Butterick Pattern Company in October 1899. The envelope measures 8½" x 5½". The original price was ten cents. The pattern is for a doll 14" in height. The pattern came in 12" to 30" in two-inch increments. The pattern contains a girls doll's underwear set: consisting of a nightgown, petticoat, princess slip, and drawers. There are 12 pieces to the pattern. All the directions and illustrations are on the back of the pattern. The pattern pieces are of white tissue paper with notches and perforation markings for matching, tucks, hems, pockets, etc. **Complete: $50.00 and up.**

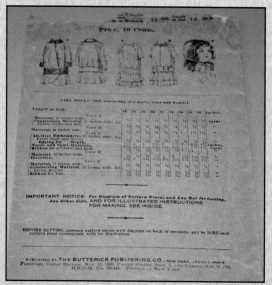

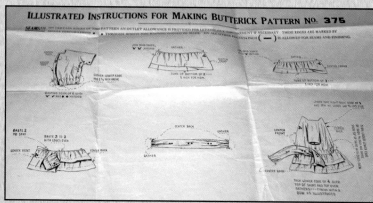

Plate 537. Butterick's Girl's Doll Set #375 was published by Butterick Pattern Company, October 1899. The envelope measures 8½" x 5½". Printed on the envelope is *IMPORTANT NOTICE: For diagram of pattern pieces and lay out for cutting, see other side, AND FOR ILLUSTRATED INSTRUCTIONS FOR MAKING, SEE INSIDE.* This is one of the first illustrated instruction sheets to be inserted in the envelope instead of printed on the outside. The pattern consists of a dress, coat and bonnet for a 14" doll. The pattern comes in size 14" to 30" in two-inch increments. There are 14 pieces of white tissue paper with notches and perforation markings for matching tucks, hems, pockets, etc. **Complete, original pattern: $50.00 and up.**

Plate 538. Doll Special 16" long is patented April 21, 1908, published by McCall's Pattern Company. The envelope is 5" x 3½". The pattern is only one size and is of a dress with a dropped waist and a large bertha, and puffed sleeves. There are six pieces to the pattern. The patterns are already cut out and have perforation, notches, dashes, large and small circles, and stars for matching, hems, folds, etc. The instructions are on the front and back of the envelope with illustrations. **Complete: $25.00 and up.**

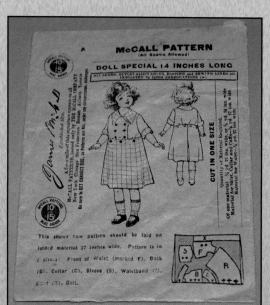

Plate 539. Doll Special #5956. Written on the envelope: *A facsimile in doll's size of Girl's Oliver Twist Dress #5956.* The pattern is patented April 21, 1908, by McCall's Pattern Company. The envelope is 5" x 3½" and contains a pattern for a 14" doll. Inside on white tissue are seven pattern pieces to make the dress shown. The pieces are already cut out and have perforation, notches, dashes, large and small circles and stars for matching hems, folds, etc. The instructions are on the front and back of the envelope with illustrations. **Complete original pattern: $25.00 and up.**

Note: There is no price on this pattern, I have seen this size with a "Sample Pattern" stamp, and they were given free.

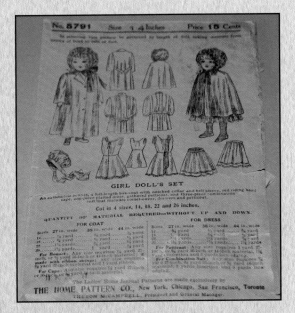

Plate 540. Girl Doll's Set #5791 circa 1911 published by the Home Pattern Co. At the top of this pattern it is written: *In selecting this pattern be governed by length of doll, taking measure from crown of head to sole of feet.* Girl Doll's Set #2895 is for an automobile bonnet, and full length box coat with notched collar and bell sleeve, red ridding hood cape, one-piece plated dress, gathered petticoat, three-piece combination that includes corset-cover, drawers, and petticoat. This pattern is for a 14" doll the pattern came in 14", 18", 22", and 26". The pattern pieces are of white tissue paper with notches and perforation markings for matching, tucks, hems, pockets, etc. The instructions and illustrations are printed on the front and back of the envelopes. **Complete: $50.00 and up.**

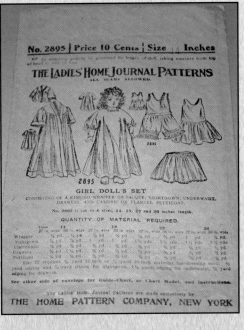

Plate 541. Girl Doll's Set #2895, circa 1911 published by the Home Pattern Co. for the *Ladies' Home Journal.* It is for a 26" doll, however the pattern also came in 14", 18", 22", and 26". The pattern envelope is 8¼" x 5" and it's original price was ten cents. There are 11 pieces to the pattern. The pattern pieces are of white tissue paper with notches and perforation markings for matching, tucks, hems, pockets, etc. The pattern consists of a kimono wrapper or sacque, night-gown, underwaist, draw-ers, and cambric or flannel petticoat. Girl Doll's Set #2895 came in four sizes 14", 18", 22", and 26". This pattern announces "All Seams Allowed." **Complete: $50.00 and up.**

Plate 543. Pictoral Review Pattern #5938, circa 1914, by Pictorial Review Pattern Co. The pattern envelope is 9½" x 4" and the original price was ten cents. This pattern is for a 20" doll but also comes in size 14" to 30" in 4" increments. The pattern contains a girl doll's set consisting of a dress with one-piece raglan sleeves, and to be slipped on over the head. Separate straight one-piece underskirt sewn to a band, a cape with "directoire" collar, and a box-plaited hat. The pattern has 11 pattern pieces. The pattern pieces are of white tissue paper with notches and perfo-ration markings for matching, tucks, hems, pockets, etc. The instructions are on the front and back of the envelope. **Complete: $50.00 and up.**

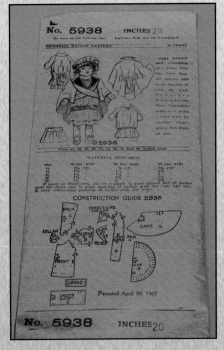

Plate 542. Pictoral Review Pattern #5362, circa 1914, by Pictorial Review Pattern Company. The pattern envelope is 9½" x 4" and the original price was ten cents. Pictoral Review Pattern #5362 is for a lady doll coat. This pattern is for a 24" doll but the pattern also came in size 16" to 32" in two-inch increments. The pattern has only one piece. The pattern piece is of white tissue paper with notches and perforation markings for matching tucks, hems, etc. The cutting and construction guides for this pattern are inside the envelope. **Complete original pattern: $25.00 and up.**

Plate 544. May Manton's Doll's Dress and Coat #6492 was published by May Manton Pattern Company circa 1915. The envelope measures 9½" x 4". This pattern is for an 18" doll but the pattern also came in 22" and 26". There are 13 pieces to this pattern. The pattern pieces are of white tissue paper with notches and perforation markings for matching tucks, hems, etc. All of the instructions and illustrations are on the front of the envelope. The back has advertising for thread, fabrics, and dyes. **Complete: $50.00 and up.**

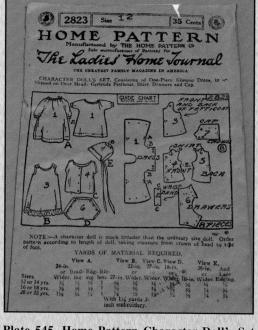

Plate 545. Home Pattern Character Doll's Set #2823 was published by Home Pattern Company, circa 1915 for the *Ladies' Home Journal*. The envelope measures 8¼" x 5". The pattern consists of a one-piece kimono dress to be slipped over the head, gertrude-petticoat, shirt, drawers, and cap. This pattern is for a 12" doll, but was also available sizes 12" to 22" in 2" increments. There is a note on the pattern that a character doll is much broader than the ordinary size doll and to order according to length of doll taking measure from crown of head to sole on foot. There are eight pattern pieces of white tissue paper with notches and perforation markings for matching tucks, hems, etc. The instructions are on the front and back of the pattern envelope. **Complete pattern: $50.00 and up.**

Plate 546. Doll Special #4524 a facsimile in Doll's size of Girl's Dress #4524 by McCall Pattern Co., circa 1915. The envelope is 5" x 3½". This pattern came in only one size 14" and has six pieces. The patterns are already cut out and have perforations of notches, dashes, large and small circles, and stars for matching, hems, folds, etc. The instructions are on the front and back of the envelope with illustrations. **Complete: $25.00 and up.**

Plate 547. Doll Special Dress, Hat and Bloomers circa 1915 by McCall Pattern Co. The envelope is 5" x 3½". The pattern is for a 16" doll. Inside on white tissue are nine pattern pieces, to make the dress shown. The patterns are already cut out and have perforations of notches, dashes, large and small circles, and stars for matching, hems, folds, etc. The instructions are on the front and back of the envelope with illustrations. **Complete: $25.00 and up.**

Note: There is no price on this pattern, I have see this size with a sample pattern stamp.

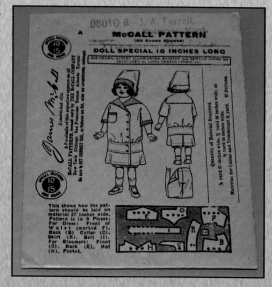

Plate 548. Das Fleissige Puppenmütterchen (The Busy Little Doll Mother) comes in an 8" x 5½" x 1½" box. There are 14 wax paper envelopes each with a pattern, instructions in German and a color picture of the outfits. There are about 50 doll patterns in all, circa 1915 style, and they fit about a 10" doll. The headings for each pattern are undergarments, nightgown, chemises, baby's outfit, morning garments, sailor suits, cape, "tobogganning" costumes, dirndl costume, "Tegernsee" boy's costume, party dresses, at the swimming pool, housecoat, empire dress, and kimono style. Also included in the box is an English translation of the instructions with a German Glossary. There are no dates, author, or maker anywhere on the box, pattern, or instruction sheets. Printed on the bottom of the box is "Verlag Marianne Cieslik." The patterns were sold for a number of years through Dollmasters. **Complete, Cieslik's reprint: $25.00 and up.**

Note: Cieslik's book German Doll Studies states these patterns come from a child's German sewing set Das Fleissige Puppenmütterchen. The dolls in the colored pictures on the pattern envelopes seem to be K* R 117.

Plate 549. The New McCall Pattern Doll's Dress and Envelope Chemise, circa 1921, was one of McCall's new printed patterns. Printed on the envelope is: *All Directions for cutting and making are clearly printed on every piece of the pattern. An exact reproduction in miniature of The New McCall Pattern "It's Printed."* The envelope measures 4½" x 3½". The pattern has six pieces and on the back of the envelope are charts on how to cut the pattern and a diagram on matching notches and closing the seams. **Complete pattern: $25.00 and up.**

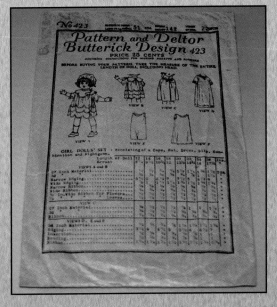

Plate 550. Pattern and Deltor Butterick Design #423 published by Butterick Pattern Co., circa 1923. The envelope is 8½" x 5¼". Girl's doll set consisting of a cape, hat, dress, slip, combination, and nightgown. This pattern is for a size 22" doll and cost twenty-five cents. The pattern comes in size 12" to 26" in 2" increments. The pattern has 14 pieces. The pattern pieces are of white tissue paper with notches and perforation markings for matching, tucks, hems, pockets, etc. The "Deltor" was a new instruction sheet now placed in the envelope with all the cutting layouts, and sewing instructions. **Complete: $50.00 and up.**

Plate 551. Butterick Pattern including Deltor #427 published by Butterick Pattern Co., circa 1923. The pattern is for a girls' doll's set consisting of a dress, cap, slip, bloomers, pajamas, and coat. This pattern is size 20", however the pattern came in size 12" to 26" in 2" increments. The pattern has 19 pieces. The pattern pieces are of white tissue paper with notches and perforation markings for matching, tucks, hems, pockets, etc. The Deltor was a new instruction sheet now placed in the envelope with all the cutting layouts, and sewing instructions. **Complete: $50.00 and up.**

Plate 552. New Butterick Pattern including Deltor #431 was published by Butterick Pattern Company, circa 1923. The envelope measures 8¼" x 5½". This is a pattern set for girl dolls with large bodies, which includes a frock and bonnet, underwear, and sleeping bag. The pattern has 16 pieces and a transfer for embroidery. This pattern is for a size 24" doll, but also came in size 12" to 26" in 2" increments. The pattern pieces are of white tissue paper with notches and perforation markings for matching tucks, hems, pockets, etc. The "Deltor" was a new instruction sheet placed in the envelope with the cutting layouts and sewing instructions. **Complete pattern: $25.00 and up.**

Plate 553. McCall's Doll Set, hat, dress, and bloomers was published by McCall's Pattern Company circa 1926. The envelope is 4½" x 3½". The size is for a 22" doll and the pattern has 10 pieces. McCall's was the first pattern company to introduce color to the pattern envelopes. This is not only a printed pattern, as it states on the front of the envelope, but it also contains the new "printo gravure" which includes cutting diagrams for laying this size on two widths of material and construction diagrams showing how to assemble. There are also suggestions for material and trimmings and photographic charts of finished details. **Complete, original: $25.00 and up.**

Plate 554. Children's Vogue Pattern Doll Set #20010 was published by The Condé Nast Publications. The envelope is 8¼" x 5¼" and is circa 1930. This pattern is for a size 19" doll, but the pattern also came in a 12", 14", 18", and 22". The original price was thirty cents. The pattern contains a party frock and bonnet, coat and hat, jumper frock, overalls, robe, petticoat, and panties. The pattern is not a printed pattern but is white tissue with notches and perforations. There is a "Practical Dressmaking" instruc-

tion sheet that shows the layout on the material and instructions on putting the garments together. **Complete: $25.00 and up.**

Plate 555. The Little Dressmaker-Dolls Patterns Set #1, for the little homemaker to be, comes in a 9½" x 7½" red folder with white writing. The *Australian Home and Fashion Journal* published it circa 1950. The folder has eight heavy card booklets, seven having two patterns each and the eighth with three patterns. The patterns range in sizes 14" to 20" for both girl and boy dolls. The patterns are not full-size patterns ready to cut out, but are pattern guides. With a ruler, paper, and pencil you make your own pattern just like a dressmaker. The pattern guides included in the folder are for a square neck dress, pleated skirt and blouse, long party dress with puffed sleeves, long party dress with ruffled sleeves, boy's and girl's beach set, girl's tennis set, overalls with ruffle straps, girl's pleated dress, boy's short pants and shirt, girl's blouse and skirt with straps, boy's short pants, shirt, and vest, sun dress, dress with yoke, bathrobe, nightgown, and pajamas. The system looks easy-to-follow and the child probably would have fun making her own patterns. This is a most interesting set of children's sewing patterns. **Complete pattern set: $25.00 and up.**

Plate 556. Learn-to-Sew #6570, #6919, #7820, and #7821 patterns for children are printed by Advance Pattern Company, circa 1950s. Each comes in a standard envelope 8¼" x 5¼". Advance made the patterns large and only a few to a package. The instructions are easy to read and understand, and eliminate as many seams and construction details as possible. Pattern #6570 has 12 pieces and makes a bunting, bonnet, slip, dress, sacque, and sleeper. Pattern #6919 has only six pieces and makes a bridal or evening dress and a short dress. Pattern #7820 has four pieces and makes baby doll pajamas, nightgown, shorts, and top. Pattern #7821 has 10 pieces and makes a blouse, skirt, petticoat, and overalls. The original price for the Learn-to-Sew patterns was thirty-five cents each. **Complete pattern, each: $5.00 and up.**

Plate 557. Little Dress Designer by Mollyé, circa 1950s. I am not sure if this came in a sewing kit, was part of a doll wardrobe, or simply a pattern, but since I have only found the pattern I have placed it in this chapter. The pattern is marked patent pending and has this message: *Lesson 1. For the little Dress Designer to learn to make and design dolls and clothes by America's Leading Doll Designer. Follow instructions carefully and you will find a lot of play and educational value in sewing and designing. For next lesson ask for Creations #2 set.* I have only found pattern pieces for style 1, panties, style 2 petticoat, and parts of style 3 dress. With the patterns I found a dress, coat, hat, and handbag made up. The clothing fits a Ginny-type 8" doll. Mollyé was the trademark of Molly Goldman. **Value, complete: unknown.**

Note: I am searching for more information about this set. If anyone can supply any information I can be contacted through Collector Books.

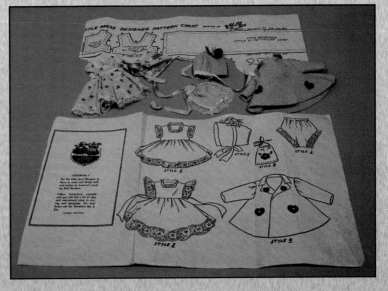

Children's Sewing Patterns

Plate 558. A Primer of Embroidry Stitches. This 9" x 6" circa 1950s envelope has no name or maker printed on it. The instructions are on the back of the envelope and on the pattern sheets. With each pattern sheet to be transferred for embroidered it gives a suggestion of what you can make with the design. There are 12 lessons, for each of project you have one or two new stitches by the time you get to the twelfth you can do 12 embroidery stitches, and you have seven projects finished for family gifts. Some of the projects are bean bag for brother, pot holder for mother, sachet case for auntie, bag for daddy's collar buttons, hanky case for grandmother, embroider a flower on a blouse, make a picture. **Complete: $10.00 and up.**

Plate 559. Kid Sew #215 & **224**, copyright 1986 by Alma Burge. The envelopes are 7¾" x 5¾". Pattern #215 is for a 15" – 20" dolls sleeping bag, it can be made at level 1, 2, or 3 depending upon how fancy you make it. Pattern #224 is for a trumpet skirt. The one-piece pattern allows sewer to choose from 6+ panels for skirt. It has an elastic waistband. Level 1 is constructed with woven fabric or stabilized knits. Level two is for softer, more difficult knits stitched with knit techniques. **Complete: $5.00 and up.**

Plate 560. Kids Can Sew #7929, #7930 & **#8335** was published by Simplicity Pattern Co. in a standard 8½" x 6" envelope. Both of the patterns are copyright 1992 and 1993 by Simplicity Pattern Company on the envelope, but on the instruction sheet they have a copyright by Simplicity Pattern Company and Carolyn Curtis. It seems Carolyn Curtis is the president of Kids Can Sew and her trademark is on the front of the envelope. Ms. Curtis has a business selling sewing kits to women who want to teach children to sew. I have not seen Kids Can Sew patterns in the Simplicity catalogs recently, however, Ms. Curtis is still on the web. The patterns in this plate are #7929 a skirt and bag, #7930 shorts and a bag, #8335 a mini blouse. They range in size of small to extra large. The original price on Kids Can Sew patterns was $4.95 to $7.50. **Complete, each: $5.00 and up.**

Plate 561. I'll Teach Myself #4535, **#DP11,** and **#DP13**. I'll Teach Myself #4535 is copyrighted by Butterick but has an I'll Teach Myself trademark by Possibilities. It is a joint venture between the two companies. The pattern envelope advertises *Easy Sewing! Just for kits! Kid Tested and Kid Approved! Fun and Colorful Instructions!* The instructions look just like I'll Teach Myself books (#106-P). The original price on pattern #4535 was $7.95. I'll Teach Myself Paper Shapes #DP11, is dated 1993 copyright by Possibilities and is sewing on paper. There are nine designs to sew with colored paper. I'll Teach Myself Soft Shapes #DP13 has six designs to sew with fabric, and is dated 1993 copyright by Possibilities. **Complete, each: $5.00 and up.**

Plate 562. Sew Young, Sew Fun Pattern Kit by Sew Young, Sew Fun, copyright 1999. This is a 11½" x 9½" x 2" soft vinyl case with a handle. It contains 14 tab dividers with an introduction and sewing 101 through 113. There is a Sew Young, Sew Fun television program and a website (www.sewyoungsewfun.com). Sew Young, Sew Fun kit represents 13 thirty-minute shows for Public TV. Included in the kit are instructions and patterns for each of the 13 feature projects as well as the notes from the "Stitches That Serve" and "Gretchen Answers It" segments. The kit recommends beginning with program 101 and following the order of the project guides. The projects are creativity kit (folding sewing kit), boxer shorts, crocheted granny square afghan, drawstring skirt, party favors, bag and autograph gecko, one piece reversible vest, robe, bean bag seat, tic-tac-toe pack, hip chenille handbag, pieced notebook cover, team pride pennant, and personalize your clothes. All the projects come with patterns including the clothing, the clothing has Kwik Sew patterns in size 8, 10, 12, and 14 included. Also included is a charity program "Stitches That Serve," you can sew comfort pillows, comfort caps for a child or adult, or serger premie gowns for your local hospitals, all the patterns are included. **Complete: $10.00 and up.**

Books written especially for children were published as early as the middle of the seventeenth century when it became evident to parents that an interesting book could not only captivate a child, but could also be used as a teaching tool. Educational books became a necessity, especially for the Victorian child.

The first instruction books for young children were alphabet books, usually based on such appealing themes as animals, trains, and flowers. Victorians, who were passionately involved in education, usually bought books for their children that would improve young minds such as geography, religion, and history. Until the mid-nineteenth century, many Victorian parents thought that books such as fairy tales, that were purely entertainment and had no moral or educational value, were sinful and immoral.

The first instruction books of games and things to make and do were directed at boys. I imagine little girls were kept busy helping their mothers cook, clean, and take care of smaller brothers and sisters and didn't require the diversions their brothers did.

However in 1831, there was one woman, Mrs. L Maria Child, who thought little girls needed their own book. Mrs. Child wrote one of the first instruction books that I've found for girls *The Little Girl's Own Book* (1-P). Mrs. Child, wanted to make sure every girl knew how to make herself useful. She writes in her books preface:

In this land of precarious fortunes, every girl should know how to be useful; amid the universal dissemination of knowledge, every mind should seek to improve itself to the utmost; and in this land of equality, as much time should be devoted to elegant accomplishments, refined taste, and gracefulness of manner, as can possibly be spared from holier and more important duties. In this country it is peculiarly necessary that daughters should be so educated as to enable them to fulfil the duties of a humble station, or to dignify and adorn the highest. This is the reason why I have mingled a little of every thing in the Girl's Own Book.

At the same time Mrs. Child was writing *The Little Girl's Own Book*, Miss. Leslie was writing her book for girls, the *American Girl's Book or Occupation for Play Hours* (2-P). The books are very much alike; both have sports and games for indoors and out, puzzles, riddles, charades, and needlework. However the authors give very different reasons for writing the same type books. Miss Leslie writes in her introduction:

I have often regretted that so many of the diversions which formerly enlivened the leisure hours of very young people should long since have become obsolete, or only to be found in

circles which are yet untouched with the folly and affectation of what is called fashion. And also that in families where the children are over educated (as is now too often the case), the parents, forgetting that they themselves were once young, allow no recreations but those of so grave a character, that play becomes more difficult and fatiguing than study. The author of this little book has not aimed at compiling a juvenile encyclopedia. It is simply an unpretending manual of light and exhilarating amusements; most of which will be found on trial to answer the purpose of unbending the mind or exercising the body, and at the same time interesting the attention.

Whatever the authors' reasons for writing their books, I am sure many a little girl enjoyed these two little books written especially for them.

In 1859, Mr. E. Landells wrote an instructional book for boys and named it *The Boy's Own Toymaker*. It was a very popular book and was reprinted in only a year's time. In that same year, Mr. Landells introduced *The Girl's Own Toymaker* (3-P) sharing the authorship with his daughter Alice. In the introduction Landells states;

Our earliest and most lasting impressions are made at home; and the object of this little work is to assist those, who have not the leisure or opportunity of leading the young mind into habits of thought and study, in a way that is most likely to benefit them.

The child that is properly instructed to make its own doll's clothes, toy-furniture, bedding, etc., will soon take a pride in making them properly, and will thus be acquiring knowledge of the most useful and practical character.

The plan and designs for the work are quite original, and I have been greatly assisted in it by my daughter, Miss Alice Landells. The directions and illustrations for dressing dolls, furnishing houses etc., as well as many of the more ornamental toys, are entirely her own production; and the way she has executed that part of the work will no doubt be appreciated, for its general utility and completeness.

Indeed Miss Alice was a talented young lady; the illustrations are beautifully drawn and the instructions are well written and easy to follow. *The Girl's Own Toymaker* was a complete success — the first edition was sold out in only a few months — and a second edition was published in the same year.

Godey's Lady's Book printed a series of articles from *The Girl's Own Toymaker* for children in 1860. These articles included doll clothing and cardboard furniture. *Godey's Lady's Book* also suggested that mothers might enlarge the doll clothes patterns to make clothing for their children.

According to François Theimer the first periodical especially written with sewing instructions for little girls in France was *Cendrillon, Journal des Petites Demoiselles* (*Cinderella, the Journal for Young Misses*) in 1861. *Cendrillon* was directed at young girls between the ages of six and seven, but only published patterns for dolls during a three-month period, between January and March of 1862. *Cendrillon* was the first magazine of its kind, reserving space for patterns and fancy work for little girls. In 1963 a new magazine was established titled *La Poupée Modèle* (4-P) (plate 563). The magazine acquired the services of Mademoiselle Jeanne Peronne, a talented seamstress, to create doll patterns and help launche *La Poupée Modèle*. Mlle. Peronne had just opened her own shop specializing in clothing and accessories for dolls and was the perfect person for their new magazine. Mlle. Peronne named the doll featured in the first issue of the magazine Lily. Lily was to be a 45cm size 4 Parisienne, and all the patterns and accessories for the dolls in the magazine were fitted to her size. A savvy Mlle. Peronne (Mme. Lavallée-Peronne after her marriage in 1865) carried a variety of dolls measuring 45cm. She had a large inventory with many styles and prices to choose from. Using *La Poupée Modèle* patterns and accessories any 45cm doll from Mme. Lavallée-Peronne could be a Lily. Mme. Lavallée-Peronne realized not every little girl could afford a new 45cm, size 4, doll so her patterns could be made larger or smaller using a method which was explained in the magazine. Lily had the most beautiful trousseau that any doll could have ever wished for. She was even blessed with many lovely accessories, but alas, it was to end. Lily the lovely Parisienne was fazed out in 1883 when the articulated bébés were beginning to replace the French fashion dolls. Mme. Lavallée-Peronne retired. A new doll, an articulated bébé with the name of Benjamin, replaced Lily, and with Benjamin came a new pattern maker, Madame Regnault. *La Poupée Modèle* lived on until it ceased publication in September of 1924.

The Young Ladies Book (6-P) written by Mrs. Henry Mackarness in 1876, also has a chapter on dressing dolls and includes drafts for doll clothing patterns and suggestions for dressing dolls in ethnic costumes. These instructions and drafts were later published in *The Ladies Guide to Needle Work, Embroidery, Etc.* and *American Girl's Home Book of Work and Play* (7-P). The instructions were slightly edited but the drafts were not changed. More than once, in these early books, I have found the same patterns repeated from book to book.

In the late 1880s and into the 1900s, Lina and Adelia Beard wrote recreation books for girls. In the Preface of *The American Girl's Handy Book* (8-P) the Beard's wrote:

"I do wish some one would write a book like that for girls," is the remark we have frequently heard when a new book of sports for boys has made its appearance; but it was not until the publication of the "American Boy's Handy Book" that it occurred to us to write a book for the American boy's neglected sisters, which should be equally original and practical.

In the "Girl's Handy Book," which it has been our endeavor to make peculiarly American, we have sought to intro-

duce original and novel ideas, and by their aid to open new avenues of enterprise and enjoyment.

We scarcely deem it necessary to point out the fact that in supplying healthy, sensible work and amusement for leisure hours, employment is given whose whole tendency is to refine the tastes and ambitions of our American girls.

Lina and Adelia Beard wrote many other girl's books including, *On the Trail An Outdoor Book for Girls*; *Things Worth Doing and How to Do Them*; *What a Girl Can Make and Do*; and *Handicraft and Recreation for Girls*. They also published articles for girls in children's periodicals such as *The Youth's Companion*, *St. Nicholas*, *Harper's Young People*, *Golden Days*, and *Wide Awake*. By the late 1890s there were quite a few children's periodicals. They were full of stories, poems, history, music, and usually offered at least one activity page. The activity page could usually be enjoyed by both boys and girls. Many times these pages were paper toys.

In 1891, a new magazine just for girls debuted on the American market. *The Dolls' Dressmaker, A Magazine for Girls* (9-P) (plate 564) by Jennie Wren. The magazine carried stories about dolls, poems, paper furniture, paper toys, and full-size patterns for dolls' clothing. The magazine was short lived; the latest copy I have found is September 1893. It was a wonderful little magazine and the only one I have found thus far for little American girls that was dedicated to sewing. However, the name of the author, Jennie Wren, is suspect for more than one reason. In my research I found that the name "Jennie Wren" came from England. The legend goes; shortly after the invention in 1764 of the Spinning Jenny that spun cotton into thread to be made into fabric, there was a great need for spinners. The mills found that they could use cheap child labor by bringing in young girls from nearby farms. The young girls who were brought to the mills for spinning were called "wrens". Thus, the name "Jennie Wren" was used when referring to any woman in England who worked at spinning or sewing for a living.

The other reference to Jenny Wren is in Charles Dickens' last novel in 1865, *Our Mutual Friend*. Jenny Wren is a crippled dwarf of a child who makes her meager living as a doll's dressmaker.

Ralphael Tuck and Sons published a booklet written in 1896, titled *Dolly's Dressmaker* (10-P) (plate 565). This booklet was both a sewing book and a paper doll book. There are full-size patterns for a wardrobe to fit a 9" doll and three color-printed pages of paper dolls. The paper dolls color printed clothing was also the illustrations of the finished garments to be made for the 9" doll. Both the child's dolly and paper doll could be dressed the same.

One little girl's periodical that lasted for a very long time was the French periodical *La Semaine De Suzette* (17-P) (plate 567). First published in 1905, it became popular in a very short time. This weekly paper offered a little doll named Bleuette to its subscribers. Bleuette was the whole reason for the periodical — she became the children's teacher. Every week, French children followed her through her adventures, read her stories, and made clothing for her from the patterns printed in the periodical. *La Semaine De Suzette* was published for 55 years. Bleuette is very popular today in America among the doll collecting/sewing population. There are Bleuette clubs and American-based periodicals dedicated to sewing just for Bleuette.

Most of the popular books up until 1900 written for little girls that included sewing were variety books. These offered many leisure pastimes and sewing was just a small part. It is interesting to note, that all of the books for girls listed in this chapter up to the date of 1905 had some sort of sewing that included dolls or doll clothing.

It is after the date of 1908, that the popular girls' sewing books started to appear. The first popular hardbound sewing book I have found is *How to Dress a Doll* (18-P) (plate 568). It probably has been the most copied book on doll dressing to date. It was originally published in 1908 and written by Mary Morgan. She wanted to write a book that a child could understand and enable her to make doll clothing by herself. In her foreword Mary writes:

To Young Dressmakers Little girl mothers have almost as much trouble as grown-up mothers about their children's clothes. It would never do if their dollies were not stylishly dressed; yet how to manage it is the bother. Mothers, big sisters, and nurses are usually too busy to make lots of dainty underclothes, dresses, coats and hats for their doll family, and there do not seem to be many doll dressmakers and milliners. This book will help you to get rid of that bother. It will show you how to have your dollies beautifully dressed without troubling big people or costing much money. How will it do it? By teaching you to make your dollies' clothes.

This little book covers everything you need to know, from tying a knot in your thread, to finishing the clothing with fancy stitching or lace. It is easy to see why it has been reprinted so many times. After 1908, *How to Dress a Doll* was just one in a profusion of doll-related sewing books on the market for little girls.

Just one year after Mary Morgan wrote *How to Dress a Doll*, a lady in Germany, Elizabeth Kölling, published a book in 1909 on dressmaking for dolls. Somehow a copy made its way to the Library of Congress in America, and 72 years later in 1981, Helen Berry found it and made a photocopy of the entire book. Helen then found a German translator who was proficient in sewing, Baerbel M.E. Sinn. The Minnesota Jamboree Council (an UFDC-affiliated doll club, made up of members of many Minnesota doll clubs) decided to sponsor and publish the English translation of the book. Baerbel Sinn and co-editors Helen Berry and Carol Finwall, along with artist Audrey Teeple, all worked together to create an English version of the original work by Elizabeth Kölling. They added explanations and a few illustrations and whatever else was necessary for clarity and in 1991 *Dressmaking for Dolls* (19-P) was published. After recouping the publishing costs the booklet and all proceeds were turned over to the United Federation of Doll Clubs. I am sure doll dressers all over America are grateful to the Minnesota

Jamboree Council.

There was yet another little girls' book published in 1909. Mary McCormack came out with a little red book called *Spool Knitting* (20-P) (plate 569). Mary McCormack opened up a whole new way of working with the knitting spool and yarn. It is surprising this book didn't get more exposure, as she taught little girls how to make something other than a round mat with the knitting spool. *Spool Knitting* not only told you how to make your own toy knitter, but also had patterns for your doll, everything from a doll's coat and hat to a doll's hammock. Just imagine, with a wooden sewing thread spool, a few nails, and a bit of scrap yarn, dolly could have a whole wardrobe. Up until this time, there were only occasional pages of knitting in children's books and periodicals but, to my knowledge, no complete knitting books just for children, particularly with doll clothes patterns. This book has surfaced only one other time in my book searches, so I would consider it rare.

In England, the Religious Tract Society launched *The Boy's Own Paper* in 1879. The paper was so successful that they followed up with *The Girl's Own Paper* in 1880. *The Girl's Own Paper* cost 1¢ and it offered a mix of stories, educational and self-improvement articles, answers to corespondents, poetry, music, needlework, cookery, and an occasional color plate. It was a great success; even more so than *The Boy's Own Paper*. The editor was Mr. Charles Peters, who remained editor until his death in 1907.

Flora Klickmann took over as editor in 1908 and was editor until 1931. She was very innovative and introduced many new themes to the paper. She added more needlework, more articles on style and dress, doll clothing, and other craft ideas. In 1915 Flora Klickmann offered three new books just for little girls: *The Little Girl's Sewing Book* (26-P), *The Little Girl's Knitting and Crochet* (27-P), and *The Little Girl's Fancy Work* book (28-P) (plate 575). All the little books had things to make for little girls, gifts to make, and doll clothing and bedding. These books became very popular among little English girls and today, original copies are collectors' items. Of the three original books, the most difficult to find today is *Little Girl's Fancy Work*. These books have all been reprinted and can be found on the Internet.

In America, Jane E. Fryer was also thinking of little girls when she wrote her first child's sewing book, *Easy Course in Sewing for Members of Household Art's Society* (24-P) (plate 574). It was copyrighted in 1913 by Jane E. Fryer and published by D. E. Cunningham and Company in Chicago. The book was republished the same year, with a new, more colorful cover and a different title, *The Mary Frances Sewing Book, Adventures Among the Thimble People* (25-P) by The John Winston Company in Philadelphia with the same 1913 copyright by Jane E. Fryer. The *Mary Frances Sewing Book, Adventures Among the Thimble People*, did not include the section of eight separately numbered pages found in the back of the *Easy Course in Sewing for Members of Household Art's Society*. This extra section was titled "The Mary Frances Combination Patterns" and stated:

This pattern is designed for cutting Night Gown, Kimono (Bath-robe), Dressing Sack, Princess Slip, Dress, Apron, Smocked Middy Blouse, Knitting Bag and Dutch Cap for Girls from Ten to Twelve Years of Age.

There were also instructions on making these items, including a smocking lesson, and the Story of Cloth. I believe the second title was more appealing to little girls, and probably would sell more books.

In 1918, *The Mary Frances Knitting and Crocheting Book* or *Adventures Among the Knitting People* (29-P) was published. Jane Fryer wrote five more books: *The Mary Frances Cook Book or Adventures Among the Kitchen People*; *Mary Frances Garden Book* or *Adventures Among The Garden People*; *The Mary Frances Housekeeper with The Doll Family*; *The Mary Frances First Aid Book and the Brave Family*; and *The Mary Frances Story Book*. The Mary Frances sewing and knitting books are well known today and have been used for many years by girls, young and old, to costume their dolls. Some of the Mary Frances books have been reprinted and can be found on the Internet.

Most of my favorite children's sewing books have been written before 1940, these books and the era both have an innocence about them. I think when a child had only one doll, or at least only a few, she was a better mother and spent more time with her dolls sewing and looking after their clothing. One of my favorite children's sewing books *Sue Sew-and-Sew* (40-P) (plate 578) was written in 1931. This book was written by a doll named Sue. Sue starts the book with a little song and dance and goes right into telling the reader that she, being a dolly herself, knows exactly what a doll really needs and what she feels most happy in. The book is written by Sue's mother Flavia, at Sue's instruction and illustrated by Sue's aunts Dehli and Asta. At the start of each lesson, Sue starts out with a little poem about the article to be made. She then gives instructions throughout the lesson and always signs off with a different closing. The drawings of Sue are throughout the book and are delightful. What fun Sue, Sue's mother, and Sue's aunts must have had putting this little book together.

This chapter lists well over 100 children's books, dating from 1831 to 2003. Most are dedicated just to children's sewing, a few of the early books are activity books with sewing chapters. In all, 1831 to 2003, 160 years, more than half of the books have dolls used in some way to introduce and teach sewing.

It is interesting to break it down through the years to see where dolls were the most popular in the children's sewing books, and this I have done.

In the years 1831 to 1900, 100%, or all, of the 11 books listed have used dolls in some way to teach sewing.

Between the years 1900 to 1920 17 out of 21 books listed, or 81%, have used dolls in some way to teach sewing.

From 1920 to 1950 nine out of 13 books listed, or 69%, have used dolls in some way to teach sewing.

During the years 1950 to 1980 24 out of 49 books listed, or 50%, have used dolls in some way to teach sewing.

The last years 1980 to 2003 seven out of 24 books listed, or 29%, have used dolls in some way to teach sewing.

What was replacing the beloved doll that the earlier girls used for a sewing model? Simple, easy-to-do projects that take only minutes to put together, a lot of the new projects are done with felt, so turnings and hems are not needed. The books are full of decorations for rooms such as pillows, banners, place mats, and wall hangings, as well as many things kids can wear, fleece mittens, scarves, bags, hair bands, and hats. Sewing is no longer considered an art or a necessity, it is now a hobby, and when children sew today it is a craft or a pleasure pastime.

There have been many wonderful sewing and needlework books written for children through the years, but the most sought-after books were written in the years between 1860 and 1931, a time when a girl child was taught and was expected to sew and knit. Children's knitting books often included items to knit and crochet for baby sister and brother and well as dolls. Children frequently did the easy knitting in the family and often made articles for the younger children in the family. In buying and collecting children's popular sewing books, I have noticed if doll clothing isn't included in the book, the price is always more reasonable. It is the early harder-to-find books with doll clothing patterns or drafts that are the most eagerly sought after and collected.

Note: There are two chapters of books in *Children's Sewing Collectibles* Popular Sewing and Needlework Books and Children's School Sewing Books. There are girls' books that were written late in the nineteenth century or early in the twentieth century that gave instruction on any number of things a lady might need to know, including sewing. Usually there is only one chapter on sewing in the *girls' books*, but I feel it is important to include these early variety books because many were part of girls sewing education. I have only included girl's variety books written before 1940. Girls' variety books will be found in this chapter.

I have included the description of the book cover, knowing that I can spot something if I know what I am looking for. On the other hand I may have put you at a disadvantage because, as I have searched these little books out I have found that the color of the cover often was changed, and sometimes even the name. The values listed are for the original copyright, unless stated differently.

1-P
The Little Girl's Own Book
Mrs. L. Maria Child
Published by Clark, Austin and Co., N.Y.
Copyright 1831 by Carter, Hendee and Babcock
228 pages with 17+ needlework projects
Hardcover, 5½" x 5 "

The Little Girl's Own Book has a brown cover with gold lettering and decoration on the front cover and spine. The front cover shows three little girls playing with a jump rope and gold scroll decoration all around the edges.

Mrs. Child wrote in the preface:

This little book was compiled with an earnest desire to make it useful, in all respects, to it's readers; but I have relied on my own judgment and experience: therefore there is little doubt of numerous imperfections.

Perhaps I have erred in trying to please all; and may thus, like the old man in the fable, succeed in pleasing none. Some will say there is too large a proportion of games; others will smile at the directions for sewing and knitting; some may complain that the frequent recommendations of active exercises will tend to make their children rude and disorderly; others will think too much is said about gracefulness and elegance: some will call the conundrums old, others will say they are silly, and others, that they should have been entirely excluded. I knew I could not avoid numerous criticisms, and, therefore, I did not write with the fear of them before my eyes.

The chapter on Needlework begins with plain sewing by stating:

There is no accomplishment of any kind more desirable for a woman, than neatness and skill in the use of a needle. To some, it is an employment not only useful, but absolutely necessary; and it furnishes a tasteful amusement to all.

The chapter talks of plain sewing and how it is done properly, but it doesn't include diagrams. Mending is the next topic in the chapter it touches lightly on stockings and patches:

Patches should always be well shaped and basted on perfectly even; a round, angular, or slanting patch, is the sure sign of a slut.

The items in the "Needlework" chapter are bags, ribbon bags, balloon bags, beaded bags, bead work, thread bag, ribbon box, pincushions, needle-books, emery bags, purses, pen-wipers, trimmings, embroidery, marking, patchwork, and knitting. For the most part the items have instructions, some have diagrams and some are just suggestions. The book is divided into four sections, "Spring," "Summer," "Autumn," and "Winter." There are crafts, games, decorating, cornhusk dolls and a plethora of things to make and do. *The Little Girl's Own Book* is a delightful little book and gives an insight into the occupations of little girls in 1831. **Condition, good: $50.00 and up.**

2-P
American Girl's Book or Occupation for Play Hours
Eliza Leslie
Published by Monroe and Francis, Boston, C. S. Francis, New York
Copyright 1831 by Monroe and Francis
431 pages with 40 sewing or needlework projects
Hardcover, 5½" x 4½"

The cover of *American Girl's Book* has applied brown marbled paper with tan leather corners and spine. The title is written in gold on the spine.

The chapters in *American Girl's Book* are "Sports and Pastimes," "Plays with Toys," "Little Games with Cards," "Riddles," "Amusing Work," "Pincushions," "Needle Books," "Reticules," and "Varieties."

The projects listed under Pincushions include a brick pincushion, flannel pincushion, heart pincushion, gored pincushion, corded pincushion, strawberry pincushion, basket pincushion, bunch of hearts pincushion, root pincushion, star pincushion, melon seed pincushion, boot pincushion, swan pincushion, doll pincushion, and guitar pincushion.

The projects included in Needle Books are a bellows needle book, thistle needle book, needle-book workbag, convenient needle book, pincushion needle book, and a three-sided needle book. Under Reticules are a doll bag, circular reticule, basket reticule, three sided reticule, pocketbook reticule, plated reticule, melon reticule, pointed reticule, halbert-shaped reticule, dimity reticule, and braided reticule.

There are also four dolls to make — a dancing doll, jointed linen doll, a common linen doll, and a black doll. The pen-wiper projects are a card pen-wiper, string pen-wiper, circular pen-wiper, and hexagon patchwork pen-wiper. The projects have instructions, but no patterns. However there are drawings for the projects in most cases. **Condition, good: $100.00 and up.**

Note: The *American Girl's Book* is rare.

3-P
The Girl's Own Toymaker and Book of Recreation
E. Landells and Alice Landells
Published by Griffith and Farran, London, England
No copyright, but Introduction dated Nov. 1859
154 pages with 20 sewing projects
Hardcover, 6" x 5"

The Girl's Own Toymaker has a dark green cover with gold decorations and lettering.

The introduction states:

The method of teaching by toys has been proved, in our infant and national schools, to be so productive of the best results, that the system has daily become more universal.

Mr. Landells said that children, when taught to construct their toys, were better off for it. He goes on to say:

But when taught to construct toys for itself, they are more likely to be valued, and the habit of preserving them ought to be carefully encouraged and promoted.

Mr. Landells gave his daughter the credit for many of the ornamental toys and the directions and illustrations for dressing dolls and furnishing dollhouses in the book, saying they were entirely her "own production." *The Girl's Own Toymaker* has paper toys, cardboard toys, doll's furniture, doll dressmaking, ornamental toys, miscellaneous toys, puzzles, and outdoor sports.

In the section on "How To Dress A Doll," the instructions and drafts are for a chemise, stays (corset), drawers, flannel petticoat, hoop petticoat, white petticoat, petticoat body (camisole), frock, pinafore, cape, hat, and night dress.

In the "Ornamental Toys" section, the sewing projects are: watch pocket, fashionable lady pincushion, dressing table pincushion, shell pincushion, shell needle book, carved needle book, butterfly pen-wiper, and witch pen-wiper. **Condition, good: $75.00 and up.**

Note: The doll clothing drafts and instructions in *The Girl's Own Toymaker and Book of Recreation* are the same word for word, diagram for diagram as *Godey's How to Dress a Doll* (69-P). The same drafts and instructions were also used in the Especially for Children pages in *Godey's Lady's Book* magazine in 1860.

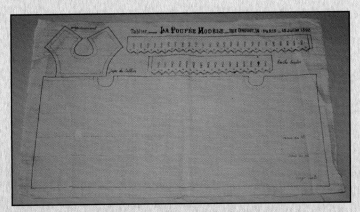

Plate 563. La Poupée Modéle (4-P) Supplement Pattern. This pattern was added to a 1898 *La Poupée Modéle* magazine as a supplement. The pattern is printed on a piece of 11" x 7¼" pink batiste. In French is printed Tablier *La Poupée Modéle*_Rue Drouot, 14 Paris_15 Juilient 1898. The pattern is for a doll apron that would be 6¼" long and measures 1½" across the bust when finished. It is trimmed with broderie anglaise that the child is to do herself following the pattern printed on the fabric before attaching.

4-P
La Poupée Modéle
Published by *Journal des Demoiselles*, Rue Drouot,
  14 Paris
Published monthly November 1863 to September 1924
Approximately 24 pages with foldout patterns for doll
  clothing and needlework
Magazine, 10" x 7"

La Poupée Modéle was a magazine published in France from 1863 until 1924. Its sole purpose was to entertain little French girls in an educational way. The periodical contained articles, stories, poems, bibliographies, legends, plays, puzzles, and, best of all, were the patterns of needlework and doll clothing. Every month there was a fold out page with doll patterns on one side and needlework patterns on the other. The patterns were superimposed using different markings. The first doll clothing patterns were for a number 4, poupée, 45cm tall (about 17¾"). In the very first issue there was instructions on making the patterns bigger or smaller to fit a doll a child might already have. The magazine hired a special lady Miss Peronne to make the patterns that were offered each month. Miss Peronne not only made the patterns, but also supplied many a little French girl with dolls and accessories from the poupée shop she opened. The magazine was to last until 1924, however the doll to dress was changed from a poupée to a bébé incassable in 1875, 25cm Benjamin. In the 1890s the magazine added pattern supplements that were printed on real cloth. **Magazine: $100.00 and up.**

Note: When obtaining the above information, I was working with a bound copy of *La Poupée Modèle* that included the years 1879 – 1880.

5-P
The Home Book of Pleasure and Instructions edited
Mrs. R. Valentine
Published by Frederick Warne & Co., London, England,
  Scribner, Welford & Co., N.Y.
No copyright, date circa 1868
567 pages with 75+ sewing or needlework projects
Hardcover, 7½" x 5½"

The cover of *The Home Book of Pleasure and Instructions* is green and black with gold lettering and decoration.

The Home Book of Pleasure and Instructions was the contribution of 17 authors who are listed on the title page. The chapters listed are "Open Air Pastimes," "Indoor Games," "Christmas Games," "Dolls and How To Dress Them," "Young Ladies' Pastimes," "Work" (Needlework), "Home Studies," "Home Amusements," and "Graver Hours of English Girlhood."

The projects in the Dolls and How to Dress Them chapter are doll's chemise, drawers, flannel petticoat, hoop petticoat, upper petticoat, stays (corset), petticoat bodice, nightgown, print frock, muslin dress, jacket, paletot (longer jacket), three pinafores, knickerbocker suit for a boy doll, jacket for boy doll, Gipsy cloak, crochet shawl, ermine muff, velvet bonnet, shoes, and boots.

There are also three pages devoted to dressing small dolls 3" to 4" tall, including crochet patterns and suggestions for lace and fabric clothing. Another portion of this chapter is on foreign dolls, their history, and how to make their costumes and dresses. There are also two dolls to make a rag doll and a dancing doll.

Under the section Plain Needlework and Useful Hints for Young Ladies, in the chapter titled Work are hints for plain sewing, trimming bonnets, sewing for the poor, and mending. There are about 50 pages in this chapter, which also includes instructions and patterns on embroidery, applique, knitting, crochet, quilting, and other needlework. The patterns given for the doll clothing and the making of dolls are drafts and instructions and occasionally only suggestions. **Condition, good: $50.00 and up.**

Popular Sewing and Needlework Books

6-P
The Young Lady's Book
edited by Mrs. Henry Mackarness
Published by George Routledge and Sons, London and
N.Y.
No copyright, but dated 1876
477 pages with 36+ projects
Hardcover, 7" x 5"

The Young Lady's Book has a dark blue cover with a gold title and embellishments.

The book is divided into six sections. Section one is "Something To Do" and has everything from cooking to amateur upholstery, the second section, is "Home Studies" and has reading, music, drawing, etc. The third section is "Indoor Occupations" and includes things like mosaic work, collections, and needlework. Section four is "Outdoor Occupations" and includes swimming, skating, gardening, and so forth. Section five is "Indoor Amusements" and lists, games, pets, etiquette, doll dressing, and the like, and section six is "Outdoor Games" which is self-explanatory.

In the Indoor Occupations section is a chapter titled Work in which we find a needle case, shoulder straps for children, bag for shoes, modern point lace (imitation of renaissance lace), knitted counterpane, knitted baby shoes, knitted gentleman's waistcoat, child's socks, gentleman's socks, knitted dish cloth, honeycomb netting, diamond netting, crochet silk purse, antimacassar (chair tidies), carriage wrapper, appliqué in cretonne, table borders, banner screen, ticking work, roman work, mantelpiece, rug braiding, beadwork, appliqué work, embroidery, patchwork, feather embroidery, and ribbon embroidery.

The doll clothing to be made includes nightgown, chemise, drawers, apron, jacket, dress for a china doll, and boy's knickerbockers, and trousers. There is also a chapter on making doll-clothing costumes including instructions for a Normandy Peasant, Italian Peasant, Spanish Dancer, and Marquise Dress.

The instructions show how to put each item together, and what type of seams to make. As the book states: *the little diagrams being only a hint for the shape.* The drafts for the clothing are small and a lot of imagination has to be executed to finish an item. Only an experienced seamstress would be able to complete the garments to satisfaction.

At the end of the Doll Dressing section in *The Young Lady's Book*, Mrs. Mackarness tells of her youth and playing with dolls and what her mother taught her:

If little girls would learn to play with and consider their dolls as if they were alive, it would really go far towards making them handy when the waxen favorites are exchanged for real "live dolls," and would be more interesting to them than using them merely as toys. The first long-clothes doll I had, my mother taught me to dress in exactly the same way as she dressed the baby. Never to set it up on any account whatever, was one thing that was early impressed on me, until it was supposed to be three months old; also to feed it at regular times;

to put it to bed at a fixed hour; and put it down for its morning sleep at regular times.

I am sure it helped to give me regular orderly habits, and such a sight as dolly flung on the ground, and left there all night, was never seen in my nursery. I should have been as much shocked, I believe, to have seen my baby brother there. The Young Lady's Book is a wonderful look into the past. **Condition, good: $100.00 and up.**

Note: The drafts for doll clothing in *The Young Lady's Book* was also published later in *The Ladies Guide to Needle Work, Embroidery, Etc.*, circa 1877, and *The American Girl's Home Book of Work and Play* (6-P) in 1883. In both books the aprons became pinafores and some text was edited out as well as a few drawings.

7-P
The American Girl's Home Book of Work and Play
Helen Campbell
Published by G. P. Putnam's Sons, N.Y., N.Y., and London, England
Copyright 1883 by G. P. Putnam's Sons
431 pages with 12 doll sewing projects
Hardcover 8" x 5½"

The American Girl's Home Book of Work and Play has been reprinted many times with different covers. Some with the complete title and others as just *The American Girl's Home Book*.

The preface states:

As yet, though boys are provided for, girls have no book that will be a trustworthy guide, either in work or play; and it is hoped that the present one will fill the "long unoccupied niche" which many authors have felt it their mission to redeem from emptiness, and become the trusted friend and advisor of all the girls who are uncertain what is best in either work or play.

The American Girl's Home Book is divided into three parts, the first part is "Indoor Plays" with paper furniture, games, parlor plays, and the like. The second part, "Outdoor Games" has listed lawn tennis, archery, boating, and camping out, etc. The third part of the book is "Occupations For Play Or Profit" and has Christmas gifts, leather work, and wax flowers among the listings. Chapter one in the third part is "Sewing and Doll's Dress-Making." The chapter begins:

Sewing as it is generally learned is always a great bugbear to a child, who is often made to sew an hour or more on a dreary "over and over patchwork square." The sewing-schools in our great cities have come to be much more cheerful places than the room at home where tired and fretful little bodies knot their thread, and grow crosser and crosser with every stitch. In the sewing-schools there are songs that describe all the things that must be done, from a hem or a fell to a patch, and a set of questions to which answers are made in concert; Mrs. Louise J. Kirkwood's little sewing primer (1-S) giving them all, with many hints that mothers or older sisters would do well to copy.

The American Girl's Home Book has drafts and diagrams of stitches used to make the doll clothing, however it is suggested we might want to purchase a pattern from the pattern manufacturers.

The items to be made are a nightgown, chemise, drawers, aprons, jacket, dress for a china doll, boy's knickerbockers, and trousers. The chapter also gives instructions for doll clothing costumes, including a Normandy Peasant, Italian Peasant, Spanish Dancer, and Marquise Dress.

In the same section are "Fifty Christmas Gifts for Small Fingers" and among the sewing projects are pen-wipers, scent cases, bureau covers, drawn work, crocheted mats, pansy pincushion, work cases, feather screen, book covers, cabin bags, work aprons, sand bags for windows, shoe cases, bean bags, pillow, sachets, baby's blanket, napkin bands, embroidered linen, glove box, and egg cozy. **Condition, good: $100.00 and up.**

Note: All the doll pattern drafts in *The American Girl's Home Book* are the same pattern drafts that are in *The Young Ladies Book* see 5-P on page 291. *The Young Ladies Book* has more text with the pattern drafts and some hints and diagrams on dressing a grown-up (fashion) doll. G. P. Putnam's Sons republished this book in 1901 with two new chapters.

8-P
The American Girl's Handy Book
Lina Beard and Adelia Beard
Published by Charles Scribner's Sons, N.Y., N.Y.
Copyright 1887 by Charles Scribner's Sons
474 pages with 15 + sewing projects
Hardcover, 8" x 5½"

The American Girl's Handy Book has a reddish brown cover with a girl in the foreground sitting on a rail fence. Overhead is a piece of fish net hanging on a canoe paddle and in the top left hand corner is a painter's palette and brushes. The title is written in gold on the cover and spine.

The preface reads:

We scarcely deem it necessary to point out the fact that in supplying healthy, sensible work and amusement for leisure hours, employment is given whose whole tendency is to refine the tastes and ambitions of our American girls.

The American Girl's Handy Book is divided into seasons. "Spring" lists wild flowers and their preservation, games, pastimes, and things to do for the spring holidays. In the "May Day" chapter, the sewing projects listed are birch bark baskets and cardboard baskets. The "Summer" section includes such things as seaside crafts, Fourth of July decorations, nature printing, cornhusk dolls, and picnics. The "Autumn" section has Halloween decorations, gourd bowls, nutting parties, drawing, etc. The "Winter" section lists Christmas gifts, scrapbooks, crafts, decorations, gymnastics, etc.

In the Winter section under Christmas gifts there are a number of sewing projects including chamois for eyeglasses, glove pen-wiper, scrap bag, doll, soft-ball, fairy dancers, and butterfly. In this same section under Old Fashioned Needlework, are plain sewing, drawn work and ribbon embroidery. A Heap of Rubbish includes a music roll and a workbasket. *The American Girl's Handy Book* would keep any girl supplied with ideas of what to do all year through. **Condition, good: $50.00 and up.**

Note: A few of the chapters are taken from articles which were written for them, and published by, "The Youth's Companion," "St Nicholas," "Harper's Young People," "Golden Days," and "Wide Awake." *The American Girl's Handy Book* has been reprinted a number of times by different publishers including David R. Godine, C.E.Tuttle, and Dearydale Press and is easy to find in a reprint.

Plate 564. The Doll's Dressmaker a Magazine for Girls by Jennie Wren, May 1891 (9-P). Dolls apron made from pattern in November 1892 issue.

9-P
The Doll's Dressmaker, A Magazine for Girls
Jennie Wren
Published monthly by Jennie Wren, N.Y., N.Y.
Copyright 1891 – 1893 by Jennie Wren
Approximately 30 pages with two projects in each magazine
Magazine, 9¾" x 7"

The Doll's Dressmaker, A Magazine for Girls, has a buff-colored cover with line drawings of Jennie Wren at her table, sewing doll clothing in the upper left hand corner and dolls spilling across the top and down the left side of the cover

The magazines contain stories about dolls, poems, paper dolls, doll furniture, toys, the Doll's Letter Box, Mother's Page, and full size-patterns for dolls clothing. Some of the clothing offered through the years were night dress, girls Reefer jacket, Quaker bonnet, drawers and under-waist, quilt pattern, chemise, boy's Fauntleroy trousers, girls guimpe, dress and sash, lady's cape, baby doll's sack, doylies for doll's table, cap, and collar, lady's skirt, Fauntleroy jacket, Zouave jacket and cap, rag doll, lady's trained costume, Puritan bonnet and combination, Easter hat, traveling Ulster, blouse waist, boy's jacket, fichu, boy's cap, shoe with buckle, baby-dolls cape, wrapper, hat, stockings, and apron.

The Doll's Dressmaker was recommended by *The New York Herald* as:

That odd and entertaining little monthly The Doll's Dressmaker grows in size and interest.

As for its value, neither books, Sunday-schools nor home training equals the doll in keeping little children out of mischief, nor is anything else so effective in developing the imaginative faculty in children as a doll. The editor is to be congratulated on having found an entirely new field that well deserved to be worked.

Another newspaper, *The St. Louis Republic* wrote:

The Doll's Dressmaker is a new magazine for girls, recently started at New York City. For a small sum of 50 cents a year gives its little readers helpful, interesting, or amusing stories and articles, with choice selections of poetry. Its great feature of course, is to instruct them in the art of sewing miniature garments for that sub-human race so beloved by the young — the dolls.

The patterns are full-size, with suggestions to make them fit smaller or larger dolls. The instructions for sewing are clear, but some previous experience in sewing is needed. It is assumed the child knows all the sewing stitches and sewing terminology. This is a delightful little magazine; one any doll dressmaker would appreciate. **Condition, each good: $25.00 and up.**

Note: I can't tell you the date of the final issue of *The Doll's Dressmaker*, but the last issue I have seen is September 1893. *The Doll's Dressmaker* was reprinted in part by Century House and edited by Ruth S. Freeman in 1969. It was an 8½" x 5½" booklet with 96 pages. Century House printed two complete issues and the basic patterns (scaled down) for the years 1891 and 1892. See plate 564 on page 293 for the apron made from a pattern in *The Doll's Dressmaker*.

Plate 565. Dolly's Dressmaker (10-P) by Raphael Tuck and Sons, Ltd., 1896. Silk frock with yoke made from a pattern in *Dolly's Dressmaker*.

10-P
Dolly's Dressmaker
Unknown author
Published by Ralphael Tuck and Sons, LTD, London, England
Copyright 1896 by Ralphael Tuck and Sons
12 pages with 7 doll sewing projects
Softcover, 10" x 8"

The *Dolly's Dressmaker* cover is a true Raphael Tuck work of art in every way; a cherub of a girl sitting on a fancy stool, with fashion pages on the wall behind her and scattered on the floor, along with her sewing supplies and doll. The girl is holding up the fruits of her labor: a lovely doll dress.

The first page declares:

This book will show you how to make new dresses for your dear Dolly, so you will now have something to do on a rainy day, and dolly will always look lovely.

Dolly's Dressmaker shows a wardrobe for a 9" doll. There are full-size patterns and instructions for each article. The articles include an apron, mantle, skirt, blouse, cape, frock with yoke, and mantle with yoke. There are three pages of color paper dolls and each paper doll has four pieces of clothing illustrating the patterns in the book, a clever way to show the finished garments.

I made the frock with yoke and found the pattern to be quite difficult, the directions give the barest of details. *Dolly's Dressmaker* is a wonderful, rare book. **Condition, good: $200.00 and up.**

Note: See plate 363 in this chapter for the frock with yoke made from a pattern in *Dolly's Dressmaker*. *Dolly's Dressmaker* was reprinted in 1971 by Barbara Whitton.

11-P
The Games Book for Boys and Girls
Unknown author
Published by E. Nister, London, England & Dutton & Co. N.Y.
No copyright date, circa 1897
192 pages with 9 sewing suggestions
Hardcover, 9" x 7"

The Games Book for Boys and Girls has a brown cover and gold lettering. On the cover is a girl playing blind-man's bluff, she is wearing a blue dress with a pink sash and shoes.

The Games Book for Boys and Girls is full of games, tricks, puzzles, occupations, collections, and pets. Among the "Occupation" are doll's dressing, crochet, knitting, and pincushions.

The needlework projects are crocheted woolen cuffs, crocheted Tam O' Shanter, and knitted stockings. Doll's dressing gives drafts or instructions for a dress, Irish peasant cloak, gathered-dress, yoked dress, and hood. The pincushion paragraph gives instructions for two pincushions: a pocket pincushion and a trinket-box pincushion. The Occupations chapter is a very small part of this book, but does give some insight into children's pastimes with the needle in the late eighteen hundreds. **Condition, good: $50.00 and up.**

12-P
The Girl's Home Companion
edited by Mrs. Valentine
Published by Frederick Warne & Co., London, & N.Y.
No copyright date, circa 1898
756 pages with 72 pages on needlework
Hardcover, 8¼" x 6"

The Girl's Home Companion is bright blue with gold lettering on the spine. The cover has black lettering and line drawings of girls playing tennis, playing the piano, cycling, and boating.

The Girl's Home Companion is a book of pastimes in work and play and has many pleasant diversions for the young lady. There are outdoor games, indoor games, pets, decorating, photography, painting, carving, gardening, domestic matters, and many more pastimes listed in this book. The section titled "Work" (needlework) lists: Crewel Embroidery, Arrasene Embroidery (a type of chenille embroidery), Silk Embroidery, Tapestry, Appliqué, Russian Embroidery, Drawn Work, Macramé Lace, Modern Point Lace, History of Lace, Methods of Making, To Clean Lace, Cretonne Work, Knitting, Crochet, Netting, and Tatting. **Condition, good: $75.00 and up.**

Plate 566. Novelties and How to Make Them (13-P) by Mildred Duff, circa 1900. The needle-book doll shown is made from instructions in this book. *Three Hundred Things a Bright Girl Can Do* (15-P) by Lilla Elizabeth Kelley, 1903.

13-P
Novelties and How to Make Them
Mildred Duff
Published by Salvationist Publishing & Supplies, Ltd.,
    London, England
No copyright or date, circa 1900
127 pages with 30 sewing projects
Hardcover, 7" x 5"

Novelties and How to Make Them has a tan or sometimes blue cover with a large paper house sitting in front of a half round window in the background. A girl in a red dress is sitting on a large table in the foreground cutting out paper. A boy is sitting in a chair at the same table painting a cutout of a house.

Novelties and How to Make Them being a collection of hints and helps in providing pleasant occupation for children. The book's name says it all. It is filled with all types of fun things for a child to do, from wood projects to paper and cardboard toys.

There are a number of needlework projects including a pig pen-wiper, union jack pen-wiper, butterfly pen-wiper, witch pen-wiper, baby shoes, ring mat, soft ball, tea cozy, cloak and dress for dolly, hassock pincushion, cardboard watch-frame, shell pen-wiper or needle book, pencil case, leaf pen-wiper, rag quilt, patchwork skirt, button mat, egg cozy, rag animals, knitted whip, letter rack, pussy pen-wiper, ribbon sewing-dolly, pincushion and thread box, pincushion shoe, wool kettle-holder, ship needle-holder and pincushion, and acorn pin-cushion. **Condition, good: $25.00 and up.**

Note: The hints and suggestions given in *Novelties and How to Make Them* appeared originally in *The Young Soldier*.

14-P
The Child Housekeeper
Elizabeth Colson & Anna Gansevoort Chittenden
Published by A. S. Barns & Company
Copyright 1903 by A. S. Barns & Company
187 pages on housekeeping, including mending
Hardcover, 8" x 5½"

The Child Housekeeper has a blue-and-white checked cover with the title in a rectangle in the center. Just under the book's title are a boiling pot, broom, feather duster, fork, spoon, and a music scroll.

This is a book on how to keep a happy home with simple lessons, and songs, stories and games. There are songs such as Housekeepers March and To Work To Work. Chapter eight covers mending and under General Directions we are told:

Directions are given for stocking darning and the sewing on of buttons, for they are usually the children's share of the weekly mending.

Stories are to be told during the sewing lessons, for example, the story of Arachne while darning, and the story of buttons and how they are made while sewing on buttons, and so forth. **Condition, good: $25.00 and up.**

Note: The girl Arachne was a wonderful weaver but she was very proud and did much boasting. Athena, the goddess of all household arts, was angry that this girl should boast so much and turned her into a spider. "Live on, Arachne," she said. "And since it is your glory to weave, you and yours must weave forever." As a spider, Arachne spends all her days weaving and weaving and you may see something of her handiwork any day among the rafters.

15-P

Three Hundred Things a Bright Girl Can Do
Lilla Elizabeth Kelley
Published by The Page Company, Boston, Mass.
Copyright 1903 by Dana Estes and Company
630 pages with 100+ needlework projects
Hardcover, 8" x 5½"

Three Hundred Things a Bright Girl Can Do has a red cover. Outlined in green is a girl in a long dress with an owl on her shoulder and a torch in her left hand. There are two angels sitting below her, one holding sports equipment and the other gardening tools. The title is written in gold on the front and the spine.

Three Hundred Things a Bright Girl Can Do boasts 33 contributors to assure that the many craft-type offerings and needlework projects offered are complete.

Chapters that contain needlework projects are Beads and Their Uses, Worsted, Thread Work, and Rug Making. Some of the projects are bags, purses, fobs, card case, belts, necklaces, afghans, sweaters, petticoats, baby clothes, bed shoes, booties, vests, slippers, and gloves. There are pages on plain sewing, embroidery, drawn work, Teneriffe, lace making, and Danish embroidery.

Three Hundred Things a Bright Girl Can Do is a wealth of information about the 1900s. **Condition, good: $50.00 and up.**

16-P

The Child's Rainy Day Book
Mary White
Published by Doubleday, Page & Company, N.Y.
Copyright 1905 by Doubleday Page & Company
215 pages with 16 sewing projects
Hardcover, 7½" x 5"

The Child's Rainy Day Book has a tan cover with the title and frame-type decorations done in red and green cross-stitch. The title is also on the spine.

Mary White wrote in her foreword:

How shall we answer the ever recurring rainy day question, "What shall I do?" Shall we not answer the question by giving the children something to do, not by entertaining them, but by helping them to entertain themselves?

The Child's Rainy Day Book has ten chapters and there are many crafts offered, such as paper toys, home made games, basket-weaving, etc. There are four chapters that cover sewing: "Simple Home Made Toys and Games," "Knots with Raffia and Cord," "What a Child Can Do with Beads," and "Gifts and How to Make Them." The sewing projects are dolls Shaker bonnet, doll bedding, doll hammock, bead-wrought Indian shirt, Indian leggings, beaded moccasins, beaded silk-bag, beaded knife-case, silk needle-book, sweet-clover bags, eyeglass cleaner, pin case, tape case, raffia mat, raffia doll-hat, beaded pin-wiper. **Condition, good: $50.00 and up.**

17-P

La Semaine De Suzette (Suzette's Week) Magazine
Published by Editions Gautier, and later, Editions Gautier/
    Languereau, Paris, France
Date 1905 to 1960
Approximately 16 pages in each magazine with 2 projects
Magazine, 13" x 9"

Plate 567. La Semaine De Suzette magazine, (17-P) October 30, 1913 issue. Bleuette simple dress No. 21, 1921 made from pattern in La Semaine De Suzette.

La Semaine De Suzette was published in a newspaper style. It was first issued in 1905 and became a very popular paper for little French girls.

The publishers of *La Semaine De Suzette* wanted a journal, specially designed for little girls (the future mothers of France), to include everything to interest the budding intelligence of little French girls between the ages of eight and thirteen.

At the beginning, a little doll 27cm tall, named Bleuette was given with each new subscription. It was originally given as an enticement to purchase the magazine, but the doll became so popular that it was later offered for purchase and became an integral part of the magazine.

La Semaine De Suzette included stories, cartoons, etiquette, poems, crafts, and sewing. The reader followed the trials and tribulations of Bleuette. *La Semaine De Suzette* was a weekly magazine and offered patterns to sew, often for Bleuette.

This little weekly paper lasted until the 1960s in France and it was always up to date with Bleuette and her changing fashions. **Condition, each good: $5.00 and up.**

Note: There are many books on the market both in English and French about Bleuette at this time, but they have been, and at present are, being sold to doll collectors and not children, so I have not included them.

18-P

How to Dress a Doll
Mary H. Morgan
Published by Henry Altemus Co., Philadelphia,
    Pennsylvania
Copyright 1908 by Howard E. Altemus
95 pages with 17 doll sewing projects
Hardcover, 6½" x 4½"

Plate 568. Original book on How to Dress a Doll (18-P) 1908 by Mary Morgan. Reprints of Original, **Costumes for Your Antique** (88-P), and **How to Dress and Old Fashioned Doll** original book is Dolly's Kimono made from *How to Dress a Doll.*

How to Dress a Doll is printed in yellow on a tan cover and shows a child and her doll each wearing a Dutch costume in yellow and blue. In the background is a lake, sailboat, and windmill.

The foreword in *How to Dress a Doll* declares:

Every girl, nowadays, wants to be a fine needlewoman, and the best way to become one is to sew your doll's clothes just as neatly as possible. Then, when you are grown up you can make yourself lovely blouses and frocks.

The first part of *How to Dress a Doll* gives general sewing hints and teaches simple-stitches, buttonholes, and scallops. The second part contains the patterns and instructions on how to adjust them to fit any doll.

The garments include an infant's outfit (coat, dress, petticoat, flannel petticoat, cap and bonnet), party dress, half-slip, undergarment, lingerie hat, street clothes (coat, everyday dress, apron), nightgown, kimono, Red Riding Hood costume, Pierrot costume, and a Japanese dress.

The patterns are simple and easy to make and both children and adults would enjoy this book when sewing for their dolls. **Condition, good: $50.00 and up.**

Note: *How to Dress a Doll* has been published twice since the original publication with different titles. Dover published it in 1973 and titled it *How to Dress an Old-Fashioned Doll* and Merrimack Publishing Company, giving no publishing date, published it under the title *Costumes for Your Antique Dolls.* Both are soft cover, have different cover graphics and are exact copies of the original text, but in a larger format. See plate 568 for all copies.

19-P
Dressmaking for Dolls
Elizabeth Kölling
Published originally in German, circa 1909 by Brandus Publishing House, Berlin, Germany
Translated and published 1991 by Minnesota Jamboree Council
Copyright 1991 by Minnesota Jamboree Council
31 pages with 9 doll sewing projects
Softcover, 11" x 8½"

Dressmaking for Dolls has a light blue cover with a center circle window showing a little girl sewing for the doll sitting next to her.

The first two pages tell of finding the original German edition of *Dressmaking for Dolls* in 1981 in the Library of Congress, and how it came to be translated into English by Baerbel M. E. Sinn, and includes notes on why and how things were changed in the translation. Because *Dressmaking for Dolls* was translated for the present-day doll dressmaker it was necessary to make the old directions and terms recognizable for modern sewers. There have been some changes made in the translation, and many explanations inserted as needed.

The garments described do not reflect the styles of 1909, but of 1906 to 1908. Many of the early doll patterns were a little behind the current styles. The original text starts with a letter to children about how important it is to learn to sew for their dolls and how it will help them learn to make clothing for themselves.

The projects include a dress, bib, apron, chemise, bonnet, drawers, underwaist, petticoat, and jacket. The garments are fairly simple and well finished, but it would be easy to add more detail and trimmings. The book shows how to make patterns for your doll and how to cut and sew the clothing. The translators did a suberb job and an adult doll dressmaker would find this book most interesting. Most children of today would need help from an adult, but with assistance could make a well-fitting garment for their doll. **Condition, good: $5.00 and up.**

Note: *Dressmaking for Dolls* was available from the United Federation of Doll Clubs.

Plate 569. Spool Knitting (20-P) by Mary McCormack 1909. Knitting things with a knitting spool for dolly and you. Doll's Little Red Riding Hood cape made from pattern in *Spool Knitting.*

20-P
Spool Knitting
Mary A. McCormack
Published by Beckley-Cardy Co., Chicago, Ill.
Copyright 1909 by A. S. Barnes and Co.
73 pages with 31 spool knitting projects
Hardcover, 7½" x 5¼"

Popular Sewing and Needlework Books

Spool Knitting has a bright red cover with black printing. The book's title is at the top and below the title is a circle with two hands working with a spool knitter.

Spool Knitting carries a lot of entertainment; it explains toy knitters, and both the round web and the flat web. All the plates are black-and-white photographs, some with bisque dolls wearing the garments.

The projects include, circular mat, ball, doll's muff, collarette, tam-o'-shanter cap, baby's rattle, toboggan cap, child's bedroom slippers, small mittens, doll's hood, doll's coat, booties, Little Boy Blue outfit, Little Red Riding Hood cape, doll's skirt, little boy's hat, child's muffler, child's hood, little girl's hat, doll's sweater, wristlets, shoulder shawl, doll's carriage robe, child's leggings, muffler, jumping rope, toy horse reins, wash cloth, school bag, chimney cleaner, and doll's hammock. The patterns are easy to follow and girls of all ages would enjoy this book. **Condition, good: $75.00 and up.**

Note: See plate 569 on page 297 for the book cover and Red Riding Hood Cape made from a pattern in *Spoon Knitting*.

21-P
When Mother Lets Us Sew
Virginia Ralston
Published by Moffat, Yard & Co., N.Y., N.Y.
Copyright 1910 by Moffat, Yard & Co.
83 pages with 9 projects
Hardcover, 8" x 5½"

When Mother Lets Us Sew has a tan, orange and blue cover with two little girls sitting in straight-back chairs, sewing. There is a small table between them and a leaded glass window behind them. The book's title is at the bottom in black lettering.

The introduction asks:

But the very best, I've kept 'til last, for wouldn't you like to learn how to cut out, sew and make all your own doll baby's clothes? To make real underclothes with real buttons and buttonholes that will button and unbutton? Just to think of being able to dress and undress your little doll baby family as often as you like! One could even make little night gowns for them to sleep in and best of all, everything they wore would be made by your own busy little hands.

The text of *When Mother Lets Us Sew* is written to the child and scattered throughout are little short poems, such as the following:

"When I'm a grown-up woman,
With my hair on my head,
I'll sit and sew 'til very late
And never go to bed!"

The first part of the book gives hints on sewing, the workbox, and simple stitches. The first projects are a beanbag, dusting cloth and bib. As the child progresses through the book and completes more projects, she learns more stitches. A little less than

half way through the book a doll named Arabella is introduced:

"Arabella needs some clothes,
Frocks and hats trimmed with bows.
Shoes so tiny, and fine silk hose,
From yellow curls to small wax toes."

The clothing for Arabella consists of a petticoat, underwaist, drawers, nightgown, everyday frock, mantle (coat), and fancy flannel sacque. Darning is the last chapter in the book. The patterns are all drafts and can be made to fit by measuring the doll. This is a wonderful book for doll dressmakers trying to duplicate homemade clothing from the 1900s. **Condition, good: $75.00 and up.**

Note: *When Mother Lets Us Sew* is a hard-to-find book.

Plate 570. *Sewing For Little Girls* (22-P) by Olive Hyde Foster, 1911 a book about sewing for dolly. Coat and hat made from a draft in *Sewing For Little Girls*.

22-P
Sewing For Little Girls
Olive Hyde Foster
Published by Duffield & Company, N.Y., N.Y.
Copyright 1911 by Duffield & Company
83 pages with 12 sewing projects
Hardcover, 7½" x 5¼"

Sewing For Little Girls has a dark blue cover with white sewing accessories stamped around the edges. The book's title, also in white, is at the center top.

A bonus in *Sewing For Little Girls* is two 1909 black-and-white photographs of three little girls sitting on a porch sewing for their bisque-head dolls, one is titled, "A busy morning," the other, "Studying out a pattern."

Sewing For Little Girls starts out with a note to mothers, saying that:

The average mother pays scant attention to her child's play with dolls, not realizing that it is possible to turn the making of the doll's outfit into the most practical of lessons.

Indeed, with the doll's clothes it is possible to make each article teach some special lesson under the guise of the most fascinating play, while having mother for a friend and helper will be another incentive to neatness. And after all, few things give a woman more satisfaction than the ability to sew.

Sewing For Little Girls enters into sewing by talking about a workbox and how it should be outfitted, by the fourth page we are making the first project a quilt for our dolly. The other projects are sheets for dolly's bed, a "polybag" for carrying thread, needles, scissors and thimble (for when you go visiting and carry your work), pin-case, needle-book, sewing apron, pencil case, dolly's drawers, dolly's petticoat, dolly's fine white dress, and dolly's coat and hat.

It is interesting that in the chapter on making dolly's drawers, the author tells us:

Making dolly's drawers so they would allow her to sit, puzzled me greatly when I was a little girl. Her jointed kid body allowed the legs to bend so much that there was never room enough in the seat, and it took me some time to figure it out for myself, but I finally did it this way: the chapter went on to give directions for the drawers pattern.

As the projects are completed the finishing touches, such as closings, feather stitching, buttonholes, and other embellishments are shown with instructions. A complete outfit can be sewn for dolly in the 1900s style. Children as well as adults would find this book useful. **Condition, good: $50.00 and up.**

Note: *Sewing For Little Girls* had three copyrights 1909 by F. M. Lupton, 1911 by The Butterick Publishing Co., and again in 1911 by Duffield and Company. See plate 570 on previous page for the book and coat and hat made from a pattern in *Sewing For Little Girls.*

Plate 571. *Goodwin's Home Course in Sewing* **(23-P)** 1912, by Emma Goodwin. Three courses in one, with 16 McCall's 5½" x 3¾" miniature patterns in the book's back pocket. See 9-S, 10-S, 11-S, and plates 572 and 573 for more information.

Plate 572. McCall's Doll Patterns from Goodwin's Home Course in Sewing. Patterns fit dolls from 18" to 21". From left top corner: #1 drawers, #2 chemise, #3 petticoat, #4 one-piece dress, #5 circular sack. #6 slipover nightgown. #7 gathered apron, #8 corset-cover, and #9 jumper dress. The envelopes measure 5½" x 3¾".

Note: These same patterns are also found in Goodwin's Course in Sewing, Book II in, Children's School Sewing Books.

Plate 573. McCall's Misses Patterns from Goodwin's Home Course in Sewing. McCall's Pattern, misses bust measurement 34" waist 24". From top left: #1 corset cover, #2 drawers, #3 petticoat, #4 dressing sacque, #5 sewing apron, #6 shirtwaist, #7 seven-gored skirt. The envelopes measure 5½" x 3 ¾."

Note: These same patterns are also found in Goodwin's Course in Sewing, Book III in Children's School Sewing Books.

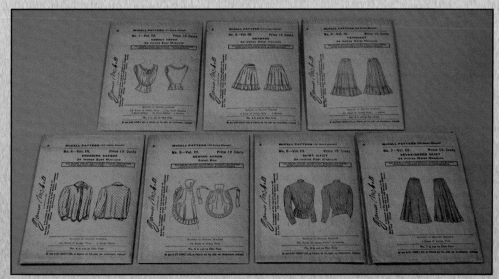

23-P
Goodwin's Home Course in Sewing
Emma E. Goodwin
Published by Frank D. Beattys & Co., N.Y., N.Y.,
Copyright 1912 by Emma E. Goodwin
54 pages with 30 sewing projects
Hardcover, 8½" x 6½"

Goodwin's Home Course in Sewing has a light brown cover, dark brown lettering and line drawings. In a square is a young girl in a wingback chair, sewing on a dress. In the background is a table with an open book and a lamp.

Goodwin's Home Course in Sewing has the same text and patterns as. *Goodwin's Course in Sewing I, II, and III* combined. **Condition, good: $200.00 and up.**

Note: See *Goodwin's Course in Sewing* (9-S, 10-S, and 11-S) *Books One, Two, and Three* in *Children's School Sewing Books* for content. These same patterns are also found in *Goodwin's Course in Sewing, Book III* in Children's School Sewing Books.

Plate 574. *Easy Course in Sewing for Members of Household Art's Society* **(24-P)** by Jane E. Fryer, 1913, 280 pages with the sewing story and eight extra pages in back for the Mary Frances Combination Pattern and The Story of Cloth. *The Mary Frances Sewing Book or Adventures Among the Thimble People* **(25-P)** by Jane E. Fryer, 1913, 280 pages with the sewing story. Both carry same story and the same 33 patterns. Romper shown is made from a pattern in the books.

24-P
Easy Course in Sewing for Members of Household
    Art's Society
Jane Eayre Fryer
Published by D. E. Cunningham & Co., Chicago, Ill.
Copyright 1913 by Jane Eayre Fryer
280 pages + 8 separately numbered pages and 33
    full-size patterns for a 16" doll
Hardcover, 9¼" x 6¾".

Easy Course in Sewing for Members of Household Art's Society has a light blue cover with a darker blue and orange band of sewing supplies printed at the top and bottom. The title is printed in the center.

This is a story about a little girl named Mary Frances who spends a summer vacation at her grandmother's and meets new friends, the Thimble People. The Thimble People show her how to sew, first for her 16" doll, Angie, and then later for a new doll, Mary Marie, also 16", that mother sends by mail.

It's a wonderful story with a singing in rhyme Sewing Bird that turns into a Fairy Lady when the words "Magic and Mystery, Give my wish to me" are spoken. There is a lot of nonsensical bantering between the Thimble People as they attempt to teach Mary Francis how to sew. The story is entertaining and instructional.

The doll clothing patterns include doll's laundry bag, apron, handkerchief, nightgown, bathrobe, kimono, dressing sack, pinafore, morning dress, flannel petticoat, underwaist, lawn petticoat, drawers, rompers, bloomers, leggings, fur-lined cape, afternoon dress, guimpe, party dress, automobile coat, automobile bonnet, bathing suit, fur muff and tippet, sun bonnet, work bag, rain coat, polo cap, and wedding dress. There are also patterns for a lady's work bag, lady's belt, baby's bib, and girl's collar.

The last eight pages are separately numbered and are called The Mary Frances Combination Pattern and states:

This pattern is designed for cutting Night Gown, Kimono (Bath-Robe) Dressing Sack, Princess Slip, Dress, Apron, Smocked Middy Blouse, Knitting Bag, and Dutch Cap for Girls from Ten to Twelve Years of Age.

Also included is *The Story of Cloth,* including wool, cotton, silk, flax and lace. **Condition, good: $75.00 and up.**

Note: *Easy Course in Sewing for Members of Household Art's Society* has the same content and patterns, word for word, as *The Mary Frances Sewing Book* or *Adventures Among the Thimble People.* However, *Easy Course in Sewing for Members of Household Art's Society* also has the eight extra separately numbered pages in the back. I believe this is the first printing of the book by the D. E. Cunningham and Co. and that the John C. Winston Co. published it a second time in the same year with a different title omitting the last eight pages.

25-P
The Mary Frances Sewing Book or Adventures
    Among the Thimble People
Jane Eayre Fryer
Published by The John C. Winston Co., Philadelphia,
    Pennsylvania.
Copyright 1913 by Jane Eayre Fryer
280 pages and 33 full size patterns for a 16" doll
Hardcover, 9¼" x 6¾"

The Mary Frances Sewing Book Adventures Among the

Thimble People has a blue cover with an applied color print of a child sewing with a doll. There are animated sewing supplies and a Fairy in the background. The cover art is signed J. A. Boyer.

See 24-P *Easy Course in Sewing for Members of Household Art's Society* in this chapter for a complete description of this book, excluding the last eight separately numbered pages. **Condition, good: $100.00 and up.**

Note: *The Mary Frances Sewing Book Adventures Among the Thimble People* has only 280 pages. The Mary Frances books were a series which included, *The Mary Frances Cook Book* or *Adventures Among the Kitchen People*, *The Mary Frances Garden Book* or *Adventures Among the Garden People*, *The Mary Frances Housekeeper with the Doll Family*, *The Mary Frances First Aid Book and the Brave Family*, *Mary Frances Story Book* and *The Mary Frances Knitting and Crochet Book* or *Adventures Among the Thimble People* (28-P). See plate 574 for the romper made from a pattern in *The Mary Frances Sewing Book Adventures Among the Thimble People*.

Plate 575. Set of three books published in 1915 by Flora Klickmann, editor of *The Girls Own Paper and Woman's Magazine. The Little Girl's Sewing Book (26-P), The Little Girl's Knitting and Crocheting Book (27-P), The Little Girl's Fancy Work (28-P).* All have clothing for dolls.

26-P
The Little Girl's Sewing Book
edited by Flora Klickmann
Published by *The Girl's Own paper* and *Woman's Magazine*, London, England
No copyright, published in 1915
114 pages with 33 sewing and needlework projects
Hardcover, 8" x 6"

The Little Girl's Sewing Book has a white background and

an applied color print of a little girl wearing a pink dress and hair bow. She is sewing for her dolls, which are scattered about her on a round window seat. The title is at the top of the cover and the print is signed MDC.

"A Word to the Grown-ups" states:
This book contains lessons in practically all the stitches used in plain needlework, as well as the more useful of the fancy stitches.

It does indeed contain a plethora of information. Included are cross-stitch, macramé, beadwork, Berlin wool-work, needlepoint, hardanger, hairpin work, hemstitching, patchwork, wool work, and rug making. The projects are shown in black-and-white photographs and drawings of darling little children are scattered thoughout the pages.

The projects are work apron, ribbon box, lambkin bag, swallow pocket, girl's pinafore, girl's sunbonnet, housewife, feeder, chair back, handkerchief sachet, hairpin lace bag, stocking bag, peacock cloth, bead work, wool-work kettle holder, butterfly pincushion, and farmyard curtain.

There is also a chapter on sewing for dolly that includes for dolly's bed: a mattress, mattress cover, sheets, blankets, pillow, pillowcase, bedspread, nightdress case, patchwork quilt, perambulator cover, and another bedspread. To complete dolly's bedroom there are curtains, carpets, and hearthrugs to make.

Dolly's wardrobe consists of a nightdress, knickers, chemise, white petticoat, flannel petticoat, frock, and coat. The instructions for putting dolly's wardrobe patterns together are printed in detail in the book, however the patterns are not included in the book. A set of paper patterns could be obtained from The Little Girl's Editor in London.

The Little Girl's Sewing Book is a lovely book with a lot of interesting items for the young miss to sew. The set of bedding for a doll is especially interesting to a doll collector. **Condition, good: $50.00 and up.**

Note: *The Little Girl's Sewing Book* is one in a series of books edited by Flora Klickmann and *The Girls Own Paper* and *Woman's Magazine*. The other two books are *The Little Girl's Knitting and Crochet Book* (26-P) and *The Little Girl's Fancy Work* (27-P). The three books were reprinted in a larger size in 2002, by Lacis Publications in Berkeley California.

27-P
The Little Girl's Knitting and Crochet Book
edited by Flora Klickmann
Published by *The Girl's Own Paper* and *Woman's Magazine*, London, England
No copyright date published circa 1915
114 pages with 29+ projects
Hardcover, 8" x 6"

The Little Girl's Knitting and Crochet Book has a white background and an applied color print of four little girls surrounded by a family of dolls, two of the girls are knitting and two are looking on while holding dolls. The print is signed

MDC and the book's title is at the top.

The Introduction to *The Little Girl's Knitting and Crochet Book* is short:

Now that every grown-up is making woolly things, the little girl will want to be doing likewise. The following pages show her how to make pretty and useful things in Knitting and Crochet, and she is taught how to do the simple stitches and easy patterns in small pieces of work that will not tire her.

The projects are shown in black-and-white photographs and there are lovely drawings of children throughout the book.

The projects are a pretty mat, kettle holder, baby's socks, baby's jacket, hood for baby, baby brother's cap, little slippers, slouch hat, girl's vest, doily, tray cloth, petticoat, blanket, pansy edging, and collar edging.

There are also things for dolly's room: bedspread, sheet, toilet cover (chest of drawers cloth), tablecloth, and window curtain. Also for dolly are a knitted pram cover, crochet coat and cap for walking, crocheted pram coat and hat, knitted jersey, crocheted muff and stole, knitted short coat and bonnet, crocheted outfit including knickers, vest, combinations, every-day petticoat, princess petticoat, dress, jacket and bonnet, and crocheted booties.

There doesn't seem to be any sizes on the doll clothing, so I am sure mother had to help measure dolly so everything would fit. This book would be an asset to an antique doll dress-maker that knows how to knit and crochet. **Condition, good: $50.00 and up.**

Note: *The Little Girl's Knitting and Crochet Book* is one in a series of books put out by Flora Klickmann and *The Girls Own Paper* and *Woman's Magazine*.

28-P
The Little Girl's Fancy Work
Edited by Flora Klickmann
Published by *Girl's Own Paper* and *Woman's Magazine*,
    London, England
No copyright date, published circa 1915
84 pages with 18 needlework projects
Hardcover, 8" x 6"

The cover of *The Little Girl's Fancy Work* has a white background and an applied color print of four girls sitting in a garden working on fancy work. One girl sits in a large brown wicker chair, another on a campstool, the other two are sitting on a footstool and the ground. Placed on the grass are a sewing basket, ball, doll, stuffed fox, and a golliwog. The print is signed MDC and the book's title is at the top.

A Word to the Grown-ups states:

All little girls love ornamentation. They like to add decoration on the household furnishings, and long for trimming on their clothing. It is a natural, healthy instinct that makes them desire to beautify their surroundings-and it is a characteristic which, if properly developed, will be invaluable to them when the time comes for Home-making in real earnest. But their taste needs training in this, as in every other form of art.

The object of this book is not merely to teach girls how to do needlework that shall be good craft as well as "fancy"; it also aims to show them how to turn their handwork to useful account, and apply it to the practical things of everyday life.

The plates are black-and-white photograph and there are wonderful drawings of children throughout the book's pages. *The Little Girl's Fancy Work* teaches needle arts such as cross-stitch, tacking, penelope canvas work, hemstitching, knitting, crochet, hardanger, needlepoint, and embroidery.

The projects include a tea cozy, duckling chair-back, little-bird cloth, bunnies on a cloth, baby's breakfast-cloth, wild-rose cloth, baby socks, mothers apron, collar, cushion cover, needle book, socks for two-year old, and a sampler.

The projects for dolls are knitted bonnet, knitted slip-on jumper, crocheted bonnet, crocheted tam-o'-shanter and chintz-covered cradle. Of interest to the doll collector/dresser are the knitted and crocheted items. **Condition, good: $75.00 and up.**

Note: *The Little Girl's Fancy Work* is one in a series of books put out by Flora Klickmann and *The Girls Own Paper* and *Woman's Magazine*. The other two books are *The Little Girl's Sewing Book* (26-P) and *The Little Girl's Knitting and Crochet Book* (27-P). The 1915 original *The Little Girl's Fancy Work* (28-P) book is harder to find than the other two books in this series. These three books have been reprinted in a larger size in 2002, by Lacis Publications in Berkeley California.

29-P
The Mary Frances Knitting and Crocheting Book or Adventures Among the Knitting People
Jane Eayre Fryer
Published by The John C. Winston Co., Philadelphia, Pa.
Copyright 1918 by Jane Eayre Fryer
270 pages with 50+ doll knitting and crochet projects
Hardcover, 9½" x 7"

The Mary Frances Knitting and Crocheting Book or Adventures Among the Knitting People has a blue cover with an applied color print of a child sitting in a window seat knitting. There is a yarn doll looking over her shoulder and a doll with a knitted hat and coat sitting beside her. The cover art is signed J. A. Boyer.

Mary Frances is left alone with her housekeeper while her mother and aunt take an emergency trip to take care of Mary Frances's father who was hurt in a railroad accident. The crochet and knitting people come to life and teach Mary Frances how to crochet and knit for her 16" doll Mary Marie and make outfits for a new infant doll mother brings back with her.

Crow Shay sings in rhyme through out the book and tells Mary Frances how to summon Fairly Flew the fairy with the magic needles, "Fairy Fairly Flew, Please come, for I need you." The doll Mary Marie comes to life in this story when she is kissed by Fairly Flew, the fairy. The fairy gave Mary Marie, the doll permission to talk until the lessons were over, as long as there were no other people around. This is another delightful story by Jane Eayer Fryer, and includes a large number of knitting and crochet items for dolls.

The projects for the doll Mary Marie include a crocheted necklace, rose scarf, shawl, petticoat, cap, turban, toque, hat, baby's ball, bedroom slippers, book bag, sweater, tam, leggings, sports hat, mittens, knitted shawl, hood, bean bag, sleeveless sweater, breakfast cap, breakfast shawl, sleeveless silk sweater, shopping bag, flower basket, aviator doll's outfit (helmet, wristlets, sleeveless sweater), sports sweater, muff, boa, and hat.

There are also instructions for a baby doll's clothing including bedroom slippers, saque, socks, cape and hood, cap, coach cover, and ball. For a baby sister or brother there are crocheted booties and a crocheted ball. For mother a crocheted necklace and a lady's sweater.

The last chapter has Red Cross knitting for the war including a muffler, wash cloth, sleeveless sweater, knitted helmet #1, knitted helmet #2, wristlets #1, Wristlets #2, medium-sized socks, bed socks, and hot-water bottle cover. **Condition, good: 100.00 and up.**

Note: The Mary Frances books were a series which included, *The Mary Frances Cook Book or Adventures Among the Kitchen People*, *The Mary Frances Garden Book or Adventures Among the Garden People*, *The Mary Frances Housekeeper with the Doll Family*, *The Mary Frances First Aid Book and the Brave Family*, *Mary Frances Story Book* and *The Mary Frances Sewing Book* or *Adventures Among the Thimble People* (25-P).

30-P
A Little Sewing Book For a Little Girl
Louise Frances Cornell
Published by The Colonial Press, Boston, Mass.
Copyright by 1918 by The Page Company
202 pages with 11 sewing projects
Hardcover, 7¼" x 5"

A Little Sewing Book For a Little Girl has a white cover with the book's title at the bottom and a black outline of a girl sitting on cushion sewing, she has a red dress and a red band in her hair.

At the beginning of *A Little Sewing Book For a Little Girl* is a lovely color picture of a little girl sitting on a stool while sewing for her bisque-head doll sitting at her feet.

The introduction declares:
The neglected art of the needle is coming again into it's own and the time to inculcate its principles is in childhood, when the mind is plastic and the fingers flexible. Any little girl may develop into a finished needlewoman if she undertakes the study of sewing with a competent teacher who can combine practical instruction with the play spirit, and make the lesson as interesting as a game. To inspire little girls with the desire to learn sewing, and to help their elders teach them, this story of Annalu was written.

A Little Sewing Book For a Little Girl is the story of Annalu and how she learns to sew. The story starts with Annalu learning to sew by making a stitch sample book.

She goes from there to completing her first project, a needle book. The other projects she makes are an apron, doll's petticoat, clothespin bag, card table cover, doll's panties, doll's chemise, doll's kimono-dress, sewing apron, straight camisole, and a collar and cuff set.

During the projects and sewing lessons Annalu goes to fairs, learns about fabric, patching and darning, how to make bias strips, visits with friends, and adds to her sample book. Eventually, she wants to become a dressmaker and open her own shop.

A cute little book, and fun to read, both children and adults would enjoy working with Annalu, especially when she is sewing for her doll. **Condition, good: $50.00 and up.**

31-P
Your Dolly's Clothes, How to Cut and Make Them
Unknown author
Published by Doll-Craft Publishers, N.Y., N.Y.
Copyright 1923 by Doll-Craft Publishers
15 pages with two doll sewing projects and many
   variations
Softcover, 11" x 8½"

The cover of *Your Dolly's Clothes, How to Cut and Make Them* has a child in a checked bloomer dress and a large hair bow holding a rather large pair of scissors. A doll and a sewing basket sit on a stool, the basket is filled with fabric and another doll.

The dedication reads:
To the mothers of our little girls who realize that the "youngsters of today" are the "women of tomorrow," and who therefore guide them from their childhood on, into channels of usefulness, this little book is lovingly dedicated by The Publisher.

The seven picture pages are in color with two patterns, a romper and a dress with bloomers. There are many variations that can be made from the two full-size patterns. There are six styles that can be used for the romper and five different styles of dresses that can be made from the dress with bloomers. There are pages of instructions for cross-stitch embroidery, shaped patches, dress ideas, and a "stitches primer."

Your Dolly's Clothes, How to Cut and Make Them is darling little book from the 1920s. Parental instruction would be needed as the instructions lack detail. An adult with sewing experience would enjoy this book for dressing dolls or maybe just dreaming. **Condition, good: $100.00 and up.**

Note: *Your Dolly's Clothes, How to Cut and Make Them* is rare.

32-P
Dolly and Her Dresses
Unknown author
Published by Knight Publishing Co., N.Y., N.Y.
Copyright 1924 by Knight Publishing Co.
14 pages with six doll sewing projects
Softcover, 11½" x 8½"

Popular Sewing and Needlework Books

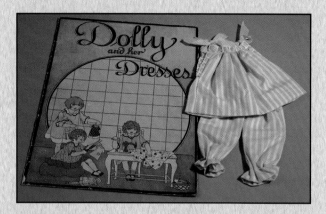

Plate 576. Dolly and Her Dresses (32-P) 1924, by Knight Publishing Co. Pajamas are from instructions in *Dolly and her Dresses.*

Dolly and Her Dresses has a gold background and a large round window with three little girls sewing dolly's clothes. One little girl is using toy sewing machine, one is cutting, and the other is hand finishing the clothing.

Dolly and Her Dresses is about making and dressing Babbette and gives instructions and a full-size pattern for making a doll. She is approximately 12", very simple with wool hair, straight-stitch embroidered eyebrows, nose and mouth, and two lazy daisy eyes.

Her wardrobe includes two pretty hats, pajamas, romper, and a dress with bloomers. There are also full-page color pictures of suggestions for the dress and romper and one page each of ribbon trimmings and patches for pockets or trimming. The instructions are easy to follow and the clothing is sweet. This little collectable book is a look back to dolls in the 1920s. **Condition, good: $100.00 and up.**

Note: *Dolly and Her Dresses* is rare. Hobby House Press reprinted *Dolly and Her Dresses* in black and white in 1980. See plate 576 for pajamas made from instructions in *Dolly and Her Dresses.*

33-P
The One-Eyed Fairies
Georgia Eldredge Hanley
Published by Lothrop, Lee & Shepard Co., Boston, Mass.
Copyright 1924 by Lothrop, Lee & Shepard Co.
214 pages with 4 sewing projects
Hardcover, 7½" x 5½"

The One-Eyed Fairies has an off-white cover with a large red tomato pincushion in the center and needle fairies stuck into and dancing around it. The title is in green at the top of the front cover.

The One-Eyed Fairies is a bit different from most of the children's sewing books, as it does not give patterns or drafts for projects and it is written in story and rhyme.

Margaret Allen has been given a workbasket for her birthday from her auntie. Margaret wishes there were fairies to help her learn to sew and suddenly she sees a line of little shining figures dancing and prancing out of her new workbasket; the Needle Fairies.

We follow Margaret as the One-Eyed Fairies teach her to sew on a doll dress (that mother has cut out) and give her directions to make a doll blanket, marble bag, and apron. Margaret also learns to mend and add to her own clothing by sewing on trims, buttons, patches, lace, tucks, rickrack, etc.

The foreword states:

I hope that mothers, teachers, and those interested in girls will find this book helpful, as my experience has been that children eagerly grasp and absorb facts presented in story and rhyme.

A number of these sewing-lesson stories have appeared in the "Modern Priscilla Magazine." Acknowledgment is here gratefully made for permission to use them. **Condition, good: $50.00 and up.**

Note: *The One-Eyed Fairies* is filled with delightful plates of the needle fairies, Margaret, her doll, and sewing projects. There is one full-color page of Margaret, her sewing basket and doll at the beginning of the story. *The One-Eyed Fairies* (plate 577) is a wonderful introduction to sewing.

Plate 577. *The One-Eyed Fairies* **(33-P)** by Georgia Eldredge Hanley, 1924. A Sewing Book in story form. *Betsy Ross First Stitches* **(35-P)** published by Charles E. Graham and Co., 1925. This is a cute little book of stitches and a sampler.

34-P
The Little Folks Knitting and Crocheting Instuction Book
Unknown author
Published by Fleming, Reid & Co., Ltd.
Copyright Fleming, Reid & Co., Ltd., date unknown
39 pages with 14 knitting and crochet projects
Softcover, 9½" x 6"

The cover is missing from my copy of *The Little Folks Knitting and Crocheting Instruction Book* however, the title of the plate on the cover is Mother Knows Best, as it is written in the index.

Contained in *The Little Folks Knitting and Crocheting Instruction Book* are simple instructions for knitting and crocheting. For knitting, the stitches are plain knitting or garter stitch, casting on, casting off, and purl stitch. The knitting projects are baby's hood, infantees (mittens), baby brother's first suit (Jersey and Knickers), baby's knitted pullover, reins, garters for daddy, scarf for a little boy, scarf for a little girl, knitted frock for a baby girl, and a baby's vest.

The stitches taught for crocheting are the chain stitch, single crochet, double crochet, and treble crochet. The projects are a frock for baby sister, and infant's slippers with pom-pons. All children's clothing is sized for eighteen months to two years. The clothing is now out of date, but scaled down it could be used for a doll. The items are all very professional looking in the photographs, but the directions seem very simple. A child who can already knit could use this book. It is strictly a teaching book, no cute drawings, or colored pictures, definitely an adult approach to knitting and crocheting. **Condition, good: $5.00 and up.**

35-P
Betsy Ross' First Stitches
Unknown author
Published by Charles E. Graham & Co., Newark, N. J. &
   N.Y., N.Y.
Copyright 1925 by Charles E. Graham & Co.
16 pages, with 1 sewing project
Softcover, 9½" x 7"

This delightful little book has two softly colored lithographs on the front and back covers. The front shows a little girl with brown curly hair wearing a mobcap sitting in a straight-back chair bending over her sewing and the back has the same girl with a bonnet holding a large bouquet of roses.

The inside of the book is in black and white. There is an index of needles and threads, how to start threading a needle and making a knot. *Betsy Ross' First Stitches* (plate 375) is just what its title says: first stitches - running stitch, back stitching, overhanding, basting stitch, stitching stitch, cross stitch, catch stitch, overhanding two-edges, overcasting, hemming stitch, blanket stitch, feather stitching, and a grand sampler to make. The plates are very simple and easy to understand. The real value in this book is its age and cover lithographs. **Condition, good: $75.00 and up.**

36-P
The Piece Bag Book
Anna La Tourette Blauvelt
Published by The Macmillan Co., N.Y., N.Y.
Copyright 1927 by The Macmillan Co.
96 pages with 8 needlework projects
Hardcover, 7" x 5½"

The Piece Bag Book has a cover of bright yellow and a black square in the center with an impression of a girl done in 1920s style. The book title is also in black at the top.

Anna Blauvelt has used a story line throughout her book about Teddy and Eleanor, two little sisters eight and six years old. It is raining and they decide to make a playhouse. Mother overhears their plans and shows up with a piece bag of scraps of fabric and worsted yarn.

First there are things to make for the playhouse, a tablecloth, chair cushion, dolls bedspread, and a cheesecloth duster. Maggie May, the girl's favorite doll, is fetched and shown her new bedspread in the playhouse. Then the girls think of other things they could make for Maggie May. The girls learn to weave worsted on cardboard looms and make her a tam-o'-shanter, worsted scarf, and muff. The weaving projects are done on cardboard looms that are destroyed in order to remove the weaving when done. This is a darling book with four-color plates of Teddy and Eleanor in delightful clothing of the period. **Condition, good: $50.00 and up.**

Note: *The Piece Bag Book* is one of four in Macmillan's The Work and Play Series, the other three books are *Your Workshop, With Scissors and Paste,* and *Playing with Clay.*

37-P
Embroidery-Plain Sewing, Knitting and Leathercraft
Unknown author
Copyright circa 1929 by W. Foulsham & Co., Limited
63 pages with 6 sections on needlework
Hardcover, 10" x 7"

The cover of *Embroidery-Plain Sewing, Knitting and Leathercraft* is dark gray with a blue spine. There are color graphics applied to the front showing some of the articles to be made using the book. Printed at the bottom is "How to make many pretty and useful articles." The title is printed on the top cover and the spine.

Embroidery-Plain Sewing, Knitting and Leathercraft has more needlework than its title implies. The chapters include "Embroidery," "Plain Sewing," "Knitting," "Crochet," "Raffia Work," "Leather-Craft," and "Miscellaneous Needlework"

Projects under "Embroidery" are pictures in wool, table runner and afternoon tea cloth in cross-stitch. Under "Plain Sewing" are a frilled lampshade and a doll's coat. The "Knitting" chapter has a doll's knitted frock, doll's bonnet, knitted doll's coat, and baby socks. In the "Crochet" chapter, are a doll hat, flowers, initials, crochet rug, and a crochet pram-cover. The ""Miscellaneous Needlework" chapter includes a tea cozy, ball, golliwog of wool, woolen flowers, envelope bag, dress ornament, book cover, slippers, and indoor coat. "Raffia Work" includes embroidered canvas bag, needle case, shopping bag, tablemats, waste paper basket, box, and flowers. Along with all the projects are instructions on each craft, such as embroidery stitches and how to knit or crochet. **Condition, good: $50.00 and up.**

38-P
When Sally Sews
Helen Perry Curtis
Published by The Macmillan Co., N.Y., N.Y.
Copyright 1929 by The Macmillan Co., N.Y., N.Y.
130 pages with 50 things to make
Hardcover, 8½" x 6½"

Popular Sewing and Needlework Books

When Sally Sews is lime green with the title printed in black on the front and spine. The dust jacket, in white and lime green, shows a teen-age girl sewing on a patchwork quilt while sitting in an easy chair. She has her sewing implements on a table at her side and a cat at her feet.

When Sally Sews was published because of the popularity of the author's craft and sewing pages for girls in various magazines, including *The American Girl*, *Modern Priscilla*, *Youth's Companion*, *The Ladies Home Journal*, and *The Woman's Home Companion*.

The story line is about a girl named Sally about 14 years old. The sewing, embroidery, and crafts are divided into sections. We follow Sally as she goes out for winter sports and needs to make a sports-dress, cape, and skating set. Sally makes her own underwear, goes to the sea shore, attends a party, makes over her own room, and creates Christmas presents for everyone in her family including the baby.

There are some crafts and embroidery, but most of the book is about Sally's wardrobe and she makes everything from underwear to a party dress. When Sally does over her room, it includes curtains, bedspread, patchwork quilt, dressing table from orange crates, and even lampshades.

When Sally Sews assumes that the child already knows how to sew and gives no diagrams of stitches, however it does tell you how to make a French seam when making the evening coat.

The instructions for each project include what type of fabric, how many yards, what notions are needed for a 14 year old girl. The drawn patterns are done by measurements:

Three yards of fabric, fold in half, measure off ten inches from the fold, below that measure six inches and mark off, with pins or basting threads, a straight line which will reach from a point under the arm down to the hem.

There is a diagram of each project with the measurements shown and the fabric waste shaded, so it isn't as difficult as it sounds.

When Sally Sews is a fun book and I can see a teen using some of the items in 1929, however today it is simply a collectable book on teen sewing at an earlier time. An adult with some sewing experience could use this book to make a wardrobe for a flapper doll by using the diagrams and adjusting them to size. The clothing is quite sophisticated and a good study of fashions in the 1920s. **Condition, good: $25.00 and up.**

39-P
The Sew-It Book
Rachel Taft Dixon
Published by Rand McNally and Co., N.Y., Chicago, San Francisco
Copyright 1929 by Rand McNally and Co.
57 pages with 20 + needlework projects
Hardcover, 10" x 8"

The Sew-It Book has a black cover with red and white sewing accessories and decorative stitching scattered across it. In the center there are two button people threading a needle from a spool of thread; the book's title is above surrounded by a cloth tape measure.

The Sew-It Book teaches sewing, embroidery, cross-stitch, raffia embroidery, tie-dye, hemstitching, and how to make crepe-paper costumes. There is a letter to the children about the book and sewing and two pages with plates of stitches to remind you how they are made.

The projects are marble or button bag, cross-stitch towel, cross-stitch bib, raffia purse, sampler, dolls luncheon set, mother's luncheon set, tie-dye handkerchief, cushion, rag doll, doll dress, doll bonnet, child's apron, tie-dyed coolie coat, smock, crepe-paper costumes, white window curtains, and chintz side curtains, and valance. The book is well written and well illustrated.

A child, as well as an adult, would enjoy using *The Sew-It Book*. The doll dress is darling and simple, very 1920s. The doll is measured and a pattern is made using the draft in the book. Different ways are shown to trim the dress, which results in three different looking dresses. The doll bonnet is also shown trimmed four different ways. A very clever little book. **Condition, good: $25.00 and up.**

Plate 578. *Sue Sew-and-Sew* (40-P) by Asta, Dehli and Flavia Gág, 1931. A doll named Sue shows you what all dolls want to wear and teaches you how to make it. *The Home Toy Shop* (41-P) by Nina R. Jordan, 1937. Twenty-one chapters on toys to make including many, sewing projects, including some dolls.

40-P
Sue Sew-and-Sew
Asta, Dehli & Flavia Gág
Published by Coward-McCann, Inc., N.Y., N.Y.
Copyright 1931 by Coward-McCann, Inc.
64 pages with 12 articles of clothing for a doll
Hardcover, 8" x 6"

Sue Sew-and-Sew has a sweet front cover with a background of red shamrocks and dots and a center picture, framed in scallops, of a little girl sewing by hand for her doll.

I love this little book with a doll named Sue who gives instructions on what clothes dolls like to wear, and showing how you can make them for your doll. It is written in such a fun way that sewing becomes a game.

I'm Sue Sew-and-Sew, come with me-
We'll pass the hours merrily.
We'll dress your doll from top to toe,
She'll be delighted, that I know.
We'll scheme and snip and stitch away,
Here is a Different way to play!

There is a quick lesson on knots, seams and hems then we get started on dressing dolly. The garments are a chemise, step-ins (panties), flowery dress, dainty dress, gingham apron, nightgown, kimono, gingham frock, hanky and purse, cape, beret, and party dress. Dolly can be any size, as the pattern drafting is done by very simple measurements and folding. There are lots of plates and drawings of the garments and dolly Sue wearing them. A delightful book any child or adult would be interested in reading, as well as using it for making doll clothing. **Condition, good: $100.00 and up.**

Note: *Sue Sew-and-Sew* is a rare book.

41-P
The Home Toy Shop
Nina R. Jordan
Published by Harcourt, Brace & Company Inc., N.Y., N.Y.
Copyright 1937 by Harcourt, Brace & Company Inc.
233 pages with 15 sewing projects
Hardcover, 9" x 6½"

The Home Toy Shop has a bright red cover decorated with black line drawings of the toys to make that are shown in the book. The title of the book is on the spine only.

The Home Toy Shop has 21 chapters, all with different toys to make — boats, cardboard figures, Noah's ark, trains, musical toys, and so on. The book was written for boys and girls from approximately 6 to 10 years of age. The first chapter gives encouragement in doing the projects, tells you the few tools that are needed and materials that are mostly odds and ends, and talks about working space and a place to keep your supplies. The sewing projects include tire tube toys, cat, bear, elephant, doll, bunny, and piglet. There are stocking dolls: a girl, farmer, Indian mother, and baby, Indian brave, and Lo Lo. Also included are spool dolls, stuffed paper dolls, clothespin dolls, and puppets. *The Home Toy Shop* (plate 578) is a delightful book with many toys to keep any child happy for hours. **Condition, good: $25.00 and up.**

42-P
The Good Housekeeping See and Sew, a Picture Book of Sewing
Mariska Karasz
Published by Frederick A. Stokes Co., N.Y., & Pa.
Copyright 1943 by Frederick A. Stokes Co.
83 pages with 6 sewing projects
Hardcover, 7½" x 10"

Plate 579. *The Good Housekeeping See and Sew, a Picture Book of Sewing* (42-P) by Mariska Karasz, 1943. A simple way to learn to sew fun and interesting thing. *My Needlework Book* (43-P) by Gladys and Bee Mc Mullen, 1947. A book about making lovely things for yourself and doll.

The cover on *The Good Housekeeping See and Sew, A Picture Book of Sewing* looks like a crazy quilt square. It is striped orange and white with a different blue embroidery stitch on each stripe and all the stitches are identified in blue lettering.

The author encourages the use of a thimble, calling it the "Magic of the Thimble." The book is printed in black and white with a smattering of orange here and there. *The Good Housekeeping See and Sew, a Picture Book of Sewing* starts with the warp and woof of fabric, the ABCs of dressmaking, types of fabrics, how to use a tape measure, and the difference between scissors and shears.

The projects are a tray cloth or doll bedspread, heart pincushion, fabric horse, first aid kit, skating cap, and skirt made with suspenders (for a 10 year-old.)

There are a lot of hints and lessons between the projects, and different ideas are suggested for each project. Some of the items are decorated with embroidery stitches, so that the child gets embroidery lessons along with the sewing lesson. This is a good teaching book, but not too exciting. **Condition, good: $25.00 and up.**

43-P
My Needlwork Book
Gladys and Bee McMullen
Published by A R. Mowbray & Co., Limited, London &
    Oxford, Great Britain
Copyright 1947 by A. R. Mowbray & Co., Limited
47 pages with 10 sewing projects
Hardcover, 9¾" x 6¼"

The cover is printed all over in a blue and green flower stripe. The title, *My Needlwork Book*, is surrounded by a blanket stitch and there are four of the sewing projects shown one in each corner.

My Needlwork Book reads like a story, Hazel wants to make clothes, and mother agrees to help her learn to sew. The first project is a pillow cover for Winnie's doll bed, then a blanket to match. Winnie then needs a bonnet, then a cloak. Hazel makes them both.

Hazel decides to make a feeder (bib) for the neighbor baby. Then for the poor children, Hazel and her mother make a petticoat, a scarf, and bonnet. They are so pleased with their items, they decide to make more clothing for poor children.

The projects are simple and easy to do, but an adult needs to help at times. The stitches are learned while making the items. It's a cute story that would promote sewing with an adult. **Condition, good: $25.00 and up**

44-P
Judy's Book of Sewing and Knitting
Muriel Goaman
Published by Faber & Faber, Ltd., London, England
Copyright 1950 by Faber & Faber, Ltd.
76 pages with 14 sewing projects and 5 knitting projects
Hardcover, 8½" x 6"

The cover of this book is blue, it probably had a dust jacket (mine does not). The book has no decoration or lettering on the front cover, *Judy's Book of Sewing and Knitting* is printed on the spine in red.

Judy's Book of Sewing and Knitting begins with simple hints for sewing and knitting. The sewing projects are a drawstring bag, dressing a puppet and a doll's bedding consisting of a mattress, pillow, pillow case, sheets, blankets, counterpane, and eiderdown.

The chapter on "Working in Felt" shows you how to make two elephants, rats, and an egg cozy. In the "Sewing" section are a cotton apron and a flannel doll. The nice thing about *Judy's Book of Sewing and Knitting* is she doesn't group all the stitches together in the front of the book, but shows you how to do each stitch as you make the items.

The "Knitting" chapter has you making baby mitts, baby bonnet, baby slippers, a tea cozy, and a doll's matinee coat. This is a book that a child, and even an adult, would enjoy, particularly the doll bedding section. **Condition, good: $25.00 and up.**

45-P
I Learn to Knit to Dress My Doll Primrose
Elaine Lamarque
Published by Laines du Pingouin, distributed in America
   by Adrien Mey & Co. N.Y.
Copyright with no date by Eliane Lamarque
32 pages with 4 doll knitting projects
Hardcover, 9½" x 7"

The cover of *I Learn to Knit to Dress My Doll Primrose* has a white background with a child in a red plaid jumper and a white smocked blouse holding her doll while knitting. The title is in black.

This book was first written in French and was translated to English by Dee T. Bass. There are no dates in the book. I am assuming it was written in the early 1950s.

The book is in story form about a little girl, Catherine, and three toys. The toys, Primrose the doll, Cyclone the plane, and a toy Penguin all live with Santa. The toys decided to go on an adventure, they get into trouble more than once and finally end up on earth where Catherine finds them cold and frightened in the rain. Primrose's dress is spoiled from the rain and Catherine promises to knit her a new warm outfit. Catherine makes Primrose four new ensembles.

The outfits are a striped skirt and bolero, skirt, sacque and bonnet, coat, leggings, pointed bonnet and a dress with pompons, bonnet, and slippers.

The doll is 16" tall. The outfits are cute and the directions seem simple; a child, as well as an adult, would enjoy dressing a doll in these little French knitting patterns. **Condition, good: $25.00 and up.**

46-P
Teaching Little Girls to Sew
Good Housekeeping Needlework and Sewing Center
No publisher listed
No copyright or date listed (clothing and projects look 1950s)
27 pages with 17 projects
Softcover, 11" x 8½"

A black-and-white photograph of a little girl sewing a piece of gingham on a small sewing machine is on the cover of *Teaching Little Girls to Sew*.

Teaching Little Girls to Sew doesn't give any instruction on stitches or how to sew, but is a book of patterns for a child to sew. Each pattern gives the listing of materials, how to trace and cut and how to make the project.

The projects include a bath mitt, key chain, coin case, turtle beanbag, glasses case, potholder, flowerpot needle-case, triangular apron, place mat, jacks or marbles bag, beanie, organdy apron, coasters, slippers, cobbler apron, doorknob decoration, hood and mittens, and a blouse.

This pamphlet has many simple projects done in felt. A child who is capable of cutting out the projects would have no trouble sewing and finishing them. **Condition, good: $10.00 and up.**

47-P
Child's Book of Sewing
Jane Chapman
Published by Greenberg Publishers, N.Y., N.Y.
Copyright 1951 by Greenberg Publisher.
65 pages with 4+ sewing projects
Softcover, 8" x 5½"

Child's Book of Sewing is a melon color with a cartoon-type drawing of a child within a pinked-edge, oblong, white patch. There are sewing implements drawn with stick arms and legs, dancing along the edges of the book.

The foreword of *Child's Book of Sewing* explains:
This book is written in words that a little girl can read, so that she can learn to sew all by herself. The text is simple, the print is large and the book is colorfully illustrated.

One clever thing *Child's Book of Sewing* instructs the child do is to make a stitch card for reference when doing the projects. The projects are a personalized bookmark, change purse, bean bag, and wrist pincushion.

This is a simple little book for a beginning reader to learn how to sew with felt unassisted. **Condition, good: $10.00 and up.**

Note: This is a Brevity Booklet, a condensation of *Child's Book of Sewing*.

48-P
4-H Club Sewing
Agricultural Extension Service, University of Tennessee
Published by Agricultural Extension Service, University of
    Tennessee
Copyright 1951 by Agricultural Extension Service,
    University of Tennessee
16 pages with 3+ sewing projects
Softcover, 9" x 6"

This 4-H pamphlet has a black-and-white photograph of a teen-age girl sitting at a sewing machine while sewing on a project. There is a curtained window behind her.

The first chapters talk about tools and preparation. Project one is to make a towel, head kerchief, apron, slip, dirndl skirt, or a simple sleeveless blouse. The chapter gives some instruction on pockets, gathering, hems, types of seams, shoulder straps, finishes, and hems for slips.

Project two is darning and patching and shows how to make a hemmed patch and how to darn hosiery.

Project three, is school frocks that accent personality. This chapter tells you how to select a pattern, how to cut it, make pockets, make hems, finish seams, set in a sleeve, put in a slashed opening, slide fasteners, or side placket openings, and how to sew on buttons and make buttonholes. This pamphlet gives a peek into 4-H and sewing in the 1950s. **Condition, good: $5.00 and up.**

Plate 580. *The Real Book About Making Dolls and Doll Clothes* (**49-P**) by Catherine Roberts, 1951. A variety of dolls to make along with their clothing. *Girl's Book of Sewing* (**51-P**) by Jane Chapman, 1952. A complete learn-to-sew book, of fun things for girls of all ages.

49-P
The Real Book About Making Dolls and Doll Clothes
Catherine Roberts
Published by Garden City Books, Garden City, N.Y.
Copyright 1951 by Franklin Watts Inc.
191 pages with 11 doll projects
Hardcover, 8" x 5½"

The Real Book About Making Dolls and Doll Clothes has a blue cover with a red and white drawing of a doll in a plaid dress.

The first chapter is a little history on the doll, how it was made, the materials used and why. The first doll to be made from this book is the cotton baby for a dollhouse. The book also has directions to make a handkerchief doll, paper dolls, crepe paper dolls, rag dolls, dolls with wire armatures, clay dolls, and marionettes.

All the dolls are dressed and completed. There are patterns for both the dolls and their clothing. This is such a fun doll-*Sewing Book*! I wanted to make some dolls as soon as I saw this little volume. **Condition, good: $10.00 and up.**

50-P
Child's Book of Knitting
Edith Jay
Published by Greenberg Publishers, N.Y., N.Y.
Copyright 1952 by Edith Jay
92 pages with 5 knitting projects
Hardcover, 8½" x 5¾"

If *Child's Book of Knitting* ever came with a dust jacket, mine has been lost. The *Child's Book of Knitting* cover is orange with cream color printing and a black-and-cream graphic of two knitted dolls, a girl and a boy. The girl doll is sitting in a chair and the boy doll is sitting on a round rug slightly beneath her.

Child's Book of Knitting is written in large print with instructions on how to knit. It introduces knitting as a game that you can play by yourself. There is a list of items needed for each project.

The text shows every step in learning how to knit, from casting on to binding off. It addresses how to read knitting patterns, how to follow graphs, shaping, measuring, and using a stitch holder.

The projects are a purse with a handle, twin dolls, hat, slippers, and a vest. It is a very complete book on learning how to knit. Any child or adult who wanted to learn to knit could benefit by using this book. **Condition, good: $10.00 and up.**

51-P
Girl's Book of Sewing
Jane Chapman
Published by Greenberg Publisher, N.Y., N.Y.
and simultaneously by Ambassador Books, Ltd. Toronto,
    Canada
Copyright 1952 by Greenberg Publisher,
95 pages with 18+ sewing projects
Hardcover, 9½" x 6"

Popular Sewing and Needlework Books

The dust jacket of *Girl's Book of Sewing* is wide green stripes with pink and black cartoon-type drawings of teen-age girls cutting and sewing fabric. The book itself is dark green with the title only on the spine.

Girl's Book of Sewing starts out with sewing hints, stitches and equipping the sewing basket. The projects start right away with a headscarf, bridge cloth, napkins, dresser scarf, place mats and napkins, snackins (napkins), and a cross-stitch picture. There are additional lessons on pressing and using the sewing machine.

The other projects are: a halter, a girl's hood, baby's hood, apron, drawstring dress-ups for your room, curtains, dressing-table skirt, lampshade cover, lining for your sewing basket, heart pincushion, turtle toy, and a rocking doll.

The last chapter has the instructions for making a blouse, skirt, and shorts from Simplicity pattern #3874 that you purchase yourself. An easy book for a teen to learn from with simple, but satisfying projects. **Condition, good: $10.00 and up.**

52-P
Sewing
Jeanette Zarchy
Published by Alfred A. Knopf, Inc., A Borzoi Book,
  N.Y., N.Y.
Copyright 1952 by Alfred A. Knopf, Inc.
45 pages with 17 sewing projects
Hardcover, 8½" x 6"

The cover of *Sewing* is bright red with a lavender and black insert of a child sewing a felt rabbit toy with her mother looking on with pride.

The title page declares it is A Daughter and Mother Activity Book. The introduction states:

You can learn to sew easily, provided you go about it in a systematic manner. Practice the different stitches, and you will be able to make many things of which you can be proud.

Young people who learn to sew always have something to do, it is a wonderful hobby, which they can turn to at any time.

Sewing is a how-to-sew book and starts with outfitting your sewing box. Then continues with how to thread a needle, types of stitches, seams, bindings and sewing on snaps, buttons and hooks and eyes.

There is also a chapter on decorative and embroidery stitches. The instructions are very clear with lots of diagrams. The articles to make are a pincushion, bath mitts, pot lifters, clothespin apron, square apron, barbecue apron, carpenter's apron, stuffed toys, shoe bag, book cover, coin purse, beach wrap, dance costume, kitchen pad, and laundry bag.

A very complete book to teach sewing to a young child that could be used successfully today. **Condition, good: $10.00 and up.**

53-P
Sewing Book (A Picture Sewing Book)
Elise M. Wollenweber
Published by Paxton-Slade Publishing Corp., N.Y., N.Y.
Copyright 1952 by Paxton-Slade Publishing Corp.
64 pages with 12 sewing projects
Softcover, 8" x 6¼"

Sewing Book (*A Picture Sewing Book*) is done mostly in yellow and red and shows a child of 8 to 12 years of age threading a needle. Her sewing box, doll, and sewing implements are in the foreground.

The introduction tells of the necessity of sewing in years past but today with ready made clothing in stores it has become a hobby. The book goes on to say that sewing is one way women can express her creative talents and thus, bring her joy and happiness.

Sewing Book (*A Picture Sewing Book*) uses dolls throughout as an encouragement to sewing, starting with filling your workbox with doll clothes patterns along with tools and equipment.

Sewing Book (*A Picture Sewing Book*) teaches the fundamentals of sewing, measurements, embroidery, using a gauge, cutting, selecting materials, hand weaving, and dressmaking.

The projects for the child includes a sewing apron, a basic dress, blouse, jumper skirt, jacket circular skirt, playsuit, cincher-belt, and bonnet cap. For dolly, a panty/slip set, and a layette for a baby doll.

The book has an interesting slant to it. In the second project the doll panty slip/ set, the book suggests you trace the model paper-doll they provide on a page, color it, paste it to cardboard and cut it out so you will have a paper doll for your dressmaking model.

There are pages with hints on pressing, color, sketching clothing, and starting sewing clubs. The patterns included in the book are drafts used by folding and measuring the fabric. This is a book that could teach a young child to sew with the help of an adult. **Condition, good: $10.00 and up.**

Note: Paxton-Slade Publishing Corporation published *Sewing Book* (*A Picture Sewing Book*) in paperback in 1960. It had the same cover and was a larger size, but had the same content. *Sewing Book* without the subtitle (*A Sewing Picture Book*) also, came out in 1960. This edition has the same content as *Sewing Book* (*A Sewing Picture Book*) with a different cover, mostly green and yellow in color with a cartoon-type child next to a dress hanging on a dress form.

54-P
How to Make Doll Clothes (A Book for Daughters, Mothers and Grandmothers)
Emily R. Dow
Published by Coward-McCann, Inc, N.Y., N.Y.
Copyright 1953 by Emily D. Eddy
96 pages with 30+ projects for a doll
Hardcover, 8½" x 6½"

How to Make Doll Clothes is plain yellow with red printing on the spine only. The dust jacket is red with black printing and black-and-white graphics of a girl hanging half off the cover along with a pair of shears and a scattering of doll garments.

How to Make Doll Clothes was written by a sewing teacher because she realized, while teaching her nieces, that a book on how to draft doll clothing was needed; a book with simple instructions and pictures easy enough for children, but one an adult would also find interesting.

The first chapter, "The Doll Dressmaker," tells how to use the book, tools needed, useful gadgets for the experienced sewer, easiest way to cut and sew, how to knot and measure your thread, and useful scraps to save for doll dressmaking. There are over 100 plates, all types of stitches from basting to fancy embroidery stitches, and drafts of clothing for dolls.

The projects include doll's underwear, dresses, sun suit, nightgown, pajamas, coats, snowsuit, jumper, pinafore, overalls, clown suit, wedding dress, hats, socks, and shoes. The book also contains a dictionary of sewing terms. This is a good book to start a child sewing for her doll with some help from an adult. **Condition, good: $25.00 and up.**

55-P
Girl's Book of Embroidery
Jane Chapman
Published by Greenberg Publisher, N.Y., N.Y.
Copyright 1953 by Greenberg Publisher
96 pages book on embroidery
Hardcover, 8½" x 6"

Girl's Book of Embroidery is baby blue with soft yellow lettering and decoration. A girl outlined in black, holding an embroidery hoop, needle, and thread is drawn among various embroidered designs.

Lots of ideas are in this book, from embroidered samplers to greeting cards. There are instructions on many of the embroidery stitches, each with variations. The *Girl's Book of Embroidery* shows you how to embroider on gingham, dots, and quilting, how to embellish ribbon, rickrack trim, and bias tape. There are patterns for alphabets, emblems, and patches, you can embroider bands on your skirt, or monogram your blouse. There are hundreds of ideas for embroidery in original designs, including some for decorating your room. A child wanting to learn to embroider would find this book a delight. **Condition, good: $25.00 and up.**

56-P
Sewing Magic for Teen-Agers
Mildred Graves Ronin
Published by The Greist Manufacturing Co., New Haven, Conn.
Copyright 1954 by The Greist Manufacturing Co.
37 pages with 14 sewing chapters
Softcover, 8½" x 6"

Sewing Magic for Teen-Agers has a soft green cover with a line drawing of a cartoon-type teenager with a ponytail holding up a ruffle that is trailing down from her sewing machine's needle.

Sewing Magic for Teen-Agers is for the teen-ager, to teach her about sewing machine attachments and how to use them.

The chapters are "Sewing Magic," "Helpful Hints," "Cloth Guide," "Zipper and Cording Foot, Scissors Cutting Gauge, Gathering Foot, Narrow-Hemmer, Hemmer, Tucker," "Quilter," "Edgestitcher," "Multiple-Slotted Binder and Ruffler." This is an interesting book for learning about 1950s attachments for sewing machines. **Condition, good: $5.00 and up.**

57-P
The First Book of Sewing
Catherine Roberts
Published by Ambassador Books, Ltd., Toronto, Canada
Copyright 1956 by Franklin Watts, Inc.
67 pages with 9 sewing and embroidery projects
Hardcover, 9" x 7"

The First Book of Sewing has a green and cream cover with a print of apples, cherries, and leaves. There is a large green patch towards the top of the cover with the title printed in cream.

The First Book of Sewing has nine chapters. They are "Hand Sewing is Fun," "First Things First," "Tools," "How to Make a Table-mat, a Napkin, and a Doll's Dirndl," "It's Easy to Embroider!" "Looped Stitches," "Working with Plain Fabrics," "Samplers," "Glamour and Glitter."

This is truly a first book of sewing it tells a child everything they would need from threading a needle to tying a knot. There are a few pages on the history of sewing that would be interesting to a child. Half of the book is in print and half is cursive with lots of diagrams of stitches. A number of pages are given to embroidery stitches. Besides the table mat, napkin, and doll's dirndl are two child's aprons, sampler, decorative pockets, ornaments, and Christmas cards. This is a cute little book sure to interest a child in sewing. **Condition, good: $10.00 and up.**

58-P
Make Your Own Teen-Age Clothes, Accessories and Gifts
Kay Hardy
Published by Funk & Wagnalls Co.
Copyright 1956 by Funk & Wagnalls Co.
213 pages with 13 chapters filled with sewing projects
Hardcover, 9¼" x 6½"

My book has a plain gray cover with a red binding. I am sure *Make Your Own Teen-Age Clothes, Accessories and Gifts* has a dust jacket, but mine is missing.

This is a serious book for the teen age miss, which teaches full sewing, with knitting and crochet instructions.

Here is you open-sesame to a closet full of smooth-fitting clothes that suit your personality and coloring-a book designed to help you, the teen-ager, build a lovely, distinctive wardrobe at very little cost and in a short time.

Although this is not a textbook, it reads like one. Everything you want to know about clothing is in this book.

Make Your Own Teen-Age Clothes, Accessories and Gifts is filled with 1950s knitting and crochet patterns, along with simple-to-make gloves, hats, handbags, dresses, and sport clothing. A look back into the 1950s is what you will find while reading this book. **Condition, good: $5.00 and up.**

59-P
Sew Easy for the Young Beginner
Peggy Hoffman
Published by E. P. Dutton & Co., Inc., N.Y., N.Y.
Copyright 1956 by E. P. Dutton & Co. Inc.
93 pages with 12 sewing projects
Hardcover, 10¼" x 7"

The cover for *Sew Easy for the Young Beginner* is plain aqua with pink printing on the front and spine. The dust jacket has a black-and-white photograph of a young girl in braids sitting at a table, busy making clothing for her dolls.

Sew Easy for the Young Beginner is primarily a book about hand sewing, although there is a brief section on using a sewing machine, with adult supervision only.

After a brief discussion about tools, proper posture, and lighting, the projects begin. Each project introduces a different sewing skill, and none seem to be too complicated. The first project is a luncheon and napkin set that really doesn't have any sewing, but shows you how to pull threads. The remaining projects are an apron, baby's bib, beanbag, change purse, doll clothes, half-slip, laundry bag, man's scarf, pajama pillow, pillowcases, ribbon headband, and halter top.

The doll clothing is for a 7" celluloid doll, however the directions say if made for a 10" doll, cut the patterns 1½ times larger, and for a 12" to 14" doll, twice as large. The doll clothing consists of a scarf (can be used as a halter), ballerina skirt, full skirt, blouse, hat, "fly-away" coat, panties, and pocketbook. The doll clothing is rather simple, but a child would enjoy making them. The little girl's halter-top, I think, would be a big hit with young girls. **Condition, good: $10.00 and up.**

60-P
Sewing is Easy
Helen Nicol Tanous
Published by Random House, N.Y., N.Y.
Copyright 1956 by Helen Nicol Tanous
64 pages with 13 sewing projects
Hardcover, 10" x 7½"

Sewing is Easy has a two-color cover of gray and green. The lower half of the cover shows a photo of three girls with a doll, sitting at a table, while sewing. The book's title is printed in green.

Sewing is Easy is very easy to understand. A beginning book, the first 26 pages talk about sewing, getting ready, learning to measure, explaining the warp and woof of fabric, hand and machine sewing and so on, giving all the correct ways to

begin sewing with good habits.

The projects are dish-towel apron, fringed table mats, plastic envelope for table mats, potholders, barbecue mitts, workshop apron, scissors case, doll hat, felt envelope-style purse, ponytail hat and scarf, gathered skirt and ruffled blouse.

The projects are easy to understand and include boys in the pictures sewing the barbecue mitts and workshop aprons. Also included is a sewing dictionary.

Even though written in the middle of the 1950s the projects would be stylish and useful today. *Sewing is Easy* is a good book that would teach a child of age 10 to 13 how to sew. **Condition, good: $10.00 and up.**

61-P
Starting to Sew
Unknown author
Published by Needlework Development Scheme, Glasgow, Great Britain
No copyright date (dated in pencil 1957)
19 pages with 3 sewing projects
Softcover, 9" x 6"

The cover of *Starting to Sew* has a blue background and a child with braids threading a needle. The title is in white at the bottom.

Starting to Sew is a picture book about a sewing class. It features black-and-white photographs of children at work, along with colorful plates showing the stitches.

The introduction begins: *Isn't it fun to make your own dolls and dress them in clothes you made by yourself? You will enjoy the help this book will give you to plan, cut out and sew the dresses and other garments you will want to make.*

This is a very simple little book on learning to sew. The chapters are "The Work Box," "Using a Thimble," "The Piece Box," "Cutting Out From a Pattern," "Start with a Double Stitch," "Sewing with Running Stitches," "Making a Hem," "Making Gathers," "Making Borders with Stitches," "Apron with Drawstring," "Joining with Oversewing," "Make a Gay Skirt," and "How to Work a Blanket Stitch." *Starting to Sew* is a cute little book for the beginning young sewer. **Condition, good: $10.00 and up.**

62-P
Sewing is Fun
Edith Paul
Published by Scholastic Book Services, N.Y., N.Y.
Copyright 1958 by The Singer Manufacturing Co.
64 pages with 12 sewing projects
Softcover, 8" x 6"

The cover of *Sewing is Fun* has a blue background with a drawing of a young girl's hand sewing on an apron.

The first chapters of *Sewing is Fun* are about outfitting your sewing box, how to sew safely, fabrics, pressing, cutting, sewing on buttons, and how to do a running stitch.

The first six projects, button-flower needle case, apple pincushion, daisy eyeglass case, oilcloth book cover, and the bunny baby bib are all done by hand. The stitches are learned as the child completes the projects.

Learning how to use the sewing machine comprises the second half of *Sewing is Fun* and the projects are a table place mat and napkins, ribbon bow belt, pinwheel pillow, collar, lampshade covers, and gingham apron. This is a good first *Sewing Book* for a child. **Condition, good: $10.00 and up.**

63-P
The See and Do Book of Dolls and Doll Houses
Helen Jill Fletcher
Published by H. S. Stuttman Co., Inc. New York, 16, N. Y.
Copyright 1959 by H. S. Stuttman Co. Inc.
128 pages with many sewing projects
Hardcover 8½" x 5½"

The See and Do Book of Dolls and Doll Houses has a blue spine and a light blue linen-look cover the title is only on the spine. The dust jacket is blue and has picture of a mother, daughter, and son working on various crafts involving dolls. The title is in white at the top of the book.

The See and Do Book of Dolls and Doll Houses has six chapters, "Making Dolls and Doll House — A Fascinating Hobby," "Designing and Making Rag Dolls," "How to Design and Make Colorful Costume Dolls," "Novelty Dolls You Can Design and Make," "Designing and Making Doll Clothes," and "The Design and Construction of Doll Houses and Doll Furniture." This little book assumes a child knows how to do basic hand sewing, it shows no stitches or instruction on the actual basic sewing.

The first chapter is finding materials for making things in the book and tells you how to start a treasure chest. Chapter two gives you hints, like suitable materials for rag doll, how to cut, stuff, making hair in different hair styles, and faces and features. In chapter three you learn how to make costume dolls such as Delores, a Spanish doll, and Colette, a little French doll, etc. chapter four is all about novelty dolls like twig dolls, baby sock doll, and all kind of animal dolls. In chapter five you learn *How to Make Doll Clothes*, how to make your own patterns, make clothing from old socks and scraps. It covers everything from hats to shoes. The last chapter is how to build your own doll house using shoe boxes to orange crates. It even tells you how to decorate and make the furniture from wooden spools, pipecleaners, boxes, etc. This is really a fun book and could keep a child occupied for hours. **Condition, good: $10.00 and up.**

64-P
Let Me Embroider
Winsome Douglass
Published by Mills & Boon Ltd., London, England
Copyright 1960 by Winsome Douglass
63 pages with 20 embroidery projects
Hardcover, 8" x 5½"

Let Me Embroider has a dust jacket that is the same as the book's cover bright red with a drawing of a girl dressed in an embroidered costume. The title is in white at the top of the book.

The author is an art teacher who learned needlework from her grandmother when she was a child. *Let Me Embroider* is simply written, with only a few words on each page and the illustrations are large and easily understood.

The projects are, a mat, square bag, pencil case, gathered bag, oven mitts, triangle bag, kettle holder, pajama case, stool pad, animal bag, hanky sachet, Christmas bird, wall panel, skating bonnet, drawstring purse, shoulder bag, book cover, and trinket box. *Let Me Embroider* has simple projects and with lots of room for to creativity. **Condition, good: $10.00 and up.**

65-P
Needlecraft for Juniors
A. V. White
Published by Routledge & Kegan Paul Ltd., London,
   England
Copyright 1960 by A.V. White
184 pages with 31 + needlecraft projects
Hardcover, 9" x 5½"

Needlecraft for Juniors is a plain, tan book with red printing on its spine. The dust jacket is orange and green plaid with a cartoon type figure sewing cross-stitch on a piece of fabric.

Needlecraft for Juniors covers a lot of material. It starts out with easy projects and ends up with making clothing for oneself. The projects are easily understood and the teaching is done while the child is making a project.

The projects are clothes pin dolls, needle case, egg cozy, pincushions, apron, handkerchief case, tray cloth, apron needlework bag, tea cozy, pinafore, toy fish, pencil case, tapestry, peg bag, spotted apron, flared apron, handy bag, pocket belt, felt mitt, hand puppet, and toy dog. Under the section on clothing to be made for yourself are gathered skirt, buttoned skirt, bolero jacket, buttoned blouse, round neck blouse, no-button blouse, collared-blouse, shorts, pajamas, and felt Juliet cap.

In chapter seven, "The Teaching of Needlecraft," the author points out:

Needlecraft provides children with an opportunity to create things for their world of make-believe. This they can do by sewing things for a dolls' house, by making the contents of a dress shop or millinery shop or by making clothes for a doll.

During this period the child is not only acquiring skill in the use of tools and the handling of materials but is also gaining a sense of colour, style, and taste and is learning to be self-reliant and accurate.

Needlecraft for Juniors contains a lot of material and ideas, it could be useful for a long period of time, either in teaching or learning needlework. **Condition, good: $5.00 and up.**

66-P
Sewing Book
Elise M. Wollenweber
Published by Paxton-Slade Publishing Co., Inc., N.Y., N.Y.
Copyright 1960 by Paxton-Slade publishing Co.
64 pages with 14+ sewing projects
Softcover, 11" x 8½"

Sewing Book has the same content as *Sewing Book* (*A Picture Sewing Book*) (53-P). **Condition, good: $10.00 and up.**

67-P
Things for Little Girls to Sew
Unknown author
Published by Singer Manufacturing Co.
Copyright 1961 by Singer Manufacturing Co.
32 pages with 10 sewing projects
Softcover, 7½" x 5½"

The cover of *Things for Little Girls to Sew* shows a picture of a little girl sewing on her child's Singer Sewhandy sewing machine. In the upper right hand corner is the Singer logo.

Things for Little Girls to Sew teaches basting, cutting, seams, gathering, hemming, and quilting. It is also an instruction book for a child's toy Singer Sewhandy sewing machine, however it was sold separately from the Sewhandy sewing machine.

The projects could be sewn with any machine or stitched by hand. The items are an apple pincushion, dusting glove, table mats and napkins, girl's collar, lamp shade covers, pillow, ribbon belt, gingham apron, quilted potholder, and cover for hot dish pad. All these projects in *Things for Little Girls to Sew* are simple for a child to sew. **Condition, good: $5.00 and up.**

68-P
Dolls' Dressmaking
Winifred Butler
Published by Oxford University Press, New Jersey, N.Y., Toronto, N.Y., & London
Copyright 1962 by Winifred Butler
142 pages with 50+ doll projects
Hardcover, 10" x 7½"

The cover of *Dolls' Dressmaking* is grass green with white printing on the front and spine. The dust cover is lime green with a photograph of two dolls and a teddy bear dressed in clothing.

Dolls' Dressmaking gives instructions and patterns in black-and-white for more than fifty garments for a baby doll, girl doll and teddy bear. Complete wardrobes for each doll are included and consist of day clothes, party dresses, nightclothes, hats, shoes, and a christening robe for the baby doll.

The full-size patterns are for a 16" baby doll, 17" girl doll, and a 17" teddy bear. In the back of the book is a chart for converting them to fit 10", 12", 14", and 20" dolls or bears. The instructions have lots of easy-to-understand diagrams. Winifred Butler has organized the book so that as the child uses it, she receives training in dressmaking, which can be used in other sewing projects.

Each new stitch becomes part of an attractive outfit for a cherished doll. A well thought-out book to entice any child to learn the art of dressmaking. Adults who like to sew doll clothing could also benefit from this book. **Condition, good: $25.00 and up.**

69-P
Godey's How to Dress a Doll and Make Cardboard Furniture 1860 Style
Published by The Dollover's Library, Scotia, N.Y.
Copyright 1964 by Grace H. Coutant
12 pages with 14 doll sewing projects
Softcover, 8½" x 5½"

The cover of *Godey's How to Dress a Doll and Make Cardboard Furniture 1860 Style* is a copy of an 1860 *Godey's Lady's Book* cover printed in sepia tone. The title, *Godey's How to Dress a Doll* is printed at the top of the cover.

Some of the first words in this sewing book are:

This is not only pleasant employment, but it is extremely useful; to be able to make your own doll clothes, you will acquire the knowledge of making your own dresses when you are older. Every little girl is fond of dolls, and to dress one neatly requires some experience. Young ladies too often depend upon others to make their doll's clothes: but with the practical Plates we propose giving for making each article of dress separately, we trust all our young friends will be enabled to make their own things. Sewing is particularly a lady's accomplishment, and it cannot be too early practiced or encouraged.

The projects are a chemise, stays (corset), drawers, flannel petticoat, pinafore, cape, hat, hoop petticoat, white petticoat, petticoat body (camisole), frock (dress), nightdress, Miss Dinah pen-wiper, bird in cage, bed with cornice, bedding, couch, armchair, bassinet, and house with fence. **Condition, good: $10.00 and up.**

Note: The doll clothing drafts and instructions in *Godey's How to Dress a Doll* are the same, word for word, diagram for diagram, as *The Girl's Own Toymaker and Book of Recreation* (3-P). The drafts and instructions were also used in pages especially printed for children in *Godey's Lady's Book* magazine in 1860.

70-P
The Lucky Set-it-Yourself Book
Camille Sokol
Published by the Scholastic Book Services, N.Y., N.Y.
Text copyright 1964 by Camille Sokol, Plates copyright 1964 by Bill Sokol
45 pages with 5 sewing projects
Softcover, 8" x 6"

The Lucky Set-it-Yourself Book white cover has a stick figure girl with a red A-line dress and two big red bows at each side of her head. She is holding a sewing box and there is a yellow cat curled up at her feet.

This book is so simple a child just learning to read can use it; it is filled with simple pictures that the child could almost follow without reading.

The first part of *The Lucky Set-it-Yourself Book* tells what is needed in order to sew and shows how to make practice stitches on gingham. The projects are also very easy, a headscarf from gingham, a little pocketbook, apron, pincushion, and a pillow for your doll. A really cute and inexpensive book to start the youngest child on her way to sewing. **Condition, good: $10.00 and up.**

Plate 581. *Dot Young's Sewing Book* (71-P) by Dot Young, 1964. Dot Young, shows high school girls how to hand sew and use a sewing machine, with fun projects. *Miss Patch's Learn-to-Sew Book (75-P)* by Carolyn Meyer, 1969. Miss Patch learns to sew and takes you right along with her and her dog Charlie.

71-P
Dot Young's Sewing Book
Dot Young
Published by J.B. Lippincott Co., Philadelphia & N.Y.
Copyright 1964 by Dot Young
62 pages with sewing instructions
Hardcover, 10¼" x 7¾"

The dust cover of *Dot Young's Sewing Book* has the same graphics as the front of the book, a teenage girl in a pinked-edge picture frame decorated with a sewing machine and assorted sewing accessories.

This book, dedicated to 4-H and junior high school girls, who in the past have struggled to sew using adult Sewing Books and adult patterns, covers only the first sewing skills and good habits needed for the construction of attractive clothes.

Dot Young's Sewing Book is a real teaching book, showing the correct equipment, how to use the sewing machine, select fabric, patterns, construction, finishes, pressing, and sewing skills. It would be a good book to have when sewing with your first pattern. **Condition, good: $10.00 and up.**

72-P
Making Far and Near Dolls
Faith Eaton
Hulton Educational Publications Ltd., 55/59 Saffron Hill,
   London E. C. 1
Copyright 1966 by Faith Eaton
84 pages with 16 dolls and 15 animals to make
Hardcover, 8¾" x 6¼"

Making Far and Near Dolls has a cover with a green background and an orange spine. There are three costume dolls on the cover and the title is in black at the top of the book.

Making Far and Near Dolls has 15 costume dolls to make and fourteen of them have an animal that goes with them. Tom has a black cat, Martin has a lamb, Tuan has a monkey, Odak has a seal, Kristin has her dog, Roberto has a calf, Nicos has a donkey, San has a baby elephant, Henri has a horse, Sawat has a buffalo, Ali has a camel, Anna has a reindeer, Pedro has a llama, and Suiko has some silkworms and a kokeshi doll. Don does not have an animal when he goes down the nine with his father, but you can make him a helmet with a lamp, and a pit prop for him to carry.

The dolls are about 7" and are made of felt with a pipe cleaner form. The instructions are clear and very detailed, down to the color of the dolls skin and hair and eye color. The animals are also made of felt. This little book could keep a sewing child busy for a long time and the toys made would be fun to collect and play with. **Condition: $25.00 and up.**

73-P
The Young Embroiderer
Jan Beaney
Published by Frederick Warne & Co., Inc., N.Y., &
   London, England
Copyright 1966 by Kaye & Ward, Ltd.
57 pages with 8+ embroidery projects
Hardcover, 11" x 8"

The Young Embroiderer has an olive green cover with black printing on the front and spine. The dust jacket is olive green and has examples of early embroidery, a jacket, a glove, and two panels. The cover is very sophisticated one wouldn't expect it to be a child's *Sewing Book.*

This is a how-it-is done book. The introduction promises:
This book is about embroidery and how you can learn to be your own designer. If you like a variety of materials, rich colour, texture and pattern, you will find this craft very exciting.

These colourful decorations, if displayed in your room, could inspire and stimulate you to go on to bigger and better things.

The Young Embroiderer starts out talking about embroidery its history, uses, threads and equipment. The book shows some fancy embroidery stitches, but not common ones such as the outline or stem stitch.

Popular Sewing and Needlework Books

The projects are a greeting card, calendar, appliqued panel, paperweight, and cushion. A large portion of the book covers designing and making sketches of designs. Free-style embroidery is emphasized and a lot of museum pieces are shown throughout the book. I would think an older, experienced child or adult would do better with *The Young Embroiderer* than the beginner. **Condition, good: $10.00 and up.**

74-P
The Co-Ed Sewing Book
Marian Ross
Published by Scholastic Book Services, N.Y., Toronto,
    London, Auckland, Sydney
Copyright 1968 by Scholastic Magazines, Inc.
128 pages with information on how to select fabric and
    sew clothing
Softcover, 7½" x 5¼"

The Co-Ed Sewing Book has a dark green cover with a burlap outline of a dress surrounded by a hat, dressmaker pins, ribbons, tapes, and thread.

The Co-Ed Sewing Book does not have projects, patterns or items to make, but is crammed full of teen-age ideas on making-over your wardrobe.

Some of the chapter titles are "Instant Fashion," "Dramatize Yourself," "Masterminding Your Wardrobe," "Hand Stitches You Should Know," "Introducing Your Sewing Machine," and "What Size Are You, Really?" It is a book that would probably answer any question a young girl might have in planning to sew a wardrobe. **Condition, good: $5.00 and up.**

75-P
Miss Patch's Learn-to-Sew Book
Carolyn Meyer
Published by Hardcourt, Brace & World, Inc., N.Y., N.Y.
Copyright 1969 by Carolyn Meyer
96 pages with 13 projects, and wardrobes for dolls
Hardcover, 9½" x 7"

Miss Patch's Learn-to-Sew Book has a pink cover with a black drawing of Miss Patch and her dog on the front. The title is in black on the spine. The dust cover is done in pink and blue with a white background and has nine patches showing sewing supplies and Charlie the dog, Miss Patch is the center patch.

Miss Patch is with you throughout the book. She and her dog Charlie romp through the book showing you how to sew. She starts out right away making a pillow for Charlie. Miss Patch gives instructions on each project as you come to it.

Miss Patch's Learn-to-Sew Book is in black and white and the Plates are clever and easy to follow. The projects are a pillow, drawstring bag, kerchief, scarf, apron, pillow and cover for a doll's bed, play skirt, half-slip, gingerbread boy doll, pincushion heart, bath or hot mitt, hand puppet, and doll clothes.

The doll clothes start out with an 11½" fashion doll. She gives two pattern graphs that make all types of clothing depending upon the lines that are chosen. The second part of the doll clothing is for a 12" to 16" and 14" to 17" doll. Again, there are two patterns graphs with different lines to choose for different garments. There are many suggestions on how to sew them. *Miss Patch's Learn-to-Sew Book* is a delightful, fun book and children and adults would enjoy using it. **Condition, good: $25.00 and up.**

76-P
Simple Sewing
Edith Paul and Barbara Zeitz
Published by Wonder Books, N.Y., N.Y.
Copyright 1969 by The Singer Co.
64 pages with 5 sewing projects
Softcover, 8" x 5"

The cover on *Simple Sewing* is a lime green pasteboard with is a little girl sitting on a stool, hand sewing with a sewing basket by her side and a kitten playing with her thread as she stitches.

Simple Sewing starts out with: *You are smart to want to sew! Did you know that surveys show boys are impressed by girls who can sew? Sewing is really "in."*

The first chapters are about tools, materials, pressing, hand sewing and plain sewing. There are chapters on how to use a sewing machine, how to take care of your clothes, how to make a dress from an easy to make pattern, embroidery, and crewelwork.

The projects are simple, felt bookmarks, felt eyeglass case, table place mats, napkins and a gingham apron. A simple, easy-to-understand book, not too challenging for the beginner child sewer. **Condition, good: $10.00 and up.**

77-P
Betsy McCall My Embroidery Book
Pages out of *McCall's Magazine* to make into a booklet
Copyright 1970 by McCall's Publishing Co.
8 pages with 6 stitches and examples of projects
Magazine pages, 10" x 6½"

The cover page of *Betsy McCall My Embroidery Book* shows Betsy McCall in a Santa suit, with sewing supplies and presents around the page. The page is dated 1970 has no month; I assume it is November or December.

The pages teach how to make embroidery stitches and the gifts that Betsy herself made for her family. The stitches are lazy daisy, chain stitch, running stitch, blanket stitch, outline stitch, and French knot. The last page is a Betsy McCall paper doll with two outfits. **Complete in good condition: $5.00 and up.**

78-P
My Learn to Sew Book
Janet Barber
Published by Golden Press, Western Publishing Co., Inc.
Copyright 1970 by The Hamlyn Publishing Group
    Limited, England
61 pages with 38 sewing projects
Hardcover, 2½" x 9"

My Learn to Sew Book has a white background and yellow-and-red paisley elephant pillow with a little girl sitting on its head. The title of the book is printed above.

My Learn to Sew Book is written for children 5 to 12. The first two pages have helpful hints and talks about your sewing box then proceeds immediately to the sewing projects.

The projects include, a shell needle-book, bookmarks, butterfly brooch, hedgehog pincushion, finger family, inside your doll house, hen egg-cozy, ghost glove-puppet, mouse, frog, cat, beanbag snake, humpers-dumpers (doll), elephant cushion, Baby Billy and Baby Billy's clothes, Polly Dolly, and Polly Dolly's clothes, doll's mattress, pillow, sheets and blankets, patchwork quilt, hearts-and-flowers mats, quilted oven glove, house with giant sunflowers, cross-stitch alphabet, rainbow fish, poncho and headband, beach bag, pencil case, shoe bag, purse belt, shoulder bag, dirndl skirt, headscarf, apron, jerkin and vest, winter hood, and lion slippers.

My Learn to Sew Book starts out with the simplest projects and works up to harder ones, in a "learn as you go" style. **Condition, good: $10.00 and up.**

79-P
Of Course You Can Sew!
Barbara Corrigan
Published by Doubleday & Co., N.Y., N.Y.
Copyright 1971 by Barbara Corrigan
127 pages with 14+ sewing projects
Hardcover, 10½" x 7 ¼ "

Of Course You Can Sew! has a green and blue print cover, with a running stitch in black thread around the edges and the title in white. The dust cover is exactly the same.

Of Course You Can Sew! is a book on the basics of sewing for the young beginner. It is intended for girls with no prior sewing experience. The text is in black and white with punches of orange and green in the plates.

The first chapters go over the equipment, fabrics and basic stitches, including the use of the sewing machine. The beginner is shown how to make clothes from start to finish without a pattern. The last chapters introduce commercial patterns for dresses and blouses, how to lay and cut them out and seam them up.

The projects are accessories from a straight piece of fabric, ponchos and capes, shift or robe from Turkish towels, gathered skirt and things to do with sheets. The plates are easy to understand and the text complete.

Of Course You Can Sew! is a good basic book on learning how to sew clothes and accessories for any beginning sewer. **Condition, good: $10.00 and up.**

80-P
A Ladybird Book Learning to Sew
Noreen Davis
Published by Wills & Hepworth Ltd., Loughborough,
    Leicestershire, England
Copyright by 1972 by Wills and Hepworth, Ltd.
52 pages and 17 sewing projects
Hardcover, 7" x 4½"

The cover of *A Ladybird Book Learning to Sew* is multicolored with crochet cotton, embroidery floss, sewing thread, a thimble, and needle at the top and stitches and a finished pincushion at the bottom.

A Ladybird Book Learning to Sew begins with making a table mat using a straight stitch with different colored yarns on binca canvas (aida cloth).

The rest of the projects include two different tablemats, pincushion, gingham tray cloth, jewelry pack, dressing table set, felt fish, comb case, hair band, round pincushion, needle case, felt toy, felt purse, doll's bonnet, doll's skirt, collage picture, and sewing card.

There are pages that show how to make decorative stitches, sew on a button and turn a hem. Excluding the table mats and doll's skirt, all the projects are done with felt, making it possible for the youngest sewer to complete a presentable sewing project.

A Ladybird Book Learning to Sew is a simple and rewarding all-color little book that any child learning to sew would enjoy. **Condition, good: $5.00 and up.**

81-P
A Ladybird Book About Knitting
Maureen and Michael Harvey
Published by Ladybird Books Ltd., (formerly Wills &
    Hepworth, Ltd.) Loughborough, England
Copyright 1972 by Ladybird Books Ltd.
52 pages with 9 knitting projects
Hardcover, 7" x 4½"

A Ladybird Book About Knitting has a gray cover and shows a pair of hands knitting a square, in the background are a pair of knitting needles, yarn, pencil case, and egg cozies.

This is an all-color book and starts out with knitting hints and supplies. There are instructions on casting on and knitting stitches with clear, precise pictures.

The projects are a hair band, pincushion, change purse, balls, egg cozies, doll's pram-blanket, pencil-case, drawstring bag, and a man's tie.

There are lessons on changing yarn and different ways to sew your knitting together. *A Ladybird Book About Knitting* is a

Popular Sewing and Needlework Books

comprehensive little book with simple projects for the beginner knitter. **Condition, good: $5.00 and up.**

82-P
Let Yourself Sew
Simplicity Pattern Co., Inc.
Published by Simplicity Pattern Co., Inc.
Copyright 1972 by Simplicity Pattern Co., Inc.
96 pages with sewing hints
Softcover, 10" x 8"

The cover of *Let Yourself Sew* has a teen-age girl in a red gingham dress trimmed with eyelet. She has her hand extended showing a sewing bird pincushion.

This is a *Sewing Book* for teen-agers. The Introduction reads:

Let yourself sew can be your "Open Sesame." How you express yourself is what Let yourself sew is all about. It's an indispensable guide to sewing and fashion and how to put them together. Your big-and little-questions are answered, with lots of pictures, tips, explanations and more to show you the way.

Let Yourself Sew has a little of everything in it, including wardrobe planning, trimmings, crochet, embroidery, applique, sewing techniques, marking and cutting patterns, fitting, operating a sewing machine and its accessories, and making your own sewing space, just to name a few. *Let Yourself Sew* would a wonderful book for the teen-age girl learning to sew. **Condition, good: $10.00 and up.**

83-P
Make It with Felt
Arden J. Newsome
Published by Lothrop, Lee & Shepard Co., N.Y.
Copyright in 1972 by Arden J. Newsome
96 pages with 37 felt projects
Hardcover, 9½" x 6½"

The cover of *Make It with Felt* is bright orange with a line drawing of a blue pumpkin mobile on the front cover. The lettering is on the spine in blue. I assume the book originally had a book jacket.

The chapters listed in the book include "Materials," "General Instructions," "For School," "Toys and Games," "For You and Your Room," "Gifts and Things," "For Holidays and Parties," and "Sources of Supplies."

The projects listed are, flower bookmark, whatsits pencil-case, school pennant, book cover, pencil topper, charming snake, monkey bean bag, ring puppet, bean-bag toss, building blocks, ball, bean-pole doll, Indian feathers, Indian tom-tom, beautiful bobby-pins, link belt, wampum pouch, bulletin board, flower tacks, pretty pillow, pear pot-holder, dog collar, kitty catnip-mouse, four seasons wall hanging, holiday place-cards, valentine heart-sachet, Easter egg, Easter pals, pumpkin-man mobile, Christmas napkin-rings, doorknob Christmas-tree,

Christmas stocking, and Christmas angel. The projects are clear with lots of patterns and illustrations. **Condition, good: $5.00 and up.**

84-P
Sew Your Own Accessories
Joellen Sommer with Elyse Sommer
Published by Lothrop, Lee & Shepard Co., N.Y., N.Y.
Copyright in 1972 by Joellen Sommer and Elyse Sommer
91 pages with 45 sewing projects
Hardcover, 9½" x 6¾"

The white dust jacket of *Sew Your Own Accessories* shows a teen-age girl wearing a yellow dress while showing off her orange accessories that were made using the book. The book itself is orange with a line drawing in the bottom left hand corner of a girl wearing slacks and suspenders. The title is on the spine only.

Joellen, a 15-year-old high school student wrote this book. Joellen learned to sew in junior high and has been sewing ever since, she especially likes to make accessories, as they are quick and inexpensive, requiring only small amounts of fabric.

Sew Your Own Accessories gives an introduction to the value of accessories in your wardrobe. The first chapters of the book are about tools, stitches and techniques. The projects listed in the other chapters are belts, hats, bags, jewelry, gifts, and room accessories.

There are some cute projects. I especially liked the patchwork-belt, shoulder bag made from an old pair of pants, and the Mexican burlap necklace. I can see a beginning teen-age sewer enjoying some of the projects in *Sew Your Own Accessories*, even today. **Condition, good: $10.00 and up.**

85-P
Yarn, the Things it Makes and How to Make Them
Carolyn Meyer
Published by Hardcourt Brace Jovanovich, Inc., N.Y., N.Y.
Copyright 1972 by Carolyn Meyer
125 pages with 25 projects
Hardcover, 9¼" x 7"

Yarn, the Things it Makes and How to Make Them has a plain green cover with its title in black only on the spine. The dust jacket is white with two knitting needles, a crochet hook and a sewing needle threaded with a piece of purple yarn winding around the title.

If you want to learn the yarn arts, this is the book for you. It is a guide to crocheting, knitting, weaving and macramé. Carolyn Meyer starts at the elementary level and introduces the projects so that each project builds on the previous one. Every step is illustrated with diagrams; as you master the techniques, she gives ideas and suggestions to be more creative.

The projects are divided into the four chapters. In the "Crochet" chapter are a yarn necklace, headband, belt, sunflower pillow, round mat, and granny skirt. Projects in the "Knitting"

318

chapter are a glass case, baby bunting, scarf, stocking cap, mittens, shoulder bag, blanket or scarf, and a poncho. The "Weaving" chapter has a bookmark, place mat, scent cushion, pillow, and a wall hanging. The "Macramé" chapter shows a watchband, belt, mat, suspenders, vest, and a sampler yarn bag.

The projects are easy, and most could still be used today.

Yarn, the Things it Makes and How to Make Them is a good book to introduce a child to the fiber arts. **Condition, good: $10.00 and up.**

86-P
Look! I Can Sew and Tie-Die and Batik Too!
Angela Burduck
Published by Octopus Books, Limited, London, England
Copyright 1973 by Angela Burduck
64 pages with 35 sewing projects
Hardcover, 12½" x 9½"

The cover of *Look! I Can Sew and Tie-Die and Batik Too!* has a blue and yellow background with three children holding projects made from the book that include hand puppets, a soft toy and dolls.

Look! I Can Sew and Tie-Die and Batik Too! was originally written in for British children, so there might be a bit of confusion about the wording. At times they have used both the British and American terms.

Look! I Can Sew and Tie-Die and Batik Too! has a cartoon-type drawings of three children, two boys and a girl, Dominic, Angela Grey, and Linus.

The first 11 pages give the introduction, 12 sewing stitches, including some embroidery stitches, equipment, cutting, pinning, and hints.

The projects include a needle book, freaky pig pin-cushion, lazy daisy egg-cozy, wrist band, baby-chick bib, hair band, wash cloth, reversible headscarf, see-how-you-grow chart, mobcap sun hat, snug muff, happy dolly, curly-haired doll, long-haired doll, doll's dress, pants and boots, doll's trouser suit and booties, wrap around skirt, calico cat and dog puppets, apron, cookie crocodile oven-glove, boy's shorts and tie, panda pajamas-case, jockey cap, patchwork bag, vest and pants, tee-shirt, pillowcase, apron, nightdress, place mats, toddler's tunic-top, and a table centerpiece.

The projects are cute and most can still be used today. I found some of the instructions a little confusing, even though the cover says the book is for kids, ages 6 to 16. I might give it to a 12-year old with some supervision, especially in the tie-dye and batik section. **Condition, good: $10.00 and up.**

87-P
My First Sewing Book
Edited by Helen Frazer
Published by Dean & Son, Ltd., London, England
Copyright 1973 by Paul Hamlyn, Pty., Limited
45 pages with 15 projects
Hardcover, 10½" x 8"

Plate 582. *My First Sewing Book* (87-P) Edited by Helen Frazer, 1973. A book for girls between the ages of 10 and 14 to learn to sew by hand and machine. *Fun Time easy sewing projects* (93-P) edited by Cameron and Margaret Yerian, 1975. A hand and machine *Sewing Book* with clever projects.

The cover of *My First Sewing Book* has a white background and a yellow insert with two young girls, one at table using a sewing machine the other girl standing threading a hand-sewing needle. A cat sleeps on the table and a dog sits on the floor.

The book is written for girls between ten and fourteen. It is all in color and the Plates are fun and interesting. The first pages are about sewing, hints, materials, measuring, cutting, hand-stitches, patterns and sewing machines. The first four projects are done by hand, the others by machine.

The projects are a pincushion wristwatch, table mats, egg cozy, covered coat hanger, pencil case, knitting-needle tidy, skirt, midi top, head scarf, apron, poncho, beach bag, make-up purse, Bob cap, and scuffs. *My First Sewing Book* is a cute book; one any young girl might enjoy. **Condition, good: $10.00 and up.**

Note: *My First Sewing Book* was first published in 1973 by Paul Hamlyn Pty. Limited. Text and plates were previously published in *Cooking, Knitting, Sewing for Girls.*

88-P
Costumes for Your Antique Dolls
Mary Morgan
Published by Merrimack Publishing Corp.
Original copyright 1908 by Henry Altemus & reprinted by
   Merrimack Publishing Corp., sometime after 1963
95 pages with 17 projects
Softcover, 8½" x 5½"

See original 1908 copy *How to Dress a Doll* (18-P)

Costumes for Your Antique Dolls. **Condition, good: $5.00 and up.**

Note: *How to Dress a Doll* was also published in 1973 by Dover Publications, Inc., and titled, *How to Dress an Old-Fashioned Doll* and has the same content.

Popular Sewing and Needlework Books

89-P
How to Dress an Old-Fashioned Doll
Mary Morgan
Published by Dover Publications, Inc.
Original Copyright 1908 by Henry Altemus and reprinted
    by Dover Publications, Inc. 1973
95 pages with 17 projects
Softcover, 8½" x 5¼"

See original 1908 copy *How to Dress a Doll* (18-P)
How to Dress an Old-Fashioned Doll. **Condition, good: $5.00 and up.**

Note: *How to Dress a Doll* was also published by Merrimack Publishing Corp. with no date and titled, *Costumes for Your Antique Doll* and has the same content.

90-P
How to Have Fun Sewing
Editors of Creative Educational Society
Published by Creative Education, Mankato, Minnesota.
Copyright 1974 by Creative Educational Society
31 Pages with 1, sewing project
Hardcover, 9¾" x 7½"

The cover of *How to Have Fun Sewing* has a red gingham top half and a red and pink stripe bottom half and there are two girls are sitting on the top edge of an oversized purse, one girl is sewing.

How to Have Fun Sewing is a simple book that gives a short history about sewing. The first part of the book shows how to tie a knot, do the running, basting, back, and overcast stitches, and sew-on a button.

The project is a small, fold-over purse, closing with a button. A primary school beginner sewer would find this book useful. **Condition, good: $10.00 and up.**

91-P
I Love to Sew
Barbara Corrigan
Published by Doubleday & Co., Inc., Garden City, N.Y.
Copyright 1974 by Barbara Corrigan
139 pages with 19 sewing projects
Hardcover, 9½" x 6½"

The cover of *I Love to Sew* is plain dark blue with red lettering on the spine only. The dust jacket has the title printed in yellow with a dark blue background. There are five pictures of things to sew from the book placed around the edges.

The book is written for children ages 9 through the teens. The beginning of *I Love to Sew* shows how to thread a needle, make a knot, various hand-sewing stitches and a very short lesson on the sewing machine. The projects are well written and illustrated.

The projects include fringed place mats and napkins, fringed table runner, drawstring bag, envelope bag, belt, scarf,

hat, curtains, pillows, wall hanging, stuffed toys, hand puppets, gathered skirt, ankle-length skirt, wrap around skirt, pants, tops, apron, and 11½" teen doll clothes.

Some of the projects are dated the but younger children would still like them. The 11½" teen doll clothing is simple and attractive and has full-size patterns. **Condition, good: $10.00 and up.**

92-P
Dolls for Children to Make
Suzy Ives
Published by B T Batsford, Limited, Great Britain
Copyright 1975 by Suzy Ives
96 pages with 24 doll projects
Hardcover, 9" x 5½"

Dolls for Children to Make has a black cover with a gold title on the spine. The dust cover is brown, green and pink with a stylized Red Riding Hood doll in the center.

Dolls for Children to Make is an interesting book with the pattern for one standard doll that can be made into 24 different characters. The doll is about 5" tall and 3" wide, is dome shaped, has no arms and legs, but does have feet.

The characters include Little Red Riding Hood, Granny, Grandpa, Blushing Bride, Thorgrimmor Irontoe the Viking Chieftain, Carmen Miranda, Bill the Burglar, Lieutenant Ffyfe-Smith, Blodwyn Jones, Lotus Blossom, Sister Florence, Black Jack the Highwayman, Poppy Fothergill the Flapper Girl, Batman/Superman, Minnie Ho Ho the Squaw, Witch, Slim Jim the Cowboy, Ballerina, Monsieur Flambé the Chef, Mexican Pete, Robin Hood, Queen Philomena, King Egbert, and The Angel.

The dolls are cute and are simple to make most little girls would love to make them for a shelf or dresser. There are many possibilities and the variety could be endless. **Condition, good: $10.00 and up.**

93-P
Fun Time Activities Easy Sewing Projects
Edited by Cameron and Margaret Yerian
Published by Childrens Press, Chicago.
Copyright 1975 by Regensteiner Publishing Enterprises, Inc.
47 pages with 15 sewing projects
Hardcover, 9½" x 8"

Fun Time Activities Easy Sewing Projects is a "Fun Time Activities book." The cover is green and white with a white ghost like thing, sitting on a stool and sewing on a striped toy cat while a real cat sits by snarling at the toy cat.

Fun Time Activities Easy Sewing Projects has two-parts, "Finger Work" and "Stuffies." In the "Finger Work" section are six projects, a stitch dictionary (stitch sample card), letter-perfect pencil holder, strip quilt, fringed place mats, napkins and picture stitchery.

The "Stuffies" section projects are, pillows, punchy-pairs pillows, Tubby T pillows, Manfred mouse, people pals, puzzle pillow, fabric tube, beach flip-flop, and Percy pop-up puppet.

Fun Time Activities Easy Sewing Projects is all in color and the projects are easy with lots of diagrams. **Condition, good: $10.00 and up.**

Note: The Childrens Press also published a book named Fun Time macrame, knitting & weaving.

94-P
Simple Sewing
Gretchen Beede
Published by Lerner Publications Co., Minneapolis, Minn.
Copyright 1975 by Lerner Publications Co.
32 pages with 6 sewing projects
Hardcover, 7½" x 7½"

Simple Sewing has a yellow cover with a child sewing sitting, cross-legged on the floor with a sewing basket in the foreground and a calico cat looking on.

The contents of *Simple Sewing* include "Why People Sew," "Tools and Materials," "Using a Pattern," "Learning the Basic Stitches," "A Stuffed Animal," "A Beach Coat," "A Matching Tote Bag," and "Making an Apron."

In the "Using a Pattern" chapter, a needle book is made and in the "Learning the Basic Stitches" chapter, a bookmark is made. The apron project is suitable for a boy as well as a girl to make, as it can be a tool or barbecue apron.

Simple Sewing is written simply and would be helpful in teaching a child how to sew; the projects are fun and up to date. **Condition, good: $10.00 and up.**

95-P
Dolls for Ages 8 and Up
Molly Ziemer and Jean Sperry
Published by Taurus Publications & Design Center,
 Pleasanton, Calif.
Copyright 1977 by Taurus Publications
19 pages with 7 doll projects
Softcover, 10" x 8½"

The cover has a white background with *Dolls for Ages 8 and Up* printed in red. The cover art shows a little girl in a big hat in front of a dressing table. There are two dolls on the table, one on a stool and two more on the floor.

Dolls for Ages 8 and Up is one of a series of books for ages 8 and up. The first page gives all the stitches needed for making the seven dolls. The dolls included are a powder puff doll, helper doll, Sally sock-doll, Carolyn crayon, Gina the glamour doll, Pollyanna the pajama doll, and clothespin people.

Although the title says ages 8 and up, I think an eight-year-old would have some problem in following the instructions and patterns without adult assistance. The dolls are cute, and with the help of an adult would be fun to make. **Condition, good: $10.00 and up.**

Popular Sewing and Needlework Books

96-P
It's Easy to Sew with Scraps and Remnants
Carol Inouye
Published by Doubleday & Company, Inc., N.Y., N.Y.
Copyright 1977 by Carol Inouye
123 pages with 34+ sewing projects
Hardbound 8½" x 5½"

It's Easy to Sew with Scraps and Remnants has a blue cover and green binding with its title printed in gold. The dust jacket is a patchwork print with a denim pocket and an appliquéd flower under the title.

The book has a lot of ideas crammed into it. The introduction states:

Whether you are a beginner or an accomplished sewer, you can design your own clothes and create you own accessories. This book will show you how you can have fun and sew something out of recycled fabrics or remnants for practically nothing! Use this book only as a steppingstone to create your own things. Let your imagination soar and don't be afraid to experiment.

It's Easy to Sew with Scraps and Remnants teaches about fabrics, patterns, tools and finishing stitches. It also covers how to remodel old clothing, make accessories, toys and games, things for the house, and holiday gifts all from recycled fabric or scraps and remnants.

The projects include, tank tops, T-shirts, sweaters, blouses, pants, skirt, halter top bikini top, bikini bottom, blouse, patchwork skirt, peasant dress, towel caftan, towel slippers, barbecue apron, hostess apron, poncho, patchwork stole, ribbon belt, ribbon-weave tote bag, beach bag, old-fashioned cap, pendants, chess board, beanbag frog, stuffed shark, hand puppet, pocket place-mat, potholder, pocket organizer, patchwork bedspread, heart pillow, lion's mask, zodiac hanging, Christmas ornaments, and a Christmas stocking.

It's Easy to Sew with Scraps and Remnants is an interesting book with lots inexpensive creative possibilities for a beginner as well as an experienced sewer. **Condition, good: $10.00 and up.**

97-P
Sewing with Yarn
Barbara C. Schwartz
Published by J. B. Lippincott, Philadelphia & New York
Copyright 1977 by Barbara C. Schwartz
80 pages with 15 sewing projects
Hardcover, 9¼" x 7"

Sewing with Yarn has a bright blue cover with a white patch trimmed in a red blanket stitch and the book's title spelled out in red, black and blue yarn.

An introduction to *Sewing By Hand* is printed under the title.

Big needles and big thread are easy for youngsters to handle. Yarn sewing can be done quickly, enabling a child to finish a project before they become bored.

The projects are pillows, pincushion, potholder, sweatband,

321

Popular Sewing and Needlework Books

drawstring bag, chef's apron, carpenter's apron, lion cub pillow, owl pillow, dog pillow, halter, eye mask, stocking cap, place mat, and a wall hanging. The items are simple and so very seventies, a lot of burlap and felt is used. **Condition, good: $10.00 and up.**

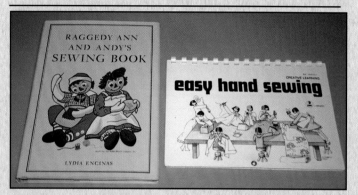

Plate 583. *Raggedy Ann and Andy's Sewing Book* (**98-P**) by Lydia Encinas, 1977. A romp with Raggedy Ann and Andy as they teach you how to sew, make presents and neat things for your room. *Easy hand sewing* (**99-P**) by DMC library, 1978. How to embellish and decorate with hand sewing.

98-P
Raggedy Ann and Andy's Sewing Book
Lydia Encinas
Published by The Bobbs-Merrill Co., Inc., Indianapolis & New York
Copyright 1977 by The Bobbs-Merrill Co., Inc.
125 pages with 12 sewing projects
Hardcover, 9½" x 6½"

Who else but Raggedy Ann and Andy would be on the cover of *Raggedy Ann and Andy's Sewing Book*? Raggedy Andy is stitching a patch on a pillow and Raggedy Ann is doing cross-stitch in a hoop. The background is a mint green with black lettering.

Raggedy Ann and Andy's Sewing Book is a cute book with clear and easy sewing diagrams done in black and white. The real treat is the 15 color Raggedy Ann and Andy pictures, mostly from the early books, 1917 to 1939 but also including a Christmas one with Santa from 1975. The pictures are scattered throughout the book, relating to the sewing projects.

The book starts off with sewing tips, helpful hints, and home safety tips and then goes right into the projects. The projects are a square purse for your belt, happy face pajama bag, work apron, drawstring toy bag, multicolor floor cube, toss game, tic-tac-toe game, star eyeglass case, puppet bath mitt, patchwork pillow, black cat costume, and Robin Hood costume. The projects are cute and seem fairly easy for a child to make. **Condition, good: $25.00 and up.**

99-P
Easy Hand Sewing
Unknown author
Published by Arts Graphiques DMC-Mulhouse, France

Copyright 1978 by DMC Library
63 pages with sewing ideas
Softcover, 6" x 8½"

A drawing of a large sewing table with eight little girls sewing is the artwork on the cover of *Easy Hand Sewing*. A delightful little book packed full of fun stitches and ideas.

Easy Hand Sewing makes into an easel and has a spiral spine for ease in using, so it can be set up to be referred to when learning a stitch. The chapters consist of basic stitches, joining pieces together, pretty edgings, and adding fullness and openings.

For instance the fullness chapter in *Easy Hand Sewing* suggests that instead of just gathering the fabric and securing it in a seam you might mount the gathers on the outside with back stitches in pretty thread. Or you might do a wavy gather with colored thread that looks like smocking, or honeycomb, or ribbon smocking.

If you want to make your garments special using hand sewing, this is the book for you. An adult as well as a child would enjoy this book. **Condition, good: $25.00 and up.**

100-P
My First Show Me How Sewing Book
Jill Wallis
Published in 1981 by Dean and Son, Ltd., London, England
Copyright 1973 by Paul Hamlyn, Pty., Limited
45 pages with 15 projects
Hardcover, 10½" x 8"

My First Show Me How Sewing Book has the same text and plates as *My First Sewing Book* the only difference is this books cover has a bright green background instead of white. See 88-P for content. **Condition, good: $5.00 and up.**

Plate 584. *Busy Little Hands Sewing* (**101-P**) edited by Editor Rona Kemp, 1988, A parent-and-child workbook on the craft of sewing. *Learning to Sew Can Be Fun* (**102-P**) by Judy Schenck, 1989. A workbook of step-by-step lessons designed especially for children.

101-P
Busy Little Hands Sewing
Edited by Rona Kemp

Published by The Hamlyn Publishing Group Limited,
    London, England
Copyright 1988 by Robert Mathias Editions
30 pages with 12 sewing projects
Hardcover, 10½" x 8"

The cover of *Busy Little Hands Sewing* has a white background with two dressed rabbits, a girl and boy. The girl rabbit is looking on while the boy rabbit sews a patch on the back of a teddy bear's pants and a sewing kit is at the bottom of the drawing.

Busy Little Hands Sewing is such fun to look at. It is filled with little creatures on every page, the majority being rabbits, mice and teddy bears. It is a parent-and-child book, encouraging the parent to supervise the work; the projects are marked with a star if adult help is needed. Some of the patterns are full-size others are reduced size on a grid.

The first couple of pages of *Busy Little Hands Sewing* show how to get started and the simple stitches needed to master the projects. The projects are a leaf needle-case, prickly pincushion, butterfly mobile, pencil case and desk tidy, alphabet patches, pirate fancy dress, patchwork night-case, elephant apron, Neptune mask, jester's crown, lazy basset, and a drawstring bag.

Busy Little Hands Sewing is a delightful little book the simple cute projects are sure to entice the littlest sewer. **Condition, good: $10.00 and up.**

102-P
Learning to Sew Can Be Fun
Judy Schenck
Published by Pot of Gold, San Diego, California
Copyright 1989 by Judy A. Schenck
320 pages with 20 projects
Softcover, 11" x 9"

Learning to Sew Can Be Fun has a white and black background with an ABC bag, cloud, balloons, Christmas stocking, clown and bib on the cover.

The author Judy Schenck writes: *This book was written to be used as the "teacher."*

This book can also be used as a guide for mothers, grandmothers, aunts, neighbors, or friends or anyone who would like to assist children in their desire to learn to sew. It includes step-by-step instructions for enjoyable sewing projects and is designed to teach by progression. Each project is a little more difficult than the last, but not so hard as to discourage the student.

The projects include a fragrant sachet, sewing and fitting a book cover, measuring and sewing a fun bag, cutting out and edging an apron, remaking a potholder, fabric picture-book, pillowcase, tissue-box cover, sock rabbit, heart pillow, fabric tool-kit, Christmas stocking, wall balloons, sewing machine cover, rainbow cloud, beanbag clown, sewing basket, and skirt.

The last chapter teaches how to use patterns. *Learning to Sew Can Be Fun* is a large book with a spiral binding and lots of instructions and diagrams. **Condition, good: $25.00 and up.**

Plate 585. *Busy Bee Pack* (**103-P**) by Susannah Bradley, 1991. Learn simple sewing, embroidery, knitting, and crochet. *My Little House Sewing Book* (**118-P**) by Margaret Irwin, 1997. Eight projects from Laura Ingalls Wilder's classic stories.

103-P
Busy Bee Pack
Susannah Bradley
Published 1991 by Henderson Publishing, Ltd. & 1992
    The Mad Hatter, Inc. California
Copyright 1991 by Henderson Publishing, Ltd. & 1992
    The Mad Hatter, Inc.
30 pages with 17 needlework projects
Softcover, 11" x 8½"

Busy Bee Pack has a colorful cover with a big, bright red flower on a blue background with three bumble bees holding needles in their mouths while stitching in red the book's title.

Busy Bee Pack is a book and packet combined, it teaches sewing, embroidery, knitting, patchwork, and crochet. The book itself has 15 pages and on the back cover is a pocket that holds the Busy Bee Project Book, a transfer sheet for embroidery, pattern sheet, quilting templates, window card mount, and a Busy Bee ruler marked in inches and centimeters.

The Busy Bee Project Book has color pictures and diagrams on how to accomplish each needle-art with tips and lists of what you need. It also gives you the patterns and tools to make the projects.

The projects are a Busy Bee emblem, sewn hair-scrunchie, pincushion, knitted scarf, crochet square, crochet bag, knitting brooch, bookmark, sparkly hair-bow, cotton cat, quilted booties, braided rag rugs, crochet choker, knitted finger puppets, baby's door hanging, personal patchwork cushion cover, and a patchwork pincushion.

The instructions and projects in *Busy Bee Pack* are simple and easy to understand and would help any child to learn all five needle-arts. **Condition, good: $10.00 and up.**

104-P
Make Clothes Fun
Kim Solga
Published by F. & W. Publications, Inc., Cincinnati, Ohio
Copyright 1992 by F. & W. Publications, Inc.

Popular Sewing and Needlework Books

48 pages with 10 needlework projects
Hardcover, 11" x 8½"

A white background with felt squares, buttons, decorated tennis shoes, and sweatshirt is on the cover of *Make Clothes Fun*.

Both boys and girls are introduced to ways of decorating their clothing and sewing is sometimes involved, along with craft type projects. In a Note to Grownups the author states:

The emphasis is on fun. Kids will love working with fabrics and fabric paint, sewing, weaving, embroidering, tie-dyeing, decorating with materials from buttons, to lace, to studs, and designing caps and team insignia patches.

In *Make Clothes Fun* there are pages on work habits such as asking permission from an adult to do the project, following directions, cleaning up, how to treat your tools, etc.

The projects include decorating shoelaces, painting T-shirts, button designs, design patches, soda-straw weaving, critter caps, towel tops, cloth collage, jacket jazz, and tie-dye. A fun and creative book for the 6 to 11 ages group. **Condition, good: $10.00 and up.**

105-P
My First Sewing Book
Winky Cherry
Published by Palmer/Pletsch, Inc., Portland, Oregon
Copyright 1992 by Palmer/Pletsch, Inc.
40 pages with 2 sewing projects
Softcover, 8½" x 8½"

My First Sewing Book has a white cover with black lettering. There is a red tomato pincushion in the right hand corner and a needle with thread circling the title.

My First Sewing Book was written in rhyme for 5 to 11 year-olds. It comes in a plastic bag with pre-cut felt materials to make two projects. The projects, complete with thread, are a large and small bird to sew and stuff.

An item list is given to complete the projects such as fiber-fill, needles, etc. There is a complete page with 18 more shapes to be enlarged and copied on a copy machine for the child to sew around and stuff. *My First Sewing Book* is a simple and fun way to teach a young child sewing. **Condition, good: $10.00 and up.**

Note: "My First" is a series of books put out by Winky Cherry to teach children to sew. The others are *My First Doll Book* (110-P), *My First Machine Sewing Book* (111-P), *My First Embroidery Book* (109-P), *My First Patchwork Book*, and *My First Quilt Book*. Finding these books on the secondary market means you may not get them with the supplies listed, however the supplies are easy to find in any craft store and the books can be used with your own supplies.

106-P
I'll Teach Myself 1 — Sewing Machine Fun

Nancy Smith & Lynda Milligan
Published by Possibilities, Denver, Colorado
Copyright 1993 by Lynda Milligan & Nancy Smith
71 pages with 10 sewing projects
Softcover, 9½" x 7½"

I'll Teach Myself 1-Sewing Machine Fun has a bright blue cover with a red, yellow, and orange sewing machine and a green and yellow checked border at the bottom.

This is sewing today. It's a fun book that teaches the parts of the sewing machine and how to use them. There are games and puzzles to test your skill on the sewing machine that are not only fun, but you learn as you play.

I'll Teach Myself 1-Sewing Machine Fun has you stitching without thread, using paper, to play games of skill using curves and pivots. There are crossword puzzles and guessing games, even jokes.

The first sewing is thread pictures, dot to dot, then brown paper shapes. The rest of the projects are greeting cards (two kinds), custom envelopes (no sewing), soft shape heart, soft shape bunny, button-up dog or cat, and "possibilities pocket."

If there is a project that you really enjoy doing, you can send for more patterns or kits. *I'll Teach Myself 1-Sewing Machine Fun* is a fun way to get your child interested in the sewing machine. **Condition, good: $10.00 and up.**

Note: *I'll Teach Myself 1-Sewing Machine Fun* is book one in a series of 5 I'll Teach Myself Sewing Books. *I'll Teach Myself 2 — More Sewing Machine Fun* (107-P), *I'll Teach Myself 3 — Step Into Patchwork* (108-P), *I'll Teach Myself 4 — Gifts to Give* (116-P), *The Best of Sewing Machine Fun for Kids* (125-P).

107-P
I'll Teach Myself 2 — More Sewing Machine Fun
Nancy Smith & Lynda Milligan
Published by Possibilities, Denver, Colorado
Copyright 1993 by Lynda S. Milligan & Nancy J. Smith
71 pages with 7 sewing projects
Softcover, 9½" x 7½"

I'll Teach Myself 2 — More Sewing Machine Fun has a black background with a tomato pincushion, spool of thread, a pair of sewing shears, and an orange-and-yellow checked border at the bottom.

This book is an extension of *I'll Teach Myself 1 — Sewing Machine Fun*. It reinforces skills learned in the first book and introduces new techniques and more games, jokes, puzzles, mazes, and fun.

The projects are button-up Bossie cow, character pillow or picture, book covers, hair bunchies, lunch bags, burger bites, and a treasure pouch. This is another book of fun with the sewing machine. **Condition, good: $10.00 and up.**

Note: *I'll Teach Myself 2 — More Sewing Machine Fun* is book two in a series of 5 I'll Teach Myself Sewing Books,

I'll Teach Myself 1 — Sewing Machine Fun (106-P), *I'll Teach Myself 3 — Step Into Patchwork* (108-P), *I'll Teach Myself 4 — Gifts to Give* (116-P), *The Best of Sewing Machine Fun for Kids* (125-P).

108-P
I'll Teach Myself 3 — Step Into Patchwork
Nancy J. Smith & Lynda S. Milligan
Published by Possibilities, Denver, Colorado
Copyright 1994 by Lynda S. Milligan & Nancy J. Smith
71 pages with 8 sewing projects
Softcover, 9½" x 7½"

A bright purple background with red and green squares and a black-and-white check border at the bottom adorns the cover of *I'll Teach Myself 3 — Step Into Patchwork.*

This book explains the parts of a quilt, types of blocks, and templates. It starts the patchwork with paper strips to create "write-ons," including a message board, card, and door hanger. More paper squares create fun notes, sunshades, and game boards.

The fabric projects are beanbags, a cover up (small quilt), and cozy pillows. There are lots of games and jokes, mazes, searches, and fun. A very creative way to teach patchwork. **Condition, good: $10.00 and up.**

Note: *I'll Teach Myself 3 — Step Into Patchwork* is one book in a series of 5 I'll Teach Myself Sewing Books. *I'll Teach Myself 1 — Sewing Machine Fun, I'll Teach Myself 2 — More Sewing Machine Fun* (107-P), *I'll Teach Myself 4 — Gifts to Give* (116-P), *The Best of Sewing Machine Fun for Kids* (125-P).

109-P
My First Embroidery Book
Winky Cherry
Published by Palmer/Pletsch Publishing, Inc. Portland,
  Oregon
Copyright by 1994 by Palmer/Pletsch Publishing, Inc.
40 pages with 1 project (name sampler)
Softcover, 8½" x 8½"

My First Embroidery Book has a white cover with black lettering. There is a blue gingham sampler in a hoop at the top and green stitches surround the title.

It is written in rhyme for 7 to 11 year-olds and teaches straight-stitch embroidery on gingham. The project included is a sampler with embroidery stitches and the child's name. There is a shopping list for items needed to complete the sampler. Included with the book are an 8" wooden embroidery hoop, gingham fabric, flannel-backing fabric, and five colors of crochet floss.

My First Embroidery Book teaches children to embroider their name on a sampler using horizontal, vertical, and diagonal straight stitches, cross-stitch, and satin stitch. **Condition, good: $10.00 and up.**

Note: "My First" is a series of books put out by Winky Cherry to teach children to sew. The others are *My First Sewing Book* (105-P), *My First Doll Book* (110-P), *My First Machine Sewing Book* (111-P), My *First Patchwork Book,* and *My First Quilt Book.* Finding these books on the secondary market means you may not get them with the supplies listed, however the supplies are easy to find in any craft store and the books can be used with your own supplies.

110-P
My First Doll Book
Winky Cherry
Published by Palmer/Pletsch Publishing, Inc., Portland,
  Oregon
Copyright by 1994 by Palmer/Pletsch Publishing, Inc,
40 pages with 4 doll projects
Softcover, 8½" x 8½"

My First Doll Book has a white cover with a cookie-shaped doll wearing a blue dress in the upper left corner. The lettering is black with blue stitches surrounding the title.

The book is written in rhyme for 5 to 11 year-olds. It gives instructions to make a felt doll, complete with embroidered face, yarn hair, and clothing. Included with the book are two felt cutout dolls (two different skin tones,) crochet thread and yarn for hair. There is also a shopping list for supplies needed to complete your dolls.

My First Doll Book shows you how to cut out your dolls, mark them, sew, attach yarn hair, and make clothing for them. There are four full-size patterns in the book for the dolls — Mom, Dad, Child, and Baby — and patterns for clothing for the child doll. The other size dolls have instructions on making patterns for them. **Condition, good: $10.00 and up.**

Note: "My First" is a series of books put out by Winky Cherry to teach children to sew. The others are *My First Sewing Book* (105-P), *My First Doll Book* (110-P), *My First Sewing Machine Sewing Book* (111-P), *My First Patchwork Book,* and *My First Quilt Book.* Finding these books on the secondary market means you may not get them with the supplies listed, however the supplies are easy to find in any craft store and the books can be used with your own supplies.

111-P
My First Machine Sewing Book
Winky Cherry
Published by Palmer/Pletsch Publishing, Inc., Portland,
  Oregon
Copyright by 1994 by Palmer/Pletsch Publishing, Inc.
40 pages with 2 sewing projects Softcover, 8½" x 8½"

My First Machine Sewing Book has a white cover with a gold sewing machine in the upper left corner. The lettering is black with a purple dotted line around the edges of the cover.

My First Machine Sewing Book is written for ages 7 to 11.

Popular Sewing and Needlework Books

It introduces them to the sewing machine as they first use practice papers and then fabric to sew a star. Basic sewing concepts are taught such as seam allowances and turning right side out. Rhymes and silly names for machine parts help children remember information and rules.

There is a full page to be enlarged and copied on a copy machine of more shapes to sew and stuff. Included with the book are seven practice sewing sheets and fabric for two stars. **Condition, good: $10.00 and up.**

Note: "My First" is a series of books put out by Winky Cherry to teach children to sew. The others are *My First Sewing Book* (105-P), *My First Embroidery Book* (109-P), *My First Doll Book* (110-P), *My First Patchwork Book* and *My First Quilt Book*. Finding these books on the secondary market means you may not get them with the supplies listed, however the supplies are easy to find in any craft store and the books can be used with your own supplies.

112-P
Sewing by Hand
Christine Hoffman
Published by Scholastic Inc., N.Y., Toronto, London,
    Auckland, & Sydney
Copyright 1994 text by Christine Hoffman
29 pages with 3 sewing projects
Softcover, 10½" x 8½"

A white background, a dancing red cat with yellow spots, stork scissors, a tomato pincushion, and two spools of thread are scattered on the cover of *Sewing by Hand*.

Sewing by Hand is a very simple, easy-to-read Sewing Book. There are lots of easy diagrams and the print is large for beginners to read. The first three chapters are "Tools," "Materials," and "Sewing Skills."

The projects are circle pillow, beanbag cat, and a flower girl doll. All the items are sewn with either a running, back or overhand stitch. The projects are cute and the book is interesting enough to keep a child busy. **Condition, good: $5.00 and up.**

Note: *Sewing by Hand* is a Scholastic Edition and is only available for distribution through school and on the secondary market.

113-P
Starting Needlecraft
Ray Gibson
Published by Usborne Publishing, Ltd., London, England
Copyright 1994 by Usborne Publishing, Ltd.
32 pages with 13 needlework projects
Softcover, 9½" x 8"

The cover of *Starting Needlecraft* has a white background with red lettering. In the center is a brown teddy bear with his hot water bottle and around the edges are sewing supplies.

The first page of this book starts out with the projects which include Christmas tree wall-hanging, large net-fish,

pom-pon bug, wizard puppet, Dracula puppet, frog pincushion, pocket mice, juggling bags, teddy's sleeping bag, hair scrunchy, tiger needle case, cross-stitch card, and clown.

The projects are easy and simple, yet they are very rewarding when finished. The book is very colorful and contains all the patterns and instructions to make each project. *Starting Needlecraft* is a book that any youngster who wants to learn sewing should own. **Condition, good: $10.00 and up.**

Note: *Starting Needlecraft* is also sold with a sewing kit to make four of the projects: the frog pincushion, teddy bear sleeping bag, pocket mouse, the three juggling bags plus a bonus project, a friendship bracelet.

114-P
Dolls Kids Can Make
Sheila McGraw
Published by Firefly Books, Buffalo, N.Y.
Copyright 1995 by Sheila McGraw
72 pages with 11 doll projects
Softcover, 11" x 8½"

The cover of *Dolls Kids Can Make* has photos of four colorful dolls on a white background with the title in block letters in black.

The projects are cute and fairly quick, but do need some sewing skill. There are step-by-step instructions for each project and a sewing glossary in the back of the book with some stitches and explanations.

The projects are a stretch glove doll, terry facecloth doll, sock baby, walnut head angel, paper angel, stocking-face witch, potpourri lace doll, granny mop doll, panty-hose doll, rag dudes, and a Little Red Riding Hood and wolf double doll.

A child needs a fair amount of sewing experience to be able to use this book. I think *Dolls Kids Can Make* would make a good gift for a teen-ager or an adult, but it's not for a beginner sewer. **Condition, good: $10.00 and up.**

115-P
A Kid's First Book of Sewing
Alison Snepp
Published by Murdoch Books, Sydney, Australia
Copyright 1995 by Murdoch Books
63 pages with 21 sewing projects
Softcover, 10" x 8¼"

A Kid's First Book of Sewing has a cover with a white background and a girl of about 10 wearing a print backpack, behind her is a trimmed towel, washcloth, and jewelry tote, all items included in this book. There is a *Family Circle* magazine logo in the upper right hand corner.

A Kid's First Book of Sewing is a book for a child of 10 to 13 years of age. The projects include gifts, as well as simple clothing a girl would love to wear. The first chapter discusses sewing with a machine and finishing articles by hand. Hand sewing stitches are shown in each chapter when they are appropriate to the project. All patterns are done in centimeters.

The projects are a midriff top, long pants, dirndl skirt, scrunchie, potholder, oven mitts, Eco bag, teddy-bear bed linens, backpack, lavender sachet, pincushion and needle case, stationery holder, pencil case, cross-stitch napkins, face cloth, hand towel, patchwork cushion, glasses case, slumber-party bag, pillowcase, and jewelry roll up.

The items are modern and cute and a color photograph is shown of each project. A child as well as an adult would enjoy using *A Kid's First Book of Sewing*. This would be a good book for fast bazaar items or gifts. **Condition, good: $10.00 and up.**

116-P
I'll Teach Myself 4 — Gifts to Give
Nancy J. Smith & Lynda S. Milligan
Published by Possibilities Publishers, Denver, Colorado
Copyright 1996 by Nancy J. Smith & Lynda S. Milligan
71 pages with 12+ sewing projects
Softcover, 9½" x 7½"

I'll Teach Myself 4 — Gifts to Give is printed on a yellow cover with three stylized gift boxes decorated in stripes, stars, and checks.

This book is a hand-sewing book and all the projects are done with just three stitches: running, overcast, and blanket.

The projects are felt magnets, button magnets, greeting cards, place mats, calendar quilt, holiday stockings, snowmen, snowmen wall hanging, "warmies" headband, "warmies" mittens, and "warmies" scarf.

There are lots of full-size patterns and games to play as you work through the book. The projects are simple, yet satisfying. **Condition, good: $10.00 and up.**

Note: *I'll Teach Myself 4 — Gifts to Give* is the forth in a series of 5 I'll Teach Myself books. *I'll Teach Myself 1 — Sewing Machine Fun Book* (106-P), *I'll Teach Myself 2 — More Sewing Machine Fun* (107-P), *I'll Teach Myself 3 — Step Into Patchwork* (108-P), *The Best of Sewing Machine Fun for Kids* (125-P).

117-P
Kids Can Quilt
Barbara J. Eikmeier
Published by That Patchwork Place, Brothell, Washington
Copyright 1997 by Barbara J. Eikmeier
79 pages with 4 sewing projects and 13 block patterns
Softcover, 11" x 8½"

The cover of *Kids Can Quilt* shows an adult supervising and two children sewing — a girl at a sewing machine and a boy sewing by hand. In the background is a twelve-patch quilt wall hanging.

The book was written with the focus on teaching a child to stitch. The instructions are written for a one-on-one teaching. The projects are intended to be made in partnership with an adult, however there is a chapter on teaching kids in a group.

The blocks are simple, yet interesting to put together. The block patterns are snowman, heart, clover, rabbit, tulip, beach ball, flag, watermelon, apple, cat, pumpkin, Santa, and basket. The projects are bottle-cap pincushion, sewing bag, pillow, and an ornament.

Kids Can Quilt covers such things as techniques, quilt plans, and finishing. I would love to try some of these projects myself. This book is interesting enough for an adult as well as a child. **Condition, good: $10.00 and up.**

118-P
My Little House Sewing Book
Margaret Irwin
Published by Harper Festival, a division of Harper Collins
   Publishers, Inc.
Copyright 1997 by Margaret Irwin
60 pages with 8 sewing projects
Softcover, 10" x 8"

The cover of *My Little House Sewing Book* is edged in pink-and-cream gingham. In a cream-colored background is a prairie sunbonnet in purple, a doll with an apron and a needlebook; all projects found in the book.

The first three chapters are "Sewing Supplies," "Sewing Skills," and "Good Basics for Sewing." Each project includes a short story telling why it was made and who made it for whom.

My Little House Sewing Book, named after, Laura Ingalls Wilder's classic stories has entwined the sewing projects with the characters we know so well. The projects include Ma's needle book, Laura's nine patch pillow, Carrie's lace-edged handkerchief, Mary's braided rug, Laura's embroidered picture frame, Alice's embroidered sampler, Laura's doll apron (fits an 16" to 18" doll), and Laura's prairie sunbonnet.

In the back of *My Little House Sewing Book* is a pocket with a flap to keep the full-size patterns. The book is fully illustrated with color pictures and the projects are simple and attractive. This is a nice first *Sewing Book* for a little girl. **Condition, good: $10.00 and up.**

119-P
Kids Knitting
Melanie Falick
Published by Artisan, a division of Workman Publishing Co.,
   N.Y., N.Y.
Copyright 1998 by Melanie Falick
127 pages with 15 knitting projects
Hardcover, 9" x 8½"

The cover of *Kids Knitting* is a shiny purple with the title in white on the spine. One word describes the dust cover of this book: color! *Kids Knitting* is spelled out in bright colors, there are six squares three show kids knitting and three show projects from the book.

The book starts out with learning about tools and yarn. Very shortly we are learning how to finger knit, and spool knit, dye our yarn with Kool-Aid and making knitting needles from dowel sticks and decorating them with polka-dots and acorn caps.

The projects are a basic beanbag, pocket scarf-and-hat set, patchwork afghan, kids knitting tote-bag (fabric), garter-stitch dolls, owl and pussycat bath puppets, crazy caterpillar, wrap-around ribbed scarf, backpack, eyeglass case, purse, wizards cap, spiral tube-socks, swatch scarf, fuzzy-felt balls, and curly-edge pullover sweater.

All through *Kids Knitting* there are suggestions, tips, new stitches, and patterns. This book teaches all types of knitting, including three-needle and circular knitting.

In the back of the book are common abbreviations for knitting terms and how to read a pattern. *Kids Knitting* is a very complete book for a beginner knitter, child or adult. **Condition, good: $10.00 and up.**

120-P
Sewing with Kids from Country Stitches
Anita Covert PhD and Deb Lathrop VanAken
Published by Country Stitches Ltd.
Copyright 1998 by Country Stitches Ltd.
96 pages with over 50 projects
Softcover, 11" x 8½"

The cover of *Sewing with Kids from Country Stitches* is purple fading to red with a diagram of a modern sewing machine in yellow and white. The lettering is done in white.

The book starts with an introduction, guidelines, and the Golden Rules of sewing. There is a sample class for beginners and learning about the sewing machine. But best of all is the projects they are too numerous to list except for the subtitles. The subtitles include bags of all kinds, clothing and accessories, gifts for mom, dad, and others, stuffed animals, dolls and their accessories, things for your room, and miscellaneous. There are drawn patterns and how to measure to make your own.

The projects seem to be easy and there are so many to choose from there should be something to please every child. The projects are all listed in the contents and the easy projects are marked. Some of the projects are water bottle cover, mittens, shirt-dress, stuffed cat, doll quilt, holiday ornament and zippered purse, Duffel bag, fleece scarf, crazy novelty shirt, patch vest, log cabin photo block, quilted potholder, stuffed bear, stuffed cat, sleeping bag liner, summer blanket, windsock, and tooth fairy pillow.

At the end of the book are sewing techniques, sewing terms, troubleshooting tips, and sources. The book is recommended for children ten and up. **Condition, good: $10.00 and up.**

121-P
Simple Sewing
Editors of Klutz
Published by Klutz Publishing Co., Palo Alto, California
Copyright 1999 by Klutz
46 pages with 7 projects
Softcover, 9" x 9½"

The cover for *Simple Sewing* has a background of blue denim with a dotted ribbon and a small felt flower at the corner of a small picture of two girls sewing. Attached to the cover is a see-through zipper pouch that contains sewing materials.

The first chapter of *Simple Sewing* starts out with sewing basics, pinning on a pattern and cutting it out, threading the needle and tying a knot and three basic stitches, straight, hem, and whip.

The projects are a scented sachet, needle book, strawberry pincushion, drawstring pouch, dishtowel apron, felt mouse, and fat cat.

Simple Sewing has nine pieces of felt in the back of the book bound in with the pages, and the zipper pouch has all the other materials needed to make all the projects except the scissors, fiberfill, and dishtowel for the dishtowel apron. These items must be purchased separately.

The instructions are simple and easy to understand, and are followed by lots of colorful plates. I would highly recommend *Simple Sewing* for someone who wants to learn to sew. **Condition, good: $5.00 and up.**

Plate 586. *Kid's Easy Knitting Projects* (122-P) by Peg Blanchette, 2001. Quick Starts in Knitting for Kids 10 to adult. **Stitches & Pins (123-P)** by JoAnn Gagnon and Corrie Gagnon, 2001. A beginning sewing book for girls, written by a mother and her daughter.

122-P
Kid's Easy Knitting Projects
Peg Blanchette
Published by Williamson Publishing, Charlotte, Vermont
Copyright 2001 by Peg Blanchette
64 pages with 7 projects
Softcover, 10" x 8"

Kids' Easy Knitting Projects has a cover with a cartoon-type boy, girl, and cat. The girl is holding up two different colored socks, the boy is all smiles with a new stocking cap and scarf. Knitting is spelled with two knitting needles as the letters T.

Cartoon children and animals run through *Kids' Easy Knitting Projects* in a black-and-white format. The first 18 pages explain all about yarns, casting on, and knitting stitches.

The projects start easy and, as the child progresses, get a little harder. The projects are quick-start coasters, wool scarf with beaded fringe, cozy toe slippers, Mama and little Baa, perfect purse, sox and stripes, and a tassel-top hat.

The last pages of *Kids' Easy Knitting Projects* make up a "how-to" stitch dictionary. The plates are easy to understand and there is lots of encouragement throughout the book. With the help of an adult now and then, a child would surely learn to knit. **Condition, good: $10.00 and up.**

123-P
Stitches & Pins
JoAnn Gagnon & Corrie Gagnon
Published by Bunkhouse Books, Waitsburg, Washington
Copyright 2001 by Bunkhouse Books
68 pages with 14 sewing projects
Softcover, 11" x 8½"

Stitches & Pins, a beginning sewing book for girls, has a blue and yellow cover with a photograph of a family, a mother and two daughters. They are gathered around a sewing machine with Raggedy Ann fabrics and Raggedy Ann and Andy dolls. The mother and older daughter in the picture are co-authors of this book.

Stitches & Pins is a serious book about sewing for ages 8 to 16. It gives you everything you need to know about the sewing machine, sewing supplies, fabric, patterns, and pinning.

A color picture of each project modeled by the sisters is shown on the inside front and back cover. The rest of *Stitches & Pins* is printed in black and white with lots of easy to understand Plates. There are 14 different projects to complete as you learn and master different sewing techniques. All the patterns, girls' sizes 8 to 16, are full-size and are included in the back of the book.

The sewing projects are pillowcase, book cover, tote bag, laundry bag, house potholder, doll quilt, hostess apron, bound blanket, circle potholder, elastic waist skirt, reversible vest, matching purse, pajama bottoms or shorts, and pajama top or nightshirt.

Raggedy Ann fabrics are used profusely throughout the book. As for the Raggedy Ann and Andy dolls on the cover, the parting words are:
Once you've completed the projects in this book, you should have enough skill to tackle these dolls. They come as a preprinted panel with directions, and are available at fabric stores.

Stitches & Pins is a well-thought-out book and one that would encourage a teen-ager to sew. **Condition, good: $25.00 and up.**

124-P
Traditional Quilts for Kids to Make
Barbara J. Eikmeier
Published by Martingale and Company, Woodinville, Washington
Copyright 2001 by Barbara J. Eikmeier
79 pages with 8 plans and 15 traditional blocks
Softcover, 11" x 8½"

Traditional Quilts for Kids to Make has a red, blue, and yellow patchwork quilt on the cover. The title is in black on a yellow rectangle.

The book takes the child through the basic techniques of making a quilt with easy-to-understand language and plates. The blocks shown include Double Nine Patch, Fair and Square, Flag, Butterfly, House, Indian Hatchet, Saw-Tooth Star, Basket, Friendship Star, Pinwheel, Flower, Leaf, Pine Tree, Railroad Crossing, and Sailboat.

The quilts are Becky's Stars, Blue Sampler, Butterflies 11, Cousins by the Row, Irish Chain, Patch Quilt, Ranger's Cabin, and Sarah's Sampler.

Everything you need to know is shown in this book. It is a great first book for the budding quilt maker. **Condition, good: $5.00 and up.**

125-P
The Best of Sewing Machine Fun for Kids
Nancy Smith and Lynda Milligan
Published by C&T Publishing, Inc.
Copyright 2003 by Lynn Mulligan and Nancy Smith
128 pages with 17 sewing projects
Softcover 9½" x 8"

A bright red background with a blue sewing machine, yellow star and multi-colored and yellow lettering makes *The Best of Sewing Machine Fun for Kids* easy to spot.

The Best of Sewing Machine Fun for Kids is a reprint of books *I'll Teach Myself 1 — Sewing Machine Fun* (106-P) and *I'll Teach Myself 2 — More Sewing Machine Fun* (107-P). Just like the other two it's a fun book that teaches the parts of the sewing machine and how to use them. There are games and puzzles to test your skill on the sewing machine-that are not only fun-but you learn as you play.

I'll Teach Myself 1 — Sewing Machine Fun has you stitching without thread, using paper to play games of skill using curves and pivots. There are crossword puzzles and guessing games, even jokes. The first sewing is thread pictures, dot to dot, then brown paper shapes, greeting cards (two kinds), custom envelopes (no sewing), soft shape heart, soft shape bunny, button-up dog or cat "possibilities pocket" the same projects as in *I'll Teach Myself 1 — Sewing Machine Fun*. The rest of the projects are character pillow, cover-ups, hair bunchies, lunch bags, hamburgers, and treasure pouch that were found in *I'll Teach Myself 2 — More Sewing Machine Fun*.

Note: *The Best of Sewing Machine Fun for Kids* is book one in a series of five, I'll Teach Myself *Sewing Books*. *I'll Teach Myself 1 — Sewing Machine Fun* (106-P), *I'll Teach Myself 2 — More Sewing Machine Fun* (107-P), *I'll Teach Myself 3 — Step Into Patchwork* (108-P), *I'll Teach Myself 4 — Gifts to Give* (116-P).

Children's School Sewing Books

In the nineteenth century, sewing was an integral part of a girl's education. Her mother, aunt, or another female family member often taught the sewing lessons. It was essential to the family to have the children learn to sew in order to help with the mending and weekly sewing chores. Families often relied on their children to do small mending jobs such as stitching seams, sewing on buttons and darning stockings. Because sewing was so essential, expert needlework was considered a very important part of a lady's education. Those families that could afford it sent their girls to young ladies' academies where needlework was taught.

Many of these academies, including the Mary Anna Longstreth School in Philadelphia, taught model sewing. Each girl made a model sewing example of the stitch or construction process being taught on either a small square of fabric or sometimes an actual miniature (doll) garment such as *Plain Sewing Book of Lucy Riechel* (plate 239). These models were then secured in the girl's sewing notebook for the teacher to grade. The graded notebook was then given back to the student. This had a twofold purpose; it reassured the teacher that the stitch or construction was properly executed and the student had a sewing book to use for future reference. This practice of model sewing was carried on into the 1900s. See *Hand Sewing Lessions* (plate 589) and (4-S) and *Manual of Exercises in Handsewing* (6-S).

In 1901 Sarah Krolik the author of *Hand Sewing Lessions* writes in her preface:

"Hand Sewing Lessons" is a book for those who wish to learn sewing and how to teach it to others. It gives a practical course for normal and high school classes and supplies trained teachers with printed instructions for pupils in place of written ones that take so much time and that over-lap the work of other departments. The stitches are combined for practice while new ones are being learned, so as to form a continuous line of progress and carry out the principle of bridging the way from the known to the unknown, and of making a pleasant road to knowledge, which will become a part of daily life in after years.

One of the first books written for children exclusively for sewing drills was *Sewing Illustrated Primer* (1-S and plate 587). Written in 1881 by Louise Kirkwood, it was the outcome of studying the large sewing classes at industrial schools. She states in the preface:

Portions of these lessons have existed in various forms for several years, first as leaflets, and later in the "Little House-keeper," published by Randolph, and have proved their practical value, by a widely extended circulation.

Kirkwood compiled and enlarged the lessons on sewing, music, and songs and published them in *Sewing Illustrated Primer*. It included plain sewing stitches and also carried the songs, music, and instructions on holding large classes.

Eighteen years later in 1899, the *One Stitch Dropped* (3-S) by Mary Dunham was written for children just out of kindergarten and starting their elementary sewing classes. While the children learned their stitches, they sang simple little verses such as *In and out, in and out, this is the way we baste about.*

The book utilized jointed dolls as models and the children learned to make a complete outfit from underwear to cape and hat to fit the dolls. See plate 588 for book cover and drawers and underwaist made from instructions in the *One Stitch Dropped.*

In the mid-1800s, free public education for children in the United States was introduced. By the 1860s public schools had expanded the curriculum beyond reading, writing, and arithmetic to include personal development studies, and secondary schools (high schools) were now open to all who wanted to further their education. Secondary schools not only prepared a student for college, but also provided terminal education for those not attending college. Even though the public schools admitted both boys and girls into the elementary and secondary schools, for the most part it was still a man's world in the colleges and universities.

Writers such as Catherine Beecher fought for education for women to become teachers and mothers. Miss Beecher felt that women alone could no longer prepare their daughters to become proper homemakers, wives, and mothers in the fast changing world. She theorized that to have a well managed and balanced home, young ladies must be schooled and taught. She believed that women's talents were largely wasted and should be cultivated. In her speech, Suggestions Respecting Improvements in Education, Catherine Beecher stated:

If all females were not only well educated themselves but were prepared to communicate in an easy manner their stores of knowledge to others; if they not only knew how to regulate their own minds, tempers, and habits but how to effect improvements in those around them, the face of society would be speedily changed.

In 1862, The Morrill Land Grant Act donated land to each state to support colleges to teach agriculture and mechanical arts to further education of the industrial classes. It was this act that gave many the opportunity to obtain a higher education and further the development of agriculture, engineering and home economics. In May of 1868, by a vote of 4 to 3, the board of Iowa State College furthered the cause of home economics by allowing women to attend the college. On March 17, 1869, the college building was dedicated and Adonijah S. Welch was inaugurated as president. The college had enrolled 253 students, 97 of them were women.

Benjamin Gue, president of the Board of Trustees, was strongly in favor of home economics and the admission of women. In his speech at the inauguration of Iowa State College, Mr. Gue stated:

In this people's college dedicated to the encouragement and promotion of industry, we must aim to make labor attractive not only to the boys who are seeking knowledge in their department but to the girls who can never become accomplished and thoroughly educated women without the knowledge of the art of housekeeping and the best methods of conducting every household occupation with system, intelligence and womanly grace.

In that same year of 1869, Mary B. Welch, the wife of the new president A. S Welch was the asked to teach home economics. Mary had attended various institutions, toured many cooking schools along the East Coast, and had her own ideas and experiences to give to the new course. Mary Welch is said to have been the first woman to teach college home economics.

In 1870, a year after Mary Welch started teaching home economics, Ellen Swallow petitioned to enter Massachusetts Institute of Technology. She was denied because they didn't accept females. Striking a deal with MIT, she was allowed to sit in on classes. Ellen received her degree in chemistry in 1873 and stayed on as a chemistry assistant. It was around this time that Ellen Swallow married a mining professor, Robert Richards. In 1876 Mrs. Swallow Richards, always with the thought of improving women's education, convinced wealthy Boston society families to donate money for women's studies. With this money she set up a correspondence school for homebound women and a New England Kitchen for working class people.

Also in 1876, Mary Welch was instrumental in establishing an experimental kitchen at Iowa State College. In Iowa's State Register, Father Clarkson wrote:

Mrs. Welch is doing more to improve and elevate domestic economy than all other influences in the State.

By 1877, Iowa State College had enlarged its home economics curriculum by adding care and arrangement of the house, plan of the week's work, training of children, sewing and mending. Mrs. Welch gave lectures on and off the campus for 15 years, teaching students and housewives about cooking, sewing, house furnishings, health, care of the sick, ventilation, water supply, courtesy, entertaining, and hospitality.

Ellen Swallow Richards eventually won her battle with MIT in 1882 and women were admitted into the regular programs at Massachusetts Institute of Technology. Two years later, Ellen Richards received the honor of being the first woman to become a MIT faculty member.

In the late 1800s, the United States began to formalize sewing in schools. In 1892, Amy Smith published *Needlework for Student Teachers* (25-S) and in 1893, Mary Woolman published her book, *A Sewing Course for Teachers* (18-S), these were among the first books written for teaching sewing in public schools.

By the end of the 1800s, domestic courses were being offered to women in some land grant colleges and by the beginning of the 1900s there was such a demand for domestic science teachers that training began not only in land grant colleges, but also in private colleges.

By the early 1900s, sewing classes were taught in schools throughout the United States. Amy Smith wrote in 1893, less than a year after her book, *Needlework for Student Teachers*, had been published:

The first edition of this book has been exhausted in rather less than a year.

During the year this text-book has been used by about 800 teaches preparing for Scholarship and Certificate examinations.

Home sewing was still an indispensable practice for the average family since factory-made clothing was more expensive and still not easily available, especially in the rural areas.

The instructor of sewing in the School of Agriculture at the University of Minnesota, Margaret Blair wrote the *Manual of Exercises in Hand Sewing* in 1904 (6-S). In the introduction she states:

To introduce sewing successfully in the public schools, three important points must be considered. First, the merit of the system. Second, the effect upon the school work and upon the pupil. Third, the ability or efficiency of those who superintend or teach the sewing.

To teach sewing successfully the teacher must be able to adapt the system to her pupils and to the time she has at her disposal. Much can be accomplished even in a limited period if the essentials are properly chosen from the elementary work here outlined.

In 1899, at Lake Placid, New York, Ellen Swallow Richards organized a small group that was involved in home economics. Their goal was to expand the field to deal with environmental, sociological, and economic problems of the home and to define the standards for teacher training and certification in the field of home economics. It was during one of these conferences in 1908 that the American Home Economics Association was founded. Ellen Swallow Richards was elected president. In 1910 she was named to the Council of the National Education Association and she held the position of overseeing the teaching of home economics in public schools.

The early teaching of home economics at the college level followed the model sewing method, as in the early books *Needlework for Student Teachers* (25-S), *Hand Sewing Lessions* (4-S), and *Manual of Exercises in Handsewing* (6-S).

By the early 1900s methods were starting to change. Ellen Swallow Richards published the *Journal of Home Economics* in 1910 and starting with the introductory issue a new method of teaching was introduced. More and more articles were urging the problem method of teaching. Educators were against teaching needlework solely as a skill of the hand. They thought sewing should involve more creativity and problem solving.

Instead of having everyone produce the same size piece

Children's School Sewing Books

with the exact same stitch done to perfection, a newer way of sewing was proposed in the problem method. The teacher would choose a garment, and each girl would be responsible for securing a proper pattern, fabric suitable for the garment both in type and durability, and then cutting it out and constructing it using the correct sewing techniques in a neat and pleasing manor. The student could work at her own pace and learn from her own successes or mistakes. The problem method is reflected in the book *School Sewing Based on Home Problems* (19-S).

This new way of sewing was also being taught in the younger grades. In 1905 Elizabeth Sage and Anna Cooley wrote *Occupations for Little Fingers* (*A Manual for Grade Teachers, Mothers and Settlement Workers*) (7-S). The book was dedicated:

To the many little people who will find joy through expression.

In the Introductory Note, Mary Woolman writes:

Mothers, who were the earliest and should be the best teachers, long ago found that the happiest child was the busy one. They discovered also that to keep him at work he must be interested in the thing he is doing. To accomplish this they must provide that which he feels to be worth the effort. It must be something which he understands and which he can finish in a short time. A stupid, difficult "stint" such as poor Little Prudy had to finish daily is not calculated to increase a love for work.

Handwork has its place in education as well as in the daily life. It should ever be "a blessing, not a doom."

I imagine "poor Little Prudy" was working on a sampler, as many a young girl complained in their journals about the boredom of such tasks. *Occupation for Little Fingers* is full of interesting projects and most assuredly would lead to a creative child.

Another set of books came on the market in 1910, not only mirroring the new thought in sewing, but also using store-bought patterns that were now plentiful and easy to find. This three-book set was *Goodwin's Course in Sewing*, Books I, II, and III (9-S), (10-S), and (11-S). Emma Goodwin, an experienced dressmaker and teacher, realized the need of a more thorough training for the students in the primary principles of needlework. She wrote in her preface:

I have formulated a definite, practical outline of the work that should give a foundation for an advanced technical training, fitting for the trades, or enable the pupil to do all necessary household sewing.

Book I was designed to provide a two-year course on plain sewing. Instead of requiring sewing models she adopted articles such as needle books, receptacles, lamp mats, and a dolls apron; projects that could be used and enjoyed when completed. Book II covered the sewing of doll clothes. Emma Goodwin felt that sewing with a pattern was an important step in learning dressmaking. In the Introductory Note to Book II she states:

The drafting of garments properly belongs to a more advanced technical course, and will be much more readily and intelligently acquired when the method of putting the garments together has been thoroughly mastered. The miniature patterns accompanying this book were designed especially by The Mc-Call Company of New York, and are uniform with full-size patterns.

Included in the book were four sewing projects and in a pocket in the back of the book were nine doll clothes patterns with instructions in the book on how to execute them properly. See Doll Patterns from *Goodwin's Home Course in Sewing* plate 572.

Book III was for the sewing of full-size articles. Emma Goodman again used McCall's patterns in her book, supplying a size 34 bust and a 24 waist. In her introductory note she says:

The use of these patterns as shown in the diagrams will enable the pupil to make intelligent application of patterns to the cutting of garments. This is a method far more practical for the untrained than the partial mastery of a system of cutting, which has its place in the trade schools, where a thorough technical training may be had.

See *Misses Patterns from Goodwin's Home Course in Sewing* (plate 573) for patterns. With sized paper patterns now on the market and readily available there really was no need to learn drafting and cutting unless one was going into the trade.

By 1917, public schools in every state of the union had a home economics class that included sewing. Before World War I, 63 percent of students taking home economics were preparing for homemaking, five percent were preparing for administrative positions and the remaining 35 percent would go on to teach home economics.

The 1920s were years of relative prosperity. Clothing was plentiful and easy to find. Women were buying manufactured clothing more than ever before. However there was still a stigma attached to manufactured clothing. Many women still insisted that the clothing was made with shoddy construction and cheap materials. The lack of quality workmanship in store-bought clothing motivated women to go back to their sewing machines.

The Great Depression hit the United States in 1929 and sewing became a tool for saving money. Women who knew how to sew could keep their families well clothed. Knowing how to sew allowed housewives to patch, mend, let out, and make over garments. Many people were unemployed and trying to keep homes and family together was a constant worry. New clothing was simply out of the question for many. The emphasis was on durability making over, care, and repair.

There were only a few sewing books published in the 1930s, however needlework magazines were abundant. Fashion Service put out by the *Woman's Institute Magazine* showed the new styles with a lot of hand detail such as trimming in cross-stitch and smocking. There was an article on *Economy Frocks of Smart Design* reminding women of the modest price of the new fabrics. But of more interest were the ads for making money at home with titles such as:

"I Have Kept My Home Intact For My Children" and "How I Made Up For John's Shrunken Pay Check."

By the late 1930s, new avenues were opening up for young women and there were new important positions in the clothing industry. Young women realized they could have careers, and courses in the clothing and textile field could prepare them for positions such as department store buyers, fashion illustrators, fashion editors, stylists, or even dress designers. The study of textiles and clothing became a well-established field and provided careers for many women. By the end of the 1930s, more than 90 percent of schools in towns and cities with a population of 2,500 or more offered home economics classes and more than half required home economics in high school.

The 1940s brought World War II and consumer goods were needed for the war. Again, sewing became a way of saving not only money but also goods.

"Use it up; Wear it out; Make it do or Do Without!"

This was the slogan of the war and most women followed it. During World War II, Nina R. Jordon's book, *How to Sew*, not only encouraged sewing with old fabric saying it was softer and easier to sew with, but it also gave instructions on mending and patching. Many women took on the jobs left by the servicemen gone to war, and worked outside of their homes. Women who stayed at home joined the war effort by making over clothing from their own closets. Mothers made coats for children out of discarded men's suits and nightgowns for girls out of men's old shirts. Nothing should be wasted. Women who knew how to sew during this time were fortunate, not only were they providing for their families but they also had a hand in helping with the war effort and the government encouraged and acknowledged it.

After the war, most women were happy to have their men at home and to once again be housewives. They embraced the life of cooking, cleaning, and sewing. Meanwhile home economics in the schools had changed with the times. Where the older books taught sewing and caring for the family and home, the new books addressed more the fashion end of sewing and personal health. There were chapters on grooming, hairstyles, studying about color, style, etc.

How You Look and Dress (29-S) was written in 1948. The first seven chapters are Your Grooming, Care of Your Clothes, The Design of Your Clothes, The Color of Your Clothes, The Textiles of Your Clothes, The Right Clothes for You, and Buying Your Clothes. Almost half the book is about "you"! Of course there are chapters on sewing and they are very complete. These new home economic books showed how society was changing now that the war was over and stores were once again filled with manufactured clothing. Garment construction was still taught, but the emphasis was on grooming and fashion.

Clothing Construction and Wardrobe Planning (30-S) written in 1960 has seven parts, only one is on the construction of clothing. In the introduction Dora Lewis writes:

The authors of "Clothing Construction and Wardrobe Planning" have sincere convictions about the personal, social,

and economic significance of clothing. Equitable sharing of the family's clothing money and the responsibilities of the consumer-buyer are both stressed throughout the text.

In the preface, Mabel Bowers and Marietta Kettunen write:

Starting with simple grooming procedures, and the art of choosing becoming lines, textures, and colors, we have gone on to show how to choose clothes and accessories that create harmonious costumes. Most families have limited funds for clothing, and girls must be resourceful and intelligent in meeting their clothing needs if they are to be well dressed. It is quite a trick for them to assemble a wardrobe that provides plenty of changes for school wear, for working or lounging at home, for parties, and for other occasions.

Clothing Constuction and Wardrobe Planning devotes only one third of the book to the actual construction of garments.

Home Economics lost some of its credibility in the 60s as an academic subject. It was seen as an easy course and many students took it for easy credit. Sewing had become more of a hobby and less a part of domestic life. Most girls wanted the latest clothing styles in the stores and took after-school or weekend jobs to earn the money that allowed them the freedom to buy the clothing they wanted.

Dress (36-S) written in 1975 is one of the last of the home economics books that I have found. Approximately one-fourth of its 672 pages are dedicated to sewing. *Dress* is a very complete book of what we were teaching our children in home economics in the 1970s. I have found only one other book written later, *Creative Living* (37-S). It was written in 1990 and is a very interesting home economics book, written for both boys and girls. It is packed full of today! It covers relationships, life management, consumer skills, technology, career exploration, family, cooking, and life in general. It has a very basic chapter on sewing. Sewing is a small part of *Creative Living* and of young people's lives today.

Home economic books bring back the fascinating history of sewing in America, the impact of the women's movement and the entrance of American women into the labor market.

Sewing in the late 1800s was a necessity for young girls; it was needed in order to keep a happy and productive home. Sewing in 2000 is a leisure hobby for young girls, as well as their mothers. A hobby that provides not only a creative outlet but for many, it is therapeutic, promoting well being and relaxation.

Note: The books in this chapter are listed by publishing date the oldest book being number 1. I have used the copyright date of the book listed, when known. If the book had been published earlier I will record it in the copyright line. There is also an alphabetical index of both popular and school sewing books at the end of this book.

Children's School Sewing Books

1-S
Sewing Illustrated Primer
Louise J Kirkwood
Printed by Wumkoop & Hallenbeck N.Y., N.Y. U.S.A.
Copyright 1881 by Louise J. Kirkwood
67 pages with sewing diagrams and music
Hardcover, 6½" x 5"

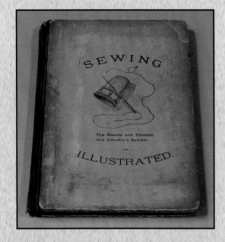

Plate 587. *Sewing Illustrated Primer* by Louise Kirkwood, copyright 1881. *Sewing Primer with Songs and Music for Schools and Families.*

Sewing Illustrated Primer has a light green cover. *The Needle and Thimble Are Industry's Symbol* is printed under a black line drawing of a fancy thimble and threaded needle. The title page states:

Sewing Illustrated Primer with songs and music for schools and families.

The preface states: *Numerous inquiries regarding the plan of conducting large classes in sewing in Industrial Schools, have induced the publication of the Sewing Primer, the lessons of which have been, from time to time, worked out for the benefit of such classes. Portions of these lessons have existed in various forms for several years, first as leaflets, and later in the "Little Housekeeper," published by Randolph, and have proved their practical value, by a widely extended circulation. The Primer is but an enlargement of these publications; and although not claiming to be exhaustive, it includes what seems to be the most needful instruction in plain sewing. The Songs, set to popular airs, are designed to awaken enthusiasm in what may sometimes seem to the child a prosaic subject; at the same time they embody rules and suggestions which will be of use in later life.*

Louise J. Kirkwood felt that it was important to teach our young girls to "ply the needle." She felt sewing was an art that:

Would prove an armor of defense against temptation to idleness, which leads to want and so often to crime.

Sewing Illustrated Primer has "Hints to Teachers," "Preparation for Sewing," "The Workbasket," "Cutting," "Needles and Thread," and all the plain sewing stitches. The lessons, are set to music:

Try O Try Air-Buy a Broom

O Stitching is witching
And hemming as well,

But what is distressing
Is turning a fell.
I'm sick of such screaming,
And ready to cry,
But I hear the word ringing,
"Try, little one, try;
Try, O try; try, O try;"
I hear the word ringing,
"Try, little one, try."

There are twenty-two songs with names like "Swift Flying Needle," "Stitching Firm and Fast," "The Idle Girl's Serenade," etc. *Sewing Illustrated Primer* is a delightful little piece of sewing history. **Good condition: $75.00 and up.**

2-S
School Needlework
Olive C. Hapgood
Published by Ginn and Company New York and London
Copyright 1892 by Olive C. Hapgood
254 pages with 12 projects including doll clothes
Hardbound, 7½" x 5".

School Needlework has a brown cloth cover with the title printed in gold on the front and spine.

Olive Hapgood was a sewing teacher in the Boston Public Schools. On the inside fly page she quotes John Ruskin:

"Learn the sound qualities of all useful stuffs, and make everything of the best you can get, whatever its price...and then, every day, make some little piece of useful clothing, sewn with your own fingers as strongly as it can be stitched; and embroider it or otherwise beautify it moderately with fine needlework, such as a girl may be proud of having done."

In the preface Olive Hapgood writes:

The importance of instruction in sewing in the Public School is now generally recognized. As manual training comes into greater prominence, new methods and helps are necessary. The demand for these was felt by the author, and this book is the result of practical experience in the class-room. Its purpose is to assist both teacher and pupil; lightening the teacher's labors by saving constant repetition, and giving the pupil a manual for reference, with the hope that the information thus acquired will assist in fitting her for the duties of life. Simplicity with completeness has been the aim throughout.

The first part of the book contains all the plain sewing stitches and models along with embroidery. The second half covers "Drafting," "Cutting," and "Making Garments." The items to be made are two-breadth apron, child's bib, child's drawers, night-dress yoke, child's sack tier, gored skirt, drawers, child's waist, and misses' waist. These are all done on graph paper using your own measurements. There is also a page of doll patterns on graph paper with instructions on how to make them larger to fit a ten-inch doll. The patterns include underwaist, sack, drawers, and wrapper. This book is the teachers' edition and in the back includes the "Teachers' Supplement." It gives instruction to teach from the first to the sixth year. There is an illustration of a sampler in the shape of a pair of pantaloons using all the plain stitches learned, such as shirring on the leg ruffles, gusset in the crotch and buttonhole on the band. There are a lot of hints and suggestions, and for the first grade there are sewing cards to be copied. *School Needlework* is a wonderful little book. **Good condition: $75.00 and up.**

3-S
The One Stitch Dropped Doll Dressing
Mary E. Dunham
Published by Columbia Book Co., Philadelphia,
    Pennsylvania, U.S.A.
Copyright 1899 by Mary E. Dunham
62 pages with 22 doll sewing projects
Hardcover, 7½" x 5½"

Plate 588. *The One Stitch Dropped Doll Dressing* by Mary E. Dunham, copyright 1899. Mental Development and Manual Training Combined taking up The One Stitch Dropped in Sewing by Drills to Sound-Singing. Drawers and underwaist #1 made from instructions in The One Stitch Dropped Doll Dressing.

The One Stitch Dropped Doll Dressing has a plain brown cover with the title printed in a darker brown.

The inside fly page has the book's full title, *Mental Development and Manual Training Combined.*

Taking Up *The One Stitch Dropped Doll Dressing* In Sewing by Drills to Sound-Singing. At the bottom of the page is a little poem:

> Then the one stitch dropping pulled the next stitch out,
>   And a weak place grew in the fabric stout,
>   And, the perfect pattern was marred for aye
> By the one small stitch that was dropped that day.

This book is meant to be used immediately after kindergarten, thus leaving no gaps in the child's education. The work is planned to cover a period of two years, giving two 45-minute lessons per week for ten months in a year. There are 16 drills, seven garments are to be made of paper, eight of cloth, and

seven shaped garments. All the sewing drills have little rhyming songs to be sung while working, such as:

> Right hand, we will give you a lesson,
>   One thumb and fingers four;
>   Long finger must wear the thimble,
>   Or with sewing you will be sore.

Two sizes of jointed dolls are used for the doll dressing, 11" and 16". The paper garments including an apron, underskirt, apron with straps, underwaist #1 with shoulder straps, underwaist #2, cape, and hat are made in manila paper because of its adaptability for folding and cutting lessons and stitch making practice. These paper garments are for an 11" doll. The book goes on to say:

The skill and knowledge gained in the previous lessons can now be applied to actual garment making. The measurements given are correct for the 11" doll. Use soft unbleached muslin for the underskirt, drawers and underwaist; gingham of small plaid for the apron and dress, and plain cotton cloth for the cape and hat.

Shaped garments fit a 16" doll and consist of an underwaist, gored underskirt, shaped drawers, sacque nightgown, blouse-waist dress, and cloak and hat. The patterns for the doll clothing are all drafts for folding and measuring and cutting to the doll's size. This is one of my favorite books, giving a glimpse back in time to the child's first sewing lessons. The garments are simple in looks but sturdy and strong, surely some of them have survived to this time. **Good condition: $100.00 and up.**

Note: *The One Stitch Dropped Doll Dressing* is a rare book.

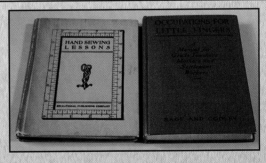

Plate 589. *Hand Sewing Lessons* by Sarah E. Krolik, copyright 1901. Pupils are taught that only by careful practice can they hope to excel. **Occupations for Little Fingers** by Elizabeth Sage and Anna M. Cooley, copyright 1901. A Manual for Grade Teachers, Mothers, and Settlement Workers. See (7-S) for content.

4-S
Hand Sewing Lessons
Sarah Ewell Krolik
Published by Educational Publishing Co., unknown
    address
Copyright 1901 by Sarah Ewell Krolik
101 pages with 32 models and 8 projects
Hardcover, 8" x 6"

Hand Sewing Lessons has a green cover with a black title and graphics. The graphics consist of a frame of rulers surrounding a tape measure, a pair of shears, and the title.

The frontispiece is a photograph of a young girl sitting in a wicker chair, sewing. The caption reads: *A skillful hand is a helpful hand.*

The preface explains the need for this book:

The value of these lessons has been proven by fifteen years of experience in the "Self Help Circle," a school organized to instruct girls in the domestic arts. At first they were taught on clothing for themselves.

It was found that while all learned to make garments for home use, few became expert needlewomen. Haste to complete wearing apparel resulted in inferior workmanship. A combination course was adopted which gives variety with continuity.

Pupils are taught that only by careful practice can they hope to excel, that these models are the way marks of their progress, and will be treasured by them in the future as their own handiwork. With the text, they form a book of reference on making and mending garments that is highly prized.

Hand Sewing Lessons is about model sewing. In the back of the book are blank pages that are to be filled with models (samples) of the child's sewing so that the child might return to the model page to review her stitches in the future. There are three parts, 12 divisions, and 32 models. The first part of the book is all model sewing and is added to the blank pages in the back of book when completed.

In the second part a doll is introduced. Garments are fitted to the doll and are given to the student when finished. The garments for the doll are models 28 through 32, a gored skirt, underwaist, drawers, flannel skirt, and dress. There is a draft for the doll's dress. Also included in the book are patterns for a child's waist and two pillow tops. The book also gives lessons on cross-stitch embroidery and has a bonus chapter on American Indian beadwork and basketry. **Good condition with no model sewing: $50.00 and up (samples). Good condition with original model sewing in the book: $100.00 and up.**

5-S
Home and School Sewing
Frances Patton
Published by Newson and Company, N.Y., N.Y., U.S.A.
Copyright 1901 by Frances Patton
234 pages with sewing instruction
Hardcover, 7½" x 5"

The cover of *Home and School Sewing* is green with black lettering and the title is on the front and spine.

The preface says that sewing was introduced into the Philadelphia Public Schools in 1884 and *Home and School Sewing* was the result of practical suggestions from teachers over the seventeen years since the book was first introduced.

Home and School Sewing is a book devoted entirely to plain sewing, the entire book is practice, leaving the child with a model of sewing to which she can refer when making a garment. The model chapters are "Preparation," "Basting," "Hemming," "Overseaming," "Running Seams," "Backstitching," "Overcasting," "Facings," "Slip Stitching," "Gussets," "Plackets," "Cording," "Piping," "Bindings," "Mitered Corners," "Bias," "Gathering," "Bands," "Darning," "Patching," "Tucking," "Fastenings," "Decorative Stitches." Every stitch is covered with complete instructions. There are also chapters on "Economy," "Color," "Materials," and "Tools." **Good condition: $25.00 and up.**

6-S
Manual of Exercises in Hand Sewing
Margaret J. Blair
Published by Webb Publishing Co., St. Paul, Minnesota, U.S.A.
Copyright 1904 by Webb Publishing Co.
105 pages with 39 models
Hardcover, 8½" x 5¾"

Manual of Exercises in Hand Sewing has a green cover with the title in gold on the cover and spine. The introduction states:

All educators agree that the beginning and successive steps of education must harmonize with the corresponding stages of the child's development. This gives sewing, cutting and fashioning garments one of the first places in the succession of studies to be taken up. The child has scarcely a point of contact with the world that he so readily perceives as that made by his own garments.

But if the child is trained along wholesome natural lines, his taste will develop individuality very early.

All of the plain stitches along with darning are addressed in this manual with illustrations. The first stitches are done on canvas. Along with the usual sewing models done on a square of fabric. There are some models that could be used as doll clothing or accessories. These items are a sheet, pillowcase, apron, hemstitched towel, and doll's skirt. There are 39 models in all. This little book shows exactly what was taught in the primary grades in the early 1900s. **Good condition: $25.00 and up.**

7-S
Occupations for Little Fingers
Elizabeth Sage and Anna M. Cooley
Published by Charles Scribner's Sons, New York, Chicago, Boston
Copyright 1905 by Charles Scribner's Sons
154 pages with 13 chapters of projects
Hardcover, 8" x 5½"

Occupations for Little Fingers has a red cover with black

lettering. The title is printed on the spine and is also on the front cover along with its subtitle *A Manual for Grade Teachers Mothers and Settlement Workers*.

There is a photograph at the beginning of the book titled "Indian Life, First Grade, Horace Mann School, Teachers College, New York City." It shows children at their school desks, some with Indian headdress. In the introductory note Mary Woolman writes:

The child is naturally a worker. He will destroy if he does not know how to make. Destruction interests him as much as construction.

Mothers, who were the earliest and should be the best teachers, long ago found that the happiest child was the busy one.

Handwork has its place in education as well as in the daily life. It should be a blessing, not a doom.

This book considers the needs of both the mother and the teacher.

This little book should therefore increase the helpfulness and happiness of many little workers in the school, the settlement, and the home.

The book has 13 chapters, and all of them are filled with projects for both boys and girls. The sewing chapter is "Coarse Sewing" which uses large needles and thread. The projects in this chapter are a pen-wipe, blotter, match-scratcher, napkin ring, hair-receiver, pencil case, blotter corners, letter case, iron holder, book cover, doll's table-cover, pin ball, and bag.

There are two chapters on raffia. The first chapter includes a doll umbrella, round picture frame, oval picture frame, splint-and-raffia mat, needle book, napkin ring, doll hats, broom holder, and a Solomon's knot bag. The second chapter on raffia offers another splint-and-raffia mat, string ball, another string ball, braided mat, braided basket, coiled basket, shopping bag, doll raincoat and hat.

The chapter on weaving has paper weaving, a doll's hammock, mat, raffia mat, miniature Indian blanket, doll size rugs, circular mats, circular pocket, and bags. It also explains how to make different weaving looms. The chapter on crochet and knitting has a washcloth, doll's hood, wristlets, and a doll's sweater. See plate 589 in this chapter for book cover. **Good condition: $50.00 and up.**

8-S
Sewing Handicraft for Girls
Idabelle McGlauflin
Published by The Manual Arts Press, Peoria, Ill., U.S.A.
Copyright 1910 by Idabelle McGlauflin
116 pages with 28 projects
Hardcover, 9" x 6"

Sewing Handicraft for Girls has a green cover with black lettering. The title is on the front cover and spine.

Sewing Handicraft for Girls is a graded course for city and rural schools. The exercises in this five-year course are based upon an estimated time of one hour per week in the first two

years and one-and-one-half hours per week in the last three years. The school year consisted of 38 weeks.

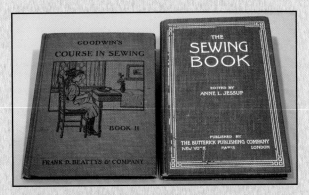

Plate 590. *Goodwin's Course in Sewing, Book II* by Emma E. Goodwin, copyright 1910. Practical Instruction in Needlework for Use in Schools and at Home. See 10-S for book and plates 572 and 573 for patterns in the book. *The Sewing Book* by Anne Jessup, copyright 1913. The right training of the child is training for life. See 13-S.

Chapter one offers "Suggestions to Teachers." Chapters two, three, four, five, and six are all "Course of Instructions" starting with grade three and ending with grade seven. Chapter seven is a "Description of Stitches," chapter eight covers "Textile Fibers and Fabrics," chapter nine is "Costume," and chapter ten is "Basketry."

The projects are a doll's embroidered-quilt, hemming a towel, pincushion, child's picture-book, emery balls, bag, doll's sofa-pillow, a pair of doll's pillowcases, doll's kimono, basket, napkin, pair of sleeve protectors, embroidered pincushion, doll's rag rug, ruler and pencil case, book cover, book bag, apron, hemstitched handkerchief, round pin-holder and case, petticoat or princess slip, hemstitched pin cushion, round bag with raffia covering, pillow case, guest towel, wash dress, and eyelet napkin-ring. The petticoat, princess slip, and wash dress are made from purchased paper patterns. This is the first sewing book I have seen that includes basketry. The doll's quilt is an especially interesting project; it has designs of children in native costumes to embroider on squares. **Good condition: $50.00 and up.**

9-S
Goodwin's Course in Sewing, Book I
Emma E. Goodwin
Published by Frank D. Beattys & Co. N.Y., N.Y., U.S.A.
Copyright 1910 by Emma E. Goodwin
46 pages with 8 projects
Hardcover, 8½" x 6½"

Goodwin's Course in Sewing, Book I has a drab green cover with black lettering and a line drawing of a tree and house. In the foreground is a girl dressed in an orange coat and hat, walking with her sewing bag and book in her arms.

Children's School Sewing Books

This is the first of three books by the same name. It was written for "Practical Instruction in Needlework for Use in Schools and at Home."

Goodwin's Course in Sewing, Book I is designed to be used for a two-year period. The projects include needle book, receptacle, lamp mat, draw string bag, pencil case, dolls apron, kitchen towel, and gathered bag. This is sewing as it used to be taught; sit up straight, feet on the floor, and always use a thimble.

The first projects are done on burlap canvas with worsted thread. Between the projects are practice pieces. By the end of the book a child should be able to make hemmed towels, laundry bag, string bags, wall pockets, slipper case, dusting caps, sleeve protectors, children's bibs, kitchen aprons, and other simple and useful article.

This volume is a little piece of sewing history and a delightful book that teaches a child the fine art of practical sewing. **Good condition: $100.00 and up.**

Note: *Goodwin's Course in Sewing, Book I* is hard to find. See S10 and S11 for *Goodwin's Course in Sewing, Book II* and *III*. See also *Goodwin's Home Course in Sewing* (P-23).

10-S
Goodwin's Course in Sewing Book II
Emma E. Goodwin
Published by Frank D. Beattys & Co. N.Y., N.Y., U.S.A.
Copyright 1910 by Emma E. Goodwin
50 pages with 12 projects and 9 separate patterns
Hardcover, 8½" x 6½"

Goodwin's Course in Sewing Book II has a drab green cover with black lettering and a line drawing of a room with a table and a young girl sitting in a straight back chair. She is wearing an orange dress and sewing.

This is the second of three books by the same name. It was written for "Practical Instruction in Needlework for Use in Schools and at Home."

The first book, number I in this series was designed to be used in a two-year period. Book II doesn't have a suggested time line.

Emma Goodwin included McCall's miniature doll patterns in *Goodwin's Course in Sewing Book II* because she thought:

The drafting of garments properly belongs to a more advanced technical course, and will be much more readily and intelligently acquired when the method of putting the garments together has been thoroughly mastered.

There are three items to be made that do not require patterns; they are a work bag, pin disk, and book cover. The rest of the items in the book are doll clothing. There are nine patterns for doll clothing, seven are for an 18" doll. These are drawers, chemise, petticoat, one-piece dress, circular sack, slipover nightgown, and jumper dress. For a 20" doll are a gathered apron and a corset cover.

The patterns are all identified as McCall's and have a price of ten cents printed on the envelopes. The envelopes are all numbered, one through nine, and each has the McCall's instructions printed on the back. Stated in the introductory note:

The miniature patterns accompanying this book were designed especially by The McCall Company of New York, and are uniform with full-sized patterns.

The book has instructions for each pattern printed in detail with many illustrations and pictures. Between projects, there are practice pieces such as buttonhole samples and sewing on snaps, etc.

A wonderful book, useful to those who would like to learn to make clothing from paper patterns. The patterns are a step back into the year 1910 and show what the well-dressed doll wore. **Good condition: $200.00 and up.**

Note: *Goodwin's Course in Sewing Book II* is extremely rare, especially with the patterns intact. See plate 572 for the doll clothing patterns from this book. See 9-S and 11-S for *Goodwin's Course in Sewing Book I* and *Book III*. See *Goodwin's Course in Sewing* 23-P.

11-S
Goodwin's Course in Sewing Book III
Published by Frank D. Beattys & Co. N.Y., N.Y., U.S.A.
Copyright 1910 by Emma E. Goodwin
54 pages with 10 sewing projects and 9 separate patterns
Hardcover, 8½" x 6½"

Goodwin's Course in Sewing Book III has a drab green cover with black lettering. I am not sure what the cover looks like on this book, as I have yet to find it. However I have the information as to what was in it because it was the same as the third part of *Goodwin's Home Course in Sewing* 23-P, plate 571.

The introduction states:

The third book of this course is designed to apply to full-sized garments the principles given in the first and second books, and to complete a knowledge that shall enable the pupil to construct all simple, unlined garments and many articles of household utility, as well as to repair them and keep them in order.

The patterns accompanying this book are designed especially for this work by The McCall Company of New York.

The use of the sewing machine, if practicable, for stitching up the seams of the garments is desirable, though the work given may be entirely done by hand if time permits.

The projects without patterns are table napkin, doily, hemstitching on linen, towel. The projects using McCall's patterns are corset cover, drawers, petticoat, dressing sacque, sewing apron, shirtwaist, and seven-gored skirt. The last two patterns, shirtwaist, and gored skirt, makes a shirtwaist dress and the same two patterns may also be used to make a trimmed dress. The instructions are given in the book. **Good condition: $200.00 and up.**

Note: *Goodwin's Course in Sewing Book III* is extremely rare, especially with the patterns intact. See 9-S and 10-S for *Goodwin's Course in Sewing Book I* and *II*. See *Goodwin's Home Course in Sewing* 23-P plate 573 for patterns from book III.

12-S
Sewing Tablet No. 1, A new and Practical Course of
  Graded Sewing Texts
Margaret J. Blair
Published by Webb Publishing Co., St. Paul, Minn., U.S.A.
Copyright 1911 by Margaret J. Blair
33 pages with 3 sewing projects
Softcover, 10" x 6½"

Sewing Tablet No. 1, A new and Practical Course of Graded Sewing Texts has a tan cover with black lettering and a line drawing of a hand holding a torch.

Tablet number one, has eight parts: "Stitches On Canvas," "Running and Basting On Cloth," "Hemming," "Making a Bag," "Making a Towel," "Sewing a Seam," and "Making an Apron." This book is in tablet form and is just one in a series of tablets. There are seven tablets, each one teaching a series of stitches and exercises. The higher the number of the tablet the more difficult the sewing. The note to the teacher reads:

Each lesson is a unit of work. This does not necessarily mean that all the work outlined under a given lesson is to be done in one recitation period. On the contrary, the work of a single lesson often covers several recitation periods. **Good condition: $25.00 and up each tablet.**

13-S
The Sewing Book
Edited by Anne L. Jessup
Published by The Butterick Publishing Co., New York,
  Paris and London
Copyright 1913 by The Butterick Publishing Co.
120 pages with 20+ projects
Hardcover, 9" x 6"

The Sewing Book has a green cover with the title in white on the front cover and spine.

The introduction states: *When sewing, as a branch of manual training, was first made a part of the course of study in our schools, the aim was largely educational: a training of hand and eye with no very definite industrial value. Principals and teachers looked with small favor on the introduction of new subjects into the curriculum. To-day the pendulum has swung far in the opposite direction. Every true educator realizes that the right training of the child is the training for life, and that this training must equip the pupils to meet the practical problems in the everyday world.*

The projects in this book with drafts or instructions are needle book-1, pincushion-1, hair receiver, card case, pencil case, bean bag, pincushion-2, pin ball, needle book-2, iron holder, small doll apron, doll cap, gathered doll apron, work bag, doll dress with shoulder straps, dolls fancy apron, dolls night dress, and dolls kimono. There are also projects to be made using purchased patterns for which just the instructions are given. These are sewing apron, flannel petticoat, white petticoat, gored petti-

coat, nightgown, drawers, princess undergarment or slip, cooking apron, and middy blouse. *The Sewing Book* is a wonderful reference book for dressing dolls in the early 1900s style. **Good condition: $50.00 and up.**

14-S
Shelter and Clothing
Helen Kinne and Anna M. Cooley
Published by The Macmillan Co., N.Y., N.Y., U.S.A.
Copyright 1913 by The Macmillan Co.
377 pages with 12 chapters on sewing and garment making
Hardcover 7½" x 5"

Shelter and Clothing has a green cover with the title printed in black on the front cover and spine.

Shelter and Clothing was intended for the girl pursuing any type of high school or normal school course, as well as for the homemaker. The preface states: *The authors feel that household arts in high schools should not be confined to problems in cooking and sewing. They are only a part of the study of home making. The questions of home organization, management, care, repair, home sanitation, and decoration, are also important, and should find a place in the household arts course of study in every high school.*

The book has two parts, the first being "The Home" and the second "Textiles and Clothing." The first five chapters of part two are on textile materials and how they are made. This includes cotton, flax, wool and silk, with a comparison of chemical differences and varying characteristics and properties.

The last twelve chapters are on sewing and garment making and include "Undergarments," "Patterns," "Drafting," "Cutting," "Embroidery," "History of Costume," "Costume Design," "Hygiene of Clothing," "Economics of Dress," "Care and Repair," "Construction and Millinery."

The sewing chapters throughout the book emphasize the ease of using a sewing machine with praises for its speed in doing long seams, but also points out the dainty light touch of hand finishing. There is also a warning not to buy cheap machine-made goods with coarse stitching which were manufactured in unsanitary conditions. It is evident that the use of the sewing machine at this time was not universally embraced.

Shelter and Clothing is an interesting textbook and well worth reading. **Good condition: $25.00 and up.**

15-S
Sewing, Manuals for Public and Separate Schools
Published by Ontario Department of Education, Canada
Copyright 1914 by The Minister of Education for Ontario
130 pages with sewing lessons
Hardcover, 10" x 6½"

The cover of *Sewing* is plain blue with black lettering. The title, *Sewing, Manuals for Public and Separate Schools*, is printed on the front cover.

In the introduction it is stated: *This manual is intended*

to assist teachers in giving instructions in Sewing, and its use should be supplemented, when necessary, by reference to the books mentioned in the Bibliography.

Educators have realized for some time, that, because of this instinctive tendency in every child to do something, an opportunity should be given to develop the creative side of the child's nature. For this reason, it is now generally recognized that it is necessary to make provision in the elementary schools for some form of handwork, in order that the child may find an avenue for self-expression through the hands. A course in sewing, which is one branch of manual training, is an excellent means by which this need may be met in educating girls. In introducing this work into our schools, we have in view, not only its ultimate practical use, but also its cultural and educational value in training the child.

Woolman says: "Outside of the practical advantage of being able to use the needle, the mental training through eye and hand has been proved to have a permanent effect on the character."

Sewing is a manual of practice sewing. The illustrations are photographs of sewing samples to be done by the student. The projects are at the end of each lesson and are just suggestions. In the early lessons at the beginning of the manual the suggestions are a doll's blanket, bags, aprons, mats, etc. The projects at the end of the manual are a shoe bag, drawers, nightgown, etc. Sewing is an interesting peek into the past and the sewing classrooms of 1914. **Good condition: $25.00 and up.**

Note: Four books in this chapter that were suggested as a supplement to Sewing are School Needlework (2-S), Shelter and Clothing (14-S), Sewing Handicraft for Girls (8-S), and Occupations for Little Fingers (7-S).

16-S
Handbook of Elementary Sewing
Etta Proctor Flagg
Published by Little Brown & Co., Boston, Mass., U.S.A.
Copyright 1915 by Little Brown & Co.
72 pages with 33 sewing projects
Hardcover, 7½" x 5"

Handbook of Elementary Sewing has a tan cover with dark brown lettering. The title is printed on the front and spine

This book was written for elementary school including fourth through seventh grades. The projects for fourth grade are needle case, sewing bag, pinwheel (pin holder), and doll's comfortable (tied blanket). Fifth grade projects are a doll's sunbonnet, laundry bag, potholder, doily, pincushion top, sock darning, and sewing apron with directions for drafting. Sixth grade projects are a bookmark, cooking apron with instructions on drafting, cross-stitch bag, princess slip with purchased pattern, one-piece dress with purchased pattern, and dusting cap made from a draft. The projects for seventh and eight grades are just suggestions and include a full set of underwear with hand decoration and a simple wash dress using purchased patterns.

Supplementary work includes a skirt for a small doll, a doll apron, magazine cover, laundry bag, rubber bag, sewing case, sewing apron, towel, Swedish weaving, doily, corset cover, waist protector, table cover, kimono, fancy apron, and underskirt. The projects all have instruction on stitches and assembling. **Good condition: $50.00 and up.**

Note: A few of the suggestions for seventh and eighth grade had been printed in the School Arts Magazine and were reprinted in this book through the courtesy of the publishers.

17-S
Practical Methods, Aids and Devices for Teachers, Vol. II
Teachers
Published by F. A. Owen Publishing Co., Dansville, N.Y., U.S.A.
Copyright 1915 by F. A. Owen Publishing Co.
256 pages with 7 pages on sewing
Hardcover, 12" x 9"

Practical Methods, Aids and Devices for Teachers, Vol. II has a black cover with gold lettering and the title is on the front cover only.

There are only seven pages of sewing projects in this large book, however there are a number of wonderful black-and-white photographs of children's sewing classes and things they have made. The author of the sewing section Ida Hood Clark, gives outlines for teaching sewing in all the grades and a four-week course in sewing. The rest of the book is on penmanship, drawing, nature, etc. **Good condition: $50.00 and up.**

18-S
A Sewing Course for Teachers
Mary Schenck Wollman
Published by Frederik Fernald, Washington D.C., U.S.A.
Copyright 1893 and 1908 by Mary Schenck Wollman
Revised Fifth Edition 1916
141 pages, a course for teachers
Hardcover, 9½" x 7"

A Sewing Course for Teachers has a plain brown cover with the title in gold on the spine.

In the preface of the first edition of A Sewing Course for Teachers in 1893, Mary Woolman wrote:

The introduction of manual training as a necessary part of education has raised sewing to an art of great importance. Outside of the practical advantage of being able to use the needle, the mental training through hand and eye has been proved to have a permanent effect on the character.

Attention and the power of observation are increased by giving the lesson to an entire class at one time instead of by the old method of showing each pupil separately.

An enthusiastic and progressive teacher can, through sewing, make freer and more capable beings of her pupils and help round out their characters.

By the time the 1916 edition had been published, the preface written by Mary Woolman stated:

The fourth edition of the Sewing Course has been entirely rewritten and contains almost a new volume on teaching.

The book was originally written for the College Students to supplement their instruction by technical data. It is now in use throughout the United States. Since it was first issued in 1893, there has been a great evolution in educational thought and still further changes are imminent. Interest in manual training has grown and is gradually being supplemented by enthusiasm in many new phases of industrial and trade education.

A Sewing Course for Teachers is written for teaching first through eighth grades and projects are too numerous to list, but I will give an example of three for each grade.

First grade: needle book of cardboard, broom cover, canvas bag.

Second grade: doll's blanket and bedspread, clothespin bag, curtains for dollhouse.

Third grade: sunbonnet, coarse work apron, trimmed hat of raffia.

Fourth grade: table covers, book covers, toys.

Fifth grade: articles for doll's house, doll clothing, pattern making for doll or baby.

Sixth grade: simple underclothing, night dresses, gloves.

Seventh grade: sewing and machine work, baby clothing, table and tray covers.

Eight grade: sewing and machine work, summer blouse, graduating dress, baby clothes.

This list is just a sample of projects the teachers should consider. There are no patterns or instructions in the book. The body of the book is on plain sewing and construction. In 1893 *A Sewing Course for Teachers* was one of the first published books for student teachers and set a precedent for many teacher manuals that followed. **Good condition: $75.00 and up.**

19-S

School Sewing Based on Home Problems

Ida Robinson Burton B.S. and Myron G. Burton, A.B.
Published by Ginn & Company, U.S.A. and London
Copyright 1916 by Ginn & Company
393 pages with 60 needlework projects
Hardcover, 9" x 6"

School Sewing Based on Home Problems has a green cover with black line drawings and title. There is a small square in the center of the cover with a young girl sitting at a table in a straight back chair and sewing with the aid of a hoop.

The author writes about the projects in the preface:

In order to meet the widely different conditions of mind, which must necessarily exist in the children who come from homes of varying conditions, a very extensive list of projects has been presented in each section. Kindred ones have been suggested, thus making it possible to claim the interest and attention of every normal girl, allowing her to make articles which are of practical value in her daily experience, and at the same time, enabling her to develop her latent talent for artistic expression.

The book is divided into six sections.

Section 1 projects are needle book, wash cloth, hand towels, handkerchief case, sewing apron, book cover, button bag, hair receiver, and a child's bib.

Section 2 projects are filing pocket, sleevelets, cap, silver case, school bag, broom cover, crocheted turban, darned towel, dresser scarf, and a kitchen apron.

Section 3 projects include traveling case, embroidered napkin, shop apron, ironing board cover, clothespin apron, scalloped towel, fancy apron, bedroom slippers, handmade handkerchief, and an embroidered corset cover.

Section 4 projects are sash curtains, laundry bag, sofa pillow cover, table cover, guest towel, bungalow apron, cooking apron, baseball suit, and a plain petticoat.

Section 5 projects include a coming jacket, nightgown, kimono, princess slip, ruffled petticoat, cambric corset cover, drawers, pajamas, boy's shirt, and embroidered luncheon set.

Section 6 projects are middy blouse, tailored waist, tailored skirt, housedress, school dress, wool dress, silk dress, lingerie dress, gymnasium suit, and coat.

The instructions for the projects include learning the hand stitches, using a sewing machine, and cutting and assembling. **Good condition: $50.00 and up.**

Note: Many projects throughout the book are done from measurements, some from drafts and most in the last chapter from purchased patterns. The early patterns had few instructions and an important part of the sewing lessons was drafting and how to use and alter a commercial pattern.

20-S

Household Arts for Home and School

Anna M. Cooley and Wilhelmina H. Spoh
Published by The Macmillan Co., N.Y., N.Y., U.S.A.
Copyright 1920 by The Macmillan Co.
433 pages with numerous sewing projects
Hardcover, 7½" x 5½"

Household Arts for Home and School has a dark blue cover with a black windowpane design and gold circles surrounding the edge. Inside the circles are line drawings of homemaking items. The title is printed in gold on the front cover and the spine.

Household Arts for Home and School was intended for use in the elementary school or junior high. It was planned for use in schools of all descriptions, except distinctly rural schools.

The book has a story line starting with the eighth grade class at a new school named after Ellen H. Richards, a pioneer in home economics. Miss Ashley the teacher of home economics let the girls help her decorate her new apartment so they could learn about home and management. In the second part, chapter one, the sewing begins.

The girls learn about fabrics, curtains, towels, plain-sewing stitches, how to measure for pillow covers, table covers, bags, and potholders. The girls learn to use the sewing machine and make aprons with work caps and a simple petticoat from patterns.

Some of the projects made from this book are cross-stitch workbag, pin case, thread holder, cotton holder, sewing case, workbag, lettuce bag, hemstitched towel, traveling case, folding sewing bag, and sewing apron. After some of the lessons, it is suggested that some of the items might be made again, for sister's doll.

Interspersed among the sewing projects are lessons on types of fabrics, how they are made and what they are used for. There are also chapters on mending, making over clothing, and taking care of baby. I found this a very interesting, easy-to-read book. **Good condition: $25.00 and up.**

21-S
Sewing and Textiles
Mary L. Matthews
Published by Little Brown and Co., Boston, Mass., U.S.A.
Copyright 1921 by Little Brown and Co.
155 pages with 8 sewing projects
Hardcover, 7½" x 5"

Sewing and Textiles has a plain green cover with the title printed in black on the spine and cover.

The preface states:
This volume is intended for use in places beginning the study of sewing and textiles. It has been arranged for use in the elementary schools and does not presuppose and training in general science.

The projects listed are: sewing apron, nightgown, gift towel, under slip, wash dress, garment bag, linen moneybag, and stove holders. The sewing chapters teach all of the plain sewing stitches and explain how different textiles are made and used. **Good condition: $25.00 and up.**

Note: *Sewing and Textiles* has been republished as the second part in *Elementary Home Economics* see 24-S in this chapter for more content. The wording and photographs were changed a little and a few things were added but it is essentially the same text.

22-S
Essentials of Sewing
Rosamond C. Cook
Published by The Manual Arts Press, Peoria, Illinois, U.S.A.
Copyright 1924 by Rosamond C. Cook
238 pages with 16 sewing chapters
Hardcover, 8" x 5½"

Essentials of Sewing has a green cover with a pair of scissors and the title in black on the front and the title only on the spine.

The chapters include "Sewing Equipment," "Patterns, Hand Stitches," "Plain and Decorative Seams," "Finished Edges,"

"Neckline Finishes for Undergarments," "Plackets, Fastenings," "Ruffles," "Uses of Lace and Insertion," "Pockets," "Mending," "Waistline Finishes," "Neckline Finishes for Outer Garments," "Methods of Placing and Joining Sleeves," and "Methods of Finishing the Bottoms of Sleeves." *Essentials of Sewing* is a great resource for those interested in historical construction of garments. It is well illustrated throughout with photographs. It seems to be the "how-to" book of its time. **Good condition: $25.00 and up.**

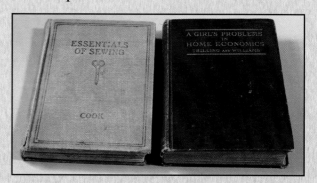

Plate 591. *Essentials of Sewing* by Rosamond C. Cook, copyright 1924. The material in this book has been prepared to aid girls in solving the problems of garment making in school and home. *A Girls Problem in Home Economics* by Mabel Trilling and Florance Williams, copyright 1926. Healthful Clothing, Dress Design, Clothing Constuction, Interior Decoration, Household Textiles, Care of the Home. See (23-S) in this chapter for content.

23-S
A Girl's Problems in Home Economics
Mabel Trilling and Florence Williams
Published by J. E. Lippincott Co., Philadelphia, London, and Chicago
Copyright 1926 by J. E. Lippincott Co.
314 pages with 6 sewing chapters
Hardcover, 7½" x 5½"

A Girl's Problems in Home Economics has either a plain blue or red cover (I've seen both) with the title in gold both on the front and spine.

A Girl's Problems in Home Economics is designed to use as a text for either junior high or the beginning of high school. It is divided into two parts, the first on clothing, the second on house and care. Each chapter has been put into sequential order of increasing difficulty. At the end of each chapter is a test.

The chapters on sewing are "The Sewing Machine and Some Things to Make," "What You Can Make From the Kimono Pattern," "How to Make Bloomers," "How to Dress In Good Taste," "Fabrics That We Use Every Day," and "Making A Dress." The chapter on the kimono pattern tells you how to draft the pattern and make either a kimono, nightgown, or apron dress. The book has 148 plates including many garments from the 1920s that would be helpful in dressing a doll of the period. **Good condition: $50.00 and up.**

24-S
Elementary Home Economics
Mary Lockwood Matthews, B.S.
Published by Little, Brown & Co., Boston, Mass., U.S.A.
Copyright 1926 by Little, Brown & Co.
272 pages with sewing lessons and 11 sewing projects
Hardcover, 7½" x 5"

Elementary Home Economics has a brown cover with two center ovals, each shows a girl, one is cooking, the other being measured for sewing. The title and graphics are dark brown and are on both the front and spine.

The preface states:

This volume is intended for use in classes beginning the study of Home Economics in schools where one book is desired to cover the entire course. It is strictly an elementary treatment of the subject and presupposes little training in general science.

The book is divided into two parts: foods and cookery, and clothing and textiles. The chapters on sewing suggest that the class should have sewing machines. The preliminary lessons are "The Sewing Basket," "Implements For the Sewing Basket," "The Sewing Machine," and "Other Things to Use when Sewing."

The projects are a pincushion, pillowcase, laundry bag, nightgown or pajamas, apron, hemstitched towel, under slip, wash dress, garment bag, linen moneybag, and stove holders. The sewing chapters show all of the plain sewing stitches and explain about different textiles and how they are made. **Good condition: $25.00 and up.**

Note: *Elementary Home Economics* part two, "Clothing and Textiles," is a rewrite of the book *Sewing and Textiles* see 21-S. The wording and photographs were changed a little and a few things were added, but it is essentially the same.

25-S
Needlework for Student Teachers
Amy K. Smith
Published by Sir Isaac Pitman & Sons, LTD., Toronto, and New York
Copyright 1893, 1st edition
Revised 1929, 10th edition
225 pages with instruction on plain sewing
Hardcover, 8½" x 5½"

Needlework for Student Teachers textbook cover is pea-green with black lettering on the front cover and spine.

The revised edition of *Needlework for Student Teachers* described here. Giana Wolverton states in the introduction:

No one can rejoice more than I do over the change that has taken place in the treatment of girls as regards their education.

I am, therefore, very glad to be allowed to say my little say

on this subject as an introduction to this most valuable addition to our plain needlework literature. It deals with the work, common, possible, essential to us all. No woman's education is complete without it. I don't care how fine a scholar she is, how good a musician, how grand an artist, if she cannot cut out and make her own, her husband's, or children's clothes, if required of her — and a time may come to require it in any of us — I do not call her a "perfectly educated" woman.*

The first part of the book deals with stitches and the process used in the making of garments, seaming, hemming, gathering, buttonholes, binding, pleating, and piping. The second part includes patching and hints on practical mending. The third and final part is on darning. There are no projects except the sample pieces one might make learning the stitches and methods of construction. *Needlework for Student Teachers* is a wonderful book for anyone wanting to learn how to construct a garment when sewing by hand. **Good condition: $25.00 and up.**

Note: *Needlework for Student Teachers* was first published in 1892 and revised in years 1893,1894, 1896, 1899, 1905, 1909, 1912, 1914, 1924, and 1929.

26-S
The Home Economics Omnibus
Harris & Huston
Published by Little, Brown & Company, Boston, Massachusetts, U.S.A.
Copyright 1935 by Little Brown and Company
617 pages with 12 sewing chapters
Hardcover, 8" x 5"

The Home Economics Omnibus has a black cover with a large orange circle on the front of the book; the title is printed inside the orange circle in black and on the spine.

The Home Economics Omnibus was written because it was thought that there was a need for a single textbook covering all the phases of home economics as taught in the senior high school. The book was written with seven divisions: "Foods and Nutrition," "Clothing, House Planning and Furnishing," "Home Management," "Child-Care and Development," "Health and Family," and "Other Social Relationships."

The chapter on "The Well-Dressed Girl" is more on how to choose and purchase clothing than to make it. The subtitles are "Good Lines and Proportions," "Basting and Marking Stitches," "Seams," "Setting In of Sleeves," "Buttonholes," "Stitches Combined to Make Embroidery," "Handmade Stitchery," "Children's Clothes," "Darning and Repair of Knitted Underwear," "Repairing Lace," and "Lengthening Clothes." It is obvious by the time this book was written that purchasing clothing was as important as making it. **Good condition: $5.00 and up.**

Plate 592. *Fundamentals of Home Economics* by Milton B. Jensen, Mildred R. Jensen, M. Louisa Ziller, copyright 1935. Designed to present in one volume a series of units from basic home-economics subject matter-knowledge, skills, judgments, appreciation's etc., about one's self, one's home, and one's family. *Fabrics and Dress* by Rathbone & Tarpley, 1948. To help pipils to develop and appreciation of the artistic, economic, and hygienic values involved in the selection of clothing and household fabrics and to help children develop high standards for the construction and care of clothing. See 28-S for content.

27-S
Fundamentals of Home Economics
Milton B. Jensen, Mildred R. Jensen, and M. Louisa Ziller
Published by The Macmillan Co. N.Y., N.Y., U.S.A.
Copyright 1935 by The Macmillan Co.
417 pages with 7 sewing chapters
Hardcover, 9½" x 6½"

Fundamentals of Home Economics has a two-toned green cover. It is divided up into 2" squares with stencils of home-making products in each square. The title is printed on the front and the spine.

The preface states:
This book is designed to present in one volume a series of units from basic home-economics subject matter-knowledge, skills, judgments, appreciation's, etc., about one's self, one's home, and one's family. It has been designed for the junior high-school level with appropriate vocabulary and problems.

The book suggests not using the sewing unit until the eighth grade, however the care of clothing and mending was to be taught in the seventh grade. The sewing chapter shows what tools are needed and how to use them. In section 2 there is information on using the treadle sewing machine. The book suggests using a paper with lines on it to practice straight lines, curves, and corners. Hand sewing is also included such as hems, plackets, trimming and. buttonholes. Section 3 includes making underwear. Section 4 covers making a dress including making your own pattern. Section 5 is making a dress from a purchased pattern, fitting and how to adjust the pattern to fit. Included in Section 6 is children's clothing, with featherstitching, closures, plackets, hems and trimmings. The last, section 7, is a suggestion of gifts you should be able to make after

finishing this book. The list includes candy, jelly, jam, mending kit, shoe-shining kit, hangers, shoe-trees, hat holders, pressing pads, cushions, towels, sheets, pillowcases and dresser scarves. This section also teaches hemstitching. The sewing portion of this book is a very small part of what is offered in this 417-page home-education course. **Good condition: $50.00 and up.**

28-S
Fabrics and Dress
Rathbone and Tarpley
Published by Houghton Mifflin Co., Cambridge,
   Massachusetts, U.S.A.
Copyright 1948 by Lucy Rathbone and Elizabeth Tarpley
419 pages with 20+ sewing chapters
Hardcover, 9" x 6"

Fabrics and Dress has a gray cover with a red outline of a pair of scissors, a tape, measure, and a dress form. The title is printed in black on the front and spine.

The preface states:
The New Revised Edition of Fabrics and Dress has been written with a twofold purpose: (1) to help pupils develop an appreciation of the artistic, economic, and hygienic values involved in the selection of clothing and household fabrics and (2) to help pupils develop high standards for the construction and care of clothing.

In the sewing unit there are chapters on "Fashion, Equipment," "Patterns," "Fabrics," "Buying," "Foundations," "Underclothing," "Sleeping Garments," "Design," "Color," "Making Dresses," "Making Coats," "Baby Clothing," "Children's and Infant's Clothing," "Care and Repair," "Curtains and Draperies," "Upholstery, Rugs, Bedding, Table Linens and Towels." The last 20 pages are on knitting, showing all the knitting stitches, tools and giving the Red Cross directions for knitting two sweaters, socks, and hat. There is a little of everything in "Fabrics and Dress"; all the stitches you need to know to construct a garment, how to cut a pattern and choose your fabric. This is definitely a good teaching book. **Good condition: $10.00 and up.**

29-S
How You Look and Dress
Byrta Carson
Published by McGraw-Hill Book Company, Inc.,
   New York, Toronto, & London
Copyright 1949 by McGraw-Hill Book Company, Inc.
394 pages with 3 projects
Hardcover, 8" x 5½"

How You Look and Dress has a gray cover with green and yellow lettering and graphics, which shows a needle with thread looped around. The title is printed on the front cover and spine.

The book was written for the beginning sewer and has 17 chapters. The first seven chapters are devoted to grooming and choosing clothing. Chapters dedicated to the basic principles of clothing construction are "Using the Sewing Machine," "Sewing By Hand," "Taking Measurements and Altering Patterns," "Cutting and Fitting," "Making a Skirt," "Making a Blouse," "Making a Dress," and "Remodeling Your Clothes."

Other chapters in the book address textiles and remodeling. *How You Look and Dress* is an interesting book and gives an idea of what was important to a teenager in the 1940s. **Good condition: $5.00 and up.**

30-S
Clothing Constuction and Wardrobe Planning
Dora Lewis, Mabel Godde Bowers and Marietta Kettunen
Published by The Macmillan Company, N.Y., N.Y., U.S.A.
Copyright 1955 by The Macmillan Company
565 pages with 19 techniques in sewing
Hardcover, 9½" x 6½"

Clothing Constuction and Wardrobe Planning has a green cover with black and white graphics of a dress form, pattern, scissors and iron. The title is on the front cover and spine.

This is a home economics book about your wardrobe. There are six parts: "Personal Grooming," "Design," "Planning and Budgeting," "Consumer Information," "Care of Clothing," "Sewing Techniques," and "Careers in Clothing." The chapter on "Sewing Techniques" takes you through the steps of constructing a garment, including altering the pattern and fitting the garment, cutting and marking, interfacing, linings, seam finishes, darts, pleats, tucks, gathers, and finishing. The last chapter, "Careers in Clothing," tells of the many careers opportunities open to a person who has studied clothing, such as teaching, home demonstration, dressmaking, designing, etc. **Good condition: $5.00 and up.**

31-S
Teaching Children Embroidery
Anne Butler
Published by Studio Vista, London, England
Copyright 1964 by Anne Butler
56 pages with 7 chapters on free embroidery
Hardcover, 12½" x 7½"

Teaching Children Embroidery has plain red background with a red-and-white photograph of a child's embroidered piece depicting a school. The title printed in gold on the spine.

The emphasis in this book is on "free embroidery." The author feels that using a free approach will bring out a child's creative ability. Young children are encouraged to play with materials with color and texture to gain inspiration. The child starts out by gluing yarn to fabric forming different shapes, or gluing small fabric shapes into pleasing arrangements. As the child progresses he learns to use thread and yarn to attach the shapes.

There are suggestions of projects to keep the child interested, such as cushions, tray cloths, containers, hair bands, dolls, bags, etc. There are black-and-white photographs of embroidered pic-

tures done by groups of children at different ages. *Teaching Children Embroidery* is intended to instruct the child from primary school through junior high. **Good condition: $5.00 and up .**

Plate 593. *Clothes: Clothing Construction and Wardrobe Planning* by Lewis, Bowers and Kettunen, copyright 1955. The authors and editors have taken into account the dramatic changes that have taken place in home and community living in the past decade. See 30-S for content. *Part of Your World* by Margil Vanderhoff, copyright 1968. *Clothes—Part of Your World* is designed to serve as a guide for the study of clothing. It is planned particularly for secondary school girls, but other persons may find it useful as a reference.

32-S
Clothes: Part of Your World
Margil Vanderhoff
Published by Ginn & Company, Boston Massachusetts, U.S.A.
Copyright 1968 by Ginn & Company
Pages 275 with 2 units on sewing
Hardcover, 19½" x 8¼"

Clothes: Part of Your World is a yellow book with cover artwork depicting seven teenage girls wearing stylish 1960s clothing. The title is on the front and spine.

Written in the preface is *"Clothes-Part of your World" is designed to serve as a guide for the study of clothing. It is planned particularly for secondary school girls, but other persons may find it useful as a reference.*

There are nine units in this book but only three deal with sewing. By the 1960s, the influence in home economics was on buying clothing rather than making it. A good portion of the book is devoted to the study of clothing, planning a wardrobe, selecting fabrics, reading labels and hang tags, storing clothing, washing and ironing. Unit 7 chapters are "Why Learn to Sew?" "How to Develop Sewing Skills," "Equipment," "Patterns," "Alterations," and "Fabric and Thread." There are seven projects that help you to learn: a simple blouse, A-line skirt with waistband, blouse with attached collar, set-in sleeves and buttonholes, jumper with waistline seam and long back-zipper placket, underlined skirt and blouse (separates or an outfit), and a one-piece dress. Each project takes you through the entire process while using a purchased pattern. Unit 8 chapters are "Alterations" and "Repairs." The last unit in the book covers "Vocations Which Require Clothing and Textile Knowledge."

Children's School Sewing Books

Clothes: Part of Your World is a good reflection of home economics in the 1960s. **Good condition: $5.00 and up.**

33-S
Stitchery for Children
Jacqueline Enthoven
Published by Van Nostrand Reinhold Co., New York, Cincinnati, Toronto, London and Melborne
Copyright 1968 by Jacqueline Enthoven
172 pages with stitchery suggestions and instructions
Hardcover, 10½" x 7"

The book *Stitchery for Children* has a plain-red cover with the title printed in gold on the spine. The book jacket has a blue-and-white background and a brown burlap picture with a pink yarn bear stitched in the center.

Stitchery for Children is a manual for teachers and parents. It has five chapters: 'Stages of Development," "Learning Stitches," "Designing Stitcheries," "Children with Special Needs," and "Suggested Materials." There is also an index of stitches.

The author recommends starting children as young as two-and-a-half with spontaneous stitching. The book progresses through each age in a child's life with what might be expected in creativity and interest. Suggestions are given as to size and materials. In chapter two there are descriptions of stitches and their variations and chapter three, covers planning, designs on paper, use of stitches in design, and the use of color.

The book is filled with children's work from the ages of two-and-a-half through high school. There are no patterns; the book is intended to teach creativity and, if used correctly, it certainly would. **Good condition: $5.00 and up.**

34-S
Introduction to Fashion Dressmaking
Department of Sewing Education
Published by The Singer Co., U.S.A.
Copyright 1971 by The Singer Co.
80 pages with 6 chapters on sewing
Softcover, 9" x 7"

Introduction to Fashion Dressmaking has a white cover with a brown print in the shape of a sewing machine. The title is in red and black on the front of the cover. This is a dressmaking I student's book.

There are six chapters: "Design elements-figure-types-pattern and fabric selection." "Your pattern and how to use it," which includes marking, fitting, alterations, etc. "Cutting-marking-getting to know your sewing machine." "Fitting-permanent stitching-pressing-zipper application." Second fabric fitting-seams-facing-interfacings." The last chapter VI is "The Finishing Touches."

Introduction to Fashion Dressmaking also features charts;

there are charts on fibers, figure type, pattern alterations, sewing equipment, fabrics, threads, needles, and stitch lengths. There is a Glossary in the back of the book as well as an Index. **Good condition: $5.00 and up.**

Note: See 35-S for *Fashion Dressmaking*, *Dressmaking II Student's Book.*

35-S
Fashion Dressmaking
Department of Sewing Education
Published by The Singer Co., U.S.A.
Copyright 1971 by The Singer Co.
126 pages with 6 chapters on sewing
Softcover, 9" x 7"

Fashion Dressmaking has a white cover with a blue print in the shape of a sewing machine. The lettering is in blue and black on the front of the cover. This is a dressmaking II student's book.

This book is the second in a series of dressmaking books by Singer. The first book taught the basic sewing techniques and this second book provides more sophisticated sewing methods that will take you toward the goal of mastering the art of sewing.

There are six chapters: "Selecting your pattern, fabric, underlining and interfacing." "Fitting and altering your pattern, cutting and marking your fashion fabric." "Fitting, underlining, pressing, constructing darts, seams and buttonholes." "Fitting and joining your bodice and skirt-applying the zipper and neckline finish." "Constructing sleeves and cuffs, patch pockets and flaps." The last chapter, VI includes "Constructing Belts and Hems — Applying Finishing Touches."

There is a Glossary in the back of the book as well as an Index and a bonus chapter at the end that covers sewing with knits. **Condition: $5.00 and up.**

Note: See 34-S for *Introduction to Fashion Dressmaking*, *Dressmaking I Student's Book.*

Plate 594. *Dress* by Gawne and Oerke, copyright 1975. Most of the book will be of equal value to young men and young women. *Creative Living* by Glencoe, copyright 1990. From the fundamentals of relationship skills to the latest in microwave techniques, *Creative Living* provides a complete home economics program. See 37-S for content.

36-S
Dress
Eleanor Jerner Gawne and Bess V. Oerke
Published by Chas. A. Bennett Co., Inc., Peoria, Illinois
Fourth copyright 1975 by Eleanor Jerner Gawne and
  Bess V. Oerke
672 pages with chapters on clothing, fabrics and careers
Hardcover, 9½" x 7"

Dress has a pink and white cover with the title printed in yellow and white. There are suggestions of line drawings of young people in various fashions along the bottom of the cover. The title is also printed on the spine.

Dress was first written in 1956, for high school students and this 1975 edition has been revised to reflect the changes in society. There are chapters for men as well as women. The preface states:

Most of the book will be of equal value to young men and young women.

The book is divided into five parts: "Personal Clothing Needs," "Clothing the Family," "Textile Fabrics," "Clothing Construction and Alterations," and "Looking-Ahead." *Dress* is crammed full of information, everything from the history of dress to make-up, storage, fabrics and careers. **Good condition: $5.00 and up.**

Note: *Dress* was Copyright in 1956, 1960, 1969, and 1975.

37-S
Creative Living
Published by Glencoe, a division of Macmillan/McGraw-
  Hill

Copyright 1990 by Glencoe, a division of Macmillan/
  McGraw-Hill
704 pages with 1 unit on clothing and textiles
Hardcover, 10½" x 9½"

Creative Living has a dark blue cover with a young girl and boy holding hands and running with pink reflecting outlines behind them. The title is on the front and spine.

The book shown here is the teachers' edition and the introduction states:

The primary goal of the "Creative Living" text is to offer comprehensive coverage that will fit your home economics curriculum. From the fundamentals of relationship skills to the latest in microwave techniques, "Creative Living" provides a complete home economics program. The second objective is to encourage critical thinking. "Creative Living" does much more than presents the facts. Students become actively involved-through discussions and activities-in responsible decision making as reflected in their daily life choices.

Creative Living is written for boys and girls. The unit on clothing is quite comprehensive. The chapters are "Clothing and You," "Design and Your Appearance," "Clothes and Fashion," "Fibers and Fabrics," "Planning Your Wardrobe," "Shopping For Clothes," "Selecting Patterns," "Fabrics and Notions," "Sewing Equipment," "Lay Out, Cut and Mark," "Basic Construction," "Adding the Details," "Clothes Care," "Redesigning and Recycling," "Careers in Clothing and Textiles," and "Teen Tips." *Creative Living* gives a good history of home economics in the 1990s. **Good condition: $5.00 and up.**

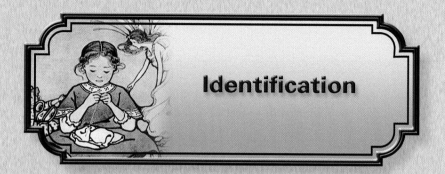

Identification

Information shared on children's sewing sets

I have tried to show all the dolls, patterns, and implements found in various types of doll sewing and embroidery sets in this chapter. In some cases the articles were securely fastened to the sets and I did not want to remove any items that would take away originality, only those that were loose or easily removed.

I feel it is important to preserve these sets in the way they were originally manufactured if possible. All of the contents have been listed in the captions of the sets in previous chapters and hopefully they can all be seen. If you are missing a pair of scissors, card of thread, etc., this chapter should be able to help you find the suitable replacement.

Oh You Beautiful Doll
An identification guide to dolls found in sewing sets.

Plate 595. Dolls found in bisque doll sewing and embroidery sets.

A. 5½" bisque head doll marked "SFBJ/302/Paris" with a mohair wig, stationary glass eyes, open mouth with teeth, and a five-piece composition body, blue painted shoes, and white socks. Found in French Doll with Machine bisque doll sewing set.

B. 7" bisque head marked "S & H" on head (Simon & Halbig Germany). Doll has a silk fiber wig, glass sleep eyes, open mouth with teeth, five-piece composition body with two strap orange shoes, and white socks. Found in Dolly Dress makers Sewing Set bisque doll sewing set.

C. 3¾" All bisque German doll with numbers too faint to read. Doll has molded painted hair, painted features, is joined at

shoulders with wire, and painted blue boots and green banded socks. Found in My Dolly's Workbox bisque doll sewing set marked "Germany."

D. 4" unmarked German bisque head doll, with a mohair wig, stationary glass eyes, and a five-piece composition body with two strap shoes. Found in an unmarked bisque doll sewing set.

E. 3½" all bisque doll marked "Germany" with painted hair, headband and features, jointed only at the shoulders. Found in My Dolly's Workbox bisque doll sewing set marked "Germany."

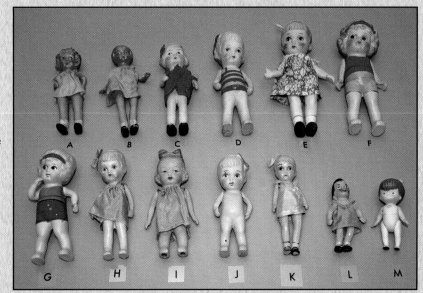

Plate 596. More dolls found in bisque doll sewing and embroidery sets.

A. 6" marked "Made in Japan" painted all bisque doll (Shirley Temple lookalike), jointed at arms and hips with painted hair, features, shoes and socks. Found in Standard Toykraft bisque doll sewing set.

B. 6" marked "Made in Japan" painted all bisque doll (Patsy look-alike), jointed at arms and hips with painted hair features, shoes and socks. Found in Standard Toykraft bisque doll sewing sets.

C. 6" marked "Made in Japan" all bisque doll jointed at arms with painted hair, hair-bow, features, and shoes and socks. Found in Transogram Co. bisque doll sewing sets.

D. 6½" marked "Made in Japan" all bisque doll, jointed at arms with painted features, sunsuit, and hair bow. Found in American Toy Works bisque doll sewing sets.

E. 7½" marked "Made in Japan" all bisque doll with a five-piece jointed body, molded loop for hair bow, painted hair, features, shoes and socks. Found in American Toy Works and Standard Toykraft bisque doll sewing sets. Either with or without painted clothing.

F. 7¾" marked "Made in Japan" all bisque doll jointed at arms with painted hair, hair-band, features, and sunsuit. Found in Pressman Co. and Gropper Toy bisque doll sewing sets, sometimes painted differently.

G. 5½" marked "Made in Japan" all bisque doll, jointed at arms, painted hair, hair band, features, and sunsuit. Found in Transogram Co. and American Toy Works bisque doll sewing sets.

H. 5½" marked Made in Japan all bisque doll jointed at the arms with a molded bow loop, painted hair, and features. Found in American Toy Works bisque doll sewing sets.

I. 5¼" all bisque doll, marked "NIPPON" molded and painted hair bow, hair, and features, open/closed mouth, jointed at arms only. Found in Standard Toykraft sewing sets.

J. 5½" marked "Made in Japan" all bisque doll, jointed at arms with painted features and hair bow. Found in Pressman Co. and Standard Toykraft bisque doll sewing sets. Either with or without painted clothing.

K. 5" marked "Made in Japan" all bisque doll, hair bow loop on head, jointed arms and hips with painted hair, features, shoes, and socks. Found in Transogram Co. bisque doll sewing sets.

L. 3½" marked "Made in Japan" painted all bisque, jointed at arms and hips with slightly bent legs, painted hair features, shoes, and socks. Found in Transogram Co. bisque doll sewing sets.

M. 3½" marked 1968 Joan Walsh Anglund all bisque, jointed at arms and hips with painted hair, eyes, and underwear. Found in Joan Walsh Anglund bisque doll sewing sets.

Note: Many of these dolls were made in different sizes and purchased to fit the sets.

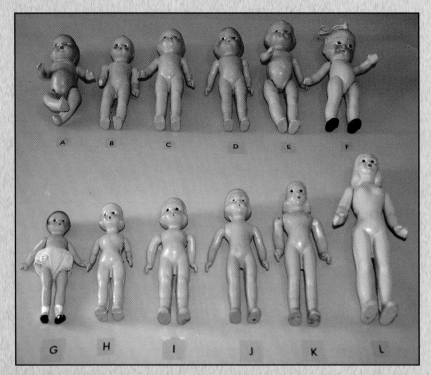

Plate 597. Dolls found in composition doll sewing and embroidery set.

A. 7" unmarked bent limb baby jointed at arms and legs, molded painted hair and features. Found in Victor Eckhardt Manufacturing Co. composition doll sewing sets.

B. 7" unmarked, jointed at arms only, molded painted hair and features. Found in American Toy Works composition doll sewing sets.

C. 7¾" unmarked, jointed at arm only, molded painted hair and features, molded shoes and socks. Found in J.Pressman & Co. composition doll sewing sets.

D. 8" unmarked jointed at arms only, molded painted hair and features, molded shoes and socks. Found in American Toy Works composition doll sewing sets.

E. 8½" unmarked, jointed at arms and legs, molded painted hair and features. Found in Transogram Co. composition doll sewing sets.

F. 8" unmarked, jointed at arms and legs, molded painted hair and features and shoes, molded loop in hair for bow. Found in unknown composition doll sewing set Doll and Sewing Machine.

G. 6" Effanbee//Wee Patsy incised on dolls back, jointed at arms and legs, molded painted features and hair, painted shoes and socks. Found in Effanbee Play Products composition doll sewing sets.

H. 6" & 7½"unmarked, jointed at arms only, molded painted hair and features, molded shoes and socks. Sometimes found with plastic arms. Found in Minerva Toy Co. and Standard Toykraft composition doll sewing sets.

I. 6¼" unmarked, jointed at arms only, molded painted hair and features, molded shoes and socks. Sometimes found with plastic arms. Found in Transogram Co., Standard Toykraft, Progressive Toy Corp., New York Toy & Game Co., Concord Toy Co., J. Pressman & Co., and Rosebud Art Co. composition doll sewing sets.

J. 7" unmarked, jointed at arms only, molded painted hair and features, molded shoes. Found in Toy Creations, Inc., Tran sogram Co., and J. Pressman composition doll sewing sets.

K. 7½" unmarked, jointed at arms only, molded painted hair and features, molded shoes and socks. Found in Standard Toykraft composition doll sewing sets.

L. 10" embossed Pressman Toy (faintly) on back, jointed at arms only, molded painted hair and features, molded shoes and socks. Found in Pressman Toy Corp. composition doll sewing sets. The same mold only 9½" and embossed (faintly) on back Transogram Co.//New York is found in Transogram Co. composition doll sewing sets.

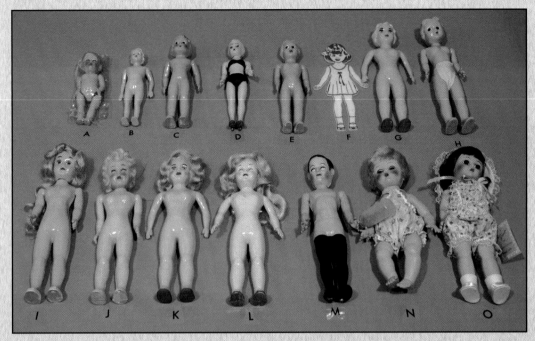

Plate 598. Dolls found in hard plastic sewing and embroidery sets.

A. 4½" jointed at head, arms, and legs, moving eyes, bare feet, marked "Hong Kong." Found in Samuel Gabriel & Sons Co. hard plastic doll sets.

B. 5" jointed at arms only, painted eyes, molded shoe, no markings. Found in Hasbro Bros., and Standard Toycraft hard plastic doll sets.

C. 6" jointed at arms only, painted eyes, molded shoe, no markings. Found in DeLuxe Game Corp. hard plastic doll sets.

D. 6" jointed at head and arms, moving eyes, molded shoe with heel painted red, marked "Hong Kong." Found in Transogram hard plastic doll sets.

E. 6" jointed at arms only, painted eyes, molded shoe, no markings. Found in Transogram, and Standard Toykraft hard plastic doll sets.

F. 6" tall ⅛" thick, unjointed, painted eyes, molded shoe outlined in red, no markings. Found in Hasbro Bros. hard plastic doll sets.

G. 7" jointed at arms only, painted eyes, molded shoes painted red, marked "Hasbro." Found in Hasbro Bros. hard plastic doll sets.

H. 7½" jointed at arms and head, painted eyes, molded shoes, no markings. Found in J. Pressman hard plastic doll sets.

I. 7½" jointed at arms and head, moving eyes, molded shoes painted white, no markings. Found in Empire Plastics hard plastic doll sets.

J. 7½" jointed at the arms and head, moving eyes, molded shoes painted white, marked "Transogram." Found in Transogram hard plastic doll sets.

K. 7½" jointed at arms only, painted eyes, molded shoes painted red, marked "Hasbro." Found in Hasbro Bros. hard plastic doll sets.

L. 7½" jointed at arm and head, painted eyes, molded shoes painted red, marked "Hasbro." Found in Hasbro Bros. hard plastic doll sets.

M. 7½" jointed at arms and neck, moving eyes, molded shoes and legs painted black, unmarked. Found in Transogram hard plastic doll sets.

N. 8" jointed at arms, head, and legs, moving eyes, bare feet, marked "Madame Alexander" on clothing only. Found in FAO Schwarz hard plastic doll sets

O. 8" jointed at arms, head and legs, moving eyes, bare feet, marked "Alexander" on back, "Wendy Loves to Sew" on sunsuit. Found in Madame Alexander hard plastic doll sets.

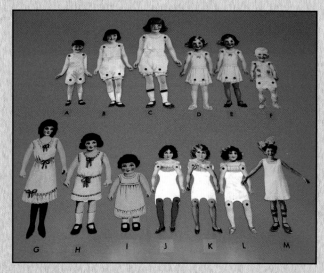

Plate 599. Dolls found in paper doll sewing and embroidery sets.

A Bobbie 7½" with jointed arms and legs. Found in Dennison Little Tots crepe paper doll outfit and crepe paper doll outfit #36.

B. Betty 8" with jointed arms and legs. Found in Dennison Little Tots crepe paper doll outfit and crepe paper doll outfit #36.

C. Eleanor 10" with jointed arms and legs. Found in Dennison Little Tots crepe paper doll outfit and crepe paper doll outfit #36.

D. Embossed 7½" blonde little girl with jointed arms and legs. Found in Dennison's Crepe and Tissue Paper Doll Outfit #33.

E. Embossed 7½" brunette little girl with jointed arms and legs. Found in Dennison's Crepe and Tissue Paper Doll Outfit #33.

F. Embossed 6¼" blonde baby with jointed at arms and legs. Found in Dennison's Crepe and Tissue Paper Doll Outfit #33.

G. Big sister, 9½". Found in Bradely's Tru-Life Paper Dolls.

H. Little Sister, 8". Found in Bradely's Tru-Life Paper Dolls.

I. Baby Sister, 6". Found in Bradely's Tru-Life Paper Dolls.

J. Embossed 7" brunette jointed at arms and legs. Found in Dennison's Crepe and Tissue Paper Doll Outfit#31.

K. Embossed 7" blonde jointed at arms and legs. Found in Dennison's Crepe and Tissue Paper Doll Outfit #33.

L. Embossed 7" brunette jointed at arms and legs. Found in Dennison's Crepe and Tissue Paper Doll Outfit, 1905

M. Pastboard, 7½", hand painted unjointed blonde doll. Found in Dollies Sewing Box.

Plate 600. More dolls found in paper doll sewing and embroidery sets.

A. Blonde, 10½" heavy board. Found in *The Sewing Book of the Roundabout Dolls* by McLoughlin Brothers.

B. Brunette, 10½" heavy board. Found in *The Sewing Book of the Roundabout Dolls* by McLoughlin Brothers.

C. Redhead, 10" posterboard. Found in American Toy Works paper doll sewing sets.

D. Blonde, 10" posterboard. Found in American Toy Works paper doll sewing sets.

E. Brunette, 10" posterboard. Found in American Toy Works paper doll sewing sets.

F. Joy, 10" cardboard. Found in Minerva Toy Co. paper doll sewing sets.

G. Margie, 10" pasteboard. Found in Ruth's Hand Painted Front and Back Doll paper doll sewing sets.

H. Girls, 5¾" pasteboard. Found in American Toy Works paper doll sewing sets.

I. Girls, 5½" pasteboard. Found in American Toy Works paper doll sewing sets.

J. Girls, 5¾" pasteboard. Found in Transogram Co. paper doll sewing sets.

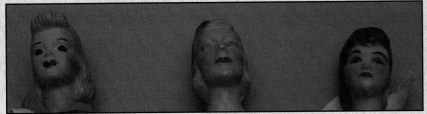

From left to right:

A. Peggy McCall's 13½" doll. Found in all McCalls Sewing Sets.
B. Junior Miss, 13½" doll. Found in all Junior Miss Fashion Designing Sets.
C. Simplicity 12½" doll. Found in Simplicity Fashiondol, Miniature Fashions #102, Marianne's Fashion Designing Set #100, Vivianne's Fashion Designing Set, and Simplicity Miniature Fashions Set.

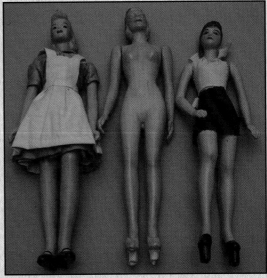

Plate 601. Composition dolls found in mannequin sewing sets.

From left to right:

A. Fashiondol 15½" doll. Found in Fashiondol #705 sets.
B. Butterick 12½" doll. Found in Singer Sewhandy Mannikin Set, Singer Mannikin Doll Set, and Ideal Butterick Sew Easy Designing Set.
C. Fashiondol 12" doll. Found in Fashiondol #503 Sets.
D. Susanne 11½" doll. Found in Susanne's Fashion Show Sets.

Plate 603. Rubber and vinyl type dolls found in mannequin sewing sets.

A. The tallest doll is 10" has a mohair glued on wig, painted eyes and shoes and socks. Found in French celluloid outfit, circa 1920. The very same doll but smaller (not shown) is found in the french 8" doll set.
B. The doll in the middle is 7", has a glued on mohair wig, painted eyes and shoes and socks. Found in Jouet De France.
C. The last doll is 7½", and she has a synthetic glued on wig, painted eyes and shoes and socks. Found in Poppeto.

Plate 605. Celluloid dolls found in sewing and embroidery sets for dolls of various materials.

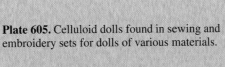

Identification

Snip and Sew

Tools and supplies including cards, ropes, skeins and balls thread found in children's sewing and embroidery sets.

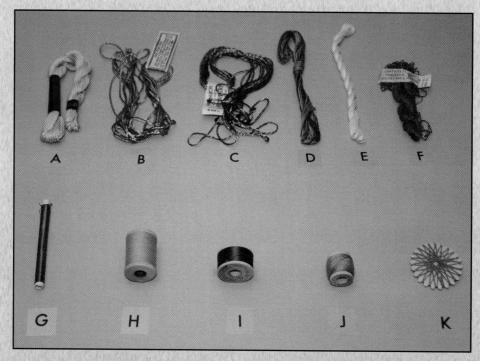

Plate 606. Thread found in bisque doll sewing & embroidery sets.

A. Royal Society perle cotton. Found in J. Pressman bisque doll sewing and embroidery sets.

B. Coats & Clarks silk floss. Found in J. Pressman bisque doll sewing and embroidery sets.

C. Premer rayon embroidery floss. Found in Transogram Co. bisque doll sewing and embroidery sets.

D. Unmarked multicolor cotton floss. Found in American Toy Works, and Minerva Toy Co. bisque doll sewing and embroidery sets.

E. Unmarked ropes of cotton embroidery floss. Found in Standard Toykraft bisque doll sewing and embroidery bisque doll sets.

F. Corlicelli silk-floss. Found in Transogram Co. bisque doll sewing and embroidery sets.

G. Cardboard tubes with silk or cotton thread. Found in early unmarked bisque doll sewing and embroidery sets.

H. Wooden spools of cotton thread. Found in early unmarked bisque doll sewing and embroidery sets.

I. Buttonhole twist. Found in Transogram Co. bisque doll sewing and embroidery sets.

J. Cotton darning thread. Found in Gropper Toy Co. and Standard Toykraft bisque doll sewing and embroidery sets.

K. Cardboard thread wheels. Found in early unmarked bisque doll sewing and embroidery sets.

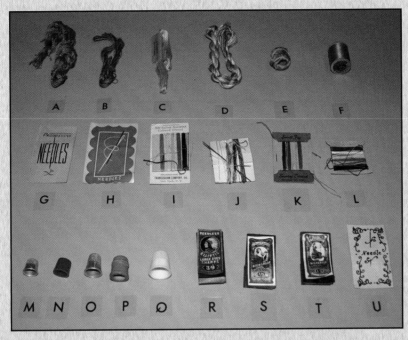

Plate 607. Thread and tools found in composition doll sewing and embroidery sets.

A. Hank of twisted silk like floss. Found in Doll and Machine composition doll sewing set.

B. Multicolor thread. Found in American Toy Works, Standard Toykraft Poducts, Concord Toys, and Progressive Toy Corp. composition doll sewing and embroidery sets.

C. Skein of cotton embroidery floss found in Victor Eckhardt Co. composition doll sewing and embroidery sets.

D. Multicolor twisted heavy floss. Found in Toy Creations Inc. composition doll sewing and embroidery sets.

E. ¾" cardboard spool of thread. Found in Pressman Co., Victor Eckhardt, and Standard Toykraft composition doll sewing and embroidery sets.

F. Wooden spool of thread. Found in Doll and Machine composition doll sewing sets.

G. Needle paper marked "Progressive." Found in Progressive Toy Corp. composition doll sewing and embroidery sets.

H. Needle paper. Found in J. Pressman Toy Corp. composition doll sewing and embroidery sets.

I. Thread card marked Transogram. Found in Transogram Co. composition doll sewing sets.

J. Unmarked thread card. Found in Standard Toykraft Products, Inc. composition doll sewing sets.

K. Small Fry thread card. Found in J. Pressman Co. composition doll sewing sets.

L. Spool shaped thread card. Found in J. Pressman Co. composition doll sewing sets.

M. ½" high aluminum thimble. Found in Transogram Co., Standard Toykraft Products, J. Pressman Co., Progressive Toy Corporation, and Doll with Machine composition doll sets.

N. ½" high blue plastic thimble. Found in Transogram Co. composition doll sewing and embroidery sets.

O. ¾" high aluminum thimble. Found in American Toy Works and Victor Eckhardt composition doll sewing and embroidery sets.

P. ¾" high pink wooden thimble. Found in Transogram Co. composition doll sewing and embroidery sets.

Q. ⅞" tall white plastic thimble. Found in Pressman Co. composition doll sewing and embroidery sets.

R. Peerless Elleptic needles. Found in Doll and Machine composition doll sewing and embroidery sets.

S. Dix and Rands needles. Found in American Toy Works composition doll sewing and embroidery sets.

T. Standard Sharps needles. Found in Standard Toykraft Products, Inc. composition doll sets.

U. Decorated needle card. Found in Concord Toys composition doll sewing and embroidery sets.

Identification

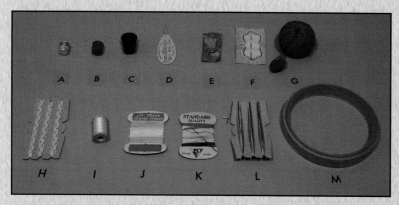

Plate 608. Accessories found in hard plastic doll sewing and embroidery sets.

A. Metal thimble ½" high. Found in Hasbro Bros., De Luxe Game Corp., and Standard Toykraft Products sewing and embroidery sets.

B. Colored plastic thimble, ½" high. Found in Hasbro Bros., Pressman & Co., Transogram, and Empire Plastics sewing and embroidery sets.

C. Colored plastic thimble, ¾" high. Found in Samuel Gabriels & Sons & Co., FAO Schwarz, and Hasbro Bros. sewing and embroidery sets.

D. White oval needle threader with printed instructions. Found in Hasbro Bros. sewing and embroidery sets.

E. Silver needle threader. Found in Pressman & Co., Lisbeth Whiting, and Hasbro Bros. sewing and embroidery sets.

F. Needle paper. Found in Hasbro Bros. sewing and embroidery sets.

G. 1¾" dia. tomato pincushion with emery. Found in Hasbro Bros., Pressman & Co., Lisbeth Whiting, and FAO Schwarz sewing sets.

H. 3⅛" x 1¾" trimmings card. Found in Hasbro Bros. sewing sets.

I. 1" wooden spool of thread. Found in Hasbro Bros., Pressman & Co., and Transogram Co. sewing sets.

J. Jr. Miss thread card. Found in Hasbro Bros. sewing sets.

K. Standard Quality thread card. Found in Standard Toykraft sewing sets.

L. Unmarked thread card. Found in Hasbro Bros. sewing set.

M. 4" cardboard hoop. Found in Hasbro Bros. and Lisbeth Whiting sewing and embroidery sets.

A. Thread card. Found in Trim Dotty's Dresses, Whitman Publishing Co. paper doll sewing and embroidery sets.

B. Thread card. Found in Transogram Co. paper doll sewing and embroidery sets.

C. Thread skein. Found in Minerva Toy Co, Cardinal Games, American Toy Works, Concord Toys, and Progressive Toy, Corp. paper doll sewing and embroidery sets.

D. Skein of thread with Standard wrap. Found in Betsy McCall and Standard Toykraft paper doll sewing and embroidery sets.

E. Thread card. Found in Ontex paper doll sewing and embroidery sets.

F. Thread spools. Found in Peter Austin paper doll sewing sets.

G. Thread card. Found in Ontex paper doll sewing and embroidery sets.

H. Thimble ½" medal. Found in Transogram Co., Progressive Toy Corp. and Hassenfeld Brothers paper doll sewing and embroidery sets.

I. Wooden thimble. Found in Peter Austin and Transogram paper doll sewing and embroidery sets.

J. Thimble, ⅞". Found in Standard Toykraft and Advance Games paper doll sewing and embroidery sets.

K. Scissors, 3¼". Found in American Toy Works, Advance Games, Transogram Co., Minerva Toy Co., Peter Austin, Standard Toykraft, Progrossive Toy Corp., and Hassenfeld Brothers paper doll sewing and embroidery sets.

L. Scissors, 4". Found in McLoughlin Brothers and Ontex paper doll sewing sets.

M. Scissors, 4". Found in Cut and Sew Handicraft (Sosaku) paper doll sewing and embroidery sets.

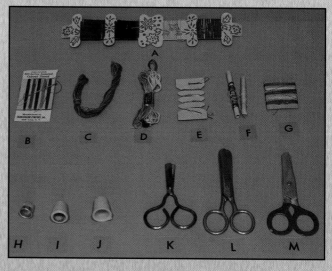

Plate 609. Accessories found in paper doll sewing & embroidery sets.

A. Twisted rope. Found in Transogram Co. embroidery sets.

B. Transogram thread card. Found in Transogram Co. embroidery sets.

C. Coats & Clark's embroidery floss. Found in Hasbro and Whitman Publishing Co. embroidery sets.

D. H.D. embroidery floss. Found in H. Davis Co. embroidery sets.

E. Twisted floss. Found in Standard Toykraft embroidery sets.

F. Royal Society rope. Found in American Toy Works embroidery sets.

G. Hank of various sizes threads. Found in American Toy Works embroidery sets.

H. Cardboard spool. Found in Multiprint Co., Italy embroidery sets.

I. Twisted string-like floss. Found in Concord Toy Co. and Borgfeldt embroidery sets.

J. Silk like floss. Found in Transogram Co. embroidery sets.

K. Menda mending thread. Found in Chad Valley embroidery sets.

L. Royal Society cotton yarn. Found in H. Davis Co. embroidery sets.

M. 1" thread ball. Found in Spears Games embroidery sets.

N. Standard Quality thread card. Found in Standard Toykraft embroidery sets.

O. Kolester Floss. Found in Transogram Co. embroidery sets.

P. ¾" cardboard thread spool. Found in Standard Toykraft embroidery sets.

Q. Twisted rope. Found in Concord Toy Co. embroidery sets.

R. Hasbro floss. Found in Hasbro embroidery sets.

S. Lilly floss. Found in Golden Needle embroidery sets

T. Royal Society floss. Found in Ullman Co. embroidery sets

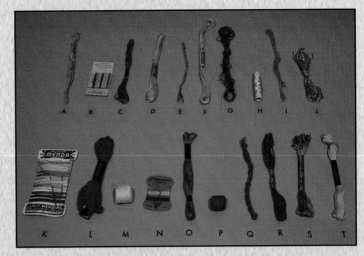

Plate 610. Thread and yarn found in children's embroidery sets.

A. 2⅝" metal pointed scissors. Found in Joan Walsh Anglund sewing set.

B. 3¼" metal blunt nose scissors. Found in J. Pressman, American Toy Works, Gropper Toys, Standard Toykraft, Transogram Co., and Minerva Toy Co. sewing and embroidery sets.

C. 3½" metal pointed scissors. Found in Transogram Co. sewing and embroidery sets.

D. 3½" decorated metal pointed scissors. Found in German sewing sets.

E. 4" metal blunt nose scissors. Found in Gropper Toy's sewing and embroidery sets.

F. ½" metal thimble. Found in J. Pressman sewing and embroidery sets.

G. ½" metal thimble marked "To a Good Girl." Found in Transogram Co. sewing and embroidery sets.

H. ⅝" metal thimble with a blue band, marked "Japan." Found in American Toy Works sewing and embroidery sets.

I. ¾" plastic thimble. Found in Transogram Co. sewing and embroidery sets.

J. Dix & Rands High Grade sharps. Found in J. Pressman bisque doll sewing and embroidery sets.

K. Standard Highgrade sharps found in Standard Toykraft sewing and embroidery sets.

L. Peerless Elliplic large eye sharps. Found in Transogram Co. sewing and embroidery sets.

M. Superior Imperial sharps. Found in American Toy Works bisque doll sewing and embroidery sets.

Note: I have not listed scissors for the early sewing sets, for the most part they didn't seem to have scissors, and when they did they were usually fine adult sewing scissors. The most prevalent scissors found in the bisque doll sets is scissors B. This type of scissors was advertised in the back of toy catalogs such as Playthings. Companies such as E.L. Sommers, Eastern Tool & Mfg. Co., or Michigan Wire Goods Co. would advertise toy parts in stock or made to order.

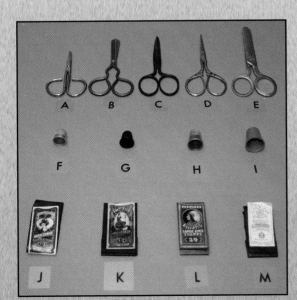

Plate 611. Accessories found in bisque doll sewing and embroidery sets.

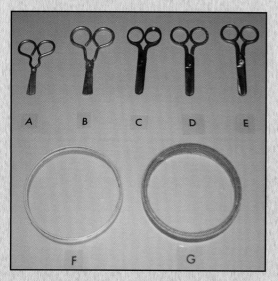

Plate 612. Accessories found in composition doll sewing and embroidery sets.

A. 3¼" wire blunt-nose scissors. Found in Transogram Co., New York Toy & Game Co., Victor Eckhardt Co., Standard Toykraft Products, Transogram Co., Minirva Toy Co., Progressive Toy Corp., J. Pressman & Co., and American Toy Works composition doll sewing and embroidery sets.

B. 4" wire blunt-nose scissors. Found in Transogram Co. composition doll sewing and embroidery sets.

C. 4" metal blunt-nose scissors with painted handles. Found in American Toy Works composition doll sewing and embroidery sets.

D. 4" metal blunt-nose scissors with flat pressed handles. Found in Standard Toykraft Products composition doll sewing and embroidery sets.

E. 4⅛" metal blunt-nose scissors rounded handles. Found in Doll with Machine composition doll sewing set.

F. 4" wooden hoop. Found in Toy Creations, Progressive Toy Corp., Concord Toys, and Standard Toykraft Products composition doll sewing and embroidery sets.

G. 4" cardboard hoop. Found in Doll with Machine composition doll sewing sets.

A. 3⅛" scissors. Found in Standard Toykraft, Hassenfeld Bros., Transogram Co., J. Pressman Co., and De Luxe Game Corp. hard plastic doll sewing and embroidery sets.

B. 4" painted handle scissors. Found in Little Miss Sew It Empire Plastic Corp. hard plastic doll sewing sets.

C. 4½" plastic handle scissors. Found in Jr Miss Sewing Kit #535 Hassenfeld Bros. hard plastic doll sewing and embroidery sets.

D. 4⅛" scissors. Found in Little Miss Seamstress Set featuring Toy Necchi Sewing Machine Hassenfeld Bro. hard plastic doll sewing sets.

E. 4⅛" scissors. Found in Jr. Miss Sewing Kit #1522 Hassenfeld Bros. hard plastic sewing and embroidery sets.

F. 5¼" plastic handle Friskars. Found in Wendy Loves to Sew Madame Alexander sewing sets.

G. 4". Found in Little Genius FAO Schwarz sewing sets.

Note: The most prevalent children's scissors found in the plastic doll sewing sets are scissors A. This type of scissors was advertised in the back of toy catalogs such as Playthings. Playthings *carried an ad for Sommer Metalcraft Corp. Both A and E scissors above were featured in the advertisement along with hooks, handles saws, and all sorts of wire forms. Their advertisement read: "We're equipped and ready to make wire parts for toys and games. Complete facilities for forming, stamping, cut-threading, butt and spot welding. Nickel, cadmium or zinc plating, bonderized enamel, parkerized or copper coated finishes. Prompt service, satisfaction guaranteed. Send us a sample, blueprint or drawing."*

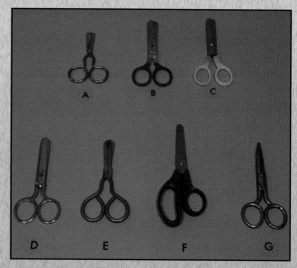

Plate 613. Scissors found in hard plastic doll sewing and embroidery sets.

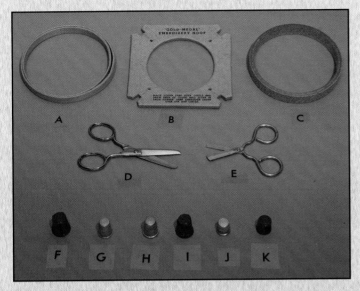

Plate 614. Tools found in children's embroidery sets.

Plate 615. Knitting spools found in children's knitting sets.

A. 4" wooden embroidery hoop. Found in Ullman Co., Standard Toykraft, Concord Toy Co., Chad Valley, American Toy Works, Milton Bradley Co., Transogram Co., Parker Brothers, and J. Pressman Co. embroidery sets.

B. 4½" square cardboard embroidery hoop. Found in Transogram Co. embroidery sets.

C. 4" cardboard embroidery hoop. Found in Transogram Co., Golden Needle, Spears Games, Standard Toykraft, Hasbro, Make Believe Playsuits Inc., Ontex, and Borgfeldt embroidery sets.

D. 4" blunt nose metal scissors. Found in Standard Solophone Co. (Hasbro) embroidery sets.

E. 3¼" blunt nose metal scissors. Found in all embroidery sets in this chapter except for Standard Solophone Co.

F. ⅝" high plastic thimble. Found in Golden Needle, Chad Valley, Make Believe Playsuits Inc., and Samuel Gabriel embroidery sets.

G. ⅝" high metal thimble. Found in Transogram Co. and Ontex embroidery sets.

H. ⅝" high metal thimble. Found in Standard Solophone Co. embroidery sets.

I. ⅝" high plastic thimble. Found in Hasbro, H. Davis, New York Toy and Game Mfg. Co., Standard Toykraft, Ontex, and J. Pressman Co. sets.

J. ½" high metal thimble. Found in Milton Bradley Co., Hasbro, Standard Toykraft, American Toy Works, Concord Toy Co., Transogram Co., Minerva Toy Co., Parker Brothers, and Ullman Co. embroidery sets.

K. ½" high plastic thimble. Found in Transogram and Hasbro embroidery sets.

Note: Not shown, 4" metal adjustable hoop. Found in Samuel Gabriel embroidery sets.

A. Red wooden 2" spool with eight wire loops and a yarn feeder spring. Found in Parker Bros. spool knitting sets.

B. Red wooden 1¼" spool with four wire loops and a yarn feeder spring. Found in Parker Bros. spool knitting sets.

C. Brown wooden 1¾" spool made from a branch with four brad posts. Found in Flights of Fancy spool knitting sets.

D. Red wooden 3¾" spool with four wire loops. Found in Whitman Publishing Co. spool knitting sets.

E. Red wooden 3" spool with four brad posts. Found in Peter Austin Mfg. Lt. spool knitting sets.

F. White wooden 2¾" spool with six brad posts. Found in H. Davis Co. spool knitting sets.

G. Red wooden 1¼" spool with four brad posts. Found in Parker Bros. spool knitting sets.

H. Green and blue plastic 2¼" spool with four plastic posts. Found in Lido Toy Co. spool knitting sets.

I. Pink plastic 2¼" spool with six plastic posts. Found in Avalon Division of Craft House Corp. spool knitting sets.

J. Pink plastic 2" spool with four plastic posts. Found in Pastime Activities spool knitting sets.

K. Yellow plastic 2¾" spool with four plastic posts. Found in Lisbeth Whiting spool knitting sets.

L. Wooden soldier 4¾" spool with six wire loops. Found in American Toy Works spool knitting sets.

M. Wooden doll 4" spool with four wire loops. Found in circa 1940s Spears Games spool knitting sets. Note. More shaped than letter N wooden doll.

N. Wooden doll 4" spool with four wire loops. Found in 1950s Spears Games spool knitting sets.

O. Plastic mushroom 3" spool with four wire loops. Found in a Parker Bros. Inc. spool knitting sets.

P. Wooden mushroom 3" spool with four wire loops. Found in a RL Germany spool knitting set.

Q. Wooden penguin 3¾" spool with four brad posts. Found in unmarked spool knitting sets.

R. Wooden doll 3¼" spool with four wire loops. Found in unmarked spool knitting sets.

Identification

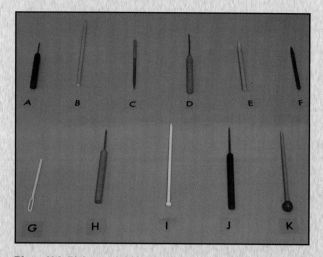

Plate 616. Picks used with spools found in children's knitting sets.

A. Painted wood and wire 3¼" pick. Found in Parker Bros. spool knitting sets.
B. Natural wood 5" pick. Found in Flight of Fancy spool knitting sets.
C. Painted and natural wood 3½" pick. Found in Whitman Publishing Co. spool knitting sets.
D. Natural and wire 4½" pick. Found in American Toy Works spool knitting sets.
E. Natural wood 3½" pick. Found in H. Davis Co spool knitting sets.
F. Red plastic 3" pick. Found in Lido Toy Co. spool knitting sets.
G. Pink 3" plastic needle. Found in Avalon Division of Craft House spool knitting sets.
H. Natural wood and wire 4" pick. Found in Peter Austin Mfg. Lt. spool knitting sets.
I. White plastic 4½" pick. Found in Spears Games set circa 1950s spool knitting sets.
J. Painted and wire 4¼" pick. Found in Spears Games circa 1940s spool knitting sets.
K. Natural wood 4" pick. Found in RL Germany spool knitting sets.

A. White plastic 9¾" knitting needles. Found in Miner Industries knitting sets.
B. Natural wood 6" knitting needles. Found in H. Davis Toy Corp. knitting sets.
C. White plastic 8" knitting needles. Found in Parker Bros. Inc. knitting sets.
D. Yellow plastic 6" knitting needles. Found in Hasbro Bros. knitting sets.
E. Orange plastic 6" knitting needles. Found in Lizabeth whiting knitting sets.
F. Pink plastic 8" needles. Found in Kekkertoys knitting sets.
G. Natural wood 9¾" needles. Found in H. Davis knitting sets.

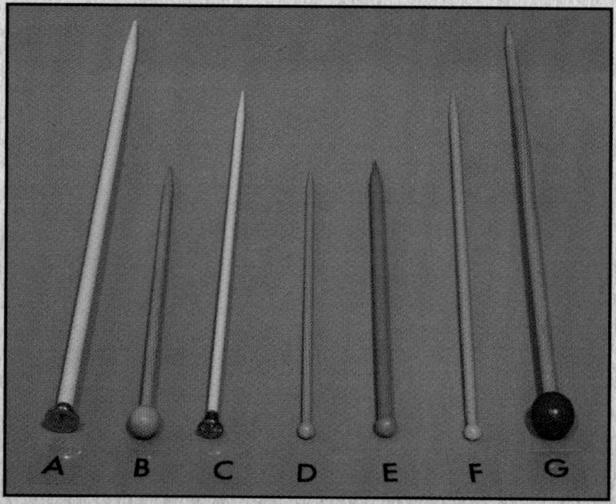

Plate 617. Knitting needles found in children's knitting sets.

Plate 618. Stands found in mannequin sewing sets.

Starting at top left:
A. Black painted oblong wood with one brad. Found in Peggy McCall mannequin sets.
B. Red or blue painted square wood with two holes. Found in Marianne's Fashion Designing Set #100, Vivianne's Fashion Designing Set, Simplicity Miniature Fashion Set, and Miniature Fashions #102.
C. Blue painted square wood with three holes. Found in Simplicity Fashiondol and Fashiondol #503 mannequin sets. With two extra holes for dowels, as pictured the middle hole is for the dress form.
D. Red diamond shape wood stand with brads. Found in Susanne's Fashion Show mannequin sets.
E. Silver metal round dome stand. Found in Singer Mannikin Doll.
F. Round dome painted metal stand. Found in Ideal Butterick Sew Easy Designing Set.
G. Composition, round dome stand. Found in all Peggy McCall mannequin sets.
H. Composition, round dome stand. Found in Deluxe Fashion Craft mannequin sets.

A. Blue flocked form. Found in Fashiondol #705 mannequin sets.
B. Bright blue composition form. Found in Large Susanne's Fashion Show mannequin sets.
C. Plaster flesh painted form. Found in Double Door Peggy McCall Fashion Model and (hatbox) Peggy McCall mannequin sets.
D. Blue painted composition form. Found in Simplicity Fashiondol mannequin sets.
E. Blue painted composition form. Found in Fashiondol #503 mannequin sets.

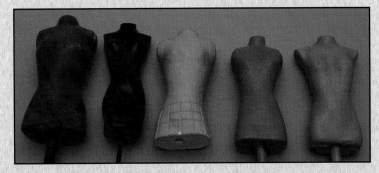

Plate 619. Dress forms found in mannequin sewing sets.

German Muller sewing machine marked Muller/Kinder Nahmashine/ DR Pat. No.4: 157. Black painted metal with gold trim, red and blue flowers, 4¾" long and 6" high. It has two clamps for securing it to a tabletop. It came in a French Doll sewing set.

Plate 620. Sewing machine found in bisque doll sewing set.

A. Marked "Sew Rite Sewing Machine, Hasbro U. S. A., #1500," 7" x 5½". Found in Hasbro's Alice In Wonderland Sewing Kit #1545 and Jr. Miss Sewing Kit #1541.
B. Marked "Necchi Supernova made in U.S.A." 7½" x 5½". Found in Hasbro's Little Miss Semstress Set #1542, Deb-U-Teen Sewing Kit #1546 and Little Miss Seamstress Sewing Case #1542.

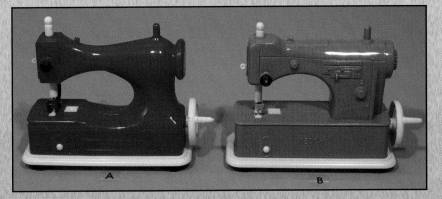

Plate 621. Sewing machines found in hard plastic doll sewing sets.

Plate 622. Sewing machine from La Petite Couturierel sewing set. The paper reads: "Muller Machin à Coudre pour enfants. Mode d'Emploi." The machine measures 6" high from base to top of thread holder, 5" long and 2¼" deep. It is black painted metal with gold trim, pink and white daisies and green leaves. The C-clamp is to attach the machine to a table while sewing. Turning the knob in the front operates the machine. Numbers 568797 are incised in the stitch plate.

Plate 623. Sewing machine from La Machinea Cord sewing set. The black metal machine is decorated with gold and red and green flowers. It measures 6¾" high, 6" long and 3½" deep. It comes with a metal clamp for attaching it to a table, and is operated by a knob in the front. Numbers "7218" are incised in the stitch plate.

Dolls Closet

Printed goods and printed clothing found in children's sewing sets including early stamped goods found in children's embroidery sets.

Plate 624. Types of pre-printed clothing found in American Toy Works sewing and embroidery sets. The smaller items at top consists of Dolly's Apron, Dolly's Pretty Dress, Dolly's Dress, and Dolly's Sweater Dress. They are printed in red yellow and green. The five larger items are all stamped in blue, and are named Dolly's Dress, Dolly's Party Dress, Dolly's Famous Sports Jacket, Dolly's Costume "Miss America," and Dolly's Dress. The name of the outfit is printed in the center neck opening and is cut away when making the outfit.

Plate 625. Pre-printed doll and clothing in J. Pressman's Little Orphn Annie sets. Clothing found in Orphan Annie and other sewing and embroidery sets by J. Pressman. The dolls have "J. Pressman" stamped along the salvage. The clothing is printed with "J. P. & Co." along the edge. All pieces are printed in red yellow and blue.

Plate 626. Stamp goods found in Art Embroidery Outfit #920 manufactured by J. Pressman & Co. circa 1920. Stamped on cotton fabric are three different style dresses, a laundry bag, two doilies, one round, and the other square.

Plate 627. Stamped goods found in Art Needlework Outfit #100S, unknown manufacture circa 1920. Stamped on cotton fabric are three different style dresses that have been embroidered, but not finished by a previous owner. All are stamped in the salvage "SOLOMCO #8."

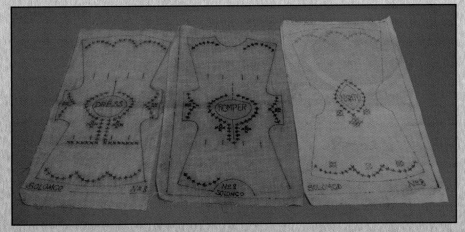

Identification

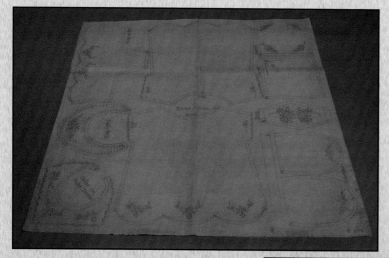

Plate 628. Stamped goods found in Gold Medal Art Embroidery Outfit, plate 193, manufactured by Transogram Co. circa 1920. Sheet of white cotton, stamped for cutting and embroidery contains 8" baby dress, with matching cap and collar, baby bib, booties, carry bag, and two hankies.

Plate 629. More **stamped goods** found in Gold Medal Art Embroidery Outfit, plate 193, manufactured by Transogram Co. circa 1920. Sheet of white cotton, stamped for cutting and embroidery contain 5½" dress with a pocket, bed spread that is stamped "My Pet" pillow cover stamped "Dolly," laundry bag and a hankie bag stamped "Dolly's Hankies."

Plate 630. Stamped goods from children's embroidery sets.

Note: It is not unusual, especially in the early sets to find the same prints in different sets, which leads me to believe they sometimes were purchased from a supplier.

A. Stamped 4½" x 3½" pillowcase. Found in Parker Brothers Embroidery Set.

B. Stamped 4" x 4" square doily. Found in Parker Brothers Embroidery Set.

C. Stamped 3" round doily. Found in Parker Brothers Embroidery Set.

D. Stamped 4" x 3½" camisole. Found in Parker Brothers Embroidery Set.

E. Stamped 3" x 2½" baby bib. Found in Parker Brothers Embroidery Set.

F. Stamped 7" x 6½" Jean Darling picture. Found in Jean Darling and Her Embroidery Outfit by Standard Toykraft Co.

G. Stamped 5½" x 5½" Peter Rabbit. Found in Gold Medal Needlework Set by Transogram Co.

H. Stamped 6" x 6" Little Housekeeper. Found in Embroidery and Needle Work by American Toy Works.

I. Stamped 4". Doily found in Bradley's Needlework by Milton Bradley Co.

Pin and Cut

Patterns that have been found in children's sewing sets.

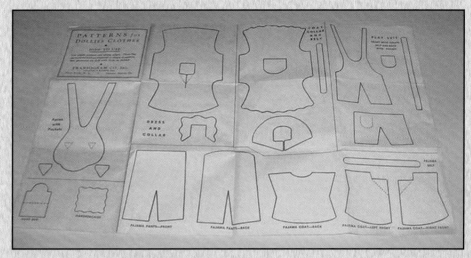

Plate 631. Transogram's patterns for 5" bisque dolls. Patterns for Dollies Clothes, includes an apron with pockets, dress with a collar, coat with a collar and belt, play suit with a pocket, pajamas with a belt, handkerchief, and handbag for a 5" doll. Found in Transogram Co. sewing sets.

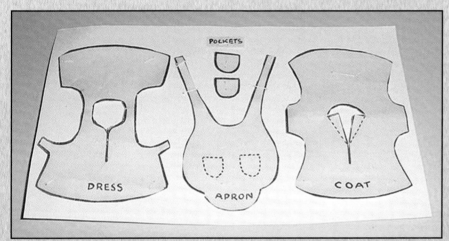

Plate 632. Transogram's patterns for 3½" bisque dolls. Pattern including a dress, apron with pockets, and a coat. Found in Transogram Co. sewing sets.

Plate 633. Gropper Toys pattern for 4½" bisque dolls. Complete Dress Patterns For Doll, includes a dress with a belt, collar and pocket, a hat with tassel, cape with a belt and pocket, nightgown with a ribbon band, and an apron with a pocket. Found in Gropper Toys sewing sets.

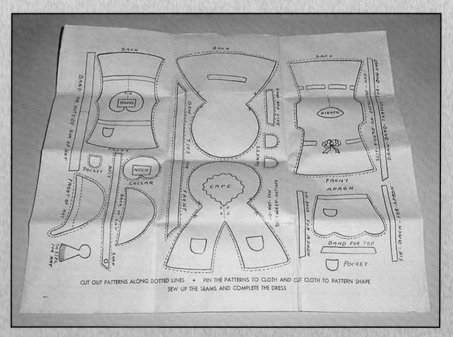

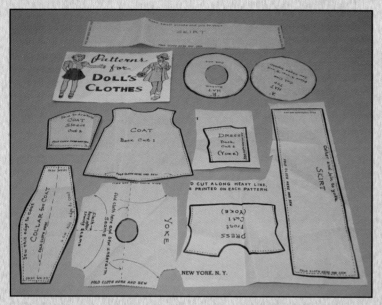

Plates 634. J. Pressman's 7½" composition doll patterns. Patterns for Doll's Clothes is found in Sewing for Every Girl #1235 manufactured by J. Pressman Co. Circa 1940, the pattern is for a 7¾" composition doll. The pattern contains patterns for two dresses and a coat and hat

Plate 635. J. Pressman's 7" composition doll patterns. J. Pressman Toy Corp. made Small Fry Trousseau #2206 in the late 1940s. The composition doll in the set is 7". Printed on only one side, the pattern booklet has information on making a trousseau bonnet, dresses, apron, knitting a scarf, and the bridal costume.

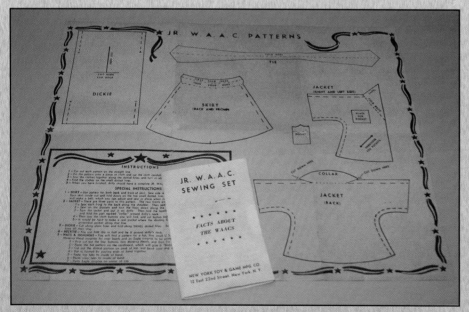

Plate 636. New York Toy & Games 6¼" composition doll patterns. World War II was the reason this pattern was made. Jr. W.A.A.C. Patterns is found in Junior W.A.A.C.'s Sewing Set made by New York Toy & Game Company. The composition doll in the set is 6¼" high. The pattern includes a dickey, tie, skirt, and a jacket with a pocket. The smaller paper is the fact sheet about the W.A.A.C.

Plate 637. Progressive's 6½" composition doll patterns. Progressive Doll Patterns is found in Progressive Sewing Set #1002 copyrighted in 1941. The composition doll is 6½" tall. The pattern is for a dress with a collar, pocket and belt, and a coat.

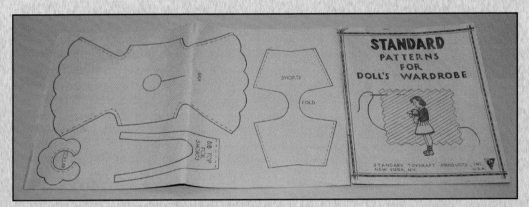

Plate 638. Standard Toykraft's 7½" composition doll patterns. Standard Pattern for Doll's Wardrobe is found in Jean Darling Sewing Outfit #1100 made by Standard Toykraft Products in 1936. The set has a composition doll that measures 7½". The pattern is printed on two sides and consists of a dress with a scalloped collar, shorts with a bib, coat, hat, and bag.

Plate 639. Toy Creation's 7" composition doll patterns. There is no title for these patterns but they are found in Sewing Set #26 produced by Toy Creations, Inc., circa 1940. The doll in the set is 7" tall. The pattern is printed only on one page and contains pattern for a party dress, coat, and a three-piece playsuit.

Plate 640. Transogram's 8½" composition doll patterns. This pattern is found in Dolly Dear Sewing Kit #5321 made by Transogram Company, circa 1939. The set has a composition that measures 8½". The pattern is printed on both sides and includes four dresses, overalls, a blouse, and a playsuit.

Plate 641. Transogram's 7" composition doll patterns. Gold Medal 4 Dolly Dress Patterns are found in Little Travlers Sewing Kit, Fairy Tin, Little Travlers Sewing Kit #1567, and Designer's Wardrobe Trunk Sewing Set all by Transogram Company, Inc. The composition dolls in the sets measures 6¼" to 7". The pattern is printed on both sides and includes a party dress (pink), school dress (red, yellow, and blue), overalls (blue), and play dress (not shown).

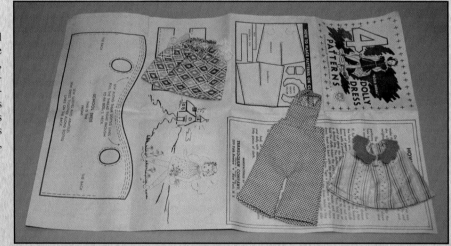

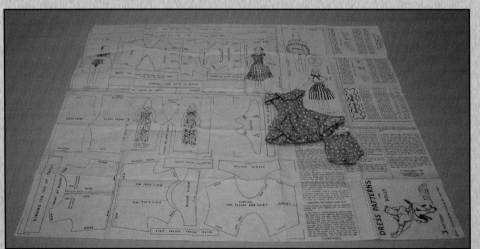

Plate 642. Transogram's 10" composition doll patterns. This pattern is found in the composition doll, sewing set Little Travler's Sewing Kit #1580. The composition doll is a full 10" tall. The Transogram Company, Inc. made the set in 1947. Dress Patterns for Dolly contains a party dress and panties, blouse, skirt, and panties, and a pants set.

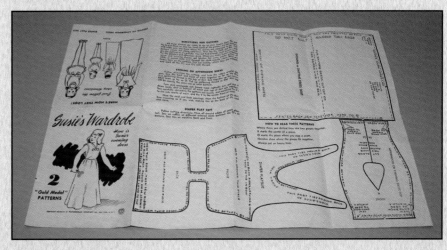

Plate 643. More of **Transogram** 10" composition doll patterns. Transogram Company manufactured Little Travler's Sewing Kit #1579 in 1942. The composition doll measures a full 10". We assume her name is Susie for her pattern is titled Susie's Wardrobe. The pattern contains two outfits an evening or afternoon dress and a "diaper" playsuit.

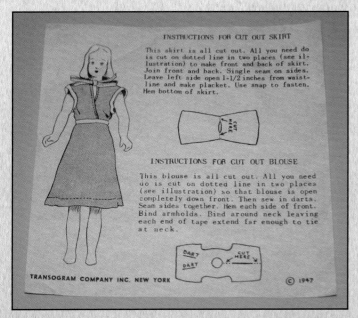

Plate 644. Transogram's instruction sheet for composition doll clothing. Transogram sewing kits Little Travler's Sewing Kit #1579 and #1580 put this little instruction sheet instructions for cut out skirt and instructions for cut out blouse in their sets in the late 1940s and early 1950s. The skirt and blouse was already cut out and binding was included to finish the edges. The composition dolls were 10" tall.

Plate 645. Lisbeth Whiting's 6" hard-plastic doll clothes pattern. Sewing Set Lisbeth Whiting includes a three-piece suit blouse, jacket and skirt and a dress.

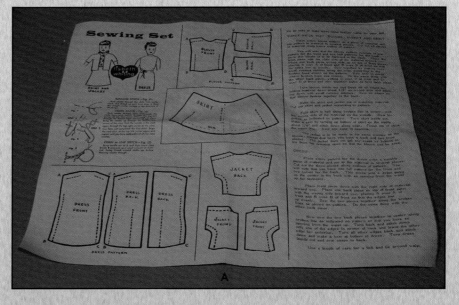

Plate 646. Trousseau patterns for 8" hard-plastic doll. Pattern includes a wedding dress and going away outfit. Found in Pressman Co. Sewing sets.

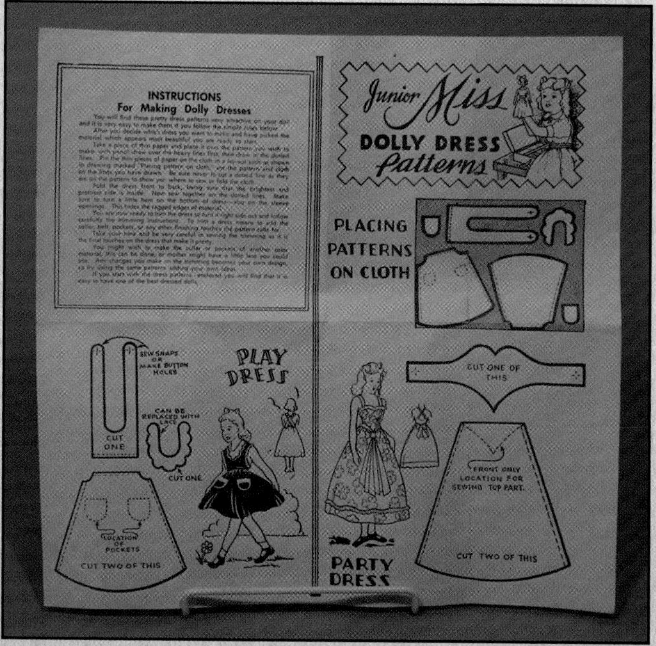

Plate 647. Hasbro's Junior Miss 7" hard-plastic doll patterns. Junior Miss Dolly Dress Patterns including a Play Dress and Party Dress.

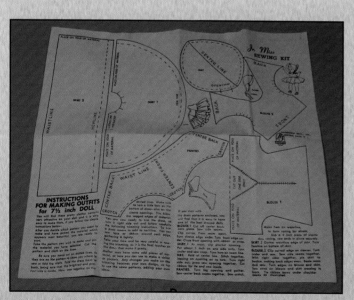

Plate 648. Jr. Miss Sewing Kit pattern for Hasbro 7½" hard-plastic dolls. Jr. Miss Sewing Kit includes a skirt, blouse, panties, dress, and hat for 7½" dolls.

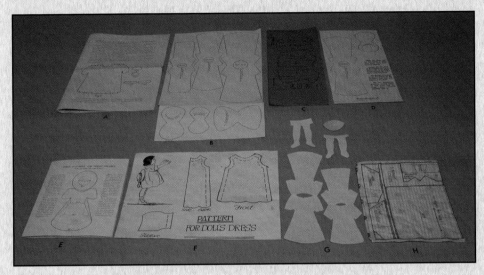

Plate 649. Patterns found in paper doll sewing and embroidery sets.

A. Pattern for 8" girls. Found in Tru-Life Paper Doll sets by Milton Bradley Co.

B. Pattern for 10", 8½", 7½" dolls. Found in Little Tot's Crepe Paper Doll Outfit #36 and crepe paper doll outfit #36 sets by Dennison manufacturing Co.

C. Pattern for 8" Little Sister. Found in Bradley's Tru-Life Paper Dolls by Milton Bradley Co.

D. Pattern for 8½" Nancy. Found in Nancy Crepe Paper Doll Outfit #38 by Dennison Manufacturing Co.

E. Pattern for 7" doll. Found in Dennison's Crepe and Tissue Paper Doll Outfit, circa, 1905 by Dennison manufacturing Co.

F. Pattern for 7½" doll. Found in Dollie's Sewing Box, unknown maker.

G. Pattern forms. Found in Dennison's Crepe and Tissue Paper Doll Outfit #33 by Dennison manufacturing Co.

H. Pattern for 8½"doll. Found in Make Mary's Clothes by Whitman Publishing Co.

Plate 650. Concord Toy Company Pattern for 10" paper dolls. A pattern found in a combination composition and paper doll sewing set made in 1942. Stitchcraft Sewing Set #204 has a composition doll with cut out clothing and the paper doll has only one outfit and it is this coat and hat. The heavy cardboard paper doll measures 10". The previous owner stitched the coat and hat as shown.

Plate 651. Patterns found in mannequin sewing sets.

From upper left:

A. Simplicity Patterns. Found in Vivianne's Fashion Designing Set, Simplicity Miniature Fashions, Miniature Fashions Set #102, Fashiondol Set #705, Simplicity Fashiondol Patterns, and Fashiondol Set #503.

B. Fashiondol. Found in Susanne's Fashion Show and Fashiondol Sets.

C. Susanne's Patterns. Found in Susanne's Fashion Show sets.

D. Marianne's Patterns. Found in Marianne's Fashion Designing Sets.

E. McCall's Pattern 6600-1-3. Found in McCall's Sets.

F. Butterick envelopes of three patterns Fashion Craft Patterns for the Singer Manikin Doll Groups 1 – 2. Found in Singer mannikin doll with machine and Singer mannikin doll sets.

G. Butterick envelopes of three Patterns to Make for the Fashion Mannequin Sets #8 and #9. Found in Ideal Butterick Sew Easy Designing Sets

H. Butterick enveloped of three patterns. Found in Junior Miss Manikin Sets #1 – 4.

I. Pattern for 11½" doll. Found in the Debutante Doll Sewing Kit.

Plate 652. Pattern found in Snip 'N Stitch sewing set by Dot & Peg Productions in 1947. There are eight outfits for a doll measuring 12½". Included are a playsuit, slip, pajamas, bathrobe, dress, bonnet, pinafore, and coat. The set also included the same fabrics as shown in the illustrated paper. The patterns are easy to sew, and included many diagrams for construction.

Plate 653. Doll knitting patterns found in children's knitting sets.

A. Outfit for 11½" Barbie dolls including sleeveless jacket, tube dress, bag, long dress, hat, and tube top. Found in Barbie Knit Magic by Mattel Inc.
B. Outfit for 8½" dolls including jacket, dress, vest, poncho, boots, bag, and scarf. Found in Knitting Pretty by Dekkertoys.
C. Outfit for 11" baby dolls including saque, bonnet, and booties. Found in Bear Brand Baby Doll Kit by Bernhard Ulmann.
D. Outfit for 13" dolls including sweater, skirt, headband, and a sweater vest, skirt and headband for a seven-year-old child. Found in Knitting Fun Doll and Me Knitting #2923
E. Outfit for 7½", 12", 15", 18" dolls including blouse, skirt, panties, and stole. Found in Jr. Miss Knitting sets by Mattel Inc.
F. Barbie dolls two-piece skating outfit including turtleneck sweater and skinny pants. Found in Knitting for Barbie #8012.
G. Outfit for 15" – 16" dolls including dress, nickers, scarf, jacket, beret, shorts, sports pullover, skirt, jumper, and cardigan. Found in Kwiknit by Spears Games.
H. Barbie dolls outfits; including striped scarf, leg warmers, hat and mittens, evening gown, shawl, fringed collar, mini dress, and fingerless long gloves. Found in Barbie Glitter Knitting kit #12588.

Following the Rules
Instruction sheets and booklets found in children's sewing and embroidery sets.

A. Davis Embroidery Instructions. Found in H. Davis sets.
B. Princess Instructions. Found in Ullman Mfg. Co. sets.
C. Directions. Found in Hassenfeld Bros. Inc. sets.
D. How To Embroider An Old-Fashioned Sampler. Found in Transogram Co. sets.
E. Directions. Found in Transogram Co. sets.
F. Embroidery Set. Found in Hassenfeld Bro. Inc. sets.
G. Small Fry Embroidery Instructions. Found in Pressman Toy Co. sets.
H. Instruction Chart of Popular Embroidery Stitches. Found in Ontex and Spears Games sets.
I. Make Your Own Luncheon Set. Found in Anne Orr sets.
J. Priscilla How To Embroider. Found in Standard Toykraft sets.
K. My First Lesson in the Art of Embroidery. Found in Transogram Co. Inc. sets.

Plate 654. Instruction sheets and booklets found in children's embroidery sets. *Note: Some of these direction sheets were used for years, going from one set to another in a company. Occasionally the directions were confusing because they did not entirely relate to the sets they were placed in. The instruction sheets that are seen most often are F and K.*

Identification

Plate 655. Instruction booklets found in paper doll sewing sets.

A. Three-page foldout Instructions and Patterns for Doll Costumes. Found in Dennison Crepe and Tissue Paper doll outfit #1905 by Dennison Manufacturing Co.
B. Eight-page Dennison's Fashions for Dolls. Found in Dennison Crepe and Tissue Paper doll outfit #33.
C. Three-page foldout Dennison Crepe and Tissue Paper Doll Outfit. Found in Little Tot's Crepe Paper Doll Outfit #36 and Crepe Paper Doll Outfit #36.
D. One-page Nancy Doll Outfit. Found in Nancy Crepe Paper Doll Outfit #38.
E. Six-page Dennison Fashions for Dolls, Vol.1. Found in Dennison Crepe and Tissue Paper Doll Outfit #31.
F. Six-page Dennison Fashions for Dolls, Vol.1. Found in Dennison Crepe and Tissue Paper Doll Outfit #31.
G. Four-page Bradley's Tru-Life Paper Dolls. Found in Bradley Tru-Life Paper Dolls.

Note: Both E and F Dennison Fashions for Dolls, Vol.1 were found in Dennison Crepe & Tissue Paper doll outfit #31.

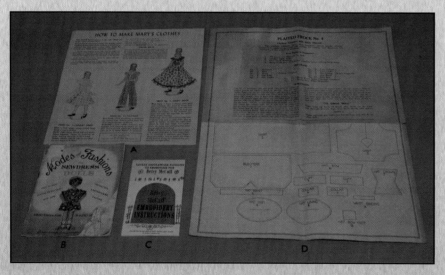

Plate 656. Instruction booklets found in paper doll sewing and embroidery sets.

A. Two-sided How to Make Mary's Clothes. Found in Make Mary's Clothes by Whitman Publishing Co.
B. Sixteen-page Modes and Fashions. Found in My Complete Sew Dress Box by Samuel Gabriel & Co.
C. Three-fold-out sheet Betsy McCall's Embroidered Instructions. Found in Betsy McCall's Fashion Shop Embroidery Sets by Standard Toykraft Products.
D. One-sheet Plaited Frock #4 by Emmy Lou Specialties, Charles Bloom.

Plate 657. Pamplets found in millinery sets. La Mille millinery designer from The Bonnet Box for a Small Miss circa 1940. Bébé Mode is from La Mode and also from Modiste millinery sets.

Plate 658. Instruction books found in mannequin sewing sets.

A. Simplicity Sewing Book for Fashiondol (green) copyright 1945, 66 pages. Found in Miniature Fashion sets, Fashiondol #705 sets, Simplicity Fashiondol sets, and Fashiondol #503 sets.
B. Miniature Fashions Simplicity Hints for the Young Designer (blue) copyright 1943, 14 pages. Found in Simplicity Miniature Fashion Set.
C. Butterick Dressmaking Book (orange) copyright 1941, 84 pages. Found in Delux Fashion Craft sets.
D. Miniature Fashions Simplicity Sewing Book for Young Fashion Designers (orange and blue) copyright 1943, 64 pages. Found in Marianne's Fashion Designing Set.

Plate 659. Instruction pamplets found in mannequin sewing sets.

A. Sewing Handbook for the Singer Manikin Doll Set. Found in Singer Sewhandy Mannikin set.
B. How to Use Your Singer Sewhandy Model 20 Sewing Machine. Found in Singer Sewhandy Mannikin set.
C. How to Remove Peggy's Arm pamphlet. Found in McCall's sewing sets.
D. Peggy the Modern Fashion Doll has a knitted sweater pattern. Found in Hat Box Peggy McCall Sewing Sets.
E. McCall Tricks in Sewing. Found in Peggy McCall (hat box), and Peggy McCall Fashion Model.
F. Susanne's Fashion Show (center). Found in Susanne's Fashion Show sets.

Commercial Patterns

This chapter contains two lists, "Dolls Named on Commercial Pattern" (these are dolls that are listed on a pattern with other popular dolls) and "Dolls with Commercial Patterns Made Exclusively for Them" (dolls with only their name on the pattern.)

You will find patterns that will include the dolls that also had patterns especially made for them in the "Dolls Named on Commercial Patterns." This is because their names are also on the patterns with other doll names. I have spelled the doll names as they are printed on the patterns.

In some cases the same pattern number was given to two entirely different patterns as in the case of Simplicity pattern number 1809. It was used for a 1956 pattern listed as "Doll's Wardrobe" with a sunsuit dress, slip, panties, nightgown coat, and hat to fit dolls 12" to 22". The same number 1890 was also printed on an undated Simplicity pattern for an 8" dolls wardrobe for Alexander-kins, Ginny, and Muffie with entirely different clothing. I have also seen different numbers on the same exact pattern.

Sometimes dolls named on commercial patterns come in multiple sizes, others come in a size range; be sure to get the size that fits your doll. Some popular dolls such as Shirley Temple came in a range of sizes.

There are many commercial patterns made that only have dolls sizes and do not mention any doll names. These patterns are not included in either list.

Dolls Named on Commercial Patterns

Doll	Brand	Pattern Numbers
Alan, 12"*	Butterick	3317
Alexander-kins, 8"	Simplicity	1372, 1809, 2294
	McCall's	2150, 2084
Alice	McCall's	1717, 1809, 1983
American Girl, Addy	Pleasant Company Addy's Pretty Clothes McCall's	7435, 7436
American Girl, Felicity	Pleasant Company Felicity's Pretty Clothes McCall's	7435, 7436
American Girl, Kirsten	Pleasant Company Kirsten's Pretty Clothes McCall's	7435, 7436
American Girl, Molly	Pleasant Company Molly's Pretty Clothes McCall's	7435, 7436
American Girl, Samantha	Pleasant Company Samantha's Pretty Clothes McCall's	7435, 7436
Andy, 12"	Butterick	2519, 3317
	McCall's	6901, 6992
Angel Baby	McCall's	2124, 8564, 9449
Annabelle	McCall's	1717, 1809
Annette, 11½"	Butterick	2519, 3088, 3317, 3385
	McCall's	2123, 6091, 6901, 6992, 9099
	Simplicity	5673, 5731, 6208
Annette	McCall's	2182, 9605
April Showers	McCall's	2124
Babe	Simplicity	5215
Babette, 11½"	Butterick	2519, 3317, 3385
	McCall's	6260, 6901, 6992
	Simplicity	4191, 4422, 4510, 4700, 5215
Babs, 11½"	Butterick	2519
	McCall's	2123, 6091, 9099, 9605
	Simplicity	4422, 4510, 5673, 5731, 6208
Baby Alive	Simplicity	7208, 8817, 9753
Baby Bevi	McCall's	2157, 8564, 9061
Baby Brother	Simplicity	7931
Baby Buttercup	McCall's	2124, 2157, 6513, 6993, 7913, 8125, 9449
Baby Cheryl	McCall's	7913
Baby Coos	McCall's	1549, 6513
Baby Crawl-along	Simplicity	7970
Baby Cry and Dry	Vogue	2592, 2868
Baby Cupcake	McCall's	6993, 8564
Baby Dear	McCall's	2124, 2157, 906, 9449
	Simplicity	4723
Baby Face	McCall's	2124, 9449
	Butterick	5743
Baby First Love	Style	2536
Baby First Step	Butterick	4169, 3385
	McCall's	2124, 2157, 856, 9449
	Simplicity	6768
Baby Giggles	McCall's	2157
	Simplicity	7970
Baby Heather	McCall's	2157
Baby Hungry	McCall's	2157
Baby Joy	McCall's	8295, 8563
Baby Kicks	McCall's	2124, 2157
Babykin	McCall's	6993, 8125, 8295
Baby Lisa	McCall's	2157
Baby Magic,	McCall's	2157, 8564, 9061
Baby Marie	McCall's	8295
Baby Pattaburp	McCall's	2124, 7913, 8125, 9449
Baby Pebbles	McCall's	2349, 6993, 7913
Baby Smile 'n Frown	McCall's	2124, 2157

Dolls Named on Commercial Patterns

Cream Puff   McCall's   6513

Crissy   Simplicity   5276, 6061, 9138,
                                          9698

Cricket   McCall's   4716

Cuddlee Babee   McCall's   2157, 9061
                    Simplicity   4723

Curtis, 12"   Simplicity   7737

Daily Dolly,   McCall's   1898, 1965, 2057,
                                  2084, 2150

Daisy Kingdom Daisy Dolly Simplicity   7497, 8245

Dancerina   McCall's   2182

Darcy, 12½"   Simplicity   5356, 8333

Dewees Cochran Portrait
  Dolls   McCall's   720

Dina   Simplicity   5276, 6061

Diana Ross   McCall's   2182

Dollikin   Simplicity 2293, 2745, 9697

Dolly Darlings   McCall's   8295, 8563

Dolly Dress Up   Simplicity   5275

Dusty, 11½"   Simplicity   6697, 7737

Don, 12"   McCall's   6901, 6992

Dy-Dee Baby   Butterick   444
                    McCall's   353, 513, 632, 713,
                        1493, 1900, 2001, 2183, 2261,
                             2349, 2657, 3412
                    Simplicity 2659, 4129, 5615

DyDee Darlin,   McCall's   2157

Elf   Simplicity   8207

Elise   McCall's   2182

Farrah   Simplicity   8281, 9194

Film Star Dolls   See Movie Dolls

Flower Kids   Simplicity   6823, 8838

Francie, 11⅔"   McCall's 2123, 4716, 9099, 9605

French Doll see also Boudoir Butterick   441
                    McCall's   1738, 1765

Gabby Linda   McCall's   6465

Gene   Vogue   V312, 615, 741, V766,
                        1417, 7105,7106, 7223, 7224,
                        7324, 7366, 7381, 7466, 7676,
                           V7844, V8055, 9105, 9106

Gerber Baby   Butterick   5229
                    Simplicity   7430

Ginette   McCall's   2183, 2261, 2349,
                                  8125, 8295

Ginger   Butterick   7972

Giggles   McCall's 2124, 2157, 9061, 9449
                    Simplicity   7971, 8561

Gigi, 7½"   McCall's 1898, 1965, 2057, 2084,
                                    2150

Gigi's Li'l Sister McCall's   2183, 2261, 2349

G.I. Joe, 12"   McCall's   4716
                    Simplicity   5807, 7737

Gina, 11½"   Butterick   3088, 3317, 3385
                    McCall's 2123, 6091, 6992, 9099
                    Simplicity   4422 5673, 6208

Ginny, 8"   Butterick   7972
                    McCall's 1898, 1965,2057, 2084,
                                  2150, 8295
                    Simplicity 1372, 1809, 2294,
                                          8151

Ginny Baby   Simplicity 5275, 5730, 6817,
                        7208, 7931, 4510, 4700, 5673,
                                    6208

Gloria, 11½"   Butterick   2519

Godey Little Lady doll, 7" Godey's Little Lady Patterns
                        #1 & #2 on doll box or in booklet
                        (same)

Goody Two Shoes   Butterick   4169, 3385
                    McCall's 2124, 8564, 9061, 9449
                    Simplicity   6768

Gotz Dolls, 18"   McCall's 2506, 2609, 3040, 3216,
                        3275, 4125, 7435, 7436, 8555,
                             9066, 9067, 9618

Gnome   Simplicity   8207

Harriet Hubbard Ayer Advance   6919
                    Butterick   6759, 7155, 7156
                    McCall's   1812, 1983, 1894

Honey   Butterick   5090

Honey Ball   McCall's   2157
                    Simplicity   7400

Honeybun   McCall's   2124, 9449

Honeybunch   McCall's   2084

Honeysuckle   McCall's   2084

Itsy Bitsy   McCall's   8295, 8563

Jan, 12"   McCall's   6987
                    Simplicity   6244. 5214, 5446

Janie   McCall's   8125

Jenny FP   McCall's   705, 737

Jesse James   McCall's   4716

Julia, 11½"   McCall's   2123
                    Simplicity   5330, 6697, 9054,
                                   9097, 9697

Jill   Butterick   8353
                    Simplicity   2744

Junior Miss   McCall's   2255, 2342

Kathy   McCall's   1717, 1900, 2001

Kay, 11½"   Butterick   3088, 3317, 3385
                    Simplicity   4422, 4510, 4700,
                        5215, 5673, 5731, 6208

Ken, 12"   Advance   2899 or Group E
                    Butterick   2519, 3317
                    McCall's   4716, 6901, 6992.
                    Simplicity   4422, 5330, 5807,
                        7737, 7928, 9054

Kerry, 17½"   Simplicity   9698

Kissy   Butterick   2520
                    McCall's   2468
                    Simplicity   4210

Leslie   McCall's   2182

Lingerie Lou, 7½"   Doll Bodies Inc.
                    pattern A #101   108
                    B #109   116,
                    C #117   124,
                    D #125   132

378

	McCall's	1898, 1965, 2057, 2150, 2270, 2323
Li'l Darlin	McCall's	2124, 9449
Li'l Dear	McCall's	8295
Lilly	McCall's	2084
Liza	McCall's	6260
Li'l Miss Fussy	McCall's	2084, 2124, 2157, 6260, 9061, 9449
Lilo	Butterick	8354
Li'l Softee	McCall's	2124
Lil Sister	Simplicity	5861, 6275
Li'l Susan	McCall's 2157, 6993, 8564, 9061	
	Simplicity	2292
	w/matching child's pattern, 2294	
Little Baby Water Babies	McCall's	7982
Little Kiddles	McCall's	8295, 8563
Little Huggums	McCall's	2124, 9449
Little Lady	McCall's	720, 918, 1015, 1089, 2342
Little Lucy	Simplicity	7931
Little Me	McCall's	8295
Littlest Angel	Butterick	7971
	McCall's	2124, 6993
	Simplicity	2292
	(w/matching child's pattern), 2294, 7400	
Little Huggums	McCall's	9449
	Vogue	9021
Little Miss Revlon	Advance	8453
	Butterick	8353
	Simplicity	2254, 2744
Little Women	McCall's	8295, 1809
Liza, 11½"	McCall's	6901, 6992
Look Around Velvet	Simplicity	5276, 6061
Look Around Crissy	Simplicity	5276, 6061
Love-Me	McCall's	2084
Lullaby Baby	McCall's	2157, 8564, 9061
Madame Alexander, 8"	Vogue	8709
Madame Alexander, 12"	Vogue	9021
Madeline	McCall's	1809
Mademoiselle Eugene, 11½"	Simplicity	6097
Maddie Mod, 11½"	McCall's	2123, 4716
	Simplicity	5330, 6697, 8466, 9054, 9097, 9697
Maggie	McCall's	1983
Magic Attic Club	Simplicity	8460, 8541, 8549, 8998, 9066
Maggie	McCall's	1717, 1809
Mandy FP	McCall's	705, 737
Manikin Models	McCall's	1058
Marcie, 7½"	McCall's	1653
Marie Osmond, 12"	Butterick	6664
Mary Hartline	Butterick	7155, 7156
Mary Hoyer	McCall's	1564, 1646, 1891
Mary Lou, 7"	McCall's 1898, 2057, 2084, 2150	
Mary Mine	Vogue	2592. 2868
Mary Poppins	McCall's	2182

Maxie, 11½"	McCall's	632
Mera, 11½"	McCall's	2123, 9099, 9605
Mia, 14½"	Simplicity	9698
Midge, 11½"	Butterick	3088, 3317, 3385
	McCall's	2123, 4716, 6992, 9099, 9605
	Simplicity	5215, 5673, 6208
Mikey FP	McCall's	705 737
Mini Mod, 11½"	Simplicity	6097
Miss Chips	McCall's	2182
Miss Curity	Butterick	1812, 6759
	McCall's	1812, 1894
Miss Debutante, 12"	McCall's	6987
Miss Flora McFlimsey	McCall's	1809
Miss Ginger	Butterick	8353
	Simplicity	2254, 2744
Miss Ginny	McCall's	2182
Miss Jill	McCall's	2182
Miss Merry	McCall's	8295, 8563
Miss Revlon	Butterick	8354
	Simplicity	3252
	also see Revlon Doll	
Mitsy 11½"	Butterick	2519
	Simplicity	6208,6244
Mitzi, 11½"	Butterick	3088, 3317, 3385
	Simplicity	4422, 4510, 4700, 5215, 5673, 5731, 6208
Modern Miss	McCall's	2182
Movie Dolls Shirley Temple, etc.	Butterick	5229
Hollywood 1913	McCall's 355, 418, 525, 579, 633	
	Simplicity	2240, 2243
Missy	McCall's	2162, 2255, 2342
My Baby	McCall's	6993
	Simplicity	4723
My Fair Lady	Butterick	8354
Munchkin	Simplicity	8207
Muffie, 8"	Butterick	7972
	McCall's 1898, 1965, 2057, 2150	
	Simplicity	1372, 1809, 2294
Nanette	McCall's	2270
New Born Thumbelina	McCall's	2124
Pampered Baby	Simplicity	5275
Patsy, 14"	Butterick	442
	McCall's	45,118, 119, 243, 445, 1918, 1919, 2443
	Sew-Easy no number	
	Good housekeeping	N-21
Patsy Ann, 19"	Butterick	443, 335
	McCall's	45, 1918, 119, 243, 2466
Patsy Babykin, 10"	Good Housekeeping	M-30
Patsyette, 9½"	Butterick	443, 445
	McCall's	10
Patsykins, 11"	Butterick	443, 445
	McCall's	45, 118, 119, 243
Patsy Joan, 16"	Butterick	443, 445

Doll	Brand	Pattern Numbers
	Good Housekeeping	N-29
	McCall's	45, 1918, 1919, 243
Patsy Lou, 22"	Butterick	443, 445
	McCall's	45, 118, 119, 243
Pebbles	McCall's	6993, 8125, 8564
Pee Wee	McCall's	8295, 8563
Peggy	McCall's	2084
Peggy Petite	McCall's	2084
Penny Brite	Simplicity	6207
Pepper, 9"	Simplicity	5771
Pittie Pat	McCall's	6513
Playpal	Simplicity	3661
Polly Jr., 11½"	McCall's	6260 6901, 6992
	Simplicity	4422, 4510, 4700, 5215, 5673, 5731, 6208
Portrait Doll	McCall's	2182
Pooty Tat	McCall's	2157
Posie	Butterick	7563
	McCall's	1892, 2084
	Simplicity	1785-w/matching child's pattern
Powder Puff	Simplicity	5275, 7208
Puddin	Vogue	2592, 2868, 8495
Pussycat	McCall's	2124, 9449
	Vogue	8495
Pretty Penny	McCall's	8125
Princess Bride	McCall's	2182
Princess Mary	Butterick	7155
Queen for A Day	Butterick	8353
Real Live Lucy	Butterick	4169, 3385
	McCall's	2124, 9449
Revlon Doll	Advance	8453, 8814
	McCall's	2162, 2255, 2293, 2342, 2397
	Simplicity	1808, 2293, 2745, also see Miss Revlon
Rock A Bye Baby	McCall's	7398
Rosamund	McCall's	1717
Rub-a-Dub Dolly	Simplicity	8817, 9753
Ruthie	McCall's	2157, 2182, 2466, 6465, 8564, 9061
Sasha	McCall's	2182
Sara Ann	Butterick	7155
Saucy Walker	Butterick	7563
	McCall's	1892, 2084, 8564
	Simplicity	1785
	w/matching child's pattern	4509, 4870
	w/matching child's pattern	4908
Shirley Temple	Advance	8813, 9603
	Du Barry	1616B
	McCall's	525, 579, 2270, 8813
	Simplicity	2717, 3217, 8813, 9603
Singin' Chatty	McCall's	7913
Skipper	McCall's	4716, 7480, 7716, 7841
	Simplicity	5771, 5861, 6275, 7600
Skippy, 14"	McCall's	1932
Skye, 11½"	Simplicity	7737
Snoozie	Butterick	4202
Snuggle Softee	McCall's	2124, 9449
Snugglebun,	McCall's	2157, 8564, 9061
Softina	McCall's	2124, 9449
Softee Baby	McCall's	9449
Sparkle Pleanty	McCall's	1549
Stacey, 11½"	McCall's	2123, 4716
Star Bright	Simplicity	7971
Star Dolls	Hollywood	1913
Sunshine Family (photo)	McCall's	4716
Supergirl, 11½"	McCall's	2123, 9099, 9605
Susan Stroller	Butterick	7563
Susie Sunshine	McCall's	2157, 7913, 8125
	Simplicity	4839, 6768
Suzy, 12"	McCall's	6987
Suzy Cute	McCall's	8295
Suzette	Simplicity	5215
Sweetie Pie	McCall's	1362
	Simplicity	4727, 5730, 6817
Sweet Sue	McCall's	1336, 1720, 1745
	w/matching child's pattern	1823, 1983, 2162, 2412, 8125
	Simplicity	1336, 1779
Sweet Sue Sophisticate	McCall's	2162, 2255, 2342, 2397
	Simplicity	2293
Swingy	McCall's	2124
Talky Crissy	Simplicity	5276, 6061, 9698
Talky Velvet	Simplicity	5276, 6061, 9698
Tammy, 12"	Butterick	2931
	McCall's	2123, 4716, 6987, 7673, 9099, 9605
	Simplicity	4883, 5214, 5446, 5771, 5852
	w/matching child's dress	5859
	w/matching child's dress	5899
	w/matching child's outfit	5941
	w/matching child's outfits	6107
	w/matching child's dress	6150
	w/matching child's dress,	6244
Tassy, 12"	McCall's	6987
Teenie Weenie Tiny Tears	McCall's	7592
	Simplicity	5275
Teenie Tiny Tears	McCall's	7592
Tearie Betsey Wetsey	McCall's	2157, 5275
Teensie Baby	McCall's	2157
Teensie Tot	McCall's	6993
Terry, 12"	Simplicity	5446, 6244, 6987
Thirstee Babee,	McCall's	2124, 2157, 9449
Thirstee Cry Baby	McCall's	6513
Thumbelina	Butterick	4202
	Simplicity	4191, 4723
Tina, 11½"	McCall's	6260, 6901, 6992

	Simplicity	4510, 4700, 5215, 5673, 5731
Tina Marie, 11½"	McCall's	6260
	Simplicity	4510, 4700, 5215.
Tiny Chatty Baby	Butterick	4202
	McCall's	8564
	Simplicity	4128, 4839
Tiny Talker	Simplicity	4723
Tiny Tears,	Butterick	2520
	McCall's	1657, 1900, 2001, 2183, 2261, 2349, 2412, 3218, 5615, 6513, 7592, 7913, 8125, 8564, 9061
	Simplicity	1402
	w/matching child's pattern, 1406, 1844, 3218, 3669, 5275, 5615, 8376	
Tiny Tubber	McCall's	6993
Tippee Toes	McCall's	2157
Tippy Tumbles	Simplicity	8561
Toni	Advance	6919
	Butterick	969, 5092, 5969, 6316, 6759, 7155, 7156
	McCall's	1561, 1646, 1657, 1706, 1812, 1894, 1983
	Simplicity	2745, 3728, 4128, 4218
Toni Sophisticate	McCall's	2255, 2342, 2397
Toni Walker	Butterick	7155, 7156, 7975
	Simplicity	1405, 4909
Toodles	Butterick	2520
	McCall's	2349
Tressy	Simplicity	5731
Trolls, 3"	McCall's	7589, 8563
	Simplicity	8207
Trolls, 4½"	McCall's	8563
Trolls, 6"	McCall's	7589
	Simplicity	8207
Tubsy,	McCall's	2157, 9061, 9449
	Simplicity	7970
Tumbling Tomboy	Simplicity	8561,
Twinkie	Simplicity	5730
Velvet, 14½"	Simplicity	5276, 6061, 9138, 9698
Victoria	McCall's	2124, 9449
	Vogue	8495
Walking Honey Baby	McCall's	6465
Walking Toodles	McCall's	2412, 6465
Water Babies	McCall's	789, 811, 5276, 6277, 6772, 7982, 9117
Wendy, 8"	McCall's	1898, 1965, 2057
Wendy, 15-18"	McCall's	1717, 1809
Wendy-kin	McCall's	8295
Wild Bill Hickock	McCall's	4716
Winking Winnie	Simplicity	7971
Wonder Woman, 11½"	McCall's	2123, 9099, 9605
Wyatt Earp	McCall's	4716

Dolls with Commercial Patterns Made Exclusively for Them

American Girl, Addy	Pleasant Company Addy's Pretty Clothes McCall's	7435, 7436
American Girl, Felicity	Pleasant Company Felicity's Pretty Clothes McCall's	7435, 7436
American Girl, Kirsten	Pleasant Company Kirsten's Pretty Clothes McCall's	7435, 7436
American Girl, Molly	Pleasant Company Molly's Pretty Clothes McCall's	7435, 7436
American Girl, Samantha	Pleasant Company Samantha's Pretty Clothes McCall's	7435,
Baby Face	Butterick	5743
Baby First Love	Style	2536
Barbie	Advance or Group A	9938
	Group B	9939
	McCall's	7137, 7162
	w/matching child's pattern,	7421, 7428, 7429, 7545
	w/matching child's pattern	
	Simplicity	7046, 7362, 7601, 7712, 8157
Becky FP	McCall's	705, 737
Betsy McCall, 8"	McCall's	2239, 2300, 2323, 2331
	w/ matching child's pattern,	2457
Betsy McCall, 11½"	McCall's	2323, 2336, 7673
Betsy McCall, 14"	McCall's	1728, 1729, 1812, 1894, 2300, 2323
Betsy McCall, 16" cloth	McCall's	3423
Betsy McCall 18" cloth	McCall's	1812, 7933, 7934, 8139
Betsy McCall, 30"	McCall's	2457
Betsy McCall, Tonner, 8 & 14"	McCall's	M4334, M4743
Brandi, 17½"	Simplicity	5276, 6061
Brook Shields	McCalls	8727
	w/ matching child's pattern	9092
Cabbage Patch Kids	Butterick 330, 340, 347, 405, 408, 3270, 5357, 3558, 5422, 6507, 6508	
	same as-330	6509, 6511, 6662, 6826, 6827
	same as 340	6934, 6935, 6981, 6984
	same as 347 Simplicity	8838
Cabbage Patch Premmie	Butterick 342, 346, 437, 3921, 6981-same as-(346)	

Dolls with Commerical Patterns Made Exclusively for Them

Charmin' Chatty — McCall's — 7269

Chatty Cathy — Advance or Group F — 2897
Group G — 2898
McCall's — 7181
Simplicity — 4652

Crissy, 17½" — Simplicity — 5276, 6061, 9138, 9698

Dina 15½" — Simplicity — 5276, 6061

Dy-Dee — Butterick — 444
McCall's — 353, 513, 632, 713, 1493, 2657
Simplicity — 2659, 4129

Gene, 15½" — Vogue — V312, V615, V704, V741, V766, V1417, V7105, V7106, V7223, V7224, V7324, V7327, V7366, V7381, V7466, V7676, VV7844, V8055, V9105, V9106,

Ginny — Simplicity — 8151

Godey's Little Lady, 7" — Pattern on doll's box or in a booklet (same pattern)

Jenny FP — McCall's — 705, 737

Honey — Butterick — 5090

Katie, 14" — American School of Needlework booklets — 8401 through 8412

Ken — Advance — 2899 or Group E

Kerry, 17½" — Simplicity — 9698

Kissy — Simplicity — 4210

Lingerie Lou, 7½" — Doll Bodies Inc. patterns
A #101 — 108,
B #109 — 116,
C #117 — 124,
D #125 — 132

Little Baby Waterbabies — McCall's — 7982

Little Lady — McCall's — 918, 1015, 1089

Littlest Angel — Butterick — 7971

Madame Alexander, 8" — Vogue — 8709

Madame Alexander, 12" — Vogue — 9021

Mandy FP — McCall's — 705, 737

Manikin Models — McCall's — 1058

Marcie 7½" — McCall's — 1653

Marie Osmond, 12" — Butterick — 6664

Mary Hoyer — McCall's — 1564, 1646, 1891

Mia, 14½" — Simplicity — 9698

Mikey FP — McCall's — 705, 737

My Friends Dolls — McCall's — 705, 737

Patsy, 14" — Butterick — 442

McCall's — 45, 118, 119, 243, 1919
Sew-Easy no number

Patsy Ann, 19" — Good Housekeeping — N-21
Butterick — 443, 445
McCall's — 45, 118, 119, 243

Patsy Babykin, 10" — Good Housekeeping — M-30

Patsyette, 9½" — Butterick — 443, 445
McCalls — 10

Patsykins, 11" — Butterick — 443, 445
McCall's — 45, 118, 119, 243

Patsy Joan, 16" — Butterick — 443, 445
Good Housekeeping — N-29
McCall's — 45, 118, 119, 243

Patsy Lou, 22" — Butterick — 443, 445
McCall's — 45, 118, 119, 243

Penny Brite — Simplicity — 6207

Pepper, 9" — Simplicity — 5771

Revlon Doll — Advance — 8453, 8814

Shirley Temple — Advance — 8813
Simplicity — 2717, 3217, 8813, 9603

Skipper — McCall's — 7480, 7716, 7841
Simplicity — 5771, 5861

Skippy 14" — McCalls — 1932

Sunshine Family (photo) — McCall's — 4716

Sweetie Pie — McCall's — 1362,

Sweet Sue — McCall's — 1336, 1720, 1823

Tammy 12" — Butterick — 2931
Simplicity — 4883, 5771, 5852
w/matching child's dress — 5859, 5899
w/matching child's outfits — 5941, 6107
w/matching child's dress — 6150

Tiny Tears — McCall's — 1657

Toni — Butterick — 5092, 5969, 6316
McCall's — 1561, 1646, 1706
Simplicity — 3728, 4218

Tressy — Simplicity — 5731

Trolls, 3" — McCall's — 7589
Simplicity — 8207

Trolls, 6" — McCall's — 7589
Simplicity — 8207

Velvet, 15½" — Simplicity — 5276, 6061, 9138, 9698

Water Babies — McCall's — 789, 811, 5276, 6277

Bibliography

Adams, Margaret ed, *Collectible Dolls and Accessories of the Twenties and Thirties* from Sears, Roebuck and Co. Catalogs. Mineola, NY: Dover Publications, 1986.

Bachmann, Manfred, ed, *Der Universal Spielwaren Katalog, 1924/26*. Cumberland, MD: Hobby House Press, 1985.

Barlow, Ronald S, *The Great American Toy Bazarr 1878-1945*. El Cajon CA: Windmill Publishing Co., 1998.

Buchhotz, Shirley, *A Century of Celluloid Dolls*, Cumberland, MD: Hobby House Press, 1983.

Burdick, Loraine, *Child Star Dolls and Toys*, Puyallup WA: Quest-Eridon Books, 1970.

Burman, Barbara, ed. *The Culture of Sewing*. Oxford, NY: Berg, 1999.

Calvert, Karin. *Children in the House*. Boston: Northeastern University Press, 1992.

Child, Mrs. *The Mothers Book*. Bedford, MA: Applewood Books, 1831.

Cieslik, Jürgen and Marianne. *German Doll Studies*. Annapolis, MD: Gold Horse Publishing, 1999.

Coleman, Evelyn; Elizabeth; and Dorothy. *The Age of Dolls*. Self-Published. 1965.

Coleman, Evelyn Jane, fd.. Marshall Field & Co. *Kringle Society Dolls*. Cumberland, MD: Hobby House Press, 1980.

Creekmore, Betsey B. *Traditional American Crafts*. New York: Hearthside Press Inc., 1968.

Cross, Gary. *Kids' Stuff, Toys and the Changing World of American Childhood*. Cambridge, MA: Harvard University Press, 1977.

Curtis, Anthony. *Memories of Childhood*. Secaucus, NJ: Chartwell Books, Inc.,1990.

Darling, Jean. *A Peek at the Past*. Jügesheim, FRG: Hamling, 1995.

Dillmont, Thérèse de. *Encyclopedia of Needlework*. Mulhouse, France: Dollfus-Mieg & Co.,n.d.

Fawcett, Clara Hallard. *Collector's Guide to Antique Paper Dolls*. Mineola, NY: Dover Publications, 1989.

Fox, Sandi. *Small Endearments*. Nashville, TN: Rutledge Hill Press, 1994.

Gernsheim, Alison. *Victorian and Edwardian Fashion*. New York: Dover Publications, Inc., 1981.

Green, Harvey. *The Light of the Home*. New York: Pantheon Books, 1983.

Groves, Sylvia. *History of Needlework Tools and Accessories*. Felthem, Middlesex: Hamlyn Publishing Group Ltd., 1968.

Heininger, Mary Lynn Stevens et al. *A Century of Childhood*. Rochester, NY: Margaret Woodbury Strong Museum, 1984.

Hewitt, Emma Churchman. *Queen of Home*. Philadelphia: Miller Megee Co., 1888.

Hodges, Felice. *Period Pastimes*. New York: Weidenfeld & Nicolson, 1989.

Holland, Thomas. *Girl's Toys of the Fifties & Sixties*. Sherman Oaks, CA: Windmill Press, 1997.

Hunter, Eleanor A. *Talks to Girls*. New York: American Tract Society, 1891.

Izen, Judith. *Ideal Dolls*. Paducah, KY: Collector Books, 1994.

Izen, Judith. *American Character Dolls*. Paducah, KY: Collector Books, 2004.

Judd, Polly and Pam. *Hard Plastic Dolls*. Grantsville, MD: Hobby House Press, 1985.

Judd, Polly and Pam. *Hard Plastic Dolls II*. Grantsville, MD: Hobby House Press, 1985.

Judd, Polly and Pam. *Hard Plastic Dolls*, 3rd Revised. Grantsville, MD: Hobby House Press, 1993.

Kahler, Atha, *Daisy's Album, Lettie Lane's Daisy, The Doll That Really Came to Life*. 9605 N.E. 26th, Bellevue, Washington, 98004.

Kybalová, Ludila, Herbenová, Olga and Lamarová, Milena. *The Pictorial Encyclopedia of Fashion*. London, England: Paul Hamlyn, 1968.

Laboissonniere, Wade. *Blueprints of Fashion Homesewing Patterns of the 1940s*. Atglen Pa: Schiffer Publishing, 1997.

Bibliography

Lady, A. *The Workwoman's Guide 1838*. Easton CT: Piper Publishing, LLC, 2002, reproduction.

Lane, Rose Wilder. *Woman's Day Book of American Needlework*. New York: Simon and Schuster, 1963.

Van Ausdall, Marci. *Betsy McCall A Collector's Guide*. Hobby House Press, Inc., 1999.

McClinton, Katharine Morrison. *Antiques of American Childhood*. New York: Bramhall House, 1970.

McConnel, Bridget. *The Story of Antique Needlework Tools*. Atglen, PA: Schiffer Publishing Ltd. 1999.

McGonagle, Dorothy A. *A Celebration of American Dolls*. Grantsville, MD: Hobby House Press, 1997.

Mertz, Ursula. *Collector's Encyclopedia of American Composition Dolls 1900 – 1950*. Paducah, KY: Collectors Books, 1999.

Pardella, Edward R. *Shirley Temple Dolls and Fashions*. West Chester, PA: Schiffer Publishing, 1992,

Picken, Mary Brooks. *The Fashion Dictionary*. New York: Funk & Wagnalls, 1957.

Schroeder, Jr., Joseph, ed. *The Wonderful world of Toys' Games & Dolls 1860 – 1930*. Northfield, IL: DBI Books, Inc., 1971.

Spero, James, ed. *Collectible Toys and Games of the Twenties and Thirties from Sears, Roebuck and Co*. Catalogs. Mineola, NY: Dover Publications, 1988.

Strasser, Susan. *Never Done*. New York: Pantheon Books, 1982.

Taunton, Nerylla. *Antique Needlework Tools and Embroideries*. England: Antique Collectors' Club LTD, 1997.

Theimer, François. *Les Catalogues d' Extrennes de Grands Magasins, 1875 – 1889*. Paris France: Editions Polichelle, 1996.

Thomas, Glenda. *Toy and Miniature Sewing Machines*. Paducah, KY: Collector Books, 1995.

Thomas, Glenda. *Toy and Miniature Sewing Machines Book II*. Paducah, KY: Collector Books, 1995.

Thomas, Mary. *Mary Thomas's Knitting Book*. London England: Hodder and Stoughton, Ltd., 1938.

Parry, Crooke, Charlotte. *Toys Dolls Games Paris 1903 – 1914*. Hastings House Publishers, 1981

Walker, Frances and Whitton, Margaret. *Playthings by the Yard*. South Hadley, MA: Hadley Printing Co., Inc., 1973.

Weissman, Judith Reiter and Lavitt, Wendy. *Labors of Love*. Avenel NJ: Wings Books, 1987.

Whitehill, Bruce. *American Boxed Games and There Makers 1822 – 1992*. Radnor, PA: Wallace Homestead, 1992.

Whiting, Gertrude. *Old-Time Tools & Toys of Needlework*. New York: Dover Publications, Inc., 1971.

Young, Mary. *Collector's Guide to Paper Dolls*. Paducah, KY: Collector Books, 1980.

Young, Mary. *Collector's Guide to Paper Dolls, Second Series*. Paducah, KY: Collector Books, 1984.

Hobbies, Gelber, 1999, Gelber, Columbia University Press, New York

Pamplets

Make and Mend for Victory. Spool Cotton Co., 1942

Periodicals

Antique Doll Collector
July 2005

Doll News
Summer 2005

Doll Reader Magazine
1981   April/May
1982   October
1991   August/October

La Poupée Modéle
1879 – 1880

McCall Sewing Corps
1943 Lessons 1 – 6

Mother's Magazine
1913   November

National Doll World
1979   July/August
1986   July/August

Parents Magazine
1949   June/July/August
1951   November/December
1953   December
1954   December
1955   December
1956   December
1957   November/December
1958   December
1959   November/December
1960   November/December
1968   December
1969   December
1971   January

Playthings Magazines
1908   June
1917   June
1923   June
1924   June, July
1925   June, December
1926   January
1928   Febuary, May, November, June
1929   January, February
1930   August
1931   January, May
1933   April, June
1935   July
1936   April
1938   September
1939   January – December
1942   March, December
1943   January, April, August, October, December
1944   January, June, September, November
1945   January, February, April
1946   March
1948   March
1949   January – December
1950   January, February, March, September
1951   March
1953   April
1963   September – November
1970   March
1984   March

Youths Companion
1888   December

Catalogs

Aunt Ellen's Art Needlework
1950   Needlework book
1951   Needlework book
1957   May catalog #8

Butler Brothers Catalog
1908   October

Dennison Crepe Paper
1892   Art and Decoration Tissue Paper
1905   Art and Decoration Tissue Paper
1906   Art and Decoration Tissue Paper
1907   Art and Decoration Tissue Paper
1912   Art and Decoration Tissue Paper
1921   Art and Decoration Tissue Paper
1922   Art and Decoration Tissue Paper
1924   Art and Decoration Tissue Paper
1924   Dealers Catalogue
1925   Dealers Catalogue
1926   Dealers Catalogue
1931   Art and Decoration Tissue Paper

F.A.O. Schwartz
1950   Christmas
1951   Christmas
1952   Christmas
1953   Christmas
1954   Christmas
1955   Christmas
1956   Christmas
1957   Christmas
1959   Christmas
1961   Christmas
1962   Christmas
1963   Christmas
1964   Christmas
1966   Christmas
1967   Christmas
1968   Christmas
1969   Christmas
1975   Fall/Winter
1976   Fall/Winter

McCall Style News
1942   May

Montgomery Ward Catalog
1942   Christmas Book
1955   Christmas Book
1957   Christmas Book
1967   Christmas Book
1972   Christmas Book
1974   Christmas Book
1976   Christmas Book

Rockwell's Toyland Basement Store, Corning NY
1960

Sears Roebuck and Co.
1954   Christmas
1955   Christmas
1956   Christmas
1971   Christmas
1972   Christmas
1973   Christmas
1978   Christmas
1979   Christmas
1985   Christmas

Toys and Novelties
1930   Edition
1932   Edition
1942   August
1953   May, June, July, October
1954   February, April, August, November, December
1964   March

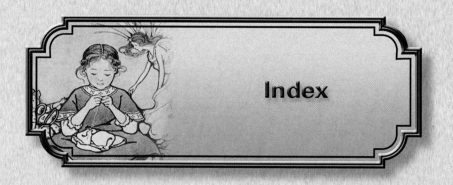

Index

Index

Index

Index

Publishers and Pattern Companies

Advance Pattern Company Incorporated

Alexander Brothers PDT.LTD

Alma Burge

Butterick Publishing Company LTD.

Index

Index

Index

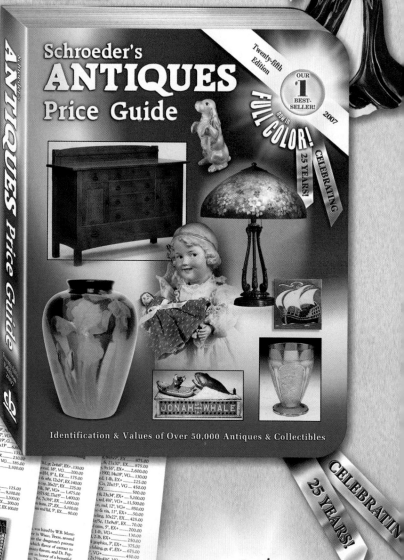